THE HOLLYWOOD CELEBRITY DEATH BOOK

JAMES

From Theda Bara and Rudolph Valentino to Marilyn Monroe and James Dean to Marlene Dietrich and Brandon Lee, the strange, often tragic, deaths of over one hundred of America's screen idols.

Library of Congress Cataloging-in-Publication Data
James Robert Parish
        The Hollywood Celebrity Death Book

        1. The Hollywood Celebrity Death Book (popular culture)
I. Title

Published by Pioneer Books, Inc., 5715 N. Balsam Rd., Las Vegas, NV, 89130.

First Printing, 1993

> They've great respect for the dead in Hollywood, but none for the living.
> —Errol Flynn

Dedicated To All Our Movie Favorites Who Have Passed On

ACKNOWLEDGEMENTS:

The author wishes to gratefully thank the following individuals and institutions for their generous assistance in the writing of this book.

Michael Gene Ankerich
Kathy Bartels
George Baxt
Bill Becker
Larry Billman
Richard A. Braff
Jeffrey Carrier
Melody Cecko (Peter Duel Remembrance Club)
John Cocchi
Richard DeCroix
Karin A. Fowler
Alex Gildzen
Richard Hayes
David Hofstede
Kim Holston
Lois Kibbee
Jane Klain
Larry Edmunds Book Shop (Peter Bateman)
Garry Lassin (3 Stooges Fan Club)
Alvin H. Marill
Doug McClelland

Jim Meyer
Photofest (Howard Mandelbaum)
Michael R. Pitts
Howard H. Prouty
Jerry Roberts
Brenda Scott Royce
Arleen Schwartz
Margie Schultz
William Schultz
Don Stanke
Tyrone Steverson
Kevin Sweeney
Vincent Terrace
Roi A. Uselton
Don Wigal
Robert Young, Jr.

Editorial Consultant: Allan Taylor

Publisher and Designer: Hal Schuster   *Editor: David Lessnick*

CONTENTS

THE CAR IN WHICH JAMES DEAN DIED

photo courtesy Photofest

Gwili Andre

February 24, 1908 - February 5, 1959

As a model, Danish-born Gwili Andre was so alluring that she became tops in the New York fashion industry. David O. Selznick, then head of RKO Pictures, brought "America's most beautiful model" to Hollywood where she was cast immediately opposite studio star Richard Dix in *Roar of the Dragon* (1932). But in that film, as in her next feature, *Secrets of the French Police* (1932), she proved to be a physically striking but dramatically wooden mannequin. By the time of her final movie, *The Falcon's Brother* (1942), she was cast in a very supporting role.

By the late 1950s, Gwili's acting career was but a memory as were her two marriages. (Her second husband had gained custody of their only child.) On February 5, 1959, a fire swept Andre's shabby apartment on Ocean Front Walk in Venice, California and she was burned to death. Her landlady admitted later that Gwili had been a heavy drinker, adding, "She's found peace at least. Something she never knew on this earth." Found in the ruins of the actress's apartment were several empty whiskey bottles plus a box of old magazines in which she had been featured as the cover girl.

Jack Cassidy

[John Edward Joseph Cassidy]

March 5, 1927 - December 12, 1976

Some smooth performers like Jack Cassidy are so multi-talented that they continually work in all mediums. His career end was not induced by professional burn-out; rather he burned to death tragically in an apartment fire.

He grew up in the Richmond Hill area of Queens, New York, the youngest of five children in an Irish-American household where the father was a railroad engineer. As a child he thought of becoming a priest, but changed his mind by age eleven. With the guidance of an uncle, entertainer Ben Dora, he decided upon a show business career. By age sixteen, he had a chorus job in Ethel Merman's musical, *Something for the Boys* (1943). When that closed, he took odd jobs—bellhop, chauffeur—to fill in between Broadway chorus work. In 1948, he had a tiny role in *Small Wonder* and was with Bobby Van in *Alive and Kicking* (1950). By now he had married TV actress Evelyn Ward and their son David was born in 1951. He enjoyed a solid success with the musical *Wish You Were Here* (1952) and went dramatic in *Sandhog* (1954). By now he and Evelyn were divorced.

Long at odds with his pretty boy image and hating being branded a lightweight actor who got by on his wit and his sharp wardrobe, he had grave doubts about his talents. However, at the same time he exorcised some of his demons by writing an autobiography, his life took another positive jump. He re-met Shirley Jones who co-starred with him in a 1956 European tour of *Oklahoma!*. They married that same year and performed together in *The Beggar's Opera* and later in a supper club tour. In 1959, the first of their three sons, Shaun was born, followed by Patrick (1962) and Ryan (1966). In 1970, debonair Jack won an Emmy for playing the defense counsel on TV's *"The Andersonville Trial."* He earned a Tony for being the dashing Hungarian fop, Mr. Kodaly in the musical *She Loves Me* (1963). He seemed to turn up everywhere—in magazine ads, on TV quiz shows, back on Broadway (with Carol Burnett in *Fade Out-Fade In*, 1964; with Shirley in *Maggie Flynn*, 1968), in movies: (*The Chapman Report*, 1962, *FBI Code 98*, 1964, *Bunny O'Hare*, 1971). On TV. he co-starred in the sitcom "*He & She*" (1967-68). In England, he and Shirley were paired for the TV series, "*Date with Shirley and Jack.*"

As their careers and lives increasingly diverged, he and Shirley parted in 1974 and their divorce was finalized in early 1975. (In 1977, she married actor-promoter Marty Ingels.) In the mid-Seventies, Jack's screen career took an upward turn: as the homosexual villain in Clint Eastwood's *The Eiger Sanction* (1975), as the aged John Barrymore in *W. C. Fields and Me* (1976). Also in 1976 he was on Broadway with Janet Leigh in the comedy-mystery *Murder Among Friends*, playing his typecast speciality—the arrogant ladies' man.

JEFF CHANDLER

Then on December 12, 1976, it all ended in a blaze of terror in his West Hollywood penthouse apartment at 1221 North Kings Road. As the arson squad later determined, Cassidy had hosted a party on Saturday night, December 11. Several cigarette butts were strewn over the floor. A fire was started by a still-lit cigarette left carelessly on or by a couch. Meanwhile, Cassidy had fallen asleep on the couch and when the flames burst out he was overwhelmed by the smoke and heat. The five-alarm inferno caused the evacuation of 100 tenants in the four-story building. Because his car was missing (later found to have been borrowed by a friend), it was not immediately known if the badly-charred body in the living room was that of Cassidy. It was hoped he had driven to Palm Springs as originally planned, and that perhaps, the victim was someone else. However, the corpse was later identified as Jack's through dental records and personal jewelry.

The finest tribute to Jack came from his ex-wife Shirley, "He was an extraordinary man with an uncanny sense of humor and a gifted talent. He was one of a kind and the world suffers a great loss that he was taken from it so soon." (Ironically, Jack left none of his $150,000 estate to Shirley Jones, Evelyn Ward, or David Cassidy. His will left everything to certain friends and relatives, as well as to the Actors Equity Fund and the Motion Picture Country House.) Jack's last movie, *The Private Files of J. Edgar Hoover*, in which he played writer Damon Runyon, went unreleased until 1978.

Jeff Chandler

[Ira Grossel]

December 15, 1918 - June 17, 1961

Ruggedly handsome, 6' 4" Jeff Chandler was only 42-years old when he died. The square-jawed hunk with prematurely gray, curly hair, was the picture of health until he suffered a slipped disc while making *Merrill's Mauraders* (1961), a World War II combat movie. Simple corrective surgery was performed at a Culver City, California hospital. The strapping patient should have been up and around in no time. However, due to medical misadventure, he died.

The future actor was born Ira Grossel in Brooklyn, where he attended

8

Erasmus Hall High School. Convinced he wanted a career in the creative arts, he took art courses and then enrolled at the Feagin School of Dramatic Art in New York City. He landed a job with a Long Island stock company, first as a stage hand and then as an actor. In 1941, he and a pal began a little theatre company in Elgin, Illinois. However, after Pearl Harbor brought the U.S. into World War II, he joined the Army, where he was stationed mostly in the Aleutians.

As of December 6, 1945, he was a civilian and headed towards Los Angeles. It was while doing a radio job that he was discovered by Dick Powell and given a small role in Powell's *Johnny O'Clock* (1947). By now he was known as Jeff Chandler and spent much of the next two years on radio: *"Mr. Dana," "Michael Shayne, Detective"* and as Eve Arden's love interest in *"Our Miss Brooks."* Universal Pictures cast him as an Israeli leader in *Sword in the Desert* (1949), and his masculine looks registered with moviegoers. He joined the studio's roster of contract young leading men, which included Tony Curtis and Rock Hudson.

With his high cheek-bones he was cast in the first of several Indian roles in *Broken Arrow* (1950), starring Jimmy Stewart, and Chandler was Oscar-nominated. As a Universal contract player, he careened through a stack of action picture: sometimes as an athlete (*Iron Man*, 1951), a swashbuckler (*Yankee Buccaneer*, 1952), or a serviceman (*Away All Boats*, 1956). Along the way, he developed a real screen magnetism, and played opposite several smoldering leading ladies: Jane Russell (*Foxfire*, 1955) Jeanne Crain (*The Tattered Dress*, 1958) and Susan Hayward (*Thunder in the Sun*, 1959).

Always ambitious, Jeff was constantly proving himself. Having shown he could play a range of roles on screen, he signed a recording contract in 1954 with Decca Records, doing several singles and an album. In May 1957, he appeared at the Riviera Hotel in Las Vegas as a singer. In addition, Chandler, who played the violin and wrote music, started his own music publishing company. Likewise, as many stars in the 1950s did, he formed his own production company to produce movies such as *Drango* (1957).

Jeff had married actress Marjorie Hoshelle in 1946 and they had two daughters (Jamie, Dana). The couple split in 1954 but reconciled. In late 1957 Jeff and aquatic movie star Esther Williams (herself recently divorced) became very good friends and together co-starred in *Raw Wind in Eden* (1958). They saved most of their passion for off camera and, in 1959, Marjorie Hoshelle sued Chandler for divorce. Ironically, by 1960 when the decree had become final, Jeff and Esther had drifted apart.

Chandler continued to turn out movies (*The Plunderers*, 1960, *Return to Peyton Place*, 1961). Then he went on location to the Philippines for *Merrill's Marauders* in early 1961. When he returned to Los Angeles, he underwent surgery on May 13 for the slipped disc. Following the uncomplicated operation, he suffered internal hemorrhages and infection. During an emergency follow-up operation that lasted 72 hours to repair a ruptured artery, he was given 55 pints of blood. He survived that and further surgery. However, another hemorrhage and more infection weakened him. He took a turn for the worse on Friday, June 16 and died the next day of a generalized blood infection further complicated by pneumonia. The needless tragedy was the talk of Hollywood.

After funeral services on June 19, 1961 at Temple Isiah in Los Angeles, his body was taken to Hillside Memorial Park for private internment. Among the pallbearers were Jeff's baseball pals, Hoby Landrith and Bill Rigney, as well as actor Tony Curtis. On behalf of their children, his ex-wife brought legal action against the medical center where Jeff was treated. Eventually, an out-of-court settlement was reached.

With Chandler's untimely passing, Hollywood had lost three major macho leading men in the course of a few short months: Clark Gable (November 16, 1960), Gary Cooper (May 13, 1961), and Jeff.

Linda Darnell

[Monetta Eloyse Darnell]

October 16, 1923 - April 10, 1965

If anyone ever had a strange premonition of her tragic future, it was Linda Darnell, the beautiful star of *Forever Amber* (1947). She had a life-long fear of fire. While shooting *Anna* and the *King of Siam* (1946), her role called for her to be burned at the stake. The scene terrified her, but it was required. While filming it, she was slightly injured. Later, she told the press, "Never again. Next time I prefer being stabbed or shot. At least that kind of dying is painless." Nineteen years later—in real life—she burned to death in a horrible fiery furnace.

Maggie Pearl Brown had grown up in Clifton, Tennessee, always dreaming of becoming an actress. Those plans were abandoned for the reality of marriage. She had two children by her first husband before they divorced. In 1915, the twenty-year-old

woman next married Dallas, Texas postal worker Roy Darnell and, in the next fourteen years, the couple had four children. Their second, Monetta Eloyse was born on October 16, 1923 (later studio press releases would push back her birth year to 1921 to make the teenager appear older). The frustrated Pearl soon fixated her show business dreams on Monetta. By age eleven, the pretty girl had physically matured enough to pass for much older and thus got department store modeling jobs. The future actress would remember, "I was going to be a movie star or Mom was going to bust in the attempt."

When her daughter was fourteen, a Twentieth Century-Fox talent scout passed through Dallas and Pearl badgered him with photos of Monetta. He brushed the woman off, but she followed him to Hollywood with Monetta in tow. The studio felt Monetta was too young and sent mother and daughter packing. Later, Pearl engineered Monetta's entry into a talent contest and soon they were back in Los Angeles. But RKO let the young girl sit out the option period, and it was back to Texas again.

Later on, Fox brought Pearl and Monetta to Hollywood and signed her to a $750 contract, renaming the starlet Linda Darnell. Linda radiated fresh beauty in *Elsa Maxwell's Hotel for Women* (1939) and was soon promoted by studio head Darryl F. Zanuck into star roles. As Hollywood's new "Cinderella Girl" she was teamed with matinee idol Tyrone Power in several features, including The *Mark of Zorro* (1940) and *Blood and Sand* (1941). To get away from her manipulative mother, Linda moved into her own apartment. But her independence was short-lived. Having long depended on the advice and kindness of veteran cinematographer Peverell Marley, she married him in April 1942 in Las Vegas. He was forty-one; she was nineteen.

Because Linda had played too many virginal heroines on screen, she was in a career rut. Thus Fox devised a fresh approach for the "new" Linda Darnell. As the smoldering vixen of *Summer Storm*, she made people take note anew. With her new speciality, she was cast as a temptress in the period thriller, *Hangover Square* (1945) in which she is strangled and her body burned. Soon she won the role of her career. When the studio shut down filming of *Forever Amber*—based on the racy best seller by Kathleen Windsor about Restoration England—Peggy Cummins was dropped from the lead and Linda was her replacement. Even in the diluted screen version, the blonde-dyed Linda was impressive as the sexy hussy. A scene in this spectacle called for Linda to be involved in the great London fire. The frightened actress-fearing the all too-real flames—had to be yanked onto the sound stage to perform.

When *Forever Amber* proved not to be a huge hit, Darnell's career stalled. Meanwhile she and Marley adopted a daughter nicknamed Lola. Her career took an upturn when she was cast opposite Rex Harrison in *Unfaithfully Yours* (1948) and then as the mercenary gal in *A Letter to Three Wives* (1948). In 1951 she and Marley divorced and the next year her Fox contract expired. She went to Italy for two movies and then was married to brewery president Philip Liebman for two years (1954-55). Linda, who was becoming a heavy drinker, tried picture-making again, but was forced to accept a Western. Her bid for Broadway stardom ended *Harbor Lights* (1956) closed after four performance. In March 1957 she married airline pilot Merle Robertson.

Her drinking problem made Linda—now approaching forty and no longer svelte—somewhat problematic on the set. After making *Zero Hour!* (1957), she didn't get another film offer until *Black Spurs* (1965) and that was a low-budget Western full of has-beens. In desperation, she did stage work, a nightclub act and TV. On November 23, 1963 she and Robertson divorced.

In March 1965, after touring in *Janus*, she visited her friend and former secretary, Jeanne Curtis, in Glenview, Illinois near Chicago. Early in the morning of April 9, Linda suggested to Jeanne and her sixteen-year-old daughter, Patricia, that they stay up and watch one of Linda's old pictures, *Star Dust* (1940). "Let's have some laughs," she urged. After the movie ended, about 2:30 a.m., the three went upstairs to bed.

About 3:30 a.m. a still-smoldering cigarette ignited on the downstairs sofa and soon the living room was aflame. The smoke and heat awoke the three women upstairs. Jeanne and Patricia managed to escape (Pat jumped from a second-floor window; Jeanne went out onto a bathroom window ledge where firemen later rescued her). However, Linda, afraid of jumping, had tried to make it down the stairs and out the front door where she was caught by the flames in the living room. A neighbor tried to smash through a downstairs window to rescue the screaming woman, but the flames were too intense. When firemen broke in, they found Darnell unconscious behind the sofa. She had second and third-degree burns over 80 percent of her upper body.

Darnell was taken to Skokie Valley Community Hospital where she underwent four hours of surgery. The prognosis was bad and later that day she was moved to Cook County Hospital's burn treatment center. A tracheotomy was performed to help her breathing. Darnell's sixteen- year-old daughter flew in from California to be at her dying mother's bedside. Linda was barely conscious during their half-hour together. However, in her distorted voice (from the tracheotomy), she kept insisting, "Who says I'm going to die? I'm not going to!" She then whispered, "I love you, baby. I love you." At 3:25 p.m., Darnell died.

Linda's body was cremated and a private service was held at the Glenview Community Church on April 11, with another memorial service conducted in Burbank, California on May 8. Darnell had wanted her ashes to be scattered over the ranch of friends who lived in New Mexico. That never happened and her remains were stored in the administration office of a Chicago cemetery for over a decade. In September 1975, when Linda's daughter was married and living with her family in New London, Pennsylvania, she arranged for Linda's ashes to be shipped to her husband's family plot at Union Hill Cemetery at nearby Kennett Square.

Linda Darnell, whose life was a perfect example of the shattered American dream, was finally at rest.

James Dean

February 6, 1931 - September 30, 1955

Few Hollywood performers have made such a charismatic impact on the world as did boyishly handsome, non-conformist James Dean. This impact is all the more impressive because he starred in only three movies during his brief, meteoric career. In both life and death, he became the symbolic rebel of his era, and amazingly, his reputation is still legendary to today's generation. Like a few chosen others—Elvis Presley and Marilyn Monroe—Dean remains as popular in death as he was in his short life. His icon refuses to fade!

He was born James Byron Dean on February 8, 1931 in Marion, Indiana, the son of Quaker dental technician Winton Dean and his Methodist mother, Mildred (Wilson) Dean. When he was nine his mother died, and he went to live with his aunt, Hortense Wilson, and her husband Marcus in nearby Fairmount. In high school (class of '49), his drama teacher (Adeline Nall) coaxed him into entering a public speaking contest, and he ended up winning the state's trophy. His father urged him to study law, and Jimmy enrolled first at Santa Monica City College and then transferred to UCLA where he majored in drama before quitting. His roommate, young actor William Bast, got him an extra's job in a TV commercial and then work as a NBC network page. Later, Dean was a movie extra in 1951 movies like *Fixed Bayonets!* and *Sailor Beware* and in the 1952 release, *Has Anybody Seen My Gal?*

At the suggestion of actor James Whitmore, Dean moved to New York in the fall of 1951 to find himself. Always a loner, he became more so in Manhattan. However, he knew how to seize on opportunities and, through friends, auditioned for *See the Jaguar* (1952) in which he made his Broadway debut. Between that flop and his next Broadway assignment, *The Immoralist* (1954)—in which he was the corrupt Arab houseboy—he did a great deal of live TV. For *The Immoralist*, he received the Theatre World Award as "Most Promising Newcomer" of the year.

While on the East Coast, Dean studied at the Actors Studio where director Elia Kazan hired him for his upcoming movie, *East of Eden* (1955). As Raymond Massey's tormented son, Jimmy struck a cord with teenage filmgoers everywhere and immediately became their new hero. While shooting *Eden*, for which he was Oscar-nominated, Jimmy fell in love with young Italian import, Pier Angeli, then a rising MGM star. She was as moody and mercurial as he. She broke off their intense engagement and, in November 1954, when she married singer Vic Damone, Jimmy sat brooding in his car across the street from the church. Thereafter, the reportedly bisexual Dean dated a host of movie starlets and became even more obsessive about acting ("Acting is the most logical way for people's neuroses to express themselves" he said). He was also an avid gun collector, motorcyclist, and liked to snap photographs with his camera, especially of himself.

Nicholas Ray, who directed Dean and Natalie Wood in the juvenile delinquency study, *Rebel without a Cause* (1955), said of the fair-haired, brooding Dean who had a trade-mark mumble: "My feelings were that he could have surpassed any actor alive." With *Rebel*, Jimmy became a major Hollywood star. He was the new voice for the teenage generation, who had earlier worshipped Marlon "The Wild One" Brando. Director George Stevens hired Dean for the big-budgeted Texas epic, *Giant* (1956), in which Jimmy's character of Jed Rink ages from the impoverished farm hand to the mega-millionaire middle-age oilman.

Always a daredevil, Dean's pride and joy was his silver Porsche Spyder (which he nicknamed "Little Bastard"). A week after completing

JAMES DEAN

Giant he was out for a spin—driving at 86 MPH—when at 5:59 p.m. on September 30, 1955, his car collided with another vehicle at the intersection of routes 41 and 466 near Paso Robles, California. His passenger, Porsche factory mechanic Rolf Weutherich, suffered a broken leg and head injuries and the driver (David Turnupseed) of the other car was only injured slightly. In the crash, Dean's head was nearly severed from his body. Later, a policeman reported that a few hours earlier, in Bakersfield, he had issued a speeding ticket to the reckless Dean and cautioned him to slow down. Dean had been heading to a sports car rally at Salinas. Reputedly, Jimmy Dean's last words to Rolf Weutherich before the fatal car crash were, "He's got to see us."

Dean was buried on October 8, 1955 at Park Cemetery in Fairmount, Indiana. (The original tombstone, as well as a later bust of Dean on a nearby pillar were stolen and the grave marker had to be replaced.) His death touched off a wave of sorrow from fans, unequalled since Rudolph Valentino died decades earlier. Both *Rebel without a Cause* and *Giant* were released posthumously and for the latter picture Jimmy was again Oscar-nominated.

For years, rumors circulated that Dean had not died in the crash, but had been so badly disfigured that he remained in hiding. He became a cult figure whose popularity seems undiminished by the passing years. There are many James Dean fan clubs worldwide; admirers and tourists make pilgrimages to his hometown and cemetery on the anniversary of his death for the three-day annual celebration sponsored by Fairmount. There is a finely craft bust Dean at the north side of Griffith Observatory in Los Angeles where part of *Rebel* was shot. At Princeton University there is a life mask of the late actor in a collection which features likenesses of Beethoven, Thackery, Keats and other creative giants. Over the years, there has been a steady flow of movie documentaries released and biographies published eulogizing the enigmatic, dead idol.

On one occasion, Ann Doran, who had played Dean's mother in *Rebel without a Cause*, was asked about the late star. She observed, "He was kind of in limbo. He had great doubts about himself and where he was going. He was that lost." It was this telltale vulnerability, plus his extraordinary ability to communicate with his audience, that has made Dean such an enduring pop figure.

Eric Fleming

1925 - September 28, 1966

Sometimes, like a gambler, an actor has to know when to quit. Eric Fleming didn't and, by tempting fate, he died.

He was born in Santa Paula, California. From an early age, he wanted to be in show business. He gravitated to Manhattan, looking for a stage career. However, he first made his mark by starring in the title role of "*Major Dell Conway of the Flying Tigers*," a low-budget adventure series telecast live by the Dumont Network. After six weeks on the air in the spring of 1951, the show disappeared for two months. When it returned Ed Peck had replaced Fleming in the key role of the American operative. Eric reappeared on series TV in the network soap opera "*Golden Windows*" (1954-55). Next, he moved back to the West Coast, where the tall, rugged Fleming got work in *Conquest of Space* (1955) and then acted in several schlock features: *Queen of Outer Space* (1958), *Curse of the Undead* (1959), etc.

As CBS-TV's answer to the highly-successful rival network series "*Wagon Train*," the studio developed "*Rawhide*." Eric starred as cattle trail boss Gil Favor, with Clint Eastwood as his right-hand man, Rowdy Yates. The hour-long show premiered on January 9, 1959 and became a big hit. After seven years on the program, Fleming tired of the role and decided to retire to a ranch in Hawaii he had purchased with his earnings. He quit the program after the 1964-65 season, with Eastwood taking over as trail boss.

Rather than following through with his relocation plans, Eric chose to remain in Los Angeles for a movie role (Doris Day's *The Glass Bottom Boat*,

1966). Then he was a guest on two episodes of "*Bonanza.*" Next, ABC-TV persuaded him to co-star with Anne Heywood in a projected adventure series, "*High Jungle.*" He joined the cast members on location in Peru where they were filming scenes in the headwaters of the Amazon River. On September 28, 1968 the cast and crew were in a remote jungle region, 300 miles northeast of Lima. Fleming and Peruvian actor, Nico Minardos, were being filmed in a canoe on the Haullaga River when the craft suddenly overturned. Minardos managed to swim to safety, but Fleming was swept off by the strong current. The remains of his body—there were Piranha fish in the area—were not found until October 3.

If only he had gone to Hawaii as he intended originally.

Robert Francis

February 26, 1930—July 31, 1955

Screen World voted him one of 1954's most promising actors. He was under contract to Columbia Pictures and had a bright future. Then in a matter of minutes, it was all over. The single-engine, four-seat private plane, which he was piloting, took off from an airstrip in Burbank, California and then crashed and exploded. At age twenty-five, handsome Robert Francis was gone.

He had a rare distinction for movie actors—he was a native Californian. He was born in Glendale and attended local schools. One day, while soaking up the sun at a Santa Monica beach, he was spotted by a talent agent who suggested he take drama lessons and then try for a movie career. Francis followed the good advice and later was auditioned and signed for an important role in Co-lumbia's *The Caine Mutiny* (1954). In a cast of top-flight professionals (Humphrey Bogart, Fred Mac-Murray, Van Johnson, Jose Ferrer), tall, clean-cut Robert gained notice. *Variety* endorsed, "Making a splendid impression in his major screen bow is Robert Francis, playing the young Ensign Willie Keith to perfection."

May Wynn had played Francis's love interest in *The Caine Mutiny* and Columbia promoted them as a new young screen team, casting them together again in *They Rode West* (1954). Robert acquitted himself well in the Korean War prisoner-of-war melodrama *The Bamboo Prison* (1955) and was next third-cast in John Ford's tribute to West Point, *The Long Gray Line* (1955), starring Tyrone Power and Maureen O'Hara.

Robert had long been a plane enthusiast and was a licensed pilot. On Sunday, July 31, 1955 he borrowed the plane of actor pal Joe Kirkwood to go for a spin. Accompanying him were 24-year-old bit film actress, Ann Russell, and George Meyers, a mechanic. The small plane took off from the runaway at the Lockheed Air Terminal in Burbank. Then the craft experienced engine failure and nose-dived. It crashed into an unused parking lot and burned. All three passengers perished.

Robert was buried at Forest Lawn Memorial Parks in his home town of Glendale. Thereafter, the movie studios began re-enforcing a standard clause in actors' contracts—i.e., that they not engage in hazardous hobbies. Unfortunately, this safety precaution came too late to help young Robert Francis.

Janet Gaynor

[Laura Gainor]

October 6, 1906 - September 14, 1984

Sometime or another, most of us have had qualms about riding in a taxi. For Janet Gaynor, the winner of the first Best Actress Academy Award, being a passenger in a San Francisco cab in September 1984 was a fatal decision.

She was born Laura Gainor in Philadelphia. When she was eight, her mother divorced and Laura, with her slightly older sister Helen, moved with her to Chicago. When Mrs. Gainor remarried, the family relocated again—first to Florida and then to San Francisco. In 1923, Laura graduated from high school. The next year, the family visited Los Angeles where the Gainor sisters found work as movie extras in comedy shorts at Hal Roach Studios and elsewhere.

Sweet-faced Laura—now known as Janet Gaynor—got her first important film assignment when she was cast in *The Johnstown Flood* (1926) at Fox. Studio production chief, Winfield Sheehan, took a particular liking to Janet and hired her at $100 a week. It was in *Sunrise* (1927), with George O'Brien, that petite Janet gained important recognition. She was rewarded with a studio raise to $300 weekly and, as the Parisian waif, was cast opposite Charles Farrell for the first time in *Seventh Heaven* (1927). It was for a combination of *Sunrise*, *Seventh Heaven* and *Street Angel* (1928—also with Farrell) that she was named best actress at the first Academy Award ceremony on May 16, 1929.

Despite a limited vocal range and a bit of a twang to her voice, five-foot high Janet was a success in her first all-talkie movie, *Sunny Side Up* (1929). That same year she married San Francisco attorney Lydell Peck. Years later, she would admit that she and co-star Farrell were off-screen lovers and that "Charlie pressed me to marry him, but we had too many differences." In 1930 she went on strike against the bland, sentimental roles she was getting and, in a huff, sailed with her mother for Hawaii. When she returned to the lot, she was back making more insipid pictures with Charles Farrell: *Merely Mary Ann* (1931) and *Delicious* (1931). Nevertheless, she remained big box-office. By 1934, she and Farrell made their twelfth and final movie together, *Change of Heart*. Also that year, her disastrous marriage to Peck

JANET GAYNOR

ended in divorce. When the studio merged with Twentieth Century Pictures in the mid-Thirties, Darryl F. Zanuck became head of the combined studio. He pushed Janet aside in favor of such younger actresses as Loretta Young and the studio's new bread-winner, the tyke star, Shirley Temple.

Gaynor thought of retiring, but instead went under contract to David O. Selznick who cast her as movie-struck farm girl Esther Blodgett in *A Star Is Born* (1937). The picture was a major hit and cute-as-a-button Gaynor was Oscar-nominated again. After making *The Young in Heart* (1938), she retired to marry (August 14, 1939) famed movie costume designer, Gilbert Adrian. Their son (Robin) was born in 1940. She made a few returns to acting on radio and TV in the early 1950s. Then she and Adrian moved to Brazil near Annapolis, to a 200-acre ranch. ("It doesn't have a modern kitchen. But we do have our own little jungle," Janet quipped). Her neighbor in Brazil was her long-time good friend Mary Martin (and her husband). In 1957, with much hoopla, Janet returned to her old studio (Zanuck was away in Europe) to play Pat Boone's mother in *Bernardine*. By now, she and Adrian had relocated to the States where he died of a stroke in September, 1959. At the time, she was rehearsing a Broadway-bound play, *The Midnight Sun* (which never reached New York). In December of 1964, 58-year old Janet married stage producer Paul Gregory, age forty-three and retired to Palm Springs. In 1980, fidgety for the limelight again, she tried Broadway in *Harold and Maude*, but the show flopped.

On September 5, 1982, Janet (long since out of the limelight), her husband, Mary Martin and agent Ben Washer were riding in a San Fran-cisco taxi, heading to a Chinese restaurant. A van ran through a red light and crashed into their cab. Washer was killed, while Martin was critically injured (but left the hospital after 10 days) and Gregory sustained far less serious injuries. As for Janet, she suffered a broken pelvis and collarbone, eleven broken ribs, and assorted internal injuries. She underwent two major operations at San Francisco General Hospital before being released in January 1983. She convalesced at her Palm Springs home and even managed a few public appearances. She was hospitalized again in August 1984. Then on September 14, 1984, she died at Desert Hospital in Palm Springs. The cause of death was listed as pneumonia, although her private physician stated that the actress "never fully recovered from the terrible automobile accident of approximately two years ago. There were repeated complications which compounded her chronic illness." She was buried at Hollywood Memorial Park, a few rows from the more elaborate resting spot of director Cecil B. DeMille. Janet's black-and-white marker reads: "Janet Gaynor Gregory."

Jon-Erik Hexum

November 5, 1957 - October 18, 1984

In the entertainment industry, it is not just women who must cope with being "just another pretty face." A lot of actors are locked into a rigid mold because of their exceptional good looks. They begin to lose their identities because people won't see beyond their marketable exteriors. One such victim was Jon-Erik Hexum. Jon-Erik was born in Tenafly, New Jersey in 1957, the second son of Norwegian immigrants, Thor (a chef) and Gretha Hexum. When he was seven, his parents divorced, and two years later, the father left the state. His mother, Greta, worked as a secretary by day and a waitress at night to support her children: Jon-Erik and Gunnar. Even as a youngster, Jon-Erik was stage-struck and commuted to New York for dance and music lessons. He could play the piano, organ and violin and, in the church band, he was the drum major. After attending Case Western Reverve in Ohio, he transferred to Michigan State University. There, Hexum majored in biomedical engineering, worked as an off-campus disc jockey (known as "Yukon Jack") and played an assortments of sports, including football. His sports activities led to an unwanted reunion with his dad. He had not seen his father since he was nine, but then Thor saw his son on a televised gridiron game and got in touch. Jon-Erik told him, "You blew it, guy. Go to hell."

After graduation, Jon-Erik returned to the East Coast, determined on a show business career. He worked nighttimes in restaurants so he could audition during the days. The only acting role he mustered was in an Auburn, New York stock version of *The Unsinkable Molly Brown*. One of Hexum's non-acting jobs was cleaning venetian blinds. One of his clients proved to be a friend of the manager of actor John Travolta. The manager thought 6'1", 190-pound Jon-Erik had show business potential and helped to launch his acting career. Soon the tall hunk modeled for two beef cake calendars. With the proceeds, he relocated to Los Angeles, where he worked for a time as a busboy in a Venice restaurant and shared a tiny hole-in-the wall room with two co-workers. However, within a short time of arriving, he was spotted and cast in *"Voyagers"* (1982-83) a science fiction adventure series which was cancelled after a season on network TV.

Although "established" in the industry, Hexum maintained a frugal lifestyle, living modestly in an unfurnished house in a non-exclusive section of Burbank and driving an old '54 Chevy. His romance with businessperson Debbie Davis ended and he later dated TV actress Emma Samms. In between, he was momentarily absorbed by star Joan Collins who cast him as her leading man in the TV movie *The Making of a Male Model* (1983). Next, he was hired as Pat Trammel, the cancer-ridden friend of Alabama football coach Paul "Bear" Bryant in the theatrical feature, *Bear* (1984). Hexum was pleased to be cast against type. "That's the direction I'd like to go in."

But it was back to form in *"Cover Up,"* a CBS-TV detective-spy series that premiered on September 22, 1984. He played fashion photographer Mac Harper, a former Green Beret and a weapons expert. A few weeks into the action series being filmed at Twentieth Century-Fox, Hexum was on the set one Friday (October 12), playing around with a prop .44 Magnum pistol which he had just loaded with a blank. About 5:15 p.m. he put the gun to his right temple, just like in a game of Russian roulette. As he pulled the trigger, he smiled and reportedly said, "Let's see if I got one for me." He was apparently unaware that, at close range, a blank (in reality a minimal charge packed with cotton) can cause great damage. The force of the discharge drove a quarter-sized piece of his skull far into his brain. The unconscious actor was rushed by studio station wagon to Beverly Hills Medical Center where he remained in critical condition.

Six days later, on the evening of October 18, still in a coma, he was declared brain-dead. On Friday morning, with his mother's approval, he was flown to San Francisco—still on a life-support system—where his heart was implanted into the body of a dying, 36- year-old Las Vegas businessman. The actor's kidneys and corneas were also removed and placed in organ transplant banks. Later, the body was flown back to Los Angeles for the coroner's office post-mortem.

Hexum's funeral was private and what followed was anti-climatic. The highly publicized stunt which caused Hexum's death was ruled "accidental," although several people who knew the actor said he had become more distant, brooding and reckless in the weeks before the tragedy. The episode led to an industry safety committee investigation and the establishment of new guidelines. As for the TV series, John-Erik's last episode was aired on November 3, 1984. The studio promoted a highly publicized search for his replacement, which proved to be another muscular hunk—Australian Antony Hamilton. Nevertheless, "Cover Up" faded from the air within another few months.

Leslie Howard

[Leslie Stainer]

April 3, 1893 - June 1, 1943

Moviegoers will forever remember Leslie Howard as Ashley Wilkes, Scarlet O'Hara's noble but weak love interest in Gone with the Wind (1939). That year, at the height of his movie career, he left Hollywood. The patriotic Howard flew to his native England which was already engaged in World War II. In 1943, he was aboard a civilian aircraft returning from Lisbon to London when the plane was shot down by the Germans over the Bay of Biscay. All aboard died. For years, speculations has run high that, at the time, Howard was involved in a secret government spying mission.

Born Leslie Stainer in 1893, he was one of five children of a Jewish, London-based stockbroker. Leslie was a bank clerk before World War I broke out, although he already had an interest in show business and had made a short subject in 1914. Mustered out of the service in 1918, he suffered from shell shock and took therapeutic acting lessons. He made his West End stage debut that year and, two years later, was on Broadway in *Just Suppose*. During the Twenties, he crossed the Atlantic back and forth in assorted stage vehicles. Meanwhile, he and his wife Ruth Martin, whom he had married in 1916 while on military leave, had two children: Ronald (born: 1918) and Leslie Ruth (born: 1924). Ironically, at home Howard was referred to as "that American actor," while in the U.S. he was known as the romantic British leading man.

His first American feature was re-creating his stage success in *Outward Bound* (1930). Back in England he had the lead as the dashing *The Scarlet Pimpernel* (1934) and, in 1936, he and Norma Shearer were mature young lovers in MGM's elaborate *Romeo and Juliet*. He had been Oscar-nominated for *Berkeley Square* (1933) and was nominated once more for the British-made *Pygmalion* (1938) which he co-directed. After co-producing *Intermezzo* (1939), in which he starred opposite Ingrid Bergman, he returned to war-torn England. There he produced several nationalistic features, including *Pimpernel Smith* (1941), as well as participating in fervent war broadcasts

THE HOLLYWOOD DEATH BOOK

and writing pro-war newspaper articles.

In the spring of 1943, Howard had gone to Spain and Portugal, ostensibly on a goodwill tour to lecture on filmmaking at the request of the British Council. On the morning of Tuesday, June 1, 1943, Howard and twelve other passengers boarded civilian flight #777 at the Portela airport outside of Lisbon. All four crew members of the DC-3 were Dutch. The craft took off about 9:30 a.m.—its destination was Whitechurch airport near Bristol, England. About an hour later it was attacked by six German fighter planes. At this point, its radio contact broke off. As information was later pieced together: after the DC-3 was hit, four men jumped from the plane. Only one of their parachutes opened. However, that caught fire and that man plummeted downward too. By the time the plane hit the water, it was engulfed in flames.

No trace of the plane or its victims was ever found. Although the British and German governments have both always remained silent about the mishap, there have been several theories. To begin with, at the time, Portugal was neutral and both the Allies and Axis forces used Lisbon as a center of espionage intrigue. For three years, one flight a day had gone from Portugal to England and another in the reverse direction. The Germans had never attacked these flights till now.

Prior to the June 1 mishap, Howard had arrived in Lisbon and gone by train to Madrid. There the Nazis used a beautiful spy, Baroness Miranda, to intercept the actor at the Spanish hotel where he was headquartered. When he later left Madrid for Lisbon, the Baroness was at the train station to bid him goodbye. Upon reaching Lisbon, in which he re-

mained for a few days, he encountered another female German spy whom he ignored.

One popular conjecture is that the Germans were retaliating against Howard because he was Jewish, a possible enemy agent and had done all that war-time anti-German propaganda work. Another premise holds that the Nazis thought England's prime minister, Winston Churchill, was aboard the plane. At the time, Churchill was actually in Algiers, but rumor had it that he was in Lisbon and soon to depart for London. Howard's traveling companion/financial advisor, Alfred Chenhalls, was on the trek and he was a look-a-like for the older, shorter, and flabbier British statesman. German agents may have mistaken Chenhalls for Churchill and thus ordered the deadly air attack.

The Allies conducted an air search for the missing plane, but it was called off on June 2, due to bad weather.

England and the world greatly mourned the loss of Howard. Like Carole Lombard who died in a 1942 Nevada plane crash while returning from a war bond selling tour, Leslie had given his life for his country in time of war.

Buck Jones

[Charles Frederick Gebhardt]
December 4, 1889 - November 30, 1942

His tragic finale read like a Hollywood movie script. Buck Jones, veteran cowboy star, perished in Boston's Cocoanut Grove Club fire of 1942 which killed 491 people. He had gone back into the conflagration three times to save trapped victims before he himself was felled.

He was born in Vincennes, Indiana in 1889 and was educated at Indianapolis public schools. Once on his own, he traveled to Montana where he became a cowhand. Always seeking adventure, he joined the U.S. Cavalary and served in the Philippines. Thereafter, he was hired by the Miller Brothers 101 Ranch Wild West Show and made his first movie with the outfit in 1913. In 1915, he married show rider Odelle Osborne—in the center ring during a circus performance—and they would have a daughter, Maxine. During World War I, he served with the U.S. Army's First Air Squadron in France. After the Armistice, he remained in Europe performing as a trick rider with several traveling shows. One of his performances brought him to the attention of film mogul William Fox who signed him to appear in Hollywood films. The new recruit—now known as Buck Jones—became the backup to the lot's top cowboy star, Tom Mix, for whom he once had doubled. Sometimes, in his Fox films, Buck put aside cowboy outfits to appear in non-Westerns, usually as the good-natured rube.

When his Fox contract ended in 1928, he produced his own feature, *The Big Hop* which flopped, as did a personal appearance tour about the same time. He made no movies in 1929—the year talkies blossomed in Hollywood. By 1930, Jones was working at Columbia Pictures, at a reduced salary. Surprising everyone, his new batch of Westerns proved a hit and by 1934 he was a top star again. He moved over to Universal that year, where he produced and starred in cowboy features as well as serials. When Universal wanted Buck to increase the number of films he made yearly, he rebelled. He returned to Columbia in late 1937. That same year he moved into his

new Spanish- style estate at Van Nuys in the San Fernando Valley. He had spent $110,000 to build the elaborate house with its accompanying stables and corral. At the time he was driving a $21,000 Duesenberg roadster, complete with gold-plated door handles and dashboard.

By the end of the Thirties, Buck was free-lancing again. He played a boxer in Paramount's quickie, *Unmarried* (1939), and was a dishonest (!) sheriff in Republic's *Wagons Westward* (1940). It was also that year that Buck's daughter married young actor Noah Beery, Jr. By now, Jones and Tom Mix had buried their old professional feud. In fact, Mix was a guest at Jones' home a day before he was killed in an auto crash on October 12, 1940.

In 1941, veteran producer Scott Dunlap teamed Buck with Tim McCoy and Raymond Hatton for the Rough Riders cowboy series at Monogram Pictures. *Arizona Bound* (1941) was the first and *Riders of the West* (1942) was the last featuring all three actors, as McCoy went on active duty in World War II. Jones and Hatton were then teamed with Rex Bell for *Dawn on the Great Divide* (1942). Buck was proud of the fact that he remained "an old-time cowboy, the sort the kids used to want to grow up to be like." (He disliked the new breed of singing cowboys.)

Having completed his *Rough Rider* pictures, Buck went on a war bond-selling trip and promoting Navy recruitment. His stop-over in Boston was the end of his ten-city tour. On the night of November 28, he was the guest of honor at a testimonial dinner given by area theater owners at the Cocoanut Grove Club. A fire broke out and due to inflammable decorations, the overcrowding, the lack of revolving doors, and general panic, the scene became a horrible disaster. Jones proved himself heroic in his several return trips into the fire, rescuing several panicked customers. On his third rush inside, he was trapped. He was taken to Massachusetts General Hospital where the doctors determined that he could not survive because of third and second degree burns on his face and neck, as well as the repercussions from burned lungs and smoke inhalaton. Two days later, Buck passed away. At the time of his death, his wife was en route to his bedside.

Buck Jones died like the cowboy hero he played on screen: quietly and bravely.

Grace Kelly

November 12, 1929 - September 14, 1982

GRACE
KELLY

Best Wishes Grace Kelly

The world adores fairy tale stories of beautiful commoners (even wealthy ones) who marry a sophisticated Prince and live happily ever after. In the case of Princess Grace of Monaco—better known as movie actress Grace Kelly—she made a sudden, tragic exit from her lofty Continental lifestyle. Thereafter, all the world learned that not only was her royal life imperfect, but that her Hollywood years were anything but staid.

Born in Philadelphia in 1929, she was the third of four children of construction contractor John Brendan Kelly and his wife, Margaret (Majer) Kelly, a former model. Grace's relatives included Uncle George Kelly, the Pulitzer Prize-winning playwright and Walter C. Kelly, a famous vaudevillian (who would die in 1939 after being hit by a truck in Hollywood). As a child, Grace was quite shy and was always competing with her older sister (Margaret) and brother (John, Jr.) for her father's attention. However, nothing she could do then (or even later in life) ever really impressed him. She attended a nearby convent school until the age of fourteen and then went to Stevens Academy in Chestnut Hill, Pennsylvania. One of her teachers there would recall: "she really wasn't interested in scholastic achievement—she gave priority to drama and boys."

Instead of attending college, the self-willed Grace chose a trip to Europe and then an enrollment at the American Academy of Dramatic Arts in New York City. Her disapproving parents agreed to pay for one year's tuition only. To earn her next year's fees, she became a fashion model, sometimes being selected as a cover girl. She also had an affair with a 27-year-old Academy instructor. Her parents disapproved of the relationship more because the man was

Jewish than because he was married (although separated from his wife).

With her patrician good looks and her family's show business connections, Grace had an edge over most other young aspiring actresses. She did summer stock at Bucks County Playhouse, made her Broadway debut as Raymond Massey's daughter in *The Father* (1949), and became a very active player in the blossoming TV industry then based in New York City.

Director Henry Hathaway chose Grace to join the ensemble cast of *Fourteen Hours* (1951), mostly shot in Manhattan. The studio (Twentieth Century-Fox) offered her a contract, but she rejected it. Instead, she chose to play the Quaker wife of an ex-marshal (Gary Cooper) in *High Noon* (1952). The movie, with its popular theme song, became a hit. Off camera, Grace and Cooper (older than her by 28 years) began an affair. While their relationship was short-lived, it set the tempo for subsequent liaisons with her older co-stars. She returned to Broadway briefly and then was hired by John Ford to join Clark Gable and Ava Gardner in *Mogambo* (1953). During the African location filming, Kelly and Gable became quite an item when they went on an off-screen safari together. Back in Hollywood, it was "the King" who consoled a disappointed Grace when her Best Supporting Actress nomination failed to produce an Oscar. By now, she was a MGM contract star being loaned out profitably to other studios.

During the shooting of *Dial M for Murder* (1954) it was not her director (Alfred Hitchcock—who had a penchant for beautiful, icy blondes) with whom she tangled romantically, but her 49-year-old co-star, Ray Milland. The actor left his wife to show he meant to marry Grace, but later re-

considered. Hitchcock borrowed Grace again for *Rear Window* (1954). Meanwhile, the actress had switched her affections from Milland to fashion designer Oleg Cassini and then to French actor Jean-Pierre Aumont. Grace's outspoken father was aghast. During the making of *The Bridges at Toko-Ri* (1954) Grace and William Holden became more than good friends. Next cast in *The Country Girl* (1954), Kelly's attention wavered from Holden to his co-star, Bing Crosby. However, she was not in love with the crooner and refused his marriage offer. For her on-camera dramatics, Grace won an Academy Award.

Having co-starred with Cary Grant in *To Catch a Thief* (1955) and while waiting to film MGM's *The Swan* (1956), Grace attended the Cannes Film Festival in May 1955. It was Olivia de Havilland's husband, Pierre Galante, a Paris-Match magazine editor, who engineered the meeting between Kelly and the 31-year old Prince Rainier III of Monaco. After being introduced to the movie star, the royal and very eligible bachelor informed his palace chaplain, "I've met somebody. I think she is the one." That December, Rainier came to Philadelphia to ask for her hand in marriage. The engagement was announced on January 5, 1956. (Not publicized were conditions to the marriage: i.e., Grace passing a fertility test to prove she could bear future heirs to the throne and a $2 million dowry.) Four months later, on April 18, 1956 they were married in a civil service. However, on the next day, they were united in a Catholic ceremony covered by 1,600 reporters as "the" social event of the decade.

Her royal marriage marked the official end of Grace's Hollywood years. It also began her motherhood period: Princess Caroline (born: 1957), Prince Albert (born: 1958) and Princess Stephanie (born: 1965). During her royal reign, Grace continually missed moviemaking. In 1962 she accepted the lead in Alfred Hitchcock's *Marnie*, but when the picture was made (1964), it was Tippi Hedren who played the heroine as the subjects of Monaco objected vehemently to Princess Grace making a film. In 1974, she appeared at a New York City tribute to Alfred Hitchcock and, in 1976, she joined the board of directors of Twentieth Century-Fox. She almost accepted a lead in the studio's *The Turning Point* (1976), but Rainier said no. The next year, she provided the narration for *The Children of Theatre Street*, a documentary about the Kirov School of Ballet in Russia.

When not coping with her frisky family—especially Princess Caroline—Grace worried about growing old, gaining weight (which she did—partially from drinking too much), rumors of Rainier's affairs, and her aborted film career. She did poetry readings around the world and starred in a documentary *Rearranged* (1979). By 1982, she hoped it was now time that she would be permitted to make a real feature film again.

On September 13, 1982, Grace had been staying at Roc Agel, the alternate family home a few miles from the royal palace. She had an appointment with her Monaco couturier, before going to Paris that night with Stephanie. After loading her Rover 3500 with dresses to be altered and luggage, she told her chauffeur there was no room for him in the car, and that she would, instead, drive. With Stephanie in the passenger seat, Grace set out at 9:30 a.m. A half-hour later, as the brown car reached a dangerous curve on the snaking Moyenne Corniche, it crashed past the barrier and down the 120-foot hillside. When local residents reached the accident scene, a conscious but injured Stephanie had managed to get out of the car and was yelling, "Help my mother! My mother is in there! Get her out!" The unconscious Princess Grace was removed by smashing the car's rear window. She and Stephanie were taken by ambulances to Princess Grace Hospital. After immediate surgery to clear Grace's lungs and halt internal bleeding, a CAT scan revealed that Grace had suffered a stroke prior to the accident. (Her injuries included multiple fractures of the collarbone, thigh and ribs.) It was concluded that even if she should recover, she would be a helpless invalid. The royal palace did it best to downplay the seriousness of Grace's injuries (which later led to speculations that the official explanation for the accident was fabricated).

About 10:30 p.m. on September 14, 1982, Grace died. She lay in state in her open coffin until September 17 when an elaborate funeral service was conducted at the same cathedral where she had married twenty-six years before. The Princess was buried in the Grimaldi's family vault in the church on September 21. The white marble slab is inscribed: "Grace Patricia, wife of Prince Rainier III, died the year of our Lord, 1982."

It was not the "happily ever after" finale that everyone expected for shrewd, self-sufficient Grace Kelly.

Percy Kilbride

July 16, 1888 - December 11, 1984

Tall, twangy and tight-lipped Percy Kilbride made an indelible mark as the bumpkin other half of feudin', fussin' and a-fightin' Ma Kettle (Marjorie Main) in a popular series of low brow barn yard comedies (1947-55). He spent most of his life behind the footlights, never realizing that a simple walk across a Hollywood street could and would end his life.

He was born in San Francisco in 1888 and as a teenager got employment as a callboy at the local Central Theatre. This job led to his first stage work—as a fop in *A Tale of Two Cities*—and from then on he was hooked on acting.

During World War I, Percy served in the Army (Company B, 317th Infantry, 80th Division) and then returned to stage work. He spent many years with stock companies in Albany, Boston, Philadelphia, Syracuse, and other cities, usually cast as a character actor or light comedian. The hawk-nosed actor with the squinty eyes made his screen debut in Carole Lombard's *White Woman* (1933) and did not make another picture until *Soak the Rich* (1936), which was filmed on the East Coast. He finally reached Broadway in *Those We Love* (1938).

Percy was brought back to Hollywood for a comedy relief role in Jack Benny's *George Washington Slept Here* (1942)—which he had done on Broadway— and decided to stay on the West Coast. It was in the comedy *The Egg and I* (1947) that Kilbride and Marjorie Main first played Pa and Ma Kettle who raise a flock of children on their ramshackled farm. The two supporting characters were so well received that Universal gave them their own showcasing series, which began with *Ma and Pa Kettle* (1949). Each entry was shot on the back lot and only cost $200,000-$400,000. However, each outing grossed about $3 million. After *Ma and Pa Kettle at Waikiki* (1955), 67-

year old Percy retired, while the series continued on for two more episodes. Parker Fennelly appeared in the final entry, *The Kettles on Old MacDonald's Farm* (1957).

In 1964, Percy was living in a Hollywood apartment at 6650 Franklin Avenue (although he still listed the Lambs Club in Manhattan as his permanent residence). Always well-groomed in private life, fans would rarely recognize him as he strolled around Hollywood. One evening while out walking with actor friend Ralf Belmont, they were crossing the intersection of Yucca and Cherokee near his Los Angeles home. A car hit them. Belmont was killed, but Kilbride survived. He underwent brain surgery and was convalescing in Hollywood when he finally succumbed on December 11, 1964. His body was taken to San Francisco where he was buried at the nearby San Bruno/Golden Gate National (Military) Cemetery because of his World War I service. A life-long bachelor, Kilbride left no survivors.

Ernie Kovacs

January 23, 1919 - January 12, 1962

Talented, wacky Ernie Kovacs—whose array of comedy characters included lisping poet Percy Dovetonsils—once said, "I like to be onstage because nobody can bother me there. lawyers, process servers, insurance salesmen—anyone." While he would make several movies, it was on TV that the burly Kovacs demonstrated best his rich and innovative comedy, most of which he wrote himself. As one associate described his cocky TV sketches, "Ernie was the master of the switch. He set up a picture that you felt totally comfortable with, and he took care in setting it up with great authenticity..... And then he'd switch it."

He was born in Trenton, New Jersey in 1919, the second son of Hungarian immigrants. His father was a tavern-keeper. After high school, he attended the American Academy of Dramatic Arts in New York City. He organized an acting troupe, the Contemporary Players, in Trenton. When that failed, he moved on to WTTM, a local radio station, where he remained for nine years in various capacities, ranging from disc jockey to sportscaster. Meanwhile, in 1945 he married dancer Bette Wilcox. They became the parents of Bette Lee (born: 1947) and Kippie (born: 1949). During 1949, the marriage ended when Bette left him. During subsequent years, the Kovacs battled over custody of their offspring, and the children finally settled in with Ernie after he kidnapped them from Florida in 1953.

It was in 1950 that Kovacs, needing more money, joined WPTZ-TV in Philadelphia, for the first in a long series of madcap television shows in which he would host and/or star. The next year he had "*Kovacs on the Corner*" on network television, co-starring with Edie Adams and Peter Boyle. At some point during the next TV seasons, the always busy Ernie was performing on several programs concurrently. He and Adams married in 1954 and moved into a plush seventeen-room duplex on Manhattan's Central Park West. In 1959, their daughter, Mia Susan. was born. Kovacs reached a career peak when he starred on NBC-TV's "*Saturday Color Carnival—The Ernie Kovacs Show.*" The unique program—done all in pantomime—won cigar-chomping Kovacs an Emmy.

Columbia Pictures signed him to a four-year contract at $100,000 a picture. He and his family relocated to California to a stately Los Angeles house in Coldwater Canyon. Jack Lemmon was the star of *Operation Mad Ball* (1957), while Kim Novak and James Stewart were the leads of *Bell, Book and Candle* (1958). However, Kovacs made an indelible impression in both movies. The thickly-moustached Ernie was comically fine as the villain in Doris Day's otherwise dull *It Happened to Jane* (1959). Not content to be merely a feature film star, he continued to guest on TV, sometimes in comedy specials, other times as a dramatic actor. He often had his own TV series (1958-59, 1961-62) and hosted other shows: "*Take a Good Look*" (1959- 60), "*Silents Please*" (1961). However, there were increasing problems with the networks over exploding budgets and unimpressive ratings.

Always wanting more attention and needing more money for his lavish life style and growing back tax debts, he performed in Las Vegas, where his addiction to gambling became costly. In 1960 he appeared in five features, ranging from *Our Man in Havana* to *Strangers When We Meet*. In what proved to be his last movie, *Sail a Crooked Ship* (1961), he was a menacing villain.

In early 1961, Kovacs was acting in a TV pilot ("*A Pony for Chris*" with Buster Keaton) and was discussing a movie production deal with Alec Guinness. Then came January 13, 1962, the day the laughter stopped.

The Kovacs were invited to director Billy Wilder's apartment on Wilshire Boulevard to celebrate the christening of Milton and Ruth Berle's new son, Michael. Edie drove to the party alone in her station wagon, since Ernie had been working on the TV pilot all day and was to meet her there. He drove to Wilder's in his White Rolls Royce. About 1:20 a.m.,

Ernie and Edie left the get-together. He offered Yves Montand a ride, but the French star decided to go with the Berles. Ernie, slightly drunk, drove off in the station wagon (which Edie hated to drive), asking his wife to drive the Rolls home. As he roared through the wet night, his car smacked into the concrete triangle at Beverly Glen and Santa Monica Boulevard. The impact spun the car around and it smashed into a pole. Kovacs died instantly of a basal skull fracture. He was found dead with a cigar a few inches from his hand. Had he not been momentarily distracted while trying to light the stogie, he would have been forty-three on January 23.

Unaware of the tragedy, Edie had driven home. When she heard the bad news, she refused to believe her husband was gone until Jack Lemmon went to the morgue and confirmed that he was indeed dead. In a bizarre request, Edie asked Lemmon to put several Havana cigars in Ernie's pocket before the burial.

The funeral was held on January 18, 1962 at the Beverly Hills Presbyterian Church, attended by a host of celebrities. Pallbearers included Jack Lemmon, Frank Sinatra, Billy Wilder and Dean Martin. The comedian was buried at Forest Lawn—Hollywood Hills where his marker reads: "Ernie Kovacs 1919—1962 Nothing in Moderation. We all loved him." His widow was saddled with $600,000 in gambling and tax debts that the hard-working Edie took years to pay off.

Over the decades since his death, a solid portion of Ernie's work from TV's Golden Age has been salvaged for TV syndication and video cassette distribution. It is a lasting tribute to his way-out talents. A less happy legacy occurred on May 22, 1982, when Ernie and Edie's 22-year-old daughter, Mia Susan, died in a Los Angeles auto crash. She is buried at Forest Lawn to Kovacs's left. Her marker reads: "Daddy's girl. We all loved her too."

Carole Lombard

[Jane Alice Peters]
October 6, 1908 - January 16, 1942

The same appealing qualities—directness, naturalness, gustiness—that made striking Carole Lombard so liked in private life, shone forth in her screen work. Rarely has a show business personality been so beloved by all who knew her. She was quite feminine and attracted many male admirers. However, she was also blessed with a salty down-to-earth humor and a lack of pretension—which made her "one of the boys." She was good at acting, but equally loved sports. She knew how to give or enjoy a rousing party, but was just as content when helping those in need. She was well-respected in the industry as a business person for she could cut a better movie deal than many talent agents.

Lombard was one of the first American luminaries to die in World War II. She had completed a successful war bond-selling tour and was heading back to Los Angeles when her plane crashed into the side of a Nevada mountain. If Carole could have heard the eulogies following her death, she would have disliked such extravagant praise. She would have insisted she was just doing her job.

She was born in Fort Wayne, Indiana, the third child of Frederick

CAROLE LOMBARD

and Elizabeth (Knight) Peters. When she was six, her parents divorced. The same year, Mrs. Peter and her three children visited the World's Fair in San Francisco and eventually decided to resettle in Los Angeles. One day in 1921, film director Allan Dwan was visiting one of the Peters's neighbors and spotted tomboyish Jane playing street ball. He hired her to play Monte Blue's sister in *A Perfect Crime*. It was four years later before she made another feature, this time playing a small part in *Tom Mix's Dick Turpin* (1925). By then her name had been changed to Carol Lombard.

Carol had just negotiated a five-year Fox Films contract and she was returning home from a hockey game one foggy night with her date. The car in front of theirs slid backward down a hill hitting theirs, and the sudden impact shoved Carol forward against the windshield. Her face was cut from the corner of her nose to her left cheekbone. The attending medical intern sewed up the wound with eighteen stitches. While recuperating Carol began studying cinematography. She realized she would have a facial scar, but that proper lighting and good camera angles could minimize it.

Having rcovered from her mishap, Carol accepted an opening at Mack Sennett's comedy factory for one of the director's famous bathing beauties. During the next eighteen months she made over a dozen two-reeler comedies. However, with the coming of talkies, Carol moved over to Pathe Pictures and then joined Paramount Pictures. In her first movie there she supported Charles "Buddy" Rogers; more importantly, in the credits the studio misspelled Carol, adding an "e" at the end. Carol—now Carole—didn't mind: "since they're paying me so, well I don't care how they spell my name."

Carole got plenty of on-the-job training at Paramount, appearing in five releases each in 1931 and 1932. She had already married one of her leading men, William Powell, in June 1931. He was thirty-nine; she was twenty-one. In 1932 she made *No Man of Her Own* (1932), co-starring with a rising young star borrowed from MGM, Clark Gable. By August 1933, Lombard and Powell had divorced, and one of her more constant escorts was crooner-band leader-movie personality, Russ Columbo. They considered marriage, but he died in a freak shooting accident (September 14, 1934).

By 1934, Carole had become a top-flight film personality. However, it was her performance in the screwball comedy *Twentieth Century* (1934) opposite John Barrymore that made her a legitimate screen star. She was now earning $3,000 weekly. On the recommendation of ex-husband William Powell, Universal borrowed Carole to co-star with him in the screwball comedy, *My Man Godfrey* (1936). It was a huge success and insured her stardom. By 1938 she signed a two-picture deal with David O. Selznick. Then, on March 29, 1939 she married Clark Gable, who had just completed *Gone with the Wind* (1939). The couple built a house at her San Fernando Valley ranch and soon became known as one of Hollywood's most compatible couples.

Next, Carole signed with RKO at $150,000 per movie plus a percentage of the profits. She was one of the first Hollywood stars to obtain such a deal. In 1940 she had a new ambition—to become a producer. She alternated heavy drama (*They Knew What They Wanted*, 1940) with comedy (*Mr. and Mrs. Smith*, 1941). In December 1941, she completed a black comedy, *To Be or Not to Be* (1942) with Jack Benny.

After the attack on Pearl Harbor in December 1941, Hollywood Victory Committee chairman Clark Gable (who was originally supposed to go himself) scheduled his wife Carole to lead a bond drive at Indianapolis, near her hometown of Fort Wayne. Her mother and her publicist went with Lombard when Gable cancelled out of the trek.

On January 15, 1942, Carole sold more than $2.5 million in war bonds in Indianapolis. Her parting thoughts to the crowds were, "Before I say goodbye to you all—come on—join me in a big cheer—V for Victory!" She could not decide between taking a train or a plane back to the coast. She flipped a coin and chose the plane, glad to be getting back to Hollywood and Gable. (Her mother, never having flown before was leery of flying and had been warned by her numerologist that January 16 would be an unlucky day.)

Around 4:00 a.m. on January 16, 1942, Carole, her mother and publicist Otto Winkler took off on the seventeen-hour trip to the Coast. At one of the stopovers (Albuquerque, New Mexico), several passengers were bumped off so that Army aviators could take their place. However, Carole persuaded the pilot to keep her and her party aboard. After refueling in Las Vegas, the craft took off for Los Angeles. At 7:07 p.m., that January 16, the TWA airliner slammed into Table Rock Mountain, thirty miles southwest of Las Vegas. The crash killed Carole, her mother and twenty other passengers and crew (including fifteen military personnel). It was two days before a rescue team could remove the charred bodies from the snowy death site. Carole was just thirty-three years old.

Among the many who sent condolences to grieving Clark Gable was President Franklin D. Roosevelt. The telegram said, "She brought great joy to all who knew her, and to millions who knew her only as a great artist.... She is and always will be a star, one we shall never forget, nor cease to be grateful to."

A few years before she died, Carole had provided in her will that she be buried in a white outfit and in a "modestly-priced crypt." In following Lombard's wishes, the famed Hollywood couturier Irene designed a special white gown for her and a private funeral service was conducted at Forest Lawn Memorial Parks—Glendale on January 21, 1942. She was buried in a white marble wall crypt in the Sanctuary of Trust there. In a nearby alcove, lay Russ Columbo whom Lombard privately claimed was the great love of her life.

In July 1942, Governor Henry Schricker of Indiana named the state's Naval air squadron "The Lombardians." That same year, a liberty ship was christened the "Carole Lombard" with a tearful Clark Gable attending the ceremony. Although he would marry twice again, the guilt-ridden Gable never stopped grieving for Carole. When he died on November 16, 1960 he was buried in a crypt next to hers at Forest Lawn.

Years later, Wesley Ruggles, Lombard's director and friend would say, "When Irving Thalberg and then Jean Harlow both died too young, the whole community experienced a shock of loss, but it was more industrial than personal.... But we couldn't comprehend losing Carole, and we never adjusted to it, either. She was irreplaceable, and we just keep on missing her." But the finest tribute of all, is that her solid body of film work continues to be appreciated, decade after decade.

Jayne Mansfield

[Vera Jayne Palmer]

April 19, 1933 - June 29, 1967

Bette Davis once said of voluptuous (a 40" bust) and brainy (an I.Q. of 163) Jayne Mansfield, "Dramatic art in her opinion is knowing how to fill a sweater." Columnist Earl Wilson noted of the buxom platinum blonde with the photogenic face and whispery child-like voice: "Jayne surrendered all her privacy and considerable dignity to the daily job of getting her name and picture in the papers. Her home, whether it was a house, apartment, or hotel suite, was always open to reporters, and photographers were constantly running in and out, stumbling over her dogs and cats...." Jayne's life was a constant quest for greater recognition—ironically she received the most attention when she died in a grisly car accident. If only she could have been alive to enjoy the sensational publicity.

She was born Vera Jayne Palmer in 1933 in Bryn Mawr, Pennsylvania to an attorney father and an elementary school teacher mother (Vera). When little Vera was three, her father died of a heart attack and the child was placed in the charge of one of her mother's friends so Mrs. Palmer could return to the classroom. In 1939, the mother remarried (Harry "Tex" Peers) and the family relocated from Phillipsburg, Pennsylvania to Dallas. While attending Highland Park High there, the future actress fell in love with another high schooler Paul Mansfield and they were married secretly on January 28, 1950. When Vera became pregnant, her parents hosted a second (public) marriage and on November 8, Jayne Marie was born. By now, Paul was at the University of Texas in Austin and Jayne was working as a dance studio receptionist and performing as a member of the Austin Civic Theatre. When Mansfield was called to active (reserve) duty during the Korean War, starstruck Jayne left her infant daughter with her mother and rushed off to California. She enrolled at UCLA and—keeping her marriage and child a secret—entered the Miss California Contest. She was a local finalist, but Mansfield made her drop out of the contest. Before she returned to Texas, Jayne had one movie bit part (*Prehistoric Women*, 1951).

While her husband was serving in Korea, Jayne went to college in Dallas, studied acting, and appeared on

JAYNE MANSFIELD

local TV shows. When Mansfield became a civilian again in 1954, she made him keep his promise to take her to Hollywood. Hell-bent on becoming a movie star, Jayne bulldozed her way into Paramount Pictures' talent department and was almost signed to a contract on the spot. With her brunette (then black) hair now dyed platinum blonde and an agent, Jayne made *Female Jungle*, not released until 1956. Paul Mansfield was dissatisfied with the "new" Jayne and he returned to Texas. (Their divorce became final in early 1958).

Jayne's aggressive new press agent (James Byron) did much to make his well-endowed client a known commodity, largely playing on her cleavage. Nothing was too ridiculous or insignificant for the career-hungry Mansfield. She gained tremendous press attention by wearing a much too small red bathing suit on a press junket to Silver Springs, Florida for Jane Russell's new movie (*Underwater*, 1955). Next, Jayne was a *Playboy* magazine centerfold, which led to a Warner Bros. term contract. She was cast as mistresses or molls in her celluloid assignments (*Illegal*, 1955, *Hell on Frisco Bay*, 1956, etc.). When the studio ended her contract, Jayne gratefully grabbed the lead in a Broadway sex comedy, *Will Success Spoil Rock Hunter?* which others (including Marilyn Maxwell) had rejected. The show was popular and Jayne made the most of the publicity options. Meanwhile, she met Hungarian-born muscle man Mickey Hargitay who left Mae West's act to join Jayne's entourage. Twentieth Century-Fox had long made a speciality of attractive blonde stars (Alice Faye, Betty Grable, Marilyn Monroe) and hired Mansfield as another threat (along with Sheree North) to troublesome Marilyn Monroe. Jayne's first movie there, the satiric *The Girl Can't Help It* (1956), was one of her best. The screen version of her Broadway hit was next (1957), followed by John Steinbeck's *The Wayward Bus* (1957) which stretched Jayne's talents, if not her wardrobe, to the limits. She received poor reviews for *Kiss Them for Me* (1957) which had Suzy Parker—not Jayne—winning the hero (Cary Grant) at the comedy's finale. In January 1958, Mansfield and Hargitay married. They would have three children: Miklos, Jr., Zoltan and Mariska.

Eager to keep working, statuesque Jayne played Las Vegas, trading on her dumb blonde comedy appeal. Fox shipped her to England for *The Sheriff of Fractured Jaw* (1958) and she stayed for two additional, dull quickies. In Italy, she and Mickey co-starred in *The Loves of Hercules* (1960). Obsessed with gaining publicity at any cost, Jayne made her pink, Spanish-style Beverly Hills a media delight, with its heart-shape bed and pool. However, her immodest sex life cost Mansfield her studio contract (it ended in 1962) and her marriage (Mickey divorced her in 1964). Meanwhile, she made the sleazy sexploitation movie *Promises, Promises* (1963) and posed nude again for *Playboy*. By now, her excessive publicity stunts seemed labored, old hat and not very entertaining. She made several mediocre quickie movies in Europe, and then married director Matt Cimber in 1964. Their child (Anthony) was born in 1965. Depressed over her fading career, she turned increasingly to alcohol. In addition, there were many headlines over her tug-of-war contest with Hargitay for custody of their children.

On Cimber's bad advice, Jayne rejected the Tina Louise role on the TV series, "Gilligan's Island" (1964-67). Instead she made junk, bottom-of-the-barrel movies such as *The Fat Spy* (1966), with an occasional cameo in a respectable production (*A Guide for the Married Man,* 1967). In 1966, Cimber directed his fading wife in *Single Room Furnished*, a quickie study of an innocent young woman who ends a worn-out prostitute. (It would not be completed until after Jayne's death and then came and went in theatres, promoted as Mansfield's last movie.)

In 1966, the bloated, heavily-drinking Jayne and Cimber divorced. While doing a publicity layout at the Jungleland tourist attraction in Thousand Oaks (California), her son Zoltan was mauled by a lion and underwent several operations. She became romantically attached to a San Francisco attorney (Samuel S. Brody). Jayne's tour of sleazy clubs in Stockholm, England and Ireland was a fiasco. She gained more notices for her drunken brawls with Brody and for being named in a messy divorce suit by Brody's ailing wife. Returning to California, Jayne (who had become fascinated with the Church of Satan) received additional bad publicity when her sixteen-year-old daughter (Jayne Marie) was placed in protective custody because her mother and Brody were accused of mistreating her.

In early 1967, Jayne toured Vietnam to entertain the troops. In June that year, she left for a club engagement (as a replacement for Mamie Van Doren) in Biloxi, Mississippi. She was joined by Brody and her three middle children. After performing at Gus Stevens's Supper Club in Biloxi, she left about 2:30 a.m. on June 29, 1967 for New Orleans to do a local TV interview show. The hardtop Buick car was driven by Ron Harrison (a college student who worked for Stevens) and the passengers were Jayne, Brody, as well as Miklos, Zoltan and Mariska, and four Chihuahua dogs. Some twenty miles before reaching New Orleans on windy U.S. Highway 90—known as The Spanish trail—the car smashed into the back of a trailer truck which had halted behind a city truck spraying the swamps with an anti-mosquito insecticide. The crash was so severe that the impact sheared off the car's top. Harrison, Jayne and Brody were killed immediately, their bodies thrown onto the highway. The bewildered three children who were sleeping in the back seat received only minor bruises. In the accident, Jayne was scalped, with her blonde wig thrown onto the dashboard.

After a Beverly Hills memorial service, Jayne's body was shipped back to Pen Argyl, Pennsylvania for burial in the family plot. At the Fairview Cemetery there, a weeping Hargitay threw himself on her pink-rose ladden coffin. (He would say of his ex-wife, "Nobody really understood her. Nobody knew the real Jayne.") Twenty years after Jayne's death, a pink memorial marker for Jayne was installed at Hollywood Memorial Park in Los Angeles by her devout fan club. Much of Jayne's reported $500,000 estate was lost to lawyers' fees and creditors, and her five children ended receiving less than $2,000 each from the will.

Dean Paul Martin

November 17, 1951 - March 21, 1987

Growing up in a father's shadow is difficult. When the parent is a superstar celebrity this situation can lead the offspring into oversized attention-grabbing stunts, sometimes resulting in death.

Singer actor Dean Martin—first teamed with comedian Jerry Lewis and then on his own—became a huge show business success. By his first wife. Elizabeth (MacDonald) Martin, he had four children: Craig, Claudia, Gail and Deanna. A week after Dean and Elizabeth divorced in 1949, he married Jeanne Beiggers. Before that couple divorced in 1972, they had three children: Dean Paul (known as Dino), Ricci and Gina.

By age thirteen, Dino had formed a rock group (Dino, Desi and Billy) with pals Desi Arnaz, Jr. and Billy Hinsche and had several popular recordings, including the hit single "I'm a Fool." At sixteen, Dino was licensed as a private helicopter pilot and graduated to jockeying jet planes. While not a football player in high school or college (he took pre-med courses at UCLA), he was later drafted by the World Football League and tried out for the Los Angeles Rams. In the early 1970s, Dino, a long-time gun collector, was arrested for (illegal) possession of an anti-tank and a machine gun. Insisting he had misunderstood the federal gun ownership law, he was fined $2,000 and placed on probation.

In the mid-1970s, Dean Paul turned from football to his long-favorite sport of tennis and played in several big-scale tournaments, including Wimbleton. By then, the tall blond playboy (who had dated such personalities as Tina Sinatra and Candice Bergen) had been married and divorced from skating champ Dorothy Hamill and was married once more, this time to actress Olivia Hussey. (He and Olivia would have a son, Alex; the couple would later divorce).

Dean Paul next turned to acting, playing an amorous tennis pro in *Players* (1979) opposite Ali MacGraw. In 1985-86, he co-starred in the short-lived adventure series "*Misfits of Science*." In line with his continued delight in flying, Martin had been piloting F-4 Phantom jets as an Air National Guard captain. On March 23, 1987, with his twelve-year-old son watching, Dean Paul took off from March Air Force Base in California in a F4-C Phantom with his weapons officer, Captain Ramon Ortiz, aboard. About ten minutes after takeoff, the craft disappeared from the radar screen as it neared the top of Mount San Gorgonio. It crashed into the snowy mountain and there were no survivors. It was six days before rescue workers could locate and retrieve the remains of the two victims in the rugged mountain area. (Later it was determined that an incorrectly given air traffic controller's warning about the location of Mount San Gorgonio may have contributed to the crash.) After a private memorial service for family and friends (including Sammy Davis, Jr.), Dean Paul Martin was buried at Los Angeles National Cemetery in Westword.

Although only thirty-five when he died, Dean Paul Martin had done a great deal of living during those years.

Vic Morrow

February 14, 1932 - July 23, 1982

Paradoxically, gritty Vic Morrow is best remembered not for his years of solid film and TV performances, but for his bizarre death. He died in a filming mishap during the making of *Twilight Zone—The Movie* (1983), in which he and two young child actors were struck and killed by the rotor blade of a crashing helicopter on the outdoor film set.

Born and raised in the Bronx, tough-looking Vic made his motion picture

VIC MORROW

debut in *The Blackboard Jungle* (1955), playing a vicious punk. He gave such a vivid performance he was typecast immediately in such surly roles: *Tribute to a Bad Man* (1956), *Hell's Five Hours* (1958), *Portrait of a Mobster* (1960), etc. Wanting a change of pace, he abandoned movies for over a decade, focusing on television and stage, both as actor and director in the U.S. and abroad. He was the tough but sympathetic Sergeant Chip Sanders in the World War II TV series *"Combat"* (1962-67). In the 1970s, he was in many TV movies and played a police captain in *"B.A.D. Cats"* (1980), a short-lived TV cop series. Morrow

had married actress/script writer Barbara Turner in 1957, but was divorced from her in 1964. (They had two daughters, one of them, Jennifer Jason Leigh, who became a movie star.)

On July 22 1982, Morrow was on location at Indian Dunes Park near Saugus (north of Los Angeles) for *Twilight Zone—The Movie*, a quartet of largely remade episodes from Rod Serling's Golden Age TV series, *"The Twilight Zone."* Filming for the night scenes on episode #1 (partially set in an Asian jungle) were begun by director John Landis at 7:30 p.m. After a 12:30 a.m. lunch break on July 23, the cast resumed work. At about 2:30 in the morning Landis was directing a sequence in which Morrow and two children (Renee Shinn Chen, age 6, and Myca Dinh Lee, age 7) were fleeing from a pursuing helicopter which is firing at them. "Fire balls" were detonated to make the chase more effective. One of the simulated explosions caused the chopper to spin out of control and it crashed sideways, having been hit by shrapnel. In its fall, either the tail or main rotor blade struck and killed the three performers. In the wake of the tragedy it was discovered that the two Asian-American youngsters were illegal aliens. (Before Landis and four associates were acquitted of involuntary manslaughter charges in 1987, the accident had mushroomed into a media circus.)

The Jewish-born Morrow was buried in the Mount Olive section of Hillside Memorial Park in Los Angeles. The major portion of his estate—estimated to be over $600,000—was reported left to his dog and the animal's caretaker, his older daughter, Carrie Ann. When *Twilight Zone—The Movie* opened in the summer of 1983, scenes involving the helicopter and the children were deleted. Regarding his last performance—playing a racial/religious bigot—*Variety* reported, "Morrow strongly conveys the insecurity lying shallow beneath the character's aggressive hatefulness, but dramatic payoff is thin." Faint praise for a role which cost the actor his very life.

Audie Murphy

June 20, 1924 - May 28, 1971

Before he was 21-years old, Audie Murphy became the most decorated American G.I. of World War II. He returned home in triumph. His life thereafter—as a cowboy movie star—was an anti-climax. His career spiraled downward, halting only when the small plane on which he was a passenger crashed into the side of a Virginia mountain. Then, it was all over for the American hero credited with killing 240 enemies in combat during the war. What price glory!

Audie Murphy was born in Farmersville, Texas in 1924, the sixth of nine children of extremely poor sharecroppers. As a child, he perfected his shooting skills killing jackrabbits for the family's dinner. When he was a youngster, his father deserted the family, and the mother died when Audie was sixteen. Years later Murphy reflected, "she died taking something of me with her. It seems I've been searching for it ever since."

With the family scattered and wanting to serve his country, skinny, baby-faced Audie enlisted in the Army (having earlier been rejected by the Marines and the paratroopers). After basic training in Texas and Maryland, he was shipped to North Africa, landing at Casablanca in February 1943. Before the European theater of war was over, Audie had been promoted to First Lieutenant and had participated in seven major battle thrusts in North Africa and Europe. He received the Congressional Medal of Honor for his extraordinary heroism and bravery in action near Holzwihr, France in January 1945. Among the more than two dozen medals he won were the Distinguished Service Cross, the Bronx Star, the Legion of Merit and the Silver Star with an Oak Leaf Cluster. Of the 235 men in his original Army company, Murphy was one of two who survived the war. As America's most decorated soldier, he was featured in a *Life* magazine cover story (July 16, 1945).

The snowballing effects of the *Life* story were tremendous. Back in the States, freckle-faced Audie was the focus of parades, banquets and celebrations. Among those who observed the hoopla was actor James Cagney who suggested Murphy come to Hollywood. Audie had been thinking of re-enlisting in the service or becoming a veterinarian, but accepted Cagney's encouragement for a Hollywood career. Audie went to acting school, sometimes sleeping in a gym owned by a friend. He insisted, "I aim to learn everything I can about this business. I don't want to be caught with my dukes down, see." His first movie was a small role in Alan Ladd's *Beyond Glory* (1948); his first lead was in *Bad Boy* (1949). In February 1949, he wed petit Wanda Hendrix, who had made a mark as a teen-age movie actress, but whose career was sliding. The couple co-starred in a Western (*Sierra*, 1950). They divorced in April, 1950, she charging him with mental cruelty. (Among Murphy's post-war traumas were terrible nightmares and paranoia. He often slept with a loaded gun under his pillow and once, in an

THE HOLLYWOOD DEATH BOOK

argument with his wife, placed the charged weapon in Wanda's mouth.)

In 1950, Audie was signed to a Universal-International Pictures contract at $100,000 a year and began his on-the-job training in a long stream of B Westerns. ("I made the same film twenty times.") The studio exploited Audie's war record and in 1955 made a screen adaptation of his best-selling autobiography, *To Hell and Back*. However, then it was back to horse operas, leading a disillusioned Murphy to observe: "Yeah, the face is the same—and so is the dialogue. Only the horses are changed. Some of then get old and have to be retired." Meanwhile, in April 1951, Audie married a former airline stewardess, Pamela Archer, and they had two sons: Terry (born: 1952) and James (born: 1954).

As his movie career faded, Audie tried TV. However, his cowboy detective series, *"Whispering Smith,"* was off the air four months after its May 1961 debut. The financial losses from the series forced him to sell his San Fernando Valley ranch. Universal kept him on contract, but in much lower-budget movies in the diminishing Western marketplace. By 1965, he was no longer working for the studio, and he and his wife separated (they never divorced). With increasing financial problems (including back taxes owed to the I.R.S.) Audie discovered hard truths about his industry friends, "When word gets around you're washed up, no one will touch you with a 10-foot pole. They're afraid you'll ask them for a job. Or a loan."

By the late 1960s, a much-bloated Audie had drug and drinking problems. He owed a great deal of money due to his gambling habit. He had several brushes with the law, but the assault charges were dropped against the combative ex-star. In 1969, he

found backers for a new picture, *A Time for Dying*, in which the fast-aging Audie played a cameo. It was scheduled for summer 1971 release. Because he owed over $360,000 to creditors and to the federal government, Audie accepted a front man job with Modular Management, a Georgia-based company which built pre-fabricated homes and motels. Meanwhile, the FBI, knowing of Murphy's gambling involvement, had used him as a decoy to trap certain Chicago underworld figures. Additionally, there was Murphy's tie-in with a New Orleans gangster attempting to have ex-teamster president Jimmy Hoffa paroled from prison. Audie was positioned as a liaison between the underworld and the U. S. government.

On May 28, 1971, Audie accompanied by Modular's president Claude Crosby and three other company executives left Atlanta on a chartered, twin-engine Aero Commander plane. Twelve miles north of Roanoke, during a thunder storm and a light rain, the pilot lost his way and, some time after 11:40 a.m., smacked into the side of Brushy Mountain. Because of the bad weather, it was not until three days later that the burned plane and the six bodies were located in the isolated, wooded area.

Few Hollywood figures attended the memorial services on June 4, 1971 for Audie Murphy at the Church of the Hills at Forest Lawn Memorial Park in Hollywood Hills. However, among the gathering of 600 were his ex-wife Wanda Hendrix and several Army buddies. Thereafter, his body was flown to Virginia and buried on June 7 at Arlington National Cemetery with full military honors. His grave is not far from that of the Unknown Soldier.

36

Ironically, at the time of his death, film director Don Siegel was considering Audie for the role of the psychopathic killer in Clint Eastwood's *Dirty Harry* (1971), a key assignment which might have started the trouble-prone Murphy on a whole new film career.

Rick(y) Nelson

[Eric Hilliard Nelson]

May 8, 1940 - December 31, 1985

Rick[y] Nelson was born into a prominent show business family and spent most of his life as an entertainer. His career ranged from being a rambunctious teenage heartthrob to a hit rock recording star to ending as a middle-aged family man who performed continually on the concert circuit (including restaurants and fairs). When he died in a plane crash in late 1985, he joined a galaxy of other recording notables who had perished in air fatalities.

Ricky's father, Ozzie Nelson (born: 1906), was always an overachiever: America's youngest Eagle Scout, a Rutgers honor student and star quarterback. Before he graduated from New Jersey Law School, he quit to form his own band which became very well-known. He and band vocalist/screen starlet Harriet Hilliard (born: 1914) married in 1935. Son David was born in 1936. Ricky was born in 1940 in Teaneck, New Jersey. In 1944, the senior Nelsons began a long-running radio sitcom, *"The Adventures of Ozzie and Harriet,"* with their real-life sons joining the program in 1949. When the series transferred to TV in 1952, the full clan appeared in weekly installments of the idealized American family, as well as in a full-length feature, *Here Come the Nelsons* (1952).

To prove to a girlfriend that he could

sing and make a recording, Ricky—then a Hollywood High School student—convinced Ozzie to let him record "I'm Walking" for the April 10, 1957 episode of the TV show. (Young Nelson, who had learned to play the guitar, accompanied himself, with the backing of the TV show's orchestra.) Within a month, the song had scored nationwide, with the flip side "A Teenager's Romance" rising to #2 on the charts. Ricky signed with Imperial Records and his "Poor Little Fool" became #1 on the charts in August 1958. Wholesome, smart-alecky Ricky, with the crew cut, became a confident multimedia star and made a few movies: *Rio Bravo* (1959), *The Wackiest Ship in the Army* (1960).

As Ricky grew to adulthood, his acting became more wooden. However, as long as he had the family TV series, his career was secure. On April

RICK NELSON

20, 1963, the one-time playboy—having dropped the "Y" from Ricky—married Kris Harmon, the daughter of gridiron Great, Tom Harmon, and the sister of budding actor Mark Harmon. Six months later, Tracy Kristine Nelson was born. (Rick and Kris would become the parents of twins, Matthew and Gunnar, in 1967 and their last child, Sam, was born in 1974.) Rick and Kris co-starred in a flop feature film, *Love and Kisses* (1965) and, the next year, the "*Adventures of Ozzie and Harriet*" finally went off the air.

By the late 1960s, Rick's career had faded, and efforts such as hosting a musical TV show, "*Malibu U*" (1967), didn't help. He was a guest on several TV series with bland results. However, he got a recording boost when his single, "Travelin' Man" (1971), was a top hit and the next year, he created a stir while performing in a rock 'n' roll revival show at Manhattan's Madison Square Garden. During the performance he tried new material. The disappointed audience who wanted him to perform only his old hits, booed him. He incorporated the disturbing experience into a hit recording, "Garden Party." In 1975, Ozzie Nelson died of cancer, with his hefty estate placed in trust under Harriet's control. By the early 1980s Rick, who had never learned to save his money, had lost his major record label contracts and was hardly getting by with low level concert tours (sometimes 200 gigs a year). His troublesome marriage had collapsed and, after several temporary separations, Kris filed for divorce in late 1980, which became final in 1982. In 1983, Rick played the principal on a TV movie ("*High School, U.S.A.*" in which Harriet Nelson was his secretary. In early 1985 he made a TV series pilot ("*Fathers and Sons*")

starring Merle Olson.

On December 30, 1985, Rick and his band played at PJ's Lounge in Guntersville, Alabama. They were scheduled to perform in Dallas at the Park Suite Hotel for a New Year's Eve show. (Nelson needed money to keep up heavy alimony payments.) On the 31st, the group was approximately 135 miles east of Dallas, when their forty-year-old chartered twin-engine DC-3 crash-landed at 5:15 p.m. in a hayfield due to faulty engines which then burst into black oil-smoky flames. (There was a briefly-held contention, later refuted, that Nelson and several others aboard had been "free basing," and that aerosol spray cans used to ignite the drug pipes had ignited the fires.) Killed in the crash was Rick, his 27-year-old fiancee (Helen Blair), four band members and one of the road crew. Some of the bodies were so badly burned that they could be identified only through dental records. The coroner's report noted that Nelson was a confirmed cocaine user.

More than a 1,000 people attempted to fill the 275-seat Church of the Hills at Forest Lawn Memorial Park in Hollywood Hills. (Nelson's body was not yet at the cemetery, as it had been held up by red tape involved in transporting the remains back to California). Rick's daughter Tracy eulogized: "I remember his grace, his gentleness. He was the kindest man you ever met. The man had class. He was an artist. He was wise. And he loved ice cream. Pop wouldn't want you to be sad." Eleven-year-old Sam, delivered an American Indian poem, dedicated to his dad. The twins, sang "Easy to Be Free." Brother David read a message of condolence from President Reagan. David concluded by asking the congregation to join him in reciting the Lord's Prayer, something the family had always sung each night at bedtime when Ozzie was alive and the boys were children.

Although Rick Nelson had earned over $700,000 in the last year of his life, debts, alimony, etc. had left only $43,000. There was some $1,000,000 in debts, including estate claims by Nelson's divorced wife, Chris. As to Harriet Nelson, Rick's will stated, "I have specifically failed to provide for my mother...as she is well taken-care of and comfortable at this time." Regarding his girlfriend, "I specifically fail to provide herein for Helen Blair as that is our wish." In 1990, the insurance firm representing the aviation company who reputedly had repaired the plane's malfunctioning heater several weeks prior to the crash, settled the long-standing case. Some $4.5 million was split among ten plaintiffs.

Rick Nelson left a show business legacy, not only with his own media performances, but also that of his children. Daughter Tracy became a TV series star ("*Square Pegs*," "*Glitter*," "*Father Dowling Mysteries*") and the twins, Matthew and Gunnar, became rock stars, 1990s-style. In 1987, brother David directed a special about Rick Nelson, entitled "*A Brother Remembers*" and aired over the Disney cable network.

Will Rogers

[William Penn Adair Rogers]

November 4, 1879 - August 15, 1935

Few if any performers in the annals of American show business can match the qualities of Will Rogers. Not only was he beloved as a very popular humorist and actor, but his wry commentaries on the contemporary American scene (especially politics) remain unparalleled today. He was at his career peak when

WILL ROGERS

he died in a plane crash while on an Alaskan flying expedition with the celebrated pilot Wiley Post. The shocking tragedy was front page news around the globe. The irony of Will's death was that Rogers might not have been aboard the craft, if he had not abruptly withdrawn from a motion picture commitment to make the aerial trek.

He was the eighth and final child born to a rancher and his quarter-blood Cherokee Indian wife in 1879 in the Indian territory which became Oklahoma in 1907. Will's mother died in 1890 and, after the father remarried, the family moved to Claremont, twelve miles north of the family spread. Will had too much wanderlust to remain in any school for too long. He eventually found himself in South Africa in the early 1900s, where he made his show business debut as a lasso artist and Rough Rider in a wild west circus. In 1905, he was in New York City at Madison Square Garden performing in a rodeo show. When a berserk steer careened towards the stands, he roped the animal and earned tremendous publicity—all of which helped his career. Soon he drifted into vaudeville and performed both in the U.S. and abroad. He had met Betty Blake in 1899 and, on November 25, 1908, they married in Arkansas. Homespun Rogers always claimed, "The day I roped Betty, I did the star performance of my life." They would have four children: Will Jr., Mary, James, and Fred (who died in 1919, one year after his birth).

Will graduated to "real" acting when he appeared with Blanche Ring in *The Wall Street Girl* (1913). Two years later, he started his profitable association with showman Florenz Ziegfeld by joining the latter's *Midnight Frolic*. Rogers's act usually featured him spinning a rope and spouting observations ("all I know is what I read in the papers") on the absurdities of pompous individuals and high-stepping politicians. Rogers made his movie debut in *Laughing Bill Hyde* (1918) and, the next year, authored two books (including *The Cowboy Philosopher on Prohibition*). Also in 1919, he made his first Hollywood movie (*Almost a Husband*). Throughout the Twenties he alternated between Broadway *Follies* and moviemaking, as well as writing a syndicated newspaper column, performing his monologues for recordings, and pursuing the lecture circuit. His fame was so great that whenever he traveled abroad he became the social intimate of government heads, royalty, writers and those he loved best—the average man.

Three Cheers (1928) was Rogers's last Broadway outing and *They Had to See Paris* (1929) was his first talkie, made at Fox Films where he would remain for the rest of his screen acting career. He averaged three to four features per year.

In 1934, Rogers returned to the stage in Eugene O'Neill's *Ah, Wilderness!*, in the father's role that George M. Cohan had done on Broadway. Playing his first full-fledged stage characterization, Will received rave reviews when the comedy opened in San Francisco in late April. After three hit weeks, the show moved to Los Angeles, where the sold-out engagement was extended three additional weeks. The plan all along had been for MGM to borrow Rogers from Fox to star in the upcoming movie version of *Ah, Wilderness!*. Suddenly, after Will ended his play run in late June 1934, he vetoed doing the movie scheduled for production in 1935. According to Will's long-time friend Eddie Cantor, during the comedy's run, Will received a strong letter from a clergyman. It so upset the actor that he wanted nothing more to do with *Ah, Wilderness!* The note stated that the religious man had taken his fourteen-year-old daughter to see the show. He had been so offended by the scene in which Will's character explains to his son about dealing with a shady lady that he and his child had left the theater in shame. Now freed from his stage obligations, Will took an around-the-world cruise, not returning to California until September 1934, when he returned to picture-making at Fox.

In mid-1935, Rogers, long a plane enthusiast, received an offer he couldn't refuse. Fellow Oklahoman, Wiley Post (who had broken several aviation records, including trips around the world) offered to take him as passenger on his next global jaunt, if Will would finance the flight, which he agreed to do. There was tremendous media coverage of the preparations and take-off of this trek featuring the world's most famous pilot (Post) and most popular plane passenger (Rogers). On August 15, 1935, the plane took off from Fairbanks, Alaska, and, after a stopover at Harding Lake to wait until the fog lifted, flew onward toward the North Pole. At about 8:18 p.m. Post and Rogers neared desolate Point Barrow, Alaska—some three hundred miles inside the Arctic Circle. Suddenly, their shiny red sky cruiser faltered in the sky due to a defect in the 550-horse power engine. The plane crashed head-down for fifty feet and plowed into a river bank. The impact drove the engine back into the fuselage, fatally crushing both Post and Rogers. When recovered, the bodies were flown back to California. Meanwhile, a week earlier, the crew and cast of MGM's *Ah, Wilderness!* had left for Massachusetts location filming with Lionel Barrymore in the role once intended for Will Rogers.

The world was stunned by Rogers's death. In Manhattan, a plane squadron with long trailing black streamers flew over the city; flags flew at half mast everywhere and theaters were darkened. Famed singer John McCormack expressed the loss best: "A smile has disappeared from the lips of America and her eyes are suffused with tears."

Will was initially buried at a Los Angeles cemetery. On May 22, 1944, his body was re-interred in a crypt in the gardens of the Claremont Memorial to Will Rogers in Claremont, Oklahoma. In June 1944, his wife Betty died and, along with their baby son Fred, was buried in the family crypt in Oklahoma. In later 1944, Will's surviving children donated his 300-acre Santa Monica ranch to California as a state park.

It was President Franklin D. Roosevelt who said of Will Rogers, "The American nation, to whose heart he brought gladness, will hold him in everlasting remembrance."

Trinidad Silva, Jr.

1950 - July 31, 1988

On TV's "*Hill Street Blues*" (1981-87) Trinidad Silva Jr. played the smart-mouthed Chicano gang leader Jesus Martinez. He was the one who repeatedly taunted police Captain Frank Furillo (Daniel J. Travanti) by calling him "Frankie boy." In the controversial movie *Colors* (1988) Trinidad was Frog, the older gang leader. Then one Sunday evening in July 1988, Silva had the misfortune of being in the wrong place at the wrong time. In one brief minute, his life ended due to a drunk driver.

Mexican-American Trinidad Silva Jr. was born in Mission, Texas in 1950. Moving to Los Angeles he gravitated into acting, making a strong impression in the stage play *Hijos*. He was in the movie *Alabrista!* (1977) with Edward James Olmos, who became a close friend. His other acting credits include: *Walk Proud* (1979) with Robby Benson, *Ell Norte* (1983), the Robert Redford-directed *The Milagro Beanfield War* (1987), and *The Night Before* (1988) with Keanu Reaves. Besides his recurring role on "*Hill Street Blues*" Trinidad had been in the cable-TV series "*Maximum Security*" (1985) with Jean Smart. He had formed his own production company and, with Michael Warren (another "*Hill Street*" alumnus), had co-starred in a new TV pilot, "*Home Free*" which aired on July 13, 1988.

On Sunday, July 31, 1988, Trinidad was out driving in his small pickup truck with his wife Sofia and their two-year old son, Samuel. As they pulled through an intersection in

Whittier, California at about 6:45 p.m. a sedan car (going about 45 m.p.h.) went through a red light and hit their vehicle broadside. The force of the impact spun the truck around and it hit the offending car. Trinidad and his son were thrown from the truck. Silva was hurled more than 100 feet before hitting the pavement. He died instantly and was pronounced dead at the accident scene. The dazed little boy and Mrs. Silva (who had been pinned in the wreckage) suffered minor injuries. The other driver—inebriated—was not injured at all. He had attempted to flee the crash site, but onlookers held him until police arrived.

Silva was one of a rash of *"Hill Street Blues"* actors who have died in recent years. Michael Conrad suffered a fatal heart attack in 1983; both Kiel Martin (lung cancer) and Rene Enrique (pancreatic cancer) died in 1990.

Samantha Smith

June 29, 1972 - August 25, 1985

In 1983, eleven-year-old Samantha Smith of Houlton, Maine, wrote a letter to Soviet premier Yuri Andropov expressing her concern about the risk of nuclear warfare. She asked the Communist politician, "Why do you want to conquer the whole world, or at least our country?" Touched by the girl's genuineness, Andropov replied that he had no such intention. He invited she and her parents on a special tour of the Soviet Union. With much media hoopla, Samantha and her family (her father was an English professor) accepted the offer. The trek made young but articulate Samantha an overnight celebrity. She was asked to write a book (Journey to the Soviet Union, 1985), appeared on several

TV talk shows and made a guest appearance on the TV sitcom, *"Charles in Charge"* (November, 1984).

As the result of her instant fame, she was cast as one of Robert Wagner's two daughters in his new hour-long detective/adventure series, *"Lime Street,"* which had an international backdrop. In the summer of 1985, Samantha went to England for location filming on the first episodes.

On August 25, 1985 she and her father had returned from overseas. In Boston that rainy Sunday evening, they boarded a commuter turboprop plane bound for the Auburn-Lewiston (Maine) Municipal Airport. About a half-mile from their destination, the plane crashed and burned, killing all seven aboard. Samantha was survived by her mother.

As for *"Lime Street,"* it debuted on September 21, 1985. The mixture of poor reviews and the general grief over Smith's tragic end caused the show to go off the air as of October 26, 1985.

ALCOHOL AND DRUGS

Nick Adams

[Nicholas Aloysius Adamchock]
July 10, 1931 - February 7, 1968

Compact, blond Nick Adams was the quintessential film fan, with a burning desire to become a movie star. The son of immigrant parents from the Ukraine, he grew up in Jersey City, New Jersey. Later in life he would admit, "Movies were my life, you had to have an escape when you were living in a basement. I saw all the Cagney, Bogart and Garfield pictures—the ones where a guy finally got a break. Odds against the world—that was my meat."

Not yet in his twenties, he hitchhiked to Los Angeles, where he had no luck in breaking into films. Discouraged, he joined the Coast Guards in 1952. On weekend leaves he would return to Hollywood where he finally talked his way into a role as a sailor in *Mister Roberts* (1955) engineering a 90-day leave to complete the part. For a brief part in Greer Garson's *Strange Lady in Town* (1955), he arranged a three-day pass. Once discharged from the service, he gained a role in *Rebel without a Cause* (1955) starring his pal, James Dean, and Natalie Wood (who was his lover briefly). Nick's big break came when he was cast as the bespectacled Ben, Andy Griffith's sidekick, in *No Time for Sergeants* (1958). Adams reached his show business pinnacle as the star of the TV series "The Rebel" (1959-61), playing a crusading ex-Confederate officer in the old West. His next effort ("Saints and Sinners") as a crusading reporter came and went in the 1962-63 TV season.

Returning to films, the determined Adams had a splashy role as an accused killer in Richard Chamberlain's *Twilight of Honor* (1963).He then spent $8,000 campaigning for an Academy Award nomination for that showcase role. He was nominated in the Best Supporting Actor category that year, but lost the prize. When his career downslided thereafter, he was reduced to appearing in such trashy low-budget features as *Frankenstein Meets the Giant Devil Fish* (1967) and *Mission Mars* (1968).

Off screen, high-achieving Nick—noted for being Mr. Super Nice Guy—became increasingly nervous about his wobbly career and his faltering marriage (the father of two, he and his wife had separated). On the night of February 7, 1968, he was found dead—braced against the bedroom wall with his eyes starring wide open—in his West Los Angeles home by his lawyer, Evin Roder. The cause of death was listed as an "accidental" overdose of the sedative paraldehyde, which his doctor had prescribed to calm his nerves. He was buried in Briar Creek, Pennsylvania, not far from the town (Nanticoke) where he was born.

Diana Barrymore

[Diana Strange Blyth]
March 3, 1921 - January 25, 1960

Coming from a royal lineage can be both a blessing and a curse, as Diana Barrymore discovered to her dismay.

She was the daughter of acting titan John Barrymore and his second wife, socialite Blanche Oelrichs Thomas, known better as the poet Michael Strange. Diana's famous parents were too high-strung and different to have a congenial marriage, and they divorced in 1928. Diana was pampered with material items as a clumsy child, but emotionally ignored in the tug-of-war between her artistic parents. As she grew into adult-

R.I.P. ALCOHOL AND DRUGS

43

hood—educated in private European boarding schools—it was assumed that she would follow in the family tradition of show business.

At eighteen, pudgy-faced Diana was among the many whom David O. Selznick tested but rejected for the role of Scarlett O'Hara in *Gone with the Wind* (1939). Five days later, she made a glittering debut as a New York debutante. She was briefly engaged to Anthony Drexel Duke, and then completed a junior course at the American Academy of Dramatics Arts. The Academy thought she lacked dramatic skills and did not ask her back. However, due to her illustrious family name she won a summer stock job at Maine's Oguinquit Playhouse. *Life* magazine in July 1939 devoted a cover story to her. Film studios now offered her screen tests. Instead, she toured in *Outward Bound*. While playing in *Tonight at 8:30* in Toronto, she fell in love with an eighteen-year-older actor, Bramwell Fletcher. They became lovers. She made her Broadway debut in *The Romantic Mr. Dickens* (1940). After her successful appearance on the New York stage in *The Land is Bright* (1941), she received more movie offers. Her antagonistic mother protested, "Let those machines get hold of you and they'll ruin you. Look what they did to your father!" Despite this warning, in early 1942, she went to Hollywood.

Her father, worn out by years of excesses greeted his daughter to the movie colony, but she chose to live on her own in a spacious rented mansion. Soon, Bramwell Fletcher—to whom she was now engaged — moved in with her, although she found other distractions with actor Van Heflin. Diana signed with Universal Pictures at $1,000 a week and the studio promoted her with "The Most Sensational New Screen Personality of 1942." Her first picture was *Eagle Squadron* ((1942). Her director, Arthur Lubin would recall, "She was a madcap girl; typical of the Barrymores. She went on the make for every man on the set." By the time Eagle Squadron was released, John Barrymore had died. Two months later, she and Bramwell Fletcher married in an elegant Hollywood ceremony. Her next film, *Between Us Girls* (1942), drew mixed notices for Diana. On *Nightmare* (1942), she spent more time in co-star Brian Donlevy's dressing room than on the sound stage. By *Frontier Badmen* (1943), she was looking bloated, appropriately so on camera, as the saloon hostess. She was reduced to a supporting role in *Ladies Courageous* (1944), which ended her studio contract. Before leaving the West coast, she announced, "I'm dissatisfied with the way things have worked out for me in Hollywood."

She returned to New York to co-star with her husband in a dramatization of Rebecca (1945). She admitted, "I've put Hollywood behind me." However, with her marriage to Fletcher disintegrating, she returned to Hollywood to be the burlesque foil to Jack Carson on his NBC radio show. She used her off time to dally with an assortment of Hollywood's wolf pack, gaining a reputation as a heavy drinker. Eventually, she was written off the Carson program. She and Fletcher divorced in 1946, and, by the next January, she wed professional tennis player John R. Howard who turned out to be quite sadistic. Their stormy union led to street brawls, arrests and bad publicity. They were divorced six months later. During all this time, she continued playing stock engagements. In 1950, she married Robert Wilcox, an alcoholic B movie actor. By now, she had almost run through her family money.

She and her new husband were fired from their theatrical engagements in Australia in 1952, and then toured the U.S. in a sex farce, *Pajama Tops*. She received her best notices for domestic skirmishes, promiscuous behavior and heavy drinking. In June 1955, broke and overweight in New York City, she was widowed when Wilcox died of a heart attack. In January 1956, she underwent treatment for alcoholism, and four months later, appeared successfully off-Broadway in *The Ivory Branch*. She wrote her exploitive autobiography, *Too Much, Too Soon* (1957) with Gerald Frank, which was turned into a tawdry movie (1958) starring Dorothy Malone. Again, Diana received praise in a stock version of *A Streetcar Named Desire* and toured in another Tennessee Williams's production, *Garden District*.

During these Williams's productions, Diana fell in love with the avowed homosexual playwright. She became obsessed with the idea of starring in the London production of his *Sweet Bird of Youth*. When he rejected her for the role, she was distraught, especially after he "abandoned" her to go to Key West.

On January 24, 1960, the depressed actress had another of her impromptu parties at her modest New York apartment. The next afternoon, her nude body—stretched face down on the bed—was found by a maid. There were a trio of empty liquor bottles in the kitchen and an assortment of sedatives in a nearby cabinet. After an autopsy, the coroner ruled out suicide or foul play. Among those attending Diana's funeral service at the Frank E. Campbell Funeral Chapel in Manhattan was Tennessee Williams. (He always insisted—contrary to official reports—that Diana had "blood streaming out of her mouth and that there was a heavy marble ashtray shattered against the wall and other evidence of struggle and violence.") She was buried at Woodlawn Cemetery in the Bronx in the family plot next to her mother (who before she died in 1950 told Diana just how little she liked her).

After Diana's death, Tennessee acknowledged, "She was a girl with talent but not enough talent and it haunted her and was destroying her. There was a sort of curse on the Barrymores, I think."

John Barrymore

[John Sidney Blyth]

February 15, 1882 - May 29, 1942

On stage he was known as "The Great Profile." However, in private life, he was the great indulger. Everything about handsome John Barrymore was prodigious: his talent, his thirst for drink and his love of women. His vices diminished a great talent, but ironically insured his legendary status in entertainment history.

He was born in Philadelphia, the son of illustrious stage troupers, Georgianna Drew and Maurice Blyth (who adopted the grandiloquent surname of Barrymore). There were two older siblings— Lionel (1878-1954) and Ethel (1879-1956)—both of whom would also enjoy lengthy acting careers. Hoping to escape the family tradition of actors, John sought a career as an artist. He studied art in London and Europe until his funds ran out. He then worked briefly in New York City as a cartoonist and then as a newspaper illustrator. Fired from both jobs, he accepted his fate and made his undistinguished stage debut in Chicago in *Magda* (1903), but it was a start. He was in San Francisco for a

45

JOHN BARRYMORE

show in 1906 when the great earthquake hit. By 1909 he had succeeded on Broadway with the comedy *The Fortune Hunter.* The next year he wed stage-struck socialite Katharine Harris, an unhappy union that lasted seven years. (She divorced the philandering John, charging desertion.) He continued his stage successes and reached his pinnacle with *Hamlet* (1922). Meanwhile, he appeared sporadically in films, most notably *Dr. Jekyll and Mr. Hyde* (1920).

In 1920, the aristocratic playboy wed poetress Michael Strange. Their daughter, Diana, was born the next year. The tempestuous marriage dissolved into three years of separation, during which he courted young actress Mary Astor. Barrymore and Strange divorced in November 1928. Six days later, he wed the much younger Dolores Costello, a film actress. They would have two children: Dolores Ethel Mae and John, Jr. During the 1920s, John had starred in several highly romantic silent films: *Beau Brummell* (1924), *The Sea Beast* (1926) and *The Beloved Rogue* (1927). They paid for his yachts and his multi-million dollar mansion.

Once talkies came into vogue, Barrymore, with his resonant voice was still in great demand. In contrast to playing a romantic lead opposite Greta Garbo in *Grand Hotel* (1932), he delighted in parts which disguised his still-handsome looks: *Svengali* (1931), *Topaze* (1933). There was much hoopla when John, Lionel and Ethel teamed on camera for the first and only time in *Rasputin and the Empress* (1933). The next year, John and Dolores divorced, with she gaining custody of the children.

By the mid-1930s, John's carousing had taken its toll; his looks were diminishing further and he was having problems in remembering his lines on camera. Although his presence on a sound stage had grown troublesome, he was still wanted for the subordinate role of Mercutio in Norma Shearer's *Romeo and Juliet* (1936). By now John had come under the sway of nineteen-year old Elaine Jacobs (who used the stage name of Barrie). She became his protegee. She pursued him from New York (where they met) to Los Angeles. On November 9, 1936 she and the 54-year-old Barrymore eloped to Yuma, Arizona. Hardly two months after the marriage, she filed for divorce, charging mental cruelty. However, a few weeks later they patched up their differences.

On screen, Barrymore was reduced to playing caricatures of himself, as in *Midnight* (1939). John had not been on the stage since the mid-1920s, but at Elaine's urging he agreed to co-star with her in *My*

Dear Children. The new comedy emphasized the co-stars' off-stage relationship. It toured the East coast, but the visibly aged and weary Barrymore took sick in Washington, D.C. When the tour re-opened in St. Louis, John and Elaine had a spat and she left the cast. The couple were divorced in November 1940 in Los Angeles, she insisting the great thespian had brought her "a great deal of anguish, sleeplessness, and loss of weight." Barrymore never remarried.

By now, the sickly Barrymore was accepting any sort of buffoon roles: *The Great Profile* (1940), *Playmates* (1942). By 1942, his activities were confined largely to radio, where he was the "comedy relief" on Rudy Vallee's program. When his increasing ailments forced him to miss performances, his brother Lionel, substituted for him. John's daughter Diana was now making movies in Hollywood, but he was too worn-out to discipline his profligate daughter.

On May 19, 1942, John appeared at the radio studio for rehearsal of Vallee's *"Fleishmann's Yeast Hour."* When it was time for a run- through, he staggered from his dressing room. Vallee hastened to his side. Barrymore, with tears in his eyes, said, "I guess, this is one time I miss my cue." He was taken to Hollywood Presbyterian Hospital where his condition was listed as grave. He was suffering from complications to the liver and kidneys. From years of abuse to the system, his heart had worn out. On May 29, 1942, after several hours of unconsciousness, he awoke and acknowledged Lionel's presence by saying "hello." Then he lapsed into a coma and soon died. Although he had earned an estimated three million dollars in his lifetime, he died in debt. Shortly before his death, Barrymore had granted an interview in which he said, "Die? I should say not, dear fellow. No Barrymore would allow such a conventional thing to happen to him."

The day that Barrymore died, two of his drinking buddies—director Raoul Walsh and actor Errol Flynn—were memorializing their late comrade at Flynn's house. While Flynn went out on an errand, the inebriated Walsh hatched a scheme. He went to the Malloy Brothers Mortuary on Temple Street in Los Angeles where Barrymore's body had been taken. One of the owners had been an actor who had worked with Walsh in movies. He agreed to letting Raoul "borrow" John's corpse for a few hours. The director drove the body in his station wagon to Flynn's estate. Arriving there, he told Errol's butler, "Alex, Mr. Barrymore didn't die. He's drunk. Help me carry him in the house." They propped the dead star up on a couch. When Flynn walked in, he saw Barrymore's corpse sitting there and dashed frantically from the house. A bemused Walsh shouted, "You missed the old boy and I brought him up here. At least, come in and say hello to him." When Flynn would have no part of it, Walsh and the butler returned the body to the Mortuary. Arriving there, Raoul explained to the drunken co-owner what he had done. "Why the hell didn't you tell me. I'd have put a better suit on him!" (Whether this wild tale is fully true or not, Blake Edwards used its substance in his 1981 movie *S.O.B.*)

Father John O'Donnell, a family friend presided at the requiem mass held for Barrymore at Calvary Cemetery in Los Angeles on June 2, 1942. Diana arrived escorted by Uncle Lionel. Elaine Barrie was in attendance, but neither John's third wife Dolores, nor their children, appeared at the service. Among the ac-

**JOHN
BELUSHI**

tive pallbearers were W. C. Fields, David O. Selznick, Louis B. Mayer and Herbert Marshall. Barrymore was buried in a crypt beside that of Irene Fenwick, Lionel Barrymore's actress wife who had died in 1936. In 1980, John Barrymore's remains were cremated and re-buried at Mt. Vernon Cemetery in Philadelphia, in the family plot. However, his crypt at Calvary Cemetery—bearing the inscription "Good Night, Sweet Prince" —still remains.

John Belushi

January 24, 1949 - March 5, 1982

Over the decades, drugs has wasted many Hollywood celebrities, but none so tragically as the talented, manic John Belushi. The high-voltage comedian was just thirty-three years old when he died of a drug overdose in Hollywood. His sudden death shocked his fans,

caused a highly-publicized industry scandal, and scared some of his pals into going cold turkey.

He was born in Wheaton, Illinois on January 24, 1949. His father was in the restaurant business. There was an older sister, and after John's birth, came two other boys (including Jim who also became an actor). During high school, John was a drummer for the Ravins, a rock-and-roll band, played football (hoping it would lead to a sports scholarship in college) and fell in love with acting. When he lost out on a football scholarship, he went to the University of Wisconsin at Whitewater which had a drama department, and later tried the College of DuPage in Glen Ellyn. In the summers, he had dramatic roles in stock. Then he happened on Second City Television, a Chicago-based revue whose troupe (which included Harold Ramis) specialized in irrevential improvisation. It opened the world of comedy to him. He delighted in mixing straight reality with near slapstick comedy and heavy satire.

John's high-energy revue work generated good notices and led to his being hired for the off-Broadway show, *National Lampoon's Lemmings* in 1973. (When that long-running production ended, he went on to do two other shows, *The National Lampoon Radio Hour* (for which he was both actor and writer) and then *The National Lampoon Show*. His big professional break came in 1975 when he joined the cast of a new, irreverent TV revue show, "*Saturday Night Live.*" The program debuted on NBC on October 11, 1975 and soon became a hit. In the four hectic years he remained with this landmark network program, Belushi became famous for his repertoire of characters which included the leering Samurai warrior and, with co-star Dan Aykroyd, one of the two singing, may-

48

hem-inducing Blues Brothers (which led to a top-selling record album). During this period, in 1976, John married his high school sweetheart, Judith Jacklin.

Belushi's first major movie work was the raucous *National Lampoon's Animal House* (1978), a box-office bonanza in which his gross, outrageous humor made him a screen favorite. In 1979, he left "*Saturday Night Live*" to focus fully on moviemaking. It was during this period that he became more insecure about his fluctuating weight and his ability to keep friends. Self-destructively, he turned increasingly to drugs which made him more insecure and isolated. (One of John's rules was that he did not want those "close" to him to see him under the influence.). He had a close friendship with his screen rival Chevy Chase. The latter tried to get John to quit using drugs, but Belushi always retreated to his chemical escapes.

Despite his talent and energy, Belushi made a string of generally unsuccessful pictures: *1941* (1979), *Neighbors* (1981) *Continental Divide* (1981). Several of them, like *The Blues Brothers* (1980), were made with his pal Dan Aykroyd who called John the "Black Rhino." These relative failures convinced John that the only way to survive the Hollywood jungle was to script and control his own projects. He wanted desperately to be considered not just a boorish comic, but a good actor who could handle more romantic roles. So, he wrote a screenplay called *Noble Rot*. He and his wife flew to New York to await Paramount Pictures' decision on the pending project. The studio vetoed it and wanted him to make *The Joy of Sex* instead. Furious, John returned to the coast alone, staying at the Chateau Marmont Hotel in West Hollywood.

On the night of March 4, 1982, John went out partying with friends to a private rock club, drinking very heavily. Finally returning to his hotel bungalow (#3), his new pal, Canadian-born Cathy Evelyn Smith—a backup singer for Gordon Lightfoot—joined him there. When she arrived, he was pale and sweating heavily. Nevertheless, he continued drinking and snorting cocaine.

Early in the morning of March 5, Robin Williams and Nelson Lyon (a "*Saturday Night Live*" writer) came by the bungalow, as did others. They left after a few minutes. Belushi then showered, and after complaining of the cold and turning up the heat, went to bed sometime between 6:30 and 8 a.m. It would later be alleged that it was Smith who helped calm John's depression by injecting him with a fatal speedball mix of cocaine and heroin.

She went into the living room. About an hour later, she rushed into the bedroom because she heard Belushi gasping for breath. He insisted he was fine and fell asleep again. About 10:15 that morning, she looked in on him again. He appeared okay and she left in his car to have breakfast. She was still out at noon time when William Wallace, his physical therapist who was helping him get into shape, visited the bungalow. He found Belushi in a fetal position on the bed. The room was strangely quiet which worried Wallace, for John was a heavy snorer. Wallace felt his pulse—there was none. Wallace ordered the front desk to send for a doctor. Meanwhile, he tried to revive his friend. Some fifteen minutes later, the paramedics arrived and pronounced Belushi dead.

In Manhattan, it was John's best friend, Dan Aykroyd, who rushed over to Belushi's townhouse at 60 Morton Street to tell Judy the bad news. On March 9, 1982, Belushi was buried in Abel's Hill Cemetery in Chilmark, Massachusetts on Martha's Vineyard, where Belushi and Aykroyd owned property. The procession to the cemetery plot was led by motorcycle-riding Aykroyd, clad in a leather jacket and jeans. Graveside, in the falling snow, James Taylor sang "That Lonesome Road." On March 11, 1982, a memorial service was held in Manhattan at the Cathedral of Saint John the Divine, where, out of respect for John's wishes, Aykroyd played a tape recording of the Ventures' "The 2,000 Pound Bee." Belushi's entire estate was left to Judy.

In the immediate aftermath of John's sudden death, Judy Belushi was stunned into silence. However, she later grew angry about the way it happened. It was she who convinced Watergate reporter Bob Woodward to investigate John's death. His investigation led to the best-selling book, *Wired: The Short Life and Fast Times of John Belushi* (1984) and to the later movie flop, *Wired* (1989). Although the Los Angeles County Medical Examiner's office listed John's death as due to "acute toxicity from cocaine and heroin," local authorities wanted the furor to die down. However, thanks to the turmoil stirred up by Belushi's widow, a Los Angeles grand jury was convened in March 1983. It decided that Smith's actions during Belushi's last, crucial hours were trial-worthy. Meanwhile, Smith had been permitted to return to Canada. An extradition warrant was obtained. Before the June 1986 trial actually began, Smith pleaded guilty to involuntary manslaughter, as well as to three less serious charges, in exchange for avoiding the more serious second-degree murder charge. The maximum sentence she can serve is

eight years, eight months.

Gone but certainly not forgotten, John's meteoric rise and fall is best summed up by the placard at his grave site:

"He could have given us a lot more laughs, but noooooo."

Olive Borden

[Sybil Trinkle]

July 14, 1906 - Oct 1, 1947

From being born Sybil Trinkle in Richmond, Virginia to becoming a has-been movie star on Los Angeles's skid row is a long trip. It took beautiful Oliver Borden forty years to make the harrowing journey.

She was a Southern girl born in 1907 to Irish parents in Richmond, Virginia and was educated in Baltimore convents. By 1922 she was established in Hollywood as one of Mack Sennett's famous bathing beauties and played in Hal Roach comedy shorts.

Three years later, she was chosen as a Wampas Baby Star. Her career got a boost in 1926 at Fox when she co-starred with Tom Mix in *The Yankee Senor* and *My Old Pal*. That same year the studio cast her opposite George O'Brien in the comedy drama, *Fig Leaves*.

Typed as a jazz baby, in 1927 she had the lead in five Fox features. She lived lavishly in a Beverly Hills mansion, never imagining it would all end one day. Then, in a fit of temperament, she walked out on her Fox contract and gained an industry reputation as a troublemaker. That, as well as the introduction of talkies, brought her career to a near halt.

Eventually she survived the advent of talkies with such vehicles as *Half Marriage* (1929). However, after

50

1930, she made no more movies until she appeared in the low-budget *Hotel Variety* (1933). Meanwhile, in March 1931, she married stock broker Theodore Spector. A year later she learned that he was a bigamist and the marriage was annulled.

Cashing in on her former film fame, she sailed to England to make the comedy *Leave It to Me*. She was not yet thirty, but it was the end of her career.

In the mid-Thirties she married John Moeller, a railroad electrician and the couple lived very modestly on Long Island. That marriage, however, ended in divorce in 1941. Switching from job to job, Olive popped up in the news again in 1943 when she joined the Women's Army Corps (WAC) where she was a chauffeur and drove an ambulance.

After World War II, Olive was back in Hollywood, drinking more than she was earning from her temporary jobs. In mid-1946 she was reunited with her mother who was working as a house superintendent for the Sunshine Mission for Women in Los Angeles herself having fallen on hard times.

Olive turned to religion and scrubbed floors at the Mission where she helped to stage the charity organization's Christmas "pageant." The once-upon-a-time star insisted, "I have found the one thing Hollywood couldn't give me—happiness."

Then, in early 1947, Olive began drinking heavily again and vanished into the nether zone of Hollywood. Her mother spent three months searching for her daughter, finally locating her in a run-down hotel on Main Street. Her mother brought the very-ill Olive back to the mission.

Becoming optimistic again, Olive told the press, "The whole world has fallen in on me, but the doctors will

make me well again." However, the next day—October 1, 1947—she died at the Mission, with her devoted mother at her bedside. Found among Olive's scant possessions were autographed photos of herself from her glamorous movie heyday.

Olive was buried at Forest Lawn Memorial Parks in Glendale, California, where her mother was laid to rest next to her some years later.

Montgomery Clift

[Edward Montgomery Clift]
October 17, 1920 - July 23, 1966

Sometimes the road to self-destruction is tortuously slow, filled with years of agonizing self-doubts, debilitating vices, and self-punishing acts. At some point, body and soul can't tolerate any more abuse and gives out. Such was the case with songbird Judy Garland. Another similar victim was her *Judgment at Nuremberg* (1961) co-star—handsome, talented and ever-so-moody Montgomery Clift.

He was born in Omaha, Nebraska in 1920 to William and Ethel "Sunny" (Fogg) Clift. There was an older brother, Brooks, and "Monty" (as he became known) had a few-minutes older twin sister Roberta. Because "Sunny" was illegitimate, she devoted her entire later life to legitimizing her family. The Clifts moved to Chicago in 1924 and later to New York where William proved very successful in the banking business. It allowed Sunny to indulge her fantasies of leading an aristocratic life. She frequently traveled abroad with her children, but without her husband. By age twelve, Monty was intrigued with the theater, and, after a few years of summer stock, came to Broadway in *Fly Away Home* (1935). Over the next decade, he sharpened his skills appearing in such New York productions as: *The Wind and the Rain* (1938) with Celeste Holm, *There Shall Be No Night* (1940) with the Lunts, *The Skin of Our Teeth* (1942) with Tallulah Bankhead and *You Touched Me!* (1945) with Edmund Gwenn. Never in solid physical condition, the slender, darkly-handsome Clift was rejected for World War II duty due to chronic diarrhea.

Throughout his young adult years, Clift was in constant conflict over his feelings towards his over-possessive mother, his homosexuality and his mounting insecurities about his professional abilities. Those who knew the sensitive, polite young man then would say, "Monty had a fence around himself. He told you in certain ways, 'Just don't come too close to me.'" Film director Howard Hawks had been impressed by Clift on Broadway and cast him opposite John Wayne in *Red River* (1948), for which he was paid $60,000. Before that successful movie about a cattle drive was released, Clift went into *The Search* (1948) which earned him the first of four Oscar nominations. With the period drama, *The Heiress* (1949), opposite Olivia de Havilland, Monty was earning $100,000 and considered one of Hollywood's major new finds. Branded as being unconventional, he insisted, "I'm not odd. I'm trying to be an actor. Not a movie star, just an actor." By now, he had become addicted to drugs and drink which caused escalating problems on and off the sound stages. Despite psychiatric therapy, Clift's complex nature grew more knotted.

When he appeared with Elizabeth Taylor in the prestigious *A Place in the Sun* (1951), the two began a life-long friendship. His best-liked screen assignment following this was as the trumpet- playing boxer in *From Here to Eternity* in 1953. He turned down *On the Waterfront* (1954), which won Marlon Brando an Oscar. Instead, he returned to Broadway in a revival of *The Seagull*, hoping to please his drama coach, Mira Rostova, on whom he was overly-dependent. The show's failure, plus losing the Best Actor Oscar to William Holden in the March 1954 Academy Award sweepstakes, filled the frightened actor with increasing self-doubt. For nearly two years thereafter, he rejected movies and stage work, agonizing over each (mis) decision. He lived on borrowed funds.

Finally, desperate for cash, he agreed to co-star with Elizabeth Taylor in *Raintree County* (1957), a costumed epic of the old South. Shooting began on April 2, 1956. On Saturday night, May 12, Clift attended a small gathering hosted by Taylor at her Benedict Canyon home in Los Angeles. After dinner, drug-confused Clift left the party and, shortly thereafter, smashed his rented car into a power pole. It was Elizabeth who, upon reaching the crash scene, pulled two dislodged teeth stuck in Monty's throat. Her action saved his life. Clift's nose was broken, his jaw shattered and his face a bloody mess. After painful reconstructive surgery, the "new" Clift returned to filming in late July.

Though he continued making movies, his ego was more frail than ever over his lost looks. As a result his dependencies deepened. He did a variation of his *From Here to Eternity* part in the World War II combat drama, *The Young Lions* (1958), and was mothered by older co-star Myrna Loy in *Lonelyhearts* (1959). He and Taylor reunited for *Suddenly Last Summer* (1959). The now more remote, mumbling Clift was in the jinxed *The Misfits* (1961), which was the last movie for his co-stars: Marilyn Monroe and Clark Gable. In his next feature, it was a strange twist to have perennial therapy patient Clift portray the father of psychiatry in *Freud* (1962). His behavior was so disruptive on the set that a law suit was filed against him.

With his industry reputation nearly destroyed by his non-professionalism and failing health, he went without work for four years. He resurfaced in a Cold War mess called *The Defector* (1966)— released after his death—in which he looked dreadfully pained and old. Over the years, friends, male lovers and acquaintances had come and gone, but Liz Taylor remained faithful. It was she who convinced industry money men to cast Monty opposite her in *Reflections in a Golden Eye* (1967). He never got to play the part, which

eventually went to Marlon Brando, an old show business friend of Clift's from the New York days.

On the night of July 22, 1966, Clift was in residence at his New York townhouse on East 61st Street. A friend who was caring for him asked if he wanted to watch *The Misfits* on TV. Clift answered, "Absolutely not!" Those were his last words. The next morning, he was found dead—nude—on his bed. The official cause of death was a heart attack, although it was drugs which had done him in. (In his Manhattan townhouse he had a huge customized closet/medicine cabinet to store his drug supplies.) After private funeral services at St. James Church in New York City, Monty was buried in a Quaker cemetery in Brooklyn.

It had been a long painful trail from Omaha to that cemetery in Brooklyn. However, for those around Clift, the inevitable finale was never in doubt. The question had always only been "When?"

Bobby Driscoll

March 3, 1937 - March 1968

The ugly fate of former child stars always makes good copy; far better than reports on the few who adjust to adulthood, like Shirley Temple or Ron Howard. One of the most tragic victims of the Hollywood studio system was talented young Bobby Driscoll. As a youngster, the industry couldn't get enough of him. When he turned into a gawky young adult, the system shoved him aside. He couldn't cope with the bitter rejection and escaped into drugs which killed him.

He was born in Cedar Rapids, Iowa in 1937 and moved with his parents to California in 1943. It was a Los Angeles barber, whose own son was already in pictures, who urged Mrs. Driscoll to have little Bobby try his luck in the movies. She took him to MGM where pixie-faced Bobby was hired for a part in Margaret O'Brien's *Lost Angel* (1943). By the time he was six, cooperative Bobby was making $500 a week. By 1946 he was being touted as "the greatest child find since Jackie Cooper played Skippy [1931)."

Driscoll was the first human actor Walt Disney put under contract. He and equally young Luana Patten were cast in *Song of the South* (1946) and *So Dear to My Heart* (1948), billed as the "sweetheart team." When asked what he intended to do with his weekly earnings, Bobby insisted, "I'm going to save my money and go to college, then become a G-man." His biggest success was in the thriller *The Window* (1949) and he was given a special Oscar as the year's outstanding juvenile performer. Also for Disney, he was Jim Hawkins in *Treasure Island* (1950) and provided the model and cartoon voice for the animated *Peter Pan* (1953).

By 1954, Bobby was in that awkward teenager period, gangly and acne-faced. Finding screen work scarce, he did a few TV guest shots. Away from work, he did not fit in with his peers. "I really feared people," he admitted later. "I tried desperately to be one of the gang. When they rejected me, I fought back, became belligerent and cocky and was afraid all the time." He first tried marijuana when he was sixteen, then turned to harsher drugs, finally becoming a heroine addict. He was arrested in 1956 on a narcotics charge and on suspicion of being a pusher. He tried to straighten out his life, and even had a new film role. However, the project was a trashy study of juvenile delinquents called *The Party*

Crashers (1958), featuring another Hollywood has-been, Frances Farmer, who also couldn't make a successful comeback.

Giving up on acting for the time being, Driscoll found odd jobs, but either he quit or got fired. He married (Marjorie), had a son and determined that his kid wouldn't endure what he was undergoing. When his wife divorced him, Bobby reverted to drugs. He was jailed as an addict in 1959 and in 1961 he was caught robbing an animal clinic. He was locked up at Chino Penitentiary for drug addiction and remained there for more than a year. When he was paroled, he worked as a carpenter and then drifted to New York. His mother would remember, "None of the studios in New York would hire him because he had once been on drugs."

His last months must have been desperate ones indeed. He died penniless in an abandoned Greenwich Village tenement. His body was discovered by two children playing there on March 30, 1968. Two empty beer bottles were found by the corpse and there were needle marks in on his arms. Since no one knew who he was, he was buried in a pauper's grave. The causes of death were listed as a heart attack and hardening of the arteries. Later that year, when Mr. Driscoll was himself dying, his wife tried again to find Bobby. She had no luck, and she went to the F.B.I. for assistance. Time passed and, finally, she heard from a L.A. County agency that her son was officially dead. He had been traced through his fingerprints to that unknown corpse who had been buried back in New York.

Nobody could write a better epitaph to this wasted life than the victim himself. At one point in his tormented adult life, he observed, "I was carried on a satin cushion and then dropped into the garbage can."

W. C. Fields

[William Claude Dukenfield]

January 29, 1880 - December 25, 1946

One of W. C. Fields' biographers (Robert Lewis Taylor) described the raspy-voiced, bulbous-nosed comedian with: "His main purpose seemed to be to break as many rules as possible and cause the maximum amount of trouble for everybody." On the plus side, W. C. had a sharp wit and an even sharper sense of comedy timing (developed during his years as a juggler). He was a consummate entertainer, pure and simple.

However, at the same time, the very mercenary Fields was a crotchety bigot, strongly suspicious of everyone. He was also a man of great contradictions who professed a hatred for a great many things (including children) which he secretly admired. If he was an enigma to those around him, there was no disputing he was a prodigious drinker. His attachment to alcohol surpassed that of his great friend—the legendary lush, John Barrymore. Noted for his eccentricity, W. C. had the attic of his Los Angeles home stacked with cases of liquor. One day he showed the inventory to Harpo Marx. The latter inquired, "Bill what's with all the booze?" W. C. retorted, "Never can be sure Prohibition won't come back, my boy."

However, for all the jokes made about W. C. Fields's Olympian consumption of spirits, the truth was that this dependency caused his cirrhosis of the liver which, in turn, brought about his death.

Because he was so secretive and ambiguous about his childhood, there is considerable doubt as to the day, month and year of his birth, let alone the exact place. Most likely he was born on January 29, 1880 in Philadelphia. His heavy-drinking, foul-tempered father, James Lyden Dukenfield, was a British cockney who had lost two fingers in the Civil War. His mother, Kate (Felton) Dukenfield would give birth to four other children after William Claude. In the course of his impoverished childhood, the youth taught himself to juggle and he made his debut (as "Whitey, the Boy Wonder") at fourteen at a park pavilion near Norristown, Pennsylvania. By eighteen, W. C. Fields, "the Tramp Juggler," was playing vaudeville in Bowery theaters of New York City. In 1900, he brought his mute-tramp juggling act to London, England and that same

W. C. FIELDS

ear, he wed chorus girl Harriet Hughes. Their son, William Claude, Jr. was born in 1904. It was not long, however, before the Fields separated; but the Catholic Hattie always refused to grant him a divorce. Although renown as a miser, Fields always provided well for his family. Thereafter, he had several romantic relationships, the longest-lasting and the final was with actress Carlotta Monti.

Gaining a strong professional reputation through years of touring, Fields was on Broadway in the *Ziegfled Follies of 1915* and simultaneously made his movie debut in the one-reel comedy, *Pool Sharks* (1915). After several *Follies*, he made a big hit on stage as Professor Eustace McGargle in *Poppy* (1923) which D. W. Griffith brought to the silent screen as *Sally of the Sawdust* (1925). Fields's subsequent silent movies were unremarkable. Back on Broadway, he was in Earl Carroll's *Vanities* (1928), which featured two of his greatest comedy sketches ("Stolen Bonds" and "A Episode at the Dentist")—both later made into movie shorts.

W. C. Fields made his talkie debut in a short subject (*The Golf Specialist*, 1931), but it was at Paramount Pictures that Fields really made his mark. His movies ranged from the insane antics of *Million Dollar Legs* (1931) to playing Humpty-Dumpty in *Alice in Wonderland* (1933), to being a tale-spinning lush in Bing Crosby's *Mississippi* (1935). W. C. proved his dramatic prowess in MGM's *David Copperfield* (1935) as the flavorful Micawber. Often writing his own scripts, he used aliases (e.g., Charles Bogle) almost as colorful as the names of his screen characters (T. Frothingell Bellows). The studio was tolerant when Fields insisted his actress girlfriend (Carlotta Monti) be cast in one of his pictures. However, Paramount grew irritated with his constant on-the-set drinking and his increasingly erratic behavior. Deciding his vogue had passed, they dropped his contract in 1938.

He moved over to Universal to do *You Can't Cheat an Honest Man* (1939), a movie in which he traded quips with his frequent radio co-stars, Edgar Bergen and his dummy (Charlie McCarthy). Because of that picture he had to turn down playing the Wizard in MGM's *The Wizard of Oz* (1939). However, he teamed with another unique legend, Mae West, in *My Little Chickadee* (1940). His last movies in the mid-Forties were merely guest appearances in which he rehashed old vaudeville routines. Broadway producer Billy Rose wanted Fields to star in a musical revue, but, now in his mid-sixties and suffering the ill effects of years of heavy drinking, W. C. declined the offer. When the press jibed Fields about his liquor dependency ruining his career, the entertainer took out a full-page advertisement in an industry trade paper insisting that over the decades he had never once missed a performance in any media.

In his last fourteen months, Fields was a patient at the swank Las Encinas Sanitarium in Pasadena, California. He had long vastly disliked the sentimentality of Xmas, but ironically it was on Christmas Day 1946 that Fields found himself on his death bed. Several cronies were in attendance at his cottage. Referring to the newsmen on a death watch outside, W. C. told his friends, "You know, I've been thinking about those poor little newsies out there. Peddling their papers in cold...and rain...sole support of...their mothers. I want to do something for them...." Fields lapsed into silence for a moment and murmured, "On second thought, ___ em!" Later a friend came by and found W. C. reading the Bible. "Bill, what in the world are you doing reading the Bible?" "Looking for loopholes," snapped W. C.

At about 12:03 p.m. on December 25, 1946, he died. Reportedly, just before he passed away, he put one finger to his lips, winked at a nurse standing nearby and then breathed his last. His estate was estimated to be worth $800,000. Nevertheless, he remained frugal to the end: he requested that he be cremated, buried in an inexpensive coffin, and that no fuss be made over his passing. However, his family (i.e. his wife and son) chose otherwise and he ended with three (!) funeral services.

At a non-sectarian public funeral, Edgar Bergen eulogized, "It seems wrong to pray for a man who gave such happiness to the world.... Bill knew life, and knew that laughter was the way to live it. He knew that happiness depended on disposition, not position...." After the initial funeral, Mrs. Field arranged for a Catholic mass. Next, Carlotta Monti, who had been denied admission to the first services by Mrs. Fields, held a third memorial—this one supervised by Reverend Mae Taylor, a Hollywood spiritualist.

For two years, while everyone squabbled over his money, Fields's crypt had no marker. Finally, in 1946 that was remedied. The much-delayed inscription merely lists his name and his birth/death dates. Contrary to popular belief it doesn't contain the remark he supposedly wanted on his marker: "I'd rather be here than in Philadelphia." As for his estate, Fields's estranged wife—on behalf of herself and their son—contested successfully Fields's will which had left bequests to his two sisters, two brothers, Carlotta Monti and for the establishment of the "W. C. Fields College for orphan white boys and girls, where no religion of any sort is to be preached."

W. C. Fields was asked once, "If you had your life to do over, what would you like to change, Mr. Fields?" He answered, "You know, I'd like to see how I would have made out without liquor."

John Gilbert

[John Pringle]

July 10, 1895 - January 9, 1936

"It is getting so that reviewing a John Gilbert picture is embarrassing. .. It isn't that Mr. Gilbert's voice is insufficient; it's that his use of it robs him of magnetism, individuality, and strangest of all, skill."

An early 1930s film critic wrote the above. Like many contemporary moviegoers, he had become disenchanted with John Gilbert—the silent movies' "Perfect Lover"—as he ambled unremarkably through talkie features. In his first sound movies, Gilbert's voice didn't match people's expectation of what he "should" sound like and they never forgave him. Neither did Louis B. Mayer, his MGM studio boss, who argued for years with his swaggering star and did his best to humiliate him into abandoning his lucrative contract. Unable to cope with his career slide during the 1930s, Gilbert turned increasingly to drink and reckless romantic pursuits. His dissolute lifestyle soon led to increasing disappointments. Years before his heart finally gave out in 1936, his spirit had evaporated.

He was born John Pringle in Logan, Utah in 1895, the son of touring stock company actors. As an infant, he was frequently made an im-

57

promptu cast member of his parents' productions. When he was fourteen his mother died. After the family money ran out, he was on his own (in San Francisco and Seattle, Washington), sometimes living on the street and, as he said, "hungry enough to eat out of garbage cans." Once his miserable childhood was behind him, he followed his dream of breaking into movies. Through his father's contacts, John began making films at Triangle Pictures, first in bits and then in small roles. He was in William S. Hart's Western *Hell's Hinges* (1916) and by the next year—now billed as Jack Gilbert—he was the leading man of *The Princess of the Dark* (1917). Dropped by the studio in 1918, he made a string of pictures for minor companies. Meanwhile, in August 1918, he married Olivia Burwell, a movie extra, in Hollywood.

Persistent and versatile, Gilbert pursued his film career, much more interested in script writing and directing than acting. Occasionally, he displayed his literary skills, as when he co-wrote Metro's *The Great Redeemer* (1920). He was signed to a lucrative deal directing movies on the East Coast, all of them to star Hope Hampton. However, the first (*Love's Penalty*, 1921) was a disaster and Gilbert reneged on his contract, fleeing back to Hollywood. He returned to acting (which he often stated he disliked) under a three-year (1921-24) Fox Films contract. He became increasingly popular with the public in *The Count of Monte Cristo* (1922), *Cameo Kirby* (1923) and *The Wolf Man* (1924).

Gilbert and his wife, Olivia, had long been separated when they divorced in 1921. Later that year, he wed actress Leatrice Joy. Their marriage was stormy and in August 1924 she sued for divorce, citing his bad tem-

per, cruelty and drinking. Their daughter (Leatrice Joy) was born a few weeks later. The divorce was made final in June 1926.

The newly-formed Metro-Goldwyn-Mayer hired Gilbert to exploit his dark good looks and his expressive eyes, betting that he could be their answer to Paramount's Rudolph Valentino. He was the dashing, prodigal Prince in *The Merry Widow* (1925) and—without his trademark moustache—scored a huge hit in the World War I drama, *The Big Parade* (1925). Now a major star, he made *Flesh and the Devil* (1927), the first of several features with Swedish import, Greta Garbo. There is dispute as to the seriousness or extent of their off-camera romance but rumors of their "love" affair certainly boosted their box-office appeal together. John was now earning $10,000 a week as Hollywood's highest paid star.

In 1929, Gilbert faced the inevitable—making his talkie film debut. He and Norma Shearer burlesqued the balcony scene from *Romeo and Juliet* in *The Hollywood Revue of 1929*. The sequence was shot in color, but it didn't hide John's stilted performance nor the unromantic vocal timber of his *His Glorious Night* (1929) was Gilbert's death knell. While his career was being shattered, he married stage actress Ina Claire in Las Vegas in May 1929. However, long before they divorced in August 1931, the union had soured, Claire—now doing well in talkies—insisted that he was an impossible person.

Before MGM comprehended that his screen future was bleak, Gilbert had negotiated a hefty new agreement ($250,000 a picture). However, when the studio realized how badly John was doing in talkies, they negotiated to buy out his contract (he refused) and, later, to force him take a pay cut (he again refused). If he was inept in *Way for a Sailor* (1930), he was more than acceptable as the villain of *Downstairs* (1932), based on a script he had written years before. His co-star in that little-seen picture was beautiful, young MGM actress Virginia Bruce, whom he married in 1932. Their daughter (Susan Ann) was born the next year, and in 1934 the couple divorced.

Petulant, juvenile Jack Gilbert brought out the protective instinct in women. Greta Garbo, now MGM's prestige star, rejected Laurence Olivier as her leading man in *Queen Christina* (1933). She insisted Gilbert be given the romantic role, even though the earlier *Fast Workers* (1933) had ended his studio tenure. He was listless and awkward in the new Garbo picture and, thereafter, he quietly left MGM—again.

After months without work, he signed for a secondary role (at a much reduced salary) in Columbia's *The Captain Hates the Sea* (1934), played a disillusioned alcoholic writer. During filming of the modest production, the director had trouble with hard-drinking Gilbert. Studio boss Harry Cohn said "It's too God damn bad, but if a man wants to go to hell, I can't stop him. Shoot around him as much as you can. But keep the picture moving!" When released, the movie and Gilbert were dismissed. It was his moviemaking finale.

Regardless that he brought much of his problems on himself, Gilbert's last years were as cruel as anything Hollywood could have concocted on screen. By now, he was dating the married Marlene Dietrich, who mothered the heavy-drinking ex-matinee idol. She would later say that he frequently complained of chest pains but dismissed them. Having already had a collapse while swimming in his pool six weeks earlier, Jack became quite ill on January 8, 1936. He was confined to bed at his Bel Air home and was under a nurse's care. The next day he had a full-fledged heart attack. The Fire Department's rescue squad attempted to revive him with an inhalator and adrenalin shots. It was no use, he was dead.

An Episcopalian funeral service was held on January 11, 1936. After cremation, Jack's remains were interred at Forest Lawn Memorial Parks in Glendale. He was now officially part of Hollywood's past.

Veronica Lake

[Constance Ockleman]
November 14, 1919 - July 7, 1973

As the song in the musical *Gypsy* instructs, "You gotta have a gimmick." Well 5' 2", 92-pound Veronica Lake did:—her famous peek-a-boo silver blonde hairdo which fell seductively over her right eye. It made her a famous movie star during the World War II years. Then, as her popularity evaporated, she drank to forget. Even after she withdrew from the film industry which had discarded her, she continued to drink heavily. Eventually, her habit did her in.

She was born Constance Ockleman in Brooklyn, New York in 1919. After her seaman father died in 1932, her mother married Anthony Keane, a staff artist with the *New York Herald-Tribune* and Constance adopted her stepfather's surname. For a time, the family lived in Montreal, Canada where silently rebellious Constance attended a convent school. Later, they went to Miami, Florida where she graduated from high school. In a state beauty contest she was named Miss Florida, but was later disqualified because she was underage.

In the summer of 1938, she went to California with her parents and cousin. Her demanding mother enrolled her in elocution classes and the shy daughter obliged begrudgingly. She accompanied a friend on an audition to the RKO studio, and it was Veronica who won a tiny role in *Sorority House* (1939). By the time of Eddie Cantor's *Forty Little Mothers* (1940), Constance had adopted her

VERONICA LAKE

over-the-eye hairstyle which came about by accident when it cascaded over one eye while shooting a scene.

By the summer of 1940, Constance had been hired by Paramount for an aviation drama, *I Wanted Wings* (1941). She also had a new name, Veronica Lake. By the time she returned to Hollywood from Texas locations to finish shooting the picture

she had decided to marry MGM art director John Detlie whom she had met months before. They married on September 27, 1941, not telling her mother, the studio, or anyone. Because of on-set problems, Veronica was already known as a temperamental performer at the studio. Paramount forgave her when *I Wanted Wings* was a big hit and Lake was pronounced a new love goddess. The press wrote so often about her unusual hairstyle that it became a craze throughout America. Every woman wanted to copy Veronica's sweepdown hairdo.

During the filming of *Sullivan's Travels* (1941), the studio learned she was pregnant, and almost removed her from the picture. Her daughter Elaine was born in August 1941. Paramount had had difficulty in finding petite enough leading ladies to pair with compact (5'4") Alan Ladd. This problem was a major reason she was cast opposite him in *This Gun for Hire* (1942). The thriller was extremely popular and was the start of the Ladd-Lake screen teaming. In *I Married a Witch* (1942), Veronica proved she could handle comedy. However, at home, her husband could not abide being Mr. Lake and they fought constantly, even when he joined the Army and was stationed in Seattle, Washington. She was pregnant during the making of *The Hour Before the Dawn* (1944). On the last day of shooting, she tripped over a sound stage cable and began hemorrhaging. She recovered and the child (William Anthony) was born in July 1943, but died seven days later of uremic poisoning. Before the end of 1943, she and Detlie divorced.

While the studio (only paying her $350 a week) gave her little film work in 1944, she spent her ample free time dating a variety of suitors, ranging from Howard Hughes to millionaire Aristotle Onassis. Instead of marrying any of them, on December 17, 1944 she wed Hungarian-born film director Andre DeToth. Their son, Michael, was born the next October, and their daughter, Diana, in 1948. Because of her increasing problems with her Paramount bosses, Veronica rebelled by walking through her screen parts, even when she negotiated salary raises to $4,000 weekly. Neither Lake nor DeToth were good at budgeting their incomes and, by 1948, Veronica again was having financial problems. In mid-1948, her mother sued her not only for back payments of a $200 weekly support agreement, but to increase the verbal agreement to $500 per week. Veronica settled out of court to end the media circus.

When Paramount let Veronica go in 1948, her career nosedived.. Her estranged husband got her the secondary lead in *Slattery's Hurricane* (1949), a picture he directed for Twentieth Century-Fox. By 1951, with her movie career moribund, she and DeToth declared bankruptcy. They separated in June 1951 and were divorced a year later. With no film roles coming to the ex-screen siren, she left Hollywood for New York. As she boarded the plane for the East, she told herself (as reported in her 1969 autobiography), "The Hell with you, Hollywood. And fuck you too."

Lake set up headquarters in a run-down Greenwich Village apartment with her children in tow. She did some TV (roles were few and far between), and she toured in plays (*Peter Pan*, *The Voice of the Turtle*). In 1955 she wed songwriter Joseph McCarthy, who was better as a drinking buddy than running a household full of children. (Her offspring were constantly being shunted back and forth between her home and her ex-husbands' places on the West Coast.) She and the two-fisted McCarthy divorced in 1959. An accidental fall in 1960 put her stage career on halt for many months. When she recovered, she moved to the Martha Washington Hotel for Women on Manhattan's East 29th Street. A reporter found her working as a barmaid there and the discovery made headlines worldwide, with accompanying photos of the bloated, strained Lake.

The ensuing publicity led to Veronica getting a job at a Baltimore TV station hostessing a Late Show movie program. In the summer of 1963 she was hired as a replacement—as a fading movie queen—in an off-Broadway revival of *Best Foot Forward*. Her looks were gone, but her energy was impressive. In April 1965, Lake made headlines again when she was arrested for drunkenness in Galveston, Texas (where she had gone to see a current boyfriend). After this beau died, she moved to Miami where she did stock theatre. She was paid $10,000 to do a Canadian-shot movie (*Footsteps in the Snow*, 1966) which saw little release. The Florida-shot *Flesh Feast*, her last film, was a horror movie mess that was not unleashed on an unsuspecting public until 1970.

In 1969, Lake went to England to promote her British-published autobiography and stayed to do a comedy, *Madame Chairman*, which failed to make it to the West End. She remained in England, to pursue stage work. But, as had happened so often in her past, Veronica's decisions proved to be whims and she was back the United States by 1971, promoting the American publication of her memoirs. When she visited Hollywood for the first time in two decades she hardly recognized the town. She was shocked into tears by the changes at her old studio. By the spring of 1972, Veronica was back in Florida, now accompanied by Robert Carlton-Munro (a retired British sea captain) whom she married that June. They returned to England. However, before long the two were fighting—sober or drunk—and she came back to America alone.

In late June 1973, Veronica visited friends in Burlington, Vermont. By then, the years of drinking had taken a final toll. She was hospitalized on June 26 for "acute hepatitis," and on July 7, 1973, she died at age fifty-three. Her son Michael, then a construction worker in Hawaii, heard of her death over the radio. He borrowed money to fly to Vermont where he arranged for Veronica's cremation (as she had requested). A small memorial service was held in New York at the Universal Chapel on East 52nd Street. None of her one-time Hollywood associates showed up for the services, nor did her other children, or ex-husbands. Her ashes were scattered at sea in the Virgin Islands, a locale she and a past boyfriend had enjoyed so much.

Thinking back over her movie career, Veronica said once, "I wasn't a sex symbol, I was a sex zombie." She admitted "I was never psychologically meant to be a picture star— I left to save my life."

Barbara La Marr

[Reatha Watson]

July 28, 1896 - January 30, 1926

Like another similarly named star (Hedy Lamarr), Barbara La Marr's beauty was breathtaking. She was so ravishing a young woman that a Los Angeles judge declared the young actress was "too beautiful for her own good" and warned her to leave the temptations of Hollywood and return home. A few years later, she left life—a victim of drug and liquor abuse.

She was born Reatha Watson in the desert community of Imperial, California. When she was fourteen, she was arrested when the police raided a Los Angeles burlesque joint where she was working. Although she had broken no laws, the judge advised her to return to her parents' care. When she was sixteen, she visited Yuma, Arizona where she met a ranch hand, Jack Lytell, and quickly married him. A few months later he died. In June of 1914, now using the professional name of Barbara La Marr, she made another stab at show business in Los Angeles. She soon wed Lawrence Converse, a young Los Angeles attorney. However, he was already married and had three children. He was detained on a bigamy charge, but died three days after marrying Barbara during surgery for a blood clot on his brain. Her third husband (1916-17) was dancer Phil Ainsworth. In 1918, she wed vaudeville comic Ben Deely.

By 1920, Barbara La Marr Deely was already a part of the movie industry. She had written several screenplays (mostly at Fox) and had acted in Metro's *Harriet and the Piper* (1920). In April 1921 she and Deely separated and were divorced later (although the decree was not final before her next marriage and Deely would sue her in 1923). Meanwhile, she had come to the attention of Douglas Fairbanks who cast her in *The Nut* (1920) and then as Milady de Winter in *The Three Musketeers* (1921). By 1923 she was a well-paid Metro player. During the course of making *Souls for Sale* (1923), she sprained her ankle and was given morphine to ease the pain so she could continue filming. Early in

1923 she adopted a baby boy, whom she named Marvin Carville La Marr. That May she married her fifth husband, movie actor Jack Daugherty, from whom she soon separated.

Vehicles like *Thy Name Is Woman* (1924) made exotic, gorgeous Barbara a top screen personality. However, by then she had three problems: (1) Metro executive Paul Bern (who would later marry Jean Harlow and then die mysteriously in 1932) had become obsessed with La Marr, (2) the actress had become addicted to morphine and booze, (3) she was a free-loving spirit who was becoming increasingly indiscreet in her escapades. Studio head Louis B. Mayer cancelled her contract and she went over to First National Pictures to make what proved to be her final three features.

In her last months, Barbara was no longer able to cope with her excessive life style. Suffering from drug and alcohol addiction she returned to her parents' home in Altadena near Los Angeles, having had a nervous breakdown. The ever-faithful Paul Bern was one of the few faithful admirers during her last days. When she died on January 30, 1926, the "official cause" was given as anorexia. She was buried in the Cathedral Mausoleum at Hollywood Memorial Park. Her marker reads "With God in the joy and beauty of youth." Barbara's estate included a Los Angeles home and a Malibu beach house. Her son was adopted by actress Zasu Pitts and her husband, Thomas Gallery.

With too much zest for life, "The Girl Who was Too Beautiful" proved to be a victim of her own extraordinary beauty.

Peter Lawford

September 7, 1923 - December 24, 1984

Dapper Peter Lawford was oh so handsome and charming. However, he frequently appeared bland and too elegant on screen at a studio (MGM) filled with distinctive down-to-earth stars like Spencer Tracy, Clark Gable and Van Johnson. Peter was unassuming about his show business career, and for years was a satellite member in the orbit of Frank Sinatra's rat pack. Adding to his strong feelings of inadequacy, the first of Lawford's four wives was Patricia Kennedy, the sister of John, Robert and Edward Kennedy. This marriage put Peter becoming in an almost flunky liaison position between the

PETER LAWFORD

White House and Hollywood. When Marilyn Monroe died under very mysterious circumstances in 1962, Lawford was one of those who really did know more than he wanted to or would reveal about the actress's tangled relationships with the Kennedy clan. Living in the shadow of so many more famous people, the playboy actor turned increasingly to a vigorous diet of drink and drugs. It accomplished its long-terms goals— it killed him.

Peter Aylen Lawford was born in London, England in 1923. His wealthy father, Sir Peter Sydney Ernest Lawford, was a World War I veteran. His flamboyant youngish mother, Lady May, was a strong-willed grand dame (she later wrote her autobiography: *Bitch!—The Autobiography of Lady Lawford*, 1986). Peter was educated in plush private schools and, one day, while visiting a London film set with his mother, he was hired on the spot to replace an inept child performer. Because of an arthritic condition, Lady May frequently traveled to warmer climates and the family accompanied her, with the result that Peter was generally educated by tutors. On one visit to California with his parents, Peter was hired to play a Cockney youth in MGM's *Lord Jeff* (1938) starring Freddie Bartholomew. Lawford might have begun a full-fledged film career then, but his mother wanted him to wait till he was an adult. The family was in Florida when World War II broke out, and they decided to remain in the States.

By 1942, Peter was back in Los Angeles, having worked odd jobs to bring the family to the coast. With a little persistence, he soon found himself signed to a MGM contract. With his good looks, youth and clipped British accent he was in frequent demand on the home lot and on loan-

out. He had a touching death scene in Irene Dunne's *The White Cliffs of Dover* (1944) and was recruited to sing and dance with June Allyson in *Good News* (1947) and then in Fred Astaire and Judy Garland's *Easter Parade* (1948). However, by the early 1950s, his MGM career was over. His prime time had passed, but, by then, he was part of Frank Sinatra's party group (started by Humphrey Bogart and Lauren Bacall), which included Judy Garland, Dean Martin and Sammy Davis, Jr. *After It Should Happen to You* (1954) Peter turned to TV series for work: *"Dear Phoebe"* (1954-55) and *"The Thin Man"* (1957-59).

In 1954, against the wishes of patriarch Joseph Kennedy, Lawford married socialite Patricia Kennedy and they alternated between a Santa Monica beach house and a New York City apartment on Fifth Avenue. They would have four children—a son, Christopher, and daughters Sydney, Victoria and Robin. In 1960, Lawford made *Ocean's Eleven*, his first feature in several years. When Peter and Patricia divorced in 1966 it was the first such happening in the very Catholic Kennedy clan.

Lawford had walk-through movie roles in the Sixties and produced a few of his own: *Johnny Cool* (1963), *Billie* (1965). In 1971, he was Doris Day's physician boyfriend on her TV series and he wed Mary Rowan, the daughter of TV star Dan Rowan; she was 27-years younger than Peter. That alliance lasted until June 1973 when she filed for divorce. Next, Lawford wed Deborah Gould (1976), but they quickly separated and soon divorced.

Since the late 1960s Peter's over-indulgence with drink and drugs had seriously damaged his health. He fooled himself and others by keeping trim and tan, but he had a severe pancreas problem. He occasionally worked on TV and films in the 1970s but spent most of his time feeding his addictions, watching TV game shows and soap operas and borrowing money from friends to keep up "a" lifestyle. His last movie appearance was with Orson Welles and Tony Curtis in *Where Is Parsifal?* (1983).

In December 1983, Peter followed in the path of many other celebrities: he entered the Betty Ford Center in Rancho Mirage, California. He was there to detoxify from substance abuse. Instead of taking the treatment seriously during his six weeks there, he secretly used his charge card to charter helicopters on which a drug dealer shipped him cocaine. Released from the Center, he returned home and to his old ways. In July 1984, he and long-time companion Patricia Seaton married in his hospital room at UCLA Medical Center, a day after he underwent emergency surgery for a bleeding ulcer. By the time he returned home there was no doubt that he was dying. The couple spent Thanksgiving dinner with Elizabeth Taylor, his long-time friend and fellow MGM star. She gave him a brief role in her TV movie, *Malice in Wonderland* (1985). He collapsed during production and barely completed his few lines of dialogue. Much in debt and worn out at age sixty-one, he died of cardiac arrest on December 24, 1984 at Cedars-Sinai Medical Center in Los Angeles. His body was cremated and his ashes were buried in a vault at Westwood (Village) Memorial Park, the same cemetery where Marilyn Monroe rested. In May 1988, the Lawford estate still owed $10,000 in unpaid funeral bills and the cemetery requested either the debts be settled or Peter's remains removed. Patricia Lawford had his ashes disinterred and, on May 19, 1988, they were scattered at sea by his widow from a boat named *Freedom*.

Bela Lugosi

[Bela Ferenc Dezso Blasko]

October 20, 1882 - August 16, 1956

Sometimes a star becomes so identified with a role that it is difficult to separate where the characterization stops and the actor starts. In the case of Hungarian-born Bela Lugosi, the fusion was far greater. So much of his American show business career was tied to playing that bizarre vampire nobleman from Transylvania—Count Dracula—that he often lost his own identity in the process. One of his escapes from the nether world of screen vampirism was drugs, and this dependency contributed greatly to the torment of his final years.

He was born in Lugos, a little Hungarian town in Transylvania in 1882, the youngest of five children in a well-to-do family (his father was a bank executive). As a restless young man he sought satisfaction in acting and studied at the Academy of Theatrical Art in Budapest. By 1900 he had made his stage debut and, two years later, became a member of the National Actors' Company. During this period he acquired his professional surname, adapted from the town where he was born and adding an "i" at the end to give it a flourish. From 1913 to 1919 he acted with the National Theatre in Budapest, gaining acclaim as a matinee idol and winning the admiration and favors of many female admirers, a situation that would continue for several decades. To earn extra money he made movies under the alias of Arisztid Olt, not wanting to dilute his growing stage reputation. In 1917, Bela married Ilona Szmik, a banker's daughter.

Because of the rising tide of Communism in his homeland, he fled to Germany in 1920 where he worked on stage and in movies (including, *Der Januskopf*, 1920, a variation of *Dr. Jekyll and Mr. Hyde.*). While he was in Germany, his wife divorced him. Two years later he came to New York where he starred in and produced several Hungarian-language plays. Meanwhile, he married Austrian actress Ilona Montagh de Nagybanyhegyes, a short-lasting relationship. In 1923, he made his Broadway bow in *The Red Poppy* (as an Apache dancer) and his U.S. film debut (as a German spy in *The Silent Command*). Having already appeared on stage in *The Werewolf* (1924), it was an easy transition for Lugosi to star on Broadway in *Dracula* (1927). The production was a great success both in New York and on the road. While performing as the cultured vampire in Los Angeles, MGM hired him to play the police inspector in their thriller *The Thirteenth Chair* (1929). Meanwhile, he was among the many admirers who dallied with Hollywood's "It" Girl, Clara Bow, in a reportedly torrid affair. By mid-1929, Bela had married for a third time. His new bride was Beatrice Woodruff, a San Francisco widow. The marriage lasted four days and then they were divorced.

When Universal Pictures originally purchased the screen rights to *Dracula*, they intended to borrow MGM's Lon Chaney for the pivotal role. However, Chaney was dying of cancer by mid-1930 and the studio settled on Bela to recreate his stage performance, although he was not well paid for the part. After the movie was released in early 1931 to great acclaim, the middle-aged, heavily-accented actor found himself much in demand in Hollywood. Without knowing it, he had reached

his career peak. Universal asked him to play *Frankenstein* (1931), but after doing a make-up test, he decided against the part because it would hide his profile and allow him no dialogue beyond grunts. Bela had visions of being a grand star of the American cinema. Boris Karloff was substituted in *Frankenstein* and it made him a star.

Much of the remainder of the 1930s was a back-and-forth mix of starring roles in low-budget features or supporting parts in major productions. He returned to Broadway for the musical mystery, *Murder at the Vanities* (1933) and that same year married his secretary, Lillian Arch. (Their son, Bela Jr. would be born in 1938.) Back in Hollywood, he was teamed with his genre rival, Boris Karloff in *The Black Cat* (1934), the first of their six joint movie appearances. His career and finances had reached a low ebb when Universal cast him as the deformed Ygor in *Son of Frankenstein* (1938), which again featured Boris Karloff as the rampaging monster. Now back on a career roll, Lugosi jumped from picture to picture, apparently unmindful of their quality or showcasing value. A highlight for Lugosi was his brief but effective performance as the Commissar in Greta Garbo's *Ninotchka* (1939).

By the 1940s Bela had become a staple performer in poverty row movies, occasionally leaping back to major studio projects. Because his heavy accent limited the range of parts he could play, he was typically cast as a mad scientist or a deranged criminal. In a career irony, twelve years after he rejected the Frankenstein lead, he played the monster in *Frankenstein Meets the Wolfman* (1943) co-starring with the studio's new horror king, Lon Chaney, Jr. In the satirical *Abbott and Costello*

66

Meet Frankenstein (1948) Lugosi showed up as his old self—Count Dracula.

The 1950s were a generally cruel period for the aged Lugosi. Most filmmakers in Hollywood had either forgotten him or thought of the quirky man as a camp joke. Because of painful leg problems (due to a World War I injury when he was in the military service), Bela had become drug-addicted. To revive his bank account and his self esteem, he toured in a Dracula stage revival throughout the British Isles and made the English film, *Old Mother Riley Meets the Vampire* (1952). Back in the States, his fourth wife divorced him in 1953, claiming he was over possessive and terribly jealous. The split-up separated him from his son. Lugosi's movie career continued but at a low ebb with one high point being his popular club act which played Las Vegas in 1954, terminated after several performances only because of his declining health.

Determined to beat his long-standing addiction and perhaps regain the affection of his ex-wife Lillian, the gaunt, frail Lugosi had himself committed to the Metropolitan State Hospital in Norwalk, California. He would later write of the horrors he underwent during the treatment. "My body grew hot, then cold. I tried to eat the bed sheets, my pyjamas. My heart beat madly. Then it seemed to stop. Every joint in my body ached." He was released after ninety days and announced that he was cured. One of the many fans who had written Lugosi during his highly-publicized hospital stay was Hope Lininger. On August 25, 1955, twenty days after he left the hospital, the couple married. Lugosi's fifth wife was more than thirty years his junior. With this age gap and Mrs. Lugosi's discovery that her husband was not the romantic figure of her childhood moviegoing days, the relationship was not a happy one.

Anxious for professional employment and recognition of any kind, Bela joined several other genre relics (John Carradine, Lon Chaney Jr., Basil Rathbone) for *The Black Sleep* (1956). By now, as a result of his years of drugs, he had great difficulty remembering his lines. In June of 1956 he was on stage for three performance in *the Devil's Paradise*, an anti-drug exploitation drama done on the cheap in Los Angeles. He had just started work on the excruciatingly awful *Plan Nine from Outer Space*, when his health deteriorated even further. On August 16, 1956, while his wife was out shopping for groceries, Bela passed away from a heart attack. Ironically, at the time of his death, the next movie Lugosi was to appear in was *The Final Curtain*. He was clutching a copy of the script when he expired.

As he had requested, Bela was buried in his trademark Dracula black cape and tuxedo. For the small gathering who attended the services, it was a strange yet eerily familiar sight to see the open coffin with a Dracula-dressed Lugosi lying inside. He was buried at Holy Cross Cemetery in Los Angeles where his marker was inscribed, "Bela Lugosi 1882—1956, Beloved Father." During his long acting career he had earned over $500,000, but his only asset at death was a building lot worth under $2,000. Drugs and poor career choices in his post-peak years had robbed him of any legacy for his beloved son.

The abysmal *Plan Nine from Outer Space*, with the few minutes of Lugosi's footage worked into its illogical narrative, was released finally in 1959, a golden turkey by anyone's estimation. It was a sad fade-out for the once illustrious Transylvanian Count.

Marie Prevost

[Mary Bickford Dunn]

November 8, 1893 - January 21, 1937

It was not an unusual Hollywood scenario: from silent star to talkie has-been. Brunette, toothy Marie Prevost was more talented than many who fell from grace in the late 1920s. She hung in there throughout the Thirties, mostly reduced to bit screen roles. Neglected and broke, she turned to drink for comfort. When she died, her only companion was her dachshund Maxie. It was two days before her corpse was discovered, due to the dog's whining. Some commentators say that the canine teeth marks on her arms were from her faithful pet attempting to wake her. Others insist that the starving beast had bitten her to satisfy his hunger.

She was born in Sarnia, Ontario, Canada in 1893. Reportedly educated in a Montreal convent, she attended high school in Los Angeles and worked for a short period as a law firm stenographer. By 1917, she had joined Mack Sennett's movie making company as one of his bathing beauties under the name Marie Prevost (the surname belonged to her stepfather). She was soon a leading lady and remained with Sennett until signing with Universal in 1921. (Marie's sister Marjorie "Peggy" Prevost was also appearing in movies by this time.) Marie's career peaked as the star of three wickedly delicious Ernst Lubitsch comedies: *The Marriage Circle* (1924), *Three Women* (1924) and *Kiss Me Again* (1925). Marie had been married to H. B. "Sonny" Gerke from 1918 to 1923. In 1924,

she wed screen leading man Kenneth Harlan, which ended in divorce in 1929.

Marie made a decent transition to sound. However, by the late Twenties, she was in her thirties and playing blowsy tough dames. Roles became harder to find and she began drinking heavily. She put on weight and was off the screen in the mid-Thirties. She tried a crash diet and returned in a few bits: *Tango* (1935), *13 Hours by Air* (1936), *Cain and Mabel* (1936). She had a comedy relief role in *10 Laps to Go* made in late 1936. By early 1937, Prevost was so broke, she borrowed a few dollars from her old friend Joan Crawford.

On January 23, 1937, a hallman at the Aftonian Apartments on Afton Place in Hollywood, investigated the continual howling of a dog in Marie's apartment. He discovered Marie's corpse; she had been dead for two days. Several empty liquor bottles were found as well as checks returned for insufficient funds. She had died from a combination of acute alcoholism and extreme malnutrition. Marie's body was cremated along with that of her mother (who had died in 1926 and whose remains were exhumed). Her final movie (*10 Laps to Go*), an independently-made cheapie filled with fading names and stock footage was not released until mid-1938.

Alma Rubens

[Alma Smith]

1897 - January 21, 1931

Today she is a nearly forgotten entity. However, in her movie heyday in the early 1920s, dark and beautiful Alma Rubens was very popular and quite successful in her Hollywood career. Then drug addiction took over and ruined her career and life. Unlike many, she did not leave the scene quickly or quietly. She left in a blaze of bad headlines. She was born Alma Smith in San Francisco in 1897. With her good looks and her ability to sing and dance, she began a stage career in musical comedies. By 1916 she was in movies, first as Douglas Fairbanks's leading lady in *The Half-Breed*. She remained at Triangle Pictures, starring in an assortment of popular features: *Madame Sphinx* (1918), *Restless Souls* (1919). In August 1918, Rubens wed stage and screen leading man Franklyn Farnum who was twenty-one years her senior. The marriage lasted less than a month. In her divorce suit she insisted he abused her physically. It was the beginning of "the" headlines.

She did not take her screen career as seriously as some other actresses and slowed down to only one or two features a year in the early Twenties. But pictures like *Find the Woman* (1922), *Under the Red Robe* (1923) and *Cytherea* (1924) were enough to keep her a well-known screen commodity.

Alma married Dr. Daniel Carson Goodman in August 1923. He was not only a physician, but also an author who had his own movie production company for which he directed and produced movies. The marriage started with a blissful honeymoon in the Adirondacks. However, by January 1925, Rubens was divorced. She claimed in court that her spouse assaulted her frequently, an allegation verified by her mother Theresa. Alma continued making movies, frequently at Fox, and then under contract to Louis B. Mayer's Metro-Goldwyn-Mayer studio. She always made the right connections with film executives to survive.

In January 1926, Alma married Jacob Krantz of Vienna in a ceremony at Riverside, California. Her newest mate was better known as Ricardo Cortez, the handsome actor Paramount had groomed in the early Twenties to challenge Rudolph Valentino's supremacy as the screen's Latin Lover. Prophetically one of Alma's movies that year was titled *Siberia* for her screen career was soon to slide way downhill and her popularity to grow cold. The lead role that had been planned for Rubens in *The Torrent* (1926)—opposite Cortez—went to newcomer Greta Garbo when Alma was too "sick" to perform. The movie helped to make Garbo a superstar.

There were several reasons for Alma's downfall. Some commentators have said that it began when Alma began experiencing blinding headaches and she consulted a studio-tied physician who prescribed drugs to lessen her pain. Thereafter, other doctors and contacts helped Rubens get the narcotics she felt she needed. Like Wallace Reid and Mabel Normand before her, she became addicted to drugs. (She told pal Joan Crawford, "It was only later that I learned what a terrible poison it was.") Rubens soon developed a glassy, wild-eyed look and a faulty memory. All her earnings were being funneled into her drug habit. After making *Masks of the Devil* (1928), a silent movie with sound effects, MGM didn't renew her contract. Studio head Louis B. Mayer had written her off. "Let her go," he said casually of this raven-haired women of whom he had once been so enthusiastic. It was a sharp lesson to other Metro players.

Rubens made no movies in 1930, although she went East to appear in *With Privileges*, which failed to reach Broadway. She then returned to California to defend her interests in a divorce suit begun by Ricardo

Cortez. While in San Diego, Alma gathered more notorious headlines for her involvement in a narcotics case. Her last months were a horror as her drug addiction took its toll. She was briefly committed to the California State Hospital for the Insane, and when she was released, spent her last weeks in an agony of pain. In her weakened condition she contracted pneumonia and, on January 21, 1931, died at a friend's home in Hollywood

Gail Russell

September 23, 1924 - August 26, 1961

There was always something hauntingly sad about blue-eyed, brunette Gail Russell, even in her early movie successes: *The Uninvited* (1944) and *The Angel and the Badman* (1947). After her death, the former head of Paramount's new talent department said of Gail, "A lovely girl who didn't belong in the movie industry. I believe she would have had a happy life had she become a commercial artist instead of a movie actress." However, she did become a movie star, which led this beautiful, introverted woman into self-destruction. As she herself analyzed, "Everything happened so fast. I was a sad character.... I was afraid. I don't exactly know of what — of life, I guess."

She was born in Chicago, Illinois in 1924 (some accounts say 1921). Her older brother, George, would become a musician, like their father (who later turned to selling cars). As a child, the very shy Gail was happiest when alone in her room drawing or painting. When she was twelve, the family moved to Glendale, California. In 1942, Gail was at Santa Monica Tech studying to be a commercial artist when her name came to the attention of a Paramount Pictures executive. Insecure Gail was reluctant to show up for the interview, but her movie-struck mother made sure her daughter kept the all-important appointment. Gail was signed to a seven-year contract in July 1942, starting at $50 a week. From *Henry Aldrich Gets Glamour* (1943), she jumped into a major picture, Ginger Rogers's *Lady in the Dark* (1944). Her breakthrough role was the haunted, troubled heroine of *The Uninvited* (1944). She was so traumatized by the pressures of her starring vehicle, that she had a nervous breakdown after completing the ghost movie. Upon recovering, she was back on camera, teamed with her good friend, Diana Lynn, in *Our Hearts Were Young and Gay* (1944).

By the mid-Forties, Gail had found an escape from her inferiority complex and the stress of performing. She turned to drinking, which would gradually increase over the years. Meanwhile, she developed an attachment for handsome young actor, Guy Madison. On screen she was the Quaker girl who falls in love with John Wayne in *The Angel and the Badman* (1947). While making *Calcutta* (1947), she became attracted to married director John Farrow, who had a reputation for being a womanizer and being sadistic. In August 1949, Russell and Madison finally married. She claimed to be deliriously happy, but, the next year, Paramount ended her contract. Her one free-lancing film (*Air Cadet*, 1951) was a marginal entry. Gail became increasingly moody and stepped up the drinking, thus losing several potential screen assignments.

In 1953, Mexican singer-dancer Esperanza sued John Wayne for divorce and named Gail—then separated from Guy Madison—as correspondent. The "Duke" insisted the allegations were untrue. Nevertheless, the traumatic situation led to Russell being institutionalized in Seattle, Washington for mental treatment. Hardly had she been released than she was arrested for drunk driving. The next year, she and Madison divorced, he insisting she "cared nothing for their home or marriage." John Wayne came to her rescue again, casting a mature-looking Gail in a Western (*Seven Men from Now*, 1956) that he was producing. Others tried to find her work, but the jobs never seemed to work out.

Gail developed a strong relationship with singer Dorothy Shay that lasted two years. While Shay tried to straighten out her special friend, Russell was too self-destructive to pull out of her problems. In 1957, while inebriated, Russell drove her car through a Los Angeles coffee shoppe window, for which she was put on three years' probation. She did some low-budget pictures in the late Fifties and had an occasional TV assignment, but casting directors felt she was too unreliable. When she was signed for an episode of "*Manhunt*," the once-star told the press, "My morale is high. All you need is a little sunshine and a pat on the back now and then. I have peace of mind for the first time in my life, and I'm happier than ever before."

But things didn't remain that way, as no further work offers came. On August 27, 1961 Gail was found dead in her modest Brentwood apartment on South Bentley Avenue. The place was littered with empty vodka bottles. One neighbor stated she had last seen Russell four days earlier when she had pleaded for a drink. Thereafter, Gail had locked herself in her apartment and refused to come out, despite the urging of neighbors. Eventually, the police were notified and they broke into Russell's place.

The autopsy confirmed that Gail Russell had died of liver disease brought on by alcohol abuse. She had not lived to reach forty.

Among those attending the funeral services at the Westwood Village Chapel were her old Paramount friends: Diana Lynn, Mona Freeman and Alan Ladd. The ex-movie star was buried at the Valhalla Memorial Park in Burbank, California.

GAIL
RUSSELL

SHARON TATE

Judith Barsi

1977 - July 27, 1988

On July 27, 1988, Sherry Barber, the mother of a young actress herself, was one of those watching the Los Angeles TV newscast announcing that 55-year-old Jozsef Barsi had killed his wife and his eleven-year old daughter, Judith Barsi. Judith, who had appeared in episodes of "*St. Elsewhere,*" "*Cagney and Lacey,*" and "*Growing Pains,*" had ironically appeared in the fact-based telefilm *Fatal Vision* (1984) as one of the children murdered by their ex-Green Beret father.

Later in a newspaper article, Sherry wrote that she had first met Maria Barsi in 1985 when Sherry's daughter, Andrea, and Judith were playing sisters—to grandparents Joanne Woodward and Richard Kiley—in the telefilm, *Do You Remember Love?* Sherry thought Judith a happy child, although she noted that Maria barely talked about her burly husband, Jozsef, of whom she said, "When he was young he looked like Mario Lanza."

Only in retrospect did Sherry recall that over the subsequent years, Marie, who always seems so straightforward, strong and capable, was giving off hints of martial discord and fears. Meanwhile, Judith's career continued. In 1987, she appeared in the features *Slamdance* and *Jaws the Revenge*. In May of 1988, Sherry and Andrea encountered Maria and Judith in a studio parking lot. Maria mentioned she wanted to take Judith to Hungary to meet her relatives. However, she was fearful because her husband threatened to burn down their house if she did so. "He showed me where he keeps the gasoline can and told me how he intends to use it." At the time, Sherry noted that Judith had put on a great deal of weight

and that she had no eyelashes. It was the last time Sherry would see the Barsis alive.

On July 27, 1988, Jozsef shot both his wife and daughter through their heads, drenched their bodies in gasoline, lit a match, and then shot himself. In the media coverage following the murders, Judith's agent stated that his young client had once plucked out her eyelashes, along with her cat's whiskers, in a mood of stress.

Judith and her mother were buried on August 9, 1987 in a small ceremony at Forest Lawn—Hollywood Hills. That November, Judith was heard as the voice of Ducky in the animated feature, *The Land Before Time*. Her final screen work was not released until late 1989. In the animated feature *All Dogs Go to Heaven*, she provided the voice of the youngster, Anne-Marie.

Dominique Dunne

1959 - November 4, 1982

In June 1982, beautiful young actress Dominique Dunne had been praised for her appearance in the hit movie, *Poltergeist* (1982), playing the older daughter of Craig T. Nelson and Jo-Beth Williams. Five months later, with everything to look forward to, she was strangled by her 26-year-old, estranged boyfriend, John Sweeney, at her West Hollywood apartment.

Dominque was born with a silver spoon in her mouth. Her industry pedigree included being the daughter of film producer-novelist Dominick Dunne and Ellen Griffin Dunne. Her older brother, Griffin, would also become an actor. She was the niece of writers John Gregory Dunne and his wife, Joan Didion. Born in Santa Monica, California, she attended the fashionable Taft School in Watertwon,

Connecticut, the Fountain Valley School in Colorado Springs, Colorado and also the British Institute and the Michelangelo schools in Florence, Italy.

Deciding on an acting career, she had all the appropriate industry contacts to break into show business. She enjoyed roles on episodes of major TV series such as "*Breaking Away*," CHiPs," "*Fame*," "*Family*," "*Hill Street Blues*", and "*Lou Grant*" and such telefilms as *The Day the Loving Stopped* (1981). Most recently, she had been cast as a regular on the projected science fiction series, "*V*" (1983) which was then shooting a four-hour pilot.

On Saturday evening, October 30, 1982, at her apartment, she and Sweeney, a chef at the chic Ma Maison restaurant, got into a screaming argument about a possible reconciliation and his wanting to move back in with her. When she said "no!" he began to choke her in a fit of anger. Police were called to the scene of the ruckus and, found Sweeney standing over her. When taken into custody, he said, "I have killed my girlfriend." However, Dunne wasn't dead. The unconscious actress was rushed to the intensive care unit at nearby Cedar-Sinai Medical Center where she remained comatose on a life support system for five days. At about 11 a.m. on November 4, her heart stopped beating. (Hospital authorities stated later, "We did not pull the plug. She never regained consciousness and just died.") She was buried at Westwood Memorial Park where her marker, featuring a rose, was inscribed "Loved by All." Her kidneys were donated to an organ transplant bank.

At John Sweeney's subsequent trial, it was revealed that several weeks earlier, the obsessive man had tried to strangle her. Now fearful of him, she had ordered him to move out of her apartment and had changed the locks. During the court proceedings, a letter from the victim to the killer was read. It stated, "The whole thing has made me realize how scared I am of you and I don't mean just physically. I'm afraid of the next time you are going to have another mood swing." When Sweeney was convicted of only voluntary manslaughter in November 1983, the presiding judge (Burton Katz of Santa Monica Superior Court) angrily lectured the defendant: "You hung on to this fragile and vulnerable woman and squeezed and squeezed and squeezed the oxygen from her while she flailed for her life.... This is an act that is qualitatively not of manslaughter but of murder." Sweeney was sentenced to the maximum prison term of 62 years. He was released in June 1986. Such is justice.

Sal Mineo

[Salvatore Mineo, Jr.]
January 10, 1939 - February 12, 1976

With his constant baby-face, compact Sal Mineo was forever cast as the sensitive juvenile delinquent. Twice-nominated for an Oscar and an Emmy winner, he never got very much beyond his career successes in the 1950s as a teen-age idol. His career floundering during the 1970s Hollywood, which had found younger leading men for their new-style movies, Sal became more drug-dependent. Then, just as his career was taking a new path (stage directing), he was murdered one late evening in West Hollywood, killed by the type of disturbed young man he had so often played on camera.

He was born Salvatore Mineo, Jr. in 1939, one of four children born to a

Sicilian immigrant couple. His father made caskets for a living. Young Sal grew up in a rough Bronx neighborhood and by the age of eight was a gang member and a troublemaker. His mother sent him to dance classes, hoping that would change his ways. Instead, at ten he engineered the theft of gym equipment from his school. He was caught and chose going to a professional high school for acting hopefuls rather than a home for delinquent kids. With his Italian good looks, the young Sal was cast on Broadway in Tennessee Williams's *The Rose Tattoo* (1951) where he had one line ("The goat is in the yard"). He was next an understudy in the musical *The King and I*, but graduated to playing the young prince for nearly two years. He made his screen debut playing Tony Curtis as a young man in *Six Bridges to Cross* (1955). However, it was his role as Plato, the switchblade-wielding delinquent in *Rebel without a Cause* (1955), that won him an Oscar nomination as Best Supporting Actor and insured his fame. There were rumors that he and that picture's star were lovers, but Mineo later told a pal, "We could have been...just like that, but we never were."

With his new-found success, Sal bought his family a fancy home in Mamaroneck, New York. As a teenage heartthrob, he tried a recording career, and his song "Start Moving" was a hit. The rest of the Fifties saw him cast over and over again as a street rebel, occasionally going offbeat, as when he played an Indian in *Tonka* (1959) or the drum-playing musician in *The Gene Krupa Story* (1959). Sal's career peaked with his Oscar-nominated role as a Zionist in *Exodus* (1960). Having played a Jew who killed Arabs in *Exodus* cost him a role in *Lawrence of Arabia* (1962),

because the Jordanian government would not allow Sal to enter their country for location shooting. Off screen Mineo had a preference for men, but in the limelight he had publicity-engineered "romances" with assorted starlets (Jill Haworth, Tuesday Weld, Joey Heatherton).

By the end of the Sixties, his acting roles were few, and Sal turned to stage directing. He supervised a controversial new production of *Fortune and Men's Eyes* (about homosexuality and rough life in prison) in Los Angeles and then again off-Broadway in New York. His last movie was as one of the simians in *Escape from the Planet of the Apes* (1971). In the fall of 1975, he staged and starred in *P.S. Your Cat Is Dead* in San Francisco, playing a bi-sexual burglar. On the night of February 12,

**SAL
MINEO**

1976 he was returning home to his West Hollywood apartment from a rehearsal of the upcoming L.A. production of *P.S. Your Cat Is Dead* at the Westwood Playhouse which was to co-star Keir Dullea. Having parked his car in the building garage, he was waylaid by an unknown assailant. A neighbor heard him shout, "Help! Help! Oh, my God." Raymond Evans rushed to his aid, giving him mouth-to-mouth resuscitation. By the time the paramedics arrived, it was too late. According to the coroner's determination, Mineo had "died of a massive hemorrhage, due to the stab wound of the chest which penetrated the heart." A witness came forth later stating he saw a long-haired Caucasian male fleeing the scene. Robbery was ruled out as a motive since Mineo's wallet had not been taken. Other theories suggested that Sal had died as a result of

bad drug deal, or that his death was a by-product of his homosexual life style.

With the crime still unsolved, a funeral service for 37-year-old Sal was held at Holy Trinity Roman Catholic Church in Mamaroneck, New York five days after the murder. Among those attending were Jill Haworth, Desi Arnaz, Jr., Michael Greer and *Rebel without a Cause* director Nicholas Ray. Mineo was buried at the Cemetery of the Gate of Heaven in Hawthorne, New York. Two years later in a Michigan prison, 21-year-old Lionel Ray Williams, a one-time pizza delivery boy, bragged to his cellmate that he had killed Mineo and that it had been easy to do. (On the night of Sal's murder when the news flashed on TV, Williams's had told his then girlfriend, "That's the dude I killed." However, at the time there was not enough evidence to arrest Lionel for the crime.) In February 1959, Williams who had a disturbing record of arrests and brutalizing victims, was convicted of murdering Mineo and received a 51-years-to-life sentence. The trial judge categorized Williams as "a sadistic killer" who "if released, he will no doubt kill again." The case of the "midnight marauder" was finally solved.

At Sal's funeral service, his brother-in-law, Chips Meyer, had said, "He lived his life with courage, abandon, humor, style and grace. His art, what he created, will always stand. Nothing can take it away from him."

Ramon Novarro

[Jose Ramon Gil Samaniegos]

February 6, 1899 - October 31, 1968

In the 1920s, Hollywood boasted three handsome matinee idols who made women everywhere swoon:

RAMON NOVARRO

Rudolph Valentino, John Gilbert and Ramon Novarro. By the end of the Twenties, Valentino had died and Gilbert was washed up by the talkies. However, Mexican-born Ramon, with his dashing good looks, possessed a fine, if accented, speaking voice and could sing as well (his version of "Pagan Love Song" became a recording hit). As he grew older and acting styles changed, the roles grew fewer, but he continued to work on TV occasionally in the 1960s. Then, on Halloween eve in 1968, he was murdered brutally in his Spanish-style Hollywood Hills home on Laurel Canyon Boulevard. The gory bludgeoning of the once-star gave Novarro the kind of headlines he had not had since he starred in *Ben-Hur* (1926).

He was born Jose Ramon Gil Samaniegos in Durango, Mexico in 1899, the oldest of thirteen children of a well-to-do dentist. The closely-knit family later moved to Mexico City. After the Mexican revolution, the family relocated to Los Angeles in 1913. When the father died soon thereafter, Ramon became the head of the household. Scrambling for an income, he worked assorted jobs: piano teacher, grocery clerk, theater usher, and busboy at the Alexandria Hotel—all the while wanting an entertainment career. For a while, Ramon was a cafe singer and then he performed in a vaudeville ballet troupe. Eventually, he began winning small film roles. He did a dance in Mack Sennett's *A Small Town Idol* (1921) clothed only in a loincloth and turban to show off his fine physique. And then he had a bit in Rudolph Valentino's *Four Horsemen of the Apocalypse* (1921). He and Valentino had been good friends for a few years—some say lovers. Ramon's big break came when director Rex Ingram cast him in the lead of The

Prisoner of Zenda (1922). The film was a hit, and with his role in *The Arab* (1924), Novarro was the screen's new Latin lover.

In 1925, Novarro was earning $10,000 a week at MGM and was given the lead in *Ben-Hur* (1926). It was the zenith of Ramon's career. Having built a 17-room mansion, his mother and several of his brothers and sisters came to live with him. Ironically, while Novarro was the idol of million of women, he preferred the company of men. For a while, he thought of leaving pictures to become an opera star, but the talkie revolution allowed him to both act and sing. He made a successful talkie, *The Pagan* (1929) and his screen career continued, with roles opposite Greta Garbo (*Mata Hari*—1932) and Myrna Loy (*The Barbarian*—1934). Occasionally he directed a feature. Growing restless in Hollywood (as MGM was with him), he went to Europe, made a movie, and then went on a stage tour with his sister Carmen. Back in California, he tried a comeback (*The Sheik Steps Out*—1937), but the result was more burlesque than satire.

The 1940s found Ramon alternating between his 50-acre ranch near San Diego, making an occasional film abroad, touring in summer stock, and, late in the decade, doing character parts in Hollywood features. His final movie role was in *Heller in Pink Tights* (1959), although he made infrequent TV appearances in the 1960s.

By the late 1960s, gray-haired Novarro was approaching seventy. He lived an almost hermit-like existence in his Hollywood Hills home, attended by long-time friend and secretary, Edward Weber. He found distraction in alcohol (he had several drunken driving arrests) and the services of male hustlers. When Weber summoned the police to Novarro's home on the morning of October 31, 1968, they found the living room in a shambles and the bedroom a blood-bath. The former star was lying dead on his king-sized bed, nude, his body bruised from head to toe. His ankles and wrists were tied with an electric cord and there was a zigzag mark (perhaps a "N" or "Z") on his neck. On the mirror was scrawled "Us girls are better than fagits." A broken black cane had been placed across the actor's legs. Underneath the bloody corpse, the police found the name "Larry" scribbled in large letters on the sheet. (The name "Larry" was also found written on a telephone pad.) In a neighbor's yard, they found a heap of bloody clothing.

It turned out that the Larry referred to had known Novarro and had passed on the rumor (that Ramon had $5,000 in cash stashed in his house) to his 23-year-old brother-in-law, Paul Ferguson of Chicago. The latter had served time in a Wyoming prison for grand theft and was on the loose in Hollywood, his young wife having left him. Paul wanted to leave town, but needed money. Joined by his 17-year-old brother, Tom, Paul arranged for a rendezvous at Novarro's house. They arrived around 5:30 p.m. and the three began drinking. Weber returned to the house with cigarettes for Novarro at 6 p.m. However, after giving his employer the package at the door, he left without going into the house. Later, the three drunken men attempted to eat the dinner that Weber had left for his boss.

When drunk, Paul—who hated himself for having to hustle—became extremely violent. In the bedroom, Paul beat the nude actor viciously when the latter tried to sodomize him. He had Tom help drag the unconscious actor to the shower to wash off the blood. Novarro briefly regained consciousness, infuriating the drunken Paul who, then, smashed the riding cane over the actor's head and shoulders. Novarro fell to the floor and suffocated in his own blood. The brothers later dragged him to the bedroom and tied him to the bed to make it look like a robbery and that a woman had been with Novarro. It was Paul who had written Larry's name on the sheet and the note pad and had scribbled the mirror message. They even placed a condom in the dead man's hand. However, the only money they found in the house was $45. The young men tore off their bloody clothes, put on others taken from Ramon's closet, and, while fleeing, flung their bloody clothes over a fence into a neighbor's yard.

With the notoriety from his murder, more than a 1,000 people paraded by Novarro's open coffin on November 4, 1968, the day of his funeral. He was buried in a simple grave at Calvary Cemetery in Los Angeles.

Meanwhile, in following up the clues, the police checked a 48-minute phone call that had been made on the murder night from Novarro's house to Chicago and found that it had been made by Tom Ferguson. With that and other clues (including fingerprints at the scene of the crime), the police arrested the brothers in Bell Gardens (near Los Angeles) on November 6, 1968. At their July 1969 trial, the Ferguson brothers were convicted of murder and sentenced to life in prison. However, seven years later, they were paroled.

Rebecca Schaeffer

November 6, 1967 - July 18, 1989

Other Hollywood screen and TV personalities have been murdered over the decades. However, the senseless shooting of Rebecca Schaeffer in 1989 polarized public sympathy and outrage. Perhaps it was because the promising actress was twenty-one, beautiful, and already so successful, and that her assassin was a crazed fan obsessed by his unrequited love for her.

Rebecca was born in 1967 in Eugene, Oregon, the only child of a psychologist and a writer. As a child growing up in Portland, she was active in the local synagogue and thought briefly of becoming a rabbi. By age fourteen, she was modeling and thinking of an acting career. When a TV movie (*Quarterback Princess*, 1983) was shot on location in McMinnville, Oregon, she won a tiny role. At age sixteen, she took off on her own for New York City ("I know my parents went through hell," she admitted later.) She attended the Professional Children's School in Manhattan, eventually graduating. She had a small continuing role on the soap opera "*One Life to Live*" in 1984. She then went to Japan to model where her short height (5'7") wouldn't be an obstacle. Upon returning to New York, she was cast by Woody Allen in a brief part in *Radio Days* (1987).

Rebecca became a prime-time TV personality when she was hired to play Pam Dawber's sixteen-year-old sister in "*My Sister Sam*" (1986—88). When asked how she coped with the pressures of "instant" success on the network sitcom, she responded coolly, "I was never frightened. I wasn't nervous. I knew I could do it and all I felt was happiness at getting the chance." With her career as-

cending, she made the sex farce *Scenes from the Class Struggle in Beverly Hills* (1989), went to Italy for the two-part TV movie *Voyage of Terror: The Achille Lauro Affair* (1990), and back in the U.S. was directed by Dyan Cannon in a picture.

On Tuesday, July 18, 1989, at 10:15 a.m., Rebecca was at her Sweetzer Avenue apartment in Hollywood, about to leave for an audition for *The Godfather, Part III* (1990), where she was to read for director Francis Ford Coppola. The doorbell rang and, because the intercom system was broken, she answered the ring in person. Dressed in a black bathrobe, she opened the glass security door to her two-story apartment building. After talking briefly with the visitor, she went back inside when he left. However, he soon returned and when she dismissed him, the young man aimed

REBECCA
SCHAEFFER

THE HOLLYWOOD DEATH BOOK

a handgun at her. The shot hit her in the chest and she collapsed. Paramedics rushed her to nearby Cedar-Sinai Medical Center where she was dead on arrival.

On July 22, 1989, she was buried at Ahavai Sholom Cemetery in Portland, Oregon. Rabbi Joshua Stampfer eulogized that Rebecca "brought in her short life more joy to more people than most of us achieve in a lifetime." Among the two hundred attending the service were Pam Dawber and her actor-husband, Mark Harmon. As the casket was lowered into the ground, Rebecca's father, Benson, grieved, "Oh Rebecca. We're always thinking of you. We will always think of you." Then, he and other relatives tossed ceremonial shovelfuls of dirt into the grave. Schaeffer's Los Angeles boyfriend (Bradley Silberling) and her best friend (Barbara Lusch) passed out copies of Schaeffer's poems (which they had typed the night before) as memorial tokens for the mourners. Within a short time after Rebecca's murder, Los Angeles police had compiled information about a "bookish looking" suspect whom had been spotted by several neighbors in front of Schaeffer's apartment building for several hours before the shooting. The young man had been holding up a picture of Schaeffer and asking passersby where she lived. After the homicide, the suspect had fled the scene. The next day, on July 19, 1991, Tucson, Arizona police detained nineteen-year old Robert John Bardo for creating a public nuisance on the streets. At the time he made statements that linked him to the Schaeffer case.

As the facts were pieced together, it developed that Bardo, a one-time Tucson janitor, had been a devout admirer of Rebecca's and had begun writing her fan letters in 1987. (Years

earlier, he had been obsessed with Samantha Smith, a ten-year old Maine girl who gained fame by writing to the premier of Russia. Bardo had traveled to Manchester, Maine to meet her, but had been prevented by police who detained him as a runaway minor.) Bardo received an autographed picture of Rebecca in response to writing her care of "My Sister Sam" and interpreted that as an indication of a special rapport existing between he and the actress. In late June 1989, Bardo paid a Tucson detective agency $250 to trace Rebecca's whereabout (accomplished through the California Department of Motor Vehicles). Now having her address, he quit his fast-food restaurant job in Tucson and took a bus to California. Once in Los Angeles, Bardo appeared one day at the Burbank Studios with a five-foot tall teddy bear and a bouquet of flowers for Schaeffer. A security guard at the front gate tried to dissuade the young man from continuing his quest. Next, with a gun that Bardo's brother had purchased for him (and which he had then taken without permission), Bardo arrived at Schaeffer's building. He talked briefly with her, they shook hands and he left. Having forgotten to give his idol a letter and a compact disc he had for her, he returned, and rang the bell again. When she politely said, "Hurry up, I don't have much time," he became offended and pulled the .357 magnum gun from his shopping bag. While she screamed "Why? Why?" he fired and then ran away. He later testified in court that he "almost had a heart attack" when he learned that night on TV that Rebecca was dead.

In his September 1991 trial in Los Angeles, it was determined that the defendant, who had a history of mental problems, suffered from schizophrenia. However, it was ruled that he was not legally insane at the time of the killing. The Superior Court judge found Bardo guilty of first-degree murder and guilty of special circumstances (i.e. lying in wait to kill the actress). Because Bardo had waived the right to a jury, the death sentence was not an option; instead, Bardo was sentenced to life imprisonment without the possibility of parole. Rebecca's parents had attended each day of the trial. After the verdict was rendered, Mr. Schaeffer stated outside the courtroom, "I feel that Rebecca will not come back to us as a result of the verdict, but justice was done."

As a repercussion from Rebecca's death, a California law was passed shortly thereafter restricting access to Department of Motor Vehicle information. Using her daughter's needless death as an example, Mrs. Schaeffer became a vocal advocate of handgun control laws nationwide.

Carl "Alfalfa" Switzer

August 8, 1927 - January 21, 1959

In 1935, the *Our Gang* movie shorts added another young actor to its comedy roster. He was gangling, freckle-faced Carl Switzer—the one with the cow-lick and a squeaky voice that screeched off-key when he sang. Nicknamed "Alfalfa" by producer Hal Roach, the boy quickly developed into a popular screen personality. However, he had one career problem: he grew up. No longer a sought-after commodity in the industry, he turned to drinking. Then he ended up dead, shot in an argument over fifty dollars.

He was born on a farm in Paris, Illinois in 1927. Carl and his older brother, Harold, often sang at local events. When they visited their grandparents in California in early 1935, the boys decided to visit the studio where those great *Our Gang* comedy shorts were made. They had no way to get onto the lot, but the studio cafeteria was just outside the gate. One day at lunchtime, the brothers made an unscheduled appearance. Dressed in coveralls, they treated the diners to an impromtu round of hillbilly songs. Roach was impressed by their gutsiness and hastily wrote them into a comedy short (*Beginner's Luck*, 1935) then in production. Harold, known as "Deadpan" or "Slim," remained with the series for a few years, but generally as a background figure. However, Alfalfa soon developed quite a following and rivaled Spanky McFarland as the focal point of the trouble-prone on-screen kids. In a six-year period, Alfalfa bounced through sixty-one short subjects.

By the end of 1941, Switzer had left the Gang, now physically too adult to partake in the Gang's juvenile she-

"ALFALFA"

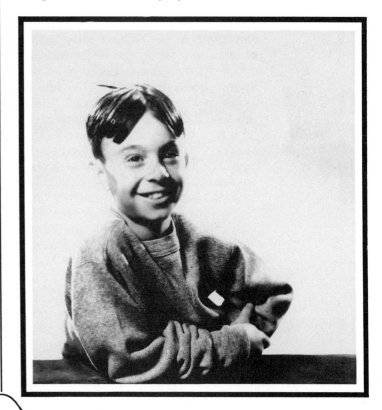

nanigans. He pounded the beat of film casting offices, where he was greeted with a constant "Didn't you use to be...? Hey, Alfalfa! Sing off-key for us!" It frustrated the young man—badly! Occasionally, he was given small movie roles: *The Human Comedy* (1943), *Going My Way* (1944), etc. He joined the low-budget Gas House Kid film series in the mid-Forties but the series sputtered out after three entries. When screen jobs were too few, he made a modest living as a bartender and sometimes as a hunting (fishing and game) guide, often in northern California. (Henry Fonda and Roy Rogers were among his clients).

In 1954, Carl married an heiress from Kansas, but the marriage was finished in five weeks. A disillusioned Switzer told the press, "Bear hunting and marriage don't mix." Irritated with life's stumbling blocks, he started drinking more frequently and heavily. When inebriated, he turned boastful and pugnacious, which frequently led to barroom brawls. Once, in early 1958, he was shot at by an unknown assailant as he left a bar. His pal Roy Rogers used him on his TV series four times between 1952 and 1955 and Switzer appeared in a segment of "*Science Fiction Theater*" in 1955. Mostly, however, Hollywood had forgotten him. When he was hired for the small role of Angus in *The Defiant Ones* (1958), he had visions of the long hoped-for comeback finally happening. Instead, the Tony Curtis-Sidney Poitier picture proved to be his swansong.

On January 29, 1959, Carl and a friend stormed over to the home of Bud Stiltz in North Hollywood. Switzer had recently lost Stiltz's hunting dog and it had cost Carl a $50 reward to retrieve the animal. Now he wanted Stiltz to reimburse him. Having failed in his efforts over the telephone, he now barged into Stiltz's living room. During the ensuing argument, the drunken Switzer grabbed a nearby heavy clock and cracked it over Stiltz's head. The blow cut Stiltz badly over his eye. While Switzer's pal remained an onlooker, Stiltz ran to his bedroom for his gun, with Alfalfa in hot pursuit. The two men fought over the weapon. It discharged, causing Stiltz's fiancee and her three children (who were huddled with her in the bedroom) to flee to a neighbor's house. Next, Carl drew his hunting knife and yelled he was going to kill his opponent. He charged the man and Stiltz fired. The bullet hit Carl in the stomach and he collapsed, dead.

Carl was buried at Hollywood Memorial Park. His marker, besides his name, carries a profile drawing of Petey (the Our Gang dog) and two Masonic symbols. At Stiltz's trial, the defendant broke down crying while reciting the facts of the case. The jury decided it was "justifiable homicide."

When Carl Switzer's father died in 1960, he was buried next to Alfalfa—the boy who couldn't take it when Hollywood turned its back on him.

Sharon Tate

January 24, 1943 - August 9, 1969

In the annals of Hollywood, there have been many shocking murders of show business celebrities. However, none was as gruesome as the wanton killing of pretty Sharon Tate and her jet-set Hollywood pals by satanic Charles Manson and his deranged clan. More than two decades after the horrendous massacre, the mere mention of the sensational case still makes even the most stoic individuals shudder, especially those who claim they were supposed to have been at Sharon's that horrid night.

She was born Sharon Marie Tate in 1943 in Dallas, Texas, the oldest of three girls. Because of her father's employment—he was a lieutenant colonel with U.S. Army Intelligence—the Tates moved a great deal as he was constantly re-posted. Throughout her childhood, the strikingly beautiful Sharon won several beauty contests, including being named Homecoming Queen at the Vicenza American High School (Verona, Italy). The stage-struck Sharon got background work in several films shot on location in Italy: *Hemingway's Adventures of a Young Man* (1962) and *Barabbas* (1962). Determined to break into the film business, Sharon was thrilled when her father was reassigned to California. Now she would be much closer to her dream city— Hollywood.

By early 1963, Sharon was Los Angeles-based, living at the Hollywood Studio Club and working occasionally in TV commercials. After being introduced to Martin Ransohoff, president of Filmways, she was assigned by him to the recurring role of Janet Trego on "The Beverly Hillbillies" (1963-65) and other bit TV roles. The producer also cast the breathtakingly attractive blonde in several of his features: *The Wheeler Dealers* (1963), *The Americanization of Emily* (1964) and *The Sandpiper* (1965). For a while, she dated French actor Philippe Forquet, then in Hollywood making *Take Her, She's Mine* (1963). However, their brief liaison was full of heated arguments. More lasting was her relationship with swinging hairstylist Jay Sebring, who enjoyed a celebrity clientele of top male Hollywood stars. It was while on location in England for *Eye of the Devil* (made in 1965; released in 1967) that Martin Ransohoff introduced her to Polish-born director Roman Polanski. Ransohoff convinced the very offbeat Polanski to cast Sharon in the female lead—as a Jewish innkeeper's daughter—of *The Fearless Vampire Killers* (1967). Polanski reluctantly agreed to use Tate instead of actress Jill St. John. Before they completed the genre parody, this most unlikely pair—the diminutive, cynical, worldly Roman and the imposing, optimistic, simplistic Sharon—had fallen deeply in love.

When Tate returned from making the Polanski horror spoof, she and Roman shared a house together in Santa Monica. Next, Ransohoff gave her the showy part of a curvaceous surfer in the Tony Curtis comedy, *Don't Make Waves* (1967). Then, one of the few highlights of the tawdry *Valley of the Dolls* (1967) was Tate's performance as sex siren Jennifer North, who commits suicide after suffering a mastectomy. Compared to her co-stars (Patty Duke, Barbara Parkins), Sharon received glowing reviews.

On January 20, 1968, in London, 24-year old Sharon wed Polanski, ten years her senior. Among those attending the ceremony were Warren Beatty, Leslie Caron and Michael Caine. After playing one of Dean Martin's girl toys in *The Wrecking Crew* (1969), Tate ended her exclusive contract with Ransohoff. With Polanski to guide her, she preferred to free-lance now that she was a rising name in the international film industry. Meanwhile, she and Polanski were part of the trendy Hollywood set, playing and dining everywhere. Before Sharon left for London to shoot *Thirteen Chairs* (1970) with Orson Welles and Vittorio de Sica, the Polanskis rented a house at

10050 Cielo Drive off of Benedict Canyon Road in Bel Air. (The prior tenants had been Doris Day's son, Terry Melcher and his girlfriend, Candice Bergen. They had moved out recently because of Melcher's need to help Day straighten out her finances after her husband's death.) Because Roman had pre-production film conferences to attend in Europe, after Sharon finished her movie, she returned alone to California in July 1969. At the time she was eight months pregnant.

Although Sharon had several new movie projects lined up (*The Story of O*, *Tess of the D'Urbervilles*), her focus was on the pending birth of her child and planning a party for Roman who was due back home before his birthday on August 18. On a hot August 7, 1969, the very pregnant Sharon went with several actor pals to a TV episode screening at Universal. The next day, actress Joanna Pettet and another friend came to Sharon's for lunch. That evening, Sharon was invited by a friend to a small dinner party. Instead, Tate changed her mind, claiming she was very tired. She insisted that she and Jay Sebring would go out for hamburgers and she would spend a quiet night at home.

On Saturday morning (August 9, 1969), when the maid arrived at the house on Cielo Drive she found a chilling sight. In the blood-drenched living room were the butchered bodies of Sharon and Jay Sebring, with a white cord trailing from Sharon's neck to a ceiling beam and extending to Sebring's neck. (He had also been shot.) The word "Pig" was written in blood on the front door. On the lawn were the mutilated bodies of a couple who had been staying with Sharon while Polanski was away: Abigail Folger (25-year-old daughter of the chairman of the Folger Coffee Company) and Wojtek Frykowski (Ro-

man's 32-year old childhood pal). Eighteen-year-old Steven Parent was found dead in his car near to the gate. He was a friend of nineteen-year old William Garretson, the estate caretaker, who had been in the out-of-the-way guest house during the entire massacre. Because Garretson had his stereo blasting music into his headphones, he had not heard the victims' screams.

Over 200 people attended the service at Holy Cross Memorial Park in Culver City. A tearful Polanski had returned in time for the services. Father O'Reilly eulogized, "Goodbye Sharon, and may the angels welcome you to heaven, and the martyrs guide your way." The casket, containing the body of Sharon and her unborn son (Paul Richard) was buried on the cemetery grounds. The white marble marker reads, "Beloved wife of Roman . . . Sharon Tate Polanski . . . Paul Richard Polanski . . . Their Baby." A few days afterwards, Sharon's movies were re-issued nationwide.

At first it was suspected that the killings were drug-related, since Sebring and some of the others murdered had been part of that culture. However, on December 1, 1969 the media reported that the police had issued homicide complaints against Charles Manson, Susan Atkins, Linda Kasabian, Patricia Krenwinkel and Tex Watson, all of whom would soon be known as the Manson Family. (The Family had killed several other people before and after the Tate massacre, but this time, had left traceable clues.)

Although the full motives may never be known, it seemed that the psychotic Manson had sent his followers to Cielo Drive for revenge. Manson had written several songs which he brought to record producer Terry Melcher who, in turn, had rejected them as being not of interest. Thinking Melcher was still living at the house, Manson had returned there asking for a second "audition" and been turned away by Sharon and Jay. The rejection led the twisted Manson to ordering the killing. At the 1971 trials of Manson and his family, all five were given death sentences. However, before they could be executed, California did away with the death penalty (in most instances) and the Family was, instead, sentenced to life imprisonment. Manson is at San Quentin Prison, while his underlings are at other state institutions. Sharon's mother became involved with POMC (Parents of Murdered Children) and each time there is talk of paroling any of the murderers, she gathers new sets of signatures to petition California officials to veto the parole of the Manson Family. When Polanski finally made *Tess* (1979) with Nastassia Kinski in the role intended for Tate, the movie was dedicated "To Sharon."

TYRONE POWER AFTER HEART ATTACK ON SET OF SOLOMON AND SHEBA

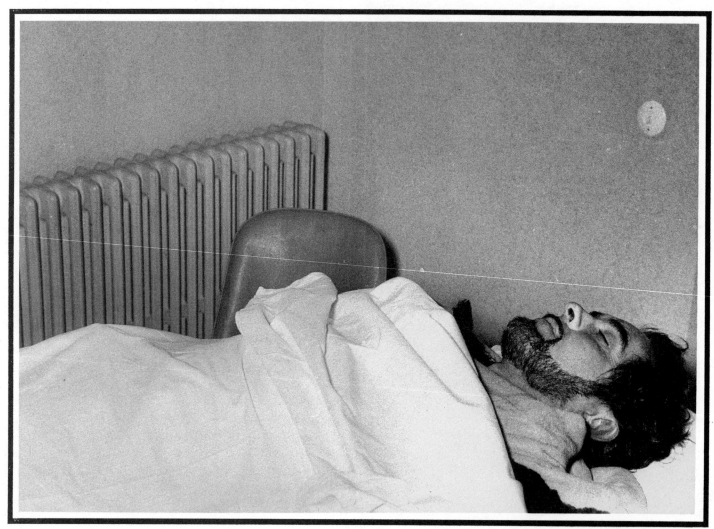

photo courtesy Photofest

Bud Abbott

[William A. Abbott]

October 2, 1895 - April 25, 1974)

During the 1940s, the daffy comedy team of Abbott and Costello were the public's favorites, helping audiences to forget the woes of World War II. Being in such high demand, the uproarious screen team made a great deal of money. However, neither actor was wise enough to invest his earnings smartly. It led to tremendous heartache, especially for Bud Abbott, who survived his chubby partner by fifteen painful and sad years.

William "Bud" Abbott was born in 1895 in Asbury Park, New Jersey, one of four children. His father (Harry) was a publicity advance man for the Barnum and Bailey Circus, his mother (Rae) was a bareback rider with the tent show. After a scattered school education, Bud began his show business career as a Coney Island amusement park barker, later becoming an assistant box-office treasurer for the Casino Burlesque House in Brooklyn. A few years thereafter, he decided he could perform standard burlesque comedy routines as well as any performer. This realization led to his performing in front of the footlights. He chose to be the straight man in his act because that role generally paid more than being the clowning partner.

The tall and thin Abbott and the short and pudgy Costello had been performing separately in burlesque when they were first teamed in 1936 on the Minsky burlesque show circuit. The funsters rose to popularity with personal appearances at Atlantic City's Steel Pier, Kate Smith's radio program and on Broadway in *Streets of Paris* (1939). They made their feature film debut in *One Night in the Tropics* (1940) and by the time of the slapstick service comedy, *Buck Privates* (1941) they were big movie stars. Throughout the Forties, whether in movies, on radio or in personal appearances, they could do no wrong with the public.

The 1950s were another matter. By then, the public had fastened onto Dean Martin and Jerry Lewis as their new favorites. Bud and Lou made their last feature (*Abbott and Costello Meet the Mummy*) for their home studio—Universal Pictures—in 1955. By then, their long run on TV's variety program *"The Colgate Comedy Hour"* was over and their half-hour comedy series was two years in the past.

As their fame diminished, their personal problems increased. Costello's poor health, a result of rheumatic fever, overweight and hypertension, deteriorated further. They reunited for one further movie, *Dance with Me Henry* (1956), a sloppy comedy done on the cheap. With their careers in the doldrums, what once had been an almost friendly rivalry between the two comedians developed nasty overtones. The team broke apart. Lou, who had come to think of himself as the major talent of the two, made solo TV guest appearances as well as starring solo in the movie, *The 30-Foot Bride of Candy Rock*. However, before that picture could be released, he died of a heart attack on March 3, 1959.

Hardly had Lou been buried, than the Internal Revenue Service intensified its pursuit of Abbott. The IRS demanded over $750,000 in overdue past taxes. Because of his freewheeling spending in the good years, the harried Abbott admitted, "I can't afford to quit working, and I certainly can't afford to die.

The taxes would wipe out my family." To appease the government, he was forced to sell his Encino, California estate as well as his 200-acre ranch at a loss. His wife sold her jewelry and furs,

BUD ABBOTT

and the actor relinquished his remaining share of profits from his and Lou's Universal movies. The frantic Abbott informed the press, "I'll have to start all over" and he begged his fans to donate 50 cents a person to help out. The appeal brought little results and the discouraged Bud teamed with Candy Candido, a show business veteran, whom he hoped could be a successful replacement for Bud's fat sidekick. After a few test engagements, Abbott had a reoccurrence of epilepsy and the attacks—when combined with his other ailments and his heavy drinking—left him too weak to pursue the comeback.

In 1964, Abbott suffered a stroke, paralyzing his left side. He partially recovered, but then had another stroke. In 1967 he was well-enough to supply one of the voices for a series of 200 five-minute Abbott and Costello TV cartoons. It was the finale to his show business career. Bud spent his final

three years confined to home. In 1972, he broke his hip and was wheelchair-bound for his remaining days. During his last year, he stopped drinking altogether, but then developed cancer and, early on the morning of April 24, 1974, he died at the age of seventy-eight. After a small funeral, his remains were cremated and the ashes scattered at sea. Betty, his wife of fifty-six years, was forced to sell their modest home to pay additional tax bills, but the debts continued to plague her until her death in 1981.

To his final days, a bereft Abbott puzzled about his late partner, "I never understood Lou. I never knew why he broke us up so suddenly."

Renee Adoree

[Jeanne de la Fonte]

September 1, 1898 - October 5, 1933

Just like a movie story, screen star Renee Adoree had a fairytale-like beginning. She was born in a tent in France where her parents (her British father was a clown; her French mother was a horseback rider) were performing in a circus. After a career as a dancer and bareback rider in her father's circus, Renee came to Hollywood where the exotic, vivacious young actress quickly became in demand. After her second American feature, *Made in Heaven* (1921), she married her leading man of that movie, Tom Moore. By the mid-1920s she was a major MGM personality and reached her zenith as the farm girl love interest of John Gilbert in the World War I epic, *The Big Parade* (1925). That same year she divorced Moore and later married a Hollywood agent, William

S. Gill, from whom she would also be divorced. In Hollywood's transition to talkies, Renee was cast opposite Gilbert again in *Redemption* (1929) and then with Ramon Novarro in *Call of the Flesh* (1930). By then, it was evident that the heavily-accented Renee was too much a product of the silent era and could not make a successful crossover to the new medium.

In 1930, when Renee discovered she had tuberculosis, she relocated to Prescott, Arizona for her health. In early 1933, deeply missing the exciting Hollywood scene, she returned to Los Angeles. However, on October 5, 1933, she died at her home in Tujunga, California as a result of her lung ailment. Renee was buried in Hollywood Park Cemetery, in the Abbey of the Psalm Mausoleum, right next to writer Gene Stratton Porter.

Jack Albertson

June 16, 1907 - November 25, 1981

He never graduated from high school. As he recalled, "I was bright but disruptive. I didn't do homework. To cover, I made wisecracks and funny faces at the teachers. They told me to take my business elsewhere." Never the less, before his lengthy show business career ended, he had become one of the few performers to have won the Oscar, Tony and Emmy awards.

Born in Malden, Massachusetts, Albertson learned his initial dance steps in local pool halls where he was first a rack boy and then a game hustler. He moved to New York City during the Depression;in due time earning chorus roles and small parts in comedy revues.Next, he tried the Catskills resorts where he developed a comedy act with Phil Silvers. After that, Jack became a straight man for such comics as Jack Benny, Milton Berle, Jimmy Durante and others. He went to Hollywood where he managed a few brief parts. However, his joining the comedy revue, *Meet the People* (1940), brought him to Broadway and led to other shows, including a revival of *The Red Mill* (1945), and are-teaming with pal Phil Silvers in the stage (1951) and film versions (1954) of the burlesque revue, *Top Banana*.

Being cast with fellow comedian Joey Faye in a West coast production of *Waiting for Godot* was a major professional turning point for Albertson. This role led to further stage work, including the tormented father in *The Subject Was Roses* (1964).Albertson won a Tony for that performance, and when the drama was translated to the screen (1968) he won a Best Supporting Oscar for recreating his remarkable delineation. He continued to make films—including *Willy Wonka and the Chocolate Factory* (1971).

Jack, who had been appearing on TV since the 1940s gained his greatest show business fame in the teleseries *"Chico and the Man"* (1974-78) playing cranky, cynical Ed Brown, the owner of a run-down garage in the barrio of East Los Angeles. While Albertson had won an Emmy in 1975 for a guest appearance on *"The Cher Show,"* he also won another Emmy in 1976 for his work on *"Chico and the Man."* Now at the height of his fame, Jack quipped, "One nice thing about achieving success at this age is that I have fewer years to become a has-been." However, his next TV series, *"Grandpa Goes to Washington"* (1978-79) was short-lived.

A constant worker, Jack remained active until the end, despite suffering from cancer. At the time of his death at his Hollywood Hills home, his latest picture—*Dead and Buried*—was in current release. His last TV work, an NBC special, *"Grandpa Will You Run with Me?"* was not aired until April 1983. Jack was survived by his third wife, as well as by a daughter, Maura Dhu, a singer-actress. His actress sister, Mabel Albertson, would die of Alzheimer's disease in 1982.

Gracie Allen

July 26, 1902 - August 27, 1964

Certainly one of the most successful marriages of the twentieth century was that of George Burns (New York Jewish) and Gracie Allen (San Francisco Irish Catholic). In one of his many autobiographies, Burns (born: Nathan Birnbaum on January 20, 1896) noted, "You know, lots of times people have asked me what Gracie and I did to make our marriage work, It's simple— we didn't do anything. I think the trouble with a lot of people is that they work too hard at staying married. They make a business out of it." Burns has always credited the on-stage daffy Gracie—known as "the smartest dumbbell in the history of show business"—as the real brains of their hugely successful act.

In his B. G ("before Gracie") show business years, Burns used a variety of pseudonyms, later claiming that he feared not getting work if managers remembered him from past (bad) performances. For a time, he had a Latin dance act and was even teamed for a spell with a trained seal. In late 1922, cigar-chomping George and petite Gracie(already an experienced if not successful performer) were introduced by mutual friends and soon became a team. At first, she played the straight man in their vaudeville act, and he delivered the comedy lines. Audience reaction led them to switching roles. They were married in 1926 and, three years later, made their first film short at Paramount's Long Island studio. Paramount soon was featuring the couple in such comedies as *Six of a Kind* (1834), with W. C. Fields, and *We're Not Dressing* (1934), with Bing Crosby.

However, starting in 1932, it was on radio that Burns and Allen gained their greatest fame with their weekly comedy program. The couple ended the decade with a final joint screen appearance at MGM in *Honolulu* (1939). Afterwards, George temporarily retired from the screen, while Gracie continued to make an occasional picture. *After Two Girls and a Sailor* (1944), she too retired from the demanding medium (they hated to get up early, put on makeup, etc.). They continued successfully in radio and, in 1950, began their long run on television with *"The George Burns—Gracie Allen Show."* By this time,their adopted children (Sandra and Ronald) were approaching adulthood, with Ronnie attempting his own show business career. In 1958, Gracie, because of a heart condition, abandoned show business permanently, allowing her to devote more time to her family, gardening and painting. George continued on, sometimes as a solo act,sometime with a new stage partner (Carol Channing, Ann-Margret) or with a new TV series co-star (Connie Stevens).

Shortly after Burns began production on his new TV sitcom, *"Wendy and Me,"* in 1964, Gracie suffered a heart attack. She died, with George at her side, on August 28, 1964. Although

Gracie was Catholic, the funeral service was held at All Saints Episcopal Church in Beverly Hills. (Burns, a Jew, could never be buried next to his wife in consecrated ground, but he could under Episcopalian rites.)

Gracie was buried in a mausoleum at Forest Lawn Memorial Parks in Glendale, California. Burns recalls, "When Gracie died, I was very upset and couldn't sleep. We had twin beds the last years she was alive because she had a bad heart. So finally I decided to change over and sleep in her bed, and it worked. There was something warm about that." To this day, the still very professionally active Burns continues to visit Gracie's crypt where he bids hello to his "sweetheart."

Jim Backus

February 25, 1913 - July 3, 1989

Veteran actor Jim Backus chased after show business fame for decades. When it finally came in the 1960s—as the cartoon character voice of the myopic old grouch Mr. Magoo—he could not shake the typecasting: "Every time I start to be a serious actor," he sighed, "I lose out because someone—usually a producer—says I'm Magoo."

Backus was born into a well-to-do family in a posh suburb of Cleveland, Ohio. His father owned a successful machinery company, but Jim had show business ambitions and moved to New York City where he attended the American Academy of Dramatic Arts. There, in 1941, he met his wife-to-be, Henny, an artist-actress. He did stage and radio work before going to Hollywood for a brief role in *The Pied Piper* (1942). After serving in World War II, he returned to Los Angeles, doing more radio work and beginning an active film career in 1949. Usually he was cast as an overly jovial businessman or a heavily scowling figure. Backus once described his movie career as a procession of "best friends—the guy who always drove the bride to the church, but never married her." A favorite role was that of James Dean's father in *Rebel without a Cause* (1955). In the late Fifties, he recorded a novelty album, "Dirty Old Man," and one cut, "Delicious" made it to the top forty charts.

It was on TV, however, that Backus became best known, playing Joan Davis's long-suffering husband in "*I Married Joan*" (1952-55). He first played the near-sighted, raspy-voiced Magoo in the animated TV special, *Mr. Magoo's Christmas Carol* (1962). This production led to the series, *Famous Adventures of Mr. Magoo* (1964-65), and to further specials, as well as theatrical and TV shorts. Adding to his laurels, Jim was cast as the pompous Thurston Howell III on "*Gilligan's Island*" (1964-67). In 1968-69, he was seen as the overbearing J. C. Dithers in the new "*Blondie*" TV series, in which his real-life wife had a recurring role.

In the 1980s Backus appeared in several TV movies furthering the adventures of the cast of "*Gilligan's Island*" and made his last acting TV appearance in 1983 in a dramatic assignment on "*Medical Center*." By the mid-1980s, Backus was suffering from Parkinson's disease. Already the author of his life story, *Only When I Laugh* (1965), he and Henny co-authored *Backus Strikes Back* (1984) and *Forgive Us Our Digressions* (1988), hilarious yet touching reminiscences dealing lightly with his debilitating disease.

On June 13, 1989 he was admitted to St. John's Medical Center in Santa

LUCILLE BALL

Monica with double pneumonia, complicated by his progressive Parkinson's disease. He died on July 3, 1989, survived by his wife. He was buried at Westwood (Village) Memorial Park.

Lucille Ball

August 6, 1911 - April 26, 1989

Hollywood movie stars have risen and fallen for years. However, few of them ever made the impact of Lucille Ball, America's favorite zany redhead. Ironically, it was not the two decades of non-stop filmmaking that did the trick for Ball. Instead, it was *"I Love Lucy"* (1951-57), the TV sitcom she engineered to bring Lucy and her off-screen husband Desi Arnaz closer to-

gether again. On the small screen, the larger-than-life Lucy proved a delightfully resourceful comedienne. Week after week, she demonstrated that she was a wonderful mixture of the best qualities that made such funsters as Milton Berle, Charlie Chaplin, Jackie Gleason and Harold Lloyd so great.

The future superstar was born in Jamestown, New York in 1911. Her father died when Lucy was four; Mrs. Ball remarried but her new marriage ended in divorce and she supported her two children (Lucy and younger Frederick) by working in a local dress shop. Mrs. Ball wanted Lucy to study piano, but her daughter was already drawn to show business. By 1926, Lucy had moved to New York City to study drama. She failed in her studies, but refused to give up. The tall, shapely blonde was fired during rehearsals for a new Broadway musical because she was a clumsy dancer. But, again, she wouldn't quit. She turned to modeling, which ended when she became severely ill and spent nearly two years recuperating in Jamestown.

Bouncing back, Lucy came to Hollywood's attention by having modeled for a cigarette ad. She became one of producer Samuel Goldwyn's "Goldwyn Girls" dressing up the background of Eddie Cantor musicals like *Roman Holiday* (1933). When that path led nowhere, she signed on at Columbia Pictures, working in their production mill for months, before finding a safer harbor at RKO Pictures. She learned her skills through a long apprentice period and was helped by the mother of studio star Ginger Rogers who gave drama classes on the lot. With supporting roles in the all-star *Stage Door* (1937) and *Having Wonderful Time* (1938) Lucy began to make her mark. Good pictures or bad, she kept turning out movies, sometimes seven a year. She was becoming RKO's B picture queen, leading one wag to quip, "she was classified with the scenery." While making *Too Many Girls* (1940), she fell in love with her co-player, Desiderio Arnaz y de Acha— better known as the bongo-playing Cuban heart throb, Desi Arnaz. On November 11, 1940, the couple eloped to Greenwich, Connecticut.

By the time Lucy left RKO in 1942, she was earning $1,500 weekly. She always knew when to jump ship and this time, moved over to MGM which transformed her into a glamorous redhead and showcased her in the musical, *DuBarry Was A Lady* (1943). However, she then stagnated at the illustrious film factory. In 1947, 36-year-old Lucy faced facts. If she couldn't be a big movie star, how about another medium. She toured on stage in *Dream Girl* and that same year took on a radio comedy series, "*My Favorite Husband.*"

By now, Lucy's marriage to Desi was sinking. It was the usual story of both parties being too career-oriented, plus hard-living Desi having a wandering eye. Nevertheless, on July 17, 1951, Lucy gave birth to their first child, Lucie Desiree. Then, to patch together their failing marriage, Lucy coaxed Desi (an astute businessman) into joining with her in the TV sitcom, "*I Love Lucy,*" which went on the air on October 15, 1951. The slapstick escapades of Lucy and Ricky Ricardo and their pals, Fred and Ethel Mertz (William Frawley, Vivian Vance), hit the nation's funnybone. When Lucy became pregnant again, it was worked into the top-ranking comedy fest. Off camera, she gave birth to Desi, Jr. on January 19, 1953. By the late 1950s the various versions of "*I Love Lucy*" had run its course and the Balls had bought RKO

for their Desilu Productions. On May 4, 1960, America's favorite couple divorced. While on Broadway doing the musical *Wildcat* (1960) Ball met comedian Gary Morton and they married in 1961. Addicted to the limelight, Lucy returned in two further comedies series, "*The Lucy Show*" (1962-68) and "*Here's Lucy*" (1968-74). As time passed, it grew harder for aging Lucy to compete with the new faces on the airwaves. Her final theatrical feature, *Mame* (1974), was a disaster. She went the path of many veteran stars: talk programs, game shows and award specials.

In the mid-1980s, Lucy's health began failing severely. Although now in her seventies, she refused to give up. She did a dramatic TV movie, *Stone Pillow* (1985), partly because, as a pathetic bag lady, she did not need to worry about how drawn she looked. Compulsive and demanding at home and work, Lucy was determined to prove she could do it again. In the fall of 1986 she returned in a new TV series, "*Life with Lucy.*" But what had been funny in the 1950s—when she was far younger—didn't work thirty-five years later. The sitcom was yanked after a few months. The humiliation did more damage than the stroke Lucy suffered in May 1988. She rallied from that crisis and appeared on the March 29, 1989 Oscar telecast trading quips with friend Bob Hope. Despite her growing catalog of ailments, Lucy still did not want to retire. She told Phyllis Diller, "I'll never take it easy. I don't want to be around when the scripts stop coming in or the phone stops ringing. I don't want a living death."

On April 18, 1989, Lucy had a heart attack, but refused to leave her Beverly Hills home for Cedar-Sinai Medical Center until she had put on her makeup. She underwent eight hours of open-heart surgery. She survived the ordeal, but the prognosis was negative. Friends and fans rallied with thousands of messages of encouragement. On the evening of April 25, as her husband Gary left her hospital room, she said, "Good night darling. See you in the morning." Those were her final words to him. She died at 5:04 a.m on April 26 of a massive heart attack. When Morton was given the bad news, he said tearfully, "I've lost my best friend."

According to Lucy's wishes, there was no funeral service. She was buried at Forest Lawn-Hollywood Hills. On Monday, May 8, 1989, a tri-city set of tributes was held for Lucy at 8 p.m., the night and time of her long-running three TV shows. At St. Monica's Catholic Church in Santa Monica, at New York City's St. Ignatius Loyola Catholic Church and at Chicago's Old St. Patrick Church, friends and fans united to memorialize the late comedienne. In December 1991, a full-sized statue of Lucy was unveiled at the Television Academy's Hall of Fame court in North Hollywood, California.

William Frawley died in 1966, Vivian Vance in 1979 and Desi Arnaz in 1986. With Lucy's passing, the last of the "I Love Lucy" gang had gone. At least, those remarkable re-re-runs are there to constantly remind us what a marvelous talent Lucy, the first lady of television, was.

Suzan Ball

February 3, 1933 — August 5, 1955

When she arrived in Hollywood as a Universal-International starlet, Suzan Ball was promoted as "The New Cinderella Girl of 1952". In the next four years, she co-starred in several Hollywood features and had a very promising career. However, at the age of twenty-two, she lost her battle to cancer and died.

She was born near Buffalo, New York. Not only was she a descendant of Massachusetts Pilgrim leader John Alden, but she was a second cousin of actress Lucille Ball. The family moved briefly to Miami, Florida in 1938, but later returned to Buffalo, and, in 1947, relocated to North Hollywood, California. During high school, Suzan was an avid choral club performer and hoped to become a professional singer. She initiated an appearance on Richard Arlen's "*Hollywood Opportunity*," a local TV show, which led to her joining Mel Baker's Orchestra for the next three years. When her parents moved to Santa Maria, California, Suzan remained in Los Angeles. She won a job as a harem girl in the low-budget *Aladdin and His Lamp* (1952) at Monogram Pictures.

Through an acquaintance, actress Mary Castle, Suzan was auditioned by Universal and was signed to a studio contract in October 1951. She had a bit in Gregory Peck's *The World in His Arms* and was officially introduced on screen as a black mailing dance hall gal in the Western *Untamed Frontier* (1952). Suzan had a brief romance with that film's co-star, Scott Brady.

During the filming of *City Beneath the Sea* (1953), Suzan fell deeply in love with older Anthony Quinn, and she pursued the married but womanizing actor relentlessly. Their publicized romance lasted a year. During the period, they co-starred in *East of Sumatra* (1953) in which she was to perform an exotic dance. Wanting to impress Quinn, she insisted that she did not need a dance double (Julie Newmar) for the scene, and did the intricate steps herself. She misjudged a step, falling to the cement floor on her right knee. It hurt a great deal, but she soon forgot about it. Later, when she was back east on a personal appearance tour, she banged the same knee again in a minor auto mishap.

By now, Suzan had broken off her romance with Quinn and was dating fellow contract player Richard Long. They became inseparable. In the course of her next film, *War Arrow* (1953), her doctor told her she had developed a tumor in her right leg. When off camera she used crutches to get around, but refused to take the throbbing pain seriously. She tried new doctors, but each of them told her that unless a miracle occurred her leg would have to be amputated. She and Long, who now planned to marry, refused to accept the diagnosis. The accident-prone Suzan slipped at home and broke her leg. She was operated on and even though surgeons thought they had removed all the cancerous tumors, the malignancy spread and the leg eventually was removed. The press chronicled the event and Suzan gained stature with the public for her bravery.

On April 11, 1954 she and Long were married in Santa Barbara. She walked down the aisle using her new artificial limb. The next month the couple acted together on a *"Lux Video Theatre"* episode, she playing a wheelchair-bound victim who walks by the finale. Director George Sherman had worked with Suzan in *War Arrow* and cast her opposite Victor Mature in *Chief Crazy Horse* (1955). When the studio wanted to replace her with Susan Cabot, Sherman insisted that Ball be kept: "She doesn't act with her legs, she acts with her face, with her mind, with her spirit."

Despite the physical pain, Suzan continued her career, going on a club tour date with Long to Palm Springs and Phoenix. While rehearsing a *"Climax"* TV show, she collapsed and was rushed to the hospital. The cancer had spread to her lungs. Now constantly heavily sedated with drugs, Suzan's personality changed drastically. Her distraught husband Richard fell into a brief relationship with Suzan's full-time nurse, Kay Biddle.

Nearing death, Suzan was only barely conscious most of the time. Some days before the end, she said: "I felt no pity for myself, nor have I any feeling of regret. Sometimes I pondered, 'Why has this thing happened to me?' But it was never in terms of a complaint, I sought a real answer. It is not an easy one to find, and perhaps I will never know." On the evening of August 5, 1955, as Long sat by his dying wife, she awoke, murmured "Tony" in reference to her past lover, Anthony Quinn and died. Funeral services were conducted at Forest Lawn Memorial Parks in Glendale, California. Pallbearers and ushers at the funeral included actors John Agar and Hugh O'Brian. Nearly twenty years later, Long, who had married actress Mara Corday, died of a heart attack on December 21, 1974.

Florence Bates

[Florence Rabe]

April 15, 1888 — January 31, 1954

Sometimes great love and great tragedy occurs to one who is not traditionally beautiful, but who possesses a remarkable inner glow and resiliency. Such was the case with Florence Bates, a short, plump character actress who was engaged in nine different careers in her lifetime. She did not make her official screen debut—in *Rebecca* (1940)— until she was past the age of fifty. One of Florence's theories of life was: "Never underestimate the intelligence of an opponent, an audience, or a child. Whenever you do, you get your comeuppance and you jolly well deserve it."

Born in San Antonio, Texas, Florence was a musical prodigy, but she injured her hand which ended a possible career as pianist. At age eighteen, she graduated from the University of Texas. She next taught school and, in her spare time, was involved in welfare work. She abandoned both careers to marry a Texan and gave birth to their daughter, Ann. The union soon floundered and she divorced him.

One day a family friend, an elderly judge, suggested that with her sharp mind she should try the law and that she could use his private law library to study at home. Six months later, at age twenty-six, she passed the bar exam—she was the first woman lawyer in Texas. Four years later, when both her parents died, she and her sister took over the family antique business. She traveled abroad finding new "treasures" to sell in the shop. With her "free" time, she became a commentator on a San Antonio radio program. In the stock market crash of 1929, the antique firm was lost and her sister soon died.

In the midst of these tragedies, in late 1929, she married Texas oil man Will Jacoby. Shortly thereafter, he lost his Texas property. They moved to Mexico to develop oil wells on his 60,000 acres there. Just as their enterprise was flourishing, the Mexican government appropriated their land. The couple eventually moved to Los Angeles where they opened a bakery on Washington Boulevard. Meanwhile, her daughter had graduated college and married a Texas lawyer.

Florence accompanied a friend to the Pasadena Playhouse where the latter was to audition for a play, *Emma*. Florence was asked to read and won the role of Miss Bates, which led her to adopting the professional name of Florence Bates. For the next four years, Florence played an assortment of parts, taking time out when her daughter in Texas died after giving birth to a daughter.

In the late 1930s, Florence had a few walk-on roles in feature films. She made her real debut in Alfred Hitchcock's *Rebecca* (1940), playing the rich and vulgar Mrs. Van Hopper. With her ability to communicate with audiences and her flair for accents, MGM put her under contract. She was a voice coach in *The Chocolate Soldier* (1941); a gypsy woman in Bob Hope's *They Got Me Covered* (1943). Frequently, she was cast as a companion/maid (*The Belle of the Yukon*, 1944) or as a dowager (*Cluny Brown*, 1946). One of her most memorable assignments was that of Florence Dana Moorehead, an aristocratic touring author in *I Remember Mama* (1948).

On October 31, 1951, while at home studying her lines for *The San Francisco Story* (1952), her beloved husband (age seventy) died of a heart attack in his sleep. When the studio offered to adjust the shooting schedule, she insisted on going on, reasoning, "Thank God I have something to do."

Six months later, she had a nervous breakdown. As she told her good friend, screenwriter and author DeWitt Bodeen, "I didn't want to give way after Will died, but now I realize I'd been existing in a state of suspended shock....I just had to let go, to give way to grief."

Florence still accepted screen and TV work, but the joy had gone out of her life. She began losing weight. She suffered several heart attacks. Finally, she agreed to be hospitalized. She died on January 31, 1954 at St. Joseph's Hospital in Burbank, California. Medical records may say differently, but Florence Bates died of a broken heart.

Louise Beavers

March 8, 1902 — October 26, 1962

Minority performers have long had a difficult time getting ahead in the film industry. Blacks have been no exception. Louise Beavers worked her way up from the bottom rung of studio jobs into becoming a respected character star. Even when stuck with a stereotypical role as a domestic, she rose to the challenge. She gave dimension to her cardboard character and provided the heroine or hero a real character with whom to trade dialogue.

She was born in Cincinnati, Ohio in 1902. When she was eleven, the family moved to California where she graduated from Pasadena High School. Her mother was a voice teacher and trained Louise from an early age. It was hoped Louise would go into concert work, but she fooled them by joining an all-female minstrel show. She had occasional vaudeville jobs and, briefly, tried nursing (she insisted she liked the white uniform), but found her tasks too depressing. Already having worked as a dressing room attendant for a celebrity photographer, she was later hired as the maid to Leatrice Joy, one of Paramount's top stars of the 1920s. When not helping her employer Louise did extra work in movies from 1923 onward.

Louise made her first real impression on audiences playing the cook in *Uncle Tom's Cabin* (1927). After Mary Pickford cast her as Mammy Julia in *Coquette* (1929), squarely-built Louise was never without movie work. She was momentarily sidetracked when chic screen personality Lilyan Tashman asked her to be her personal maid. Before long, however, Louise returned to her true love: acting. In the early Thirties Beavers usually made a dozen films a year, fighting to shine even in dull comforting servant roles. She displayed a wonderful comic timing sparring with saucy Mae West in *She Done Him Wrong* (1933).

Louise's golden moment in motion pictures came with *Imitation of Life* (1934) in which she and Claudette Colbert are friends throughout the years, helping one another to cope with survival and raising their daughters. It was the first major Hollywood movie to humanize a black individual. She should have received an Academy Award nomination for her performance; but such was the bigotry of the day that she did not. With her new success, she went on a personal appearance tour, doing a scene from *Imitation of Life*, singing songs and dancing. She was well received by audiences.

Then it was back to the grind playing maids. Her favorite such part was as Bing Crosby's wise housekeeper in *Holiday Inn*, in which she dueted "Abraham" with the crooner. She added zest to Cary Grant's *Mr. Blandings Builds His Dream House* (1948) and offered a touching interpretation as the baseball player's mama in *The Jackie Robinson Story* (1950).

"*Beulah*" had been a popular radio series starring Hattie McDaniel. For the TV version in 1950, Ethel Waters was first starred, and then McDaniel took over. However, as of April 29, 1952, it was Louise who delivered the catch phrase, "Somebody bawl for Beulah?" In February 1957 she made her live stage debut in *Praise House* which opened in San Francisco. She was the psalm-singing Mammy, but neither the role nor the play offered her much. So it was back to being a cook in *The Goddess* (1958) and for Bob Hope-Lucille Ball's *The Facts of Life* (1960) she was—you guessed it—the maid.

After years of coping with diabetes, Louise (who was 5'4" and now weighed 190 pounds) entered a Los Angeles hospital. She died on October 26, 1962, survived by her husband, Le-Roy Moore.

On February 17, 1976, Louise Beaver was posthumously inducted into the Black Filmmakers Hall of Fame at ceremonies held at the Paramount Theatre in Oakland, California.

Amanda Blake

[Beverly Louise Neill]

February 20, 1929 — August 16, 1989

In 1963, the *New York Times* declared her "the only woman character on nighttime television who is her own woman, successful in her own right and who doesn't bask in the reflection of some man." The praise was directed at Amanda Blake who from 1955 to 1974 played Miss Kitty Russell, the worldly-wise proprietress of Dodge City's not-so-proper Longbranch Saloon on the popular adult TV Western, *"Gunsmoke."*

Born in Buffalo, New York, Amanda began her acting career in a school play at the age of seven. After performing in stock and radio, she was signed to a MGM contract in 1949. However, her secondary roles in studio films—*Duchess of Idaho* (1950), *Lili* (1953), *The Glass Slipper* (1955)—were far from stellar. By 1955, she was already working in television, when she auditioned for the role of Miss Kitty.

She joined James Arness (Marshall Matt Dillon), Milburn Stone (Dr. Galen) and Dennis Weaver (Chester Goode) for what was to become one of TV's most enduring properties. In 1959 Amanda was nominated for an Emmy for Best Supporting Actress (Continuing Character) in a Dramatic Series.

By 1974, Amanda, who had been married four times, was living in Phoenix, Arizona (where she had a sanctuary for birds, ten rare cheetahs and a lion) and commuting to Hollywood for the show. Finally, she said, "God, if I have to put that damn bustle and those curls on one more time, I'm gonna snap." Withdrawing from the series (which lasted another season), she reasoned, "Nineteen years is a hell of a long time for someone to be stuck behind a bar." (She would return for a TV movie reunion: *Gunsmoke: Return to Dodge*, 1987.)

Thereafter, Amanda, an animal rights activist, was seen mostly on game shows, as a TV series guest star, etc. In 1977, the once heavy smoker (two-packs-a-day) underwent surgery for cancer of the tongue. Thereafter, she was forced to learn to talk anew and became an avid American Cancer Society spokesperson.

In 1984, President Ronald Reagan presented Amanda with the annual Courage Award of the American Cancer Society. That same year, in April, she married for the fifth and final time. Her new groom was Mark Spaeth, a

Texas real estate developer and Austin city councilman. Unknown to her, two months before their marriage, the bisexual Spaeth had been diagnosed as being HIV positive and soon developed full-blown AIDS. She and Spaeth divorced and Blake moved back to Los Angeles from Austin, Texas where they had been living. (Spaeth died in 1985.)

In 1987 Amanda was diagnosed herself as being HIV positive. To keep the news from prying reporters, she moved to a ranch near Sacramento, California, owned by Pat Derby (the animal trainer from "*Gunsmoke*"). During 1988, she suffered a severe case of pneumonia, began to lose weight, and experienced constant pain. In July of 1989, the now-bitter ("I hope the bastard burns in hell" she said of Spaeth), highly-suffering Amanda was admitted to Mercy General Hospital in Sacramento. She used her given name of Beverly Neill. She died on August 16, 1989 at 7:15 p.m., with her dog, Butterfly, at her side.

The press was informed that her passing was the result of her long battle with cancer. Only belatedly, after a media reporter came upon the true facts of her case, was the cause of death revealed as AIDS-related. Friends were asked to make donations to the Amanda Blake Memorial Fund which benefitted the Performing Animals Welfare Society (PAWS). In late November 1991, memorabilia from her estate was auctioned off in North Hollywood, California, with proceeds going to PAWS.

William Boyd

June 5, 1895 — September 12, 1972

For decades of film watchers, William Boyd will forever be associated with the beloved character of Hopalong Cassidy. In his two-fisted sagebrush series, Boyd was the gallant cowboy—sporting his distinguished white hair and a black outfit—who always rode to the rescue in the nick of time. As such, he became a role model for a generation of admirers. On screen, Hoppy was the type of guy who didn't swear, drink or smoke. He never killed the villains; he smartly captured them. Boyd's alter ego became so famous, that at times, he joked he felt he had lost his own identity.

William Lawrence Boyd was born in Hendrysburg, Ohio in 1895, the son of a laborer. The family moved to Oklahoma when he was ten and his parents died while he was in his teens. When he quit school to find work, he abandoned his dream of becoming an engineer. He plodded through an assortment of odd jobs, ranging from oil rigger to lumberjack to picking oranges. He tried to enlist in World War I, but a heart ailment disqualified him from army service. By then he was in Hollywood doing walk-ons in movies. He won a bit role in Cecil B. DeMille's *Old Wives for New* (1918), which led to increasingly larger parts in DeMille extravaganzas: *Why Change Your Wife?* (1920), *The Volga Boatman* (1926) and *King of Kings* (1927). By now, the actor had made his mark as a handsome leading man (with his distinctive silver white hair) and matinee idol. His salary escalated and he lived lavishly, buying mansions and yachts freely. Boyd made the transition to talkies successfully, as a contract leading man for Pathe (which later became RKO).

Bill was as much the playboy off screen as on. He married actress Ruth Miller in 1921 and they divorced in 1924. In January 1926, he wed actress

Elinor Fair with whom he co-starred in that year's *The Volga Boatman*; they divorced in 1929. When that decree became final, Boyd married actress Dorothy Sebastian, his leading lady in *His First Command* (1929). However, bad luck hit in late 1933 and Boyd's world collapsed. Another actor named William Boyd (later always referred to as William "Stage" Boyd to distinguish the two) was arrested during a crazy party and booked on possession of illegal whiskey and gambling equipment. In several newspaper accounts of the incident, it was suggested a sex orgy had been in progress. By error, a photo of Bill Boyd was printed with the story instead of the likeness of the lesser known Boyd. As a result, Bill's career collapsed. He lost his money and became a heavy drinker. Turned loose by RKO, he was reduced to making a few inconsequential poverty row pictures.

Finally, Boyd got a break. Veteran movie producer, Harry "Pop" Sherman was planning to shoot a batch of budget Westerns at Paramount based on Clarence E. Mulford's popular Hopalong Cassidy novels. Initially, Sherman intended to use James Gleason (or even David Niven!) in the title part, and thought of casting Bill as the major villain. However, Bill convinced Sherman to give him the lead. Part of the deal between producer and star included a promise by the actor that he would stop his boozing and abandon his wild ways.

No one anticipated that the first entry, *Hop-a-long Cassidy* (1935), would be so well received. After this debut entry, there was little attempt to conform the hero to Mulford's character (a crusty individual who had a limp. As Boyd fashioned the lead, Hopalong became a moral and gentle cowman, who treated women gallantly and bad guys roughly. He always traveled with two sidekicks (initially Jimmy Ellison and George "Gabby" Hayes). Action audiences especially liked the Hoppy Westerns because, unlike the oaters of Gene Autry and others, there were no plot delays for bothersome song interludes. In the early entries, a stunt double was used to perform Boyd's riding scenes in the long shots. Meanwhile Boyd, who initially hated horses, practiced his riding skills. Eventually, he became a decent rider although he was never a true horseman. After divorcing Dorothy Sebastian in 1936, Boyd married for the fourth and final time on June 5, 1937 to actress Grace Bradley.

Between 1935 and 1948, sixty-six Cassidy movies were made. Pop Sherman produced the first fifty-four, and Boyd supervised the last dozen on his own. Boyd said, "It's like a vacation. I ride my horse 'Topper,' chase rustlers and outlaws, shoot my six shooters and do the things that every kid—and man too—in America would want to do." In 1948, Boyd was smart enough to see the future in television. He hocked all his assets to acquire full rights to the Hoppy films and character. The Hoppy movies became a popular program in the early days of TV, and Boyd became a multi-millionaire from the merchandizing tie-ins and the new half-hour entries he produced in 1951-52. In 1952, as a favor to his long-time mentor, Cecil B. DeMille, he made a guest appearance in the latter's circus epic, *The Greatest Show on Earth*. It was to be his last movie appearance, although, at one point, DeMille was considering him for the role of Moses in his new *The Ten Commandments* (1956).

Bill sold off his interest in the Hoppy property in the late 1950s at a huge profit. He made occasional guest appearances since then, but always insisted that youngsters not be charged to see him. He donated generously to children's hospitals, insisting, "The way I figure it, if it weren't for the kids, I'd be a bum today." During the last decade of his life, the Boyds lived quietly, alternating their time between Dana Point, California in the summer and Palm Desert in the winter. By now, Bill had contracted Parkinson's disease and remained in seclusion. He wanted his fans to remember him as he was. After he had a cancerous tumor removed from a lymph gland, he refused to be photographed.

William died on September 12, 1972 at South Coast Community Hospital in South Laguna, California of a combination of Parkinson's disease and congestive heart failure. He is buried in the Sanctuary of Sacred Promise at Forest Lawn Memorial Parks-Glendale in a large marble crypt.

Bert Convy

July 23, 1933 — July 15, 1991

He sailed through five separate careers, ranging from professional baseball player to Broadway musical comedy star to the host of several popular TV game shows. As he said once, "It does help to be a moving target. If you're just an actor sitting by the phone, you can become a victim. You're no longer in control of your own destiny." One thing over which glib Bert had no power was the strange circumstances surrounding his death struggle.

He was born in St. Louis, Missouri and, at the age of seven, he and his family moved to California. At North Hollywood High School he was a star first baseman. The day after graduation, he signed with the Philadelphia Phillies who shipped him off to their farm clubs. Two years later, he realized that he would never make the grade in the big leagues. He quit and enrolled at UCLA, during which time he joined a rock 'n' roll group called The Cheers. Their "(Bazoom) I Need Your Lovin'" was a mild hit in 1954, while "Black Denim Trousers and Motorcycle Boots" in 1955 sold a million copies. The group disbanded that year and, after graduating college, Bert—who had done a bit of college acting —was hired for "The Billy Barnes Revue" which transferred from L.A. to Broadway in 1959. In the next few years, Convy was featured in several Broadway hits: Fiddler on the Roof (1964), Cabaret (1966) and a revival of The Front Page (1969).

Bert guested on several TV shows before trying his own set of TV series. However, it was in a different arena that the always-smiling Convy proved to be top notch. He had been a frequent and witty substitute host on "The Tonight Show" which led to his hosting the long-running daytime game show, "Tattletales," for which he won an Emmy in 1977. He emceed "Super Password" in 1984 and, more recently, was the celebrity host of "The Third Degree" and "Win, Lose or Draw" (the latter in partnership with friend Bert Reynolds). Along the way, he made a few theatrical features, including Semi-Tough (1974) and Hero at Large (1980).

In the mid-1960s Convy married Anne Andersen and they had three children: Jennifer, Joshua and Jonah. In 1987 he and Anne divorced. Then a strange turn-of-events began happening. On April 22, 1989, while visiting his mother at L.A.'s Cedars-Sinai

Hospital where she was recuperating from a stroke, Bert slipped, fell, and became unconscious. Doctors who initially examined him were more preoccupied with potential internal injuries. It was not until weeks later that the brain tumor was diagnosed. He underwent surgery and post-operative treatment for the cancer. In July 1990 he suffered several paralyzing strokes. Nevertheless or because of his terminal illness, on Valentine's day, 1991 he wed long-time friend, 25-year-old Catherine Hills. By then, his health was deteriorating so rapidly that the couple had to forego a honeymoon. Thanks to the ravaging disease, the 6' 1" entertainer soon dropped from 178 to 115 pounds and his remaining hair (which he hid under a baseball cap) turned white. In April 1991, he underwent more surgery at University of California Hospital in San Francisco. His weight dropped further and he was hardly able to speak. In the early morning of July 15, 1991, eight days before his 58th birthday, he died at his Brentwood home. Catherine and his three children were at his bedside, following his request, "Keep brave for the memory of me." A public funeral service was held at the Old North Church, Forest Lawn—Hollywood Hills on July 18, 1991, with private interment following.

After Convy's death, friend Bert Reynolds said, "I've often thought about what a career Bert would have had if he had been around in the MGM days of Donald O'Connor and Gene Kelly. He would have been right up there because he could act, he sang great, and he danced wonderfully."

Lou Costello

[Louis Francis Cristollo]

March 6, 1906 — March 3, 1959

"He-e-e-e-y, Ab-bott!" For years, this was the on-stage cry for help from pudgy, lovable Lou Costello, the clowning half of the hugely popular comedy team of Abbott and Costello.

Born in Paterson, New Jersey, lean and tough Lou grew up to be a superior athlete. He quit school to travel to Hollywood where he found work in the later 1920s as a stunt man and double at MGM. With the coming of talkies, he left movies and drifted into vaudeville and burlesque around the country. In 1936, now far more portly, he was teamed with ex-lion tamer and former auto racer Bud Abbott for a new comedy act on the burlesque circuit. By mid-1939 the pair were appearing on Broadway with Carmen Miranda in the hit musical revue, *Streets of Paris*.

Brought to Hollywood in 1940, the duo soon became box-office magnets with a series of service comedies, including *In the Navy* (1941) with the Andrews Sisters. While lanky, older Abbott played the straight man in the act, it was young-looking, pranksterish Costello who was considered the team's mastermind. (In fact, he demanded and received 60% of the team's salary.)

In 1943, at the height of World War II, Abbott and Costello were at the career zenith. After completing a successful war bond-selling tour, Lou became ill. His ailment was diagnosed as rheumatic fever. Lou was forced into bed rest for several months, putting their next picture on hold and causing Abbott to suspend their radio show after struggling for a few weeks as a solo act. Then, on November 4, 1943, tragedy struck. Two days before the first birthday of Costello's third child, Lou, Jr., the infant fell into the family's swimming pool at home and drowned. Later, Lou and Bud raised funds to establish the Lou Costello Jr, Youth Foundation for Underprivileged Children.

Costello eventually returned to work. However, their new movies proved less successful and the tensions off camera between the team escalated. (On one occasion, Lou poured a bottle full of beer over Bud's head and smart-mouthed, "Now you look as wet as you act!"). The two broke apart in 1945, but patched up their professional differences and went on to new box-office success with *Abbott and Costello Meet Frankenstein* (1948). As moviegoers found new screen favorites—especially Dean Martin and Jerry Lewis—the veteran comics moved over to TV successfully. By 1956, their sputtering movie and TV careers seemingly finished, the pair starred in a Las Vegas stage revue. Abbott's recurrent drinking problems were evident during the unsuccessful engagement. When the team split apart permanently thereafter, Lou said, "I worried about Bud for twenty years" and that now he intended to go it alone. His solo appearances were not reassuring. In late 1958 he starred in the low-budget *The 30 Foot-Bride of Candy Rock* at Columbia.

On February 26, 1959, Lou suffered a heart attack and was rushed to Doctors' Hospital in Beverly Hills. Family and friends were in constant attendance, but no Abbott was on the scene. Costello's health continued to decline. He was offered the last rites, but refused the ritual. On March 3, 1959, he was feeling better. He urged his long-time manag-er, Eddie Sherman, to run across the street and buy him a strawberry ice cream soda. While talking about future plans, Costello drank the soda. After finishing it, he said, "That's the best ice cream soda I ever tasted," and then died.

At the time of Costello's death, his ex-partner Bud was suing him for $222,000 regarding their joint TV series. When he learned of Lou's death, Abbott said, "Why didn't someone tell me he was sick?" Bud was among many Hollywood celebrities—including Ronald Reagan, Red Skelton and Danny Thomas—attending the requiem mass for Lou at the family's North Hollywood church. Costello was buried in Calvary Cemetery in Los Angeles in a crypt near his son, Lou, Jr. In December of that same year, Lou's grieving wife Anne died of a heart attack. Meanwhile, Lou's final picture had been released posthumously and had quickly disappeared.

Shortly before he died, Lou settled a long-standing tax problem with the Internal Revenue Service. However, his partner Bud was plagued by back taxes until his own death fifteen years later. As manager Eddie Sherman recalled of his high-earning, high-spending clients, "They thought it would never stop. They spent it all each year, forgetting that they had a partner, Uncle Sam."

Joan Crawford

[Lucille Fay LeSeuer]

March 23, 1904 — May 10, 1977

She was a lousy mother and, thanks to daughter Christina's book (*Mommie Dearest*), one can never look at a wire hanger without thinking of Joan Craw-

THE HOLLYWOOD DEATH BOOK

ford. However, she was a consummate movie star, who, once having invented herself for the silver screen, allowed that fabrication to rule her everyday life. She was compulsive on screen and off, but her magnetic strength made her fascinating to watch at any point in her movie career. Throughout life, the four-time married actress was as voracious about men as she became about vodka. Her death was listed as a heart attack. However, friends insisted she was dying of cancer, and that, tired of suffering, she had orchestrated her own finale. Seemingly, her death, as her life had been, was arranged efficiently and according to her own schedule. It was the Joan Crawford way.

She was born in San Antonio, Texas in 1904 (various sources list 1906 and 1908) to a French Canadian laborer (Thomas LeSeuer) and to Anna Bell (Johnson) of Scandinavian-Irish descent. An earlier child Daisy had died in infancy, and there was a brother named Hal. Thomas soon abandoned his family, and the mother remarried, to Henry Cassin. The household relocated to Lawton, Oklahoma where Lucille (known as Billie) became Billie Cassin. After a brush with the law, Cassin moved his family to Kansas City, but his wife soon left him. Thereafter, Billie endured a painful childhood, shunted from school to school and from one flea-bag hotel room to another. By age eleven, she was at a private school—anything to get away from her domineering mother and tyrannical brother—working as a kitchen drudge to pay her board and tuition. By 1922, she was enrolled at Stephens College in Columbia, Missouri, again the poor girl working her way through school and feeling too dumb to remain. She quit and went back to Kansas City where she took a job as a shop girl and

then was hired for the chorus of a touring show. When the production folded, she went to Chicago.

From Chicago club dancer to Broadway show chorine took a year, but by 1924, the still-pudgy Lucille was in New York in *The Passing Show of 1924*, earning $35 weekly. By the start of 1925 she had been screen-tested and signed a contract with Metro-Goldwyn-Mayer at $75 a week. After a few brief appearances in Hollywood pictures, she gained a new name—Joan Crawford—as the result of a studio publicity contest. Her career was now officially launched. She made her mark in *Our Dancing Daughters* (1928), as a vivacious flapper. Always anxious to improve herself, she married actor Douglas Fairbanks Jr. in 1929, not only because he was young and handsome, but also because he was the son of the king of Hollywood royalty, Douglas Fairbanks Sr., and the stepson of the movie colony's queen, Mary Pickford.

In the early Thirties, Joan altered her image to suit the new times, excelling in shop girl-to-riches romances like *Possessed* (1931) and *Chained* (1934). If she drowned dramatically as Sadie Thompson in *Rain* (1932), she bounced back in a musical, *Dancing Lady* (1933). Her off screen romance with co-star Clark Gable flicked off and on throughout the Thirties, but never ended in marriage. She and Fairbanks divorced in 1933 and, two years later, she married the polished Franchot Tone, a Broadway actor then under MGM contract. That mis-matched union lasted four years, although after their 1939 divorce they remained friends. In 1938, she was labeled box-office poison by exhibitors, but bounced back in a succession of strong roles: *The Women* (1939), *Susan and God* (1940) and *A Woman's Face* (1941). Meanwhile, in

1940, she adopted a three-month old child, first called Joan Jr., and then named Christina. In mid-1942, she married "rising" actor Phillip Terry. In that same year, the impossible happened: after eighteen years with MGM, the studio let her go.

If glamorous MGM had no further use for Joan, then Warner Bros., the hard-boiled film factory did—as a threat to reigning studio queen Bette Davis. It took over two years for Crawford to find the proper vehicle at Warner Bros., a project that had been rejected by Davis, Barbara Stanwyck and Ann Sheridan. Joan abandoned her famed Adrian shoulder-pad outfits for a simpler look and won an Oscar for her highly dramatic *Mildred Pierce* (1945). The next year she and Terry divorced and Crawford changed the name of their adopted son from Phillip, Jr. to Christopher. In 1947, Joan adopted two other girls, Cynthia and Cathy, whom she labeled twins even though they were born a month apart. Crawford remained with Warner Bros. until the early Fifties, her face being as well-chiseled and mannish as were her castrating roles. Then, cut loose, she made a successful thriller (*Sudden Fear*, 1952), earning her third and final Oscar nomination.

In May 1955, Joan married dynamic Pepsi-Cola president Alfred N. Steele, and developed a new career for herself as a corporate good will ambassador. She thought he would be her life's mate, but he died of a heart attack in 1959 at age fifty-seven. With few film roles being offered her, the aging actress worked hard as a Pepsi board of director executive. Some reviewers called her subsequent film the triumph

JOAN CRAWFORD

of two old bag has-beens, but *Whatever Happened to Baby Jane?* (1962) was proof that two veteran stars (Crawford and Bette Davis) could work cinema magic. The twisted horror story of a Hollywood nightmare was a tremendous box-office hit. It gave a new thrust to Joan's remaining moviemaking years in the Sixties.

By the mid-1970s, Joan, alienated from her children, lived alone in New York City in a subdued lifestyle, having been forced out of her Pepsi post. She had become a Christian Scientist and stopped drinking. She had a small circle of friends and withdrew from public appearances (one of her last was a party for MGM pal Rosalind Russell in 1974). She told a gossip columnist intimate, "I don't have to go out anymore. I don't have to be on display. I've served my time as the public Joan Crawford. Now for the first time in her life Joan Crawford is doing exactly as she pleases." No longer dying her graying hair brown, she spent much of her time watching TV soap operas and bemoaning the fact that Hollywood had so forgotten her.

The last months of Crawford's life are full of fact, fiction and legend. In early 1977, she injured her back while housecleaning (one of her favorite pastimes). In February 1977, she began giving away personal affects, items which she insisted "she would no longer need." By that May, Joan had become quite ill and had lost a good deal of weight. She needed the attention of a physician and a daily nurse. She spent Mother's Day (May 8) bed-ridden. The next day she gave her Shih Tzu dog to friends who lived in the country, asking them to care for her. According to a close associate, on Tuesday, May 10, she arose early and asked her maid and another helper if they had had breakfast. She was about to have her usual wake-up meal (tea and graham crackers). As the cup of tea was placed on her night table she quietly passed away. It was about 10:00 a.m. (Another version insists that she knew the ending was coming, and asked that her lawyer be informed.)

Many wondered why no autopsy was performed on Crawford to clear up the matter of her death. The assistant medical examiner with the New York county office would explain, "I didn't think the circumstances called for one. There was nothing in my evaluation to lead me to suspect in any way.... I do know the location of the body, in her own bed, and she appeared to be well looked after. There was no disarray, no disorder.... The replies to all the questions I asked made me feel the cause of death was natural."

According to Joan's final wishes, she was cremated (some said the rush was to hide the cause of death). Her ashes were interred in an urn next to Alfred Steele's in the Ferncliff Cemetery in Hartsdale, New York. Memorial services were held in New York (on Friday the 13) at Frank E. Campbell's Funeral Parlor in New York. Three (Cathy, Christina, Christopher) of her four children attended the simple ceremony at which Joan's Christian Science practitioner read Bible selections. A far more elaborate memorial service was held on May 17, 1977 at All Soul's Unitarian Church in New York City. Over 1,500 people attended the occasion conducted by Reverend Dr. Walter Donald Kring who read Joan's favorite essay, "Desiderata" by Max Ehrman. Eulogies were delivered by former co-stars, Geraldine Brooks and Cliff Robertson. Pearl Bailey sang "He'll Understand." Daughters Christina and Cindy attended; Christopher did not. Another tribute service was conducted in Beverly Hills.

Joan's will, made much of in Christina's book and movie, *Mommie Dearest* (1981), stated: "It is my intention to make no provision herein for my son Christopher or my daughter Christina for reasons which are well known to them." Crawford left $77,500 each in trust funds for Cathy and Cindy. Christopher and Christina contested the will and settled for a total of $55,000. As part of the compromise, a plaster bust of Joan (inscribed "To Christina") was given to the eldest daughter.

Laird Cregar

[Samuel Laird Cregar]

July 28, 1916 — December 9, 1944

Maybe if there had been a Jennie Craig Weight Reduction Clinic or a Jane Fonda Workout video in the 1940s, 6' 3" Laird Cregar would be alive today. He was a talented screen performer who became obsessed with his fatness and went on a crash diet. His Gandi-like starvation routine shocked his system and he died.

He was born in Philadelphia in 1916, the youngest of six sons of Edward M. Cregar. Like his father, Samuel Laird attended school at Winchester Academy in England where, during summer vacations, he worked as a page boy at the Stratford-on-Avon Players, sometimes used as a walk-on in their productions. These experiences whetted the boy's appetite for acting as a career. After further schooling in Philadelphia and Longport, New Jersey, he turned full-time to acting in local stock companies. He won a scholarship to the Pasadena Community Playhouse in

1936, barely making ends meet financially through his two years there. He recalled later, "whenever I went to a place for a job they seemed scared of my size." (In contrast, his brothers—all of them larger than Samuel Laird— were successful businessmen.)

Discouraged, he went East in 1938 to work at the Federal Theatre, but later returned to California to appear at the Pasadena Playhouse in the *The American Family*. Despite decent notices, no film company took notice of this massive actor. Realizing he must engineer his own showcase, Cregar found backing for a Hollywood production of *Oscar Wilde*. The drama was a hit both in Los Angeles and in San Francisco. Now the studios finally wanted him.

After a few screen bits, he accepted Twentieth Century-Fox's offer of a contract, reasoning that, in 1940, Fox had only one prominent character lead and that was tall, thin John Carradine. Cregar was a brawling fur trapper in Paul Muni's *Hudson's Bay* (1940) and in Jack Benny's farce, *Charley's Aunt* (1941), Laird revealed an excellent flair for comedy. Keeping their new contract player busy, Fox cast him as the jealous, sinister detective pathetically in love with a murdered girl in *I Wake Up Screaming* (1941). He was so effective that it sealed his fate to play screen villains from then on, usually cast as a younger version of Sydney Greenstreet.

Cregar was a conniving nightclub owner dealing with pint-sized Alan Ladd in *This Gun for Hire* (1942). Commenting on this splashy role, Laird confessed (tongue-in-cheek), "I didn't like it because it's a mammoth man who is afraid of violence. You've no idea how much physical work it requires of a large man to quake like jelly." *In Rings on Her Fingers* (1942),

107

the studio wardrobe department had the challenge of constructing a bathing suit for 300-hundred pound Cregar to wear as he dove into a swimming pool on camera.

Never slowing down (and compensating for his lack of a real social life), he found time to work as a Hollywood Canteen bus boy and to play Sheridan Whiteside in a L.A. stage edition of *The Man Who Came to Dinner*. His greatest success came in the Gothic thriller, *The Lodger* (1944), as a wily Jack the Ripper. The movie was so popular that Fox immediately repeated the formula, with *Hangover Square* (1945). This time, the corpulent star was a schizophrenic composer who commits murder and obsesses over beautiful Linda Darnell.

Having completed *Hangover Square* in late 1944, Laird zealously pursued his dieting. He dreamed of being a more traditional leading man. After losing one hundred of his three-hundred pound frame, his system rebelled and he underwent abdominal surgery. A few days later, on the morning of December 9, 1944, he suffered a heart attack and died at the age of twenty-eight in Los Angeles. He was buried at Forest Lawn Memorial Parks in Glendale in their Court of Freedom.

Too dedicated to his career, he died never having married.

Robert Cummings

[Charles Clarence Robert Orville Cummings]

June 9, 1908 — December 2, 1990

Known for his perennial youthful looks and for being a health food fanatic, handsome Robert Cummings frequently consulted astrologers to plot his future actions and believed in "mind dynamics." Despite years of fame during his heyday, he died a lonely, old man.

He was born in Joplin, Missouri, to a physician father and minister mother. By age seventeen he was a licensed pilot. (During World War II he would be an Army flight instructor). He dabbled at higher education at several colleges, including Carnegie Tech where he briefly studied engineering. He was far happier at New York City's American Academy of Dramatic Arts in 1931. He went to England and by the time he returned to the States he had a new stage name "Blade Stanhope-Conway" and a fake British accent which he thought would help him with his show business career. He worked in a magic act and had a bit in Laurel and Hardy's *Sons of the Desert* (1933). When he was on Broadway in the *Ziegfeld Follies of 1934*, he called himself Brice Hutchens. Returning again to Hollywood— complete with an adopted Texas drawl and now using his given name—he won a role in *So Red the Rose* (1935), a Civil War story. This actioner led to a Paramount Pictures contract where he performed a variety of roles, mostly in minor movies.

By the 1940s, Cummings was an established, if lightweight, leading man. He was surprisingly earnest in a dramatic role opposite Ronald Reagan in *Kings Row* (1941) and, the next year, Alfred Hitchcock cast him in am espionage thriller, *Saboteur*. He worked again for Hitchcock in *Dial M for Murder* (1953) and was still lithe enough to caper with Doris Day in the musical, *Lucky Me* (1954). However, it was on TV that Cummings—now known as "Bob" had his greatest popularity. He starred in such sitcoms as "*My Hero*"

NATURAL CAUSES

(1952-54), "The Bob Cummings Show"
and "My Living Doll." He continued in
theatrical features ranging from the
tacky The Carpetbaggers (1964) to the
dreadful remake of Stagecoach (1966).
Thereafter, he guested on TV talk
shows, did summer stock, and made an
occasional TV movie. His last TV acting was on "The Love Boat" in 1979.

Cummings always claimed vitamins
and proper nutrition kept him fit and
wrote a book How to Stay Young and
Vital (1960). (As for those who kidded
him about his regimen, Bob joked, "I'd
tell all those critics how well I feel today because of my diet. but they're all
dead.") He had a very active married
life. He first wed his childhood sweetheart, Eda Emma Myers. When that
broke up, he married Vivian Janis in
1933. They divorced a decade later and
he married Mary Elliot, with whom he
had seven children. That union ended
in 1969 and on March 27, 1971 he wed
32-year-old Regina Fong, choosing the
date and time for the ceremony after a
consensus was agreed upon by a nu-
merologist and two astrologers. In
1989, he and "Gigi" divorced and aged
Bob—now ill with Parkinson's disease—encountered Jane Burzynski, a
supermarket cashier, after she wrote
him a fan letter. Four days after he met
the 57-year old woman, he proposed.
The couple married and she moved into
his Sherman Oaks home in the San Fernando Valley. According to friends, the
marriage was never consummated; not
because he couldn't, but because she
wouldn't.

Bob's incurable disease depleted his
energy and he wasted away to 125
pounds. Finally, he was hospitalized at
the Motion Picture Country House in
mid-November 1990. In his last days,
he was unable to walk or to remember
the simplest things. On December 2,

1990, he passed away from a combination of kidney failure and pneumonia,
mostly forgotten by the legion of fans
who had once enjoyed his light-hearted
personality on screen and TV.

Brad Davis

November 6, 1949 —September 8,
1991

When actor Brad Davis died on September 8, 1991, the industry was
shocked that he had died so young (41)
and that the cause of death was AIDS-
related complications. For six years, he
had kept his illness a deep secret from
everyone except his wife so he would
not be industry blacklisted and could
continue acting. (He had even foregone
getting early treatment for the disease,
fearing industry gossip.) In a book pro-
posal written shortly before his "sudden" death, he described Hollywood's
double standards. It was an industry
"that gives umpteen benefits and charity affairs with proceeds going to research. But in actual fact, if an actor is
even rumored to have HIV, he gets no
support on an individual basis. He does
not work." Having to cope with his fatal disease in the closet, Davis worked
almost to the end. Not since Rock Hudson's death of AIDS in 1985, had the
movie business—and the world at
large—been so focused on the epi-
demic disease.

He was born in Tallahassee, Florida
and acted in high school plays. He won
a talent contest for music and moved to
Atlanta. Later, he studied in New York
at the Academy of Dramatic Arts and
made his off-Broadway debut in Crystal and Fox (1973). Over the next seasons, he performed in such plays as
The Elusive Angel and The En-

109

tertaining *Mr. Sloane*, and, years later, appeared in Los Angeles in *The Normal Heart*, as the lover of a man dying from AIDS. (That play's author, Larry Kramer, would eulogize recently of the late Brad Davis: "He brought fury and overwhelming love to the role of Ned. He was also one of the first straight actors with the guts to play gay roles.")

In 1974-75, Brad spent ten months in the TV soap opera *"How to Survive a Marriage."* After such TV productions as *Sybil* (1976) and *Roots* (1977), he made his feature movie debut in the highly-acclaimed *Midnight Express* (1978). For his impressively intense work as the American drug smuggler jailed in a horrendous Turkish prison, he won a Golden Globe Award. His career should have really zoomed upward. However, it stalled due mostly to his drug and alcohol dependency, and, as he later admitted, the sudden fame that had swelled his head. Nevertheless, when he worked, he was an impressive fireball: A *Rumor of War* (1980), *A Small Circle of Friends* (1980), *Chariots of Fire* (1981) and *Querelle* (1982). He was high-charged as the attorney general in *Robert Kennedy and His Times* (1985) and as a racist in *Chiefs* (1985), both of them television miniseries. In TV's *The Caine Mutiny Court-Martial* (1988), Davis stood out as the defense attorney. He was in the zany comedy *Rosalie Goes Shopping* (1989) and played opposite Jill Clayburgh in *Unspeakable Acts* (1990). His last work was in *Hangfire* (1991) and in the cable TV movie, *A Habitation of Dragons* (1992), the latter completed in June 1991.

When Brad died at home in September 1991, he was living in Studio City, California with his long-time wife, casting agent Susan Bluestein and their daughter Alexandra (born in 1983). The funeral service was private, but the memorial tribute was anything but quiet. Amid tremendous media coverage, it was held on September 20, 1991 at Hollywood's James A. Doolittle Theatre. Co-workers and industry figures not only reminisced about Brad's rich career, but dealt directly with the AIDS phobia in the film industry. His widow later said she was being as open as she was about Brad's illness because, "He didn't want to be one more person who said he died of something else.... He didn't want to be one more faceless person."

Sammy Davis, Jr.

December 8, 1925 — May 16, 1990

In 1989, when his new autobiography (*Why Me?*) was published, the once fast-living, fast-spending Sammy Davis, Jr. confided, "The guy from twenty-five years ago doesn't exist anymore. The guy from ten years ago doesn't exist anymore. And I hope ten years from now, I'll be able to say that this guy doesn't exist anymore. He's a better being, a more caring person." Soon thereafter, "Mr. Bojangles," a very heavy cigarette smoker, was diagnosed with throat cancer. Show business friends rallied with a lavish testimonial telecast in early 1990, but by then Davis's disease had spread.

On May 16, 1990, after months of suffering, Sammy Davis, Jr., the consummate entertainer, died. The service, one of the best attended celebrity funerals in recent times, was held at Forest Lawn Memorial Park in Hollywood Hills. The ceremony was held at the cemetery's Hall of Liberty. Rabbi Allen Freehling conducted the non-denominational service, with Reverend

Jesse Jackson delivering the eulogy. Among the honorary pallbearers were Bill Cosby, Michael Jackson, Dean Martin and Frank Sinatra. Notables attending the memorial included: Gregory Hines, Billy Crystal, Lionel Richie, Liza Minnelli, Gladys Knight, Dionne Warwick, Burt Reynolds, Angie Dickinson, Dick Gregory, Carroll O'Connor, Little Richard and Robert Wagner. After the service, Davis's bronze casket was taken to Forest Lawn Memorial Parks in Glendale where the "world's greatest entertainer" was buried in the family plot next to his father and his adopted uncle, Will Mastin.

For black, multi-talented Sammy Davis, Jr., who had spent so much of his life in an uphill struggle in the white-dominated entertainment industry, the battle was over. For his family, it was just beginning.

Lantern-jawed Davis was born in New York's Harlem in 1925. Both parents were in show business, working at the time in Will Mastin's troupe. When he was two-and-a-half, his parents split up and Sammy, Jr. remained with his dad. He soon joined Mastin's vaudeville act. Later, Sammy, his dad, and "Uncle" Will formed the Will Mastin Trio. His two years (1943-45) in World War II military service gave him fresh lessons in coping with racial bigotry. Once a civilian again, the revived Will Mastin Trio broke several racial barriers on the cabaret circuit, but always had to fight discrimination.

By 1954, Sammy was definitely the focal spot of the act, with his flashy dancing, singing, imitations, etc., and he had his own recording contract. Then, on November 19, 1954, he almost died in a car accident; he did lose his left eye. It was at this point that, encouraged by his Jewish pals (Eddie Cantor, Jeff Chandler), he converted to Judaism. Once recovered, he re-attacked his career with a vengeance—always working, always giving 110 percent. He became a member of Frank Sinatra's ring-a-ding-ding Rat Pack. He starred on Broadway in *Mr. Wonderful* (1956), *Golden Boy* (1964) and *Stop the World, I Want to Get Off* (1978). He made several films, ranging from musicals (*Porgy and Bess*, 1959, *Sweet Charity*, 1968), to gangster drama (*Johnny Cool*, 1963) to comedic junk (*One More Time*, 1970). He headlined three TV variety shows (1966, 1973, 1975-77). He was everywhere!

Hard-living Sammy's marital record was a merry-go-round. He wed singer Loray White in early 1958; they divorced fifteen months later. Much was made of his interracial marriage to Scandinavian actress May Britt on November 13, 1960. Their daughter, Tracey, was born in 1961, and they adopted two sons: Mark, Jeff. By late 1968, they were divorced, with May insisting, "there was no family life to speak of." She was given custody of their children. By mid-1970, dancer Altovise Gore was the third and final Mrs. Davis.

Having gone through several political phases (a 1960s supporter of the Kennedys; a 1970s fan of Richard Nixon), Sammy eventually dropped a lot of his glitter and glitz to display a new found social consciousness. In 1986 this new, toned-down Sammy concertized at the Hollywood Bowl, and next teamed with Frank Sinatra and Liza Minnelli in a world tour. Then in 1988, he underwent hip surgery and his father died. Several months before Davis himself passed away, he and Altovise adopted a thirteen-year-old son, Manny.

When Sammy's will was filed, there were assets of $2 million in real estate and $2 million in personal property as well as insurance polices totaling nearly $6 million. However, his debts were huge, including $5.7 million in federal taxes, which dated back to IRS tax disallowances in 1972. (Phyllis Diller once quipped, "Sammy has earned his success. He just hasn't paid for it.") The financial mess led to a great deal of squabbling between the estate's executors and various beneficiaries. In September 1991, as part of the probate sale, Davis's 22-room Beverly Hills mansion (once worth $4.25 million) was put on the depressed real estate market for $2.715 million. Later that month, at a prestigious Los Angeles auction house, much of the memorabilia Sammy had acquired over a lifetime was sold off, with items such as his

gold record, "The Candy Man," going for $10,000. About 800 people attended the sale which brought in $439,000.

If Sammy could have predicted the financial turmoil his death would generate, one wonders if he would have ever said in later years, "You have to be able to look back at your life and say, 'Yeah, that was fun.' The only person I ever hurt was myself and even that I did to the minimum. If you can do that and you're still functioning, you're the luckiest person in the world."

Nelson Eddy

June 29, 1901 — March 7, 1965

NELSON EDDY

Nelson Eddy and Jeanette MacDonald. They blended together like strawberries and cream. After eight screen musicals together, the world expected them to be always joined at the hip, whether in movie operettas or in private life. In actuality, Eddy had a professional career long before he first teamed with Jeanette, and he performed long thereafter. He even left this earth doing what he did best— singing.

Blond baritone Nelson Eddy was born in Providence, Rhode Island. His parents were choir singers in their spare time and his maternal grandmother, Caroline Kendrick, had been a successful opera singer. His parents separated when he was fourteen and Nelson moved to Philadelphia with his mother. He soon quit school to find work, including several jobs at the local newspapers. However, by the early 1920s, he had concluded he wanted to sing for his living. He debuted on the Philadelphia stage in 1922 and studied voice abroad in the mid-1920s. He returned to New York to perform opera, frequently going on the concert circuit to pay the bills. It was while performing in San Diego in 1933 that he was spotted by MGM who put him under contract.

He made three films before first pairing with Jeanette MacDonald in *Naughty Marietta* (1935). The lavishly-staged operetta was a resounding hit and set the tone for several follow-ups, including *Maytime* (1937), *New Moon* (1940) and the couple's final joint picture, *I Married an Angel* (1942). Earlier, with less success, he had been a solo star in *Let Freedom Ring* (1939) and other films. After 1942, he made others without her, such as *The Phantom of the Opera* (1943) and his last, *Northwest Outpost* (1947). Despite their now divergent careers, the public continued to think of Eddy and Mac-Donald as a love team. It didn't seem to matter that in 1937 Jeanette had married actor Gene Raymond, while in 1939, Nelson wed Ann Denitz Franklin, the divorced wife of producer Sidney Franklin.

Now past his movie leading man period, Eddy focused on radio, TV and recordings, as well as the lucrative nightclub circuit. He was frequently teamed with Gale Sherwood, both in the United States and on tour abroad. When Jeanette MacDonald died of a heart attack on July 15, 1965, Nelson sang their trademark song, "Ah, Sweet Mystery of Life," at her funeral at Forest Lawn Memorial Parks—Glendale.

On March 6, 1967, Eddy and Sherwood were headlining at the Blue Sails Room of the San Souci Hotel in Miami Beach, Florida. He had just completed one song number and was launching into another. Suddenly, his voice failed him. He asked the audience of four hundred, "Will you bear with me a minute? I can't seem to get the words out." He turned to his accompanist and said, "Would you play 'Dardanella?' Maybe I'll get the words back." After a few moments of pained silence, he blurted out, "I can't see. I can't hear" and then collapsed. He was carried off-stage while hotel employees called for medical assistance. When the city fire rescue squad arrived, Eddy was unable to talk and his right side was paralyzed. The stroke victim was rushed to Mount Sinai Hospital. There, early on the morning of March 7, he passed away. His wife was notified in their Los Angeles home of his passing. Eddy was buried in a grave adjacent to his mother's at Memorial Park in Hollywood.

A day before the fatality, Nelson—ever the polished professional—told the press, "I'm working harder than I ever have in my life. I love it. I hope to keep going till I drop."

Peter Finch

[William Mitchell]

September 28, 1916 —January 14, 1977

In his final screen role in *Network* (1976) as hell-raising TV journalist Howard Beale, Peter Finch's raving character starts a national stampede of individualism with his slogan "I'm mad and I'm not going to take it anymore!" Before the 120-minute feature concludes, the old-guard Beale is dead. A few shorts months later, so was life's own bad boy, Peter Finch.

He was born William Mitchell in London where his father was a physicist and college professor. At the age of ten, the future actor went to live with his grandmother in India, but was soon sent shipped off to Australia to be with cousins. After school Down Under, he had an assortment of jobs there during the Depression, ranging from news reporter to a baggy pants comedian. He was heard on Australian radio and made some local films. By now, he had decided fully on a show business career, reasoning, "If I was going to be broke, I decided I might as well do it with actors as anyone else." He served in World War II with Australian troops and then formed his own traveling drama troupe. The group failed, but he was spotted by Sir Laurence Olivier who was touring Australia. Olivier advised him to try the London stage and Finch went to England where he bowed on the West End in *Daphne Laureola* (1949), with Dame Edith Evans. The play was a hit and so was Finch.

Thereafter, Peter alternated between stage roles (which made him restless) and doing pictures (*The Miniver Story*, 1950, *Father Brown*, 1954). He signed a movie-making contract with J. Arthur Rank and appeared with Kay Kendall in *Simon and Laura* (1955). He made his international reputation in such Hollywood-financed productions as *Elephant Walk* (1954) and *The Nun's Story* (1959). He won the British Oscar for *The Trials of Oscar Wilde* (1960) and *No Love for Johnny* (1961) and was nominated for an American Oscar for being the bisexual doctor in *Sunday, Bloody Sunday* (1971). He took over Ronald Colman's role in the musical remake of *Lost Horizon* (1973) and played Yitzhak Rabin, Israel's Prime Minister in the TV picture, *Raid on Entebbe* (1977).

Renowned for his heavy-drinking, hard-living lifestyle, Finch was married three times; his first two ended in divorce. He initially wed ballet dancer Tamara Tchinarova, by whom he had a daughter, Anita; with South African-born performer Yolande Turner, his second wife, he had daughter Samantha and son Charles; and by his third wife, Jamaican hairdresser Eletha Barrett, he had daughter Diana.

Before moving to the U.S in late 1975 with his third wife and daughter to become permanent residents, he had resided in Italy, then Switzerland, and, for two years in the mid-1970s, operated a farm in Jamaica. On Friday morning, January 14, 1977, a very tired-looking, worn-out Peter Finch was sitting in the lobby of the Beverly Hills hotel waiting for *Network* director Sidney Lumet to fetch him for a joint appearance on TV's "*Good Morning America.*" (The previous week Finch had been nominated for a Golden Globe Award for *Network*.) Suddenly, the actor slumped over, having suffered a massive heart attack. He was taken unconscious to the intensive care unit of UCLA Hospital where the sixty-year-old star died four hours later. He was buried at Hollywood Memorial Park, where his vault was inscribed with the plaque, "Distinguished actor, loving husband and father. Forever in our hearts."

At the Academy Awards that spring, his widow accepted a posthumous Oscar for Finch for his *Network* performance as the crazed commentator. His son Charles is now a film director and screenwriter.

Redd Foxx

[John Elroy Sanford]

December 9, 1922—October 11, 1991

On his hit TV series, "*Sanford and Son*" (1972-77) one of star Redd

Foxx's recurring bits of shtick was to pretend a heart attack. Clutching his chest and wobbling bowlegged, he would shout to his dead wife, "I'm comin' Elizabeth! I'm comin'!" When he collapsed on a sound stage during rehearsals of his new series, *"The Royal Family,"* cast and crew thought he was just clowning around. He wasn't. A few hours later, the famed comedian was dead.

He was born John Elroy Sanford in St. Louis, Missouri in 1922. When he was four, his dad disappeared, leaving he, his older brother (Fred, Jr.) and his mother to fend for themselves. He grew up in the black ghettos there and in Milwaukee and Chicago. By the age of thirteen, the rascally Sanford had joined with two pals in creating a washtub band. They headed for New York in 1939, where—known as "The Bon-Bons"—they performed on subways and street corners and even won a second prize on Major Bowes's *"Amateur Hour"* radio program. Along the way, Sanford gained the nickname of "Chicago Red," because of his light skin color and his hair (and also to separate him from his pal, "Detroit Red," the young Malcolm Little who became Malcolm X). When things got tough financially, Sanford worked as a dishwasher or busboy and pushed carts in the garment district. He often slept on rooftops to survive during these scuffling years.

Sanford adopted the stage name of Redd Foxx, using the surname of baseball player Jimmy Foxx as well as to denote that he himself was a "foxy" dresser. He began his career on the Chitlin' circuit (black nightclubs and vaudeville), and made appearances at the famed Apollo Theater in Harlem. In the early 1940s, he was a master of ceremonies at Gamby's, a Baltimore club,

where he perfected his stand-up comic routines dealing with the humor of the ghettos. In the later 1940s, he teamed in vaudeville with Slappy White.

By 1951, Foxx had relocated to Los Angeles. However, because of racial discrimination in the entertainment industry, he often could not find jobs. When he was broke, he worked as a sign painter between nightclub engagements. In 1955, looking for outlets for his raucous "blue" routines, he made a comedy album, *"Laff of the Party,"* which earned him an underground reputation for his salty, wicked humor. This was the first of many hip records he made, making him a role model for many other comedians, including Lenny Bruce and Richard Pryor (who would work in Foxx's L.A. nightclub in the 1970s).

It was Hugh Downs who gave risque Foxx his big break by having him—in a toned-down format—on the *"Today"* TV show in 1964. This network appearance proved that the raunchy, black comedian could appeal to audiences of any race or social levels. Foxx was on his way and by 1970 had signed a three-year Las Vegas club pact worth almost $1 million. When he played a grouchy junk dealer in the movie *Cotton Comes to Harlem*, 1970), producer Bud York saw him and signed the raspy-voiced Foxx for a similar (but more endearing) character in the sitcom *"Sanford and Son."* After that hit program ended in 1977, Redd hosted a TV variety show in 1977-78, and returned to his irascible junk man part again for *"Sanford"* (1980-81). He continued doing his lucrative stand-up act in Las Vegas. Then, in the 1980s, Redd had highly-publicized battles with the Internal Revenue Service, which seized much of his assets for nearly $3 million in back taxes. Eddie Murphy, a long-

THE HOLLYWOOD DEATH BOOK

time admirer of Foxx, cast him in *Harlem Nights* (1989), Redd's first movie since *Norman...Is That You?* (1976). Executive producer Murphy next placed Foxx (opposite Della Reese) in a new sitcom, *"The Royal Family"* which debuted in September 1991. The ratings weren't terrific, but Foxx's return to prime time TV as a retired Atlanta mail carrier was welcomed. Part of his new salary was ear-marked to pay off his I.R.S. debts.

On Friday, October 11, 1991, when he arrived at Paramount Studios' stage 31, he told crew members that he felt funny, that he "might have a touch of something." Then he went about his business and seemed to forget about it. About 4:10 p.m., during a rehearsal break, Redd shot off one of his wisecracks and then collapsed. Everyone assumed it was a gag. After a few moments, Della Reese shouted, "Get up, Redd . . . Get up!" The unconscious star, now in cardiac arrest, was taken to Queen of Angels-Hollywood Presbyterian Medical Center where he died at 7:45 p.m., never having regained consciousness. At his bedside when he passed away were his young fourth wife, Ka Ha Cho, and his long-time stage partner, Slappy White. Most of the cast and crew were gathered in the waiting room.

Foxx's body was flown to Las Vegas for burial. At the memorial service held in the gaming capital on October 15, 1991, long-time pal and co-worker Della Reese said that at the time of his death, Foxx "was very happy . . . He was doing what he wanted to do." Among the other celebrities attending the tribute were Slappy White, boxer Mike Tyson, singer Joe Williams, and Elvis Presley's manager, Colonel Tom Parker. One of those who spoke in fond memory of Red was Flip Wilson —or

was it? It turned out to be an impersonator. "I knew it wasn't Flip," Della Reese said later, "but there were a lot of people there who loved Redd, and it would have been a mess if I had stopped the service....I have nothing against impersonators, but this was not the time or the place.... [The impersonator exhibited] absolutely no respect. And Redd Foxx deserved respect."

James Franciscus

January 31, 1934 — July 8, 1991

In his hit TV series, *"Mr. Novak"* (1963-65), James Franciscus— who bore a striking resemblance to another tall blond actor (Richard Chamberlain)—played a dedicated English teacher who inspired others to make the right moral choices. At the end of Franciscus's life, in a coma and dying from emphysema, it would be his family who had to make the difficult decision to remove the hospital life-support system from the actor and to allow him to die in peace.

The ruggedly handsome actor, who had a brother John, was born in Clayton, Missouri. James attended prep schools in Massachusetts and Connecticut before entering Yale University, where he furthered his study of acting. He authored several plays, worked in summer stock, and came to the attention of film scouts. His screen debut came in *Four Boys and a Gun* (1957). He spent one season on *"Naked City"* (1958-59) as earnest NYPD detective Jim Halloran, but wanted to work on the West Coast and surprised many in the industry by quitting the hit series. He was on TV's *"The Investigators"* (1961) before launching into *"Mr. Novak"* for which he would be most remembered. The starring role in the film feature *Youngblood Hawke* (1965) was supposed to be a turning point for the promising actor. However, when that flopped, his career floundered and other physically similar actors (Robert Redford) soon grabbed the limelight.

James made the rounds of TV series and had his own show again as the blind insurance investigator on *"Longstreet"* (1971-72). Next came two TV failures: *"Doc Elliot"* (1974) and *"Hunter"* (1977). Always known as a cerebral actor—with an abhorrence for the snooping fan magazines—he turned to TV production in the mid-1970s to bring the classics (*"Jane Eyre," "Heidi," "David Copperfield"*) to the medium. Having already played a Kennedy-like figure in *The Greek Tycoon* (1978), he starred as JFK opposite Jaclyn Smith in the TV movie *Jacqueline Bouvier Kennedy* (1981). Then he virtually retired, with his final work being the sub-par TV movie *Secret Weapons* (1985), starring Linda Hamilton.

In 1960, Franciscus had married Kitty Wellman, the daughter of distinguished film director William Wellman and they had four daughters: Jamie, Kellie, Corie and Jolie. They divorced and, in 1986, he married Carla. For years, the tennis-addicted Franciscus had been a heavy smoker and was, by now, suffering from emphysema. On June 26, 1991, his heart stopped beating at his North Hollywood home. His wife, Carla, administered mouth-to-mouth resuscitation until paramedics arrived with a respirator. By then, he had already suffered irreversible brain damage. The actor was rushed to the nearby Medical Center of North Hollywood where he was hooked up to life-sustaining machinery.

By July 2, 1991, the hospital's medical staff had nearly abandoned hope for the comatose star. When the machine monitoring brain waves showed a flicker of activity, it was decided to retain Franciscus on the life-support system. The physicians acknowledged to his family that even if he regained consciousness, he would be a vegetable.

Despite the small indication on the life-sustaining equipment, by Saturday, July 6, it was decided to remove the machinery and allow nature to take its course. The next Monday, July 8, 1991, at about 8 p.m., James Franciscus died. After he expired, his widow remained with her late husband, telling him, "I love you. I miss you so much."

Clark Gable

[William Clark Gable]

February 1, 1901 — November 16, 1960

For many—Elvis Presley to one side—Clark Gable was and always will be The King. His charming, swaggering masculinity was a trademark quality that many movie actors have mimicked, but few have equalled. He reached his zenith as the charming rogue, Rhett Butler in *Gone With the Wind* (1939). On screen he made his mark as a lady killer. Off screen he lived up to his reputation in aces. In 1960 he had just completed a very difficult movie project, *The Misfits* (1961) opposite a very trying Marilyn Monroe. He returned home to his pregnant fifth wife, Kay Spreckels, and looked forward to a peaceful future as a first-time father. Suddenly, he was felled by a heart attack and died. The legend himself had gone with the wind.

He was born in Cadiz, Ohio and began his show business career in his teens as a theater handyman. He worked as a tool dresser in the Oklahoma oil fields, but quit that task to join a Kansas City stock company. Eventually, he ended in Los Angeles where he took a job as a telephone repair man. He fixed the phone of drama coach Josephine Dillon, who took an interest in him. He married the 14-year-older older woman in late 1924. Meanwhile, he had bits in silent pictures. Then he toured with Jane Cowl in *Romeo and Juliet* and by 1930—the year he and Dillon divorced—he was making a name for himself playing Killer Mears in the L.A. company of the stage hit, *The Last Mile*. Supposedly the role was engineered by his wife-to-be, Houston socialite, Maria (Ria) Franklin Prentiss, whom he married in mid-1931. She was eleven years older than Gable.

Several studios tested Gable, but insisted he lacked charisma, especially because of his floppy ears. However, MGM had a change-of-heart and signed him in 1931. That year, in *Dance, Fools, Dance*, he teamed with Joan Crawford for the first of eight pictures together. (Off camera, they had an on-and-off love affair over the years and, later, she would graphically assess the secret of his screen appeal: "He had balls!") It was a punishment loan-out to Columbia Pictures in 1934 that won him his first and only Oscar, for the comedy *It Happened One Night*, opposite Claudette Colbert.

Gable and Carole Lombard first worked together on screen in 1932 (*No Man of Her Own*) but it was not until 1936 that they "discovered" each other. By then he was separated from wife #2

and after their divorce in early 1939, he and blonde beauty Lombard eloped to Kingman, Arizona a few months later. This was the same year in which Clark starred in *Gone with the Wind*, the saga of the old South which many authorities have rated Hollywood's most "perfect" movie. By any standard it was certainly a grand epic and did much to insure Gable's immortality.

Although Gable and Lombard were frequently described as the ideal married couple, there were rumors that Gable continued to still play around after their marriage; certainly both personalities were very strong-willed and used to being the center of attention. It was Gable who reneged on a bond-selling tour to the Midwest after the U.S. entered World War II in 1941. Carole, the good sport, went instead. Flying back to L.A., her plane crashed into Table Rock Mountain, Nevada, killing all aboard. The grieving Gable never forgave himself for indirectly causing her death.

During the war, the overage Gable, who'd been drowning his sorrow in drink over Carole's death, enlisted in the Air Force as a buck private and served as an aerial gunner in bombers. After the war, he returned to picture-making with *Adventure* (1946), a bomb, and then *The Hucksters* (1947), a hit. He married a Lombard look-a-like, Lady Sylvia Ashley (Douglas Fairbanks, Sr.'s widow), in late 1949. However, she soon grew tired of living "under a shadow" and they divorced in 1952. In 1955, when he left MGM, he returned to the Top Ten at the Box-Office with such action pictures as *Soldier of Fortune*. He also married for the fifth and final time that year to Kay Williams Spreckels, the divorcee of a sugar heir.

In the late Fifties, Clark made December-May romantic screen comedies opposite Doris Day (*Teacher's Pet*, 1958) and Sophia Loren (*It Started in Naples*, 1960). Then he found the meaty screen part he had been looking for: the aging wrangler who corrals wild mustangs in *The Misfits*. It was a prestige production: with a script by the illustrious Arthur Miller, direction by veteran John Huston, and a cast which included Marilyn Monroe and Montgomery Clift. The out-of-shape Gable was so enthused about the dramatic role and his $800,000 salary, that he embarked on a crash diet. By the time shooting began, he had slimmed down from 230 to 195 pounds.

Filming on location in the brutal Nevada heat proved to be a nightmare. The terribly insecure Monroe was feuding with her playwright husband (Miller) and became more than usual tardy and exasperating on the set. Gable, anxious to prove he was still a virile leading man, insisted on doing many of his own stunts. In the scorching heat, he allowed himself to be dragged through the dust by a wild horse. The grueling scene (with several retakes) left him rope burned, bruised and bloodied. In mid-October, he returned to Hollywood for two additional weeks of filming. When the picture was at last wrapped up, Clark told a business associate, "Christ, I'm glad this picture's finished! She [Monroe] damn near gave me a heart attack."

Two days later, on November 6, 1960, he had what he thought was stomach pains and his wife Kay rushed him from their Encino, California ranch to Hollywood Presbyterian Hospital for emergency treatment. Medical tests proved he had suffered a mild coronary thrombosis. He was hospitalized with the pregnant Kay moving into his private room to be near him. He ap-

peared to be recovering. President Dwight D. Eisenhower, himself a heart attack survivor, sent Gable a telegram: "Be a good boy, Clark, and do as the doctors tell you to do." Then, on November 16, 1960 at about 11 p.m., as he was flipping through a magazine, Clark's head nodded back. He had died from a second heart attack.

With the U.S. Air Force participating in his Hollywood funeral, Gable was buried at Forest Lawn Memorial Parks in Glendale. With his wife's approval, he was laid to rest in a crypt next to that of Carole Lombard in the Great Mausoleum. His will left everything to Kay, with the exception of a house in North Hollywood which he bequeathed to his ex-wife Josephine Dillon (who died in 1971). Five months later—on March 20, 1961—Kay gave birth to Gable's only child, a boy named John Clark Gable. Kay herself would die of a heart attack in 1983, while John would grow up to become a race car driver and then a screen actor.

Ironically, Clark Gable's last words on screen in *The Misfits* had been: "Just head for the big star straight on. The highways under it take us right home."

John Garfield

[Jacob "Julius" Garfinkle]

March 4, 1912 — May 21, 1952

For years in his movies, John Garfield successfully played society's victim, the hard-fisted anti-hero with a huge chip on his shoulder His real life eventually took a page from his own pictures in which he was "fate's whipping boy." He ended life trounced upon by the Establishment. Adding to the ironic finale is the mystique sur-

JOHN GARFIELD

briefly on Broadway in 1929 and the next year entered a Golden Gloves boxing tournament. In 1932 he played in *Counsellor-at-Law* on the road and in New York. Later, he hitched to the West Coast where he was a migrant farm worker for a time and managed his screen debut in an unbilled bit in the Warner Bros. musical, *Footlight Parade* (1933).

By 1934, Garfield (his new surname) was apprenticing with the Group Theater in New York and married to his school days sweetheart, Roberta Seidman. (They would have three children: Katharine who died of a strep throat in 1945; David Patton who would become an actor under the name John Garfield, Jr.; and Julie who would become an actress.) After playing the lead on Broadway in *Having Wonderful Time* (1937), he looked forward to starring in *Golden Boy*, but playwright Clifford Odets instead cast him in a supporting role. Frustrated by the situation, Garfield turned to filmmaking.

Warner Bros. signed him to a contract and he adopted the name John Garfield. He made a strong impression as the cynical young loner in *Four Daughters* (1938), leading to his first Oscar nomination. His impact was such that he inaugurated a new breed of Hollywood screen hero—vulnerable but tough. After several more pictures, John tried Broadway again in *Heavenly Express* (1940). A faulty heart kept him

rounding the manner in which he suffered his death-dealing heart attack.

He was born Jacob Garfinkle in 1912 to Russian immigrant parents. His early childhood was spent in poverty on New York City's Lower East Side and then in Brooklyn's Brownsville tenement district. The principal of the Bronx junior high school that "Julie" later attended diverted him from juvenile delinquency by encouraging the troublemaker to try amateur boxing and then to sample dramatics and debating. He dropped out of high school in 1929 and, instead, studied acting at the American Laboratory Theater. He was out of World War II duty, but he joined with Bette Davis in forming the Hollywood Canteen and frequently entertained the troops overseas.

In the post-war period, Garfield enjoyed some of his best screen roles: *The Postman Always Rings Twice* (1946—with Lana Turner), *Humoresque* (1946—with Joan Crawford). He was Oscar-nominated again for *Body and Soul* (1947), in which he was well-cast as the middle-aged champ who has lost his optimism. In a money dispute, Garfield rejected the Broadway role of Stanley Kowalski in *A Streetcar Named Desire* (1947). Nevertheless, he returned to the stage in *Skipper Next to God* (1948) for $80 a week because he believed so much in the production. Garfield continued to alternate between films and stage, but his career had peaked.

In 1951 he testified as a "cooperative witness" in front of the House Committee on Un-American Activities, insisting "I am no Red . . . I am no pink . . . I am no fellow traveler." While cleared of any charges, the committee's reaction to him served to unofficially blacklist him in the entertainment industry. His last picture was the low-budget *He Ran All the Way* (1951) and his final Broadway appearance was in a nine-week revival of *Golden Boy* (1952) in the title role he had coveted years before. Desperate for work, he was planning a summer stock tour of a new drama, *The Fragile Fox*, which he hoped to bring to Broadway in the fall of 1952.

By 1952, Garfield was separated from his wife. He had a long history of romancing his movie co-stars and other women as well as having suffered several minor heart attacks (in 1944, 1947, and 1950). Despite doctors' warnings, he kept to his own regimen, which included strenuous games of tennis, heavy drinking, and exertive sex. In addition, he was under great stress from worry over his failing career.

On the night of May 20, 1952 he visited a friend, Iris Whitney, at her Gramercy Park apartment in New York City. She stated later that he became ill that night and she permitted him to stay overnight in her bedroom, while she slept in the living room. In the morning of May 21, when she could not wake him, she phoned her physician who pronounced the 39-year-old actor dead at 9 a.m. The Medical Examiner's autopsy decided that John had died of cardiac arrest and there was "nothing suspicious." However, the unofficial word has always been that John died in the midst of sexual activity. Later, one Hollywood wit suggested that Garfield's epitaph should have read, "Died in the saddle."

Betty Grable

[Elizabeth Ruth Grable]

December 18, 1916 — July 2, 1973

She was that glamorous blonde with sparkling blue eyes, million dollar legs, and a luscious (34-23-35) figure. She was America's most famous pin-up girl during World War II as well as a top money-making star of the decade. She was spunky and down-to-earth and had no illusions about her acting abilities: "I am what I wanted to be. Just give me the lines that lead into a song-and-dance routine. I'm the girl the truck drivers love."

She was born in St. Louis, Missouri in 1916, the younger of two girls of truck driver and bookkeeper Conn Grable and his overly-ambitious wife,

Lillian Rose (Hoffman) Grable. One of show business's most persistent stage mothers, Lillian Grable had moved her younger daughter to Hollywood by the time she was twelve. Pretending to be older, the girl made her screen debut as a chorine in *Happy Days* (1929) at Fox. Two years later, Betty was a Goldwyn Girl decorating the background of Eddie Cantor musicals. During the making of *Palmy Days* (1931), she met the slick ex-gangster-turned-hoofer George Raft. The two developed an attraction, but the 36-year-old married Raft wanted no problems. He quipped, "I'm giving her back till she grows up."

In the early 1930s, Betty made a series of short subjects under the name Frances Dean and wandered from studio to studio making programmers. She settled in at RKO, but this sojourn led nowhere. She moved on to Fox (again) where she was in Judy Garland's first feature, *Pigskin Parade* (1936). She toured in vaudeville with ex-child star Jackie Coogan. They discovered they had lots in common; above all, both had been exploited by greedy relatives. On her twenty-first birthday, Betty married Jackie. By then, she was doing her series of Betty co-ed roles in Paramount musicals.

In 1939, Paramount dropped her option and she divorced the out-of-work Coogan. She bounced back by winning the second lead to Ethel Merman in the Broadway musical, *DuBarry Was a Lady* (1939). Darryl F. Zanuck, the libidinous studio head of Twentieth Century-Fox, signed Betty to a contract as a back-up to top star, Alice Faye.

Once back in Hollywood, Grable began her fifteen-year tenure at Fox with *Down Argentine Way* (1940) which set the successful, profitable tone for all her light-hearted pictures. Her romance with Artie Shaw ended when he wed another movie bombshell (Lana Turner). Betty renewed her "friendship" with George Raft, and then turned romantically to such co-stars as Tyrone Power (*A Yank in the R.A.F.*, 1941) and Victor Mature (*I Wake Up Screaming*, 1941, *Footlight Serenade*, 1942, and *Song of the Islands*, 1942). When she first met handsome, trumpet-playing bandleader Harry James on the set of *Springtime in the Rockies* (1942), there was no chemistry. However, that quickly changed and they married the next year. Together, they had two daughters: Victoria (1944) and Jessica (1947).

In Dan Dailey, Betty found her perfect leading man. As a team, they made *Mother Wore Tights* (1947), *When My Baby Smiles at Me* (1948), *My Blue Heaven* (1950) and *Call Me Mister* (1951). However, by the early 1950s, audience tastes were changing and the no-longer young Grable found herself playing second fiddle in *How to Marry a Millionaire* (1953) to a new blonde studio property—Marilyn Monroe. After two more pictures, Betty's movie career was over. She turned to TV guest spots, touring with James, and occasional stage work. Long before their 1965 divorce, her marriage to Harry had fallen apart. (He drank, gambled and played around heavily.)

Plucky as always, Betty returned to the limelight in a long tour of *Hello, Dolly!* that climaxed with her Broadway return in the long-running show. She attempted a musical Western, *Belle Starr* (1969), in London, but it flopped. She teamed with pal Dorothy Lamour for a 1971 summer revue in St. Louis. Next, she turned up at the 1972 Oscarcast, escorted to the podium by her one-time Twentieth Century-Fox co-star, Dick Haymes.

Returning to her modest Las Vegas

home in the spring of 1972, Betty began experiencing stomach pains. When she had a physical check-up before starting an Australian tour of *No, No Nanette*, it was discovered that heavy-smoker Grable had lung cancer. Exploratory surgery revealed that the disease had spread to her lymph glands. She should have retired right then and there. However, her industry insurance would not cover her growing medical expenses because she had earned less than $4,000 the previous year.

Therefore, Betty went back to work. As the result of the debilitating cobalt and radium treatment, her features became bloated. She lost much of her hair and had to wear a wig. By September 1972, she was re-admitted to St. John's Hospital in Santa Monica, California for further surgery. While the cancer had been arrested in her lungs, it had spread to her intestines. January, 1973 found the ailing, but determined, trouper in Jacksonville, Florida for a stock engagement of *Born Yesterday*. She suffered through the run, refueled with prescribed narcotics.

By late April, 1973, Betty was again at St. John's. The hospital announced that the 56-year old star was suffering from a duodenal ulcer problem, but gossip columnists spilled the beans to the public. Friends, like Alice Faye, visited frequently, but it was a heart-breaking experience. (Whenever Alice left, Betty would say, "I'll never see you again.") Betty returned to her Las Vegas home when the hospital could do no more. Her health deteriorated further and she again returned to the Santa Monica medical center. On July 2, 1973, just before 5 p.m., Betty started struggling for breath. By the time the emergency help rushed into her room, she was dead.

The funeral was held at All Saints Episcopal Church in Beverly Hills. Among the six-hundred celebrity mourners were: Harry James, Alice Faye, Dan Dailey, Dorothy Lamour, Cesar Romero, Patsy Kelly and Mitzi Gaynor. When June Haver MacMurray, one of Betty's 1940s Fox rivals appeared at the scene, a mutual friend snapped, "Betty sure would turn over now if she saw her here. What in hell is she doing here?" Betty's favorite song, "On a Clear Day You Can See Forever," was sung at the service.

Betty's body was cremated and her ashes interred at nearby Inglewood Memorial Park. Her crypt was inscribed: "Betty Grable James: 1916-1973." Her father's crypt drawer was beneath hers, while Betty's mother's was above. Even in death, Mrs. Grable received top billing over her daughter.

During her heyday, Betty had earned over $5 million. However, when she died she had outstanding debts and taxes. (When her bank safety deposit box was examined, a note was found in Betty's handwriting at the bottom which read, "Sorry, there's nothing more.") Her Nevada home was sold at auction to the nearby Tropicana Hotel Corporation. As for Harry James, he died on June 5, 1983 of cancer of the lymph glands. He was nearly broke at the time and worked until two weeks before the end—which occurred on the 40th anniversary of his marriage to Grable.

Edmund Gwenn

September 26, 1875 —September 6, 1959

Edmund Gwenn, that marvelous character actor with the sparkling eyes and the soft-spoken manner, won a

Best Supporting Academy Award as Kris Kringle in the Yuletime favorite, *Miracle on 34th Street* (1947). However, his reputation in Hollywood lore rests with the witty exit line he made on his death bed.

RITA HAYWORTH

He was born in Glamorgan, Wales in 1875, the oldest son of a staid government civil servant. His first career choice was to go to sea, but his parents vetoed that wild notion. His next choice was to go on the stage. "You'll die in the gutter, a rogue and a vagabond," his father thundered. When he refused to reconsider, Edmund was tossed out of the house and took the overnight boat to England. He made his stage debut in *Rogue and Vagabond*

(1895); he was just twenty. He married Minnie Terry in 1901; they divorced in 1918. He made his first British movie short in 1916 and served in France during World War I. Thereafter, he returned to the London stage and made many more British movies, usually cast in unsympathetic parts.

Nearing sixty, he came to Hollywood where his first movie was as Katharine Hepburn's dad in *Sylvia Scarlett* (1935). Occasionally, he was a villain, as the mad doctor in *The Walking Dead* (1936) or as the assassin in Alfred Hitchcock's *Foreign Correspondent* (1940). By now, Edmund had settled permanently in Los Angeles, planning to retire. However, he became one of the industry's busiest character stars. For his role as the elderly counterfeiter in *Mister 880* (1950) he was again Oscar-nominated. After *The Trouble with Harry* (1955) for Alfred Hitchcock and the wasteful *Rocket from Calabuch* (1956), his career was over.

Already in his mid-eighties, ailing and financially strapped, Edmund was helped by his long-time friend, director George Seaton, to be admitted to the Motion Picture Country House in Woodland Hills, California. Seaton would call on his friend most every Wednesday. On September 26, 1959, Seaton received an urgent message from the Country House staff. He was informed that Gwenn was failing fast and that he was drifting in and out of a terminal coma. When Seaton arrived to visit Gwenn for what would be the last time, the actor inquired if was indeed dying. Seaton admitted "yes." Then Seaton added sadly, "Oh Teddy. It's awfully tough, isn't it?" The dying man replied, "Yes, it's tough, but not as tough as doing comedy." Seconds later, Edmund Gwenn passed away. His body was cremated and his ashes are interred in a mausoleum vault at the Chapel of the Pines, Los Angeles' oldest crematorium.

Susan Hayward

[Edythe Marrener]

June 30, 1917 - March 14, 1975

Like another famous Brooklyn-born actress (Barbara Stanwyck), Susan Hayward was tough and resilient. With flashing eyes and flared nostrils, this high-voltage redhead charged through dozens of movies, always leaving a strong impression. She began her picture career as a sweet heroine, but spitfires became her celluloid speciality. After being Oscar-nominated several times, she won one for *I Want to Live!* (1958). The forthright Miss Hayward made no bones about her credo: "My life is fair game for anybody. I spent an unhappy, penniless childhood in Brooklyn. I had to slug my way up in a town called Hollywood where people love to trample you to death. I don't relax because I don't know how. I don't want to know how. Life is too short to relax." Even with her dukes up, the one battle scrapping Susan couldn't win was her death struggle with cancer.

She was born Edythe Marrenner in Brooklyn, New York, the third child (there were Florence and Walter, Jr.) of a transit company worker. When she was seven, she was hit by a car, and spent several months in a body cast, and thereafter in braces. Through a strong will, she abandoned her crutches a few years later, and learned to walk all over again. Much of her time was spent at movies and fantasizing about becoming a movie star. After high school, she became a fashion model.

One of her fashion layouts in the Saturday Evening Post came to the attention of David O. Selznick's story editor (Katharine Brown). It was arranged for Edythe to test in California for Scarlett O'Hara in *Gone with the Wind* (1939), but she didn't get the job. One day while bicycling she toppled onto the lawn of a Hollywood talent agent. He was sufficiently impressed by the accident or ploy to (1) take her on as a client (2) change her name to Susan Hayward and (3) peddle her GWTW screen test to Warner Bros. who placed her under a six-month contract.

She had several small roles at Warner Bros., but the studio soon let her go, reasoning, "she has a wonderful mind, but no heart." Next, Paramount signed her as a stock starlet. She was off the screen in 1940, but gave the performance of her young career mid-year when, at an exhibitors' convention, she turned the tables on the studio's production chief by demanding to know— in front of everyone—why she was not in more pictures. She played her first screen bitch in *Adam Had Four Sons* (1941) and got good reviews for a toss-away movie, *Among the Living* (1941). She gained the second female lead in Cecil B. DeMille's Technicolor saga, *Reap the Wild Wind* (1942) and her career was off. Never shy on or off screen, Susan had her share of romances, culminating in her marriage to actor Jess Barker in 1944. She gave birth to twin sons (Timothy, Gregory) in 1945.

She won her first Academy Award nomination as the alcoholic singer in *Smashup: The Story of a Woman* (1947). In 1949 she was Oscar-nominated again (*My Foolish Heart*) and became a Twentieth Century-Fox contract star where she remained through much of the Fifties. At one point (1954), she was earning $17,000 a month and a studio executive acknowledged, "Miss Hayward is our most valuable player." More Oscar bids followed: as singer Jane Froman in *With a Song in My Heart* (1952) and as Lillian Roth in *I'll Cry Tomorrow* (1955). Finally, for playing condemned convict Barbara Graham (*I Want to Live!*), she received the Academy Award. (Her producer, Walter Wanger, said of the victory, "Thank God, now we can all relax. Susie finally got what she's been chasing for twenty years.")

Susan ended her frequently stormy marriage to Jess Barker in 1954 and, during the next year, made headlines for overdosing on sleeping pills. A few months later, the press recorded the fight that erupted when starlet Jill Jarmyn found Susan in actor Don "Red" Barry's bedroom. Then, in 1957, Hayward married Floyd Eaton Chalkley, a former FBI agent turned lawyer and Georgia auto dealer. She now made her home with her new husband in the South.

Her 1960s roles were infrequent and in diluted vehicles such as *Valley of the Dolls* (1967). By now, she was widowed and had moved to Fort Lauderdale, Florida. She did occasional work: *Mame* on the Las Vegas stage (1968) and two 1972 TV movies. Late that year, she began experiencing severe headaches and it was discovered she had a brain tumor. In April 1973, she entered Century City Hospital in Los Angeles for cancer treatment. When she was released that May, she wore a wig (she had lost most of her hair and eyebrows) and weighed a scant 85 pounds. By year's end, she was mostly paralyzed on her right side. Refusing to give up hope, she willed herself to make a well-received appearance at the April 1974 Academy Awards, with makeup artist Frank Westmore creating a miracle of illusion.

Thereafter, the brain seizures accelerated. Susan underwent further exploratory surgery at Emory University Hospital in Atlanta. The malignant tumors were found to be spreading, and it was predicted that soon she would lose her memory and her speech. She drifted in and out of comas, but always rallied through her strong will to live. Later in the year, she flew back to California where she remained bedridden in her Culver City, California home. She had only a few visitors: Katharine Hepburn, Barbara Stanwyck and even the elusive Greta Garbo (who had learned that Hayward admired her greatly). In her last days, she was unable to swallow food. After suffering a seizure on March 14, 1975 at her home, Susan died about 2 p.m., her hand clutching a crucifix once given her by Pope John XXIII. Her body was flown to Carrollton, Georgia, where she was buried next to her husband. A pink marble tombstone marks her burial plot. The inscription reads, "Mrs F. E. Chalkley, 1917-1975." The bulk of her $950,000 estate was left to her twin sons and to her brother. (She had been estranged from her sister for years.) In the summer of 1976, her remaining effects were sold at auction in Los Angeles. Years later, reporters would link together the deaths of several members of the cast and crew of *The Conqueror* (1955)—including co-star Susan, John Wayne, Agnes Moorehead, Pedro Armendariz and director Dick Powell—all of whom had contracted cancer, the cause seemed to have been the radiation that hovered over the Utah filming site from recent government A-bomb tests.

Late in life, Susan, always the realist,

told Hollywood reporter Robert Osborne: "When you're dead, you're dead. Nobody is going to remember me when I'm dead.. Oh, maybe a few friends will remember me affectionately. Being remembered isn't the most important thing anyhow. It's what you do when you are here that's important."

Rita Hayworth

[Margarita Carmen Cansino]

October 17, 1918 — May 14, 1987

It is a strange twist of fate that two of Hollywood's most beautiful actresses—Rita Hayworth and Grace Kelly—each of whom abandoned moviemaking to become real royalty met with such tragic ends. At least Kelly's finale was swift. For Hayworth, it was a long descent into the confusion, humiliation and oblivion of Alzheimer's Disease.

She was born Margarita Carmen Cansino in New York City in 1918. Her father, Eduardo, had come to the U.S. five years earlier from Spain with his sister in a dance act. In the States he met a Ziegfeld Follies beauty, Volga Haworth, and they married. Besides Margarita, there would be two other children: Vernon and Eduardo, Jr. From an early age, Margarita was pushed by her demanding father into a dancing career, something she pursued only to please the temperamental man. As part of the family act, she made her film debut in a 1926 short subject. In 1932, Cansino acknowledged that vaudeville was dying and he moved his family to Los Angeles. By now Margarita was fourteen, and had matured into a voluptuous young woman who attracted the attention of many admirers, including her father. A victim of incest, Margarita would spend her life attempting to please dominating men and always being their abused pawn. (Rita would once observe of herself, "Basically, I am a good, gentle person, but I am attracted to mean personalities.")

Spotted by filmmakers while on the exhibition dance circuit, the dark-haired Rita Cansino made her feature debut at Fox Films as a Spanish dancer in *Dante's Inferno* (1935). Her studio contract gave her a measure of freedom, but she abandoned that when she met 41-year old promoter Edward Charles Judson. She married him in 1937, at about the same time that he maneuvered her into a Columbia Pictures contract. At Harry Cohn's studio, she went through a physical transformation (electrolysis, dying her hair auburn, dieting) and gained a new name (Rita Hayworth). Her screen career blossomed, especially on loan-out: MGM's *Susan and God* (1940), Warner Bros.'s *The Strawberry Blonde* (1941), Twentieth Century-Fox's *Blood and Sand* (1941). On the home lot, she co-starred with Fred Astaire in two musicals and her stardom was assured, especially when she was promoted as a luscious pin-up girl. By now, she had tired of the demanding, temperamental Judson and they divorced (1943). Her romance with actor Victor Mature didn't lead to marriage, but her affair with Orson Welles did in 1943. Their daughter Rebecca was born in 1944.

The genius filmmaker Welles, already a bother to the major studios, couldn't resist tampering with Rita's career whenever possible. On her own, she made the hugely successful musical *Cover Girl* (1944) and the sexy drama

Gilda (1946). Then, to appease her egotistical husband and to save their marriage, she agreed to his cutting her famous tresses and to dying the close-cropped remains blonde. He cast her in the confused drama, *Lady from Shanghai* which wasn't released until 1948—and then to disastrous results. By now, she and Orson were divorced. She fell back into the frying pan when she met Prince Aly Khan, the playboy son of the Indian Potentate, the enormously rich Aga Khan. In May 1949, the world waited breathlessly while the couple were married in a town hall in Vallauris, France. Until the next decade's Grace Kelly—Prince Rainier nuptials, it was the wedding of the century. Five months later, Princess Yasmin was born.

By the early Fifties, the royal marriage fell apart and the prodigal daughter, Rita Hayworth, returned to Hollywood, where Columbia Pictures hastily starred her in *Affair in Trinidad* (1952). By the time of the 3-D musical, *Miss Sadie Thompson* (1953), Hayworth was looking ragged around the edges; by the release of *Pal Joey* (1957), she was looking shopworn. In between, she had a short stormy marriage (1953-55) to equally unstable singer Dick Haymes, which cost her a fortune and a gre- *Separate Tables* (1958), Hayworth had matured into character leads and, that year, she wed British producer James Hill, a union which lasted three years. In 1961, she turned up in Spain with Bette Davis's ex-husband, actor Gary Merrill, and announced that—like Ava Gardner—she might relocate there. Instead, the couple returned to New York where Rita was to co-star on stage with Merrill in *Step on a Crack*. However, she never made it to Broadway, instead retreating to Hollywood alone, and in poor physical and mental shape.

Rita's final years of picture-making was an odyssey of embarrassment, ranging from *The Naked Zoo* (1966) to her final screen appearance in *The Wrath of God* (1972). She almost took over the lead from Lauren Bacall in the musical *Applause*, 1971, but left the project before her opening. She admitted to having a face-lift in the mid-1970s, and then received bad press when she disembarked "drunk" at London's Heathrow Airport in early 1976. Several announced screen projects aborted and, thereafter, Rita's only public appearances seemed to be at European film retrospectives.

In 1977, she became distraught at a Newport, California art gallery show and was hospitalized. The attending physician concluded that the ex-movie star was "gravely disabled as a result of mental disorder or impairment by chronic alcoholism." Subsequently, a petition was filed to have her estate and personal matters handled by a conservator. Her lawyer flew her out of state and the public next learned she was at a Connecticut "drying-out" hospital and that daughter Yasmin had been appointed her guardian. Rita later checked herself out of the "rest spa" and reemerged in Hollywood for a revival theater showing of *Miss Sadie Thompson*. That November she was the tribute subject for the annual Thalians charity bash.

Rita kept insisting she had given up drinking. However, her peculiar public behavior (incoherent outbursts, paranoia, memory losses, etc.) convinced observers otherwise. It was not until 1980 that doctors determined that Hayworth's problems might not be alcoholism, but rather a then relatively unrecognized brain disorder (Alzheimer's disease). Yasmin would say later, "So much embarrassment and heartache could have been saved, if at that time it had been known that Rita Hayworth was ill and not guilty of any misconduct." It was not until mid-1981 that the public learned the true nature of Hayworth's plight and that, by then, the once glamour goddess, could no longer control even her simplest basic needs.

Yasmin was appointed Rita's conservator in July 1981. Next, Rita was moved to New York City where she was established in a suite adjacent to Yasmin's at the San Remo Apartments overlooking Central Park. Most days Rita spent sitting endlessly in an armchair, gazing vacantly ahead, lost to the world. As the disease progressed, Hayworth became bedridden, too fearful to even move from the bedroom to her living room chair. Meanwhile, Yasmin who had become a spokesperson for the Alzheimer's Disease and Related Disorders Association married and, in December 1985, her son, Andrew, was born. The marriage quickly ended, but Yasmin and Andrew continued to live at the San Remo. The ailing Rita had retreated so far into the past, that she could not be made to understand that the little boy Yasmin placed on her lap was her grandson.

Rita died on May 14, 1987. She was buried at Los Angeles's Holy Cross Cemetery in the hilly area known as the Grotto. Her grave is marked with a kneeling angel and a bonsai-type tree. The marker reads "To yesterday's companionship and tomorrow's reunion."

Tim Holt

[Charles John Holt, III]

February 5, 1918 — February 15, 1973

Tim Holt was born into show business and made an easy entry in the mo-vies. After all, his father was action star Jack Holt. Tim was far more competent and versatile than his peers acknowledged. Years later, when he was dying of cancer, he demonstrated a personal courage and a public concern that verified the depth of his life-long integrity.

Soon after he was born in 1918 in Beverly Hills, his parents began calling him Tim as he would be known for the rest of his life. (His sister Elizabeth, born, in 1920, would also become a movie player under the name Jennifer Holt.) While attending Culver Military Academy, young Tim perfected his horsemanship and also appeared in one of his dad's movies, (*The Vanishing Pioneers*, 1928). While at UCLA (for two years) he met Virginia Mae Ashcroft and they married in late 1938. By then he had already attended the Westwood Theatre Guild in Los Angeles and had been in several movies. He displayed his riding ability in *Stagecoach* (1939) but was equally adept in contemporary comedy, playing with Ginger Rogers in *Fifth Avenue Girl* (1939). In 1940, his son Lance, was born.

Tim came into his own as the star of a series of well-produced RKO Westerns. Occasionally, he was given a prestige part, as when he played the wastrel son in Orson Welles's *The Magnificent Ambersons* (1942). Always modest in the face of good reviews, Holt insisted, "I'm not an actor. I'm a horse mechanic!" During World War II he served in the Army Air Corps as a bombardier; his fifty-nine missions earned him several medals and the rank of major. He and his wife had divorced in the early 1940s, and, while on service leave in June 1944, he wed Alice Harrison.

Back from the war, he was in John Ford's Western, *My Darling Cle-*

mentine (1946) and received excellent credits as Curtin in *The Treasure of the Sierra Madre* (1948). Then it was back to stock RKO Westerns, often teamed with sidekick Richard Martin. Always popular with moviegoers, Holt tired of moviemaking and quit in 1952 when his contract expired. He continued making personal appearances and touring with rodeos. A TV series pilot, *"Adventure in Java"* failed to sell. Later, he rejected the *"Wyatt Earp"* tele-series, preferring life at his Hurrah, Oklahoma ranch with his third wife (Berdee Stephens) and their three children: Jack, Jay, Bryanna. He worked as sales manager for radio station KEBC-FM Oklahoma City and later at KOPR. In 1971, he returned to the screen in the poorly-made *This Stuff'll Kill Ya,* dealing with a moonshiner.

In early 1973, Tim was diagnosed with terminal cancer. Only a few hours before his death, he appeared on KWTC-TV in Oklahoma City in conjunction with a cancer detection documentary that he had suggested the station air. Tim told the TV audience, "I've had a good life. I don't regret anything. I'm not afraid to die."

On February 15, 1973, he passed away at the Shawnee Medical Clinic in Shawnee, Oklahoma.

Rock Hudson

[Roy Harold Scherer, Jr.]

November 17, 1925 — October 2, 1985

At 6' 4" and 200-pounds, ruggedly handsome, dark-haired Rock Hudson was Hollywood's ultimate screen hunk during the Fifties and Sixties. He was everyone's favorite All American per-

sonality. Women swooned over this wholesome sex symbol, even as he matured over the next two decades of TV, stage and film work. Then in the mid-1980s, he contracted AIDS. At first he kept the facts secret, fearful that the disclosure would make known what he had been hiding for so many years—that he was homosexual. However, when his disease reached the terminal stage, he shocked the world by making the deadly diagnosis public. Too sick by this time to deliver the news himself (he was down to 97 pounds), his words—written down by Hudson's publicist Dale Olson—were read at a Los Angeles fund-raising affair by actor Burt Lancaster:

I have been told the media coverage of my own situation has brought enormous international attention to the gravity of this disease in all areas of humanity, and is leading to more research, more contribution of funds, and a better understanding of this disease than ever before. I am not happy that I have AIDS. But if that is helping others, I can, at least know that my own misfortune has had some positive worth.

As actress Morgan Fairchild said, "Rock's illness helped give AIDS a face."

The future actor was born in Winnetka, Illinois in 1925, the only son of an auto mechanic and his wife Kay (Wood) Scherer. When the boy was four, his father went to California and never returned. His mother later remarried, to ex-Marine officer Wallace Fitzgerald. Throughout childhood, Roy's mother was the boy's focal figure, as she would be in subsequent years. As a teenager he was so impressed by Jon Hall's athletic stunts in *The Hurricane* (1937), he knew that he wanted to become a movie star. After high school, Roy worked as a postal worker until he was drafted into the Navy in January 1944.

After his discharge in May 1946, Roy moved to Los Angeles where he took a truck driver job. His photograph came to the attention of talent agent Henry Willson who rechristened him Rock Hudson, later claiming the name tag came from the Rock of Gibraltar and the Hudson River. By 1949, Rock had a $125 per week Universal Pictures' contract. Along with Tony Curtis and Jeff Chandler, Hudson became a staple in that studio's action fare. By the time of the tearjerker *Magnificent Obsession* (1954), the studio was promoting Rock as the "Beefcake Baron." Hudson had long been a practicing homosexual (or bi-sexual) by the time he married Willson's secretary Phyllis Gates in November 1955. They divorced less than three years later.

Hudson gained professional credibility with his Oscar-nominated performance in *Giant* (1956). However, it was his several screen comedies—including the popular *Pillow Talk* (1959)—with Doris Day that brought Rock to his career peak. These performances led to several other romantic comedies in the Sixties with such international personalities as Sophia Loren, Gina Lollabrigida and Leslie Caron.

Hudson's studio contract days were over by the mid-Sixties and his big effort to go dramatic—*Seconds* (1966)—had failed at the box-office. However, his fading career was salvaged by a teleseries, "*McMillan and Wife*" (1971-76); known as "*McMillan*" (1976-77) after co-star Susan Saint James quit the detective program. Thereafter, he alternated mostly between stage tours (*I Do! I Do!*, 1973) and TV movies such as *The Star Maker* (1981). Just before

his fifty-sixth birthday he underwent heart bypass surgery, later insisting the strain of his flop TV series "*The Devlin Connection*" (1982) "undid me."

It was in the fall of 1982 that Rock met one-time bartender Marc Christian [MacGinnis], who was twenty-eight years Hudson's junior. The friendship developed into a romance and the musicology enthusiast moved into the star's home. B*The Ambassador* (1984) abroad, he knew he had AIDS. However, he kept the information from the world, including, according to Marc, from Christian, who was his lover. Determined to keep working despite his failing health, Rock signed for a recurring role in the nighttime soap opera, "*Dynasty*" (1984-85).

Meanwhile, in September 1984, Hudson checked into the Ritz Hotel in Paris while he underwent AIDS treatment at a local hospital. However, he quit the hospital after six weeks to return to Hollywood for his "*Dynasty*" segments, the last of his episodes being telecast in March 1985. After that, Hudson remained out of the limelight until July 1985. Then, horribly gaunt and much aged he made an agreed-upon appearance in Carmel, California on Doris Day's new cable show dealing with pets. A few days later, he returned to Paris for further AIDS treatment. On the 21st he collapsed in the Ritz Hotel lobby and, on July 25, what had been rumored for weeks was finally made public— Rock Hudson had AIDS. For $300,000, Hudson chartered a private jet to fly him to Los Angeles where he entered UCLA Medical Center. While the star was struggling with the inevitable, he worked on his autobiography with a co-writer, insisting, "there's a lot I want to say and not too much time left. I want the truth to be told, because it sure as hell hasn't been told before." (All Rock's earnings from the project went to the Rock Hudson AIDS Research Foundation.)

By the early fall of 1985 Rock was bedroom-bound at The Castle, his Spanish-style estate high up on a ridge in Beverly Hills. On September 26, he was so near the end that when Father Terry Sweeney visited the superstar, he gave him holy communion. On October 1, good friends Pat and Shirley Boone came by to pray for Rock. The next day Rock Hudson died at 9 a.m. His body was cremated and his ashes spread at sea on October 20. A day earlier, long-time friend Elizabeth Taylor was among those hosting an exclusive memorial service at The Castle. Rock's New York apartment overlooking Central Park was sold for $2 million; his Beverly Hills home was placed on the market for $4.7 million. The next April, some of Rock's belongings were auctioned off at an exclusive Manhattan gallery.

In 1974, Hudson had created a revocable trust as the beneficiary of his substantial estate, with long time friend Tom Clark in charge of all dispositions. However, in August 1984, Hudson added a codicil which revoked Clark's power in the will. Meanwhile, in late August 1985, Marc Christians had hired attorney Marvin Mitchelson. After Hudson's death, they filed a lawsuit against the estate and several other individuals for $14 million in damages, claiming that Hudson had irresponsibly failed to disclose his transmittable, fatal illness to his lover. In 1989, a Los Angeles Superior Court jury determined that Hudson had engaged in "outrageous conduct" by not advising Christian of having AIDS and continuing in a sexual relationship. It gave a $21.75 million verdict in Christian's favor. The case judge later reduced the

"excessive" award to $5.5 million. The estate appealed. In August 1991, a private settlement was reached between the two sides, and the appeal was dropped by both sides. The next time AIDS would receive so much global attention would be six years later, when sports figure, Magic Johnson, revealed that he was HIV positive.

Jill Ireland

April 24, 1936 — May 18, 1990

The expression "when the going gets tough, the tough get going" cannot fit anyone better than actress Jill Ireland. In the 1980s, she survived one tragedy after another, displaying remarkable courage and resiliency in the face of cumulative personal and family health problems that would have overwhelmed most others.

She was born in London, England in 1936, and by the age of twelve was entertaining in her country's music halls. Later, she danced and sang at the London Palladium and toured the continent with a ballet company. She was signed to a studio film contract by J. Arthur Rank and made her screen bow as a ballet dancer in *Oh, Rosalinda!* (1955). The pert blonde soon became a favorite pin-up. In 1957, she married young actor David McCallum and they would have two children: Paul and Valentine. In 1962, the year she made her last Rank feature, she and McCallum adopted a son, Jason.

By 1964, the McCallums had moved to Los Angeles where David became the star of a hit TV series, *"The Man from U.N.C.L.E."* (1964-68) and Jill appeared in the Western series, *"Shane"* (1964). By 1967, the McCallums divorced. She received custody of their children and their Bel Air home. Two years later, she married Charles Bronson, whom she and McCallum had first met when David McCallum and Bronson were on location for *The Great Escape* (1958). Action star Bronson had two children by his first marriage (1948-65) and in 1971, Jill and Charles became parents of Zuleika. Just as Ireland had guest-starred several times on "*U.N.C.L.E.*" so she began co-starring with Bronson in his pictures (*The Family*, 1970, *The Valachi Papers*, 1972, *Love and Bullets*, 1979, etc.). Bronson acknowledged that it had been Jill who had pushed him in positive career directions when his movie popularity was waning in the late 1960s.

In June 1984, Jill was diagnosed with cancer and underwent a mastectomy and then six months of chemotherapy. Having survived that trauma successfully, she was ordered to rest and avoid stress. However, life refused to allow her such indulgence. She learned the bitter truth that her son, Jason McCallum, was not only alcoholic, but a heavy-duty drug addict. (He had first experimented with drugs when he was seven and became hooked while still in his teens.) Trying to find the best way to deal with the self-destructive Jason caused many domestic fights between Jill and Charles. However, even when she began practicing "tough love," she refused to give up on her son who was unsuccessfully hospitalized for drug withdrawal. Once when he disappeared, she went searching for him through some of L.A.'s seamier areas, overcoming her own ill health to make it through the trek. As therapy for her cancer recovery, she wrote the optimistic *Life Wish* (1988), dealing with her cancer struggle, and it became a best-seller. Adding to her problems in

this period, her father, Jack, was losing his own life struggle, having suffered a debilitating stroke.

Hardly had Ireland's first book been published than Jill, who was National Crusade Chairperson for the National Cancer Society, learned her cancer had returned. When standard treatment failed, she had a special tube inserted in her heart which smoothed the flow of special anti-cancer drugs through her body. She made periodic trips to the Arlington Cancer Center near Dallas, Texas. Despite her weakening condition she authored a second book, *Life Lines* (1989), in which she dealt with her efforts to save her drug-addicted son and to keep her family intact.

Then, on November 7, 1989 she received word at her Vermont retreat, that Jason had died that day in Los Angeles of a drug overdose at his fiancee's apartment. Somehow Ireland found the strength to fly back to California for his funeral on November 11 at Forest Lawn Memorial Parks in Glendale. Because she already had one collapsed lung and the other was tumor-filled, her doctors warned that the strain of crying could kill her. Jason's birth mother, Judy Brown, appeared uninvited at the funeral, and. according to Jill, glared at the actress throughout the ceremony.

Some six months later, Jill's battle with cancer ended with her death on May 18, 1990. However, her memory was not allowed to be in peace. Before she had died, Ireland had contracted for *Life Lines* to be adapted into a TV movie. After her passing, the grieving, very private Bronson attempted to block the entertainment project, not wishing details of his pre-marriage relationship with Jill and his conflicts with her over Jason to be re-hashed publicly. He even returned the fee he and Jill had been paid for the adaptation, hoping that would end the matter. It did not. Finally, a compromise was reached between the TV film's producers and Bronson, giving him script approval. *Reason for Living: The Jill Ireland Story*—starring Jill Clayburgh and Lance Henriksen (as the Bronsons) and Neill Barry (as Jason McCallum)—was telecast on May 20, 1991. Promoted with the tag line, "Her story will live for a lifetime," the trade paper, *Hollywood Reporter*, thought the battle to air the project had been worthwhile. "...it turns out to be a surprisingly rich and complex study of how actors and others use masks to cope with tragic realities."

Michael Landon

[Eugene Maurice Orowitz]

October 31, 1937 — July 1, 1991

Michael Landon was a 5' 11" man of complex moodiness, with a tremendous drive for success. He had seen his movie publicist father turned away from Paramount Pictures in 1954 where he hoped to get a new position from industry friends. The humiliating event left an indelible impression on Landon who determined: "No matter what I did, I wasn't going to owe anybody a favor. And I didn't expect anything from anybody that had to do with business . . . I wasn't going to take any garbage from anybody, either." With his personal aggenda, the slighty-built Landon literally grew up in front of the American TV public, who took him to heart during his several decades of performing. It made his sudden death from cancer in 1991, at age fifty-four, all the more a personal loss felt by millions.

He was born in Forest Hill, New Jersey, the son of a mixed marriage. His Jewish father was an East Coast film publicist whose career was falling apart; his Irish Catholic mother had been a minor musical comedy stage actress (Peggy O'Neill) who later became suicidal and often voiced her wish that her son were dead. The future actor grew up in Collingswood, New Jersey, a predominantly white Protestant town that had scant use for a skinny little Jewish kid. Problems at school and in the tension-filled household were reflected in the boy being a bed wetter even into his teen years. (This chapter of his life would form the autobiographical background of his TV movies: *The Loneliest Runner*, 1976, and *Sam's Son*, 1985.)

Some of his frustrations dissolved when he participated in high school track events, especially javelin throwing. He developed the theory that his long hair was a symbol of strength (like the Biblical Samson) and it remained his signature throughout much of his career. His javelin-tossing ability earned him an escape from his bitter home life. He went to the University of Southern California in Los Angeles on an athletic scholarship, but a torn ligament in his arm ended his sports career during his freshman year and he quit college. He was working at a warehouse unloading freight cars when a actor friend asked him to help prepare him for an audition. However, it was Eugene who was taken on at the Warner Bros. acting school. He adopted a new name, Michael Landon, which he claimed he picked from a telephone book.

His early films were not exactly hightoned. He was the angry student Tony in *I Was a Teen-age Werewolf* (1957), which became a camp classic. He played the albino in *God's Little Acre* (1958) and was the hero-outlaw in *The Legend of Tom Dooley* (1959). He had guest-starred on several TV Westerns ("*Adventures of Jim Bowie,*" "*Frontier Doctor,*" etc.) before he got his show business break. The baby-faced actor was cast as Little Joe, one of the three sons—along with Pernell Roberts and Dan Blocker—of Ben Cartwright (Lorne Greene) on "*Bonanza,*" set at the Ponderosa ranch in 1860s Nevada. The hour-long series debuted in September 1959 and remained on the air through January, 1973. Roberts left the hit series after the 1964-65 season and burly Dan Blocker died of a heart attack in May 1972. However, Landon remained through to the end, not only acting but directing and sometimes scripting episodes shown in its last seasons. During this period he became addicted to tranquilizer pills, but later kicked the habit.

In 1956, Landon married legal secretary Dodie Fraser, seven years older than Michael. She already had a son, Mark, from a prior marriage. The couple adopted two sons, Josh and Jason. The marriage fell apart in 1962. (In 1964, Landon and his ex-wife agreed for Jason to be privately adopted by a Texas couple.) In 1963, Landon married model-actress Lynn Noe. She had a child, Cheryl, by her first marriage, and Michael and Lynn eventually became the parents of four children: Leslie, Michael Jr., Shawn, and Christopher. They divorced in 1982 and he married Cindy Clerico, a makeup artist, on Valentine's Day in 1983, with whom he had two children, Jennifer and Sean.

After overcoming several family catastrophes and his own illness (at one point he collapsed with seizures from over-work), Michael became quite religious. He was a firm believer in traditional American values and said of his next television series, "*Little House on the Prairie*" (1974-82), "I want people to laugh and cry, not just sit and stare at the TV. Maybe I'm old-fashioned, but I think viewers are hungry for shows in which people say something meaningful." For this extremely popular series about 1870s America, he produced, sometimes directed and scripted, and always starred. Landon starrng role was as Charles Ingalls, struggling to make a go of his small farm in Walnut Grove, Minnesota and to raise his family with his wife (Karen Grassle). Michael left the show in 1982, and the program—in a new format—continued on as "*Little House: A New Beginning*" for one additional season. During this period, 1981-84, Landon also produced (and sometimes directed) the TV series, "*Father Murphy*" starring Merle Olsen.

For his third successful prime time series, Michael starred in "*Highway to Heaven*" (1984-1989) as a probationary angel, Jonathan Smith, returned to Earth to help needy people. Victor French was his earthy sidekick, an ex-cop, who traveled around the country with him carrying out heavenly assignments. Although the segments were usually highly emotional, occasionally they could be joking, as in the October 1987 episode which kidded *I Was a Teenage Werewolf*.

Not content to quit the acting tread mill, Landon next began working on a new TV series, "*US.*" It dealt with a man released from prison after serving seventeen years for a crime he didn't commit. He then must deal with a father who rejected him and a son who has never known him.

Landon had been having stomach pains for several weeks when, in March

1991, he went skiing in Park City, Utah with his third wife Cindy and their two young children (Jennifer and Sean). He thought he was developing an ulcer. On April 3, he entered Cedars-Sinai Medical Center in Los Angeles for a CAT scan. He learned that he had a large abdominal tumor, and two days later, he was told he had inoperable cancer of the pancreas. On April 8, Landon held a press conference. He quipped about his illness, "I want my agent to know that this shoots to hell any chance of doing a health food commercial." He added, "Life has been good to me....I had a pretty good lick here. I am going to fight it.... Every moment gets a little more important after something like this."

Michael agreed to undergo chemotherapy, but after his first treatment, he opted for a holistic program of special exercise and diet. A second CAT scan on April 24, revealed that the cancer had spread, and he was told he had only weeks to live. On May 9, the star appeared on his friend Johnny Carson's "Tonight Show." Displaying class and bravery, Michael joked that it required lots of makeup and two blood transfusions for him to make the talk show telecast. His appearance gave the show its second highest rating since Carson took over the program in 1962.

After that, Michael remained secluded, devoting his remaining time and energy to his family. By May 13, 1991, Landon began a new round of chemotherapy and submitted to an experimental cancer treatment involving chemicals injected into the malignant tumors. When he collapsed a week later in excruciating pain, he decided to forego any further treatment. He was released from the hospital on May 25 with an intensive care unit established at his Malibu house (a 10,000-square-foot house he built in 1988 for $3 million). He insisted to friends, "I have absolutely no fear of dying." Despite his weakness, he made videos in which he read his will (concering his estimated $100 million estate) and let his final wishes be known. By June 28, Michael had grown so weak, he was down to 90 pounds and his hair had turned white. By now, the entire family was gathered at the compound, keeping a bedside vigil. On July 1, Landon was alert suddenly and, after addressing the family, asked them to leave so he and Cindy could be alone. Two hours later, about 1:20 p.m., she came downstairs to tell them that Landon was dead. By that evening, his body had been cremated.

On July 5, five hundred friends and family members gathered at Hillside Memorial Park and Mortuary in Los Angeles for Landon's funeral service. Among the attendees were Ronald and Nancy Reagan, and such actors as Ernest Borgnine, Brian Keith, Merlin Olsen, Melissa Gilbert and Melissa Sue Anderson. Michael's daughter Leslie Landon Matthews spoke at the service, "I know that dad wants us to think of him and be filled with love and happiness and laughter. She read a poem he had written for a *Little House* episode: "Remember me with smile and laughter, for that is how I will remember you all. If you can only remember me with tears, then don't remember me at all."

On September 17, 1991, a two-hour tribute to Landon, produced by Michael, Jr. and featuring family members, was telecast. *US*, the TV movie pilot for his last projected series, was shown on September 30. With Landon's consent, a March 1991 commercial he made for educational seminars continued to be aired long after his death. Perhaps the most touching eulogy to Landon came from Michael, Jr.: "My father left us with a legacy we will cherish from one generation to the next. His shows touched our hearts, our souls and our minds. He taught us the value of life and the importance of family."

Charles Laughton

July 1, 1899 — December 15, 1962

To some, distinguished Britisher Charles Laughton was a consummate actor; to others he was an unrelenting, homely ham with an obsessive ego. Still others knew him as a sensitive, overly-insecure person who masked vast inadequacies behind obnoxious egoism. Regardless of the contradictory mix, Charles Laughton was a trouper in the old-fashioned tradition. He rarely gave an unmemorable performance. That such an hefty, unattractive man should become a major star was a tribute to his magnetism. He died, as an actor should, believing that his next part was assured (in *Irma La Douce*, 1963), and that all he needed to do to start the job, was to get well again. He never did.

He was born at the end of the nineteenth century in Scarborough, England. His parents owned a middle-class Yorkshire hotel. He graduated from Stoneyhurst College, a Jesuit institution and trained at the famed Claridge's in London to learn the family trade of hotelry. During World War I, he served as a private and was gassed in the front lines (from which he never recovered fully). Demobilized, he failed at the family trade ("I would starve in the gutter first," he told his brother Tom) and enrolled in 1925 at the Royal Academy of Dramatic Arts. He earned his professional debut the next year in *The Government Inspector*, and followed it with several other dramatic roles on the West End. In 1929 he married Elsa Sullivan Lanchester, a young actress who had made a reputation with her quirky cabaret act (singing songs like "I've just danced with a man who danced with a girl who danced with the Prince of Wales").

The year 1931 was a turning point for Laughton in many ways. He had a great success starring on the British stage in *Payment Deferred*, with Elsa cast as his fifteen-year-old daughter. During rehearsals for the drama, circumstances forced him to confess to Elsa that he was bisexual at best; homosexual at heart. A young hustler harassed Laughton for more money, the police intervened, and the case came before a magistrate (who good-naturedly, or naively, dismissed it). The very Bohemian Elsa advised her concerned husband not to worry; she understood and accepted (as best one can) the situation. (Years later, she would say of their open marriage, "We both needed other company. I met his young men, and I had a young man around, and Charles didn't even argue.")

The Laughtons came to New York for Charles to play in *Fatal Alibi* (1931), which failed to make the grade. No sooner was he back in England than Charles received a film offer from Paramount. He and Elsa sailed again for America. He had made a few films before, but *The Old Dark House* (1932) on loan to Universal, gave him a taste for Hollywood filmmaking. He adored the fact that he could indulge his perfectionist desire for countless retakes. He proved himself a worthy screen presence in that spooky house classic and next tangled with Tallulah Bankhead and Gary Cooper in the shoddy melodrama, *The Devil and the Deep* (1932). He chewed the scenery as Nero in Cecil B. DeMille's *The Sign of the Cross* (1932) and was the fiendish experimenter in *Island of Lost Souls* (1932). He had found his niche in character leads. However, it was back in England that he cemented his international screen reputation by playing Henry VIII—which he also did regally on stage the same year—in *The Private Life of Henry VIII* (1933). For this film he won an Academy Award.

The much-in-demand Laughton continued alternating between the London stage films and Hollywood moviemaking. In 1935, he showed great range, going from the possessive father in *The Barretts of Wimpole Street* to the knowing butler in the comedic *Ruggles of Red Gap* (1935) to the tyrannical Captain Bligh in *Mutiny on the Bounty*. (That same year Elsa made a great impression in the title role of *The Bride of Frankenstein*.)

Thriving on the challenge of a difficult role he shone as the deformed Quasimodo in *The Hunchback of Notre Dame* (1939). He played coy as Deanna Durbin's ailing grandfather in *It Started with Eve* (1941) and sparred with that scene-stealing tyke, Margaret O'Brien in *The Canterville Ghost* (1944). During World War II, he did his part for the war effort by reading from the Bible to bedridden servicemen. From the mid-Forties onward, his performances grew increasingly exaggerated. In 1950, he and Elsa became American citizens. Always reaching for new goals, he directed and toured on stage with *Don Juan in Hell* (1951) and directed such other stage productions as *The Caine Mutiny Court Martial* (1954) with Henry Fonda. On screen he directed the very black *Night of the Hunter* (1956) and was reunited with his wife in the witty *Witness for the Prosecution* (1957). He was a fat and sly Gracchus in the spectacle *Spartacus* (1960) and overacted as a conniving southern U.S. senator in *Advise and Consent* (1962).

In the early 1960s his health deteriorated badly. His gall bladder turned bad which, in turn led to a heart attack. He underwent corrective surgery but grew depressed by his increasing ailments. He had a nervous breakdown and threatened suicide. In early 1962, he fell in his bath tub and that was the beginning of the end. He developed cancer of the spine; surgery followed and everyone hoped it had been contained. He was hospitalized in Los Angeles for much of the latter half of 1962, but was released on November 30. Director Billy Wilder promised him the role of Moustache in the sex farce, *Irma La Douce* (1963) knowing his friend would never be well enough to make the movie. Clinging to hope, Laughton grew a moustache for the part and, in great pain, got out of his sick bed, one day, to convince Wilder that he was truly on the mend.

On December 17, 1962, having been in a coma for some time, he died at home, with his wife and brother Frank at his bedside. He was buried in a black marble vault in the Court of Remembrance at Forest Lawn Memorial Parks in Glendale. When Elsa succumbed on December 26, 1986, her body was cremated and her ashes strewn at sea.

Liberace

[Wladziu Valentino Liberace]

May 16, 1919 — February 4, 1987

"Mr. Showmanship" was a more than competent pianist who found his forte in kitchy renditions of classical and pop songs. As the years passed, the broadly smiling entertainer with the wavy hair dressed up his act with increasingly outrageous gimmicks—from sequined, fur-lined capes to a performance finale which often found him flying up into the stage rafters on guy wires. He wisely learned to mock his fey, glitzy image, always chiding the sold-out audience, "Well, look me over! I don't dress like this to go unnoticed!" Whenever detractors insisted he was making a fool of himself publicly, the crafty Liberace retorted, "I cried all the way to the bank."

In the more innocent mid-twentieth century, Liberace was able to assure his middle-aged and older women fans that the real reason he hadn't married was because he hadn't found any girl as perfect as his mama. However, more worldly observers knew what Liberace would not admit publicly—that he was homosexual. Over the years, the lifelong bachelor had a long procession of boyfriends and lovers. However, to the end—when he was dying of AIDS—he refused to openly acknowledge his gay lifestyle.

He was born Wladziu Valentino Liberace in 1919 in West Allis, Wisconsin, one of twins—the other baby boy died at birth. There were three other children: Rudolph [Ralph], George and Ann. His father, Salvatore was an Italian immigrant who had once played French horn with John Philip Sousa's concert band and later with the Milwaukee Symphony. Salvatore supported his wife, Polish-born Frances (Zuchowski) Liberace and their children by running an Italian speciality grocery. Walter—as he became know—was fascinated with the piano and started lessons at age four. Early in life, he knew he wanted a career in music, despite his father's desire that he become an undertaker. (Coincidentally, Liberace later would play a coffin salesman in *The Loved One*, 1965.) When Walter was eleven, his parents separated and then divorced. Walter helped support the household by playing at local movie theatres and ice cream shoppes. He said once, "Except for music, there wasn't much beauty in my childhood."

By age seventeen, Walter had performed with the Chicago Symphony and pursued a concert career. When he played as a cocktail lounge pianist he used the name of Walter Buster Keys, indulging his sense of fantasy and illusion. It was during a 1939 concert that he blended the two contrasting sides of his performing self into a unified whole. He moved to New York where he played during intermissions at the Plaza Hotel's Persian Room. As self-protection against the rude rich audiences, he learned the knack of heckling himself as the best defense against their indifference. By the mid-Forties he was a featured performer at swank clubs nationwide (including Las Vegas), with his violin-playing brother George as his bandleader. As part of his act he used an oversized grand piano and an (imitation) Louis XIV candelabrum atop it. He attributed much of his growing success to his belief in positivism.

Walter was now called Liberace (pronounced Libber-ah-CHEE)— sometimes Lee Liberace—and made a few

Hollywood movies: *South Sea Sinner* (1950), *Footlight Varieties* (1951). However, it was TV that made him famous. His first show (1951) was a local Los Angeles program, followed by a fifteen-minute summer show (1952) and "*The Liberace Show*" (1953-55). The latter syndicated show was enormously popular and was carried by more stations than "*I Love Lucy.*" Liberace always ended his show with "I'll be looking at the moon, but I'll be seeing you." He won several Emmys and his LP albums became hit releases.

In his Sherman Oaks, California home, he had a piano top-shaped pool with 88 keys painted in black and white on the cement deck at the wide end. To appease his curious public, he wrote a fan magazine article and insisted he had been engaged three times in his life so far. Then he dated minor film actress Joanne Rio, but that quickly ended. He claimed that he feared marriage because all his family was so divorce-prone. His one professional failure during *Sincerely Yours* (1955). By the late 1950s, Liberace was considered passe to mainstream America; nevertheless, he remained a constant Las Vegas entertainer. By now, Liberace was earning over $800,000 annually and his gaudy performing outfits had reached high camp. (He always insisted he had to outdo his Las Vegas rival, Elvis Presley.) Wanting to reconquor an old medium, he returned to network TV with a summer 1969 variety show, but it was not popular.

By the 1970s Liberace was residing in Nevada for tax purposes. He had authored a cook book (*Liberace Cooks! Recipes from His Seven Dining Rooms*, 1970), an autobiography (*Liberace*, 1973) and an elaborate coffee table volume (*The Things I Live*, 1976). He pampered his weakness for fancy cars,

numerous residences (he had ten at one time) and elaborate wardrobes. The Liberace Museum in Las Vegas opened on Easter Sunday 1979 in a 5,000 square foot, one-story, Spanish-style building. (It was later expanded into a new three exhibit area complex and became the state's third most poplar tourist attraction.)

By the mid-1980s, Liberace had only one surviving close relative: his sister. Liberace's brother Ralph died in 1967, his father in 1977, his mother in 1980, and brother George (with whom he feuded in later years) in 1983. Amidst much press coverage, Liberace survived a palimony suit begun in 1982 by ex-employee (chauffeur-dancer) Scott Thorson. Thorsen, age twenty-three, claimed that the much older entertainer had reneged on an agreement to provide continued financial support in consideration for sex. The suit (for a reputed $100 million) was dismissed and a counter-claim was later settled out of court for a reported $95,000.

In 1984. Liberace enjoyed a hugely successful 14-performance run at Radio City Music Hall during Easter Week. He topped that record with 21 performances at the Hall in 1985 which grossed over $2.4 million. (His stunts included dancing with the Rockettes and being driven on stage in a chauffeured Rolls Royce). His last appearance there was in October 1986 by which time he was haggard and listless. He spent Christmas 1986 quietly at the Cloisters, his Palm Springs residence. In early 1987, despite reports that he was painfully ailing, he wrote close friends insisting he was on the road to recovery. By now, speculators contended, Liberace's symptoms indicated he had AIDS. Through his spokesmen, the showman insisted that he was suffering from a mix of anemia, emphysema and heart disease.

By early February the "word" was out that Liberace way dying. Reporters and photographers set up a vigil outside his Palm Springs home, monitoring everyone who came and went from the Cloisters. Inside, the once lively personality lay almost motionless in his bed, usually clutching a rosary. On February 4, 1987 at 11:02 a.m. he died. His doctors listed the cause of death as cardiac arrest due to congestive heart failure as the prime cause of death. However, when the Riverside County Coroner performed an autopsy, and its report was made public, it indicated, in so many words, that the entertainer had died of AIDS. Liberace was buried at Forest Lawn— Hollywood Hills in the Court of Remembrance, next to his mother and brother George. The marker on the very ornate family tombstone bears Liberace's signature and a drawing of a piano, along with the inscription "Sheltered Love." On top of the elaborate white marble tomb is a marble statue of a female holding flowers.

Liberace's last will, signed thirteen days before he died, left his sizeable estate (he had earned well over $125 million in his lifetime) to The Liberace Revocable Trust created earlier that day. The terms of that trust were confidential, but Liberace's attorney stated that a goodly portion of the estate will go to the Liberace Foundation for the Performing and Creative Arts.

Maria Montez

[Maria Africa Antonia Gracia Vidal da Santo Silas]

June 6, 1918 — September 7, 1951

Maria Montez was almost one of a kind. They don't make exotic per-

sonalities like her anymore. Not only was she beautiful and ambitious, but she was volatile and uninhibited. She was her own greatest fan and strongly believed in her destiny to succeed. Extremely superstitious, she frequently consulted astrologers. One of them warned her that her life would be short and that the end would be abrupt. A few years later, at age thirty-three, she died of a heart attack in her bath tub.

She was born in Santo Domingo in 1918, one of ten children of the Spanish consul to the Dominican Republic and his political refugee wife. Maria was educated against her will at a convent school in Santa Cruz. When she was seventeen, her father was re-posted to Belfast in Northern Ireland. There Maria married William McFeeters, a British Army officer. However, it was an ill-suited match and, before long, Maria traipsed off to New York and divorced her husband. Tired of being an oddity among Manhattan society, she arranged a screen test and signed with Universal Pictures at $150 a week. She chose her surname in honor of the nineteenth Spanish dancer, Lola Montez. Maria was put to work in bit parts which showcased her striking beauty and avoided her heavily-accented voice.

Fully attuned to promoting herself, Maria readily participated in the publicity photographic ritual. At 5' 7", with auburn hair and flashing eyes she made an eye-catching cheesecake subject. By the time of her seventh 1941 movie, *South of Tahiti,* Maria was fast becoming established as Universal's answer to Paramount's saronged Dorothy Lamour. With *Arabian Nights* (1942), Montez became a star, although still not much of an actress. She and leading man Jon Hall teamed together in several other sensual sand sagas. For some viewers, her dual roles in *Cobra Woman* (1944) is the peak of high camp; for fans, it is wonderful escapist fare. More importantly for Maria, such pictures made her a favorite with moviegoers, especially sex-starved servicemen overseas.

In October 1942, Maria met six-foot blond, blue-eyed French actor Jean-Pierre Aumont. According to Montez, "I fall in love vith heem—boom." They married on July 13, 1943. Their daughter Maria Christina was born on Valentine's Day in 1946. (She would later become actress Tina Marquand.) By 1947, the too-demanding Maria had outstayed her welcome at Universal and that year's *Pirates of Monterey* ended her contract. Maria and Jean-Pierre next co-starred in *Siren of Atlantis*. It was a costly mistake for all concerned. Begun in 1947, the United Artists' "epic" wasn't released until August 1949 and proved to be a mess.

The Aumonts moved to France, to a house in Suresnes, six miles from the heart of Paris. Jean-Pierre's brother, Francois Villiers, directed the couple in the French-made *Hans le Marin* (1949). Following several pictures in Italy, including a re-teaming with her husband, and her stage debut in *Paris in January*, 1951, Maria settled in at her Suresnes home. She complained of chest pains and joked, "I'd better watch that because eet might end up playing me a dirty trick."

On September 7, 1951, the couple dined at a chic Paris restaurant with two of Maria's sisters (Adita, Teresita) who were their house guests. The next day, as was her custom, Maria took her mid-morning bath, soaking in a mixture of extremely hot water and reducing salts. When Maria failed to come downstairs, Adita rushed up and knocked at the bathroom door. After

Montez failed to respond, Adita opened the door. She found Maria submerged in the steaming water up to her forehead. The two hysterical sisters carried Maria to her bedroom and called a doctor. Firemen arrived to perform artificial respiration. After three hours of trying to revive her, she was declared dead, a victim of a heart seizure. When Aumont reached home from his film set, he was told the bad news and collapsed.

A Roman Catholic funeral was held for Maria in the local church (Saint Pierre de Chaillot) on September 11. It was not until mid-February of 1952 that Aumont, while sorting through papers in their garage, uncovered her will. The bulk of Maria's $200,000 estate was left to Jean-Pierre and to their young daughter, with provisions made for her sisters.

Unlike most of her contemporaries, Maria Montez's popularity has not vanished into extinction. Her legend continues onward, flamed by extravagant, kitschy performances which delight and amuse new generations of movie watchers.

Edmund O'Brien

September 10, 1915 — May 8, 1985

Once when his young daughter Bridget inquired if he "minded" being a character actor, Edmund O'Brien replied, "No.... 'Cause it's me who gets a chance to do the interesting, the different, the funny, It's from me the audience expects the unusual. I like it that way." Later in life, he no longer had it his way. The Academy Award-winning actor was diagnosed as suffering from Alzheimer's disease. Like fellow victims Rita Hayworth and Arthur

O'Connell, he spent his declining years in a vacuum of lost memories and uncontrollable body functions.

He was born in the Bronx in 1915. His brother Liam would become a film/TV scripter and producer. As a child, Edmund—billed as "The Great Neirbo"—staged magic acts in his apartment building basement, relying on tricks learned from neighbor Harry Houdini. O'Brien attended high school in Westport, Connecticut, where during summers he worked backstage (and occasionally on stage) at the Community Playhouse. He focused on drama at Columbia University and made his Broadway bow in *Daughters of Atrus* (1936). For Orson Welles's modern dress production of *Julius Caesar* (1937) he was Marc Antony. He had already played a convict in Universal's *Prison Break* (1938) before his major movie break in Charles Laughton's *The Hunchback of Notre Dame* (1939). Edmund ("Eddie" to his friends) was surprised that he enjoyed screen acting so much. He made a few more. In February 1941, he eloped to Yuma, Arizona with actress Nancy Kelly—with whom he co-starred that year in *Parachute Battalion*. They separated after four months and were divorced in 1942. During World War II, Edmund joined the Army, first as a radio operator trainee, but later was given a comedy role in the Air Force's stage show, *Winged Victory*. He toured in it for two years and appeared in the screen version (1944).

After the war, the burly O'Brien, who became increasingly heavy-jowled, specialized in film noir (*The Web*, 1947, *D.O.A.*, 1949). He married actress Olga San Juan in September 1948 and they had three children: Maria, Bridget, and Brendan. He won the Best Supporting Actor's Oscar for *The*

Barefoot Contessa (1954), in which he played a glib Hollywood press agent. On radio he had starred in the detective series, "*Yours Truly, Johnny Dollar*" (1949-52) and on TV he was the lead in "*Johnny Midnight*" (1960) and "*Sam Benedict*" (1962) and was a Southern town boss in "*The Long Hot Summer*" (1965). He co-produced and directed *Man-Trap* (1961) and earned another Best Supporting Actor Oscar nomination for *Seven Days in May* (1964).

During the location shooting of *Lawrence of Arabia* (1962), the now heavyset O'Brien suffered a heart seizure and Arthur Kennedy replaced him. Despite declining health, he continued to act on TV and in movies until the mid-1970s. His last movie was *Dream No Evil* (1975). By then, he had undergone a severe personality change and could no longer remember his lines. It was later diagnosed that he had Alzheimer's disease. In 1976, Olga San Juan divorced him, but she continued to visit him at the Santa Monica rest home where he lived. He died on May 9, 1985 in Inglewood, California, and was buried at Holy Cross Cemetery and Mausoleum in Culver City, California.

Warner Oland

[Wernur Olund]

October 3, 1880 —August 5, 1938

Only in Hollywood could a Swede become famous for playing a Chinese detective. Yet, that was the case with Warner Oland who, from 1931 to 1937, played the inscrutable Oriental, Charlie Chan. Charlie Chan was the cinema's goateed detective who had a passion for cute philosophical sayings and a penchant for spawning offsprings.

143

Warner's death occurred during a secret odyssey from the film capital back to his Scandinavian homeland.

He was born of Swedish-Russian parents in Umea, Sweden in 1880. There was another brother, Carl. When Warner was thirteen, his family relocated to a farm in Connecticut. Warner went to high school in Boston and in the same city attended Curry's Dramatic School. His official stage debut was in a bit role in *The Christian* (1898) and then he toured in Shakespearean repertory around the U.S. He was noticed by the exotic Alla Nazimova who hired him to join her company performing several Ibsen dramas on Broadway in the fall of 1907. He married actress Edith Shearn in 1908 and, thereafter, his fortunes both rose and fell as he began producing his own theatrical ventures, often from his own translations of foreign classics. He toured in the title role of *A Fool There Was* (1913).

The very erudite Oland had been making occasional movies since 1909, and, by 1915, he was a frequent player in the medium. In Irene Castle's serial, *Patria* (1916) he was a dastardly foreign villain, relying on his Slavic/Mongolian genes to give the illusion of his being Oriental. However, he was not stereotyped in such roles, as he played equally as well the Jewish cantor father of Al Jolson in *The Jazz Singer* (1927).

It was his starring role as the sinister Oriental in *The Mysterious Dr. Fu Manchu* (1929), *The Return of Dr. Fu Manchu* (1930) and *Daughter of the Dragon* (1931) that set the stage for Oland to be cast as the famed Chinese sleuth in Fox's *Charlie Chan Carries On* (1931). Over the next few years, Warner would make fifteen additional installments of the series; as of *Charlie Chan in Paris* (1935) he was joined by Keye Luke as his bumbling, well-meaning #1 son, Lee. During these years, Oland also had non-series roles, such as *Shanghai Express* (1932), *Bulldog Drummond Strikes Back* (1934) and *The Werewolf of London* (1935). However, moviegoers had grown accustomed to him in the Chan series. Always eager to learn more about his craft and his characterizations, Warner made a trip to China and learned to speak some Chinese so he could authentically deliver native lines in his movies.

Distinguished as Warner Oland was, he had one vice. He was alcohol-dependent and increasingly went on drinking binges. It reached the point where his wife could take no more, and, in 1937, she filed for separate maintenance, planning on suing for divorce. That same year, during the making of *Charlie Chan at the Ringside*, the well-liked Oland left the set one day and never returned. (The studio eventually used some of the non-Oland footage in *Mr. Moto's Gamble*, 1938.) There was much speculation over the star's disappearance. Despite rumors that he had been sighted here or there, it was not until 1938 that the true story emerged.

In poor physical and mental health due to his drinking problem, Oland had quietly sailed for Italy, hoping to recoup his strength. Eventually, he made his way to Sweden where he was staying with his mother. He hoped to return to Hollywood to star in *Charlie Chan in Honolulu* (1938) and was negotiating a reconciliation with his wife. However, he contracted bronchial pneumonia and on August 6, 1938 he died at the age of fifty-seven.

When Oland died, he owned extensive real estate, including 1,000 acres on an island near Mazatlan, Mexico as well as a Massachusetts farm. As for the pending Charlie Chan film, Twentieth Century-Fox promptly cast another non-Oriental—Missouri-born Sidney Toler—to replace Oland in the movie series.

Heather O'Rourke

December 27, 1975 — February 1, 1988

On film she was the angelic little girl famous for uttering those memorable catch phrases "They're Heeere!" and "They're Baaack!" in the *Poltergeist* movies. On TV's "*Happy Days*," she was Heather Pfeiffer, the cute youngster of the nifty lady (Linda Purl) who wins Fonzie's heart. Then, at age twelve, with a bright future ahead, Heather O'Rourke died unexpectedly of repercussions from a congenital birth defect.

She was born in San Diego, California in 1975. At age five she was lunching at the MGM commissary with her mother, when filmmaker Steven Spielberg spotted her. He was intrigued by the pert youngster and asked if he might talk with her about a new movie he was planning. She said she didn't talk with strangers. However, she got permission from her mother and was soon cast in *Poltergeist* (1982), which Spielberg co-produced and co-wrote. She played Carol Ann, the young daughter who talks with strange creatures on the TV screen. The movie caught the public's fancy and was a big hit.

After a year (1982-83) on "*Happy Days*," Heather was a guest star on several other television series, including "*Webster*." In addition, she played River Phoenix's sister in a TV movie (*Sur-*

viving—1985). Naturally, there was the inevitable sequel (*Poltergeist II*—1986) to her hit movie. Then she did more television, including an episode of "*New Leave It to Beaver*" (1987). In June 1987, she finished shooting yet another follow-up, *Poltergeist III*.

On Monday, February 1, 1988, Heather, who lived with her parents both in San Diego and Big Bear, complained of stomach pains. She was rushed to Children's Hospital of San Diego. During surgery she died of cardiac and pulmonary arrest. It was identified that she had been suffering from a severe bowel obstruction, a result of a congenital birth defect. The obstruction led to an infection, which in turn caused septic shock. The shock triggered her death.

Heather was buried in Los Angeles' Westwood Memorial Park in a vault on the first outdoor mausoleum wall. Her marker reads "Star of Poltergeist One, Two, and Three." *Poltergeist III* was released four months after Heather's death and was a box-office bust. Heather was the second *Poltergeist* star to die. In 1982, 22-year-old Dominique Dunne, who had played her older sister in that movie, was strangled to death by her estranged boyfriend.

Susan Peters

[Suzanne Carnahan]

July 3, 1921 — October 23, 1952

It is rough enough to earn that lucky break which brings Hollywood stardom. But to be on the verge of screen fame and then to lose it due to a crippling accident is tragic. What followed for brave Susan Peters was even more heartache.

She was born Suzanne Carnahan in Spokane, Washington in 1921, followed in 1923 by the birth of her brother, Robert, Jr. In 1928, the family was living in Portland, Oregon when the father, a construction engineer, died in a car crash. The Carnahans moved to Los Angeles to stay with dermatologist Madame Maria Patteneaude, their French-born grandmother. As a youngster, Suzanne was athletic, excelling in swimming and horseback riding. She graduated from Hollywood High School in 1939 and, through a family friend, was introduced to director George Cukor at MGM. He suggested she take acting lessons and cast her in a small role in *Susan and God* (1940). That year Warner Bros. signed her to a contract and Suzanne insisted she would allow herself three years to succeed in pictures; otherwise she would follow through on going to medical school.

By 1941, Suzanne was performing in minor film roles and she changed her professional name to Susan Peters. However, Warner Bros. did not renew her contract. Nevertheless, she was cast at MGM in Marjorie Main's *Tish* (1942) playing Richard Quine's wife who dies in child birth. For her role as Ronald Colman's young fiancee in *Random Harvest* (1942) she was Oscar-nominated as Best Supporting Actress. Then, she had the lead opposite Robert Taylor in *Song of Russia* (1943). Later that year, on November 7, she married actor Richard Quine, who was then in the U.S. Coast Guard. She was cast in *Gentle Annie* (1944), but left the project when she suffered a miscarriage. She nearly died and was away from movies for almost a year, with an earlier-made film, *Keep Your Powder Dry*, not released until 1945.

On January 1, 1945, Susan was on a hunting trip with her husband and another couple in the Cuyamaca Mountains not far from San Diego. As it was later recounted, when she picked up her rifle, it accidentally discharged and the .22 caliber bullet lodged in her spine. Paralyzed from the waist down, she was taken to Mercy Hospital for emergency surgery. The plucky Susan recalled later, "I told myself I was going to come through this accident. I was going to walk again." However, the actress remained wheelchair-bound, with MGM continuing to pay her $100 a week salary. In December 1945, Susan's mother died of a heart attack causing Susan much distress. Adopting a baby (Timothy) in April 1946 did much to restore her spirits.

Peters kept her hand in by performing in several radio broadcasts. However, when MGM could find no realistic roles for the crippled actress, the actress ended her contract, insisting, "I won't trade on my handicap." Actor Charles Bickford brought a novel, *Sign of the Ram*, to her notice. It was custom-made for her: about a paralyzed vixen who destroys her family. Columbia Pictures agreed to make the film project, which was a strain on Susan. She was fine on screen, but the 1948 movie was mediocre. In September that year she and Quine divorced. In 1949 she played the crippled Laura in a Hollywood stage production of *The Glass Menagerie*. Then, it was two years before she re-emerged professionally, this time in "*Miss Susan*," a 15-minute daytime soap opera telecast live from Philadelphia. She was a wheelchair-bound lawyer who dispenses advice. By December 1951 she had fallen victim to the cold Pennsylvania winter and the emotional stress of doing the five-times-a-week program. The show was cancelled and Susan was hospitalized.

Susan kept being hit by continous obstacles in her life. Her engagement to an Army colonel (Robert Clark) was broken and she went to her brother farm's near Visalia, California to recuperate. She grew depressed and reclusive. She was later hospitalized for skin graft surgery and, once released, retreated again into privacy. In September 1952, *The Barretts of Wimpole Street* on stage. However, she was too physically weak by this point to fulfill the project. Not only did she had a damaged heart, but she also had developed an eating disorder (anorexia nervosa). Looking into the future, she told her doctor, "I'm getting awfully tired. I think it would be better if I did die." On October 23, 1952 she fulfilled her prophecy and passed away at a Visalia, California hospital. Officially the causes of death were listed as bronchial pneumonia, chronic kidney problems and starvation. However, the attending physician said, "I felt she had lost the will to live." Susan was buried at Forest Lawn Memorial Parks—Glendale.

A coda to Susan Peters's sad saga occurred in 1989. On June 10, 68-year old actor-turned-director Richard Quine (who had not made a film for ten years) shot himself in the head in his California home. He had been in poor health for several years.

Tyrone Power

[Tyrone Power, Jr.]

May 5, 1913 — November 15, 1958

Tyrone Power's frequent movie leading lady, Alice Faye, said it all: "He was the best looking thing I've ever seen in my life. Kissing him was like dying and going to heaven." But being beautifully handsome can also be a professional curse. Ty grew tired of the endless pretty boy and swashbuckling roles and wanted to be acknowledged as a serious actor. He fought that creative battle all his life. He died, just like his actor father before him—on a film set. At the time, Ty was shooting another of those costumed sword-and-horseplay epics he had grown so to hate.

He was born in 1913 in Cincinnati, Ohio to actors known professionally as Tyrone and Patia Power. A daughter, Ann, was born in 1915 and, two years later, the family relocated to San Diego, California because of Ty Jr.'s frail health. At age seven, the boy made his stage debut playing a monk in the annual mission play. The family later returned to Ohio where Ty graduated from high school in 1931. That year he appeared with his father in a Chicago production of *The Merchant of Venice*, did radio dramas, and was with his dad in a Broadway edition of *Hamlet*. Power Sr. went to Hollywood for a film role in late 1931. He died on the set in the arms of his eighteen-year-old son.

Ty, Jr. made his screen debut as a school boy in *Tom Brown of Culver* (1932), but didn't get another screen bit for two years. The discouraged young actor headed East, stopping off in Chicago for radio and stage work. Reaching New York, he was introduced to Katharine Cornell and understudied and/or played bit parts in three of her 1935-36 plays. A Twentieth Century-Fox talent scout saw Power on stage and this led to a studio contract. After two warm-up movies, Tyrone starred in *Lloyds of London* (1936), which set the tone for his entire career—swashbuckling adventure stories. He was the newest rival to Warner Bros.'s Errol Flynn.

147

The studio also cast Power in light fluff with Loretta Young or Sonya Henie, and sometimes, he was in big-budget period musicals with Alice Faye, such as *Alexander's Ragtime Band* (1938). However, he was so adept at costume romance films filled with swordplay, that he toiled in such productions as *The Mark of Zorro* (1940), *Blood and Sand* (1941) and *The Black Swan* (1942). Rarely was he permitted a dramatic challenge, as in *Johnny Apollo* (1940). In 1939, he wed French-born actress Annabella, but it would not stop him from having several romances during the next decade (Judy Garland, Lana Turner, et al).

Tyrone escaped the Hollywood treadmill by enlisting as a private in the U.S. Marines Corp. in August 1942. After delays to do a picture (*Crash Dive*, 1943) and an extended period at a Texas flight training school, he was stationed in the Pacific theatre of war in February 1945, flying mainly supply missions. First Lieutenant Power returned to Hollywood in early 1946, and got a new studio contract. He and Annabella separated in October and divorced two years later. His much-heralded screen return was in the idealistic *The Razor's Edge* (1946), but swashbuckling capers were still his bread-and-butter. In January 1949, he climaxed his pursuit of actress Linda Christian across three continents by marrying her in Rome. They would have two daughters (Romina and Taryn), both of whom became actresses. To break up his acting rut, he headlined in *Mister Roberts* (1950) on the London stage.

In the Fifties, Power's movie career dived as Twentieth Century-Fox promoted younger personalities, especially Gregory Peck. Frustrated by mediocre films, he toured in Steven Vincent Be-net's *John Brown's Body*. By 1955, Tyrone had left Fox, divorced Linda Christian and starred in the memorable West Point saga, *The Long Gray Line*. That same year he reunited professionally with Katharine Cornell on the road and in New York. Between those productions and doing The *Devil's Disciple* (1956) on the British stag*The Eddy Duchin Story* (1956). He had an off-camera romance with his *Abandon Ship!* (1957) co-star, Swedish-born Mai Zetterling. His last completed movie was *Witness for the Prosecution* (1957), opposite Marlene Dietrich.

Never long without a romantic attachment, Power married Deborah Minardos in May 1958. She was 26, divorced and had a daughter; he was 45. Next, he went to Madrid to play King Solomon opposite Gina Lollobrigida in *Solomon and Sheba*. On a hot November 15, while filming a difficult dueling scene with George Sanders, Tyrone suddenly turned pale and asked to rest. Back in his dressing room, he remarked on pains in his arms and chest, but insisted it was merely bursitis. At 11:30 a.m. he was rushed to the hospital, where he died within the hour. (Ironically during the summer of 1958, Power had made a educational short film sponsored by the American Heart Association in which he stressed the necessity of avoiding overwork because "time is the most precious thing we have.")

Power's body was taken from the hospital to the U.S. Torrejon Air Force Base and then flown to California. What occurred at the November 21 funeral at Hollywood Memorial Park was a circus. The crowd—many with box lunches—began queuing up at dawn to await the procession of celebrities (who as they arrived were cheered by the throng of fans). At the service Deborah sat next to the open casket holding Power's hand, while the organist performed "I'll Be Seeing You." A Navy chaplain conducted the ceremony with Cesar Romero delivering the eulogy. He read Thomas Wolfe's "The Promises of America" (which Tyrone had planned to read on Thanksgiving Day at the Air Force base in Spain). Romero then reflected on his late pal: "He constantly gave of himself until one day he gave a little too much. He was a beautiful man. He was beautiful outside and he was beautiful inside. Rest well, my friend."

Among the invited guests were Loretta Young (who arrived at the chapel wearing Oriental make-up for a TV role), Yul Brynner (hired to replace Tyrone in *Solomon and Sheba*), Henry Fonda, Clifton Webb, James Stewart and Robert Wagner. Power's widow had urged ex-wife Linda Christian not to attend (she had created an emotional scene the previous year at the Italian funeral of auto racer Alfonso de Portago). Not to be left out, Christian, who had flown in from France, arrived several hours after the service, to place a five-foot cross of white gardenias at her ex-husband's grave. Ty's aged mother, who had suffered a stroke several years earlier, was not told of her son's death. (She died in October 1959.) In France, Annabella, Ty's first wife, told the press she had seen him the previous week in Madrid and had met his "new little wife." On January 22, 1959, Deborah Power gave birth to a son (Tyrone William) at Cedars of Lebanon Hospital in Hollywood. (He would grow up to become an actor.) Linda Christian made a $200,000 claim against the estate on behalf of her daughter. Meanwhile, the court granted the plea of the estate's executor to re-

duce allowances to beneficiares because of mounting claims. In November 1962, affects for Tyrone's estate were auctioned at New York's Plaza Art Gallery. In mid-1974, Tyrone's two daughters by Linda Christian each received a sizeable inheritance from their father's estate.

These days, one of the prime tourist attractions at Hollywood Memorial Park is the Tyrone Power memorial stone bench. At one end are bookends holding a single volume which displays the masks of Comedy and Tragedy. Atop the bench is a quotation from *Hamlet*, ending with "Good night, sweet prince, and flights of angels sing thee to thy rest."

Gilda Radner

June 28, 1946 — May 20, 1989

It wasn't the way it was supposed to happen. She was America's clown princess, a quirky woman with inner beauty who had spent years mocking the absurdities of life and making a nation laugh. Then, a few years into her happy marriage to screen comedian Gene Wilder, she contracted ovarian cancer, a disease difficult to diagnose in its early stages and often not detected until it is too late to save the patient. If there is any meaning to the frightening, frustrating and painful odyssey Gilda endured, it was that her publicized plight has made the world far more sensitive to early diagnosis and treatment of this killer disease.

She was born in Detroit, Michigan in 1946, the second child (there was older brother Michael) of hotel businessman Herman Radner and his legal secretary wife, Henrietta (Dworkin) Radner. Gilda was named after the popular Rita

Hayworth movie that came out that year. When she was twelve, Herman Radner developed a brain tumor. He lingered for two years before dying, the horrifying experience leaving an indelible impression on his daughter. In 1964 she graduated from a private high school and then attended the University of Michigan. She lingered through undergraduate courses there for six years, frequently dropping out because she refused to follow the rules. When she was on campus, she was active in theater. In 1969, she fell in love with a Canadian sculptor and moved to Toronto, but that relationship fell apart sixteen months later.

Full of low self-esteem, Gilda found herself suddenly fascinated while watching a musical at a local avant-garde theater. She now knew where she belonged. She took a job at the theatre, first in the box-office and then working in pantomime shows performed for elementary school children. This experience led to a year working in the Toronto company of *Godspell* (1972). From there, the blossoming comedienne joined the local branch of the Second City, an improvisational comedy group. Her equally spontaneous co-workers included Dan Aykroyd and Eugene Levy. By 1974, she was in New York City for the *National Lampoon Show* with John Belushi, Bill Murray and Harold Ramis.

Gilda had known Canadian entertainer Lorne Michaels since her early Toronto days as a performer. When NBC-TV hired him to package the innovative "*Saturday Night Live,*" he hired Gilda to join his Not Ready for Prime Time Players, which included Dan Aykroyd, John Belushi, Chevy Chase, Jane Curtin, Garrett Morris and Laraine Newman. Working within the program's weekly onslaught of out-rageous comedy, Gilda developed into a nationally known TV personality, famous for her bawdy, physical humor and her raucous characterizations: Rosanna Rosanna-Dana, Ba Ba Wawa and Emily Litella.

She remained with "*Saturday Night Live*" through 1980. By then she had graduated to Broadway (*Gilda Radner Live,* 1979), movies (*First Family*, 1980) and assorted TV specials. While making *Hanky Panky* (1982), she and movie co-star Gene Wilder fell in love and they were married in the south of France in September 1984. During the making of their *Haunted Honeymoon* (1986), Gilda suffered a miscarriage.

Gilda's journey into hell began in January 1986 when she developed—what was thought to be—chronic fatigue syndrome. Different symptoms showed themselves and then evaporated as Radner underwent repeated testing by a battery of doctors. Finally, that October, it was discovered she had advanced ovarian cancer, stage IV. (There had been several members of her mother's family who suffered from the same disease.) When the doctors operated thirty-six hours later, they removed a large tumor. To insure that all the malignancy had been caught, Gilda underwent a course of chemotherapy. Always searching for humor even in the worst circumstances, Radner and Wilder made home videos of the progress of the treatments. Even when her hair fell out, the heart-broken comedienne learned eventually to treat it humorously.

While coping with the physically and emotionally depleting chemotherapy treatments, Gilda attended sessions of The Wellness Community, a therapy group for individuals dealing with cancer (whether recovering or not). This support group—in addition to Wilder's constant bolstering—helped her cope with her disease, which had halted abruptly her career, marriage and life.

On June 4, 1987 she underwent "second look" surgery, confident that she was well again. However, a few malignant cancer cells were detected. She endured more chemotherapy and then radiation treatment. Hoping she was now on the road to recovery, she agreed to a February 1988 *Life* magazine cover article dealing with her experiences with The Wellness Community. In April 1988, she felt well enough to make her first professional appearance in years, as a guest on TV's "*Its Garry Shandling's Show.*" Some weeks later, her doctors found that her cancer was not in remission, but was spreading. She went through carboplatin treatment, then tried a macrobiotic diet. She became increasingly fearful and angry as she grew thinner and weaker—she stopped visiting her doctor. Later, she tried chemotherapy again. In October 1988 she underwent her third surgery in three years, this time for intestinal blockage.

Contributing to Gilda's peace of mind during her last years was her authoring *It's Always Something* (1989). Originally she had intended to write about her life as an artist and housewife. On the last pages of the insightful book Gilda says, "I wanted to be able to write on the book jacket" 'her triumph over cancer'.... I wanted a perfect ending.... Now I've learned, the hard way, that some poems don't rhyme, and some stories don't have a clear beginning, middle and end."

On Saturday, May 20, 1989, 42-year-old Gilda Radner passed away in Los Angeles. That night, on TV's "*Saturday Night Live,*" Steve Martin was host and he showed a 1978 clip of he and Gilda spoofing a movie musical number. At clip's end, he said tearfully, "Gilda, we miss you."

Lee Remick

December 14, 1935 — July 2, 1991

How many times has one heard a cancer-stricken celebrity insist they will lick the disease? Sometimes, thankfully, they do, but not that often. When usually radiant but now ill Lee Remick said it in 1989, it seemed different. She was so extremely positive and self-assured that even more cynical souls wanted to believe it. However, it was not to be. Lee Remick lived her final months as she had her entire professional life: with class, authority and finesse.

She was born in 1935 in Quincy, Massachusetts, the only child of a wealthy department store owner and his actress wife, Pat Packard. Her parents divorced when she was seven and she moved to Manhattan with her mother. While attending Miss Hewitt's School in New York, she thought she would become a dancer ("I wouldn't have been that good"). Instead she decided on acting. After a brief stay at Barnard College, she debuted on Broadway in the flop, *Act Your Age* (1953). That same year she started a lengthy TV career by appearing as a guest on many live anthology series being telecast from New York. Director Elia Kazan spotted her in one of these and cast her in *A Face in the Crowd* (1957). For blonde, blue-eyed Lee, it was the first of her several predatory southern belle movie roles. That same year she wed TV director William Colleran. During their eleven-year marriage (they divorced in 1958) they had two children: Katherine Lee ("Kate") and Matthew.

THE HOLLYWOOD DEATH BOOK

Lee was nominated for an Oscar for her strong performance as Jack Lemmon's alcoholic wife in *Days of Wine and Roses* (1962). Unafraid to gamble professionally, she did a Broadway musical, *Anyone Can Whistle* (1964) with Angela Lansbury, and was Tony-nominated for her next Broadway role in *Wait Until Dark* (1966). In 1970, she married British director William "Kip" Gowens, who had two daughters by a prior marriage. This alliance began Remick's English period, during which she starred in a London production of *Bus Stop* (1974). Throughout the decade she alternated between features (*The Omen*, 1976), TV movies (*Hustling*, 1975) and mini-series (*Ike*, 1979).

By the early 1980s, Lee and her family had moved to a Brentwood, California home. She worked mostly in TV movies because it offered a versatile actress of her age far more range than movies. In 1985, she joined a Lincoln Center concert version of *Follies* and did a TV version of the musical *I Do! I Do!*

While filming the TV movie *Dark Holiday* (1989) in France, Lee developed a fever that wouldn't go away. X-rays revealed that she had a malignant tumor on one kidney and that the cancer had spread to her lungs. She underwent surgery and chemotherapy. By mid-1990 she was convinced she had beaten the disease, describing the experience as "drastic and horrible—and successful." The generally quite private actress agreed to publicize her ailment, hoping to dilute the stigma attached to it. When she accepted the Cancervive 1990 Victory Award, she admitted, "Of all the performances in my life, this one counts the most." She felt well enough to do a week of stage readings in *Love Letters* at a Beverly Hills theatre.

Then in the fall of 1990 the cancer recurred, cancelling her plans to do a TV movie, to continue more weeks in *Love Letters*, and even to co-star in the L.A. production of *A Little Night Music* in the spring of 1991. She underwent further surgery to curb the cancer which had spread to her brain. On April 29, 1991, bloated and frail from her illness, she insisted on appearing at the Hollywood Boulevard Ceremony to unveil her star on the Walk of Fame. Her husband and Jack Lemmon helped a wobbling Lee (who used a cane) from her limousine to the place of honor. She told the press, "I'm confident of beating this. I'm not finished yet. You don't recover from this overnight. But as soon as I can, I want to get back to work." She stood by her star for a brief two minutes while being photographed. Many people around Lee fought to keep back their tears. On May 4, 1991, the wheelchair-bound Remick accepted an award from the International Church Society for once having played Winston Churchill's mother on a TV mini-series ("*Jennie*," 1975).

As much as possible, during the final months, she insisted on living with dignity, even getting dressed and made up whenever possible. In the last weeks she was nearly blind and semi-paralyzed, falling in and out of a coma. Early in the morning of July 2, 1991—one day after Michael Landon died of cancer—Lee Remick passed away at her Brentwood home. At her bedside were her husband and her children—Kate (a writer) and Matthew (a rock guitarist). Funeral services were held at Westwood Mortuary on July 9. Two of Lee's former movie co-stars, Jack Lemmon and Gregory Peck, delivered the eulogies to the two-hundred attendees. Her two children sang the title song from *Anyone Can Whistle*.

Dick Shawn

[Richard Schulefand]

December 1, 1923 — April 17, 1987

Dick Shawn always hovered on the fringes of being a top banana in show business. His irreverent and wacky comedy talent warranted much more. Always an energetic actor, he got his last laugh performing what the theater audience thought was a stage pratfall. It wasn't. He'd had a heart attack and was dying.

He was born Richard Schulefand in Buffalo, New York in 1923, but he and his brother (Seymour) grew up in nearby Lackawanna where they and their Jewish parents lived in the single back room to the clothing store his father owned. To take his mind off his impoverished childhood, he dreamed of becoming a professional baseball player. He tried-out for the Chicago White Sox who signed him. However, a few days later he was drafted into the World War II Army. Already a confirmed jokster, he auditioned and was accepted for USO shows. After his discharge, he went to the University of Miami ("I heard all the rich, pretty girls were in Miami"), but dropped out to become a stand-up comic. He moved to New York where as Dick Shawn he appeared on TV's "*Arthur Godfrey's Talent Scouts*." Later, he developed his skills as the opening club act for Marlene Dietrich, Betty Hutton, and Danny Kaye. Shawn would say of his laugh-generating but thought-provoking routines, "I've always been hard to classify, I don't do mother-in-law or ugly girl jokes. In fact, I hardly tell jokes at all."

He made his movie debut in *The Opposite Sex* (1956) with June Allyson, but better displayed his idiosyncratic comedy style in *Wake Me When It's Over* (1960) and *It's a Mad, Mad, Mad, World* (1963). On Broadway, he replaced Zero Mostel during the run of *A Funny Thing Happened on the Way to the Forum* and joined with Mostel in *The Producers* (1967), a Mel Brooks's film farce where he was the lisping actor who stars in a musical about Adolph Hitler. On stage, he was in *I'm Solomon* (1968) and *The World of Sholom Aleichem* (1976). On TV, he was a regular on two short-lasting series: Mary Tyler Moore's variety program "*Mary*" (1978) and "*Hail to the Chief*" (1985). Along the way, in the 1980s, Shawn was cast in Michael Jackson's 3-D short subject, *Captain Eo*, shown as part of Disneyland's entertainment. His last film, *Maid to Order* (1987), was released posthumously.

Shawn gained a great deal of attention with his one-man show, *The Second Greatest Entertainer in the Whole Wide World* (1985) performed on stage in Beverly Hills. He said of the production, "It's surreal, but I think some of the insights are the kind of things people think about later."

On April 18, 1987, Dick was doing what he enjoyed best. He was appearing in front of a live audience at the University of California at San Diego. Before the campus performance began, he told a reporter covering the event that he had several unrehearsed surprises to try that night. Twenty-five minutes into the show, he was in the midst of a routine in which he depicted the 500 people in the theatre as the only survivors of a nuclear war. "And I would be your leader." Saying that, he fell to the stage motionless. The audience assumed it was part of the act. After nearly five minutes of silence, Shawn's son Adam—seated in the balcony—called for someone to help his father. A doctor rushed to the stage and, after turning the comic over on his back, began cardiac massage. Only then did the amazed theatergoers realize it was not an act at all. Shawn was rushed to Scripps Memorial Hospital where he died forty-five minutes later at 9:55 p.m.

The divorced comedian, survived by his son, three daughters, a brother and a granddaughter, was buried at Hillside Memorial Park in Los Angeles on the same mausoleum wall as David Janssen and George Jessel.

Two years before his death, when he was being acclaimed for his one man show, Dick Shawn said, "That's the sort of thing I'd like to do for the rest of my life.... You can't ask for a better send-off than that." He got his wish.

Kate Smith

[Kathryn Elizabeth Smith]

May 1, 1907 —June 17, 1986

For those who grew up during her lengthy heyday, singer Kate Smith symbolized everything that was good about America. Her voice was loud and pure and her patriotic image was all apple pie. If she was physically oversized—5' 10" and very hefty at times—so was her talent. Early and late in her career, comedians made fun of her weight, but no one could dispute her vocal range and capability which remained constantly on pitch throughout more than fifty years of performing. She was best known for her trademark songs ("When the Moon Comes Over the Mountain" and "God Bless America," but she was equally at ease with Sixties' pop tunes like "The Impossible Dream" or "More.") Like Al Jolson and Judy Garland, she was a distinctly American legend, the kind we used to take for granted, but can't seem to create anymore.

She was born in 1907 in Greenville, Virginia, the second of two daughters born to the owner of an independent news dealership. The family later moved to Washington, D.C. where Kate first had her performing engagements. By the time she was a teenager she was already quite heavy, but she was an extremely nimble dancer. To please her parents, she trained as a nurse, but quit after a year.

A local vaudeville job led to her being cast in *Honeymoon Lane* (1926) on Broadway. By 1930, she been on radio, made a movie short and been recording for four years. She had a popular success in another Broadway musical, *Flying High* (1930), but was unable to enjoy it. The show's star, comedian Bert Lahr, mercilessly jibed Kate about her weight on stage and off. It was a pain that never left her, although she later learned to laugh with her detractors.

During the run of *Flying High* she met recording producer Ted Collins, who began managing her career. (Throughout their many years together, their only contract was a handshake.) It was on her radio program, *"Kate Smith Sings"*—which began in March 1931—that Kate first used "When the Moon Comes over the Mountain" as her theme song. Before long, "The Songbird of the South" had become the airwaves' most popular female singer. Like other radio stars, she tried films, both short subjects and features (*The Big Broadcast*, 1932 and *Hello Every-*

body, 1933). However, because of her figure, she couldn't be a conventional movie heroine and lost interest in the medium. Over the next years, her popularity as a radio personality and recording star increased. In 1938, she introduced Irving Berlin's "God Bless America" on her radio show. When she appeared at the White House in 1939 to sing for the King and Queen of England, President Franklin D. Roosevelt introduced her with, "Your Majesties, this is Kate Smith. This is America."

During World War II, Kate sold over $200,000,000 in war bonds and was at her career height. She returned to films to sing "God Bless America" in *This Is The Army* (1943).

Her hit records included "A Nightingale Sang in Berkeley Square" and "The White Cliffs of Dover." It seemed almost impossible to turn on the radio without hearing one of her various programs (variety, musical or talk). In the fall of 1950 her *"The Kate Smith Hour"* debuted on TV and it was a weekday afternoon staple for four years. She returned with another evening show in 1960. That year, her second autobiography (*Upon My Lips a Song*) was published. By now, she was recording for RCA Records and had performed at Carnegie Hall (November 1, 1962).

It was in the early Sixties that Kate's bad times began. Her mother passed away in 1962 and Ted Collins died in 1964. That year she fell and fractured her ankle. While recovering she became a Roman Catholic and, in 1965, made her first trip to Europe, visiting the Pope at the Vatican. Trimming down and boasting a more contemporary wardrobe, she was a guest on various TV shows: ranging from Dean Martin's to Sonny and Cher's. Her religious album (*How Great Thou Art*) became a best-seller in 1966. She

KATE SMITH

tried the nightclub circuit, did TV commercials and generated a lot of attention as the good luck charm of the Philadelphia Flyers hockey team.

Ironically, it was in 1976, the year of America's Bicentennial that Kate's years of hell began. She had started the year as Grand Marshal of the Tournament of Roses Parade in Pasadena and appeared on the *"Hollywood Squares"* and other TV shows. What proved to be her final singing TV appearance was on a two-hour special (*"The Stars and Stripes Show"*) taped in Oklahoma City and aired on June 30. She sang "God Bless America."

Then, in late August 1976, everything came tumbling apart. While at her New York apartment, she went into insulin shock. It was a culmination of medical problems that had been building for years. (In 1974. Smith received radiation treatment for cancer; in recent years she had been plagued with diabetes, heart fibrillation and arthritis.) She was hospitalized in New York and later at Lake Placid (where she had had her summer home for years) and then, under an alias, at a Burlington, Vermont Hospital. As time passed, it became painfully evident that her mental faculties had been impaired permanently.

By 1979, Smith was failing badly and her family—Kate never married—had her declared mentally incompetent. Her two nieces were named estate conservators. Kate was moved to Raleigh, North Carolina to live with her sister Helena and one of her nieces. Soon the other niece and her husband appeared and before long the conservators were involved in a highly publicized court battle over the handling of Smith's assets. By now, Kate's once sizeable estate (estimated once to have been at between $10 to $35 million) had dwindled to less than $500,000. Much of her tangible assets were sold to pay for her upkeep. Her deteriorating condition was listed as a result of "organic brain syndrome, reflecting generalized cerebral arteriosclerosis."

On May 1, 1981, her *This Is the Army* co-star, President Ronald Reagan, telephoned Kate to wish her a happy birthday. She had difficulty communicating with him, but was aware to whom she was speaking. In September 1982, in a display of bad sentimentality, the frail, wheelchair-bound Kate was pushed on stage by Bob Hope during the Emmy Awards show telecast from Pasadena, California. After the audience recovered from the shock of how frail this beloved institution had become, it sang "God Bless America" in her honor. In 1983 there was continued, publicized squabbling among Kate's family regarding her estate. In January

1986, her right leg was amputated at a Raleigh hospital. On May 9, 1986, she underwent a mastectomy to remove a cancerous left breast. On June 17, 1986, about 2 p.m., her niece Kathy was visiting with her at her house when Kate, recovering from a recent fall, just stopped breathing.

A funeral mass was held in Raleigh on June 19, with a later mass on June 21 in Washington, D.C. at St. Matthew's Cathedral. Because of a dispute as to where to bury the star—she wanted to rest at the cemetery in Lake Placid; her family wanted her to be buried in Washington—Kate's body was placed in a temporary vault in North Elba, New York (where Lake Placid is located). As had become customary during Kate's last years, yet another dispute arose. Kate had requested that she be buried in a mausoleum, but the cemetery felt it would not be appropriate with the tenor of the other simpler graves. After the dispute had been aired publicly, the matter was settled and the small, tasteful mausoleum constructed. On Friday, November 13, 1987, Kate Smith, the God Bless America Girl, was laid to rest—finally.

Lewis Stone

November 15, 1878 — September 12, 1953

During his very lengthy show business career, Lewis Stone made well over a hundred feature films. However, to most movie viewers, he is best remembered for a pleasing movie series in which he was the advice-dispensing Judge—the beleaguered father of Carvel's most rambunctious teenager, Andy Hardy (Mickey Rooney). At seventy-three, Stone was still going strong as a film actor (*All the Brothers Were Valiant*, 1953) until a group of troublesome teenagers got the best of him. It cost him his life.

Lewis Shepherd Stone was born in 1878 in Worcester, Massachusetts. He abandoned college studies to serve in the Spanish-American War. Later he made his stage debut in a Canadian stock company. *Side-Tracked* (1900) brought Stone to Broadway. In 1907 he married stage actress Margaret Langham and they would have two daughters: Virginia and Barbara. (Margaret would commit suicide in 1917.) Stone's screen bow occurred in *The Man Who Found Out* (1915) and soon the tall (5' 11"), lean leading man was a popular screen player. He served as a major in World War I and then went to China where he trained local troops until the Boxer Rebellion ended his stay there.

On screen, Stone had the swashbuckling lead in *The Prisoner of Zenda* (1922), but was equally at home in domestic drama (*Old Loves and New*, 1926). He was nominated for an Oscar for *The Patriot* (1928), cast as the advisor to Russia's mad Czar Paul the First. In 1928, at the age of almost fifty, he became a full-time MGM contract star. He made several movies with Greta Garbo, including *A Woman of Affairs* (1929), *Mata Hari* (1931) and *Grand Hotel* (1932). Meanwhile, the dapper Stone, who had married and divorced Florence Pryor in the 1920s, married again in 1930, this time to Hazel Wolf, a woman in her twenties.

A flexible if somewhat straight-laced performer, the Lewis proved a distinguished asset to the Metro-Goldwyn-Mayer roster. In 1938, studio head Louis B. Mayer gave Stone a pair of silver spurs, as a gift, saying, "If it were not so impractical to close the stu-

dio down, every one of the thousands on the lot would be here to pay their tribute of affection to Lewis Stone."

It was to one of the ironic tidbits of show business history that Stone owed his greatest screen success. Lionel Barrymore had starred as the judge/father in *A Family Affair* (1937), the first of the Andy Hardy movie series. However, a hip injury (and advanced arthritis) prevented him from starring in the sequel, *You're Only Young Once* (1938). Reliable Stone took over as the small town judge and staunch family man. Over the next years, he performed in thirteen additional sagas of the beloved all-American Hardy family, ending with *Love Laughs at Andy Hardy* (1946). When asked if he ever thought of retiring, Stone responded, "Why? And miss all this." Making four to five movies a year, he found himself playing in remakes of pictures he had done years before, albeit in different roles: *Scaramouche* (1952), *The Prisoner of Zenda* (1952).

On Saturday, September 12, 1953, Stone caught three teenagers smashing the lawn furniture at his Hollywood home. While chasing the fleeing trio, he suffered a heart attack and collapsed to the sidewalk. His third wife, Hazel, was with him as he died in front of the house. Photographs of Stone's corpse sprawled on the lawn made graphic newspaper copy everywhere. He was buried in Los Angeles after private funeral services on September 16, 1953. He left a $150,000 estate.

When MGM and Mickey Rooney briefly revived the Andy Hardy series—*Andy Hardy Comes Home* (1958)—Stone was the only principal cast member unable to join the screen reunion. However, a poignant moment found the camera panning up to a portrait of the late "judge" over the living room fireplace. It was a fitting tribute to the veteran star.

Rudolph Valentino

[Rodolpho Alfonso Raffaelo Pierre Filibert Guglielmi di Valentina d'Antonguolla]

May 6, 1895 — August 23, 1926

Hollywood created Rudolph Valentino as the "World's Greatest Lover." the romantic idol famed for slicked-back dark hair, glowering eyes and flaring nostrils. However, in real life, the screen's Sheik was an elusive, simplistic individual, always involved with dominating women (one of whom gave him a slave bracelet to wear) who played upon his ambivalent sexual orientation. (It was long rumored that he had an affair, among others, with another Latin lover star, Ramon Novarro.)

Being adored by millions of palpitating women fans made Valentino a highly-paid movie star. Being scorned by envious men who labeled him a pink powder puff and fop, led him to constantly proving his masculinity to others and to himself.

Valentino's short, meteoric life—he died at thirty-one—allowed him to end his film career in grand style as it is highly likely that changing film tastes and talkies would have ruined his standing. His "romantic" death assured him a legendary status and the ensuing mass hysteria at his funeral became a high point in the annals of movie lore.

Rodolpho was born in 1895 in the south of Italy at Castellaneto to a former clown-turned-veterinarian and his French-descended school teacher wife. There was an older son (Alberto) and a younger sister (Maria). When he was twelve, his father died and the family moved to Taranto. The undisciplined youth was sent to military school, later dropping pre-med studies hopefully to join the military.

However, such dreams were too expensive for his family, and, eventually, he was schooled in the science of farming. Nevertheless, he went to Paris where he sharpened his dancing skills, indulged his spendthrift habits, and played with the Bohemian set. By late 1913, his mother had thrown him out of her house, but agreed to send him to New York— steerage class. The dreamy young man with the swarthy good looks had new realities to face in the U.S. He was a penniless immigrant. For a time he was an assistant gardener, then a busboy and a petty thief. He became a gigolo, dancing the tango with rich customers, and then performed in vaudeville and had a few East Coast film appearances en route. He went on the road with a musical (*The Masked Marvel*) which folded in Ogden, Utah and he moved on to San Francisco.

Adept at making friends and making do, Valentino was persuaded by a new acquaintance to try Los Angeles. Two New York friends, actors Norman Kerry and Mae Murray, helped him in Hollywood and he found work as an extra. When that kind of film work wasn't plentiful, he did exhibition dancing in clubs. In 1919, he married actress Jean Acker, but they quickly separated (she said their marriage was "a horrible mistake") and were divorced in 1922. Always looking for a mother image to replace his own (who died in 1919), he became friendly with scenarist June Mathis who promoted him for the lead role in *The Four Horsemen of the Apocalypse* (1921). The film made him a star for film audiences, but it also made him more temperamental and self-deluded.

Meanwhile, the exotic Russian actress Alla Nazimova picked Rudolph for her love interest in *Camille* (1921). During production, he came under the influence of Nazimova's close pal, Natacha Rambova—the former Winifred Hudnut—who was the film's costume/art designer. Having left Metro in a salary dispute, he went to Paramount where he had the lead in the heavily romantic (very absurd) *The Sheik* (1921). The movie was tremendously popular as was his role as the love-crazed bullfighter in *Blood and Sand* (1922).

In May 1922, Rudy and Natacha rushed to Mexico to marry, not realizing that his divorce from Acker was not final. He was jailed for bigamy, and later released on $10,000 bail. In March 1923, the couple re-married and his dominant bride insisted on making every artistic decision for her husband. When she alienated his studio bosses, the highly-publicized couple embarked on a cross-country dancing tour and he published a book of poetry, *Day Dreams* (1924). Eventually, a compromise was reached with the studio and he made the well-received *Monsieur Beaucaire* (1924). However, the possessive Natasha pushed him into doing such unpopular items as *Cobra* (1925). By now, she had stormed off to New York. He bought an elaborate mansion, named Falcon Lair, hoping to woo her back. Instead, she went to Paris where, in January 1926, she sued him for divorce. To bolster his manly image, he began "dating" Pola Negri, the "sexy" German actress brought to Hollywood to play temptress roles.

Now with United Artists, Rudolph made *The Eagle* (1925) and *The Son of the Sheik* (1926). The pictures did well

and his UA contract called for him to be paid $200,000 a project and twenty-five percent of the profits. However, by the time Son of the Sheik was released, he was unwell. On his way to New York to promote the film, he suffered further slurs from the press who, again, impugned his masculinity. By the time he reached New York City he was badly ill, suffering from severe stomach pains.

On Monday, August 16, 1926, he collapsed in his Manhattan hotel suite. He was admitted to Polyclinic Hospital for a perforated ulcer and it was then discovered his appendix had ruptured. By the time he had surgery, uremic poisoning had spread throughout his body. Not realizing his critical condition, the star had high hopes of going on a long fishing vacation once he was well.

By Saturday, August 21, he claimed to be feeling better, although that afternoon his fever rose to 104 degrees. On Monday, he was in such pain at 3:30 a.m., he was given a narcotic injection to ease the distress. Steadfastly, Valentino refused to deal with his perilous condition. At 6 a.m. on Monday, when Joseph M. Schenck (United Artists' chairman of the board) visited him, the actor said, "Don't worry, Chief. I will be all right." By 6:30 a.m., he was hardly conscious. Occasionally, he revived to say something in Italian. Outside on the streets, thousands awaited the latest bulletin about him. By now, his temperature had risen to 104.5 and he dropped into a coma about 8:30 a.m. Two priests were summoned at 10:00 a.m. to administer the last rites. At 12:10 p.m., on August 23, 1926, the 31-year-old star died, surrounded not by loved ones, but by three physicians and two nurses. The cause of death was listed as peritonitis and septic endocarditis. His manager insisted, "The

RUDOLPH VALENTINO

psychic drain of his emotional powers [from dealing with the bad press] had even blunted his will to live."

In death, he generated tremendous fan enthusiasm. He lay in state in a bronze coffin in the Gold Room at Frank E. Campbell's Funeral Home in New York City. Over 80,000 mourners stood in line outside to view the dead star. In the rush to see the star first hand, the crowd pressed forward, breaking a plate glass window and tramping floral displays. As a result, over one hundred people were injured. Publicity-conscious Pola Negri had rushed to New York where she said of her dead, alleged fiancee, "I loved him not as one artist loves another but as a woman loves a man." She swooned repeatedly in front of the press.

Valentino's body was shipped by train to California, after a stopover in Chicago for a public viewing. A service was held in Los Angeles where Pola Negri wore a $3,000 gown for the "occasion." Rudolph's brother Alberto announced elaborate plans for a marble memorial to signify the actor's resting place at Hollywood Memorial Park. While these expensive plans were in the "works" (and never realized because of a lack of money) he was laid to rest in a crypt that June Mathis had purchased. When she died in 1927 in a fire, Rudolph's body was transferred to her husband's more humble crypt. Later, Alberto bought the vault from Mathis's husband, Sylvano Balboni, to insure Rudolph's burial site. For years afterwards, on the anniversary of Valentino's death, an unknown woman dressed in black and carrying flowers would make a yearly pilgrimage to his final resting place.

Having earned an estimated $5 million in his lifetime, Rudolph Valentino died with $200,000 in debts. His studio (United Artists) was beneficiary of his $200,000 life insurance policy.

Jean Arthur

[Gladys Georgianna Greene]

October 17, 1901 - June 19, 1991

On screen, Jean Arthur, with that husky adolescent voice and infectious laughter, projected a winning mixture of vulnerability and forthrightness. Off camera, she was both very independent, extremely private and quite eccentric. Frank Capra, who directed her in several 1930s comedy classics, observed, "Never have I seen a performer plagued with such a chronic case of stage jitters . . . . When the cameras stopped she'd run to her dressing room, lock herself in—and cry." When asked in the mid-1960s why she had abandoned Hollywood, Jean replied, "I hated the place—not the work, but the lack of privacy, those terrible, prying fan magazine writers and all the surrounding exploitation."

Born in Plattsburg, New York, her family moved frequently during her childhood because of her father's occupation as a commercial artist. By the early 1920s, she was a New York City model, which led to a screen audition with Fox Films in Hollywood. However, after a few days starring in *The Temple of Venus* (1923) she was replaced. Jean said later, "...that is where and why I developed the most beautiful inferiority complex you've ever seen." Nevertheless, she persisted in the industry. By 1928, Jean had signed a contract with Paramount Pictures and had married photographer Julian Ancker. However, the union was annulled after one day. In 1929, she appeared in her first all-talking picture, *The Canary Murder Case*. By 1931, after fourteen unremarkable roles at Paramount, she returned to New York. In 1932, she made her Broadway debut in *Foreign Affairs* and married Frank Ross, Jr., a young actor who had played with her in Young Eagles (1930).

Back in Hollywood, Jean signed with Columbia Pictures, but it was not until *The Whole Town's Talking* (1935)—opposite Edward G. Robinson—that she made a real impact, displaying a refreshing light comic touch. In the later 1930s, she starred with Gary Cooper in *Mr.Deeds Goes to Town* (1936) and *The Plainsman* (1937); with Cary Grant in *Only Angels Have Wings* (1939); with Jimmy Stewart in *You Can't Take It with You* (1938) and *Mr. Smith Goes to Washington* (1939).Despite these screen classics, it was not until the comic *The More the Merrier* (1943) that she received her first and only Academy Award nomination. By this time, she had gained a reputation for being high-strung and temperamental on the set, and extremely aloof with reporters. Her explanation for her moodiness was "I am not an adult... Except when I am actually working on the set, I have all the inhibitions and shyness of the bashful, backward child."

When her Columbia contract expired in 1944, she did not renew it. When she was through at the studio, she ran through the back lot yelling, "I'm free. I'm free!" She hoped to become a full-time independent producer, but the RKO-co-produced *The Devil and Miss Jones* (1943) was her only such venture. Next, Arthur planned a Broadway return, but left the comedy, *Born Yesterday* (1946), before it opened. In 1948, Jean returned to movies in *A Foreign Affair*, and the next year she divorced her producer husband, Frank Ross. She was back on Broadway with Boris Karloff in a *Peter Pan* (1950) revival and, in 1953, made her final motion picture—the classic Western, *Shane*.

Subsequently, she became even more private. She broke her re-

R.I.P.

OBSCURITY

tirement in 1963 by acting in a college production of *Saint Joan*. She made her TV debut on a segment of *"Gunsmoke"* and was then lured into *"The Jean Arthur Show,"* a sitcom which lasted just twelve episodes in 1966. Her last Broadway appearance was in *The Freaking Out of Stephanie Blake* (1967) about an old lady from Illinois who gets turned on by pot. Cancelled after a few performances because of Arthur's ill health, there were rumors that the star had become impossible to deal with both on and off stage.

From 1968 to 1972 Jean taught drama at Vassar College and then joined the faculty at North Carolina School of the Arts. While in Winston-Salem she made headlines when she was arrested for attempting to stop her neighbor from mistreating his dog. She ended paying a fine and by 1974 had returned to Carmel, California. She tried the stage one more time, but shortly withdrew from *First Monday in October*, a comedy about Supreme Court justices co-starring Melvyn Douglas.

Now completely retired in Carmel, Jean moved to a smaller place there facing the ocean. Most of her attention was devoted to her pets and garden. Occasionally, she could be spotted strolling alone along the beach, or making imperious entrances into local shops.

In the spring of 1989, Jean suffered a stroke that left her an invalid. On June 19, 1991 she died of a heart attack at Carmel Convalescent Hospital. At her request, there were no funeral services. Her ashes were scattered at sea off Point Lobos. (Ironically, actress Joan Caulfield, whom Arthur's ex-husband, Frank Ross had married in 1950, died one day before Jean.)

Until the end, Jean remained firm about not granting interviews. When begged by a Los Angeles TV host in the mid-1980s to do an interview for his program, she ended the matter with, "Quite frankly, I'd rather have my throat slit."

Agnes Ayres

[Agnes Hinkle]

April 4, 1898 - December 25, 1940

Fate can push an individual into stardom and just as quickly yank it away.

Agnes Ayres was born in Carbondale in southern Illinois. By the age of sixteen, her family was living in Chicago. One day in late 1914, a girlfriend suggested they tour the local Essanay Film studio. Agnes's impressive profile and petite figure was noticed by a staff director. She was placed in a crowd scene of a feature currently being shot and was paid $3.00 at the end of the day. She was asked to return and she did. By 1916, she and her mother had moved to New York City. She received her big break when Vitagraph star Alice Joyce noted a resemblance between Agnes and herself. Ayres was hired to play Joyce's sister in *Richard the Brazen* (1917). Agnes played in twenty-five production at Vitagraph before she decided to try Hollywood. (She had married an Army captain—Frank P. Schuker—during World War I, but the couple had quickly separated; in 1921 their divorce was finalized.)

Paramount executive producer Jesse Lasky saw Agnes on screen in 1920 and quickly arranged an introduction. Although he was married and had children, Agnes soon became his mistress. Lasky starred her in the Civil War tale, *Held by the Enemy* (1920), and she received good notices. Studio director Cecil B. De-

Mille was asked to give her leading roles in *The Affairs of Anatol* (1921), *Forbidden Fruit* (1921), and *The Ten Commandments* (1923). Agnes co-starred with popular Wallace Reid in four features, including *Clarence* (1922). She became entranced with the drug-addicted star, and despite the fact that he was married, paid long and frequent visits to him at home. Finally, Reid's wife threatened to throw acid in her face if she returned again, which effectively ended the relationship.

Ayres's professional peak came in Rudolph Valentino's *The Sheik* (1921), she being the frightened English heiress he carries into his desert tent. (In the sequel, *The Son of the Sheik*, 1926, also starring Valentino, she would play the young hero's mother.) By 1923, her romance with Lasky had ended: she wanted marriage, he wanted to avoid divorce. No longer having a mentor, she stopped getting the best scripts and directors. However, she was not worried financially because she had invested wisely in real estate. She married Mexican diplomat Manuel Reachi in mid-1924 and they had a daughter born in 1925. The couple divorced in 1927.

Nevertheless, Agnes's screen career declined, with her final important movie role being the second female lead in Frank Capra's *The Donovan Affair* (1929). At the time she was worth over $500,000, but in the big stock market crash she lost everything. Now penniless, she played vaudeville, touring in one-night stands. Returning to Hollywood in the mid-1930s, she announced, "I'm still young and I see no reason why I can't get to the top again." But times had changed and the only work Agnes could get were bit roles—including an unbilled role in Janet Gaynor's *Small Town Girl* (1936).

The realization that her screen career was finished greatly depressed Agnes and she was soon committed to a sanitarium. In 1939, her ex-husband—now a film producer—gained custody of their daughter. The severely despondent Agnes died of a cerebral hemorrhage on December 25, 1950 in West Hollywood, long forgotten by her once adoring public.

THEDA BARA

Theda Bara

[Theodosia Goodman]
July 29, 1890 - April 7, 1955

In the silent movie *A Fool There Was* (1915), Theda Bara says— via title cards—"Kiss me, my fool." The *New York Dramatic Mirror* enthused, "Miss Bara misses no chance for sensuous appeal. She is a horribly fascinating woman, cruel and vicious to the core." With this trend-setting movie, Theda became a movie star. She was the first of a new type of screen leading lady—a vamp—to grace the screen.

Born in Cincinnati, Ohio, Theda was the daughter of a Jewish tailor, and a mother of Swiss descent. Upon graduating high school, Theda moved to New York to pursue a theatrical career. With her hair dyed black and an exotic makeup, she was cast in a version of Molnar's *The Devils* (1908). She toured in *The Quaker Girl* with Hedda Hopper in 1911 and by 1914 was back in New York. She came to the attention of film director Frank Powell. Although she admitted later, "my mind was set emphatically against it," she accepted movie work because of her uncertain finances.

With the release of *A Fool There Was*, Theda's stardom was insured and she helped filmmaker William Fox build the Fox Film Corporation with her string of hits—all generally variations of her innovative vamp role. The studio publicity department was at its inventive best, creating an alluring background for Theda and insisting that she was the daughter of an eastern potentate and insisting that her name was an anagram for "Arab death." For *Destruction* (1916), the studio promoted her as "The most famous vampire in her most daring role, bringing ruin and disaster to thousands." When she starred in *Cleopatra* (1917) she caused another typical Bara furor by displaying more of her shoulders than movie censors approved. Late in 1917, Theda announced grandly, "During the rest of my screen career, I am going to continue doing vampires as long as people sin. For I believe that humanity needs the moral lesson and it needs it in repeatedly larger doses."

Both studio and star realized that she could only repeat her vamp impersonations so many profitable times. However, when she was cast as *Kathleen Mavourneen* (1919), Irish groups picketed the film for presenting a Jewish girl—the queen of vamps, no less—as an innocent Irish lass. In 1919, when Theda demanded a salary raise from $4,000 to $5,000 weekly, film mogul William Fox refused—he thought she had become passe and he already had a successor to Theda in Betty Blythe.

When no satisfactory movie offers were forthcoming, Theda returned to the Broadway stage in *The Blue Flame* (1920). The supernatural melodrama was disliked by the critics and public alike and closed after 48 performances. The next year, in Connecticut, she married her long-time film director, English-born Charles J. Brabin. She retired from the screen, only to make an inconsequential comeback in *The Unchastened Woman* (1925). Her final foray was in a Hal Roach short, *Ma-*

dame Mystery (1926) which saw a heavily made-up Theda satirizing her old screen vamp image.

Theda returned to private life as a Los Angeles society matron. In the 1930s she tried a few local stage comebacks. She wrote her autobiography, *What Women Never Tell*, but it was never published. She sold her life story to Columbia Pictures in the early 1950s, but it was never filmed. In 1954 she contemplated a return to the stage in East Coast summer stock, but the project fell through.

Later in 1954, Theda was diagnosed with abdominal cancer. She entered California Lutheran Hospital on February 13, 1955. That April 7, she died, a nearly-forgotten innovator of the motion picture industry. She was buried at Forest Lawn Memorial Parks in Glendale, California. Her husband died on November 3, 1957.

Edwina Booth

[Josephine Constance Woodruff]
September 13, 1909 - May 18, 1991

As Nina, the sumptuous White Goddess with the long blonde tresses in MGM's *Trader Horn* (1931), Edwina Booth gained screen immortality. The career-making role also proved to be her professional undoing. She made a few other pictures and then disappeared from the screen entirely. For years her whereabouts remained a mystery, piquing the interest of movie aficionados. It was rumored that she had died—her demise was reported on several different occasions. However, on May 18, 1991, the truth was revealed at last. She had passed away in a Long Beach convalescent hospital of old age. "...this time she really did die," stated her brother Booth Woodruff.

She was born in Provo, Utah under the name Josephine Constance Woodruff. By 1928 she was in Hollywood appearing in Nancy Carroll's *Manhattan Cocktail* (1928) and the next year in *Our Modern Maidens* (1929). The latter picture, starring Joan Crawford, was made at MGM. That studio was embarking on a campaign to find a new face to play the unusual heroine of its jungle epic, *Trader Horn*. Twenty-year-old Edwina was hired for the role. On May 1, 1929, she and the cast and crew of the adventure film arrived in East Africa. The production endured seven months of nightmarish torment under horrible conditions: hostile natives, fierce animals, bizarre tropical diseases, primitive sound equipment. By the time the cast had returned via boat to New York, MGM head Louis B. Mayer had viewed the sent-ahead footage. He declared the project a mess and that the cast was fired. However, other studio executives convinced second-in-charge Irving Thalberg to salvage the production. So, for nearly a year thereafter, the film went through refilming in Los Angeles and in Mexico. It was done under hush-hush conditions, MGM fearing adverse reaction if it were generally known that the resultant film had not been fully shot in the African wilds. After a production cost of $1,322,000, *Trader Horn* debuted in February 1931 to critical enthusiasm. It grossed a then sizeable profit of $937,000.

Meanwhile, Edwina Booth reteamed with *Trader Horn* co-star Harry Carey in two serials—*The Vanishing Legion* (1931) and *The Last of the Mohicans* (1932)—and made a low-budget feature, *The Midnight Patrol* (1932). By the time of the latter's release she was confined to bed for what would prove to be more than a five-year recovery. She was suffering from tropical maladies she had contracted while filming *Trader Horn* in Africa. She sued Metro-Goldwyn-Mayer for over a $1 million, detailing that the studio demanded she sun bathe nude on the ship's deck on the ten-day voyage from Naples to Mombassa. Once in Africa, she claimed, they failed to provide her with necessary protective clothing adequate for the lengthy jungle stay. Her suit stated that her ailments were caused by the tropical sun and bites from unidentified jungle insects. The case was eventually settled out of court.

Once she recovered, Edwina never returned to the entertainment profession (although she continued to receive fan mail until the time of her death). She devoted most of her time to working for a Mormon temple in Hollywood. She married Rienold Fehberg, who died in 1984. When she passed away at the Medallion Convalescent Hospital in Long Beach in May 1991, she was survived by her brother, a sister (Betty Benson) and two step-daughters. A private funeral service was held on May 22, 1991.

With her death, the decades-old mystery of the elusive Edwina Booth was solved once and for all.

Clara Bow

August 25, 1905 - September 27, 1965

This petite redhead with the bobbed hair, cupid's lips and playful pout was the essence of the Roaring Twenties—she was the "It Girl" and "The Brooklyn Bonfire." Most of all, she was the vivacious jazz baby who symbolized an era. Yet, later in life, she admitted sadly to a friend, "It wasn't ever like I thought it was going to be. It was always a disappointment to me."

CLARA BOW

Clara had an unpleasant, impoverished childhood in Brooklyn, New York. Her mother, Sarah, had lost two previous daughters in childbirth and the ordeals had damaged Mrs. Bow's physical and mental health. Clara recalled that her mother "never knew a moment free from illness." Once, when Clara was a youngster, she awoke to find her mother lurching over her with a butcher knife, ranting "You'd be better off dead, than an actress!" Clara claimed she never slept a full night through thereafter.

In 1921, she borrowed a dollar from her doting father to enter a movie magazine contest and won a screen test. She made her movie debut in *Over the Rainbow* (1922). In 1923—the same year her mother died in a state mental hospital—producer B. P. Schulberg brought her to Hollywood to make pictures. Many of her early efforts were forgettable, but she made an impression playing a spirited flapper in *The Plastic Age* (1925). By the time of *It* (1927), Schulberg was entrenched at Paramount Pictures and Clara was a top star. It was the pinnacle of her career; she was the idol of shop girls and the fantasy of men everywhere. Studio chief Adolph Zukor would later recall of magnetic Clara that she "was exactly the same off the screen as on. She danced even when her feet were not moving. Some part of her was in motion in all her waking moments—if only her great rolling eyes."

Clara's popularity rose with the World War I epic *Wings* (1927) in which she played a live-wire Red Cross worker. She made her talkie debut in *The Wild Party* (1929) and the critics forgave her Brooklynese speaking voice. She was earning good money—over $2,800 a week—but she had no business sense, either to invest her earnings or to demand the higher salary she could have had from Paramount. Meanwhile, whenever the pressure got too severe, she had a nervous breakdown.

Over the years, those in the industry were well aware of the Clara's free-living, free-spending habits. She had affairs with a succession of her leading men, including Gary Cooper, Eddie Cantor, Gilbert Roland and Harry Richman, as well as other non-actors. Al Jolson even joked on radio about Clara "sleeping cater-cornered in bed." The studio did its best to play down her gambling binges, her amorous indiscretions, her abortions in Mexico, etc. Then, all hell broke loose, and all the studio's efforts went for nil. On January 13, 1931, Clara brought Daisy De Voe, her former secretary, to court on charges of blackmail and embezzlement. Going on the offensive, Daisy paraded forth in detail the wild life that her past employer was living. (It was mentioned that the USC football coach had slapped up a notice in the locker room that "Clara Bow is off limits to all members of this football team.") Daisy received a minor sentence and served only one year in prison. A bewildered Clara asked the judge, "My best friend, Daisy was. Why did she have to do me like that?"

The trauma of the scandal caused Clara to have several nervous breakdowns and she was sent to recuperate at a sanitarium. The studio dropped her contract. New film deals were "pending," but instead Clara married cowboy actor Rex Bell in Las Vegas and the couple moved to his ranch in Spotlight, Nevada. Throughout this period, Clara, who was never slim, blossomed up and down in weight. She made a brief comeback attempt with *Call Her Savage* (1932) and *Hoopla* (1933). However, moviegoers had found new screen idols, and Clara was now passe.

Clara lapsed into private life. She and Rex had two children— Rex, Jr. and George. At times her weight blossomed to a near two- hundred pounds. After Bell retired from moviemaking, they opened a Hollywood restaurant, but that failed. Later, they sold the Nevada ranch and moved to Las Vegas. There Bell operated a Western apparel store. The last time Clara was in the entertainment limelight was in 1947 when she was the mystery voice on Ralph Edwards's *"Truth or Consequences"* radio show. In 1954, Bell became lieutenant governor of Nevada and was reelected in 1958. As for Clara, like her mother before her, her mental health remained precarious. She was hospitalized in the Los Angeles area in the mid-1950s and she later retreated to a modest Culver City bungalow with a live-in companion-nurse. Although she and Bell now rarely saw one another, they never divorced. He died in July 1962 of a heart attack while seeking the governorship of Nevada. Clara emerged from seclusion to attend his funeral at Forest Lawn Memorial Parks in Glendale, California.

By 1965, Clara was living the barren life of a recluse. In a more coherent moment, she told the press, "We had individuality. we did as we pleased. We stayed up late. We dressed the way we wanted. Today, stars are sensible and end up with better health. But we had more fun."

Shortly before midnight on September 26, 1965, while watching a movie on TV, Clara died at her Culver City bungalow of a heart attack. She was buried at Forest Lawn Memorial Parks in a vault next to her husband's. At the service, Ralph Edwards read from *The Prophet*. Among those who paid their final respects to Clara were such old pals as Jack Oakie, Richard Arlen, Harry Richman and Maxie Rosenbloom.

Whitney Bolton (*New York Morning Telegraph*) offered a fitting final tribute to Clara: "She had fright in her, this girl. She had defiance that was a flower of fright. She had a kind of jaunty air of telling you that she didn't care what happened, she could handle it." Bolton also recollected that he had encountered Bow on the Paramount lot in the late 1920s. He had asked her, "Miss Bow, when you add it all up, what is 'It'?" Clara thought for a moment and replied, "I ain't real sure."

Florence Lawrence

1886 - December 27, 1938

How symptomatic of Hollywood that its first movie star—from the pioneering silent days—would end her days neglected by filmdom. Feeling rejected by the industry she helped to bolster, she killed herself by eating ant paste.

Florence Lawrence was born in 1886 in Hamilton, Ontario, Canada where her mother, Charlotte A. Bridgewood (whose professional name was Lotta Lawrence), managed a traveling stock company and was raising her two boys. At the age of three, Flo made an impromptu stage debut singing "Down in a Shady Dell" and thereafter billed as "Baby Florence, the Child Wonder," she insisted on being part of her mother's productions. By the summer of 1906, Florence and her mother were in New York City seeking Broadway work. Stage parts proved elusive, but Florence (and her mother) were hired—because she could ride a horse—by the (Thomas) Edison Company for a one-reeler film, *Daniel Boone; or, Pioneer Days in America* (1907). This job led to work at the Vitagraph Company where the main actress was Florence Turner. (In those early moviemaking days executives avoided promoting players by name fearing they would demand huge raises. Thus Turner was known merely as "the Vitagraph Girl"). Being ambitious, Lawrence soon left Vitagraph by convincing D. W. Griffith to hire her at Biograph where she became known as "the Biograph Girl." Also in 1908, she married actor-director, Harry Salter.

Because she demanded so much of her due as a popular, hard- working screen player, Biograph fired Florence in 1909. Thinking audiences would accept a substitute, they cast another actress as their new "Biograph Girl." Moviegoers, however, noted the difference and wrote strong letters of protests. While Biograph did not rehire Lawrence, Carl Laemmle's Independent Motion Pic-

ture Company (IMP) did. Florence became "the IMP Girl." In February 1910, newspaper stories (of unknown origin) insisted that "the Biograph Girl" (Florence) had died in a St. Louis streetcar accident. Laemmle wisely had Florence arrive in that city by train where crowds soon recognized her and swamped the actress. It proved she was indeed a recognizable personality worshipped by her fans. As a movie star, the softly radiant (but not beautiful) Lawrence made dozens of short movies for IMP in 1910. By 1912, she and Salter had a deal with Carl Laemmle to create their own company, with studios at Fort Lee, New Jersey. With the profits fro this venture, Florence bought a 50-acre Westwood, New Jersey estate.

While filming *Pawns of Destiny* (1915), Lawrence was injured coming down a staircase during a fire scene. When she returned to the set a month later, she had facial scars, a chronic back problem and badly frayed nerves. Somehow, she completed her studio contract, then collapsed. Thereafter, she divorced Salter, whom she blamed for forcing her do the dangerous stunt. Exhausted by the turn of events, she remained away from filmmaking for two years. In 1916, she made her first long feature, but the strain was too much. She suffered a relapse and for four months endured complete paralysis.

In 1921 Lawrence married a car salesman (Charles B. Woodring) and attempted a screen comeback. However, the industry had greatly changed during her "retirement." She went to Hollywood for the first time, but her vehicle (*The Unfoldment*, 1922) went unnoticed by the public. Frantic for screen work by the mid-Twenties, she had her nose shortened, hoping to induce a fresh career. At best, she got bit parts. She next promoted a cosmetic line, but this too failed. She and Woodring divorced in 1931 and, the next year, she wed Henry Bolton. That union ended five months later after he physically abused her. In 1936, Metro-Goldwyn-Mayer made the gesture of hiring one-time stars (at $75 per week) for bit roles, which created a lot of publicity for the studio. Among those veterans hired were King Baggott, Florence Finch, Claire McDowell and Florence Lawrence. By now, Lawrence was reduced to sharing a small West Hollywood apartment with two women acquaintances.

On December 27, 1938, convinced the public had long forgotten her, Florence did not appear at the studio for her afternoon call. Instead, at her apartment she mixed cough syrup and ant paste and drank the lethal mixture. Her screams led to an ambulance being summoned and she was rushed to a Beverly Hills hospital where she soon died. Ironically, the actress who became the first movie star the public knew by name was buried at Hollywood Memorial Park in an unmarked grave.

Mary Pickford

[Gladys Marie Smith]

April 9, 1893 - May 29, 1979

In the early twentieth century, Canadian-born Mary Pickford became "America's Sweetheart"—that smiling girl with the golden brown curls. The petite miss (barely five-foot tall) reigned supreme in an age when the movie industry was primitive, naive and optimistic. Long after she had retired from acting in the mid-1930s, she remained in the public eye as a co-owner of a major film studio, a movie producer and the social hostess ruled over Beverly Hills' legendary estate, Pickfair.

Later, the heavy-drinking Mary shrank from the limelight into a private world of alcoholism and bittersweet memories. Her ex-movie-star husband, Charles "Buddy" Rogers, became the buffer between her and the real world, always apol-

MARY PICKFORD

ogizing for, explaining away, and bringing messages from "dear Mary." When she died, a frail, detached woman of eighty-six, her passing brought back into focus a bygone era where once she and her partners—Charlie Chaplin, Douglas Fairbanks Sr. (her husband #2) and D. W. Griffith—had dominated the American film industry.

She was born Gladys Smith in Toronto, Canada in 1893, the oldest of three children to a Britisher and his Irish wife. When she was four, her father died and her mother operated a penny candy concession and took in sewing. Because money was so short, Gladys had only six or seven months of formal schooling as a child. At age five she made her stage debut, with her sister Lottie, in *The Silver King* at the Toronto Opera House. Realizing that there was money to be made in show business, Charlotte Smith became an overnight stage mother and controlled her daughter's career until Mrs. Smith died in 1928.

Between 1901 and 1906 Gladys (billed as "Baby Gladys Smith") and her family were on the road in American touring companies. Having outgrown her name tag, she determined to try Broadway. She forced an audition with austere stage impresario David Belasco. He cast her in *The Warrens of Virginia* (1907) and gave her the stage name of Mary Pickford. Later, while touring with the show in Chicago, she saw her first movie, but never thought she would have to stoop to working in the "flickers." However, needing work in 1909, she went to American Mutoscope and Biograph Company on Manhattan's East 14th Street where director D. W. Griffith hired her at $5 a day. She took any role offered, realizing "if I could get into as many pictures as possible, I'd become known, and

there would be a demand for my work." Before long, she was earning $175 a week—a very high salary in those days. By 1913, she was making features for Adolph Zucker's Famous Players-Paramount Company. It was for *Tess of the Storm Country* (1914) that she was promoted as "America's Sweetheart." She reached a peak with *Rebecca of Sunnybrook Farm* and *The Poor Little Rich Girl*, both released in 1917, and both featuring the very adult Mary as youngsters. Despite her age, she carried off the illusions wonderfully well. Meanwhile, while working at the Biograph Studio she met actor Owen Moore and they married in 1911. Her career soon outshone his by light years.

Always astute about the financial side of moviemaking, in 1919 Mary formed United Artists Pictures with Douglas Fairbanks Sr., Charlie Chaplin and D. W. Griffith. It was a pathfinding concept, leading a wag to quip, "the lunatics have taken over the asylum." The next year, she divorced Moore and on March 30, 1920 in Los Angeles, married screen swashbuckler and comedian, Fairbanks. Contrary to their fears, the legal union of Doug and Mary enhanced their mutual fame. When they toured in the U.S. and abroad, fans mobbed them everywhere. They were indeed "the most popular couple in the world." Fairbanks gave her a splendid new home in Beverly Hills, Pickfair, which became the stopping-off place for visiting celebrities from all over the world. Although she tried to break out of her mold with costume dramas—such as *Dorothy Vernon of Haddon Hall* (1924)—the public wanted Mary to stay in waif roles. She obliged, for a while. She and Fairbanks made only one feature together, the *The Taming of the Shrew* (1929).

Mary won an Oscar for *Coquette*

(1929) and made a few more movies, but, after *Secrets* (1933), she retired, insisting, "I wanted to stop before I was asked to stop." (Nevertheless, there were several aborted comeback efforts, but always it was another actress who finally played the part.) With both their careers faltering, Mary and Doug sought consolation elsewhere. Doug fell in love with British musical comedy actress Sylvia Hawkes, then wed to Lord Ashley. After a round-robin of divorces, Fairbanks married her. (He would die in 1939.) In June 1937, Mary wed Charles "Buddy" Rogers, eleven years her junior, who had co-starred with her in *My Best Gal* (1927). In the 1940s they adopted two children: Ronald and Roxanne.

As time wore on, Mary retreated further and further from the movie colony that she had once ruled. After a 1965 trip abroad, she literally took to her bed, insisting that she had worked since she was five years old and now wanted a long rest. Occasionally, she would roam the halls of Pickfair at night. Completing the surrealistic atmosphere were certain house rules. When visitors came, they could speak to Mary only through a house phone. Newspapers brought to her had any possibly disturbing story clipped out. Largely her daily diet consisted of a near-quart of whiskey.

In early 1976, the nearly forgotten Mary was persuaded to accept a special Academy Award "in recognition of her unique contributions to the film industry and the development of film as an artistic medium. For the March 29, 1976 Oscar show, the Pickford segment was pre-taped at Pickfair. Mary, with wig slightly askew, accepted her statuette and murmured a few words. The highly publicized event proved to be more Grand Guignol than the intended af-fectionate nod to an industry pioneer.

In her remaining years, Mary grew more sickly and distant, retreating further into drink and the Bible. Reportedly, in the last months, she would awake from nightmare screaming out for her mother and Douglas Fairbanks, Sr. Picford finally died of a stroke on May 29, 1979 at Santa Monica Hospital. She left an estate estimated at $50 million, with much of it going to a charity entity, the Mary Pickford Foundation. She is buried at Forest Lawn Memorial Parks in Glendale, California in an outdoor garden near the Mystery of Life section. Her mother, brother (who died of alcoholism) and sister (who died of coronary sclerosis and drinking) are buried there as well.

Two years after Mary's death, Rogers married Beverly Ricondo, a real estate agent he had known for a long time. As for Pickfair, the estate eventually ended being owned by Pia Zadora and her husband, Meshulam Riklis, with the main house virtually torn down to make way for their new showcase home. The past was gone, making way for a new future.

Norma Shearer

[Edith Norma Fisher]
August 10, 1900 - June 12, 1983

For many fans, Academy Award-winning Norma Shearer is Hollywood's ultimate movie star. Her participation in a motion picture or arrival at a social function spelled Class with a capital "C." On screen, Norma excelled at sophisticated drawing room comedy (*Private Lives*, 1931) and could handle costume drama (*Marie Antoinette*, 1938) or biting social commentary (*The Women*, 1939) with equal aplomb. The dark-haired actress was not a raving beauty and she had a trouble-

NORMA SHEARER

band, Irving Thalberg, who died prematurely in 1936. Unfortunately, there is always an end to every royal regime. In Norma's case, it was NOT "happily ever after" as in most of her films. Her final years embraced failing health, mental instability and, the worst fate of all for her, being isolated from, and forgotten by, those she loved best—her adoring fans.

She was born in a suburb (Westmount) of Montreal, Canada, the daughter of a Scottish construction company executive and an English mother whose forebears had been clergymen. There was an older brother (Douglas) and sister (Athole). As a frail child, she was persauded by her mother to become a pianist, for which she had talent. However, after winning a beauty contest at fifteen, her mother guided her toward amateur theatricals. By early 1920, when Mr. Shearer's business faltered, Mrs. Shearer escorted her daughters to New York City. Stage work failed to materialize, but the Shearer girls found extra work in silent movies, including D. W. Griffith's *Way Down East* (1920). (Athole would soon drop her show business career and later marry and divorce director Howard Hawks; Douglas would later create and supervise the MGM sound department for many years.)

some physical defect (being wall-eyed). However, with careful lighting she developed a well-bred radiance that substituted for sex-appeal.

During the 1930s, she reigned as Hollywood first lady. For much of her rule, she shared the throne with her MGM executive producer hus-

After a few years of small screen roles and modeling assignments, Norma was signed by moviemaker Louis B. Mayer and his new second-in-command, Irving G. Thalberg, for his growing film company (soon to be Metro-Goldwyn-Mayer). Shearer went to California with her mother and sister in early 1923. In this training period, she made several pictures with studio contractees Lon Chaney and John Gilbert, including *He Who Gets Slapped* (1924). On September 29, 1927 Norma, now converted to Judaism, married Thalberg at his Beverly Hills home in a lavish ceremony. Their son (Irving Jr) was born in 1930; their daughter (Katherine) in 1935.

Norma proved she could make the transition to talkies in *The Trial of Mary Dugan* (1929) and received an Oscar for *The Divorcee* (1930). Now earning $6,000 weekly, she had first refusal of the best MGM properties and talent. She gathered more Oscar nominations: *A Free Soul* (1931), *The Barretts of Wimpole Street* (1934), *Romeo and Juliet* (1936) and *Marie Antoinette* (1938). After Thalberg's death in 1936, Norma considered retiring, and then charged ahead with more pictures, such as *Idiot's Delight* (1939) with Clark Gable. She entered her "Merry Widow" social period, dating the likes of George Raft and, according to Mickey Rooney, Mickey Rooney.

In 1942, proving that times were changing, three of MGM's legendary mainstays departed the studio: Norma Shearer, Greta Garbo and Joan Crawford. Also that year, Norma married a ski instructor (Martin Arrouge), several years her junior. For years, they lived in the spacious Santa Monica beach home she had once shared with Thalberg; in 1960 they moved to more modest West Hollywood digs. Until the mid-Sixties,

Norma and Martin continued their regimen of skiing, traveling and increasingly infrequent entertaining. By 1967, Norma was experiencing the same type of anxiety attacks that had caused her sister to suffer several nervous breakdowns. Shearer underwent shock treatment to help her "adjustment" to her diminished lifestyle and social influence. To a lesser degree, Norma was suffering the same fate as Norma Desmond of *Sunset Boulevard* (1950), a role Shearer had ironically rejected. The once star became more pronouncedly suicidal and, in 1970, attempted to throw herself from a window on the top floor of a Los Angeles high-rise building.

Norma spent many months at a private sanatorium. While the shock treatments reduced her depression, its side affect was to impair her memory of current happenings. Her past became more real than the present. In the later 1970s, having already undergone corrective surgery once, her eyesight began to fade again. She clung to past times when life had been fulfilling and kept searching in the present for ties to the dead Irving Thalberg.

By September 1980, the frail, withered Norma, whose hair had turned snow white, was a permanent patient at the Motion Picture Country House in Woodland Hills, California. Once living in powerful splendor, Shearer's domain now was her small room (D133) in the hospital wing. Infrequently lucid, she generally remained wheelchair-bound or resting in bed. When she made contact at all with those about her, it was to ask the repeated query, "Are you Irving?" Irrational and confused, she would sometimes wander the hospital wing corridors dressed in her nightgown and bathrobe, not sure how to find her way back to her room. In June 1983, Norma contracted bronchial pneumonia. She died at about 5 p.m. on June 12, 1983. She was buried at Forest Lawn Memorial Parks in Glendale next to Thalberg in his marble pavilion. At last, she had come home.

Sonny Tufts

[Bowen Charlton Tufts III]
July 16, 1911 - June 5, 1970

Followers of Trivial Pursuit know that Sonny Tufts was actually a high-spirited actor, not just a nonsensical expression to evoke instant laughter.

He was born in 1911 in Boston, Massachusetts into a prominent banking family which boasted one ancestor who founded Tufts University. "Sonny," as he was known all his life, broke with the family tradition by going to Yale University (rather than Harvard) and by wanting to become a singer. By the time he graduated college in 1935, Tufts had organized several performing bands in which he was both vocalist and drummer. Thinking he wanted an opera career, he studied voice in Paris for six months. Back in New York, after more training, he auditioned for the Metropolitan Opera. However, he eventually decided the profession did not pay beginners enough. Instead, the convivial Sonny made his Broadway debut in a musical revue, *Who's Who* (1938) and then spent four years singing in East coast supper clubs. Meanwhile, in 1938, he wed dancer Barbara Dare.

A wealthy college buddy financed Tufts's expedition to California in exchange for a percentage of his potential earnings. The strapping, 6' 4", blond, blue-eyed Tufts arrived in Hollywood at just the right time. Many of the screen's younger leading men were already enlisted in the military services for World War II. Through another college connection, Tufts tested at Paramount Pictures and was hired to play opposite Paulette Goddard in *So Proudly We Hail* (1943). He was credible as the gawky Marine and Paramount signed the likeable player to a term contract. Typically in his films he was cast as a happy-go-lucky lug, opposite such star leads as Paulette Goddard (*I Love a Soldier*, 1944), Joan Caulfield (*Miss Susie Slagle's*, 1945) and Olivia de Havilland (*The Well-Groomed Bride*, 1946). Because the studio had its own resident crooner (Bing Crosby), there was little occasion to showcase Sonny in singing parts.

By the late 1940s, Tufts had left Paramount and his career tumbled downhill. Off camera in the early 1950s, he made headlines for nonsensical behavior (publicly biting a stripper on the thigh, etc.), drunken sprees, and a separate maintenance suit (his wife stopped living with him in 1950; she received a divorce in 1953). He plodded through screen trash like *Cat Women of the Moon* (1954) and was dropped from the musical *Ankles Aweigh* (1955) during its pre- Broadway tryout. After forcing himself to be sober for a year, he hoped for the role of Jim Bowie in John Wayne's *The Alamo* (1960), but the part went to Richard Widmark. By the mid-Sixties, the usually drunk Tufts had become a public joke and embarrassment. He had descended to the category of has-been and his name had become synonymous for a no-talent buffoon. Deciding to join them if he couldn't fight them, he made TV appearances on TV's "*Laugh-In*," a "*Trivia*" special, etc. poking fun of himself.

Alone and having exhausted the $2 million he claimed to have earned, Tufts died of pneumonia on June 4, 1970 at St. John's Hospital in Santa

Monica, California. On Sunday, June 7, memorial services were held for him at Beverly Hills' All Saint's Episcopal Church. He was buried the next day, another casualty of the Hollywood mill.

SONNY TUFTS

MARIO LANZA LIES IN HIS COFFIN
photo courtesy Photofest

176

Russ Columbo

[Ruggerio Eugenio di Rudolpho Colombo]

January 14, 1908 - September 2, 1934

Sometimes the causes of a particular death seem so fantastic that it is difficult to accept it as an accident—even years afterwards. Such was the case of singer Russ Columbo who, in the early 1930s, rivaled Bing Crosby and Rudy Vallee's as America's most popular crooner.

He was born in San Francisco in 1908, the youngest of twelve children. When he was five, the low-income family relocated to Philadelphia. Later, they moved back to the West Coast and, by then, Russ had learned the violin and begun studying opera. During his high school years in Los Angeles, he earned money as a violinist, often playing background music during the shooting of silent pictures. He caught the attention of exotic screen star Pola Negri who was attracted by his resemblance to Rudolph Valentino. She found Columbo more work, both playing music and doing film bits. After graduating from high school, Russ joined George Eckhart and His Orchestra and then moved on to other performing groups. With Professor Moore and His Orchestra, he played violin at Los Angeles's Roosevelt Hotel and, occasionally, got to be the group's substitute singer.

His big break came in 1928 when he was signed to join Gus Arnheim and His Orchestra at L.A.'s swank Cocoanut Grove Club. He played violin and was back-up to Bing Crosby, sometimes he and Crosby did duets. These appearances led to Russ winning small roles in talkies, starting with *Street Girl* (1929). He had a non-musical acting part in *Wolf Song* (1929) which starred Latin bombshell Lupe Velez—who took a romantic interest in him as well as in co-star Gary Cooper. In Cecil B. De-Mille's *Dynamite* (1929), Russ was a Mexican prisoner who introduced the popular song, "How Am I to Know?" By 1930 he had made his recording debut and toured the East Coast with Arnheim's group. More film roles followed.

Always anxious to improve himself, Columbo formed his own band, then he opened his own niterie, the Club Pyramid on Santa Monica Boulevard. The exposure led to a RCA recording contract and he shortly landed his own NBC network radio program. Soon he was getting stacks of fan mail and was dubbed "The Romeo of Radio." His recordings, including his theme song—"You Call It Madness (But I Call It Love)"—became best-sellers. He was a sensation on his sell-out personal appearance tours. The publicity mill insisted he was dating Greta Garbo; in actuality he romanced actresses Dorothy Dell (who died in a car crash in 1934), Sally Blane and Carole Lombard. His romance with Carole blossomed; he dedicated his song "Save the Last Dance for Me" to her. Their romance see-sawed for she suspected that his old world ways and traditional Catholic upbringing would not sit well with her freer lifestyle. Nevertheless, they were unofficially engaged to marry. By now he was frequently earning $7,500 a week. For his first major feature film role, *Broadway Thru a Keyhole* (1933), he received very positive notices (more for his pleasing personality and vocal abilities than for his dramatics).

Columbo formed a music publishing company, had a new Sunday night NBC radio program and signed a long-term deal with Universal Pictures to make a string of musicals

RUSS COLUMBO

(including a remake of *Show Boat*). As luck would have it, he made only one—*Wake Up and Dream* (1934), a song-and-dance affair about a vaudeville performer. The gleeful Columbo told the press, "I find that I have just about everything I want from life and am pretty happy about the things have worked out for me." However, by the time his breakthrough screen vehicle was released; Russ was dead.

As the "facts" have it, on Friday night, August 31, 1934, he and Carole Lombard dressed in disguise to attend a sneak preview of *Wake Up and Live*. During the weekend, he and Carole argued. On Sunday, September 2, Columbo was at 916 North Genese in West Hollywood visiting a very close pal, Hollywood portrait photographer Lansing V. Brown, Jr. The two were chatting and examining Brown's prized collection of Civil War dueling pistols. Brown supposedly struck a match on one of the firearms, which had been loaded years before. A charge exploded from the pistol. It ricocheted off a nearby desk and bounced back to hit Columbo in the left eye. He collapsed screaming as the corroded pellet lodged in his brain. He was rushed by ambulance to Los Angeles's Good Samaritan Hospital where he died two hours later, never having regained consciousness. Sally Blane was at the hospital when he passed away at the age of twenty-six.

He was buried at Forest Lawn Memorial Parks in Glendale. Among his pallbearers were Bing Crosby, Zeppo Marx, director Lowell Sherman and Carole Lombard's brother Stuart. Carole had not intended to attend the funeral, but she did, and broke down during the services. She was consoled by Bing Crosby. Later, she tried to comfort Brown who suffered tremendous guilt over causing his pal's death.

Bizarre as the recorded facts of Columbo's death, the aftermath was even stranger. His mother never learned of his death. Two days before Russ died, the nearly-blind woman had suffered a severe heart attack. The family feared the news of Russ's tragedy would finish her. They concocted—supposedly at Carole's suggestion—that he had sailed on a lengthy tour abroad. They made up letters to read to her weekly, supposedly sent by her loving son. Monthly checks were given her from his insurance policies. This deception went on for a decade until she died. (Her final words were, "Tell Russ how happy and proud he has made me.") In her will, she left part of her estate to him.

Over the years, rumors persisted as to the "real story" behind Columbo's bizarre ending. However, nothing was ever proven one way or the other. When Russ's older brother Alberto was found murdered— gangland style—in March 1954, there was fresh speculation that perhaps Russ's strange end had not been as accidental as it was made to seem back in 1934. If anyone who knows the "real" facts is still alive, he or she is definitely not talking.

Bob Crane

July 13, 1928- June 29, 1978

Were it not for the constant re-runs of his hit television series, "*Hogan's Heroes*" (1965-71), and his ghastly death, Bob Crane might just be another footnote in TV history. However, his brutal murder—still unsolved—and the constant playing of the 167 episodes of the life and zany times of Colonel Robert Hogan in a World War II Nazi prisoner-of-war camp keeps his memory very much alive.

He was born in Waterbury, Connecticut and grew up in Stamford. Early in his life, he developed an enthusiasm for playing the drums. His musical talent led to his becoming a percussionist with the Connecticut Symphony Orchestra from 1944-46; he later toured the Northeast with various bands. Next, in 1950, he turned to being a disc jockey and radio host on local radio stations, first in Hornell, New York, then in Bristol, Connecticut and, for six years, at WICC in Bridgeport, Connecticut. Meanwhile, Crane married his childhood sweetheart, Anne Terzian, in 1949. Before they divorced in 1970, they had three children: Robert David, Deborah Ann and Karen Leslie.

Crane's media experience as an ingratiating radio personality with an easy-going, clowning manner led to his coming to Los Angeles. There, on KNX radio, he hosted a celebrity interview show, displaying a sharp wit and an entertaining brashness. Before too long, he was earning well over $100,000 yearly. However, his ambition was to be an actor. "I want to be the next Jack Lemmon," he told a friend. But, his radio duties stood in the way. Industry contacts led to occasional TV guest spots ("*The Lucy Show*," "*Alfred Hitchcock Presents*"), movie roles (*Mantrap*, 1961, *Return to Peyton Place*, 1961) and a substitute host chore for Johnny Carson on the daytime quiz show, "*Who Do You Trust?*" He also turned to stage work, performing in stock shows (*Send Me No Flowers*, *Who Was That Lady?*) and being a frequent volunteer at benefit shows.

An appearance on TV's "*The Dick Van Dyke Show*" in 1963 led to Bob playing Dr. Dave Kelsey, the married next-door neighbor in "*The Donna Reed Show*" (1963-65). This role, in turn, prompted his being cast as the resourceful American colonel in "*Hogan's Heroes*." In that sitcom, it was Crane's character, along with his fellow Allied prisoners, who make monkeys out of their German captors, especially Colonel Wilhelm Klink (Werner Klemperer). The hit program lasted for six profitable seasons.

In 1970, four months after his divorce from his first wife was final, he married actress Patricia Olson. Under her stage name of Sigrid Valdis she had played Hilda, the fetching German fraulein, on "Hogan's Heroes" from 1966-70. The next year, the couple had a son, Robert Scott. When Crane's series went off the air, Bob was (over) confident that his success would lead to a prompt follow-up vehicle. He guest-starred on many TV series and made-for-television movies (*The Delphi Bureau*, 1972), and also turned down several sitcom pilots.

In 1974, Crane rejected a $300,000 a year offer to do a Los Angeles radio show four hours per weekday. Bob insisted, "I said no because that's going backward. I enjoy acting too much." Finally, he settled on doing *"The Bob Crane Show,"* which lasted two months in 1975. Its failure left the on-the-surface congenial performer, extremely bitter. By the late Seventies, he was a guest on *"Love Boat"* (a sure sign of career problems), and had only a supporting role in the Disney comedy feature *Gus* (1976) after starring for the studio in an earlier comedy, *Super Dad* (1974).

In 1978, Crane was separated from his second wife (she had filed for divorce), was hoping for a TV series comeback, and was earning a lucrative salary performing in light comedies at dinner theaters throughout the U.S.—the *"Hogan's Heroes"* re-runs had kept his name alive to audiences. (Part of Crane's reason for working so hard was that his manager had informed him that his finances were shaky; it later proved that substantial funds had been embezzled from his accounts.)

In June 1978, the glib actor was starring in a sex farce, *Beginner's Luck*, at the Windmill Dinner Theatre in Scottsdale, Arizona, a retirement community. Bob was lodged at the Winfield Apartment-Hotel in ground-floor rooms leased by the theatre for visiting star casts. A few weeks before his death, his second wife, Patricia, and their son made a surprise visit to Scottsdale. It ended in several noisy arguments before she and the boy flew back to the West Coast.

On Wednesday, June 28, 1978, after completing the evening show and signing autographs for fans in the lobby, Crane had returned briefly to his apartment with long-time friend, Los Angeles businessman John Carpenter. Before they left, Patricia had called him from Seattle, Washington (where she was vacationing) and they had argued loudly on the phone (according to Carpenter). Thereafter, Crane and Carpenter adjourned to a local bar where they had drinks with two women whom they had arranged to meet there. At about 2 a.m., the quartet went to the Safari coffee shop on Scottsdale Road. About 2:30 a.m., Carpenter left to pack for his trip back to Los Angeles the next morning. Once back at his hotel room, he called Crane one final time.

At about 2:20 p.m. on June 29, 1978, Victoria Berry, a shapely blonde Australian actress, who was in the touring cast of *Beginner's Luck* and who had become very friendly with the star, arrived at the Winfield Apartments. Bob had failed to appear for a cast lunch that noon or to keep a later appointment to help her with audition tapes to further her career. She found the front door of his two-bedroom apartment unlocked. (Crane was noted for always double-locking the door.) When she entered, the curtains were drawn and there were two bottles (one half-drunk) on a table. (Crane was not a heavy drinker.) When she went into the master bedroom she found Crane dead, hunched up in bed, lying on his side, wearing undershorts and an undershirt. His face was so battered that she, at first, didn't recognize him. When she saw his wrist watch, she knew the corpse was that of Bob Crane. She screamed and that led to the police being summoned.

The police theorized that the killer (a he or a she) was someone that Crane knew, and had left the apartment, but then had returned, having left the front door or a window unlocked. According to the Maricopa County Medical Examiner, somewhere in the early hours of Thursday, June 29, while Bob slept on his right side, he was struck a heavy blow on the left side of his head with a blunt object, and by a second, lighter one, which crushed the man's skull. A video camera electrical cord had been tied tightly around the actor's neck, but by that time, Crane was already dead. Before fleeing, the killer wiped the blood off the murder weapon onto the bed sheets and then pulled the sheet up around the victim's head. Cash was found in Crane's wallet, which seemed to rule out a robbery motive.

Investigation of the crime by the local police brought to light Bob Crane's "secret" life, which he pursued in Scottsdale as he had for several years before. He had a long-standing compulsion to videotape himself and his female sexual partner (of which there were many over the years) in various sexual acts. (It was rumors of this activity, as well as other penchants—playing drums at various topless bars in Los Angeles—which supposedly cost Crane several TV and movie acting jobs; the producers fearful of having their screen product associated with this two-sided man.) Approximately fifty such tapes were found at the Winfield apartment, as well as professional photography equipment in the bathroom for developing and enlarging still shots. A negative strip was found in the enlarger, revealing a female in both clothed and nude poses. A hefty album of similar such pornographic pictures was missing from the death scene. Several unnamed (by the police) items were missing from Crane's "Little Black Bag,"—a small, multi-zippered bag which he always carted around with him. (Berry had seen it when she first discovered the body, but later it disappeared and was never accounted for.) Because of Crane's unusual tastes, the police insisted, there could be a lot of potential suspects, including disgruntled husbands or jealous female partners. At one point, John Carpenter was considered a prime "suspect" in the case, but no official charges, to date, were ever brought against him.

On July 5, 1978—eight days before his fiftieth birthday—a funeral service was held for Bob Crane at St. Paul the Apostle Catholic Church in Westwood, California. His family (including both wives and all the children) and 200 mourners (including celebrity attendees Carroll O'Connor, John and Patty Duke Astin) attended the services. The pallbearers included several "Hogan's Heroes" alumnus: Leon Askin, Eric Braeden, Robert Clary and Larry Hovis. Crane was buried at Oakwood Memorial Park in Chatsworth, California.

Because of Bob Crane's fame, his murder was news everywhere for a long time. When the local police could not conclusively name or arrest a suspect in the case, many professionals and amateurs from around the country tried their hand at solving the puzzling, complex case. A lot of theories have been put forth, a great deal of discussion has focused on the quality of the police investigation and the jurisdictional and political controversy the case caused. However, to this date, the killer remains at large, although recurringly Scottsdale police insist that the case will soon be solved.

Dorothy Dandridge

November 9, 1922 - September 8, 1965

In early to mid-twentieth century North America show business was one of the few arenas in which a black performer was allowed to excel. But even in the entertainment field, it was difficult for a black star to find leading roles, especially in motion pictures. One of the many talented, ambitious entertainers who fought to break through the bias was sultry, coffee-colored Dorothy Dandridge. Her professional heartbreaks sustained by her in crashing the color line haunted her to the end of her relatively short life.

By the time she was born in Cleveland, Ohio in 1922, one of two children of actress Ruby Dandridge, her father had vanished. At a very early age, she and her older sister Vivian—billed as "The Wonderful Children"—performed before local church and school groups, and soon were touring. By the early 1930s, Mrs. Dandridge took her children to Los Angeles. Dorothy dropped out of high school when she began getting film roles: background parts in the Marx Brothers's *A Day at the Races* (1937) and Dick Powell's *Going Places* (1938). With Etta Jones added to the act, Dorothy and Vivian toured as the Dandridge Sisters. By now, Ruby Dandridge herself was gaining a foothold in movies (playing domestics) and hired a chaperone to be with her girls when they toured. Always idealistic and shy, Dorothy was traumatized one night when she returned home from a date and this hostile, domineering woman-in-charge accused her of sexual promiscuity. To determine if the girl was still a virgin, she tore off Dorothy's dress and probed inside the horrified girl with her finger. The nightmarish situation left Dandridge frigid for years.

In 1940, while performing with Jimmy Lunceford's Band at the Cotton Club in New York, Dorothy met Harold Nicholas, part of the popular Nicholas Brothers dance act and quite a ladies' man. Dorothy and Nicholas began dating, which continued when they both were cast in *Sun Valley Serenade* (1941) back in Hollywood. They married in 1942 and her daughter, Harolyn, was born the next year. (The infant was brain-damaged, a malady for which Dandridge never forgave herself.) Meanwhile, Dorothy continued to gain small roles in Hollywood features.

Dandridge and Nicholas divorced in the later 1940s. She admitted, "I think it was really the heartache over my child and the failure of my marriage that forced me to make a success of my career. I had to keep busy." She took acting lessons and through the guidance of musician Phil Moore, who became a romantic interest as well, she emerged a confidant, sexy chanteuse. She sang briefly with Desi Arnaz's band at the Mogambo Club in Hollywood. She took the role of an erotic jungle princess in *Tarzan's Peril* (1951) and played a sports player's wife in *The Harlem Globetrotters* (1951). With singing engagements at increasingly posh West and East Coast nightclubs, Dorothy's popularity grew. MGM cast her as a dedicated school teacher in *Bright Road* (1953) and she revealed a hitherto hidden dramatic mettle. While on a singing engagement in Cleveland, she finally met her father (Cyril Dandridge) and from this one-time-only meeting she learned she was one-quarter white.

Dorothy campaigned hard to win the temptress title role in *Carmen Jones* (1954), opposite her *Bright Road* co-star, Harry Belafonte. However, once she had won the battle, she was overwhelmed with self-doubts. A perpetual perfectionist, always striving to please everyone, Dorothy still had little faith in herself. Her doubts were reinforced when the film's director (Otto Preminger) hired a young opera student, Marilyn Horne, to dub Dandridge's voice for the difficult score. Nevertheless, Dorothy was Oscar-nominated for her fiery performance and Twentieth Century-Fox signed her to a non-exclusive contract. On screen she embarked in an interracial romance in *Island in the Sun* (1957) and played a half-caste in *Tamango* (1959). Off screen, she won a law suit against Confidential magazine for a scandalous article it published about her off camera sex life. She returned to screen musicals with *Porgy and Bess* (1959), directed by her mentor-tormentor, Otto Preminger. That year she wed her long-time romance, white restaurateur Jack Denison.

By the early 1960s Dorothy's screen career had stalled due to the lack of available roles for a black leading woman and her unhappy, costly marriage ended in divorce in 1962. Unable to cope with her growing frustrations, she began drinking heavily. When she could no longer afford to keep her retarded daughter in a private hospital she had to commit her to the Camarillo State Hospital. Dorothy tried to revive her career, but her emotional and physical health had been depleted by overreliance on liquor and pills. In April 1963 she declared bankruptcy, making public just how bad her life had become. With the assistance of her one-time manager (Earl Mills), Dorothy straightened out and made a few singing engagements, including playing Julie in a summer stock edition of *Show Boat*, starring Kathryn Grayson.

In mid-September 1965, Dorothy was scheduled to appear at Manhattan's Basin Street East. "I'm going to set New York on their ears," she insisted of her comeback club engagement. Meanwhile, she had been offered two new film projects in Mexico. The day before she went to Mexico to discuss the contracts, she twisted her ankle in a fall down the steps of a local gym and it began to pain he en route south of the border. On September 7, as soon as she returned from Mexico, she consulted a Los Angeles doctor who found that she had suffered a minor fracture. He arranged for her to return the following day to have a small plaster cast applied to the ankle. That evening she packed for the New York flight and talked with her mother on the phone. The next morning, at 7:15 a.m., she called Earl Mills asking him to postpone the hospital appointment for a few hours. "I'll sleep for a while and I'll be fine." With those final words, she hung up.

Later in the morning, Mills could not reach her by phone. He drove to her West Hollywood apartment, but there was no answer when he rang her door. He left but returned at 2 p.m. Now worried, he forced his entry into her place where he found her lying on the bathroom floor. She was naked except for a scarf wrapped around her head. When the ambulance arrived, the medics confirmed that she had been dead for approximately two hours. Strangely, a few months before her death, she had handed Mills a note—later declared her last will and testament—which stated, "In case of my death—to whomever discovers it—don't remove anything I have on—scarf, gown, or underwear. Cremate me right away. If I have anything, money, furniture, give it to my mother Ruby Dandridge. She will know what to do. Dorothy Dandridge."

The L.A. coroner's office concluded initially that Dorothy had died of an embolism, caused by fatty bits dislodged from the bone marrow in her fractured right foot which had cut off the blood flow in her lungs and brain. A few weeks later, a new medical finding was released. Further study of tissue samples revealed that Dorothy had suffered a drug overdose from Tofranil, an antidepressant, which a doctor had prescribed for her. Because of the career upswing Dorothy was undergoing at the time of her death, a psychiatric team refused to conclude definitely that she was a suicide victim. The case remains unresolved.

A funeral service was held at the Little Church of the Flowers at Forest Lawn Memorial Parks in Glendale and then her cremated body was interred. Among those in attendance was Peter Lawford, a one-time lover. Dandridge died at age forty-three with only a few dollars in her bank account. It was a melancholy finale to such a promising career.

Albert Dekker

[Albert Van Dekker]

December 20, 1904 - May 5, 1968

In Hollywood's annals, there have been many grotesque deaths and murders. However, few have been as weird as that of Albert Dekker, the distinguished, moustachioed character actor who specialized in playing polished, squinty-eyed villains.

Born in Brooklyn, New York, he graduated from Bowdoin College. He intended to follow a career in psychology, perhaps as a psychiatrist. However, he became interested in acting on campus and made his professional debut in 1927 with a Cincinnati stock company. That same year he came to Broadway in Mar-

co's Millions, followed by several other stage roles, including Grand Hotel (1930) and Parnell (1935). He married actress Esther Guernini in 1929 and they had three children: Jan, John and Benjamin. He made his movie debut in The Great Garrick (1937) and was constantly working. The 6'3", 240-pound Dekker became a highly-respected character lead, usually cast as a menacing crook or a demented scientist (Dr. Cyclops, 1940, was one of his most famous celluloid roles). He won a seat in the California State Assembly in 1944 and worked as a public servant for two years. After returning to picture-making—including The Killers (1946) and The Furies (1950)—he went back to Broadway in 1950 to take over the lead in Death of A Salesman. During the 1950s, because he spoke out against Senator Joseph McCarthy's Communist witch-hunt, he was blacklisted in the industry. On April 18, 1957, Dekker's sixteen-year old son, John, died of a self-inflicted gun wound at the family home at Hastings-on-Hudson. It was ruled accidental.

By 1959, Dekker was again making major films (Suddenly Last Summer, Middle of the Night) and he was on Broadway in The Andersonville Trial (1960) and The Devils (1965). His final role was in Samuel Peckinpah's The Wild Bunch, released after Dekker's death in 1969.

At the time of his grisly passing, Dekker had long been divorced from his wife and had been dating Geraldine Saunders for quite some time. With his $30,000 salary from The Wild Bunch and $40,000 from TV work, he and his fiancee planned to buy a house in the Encino Hills area of the San Fernando Valley. On Saturday, May 4, Saunders could not get in touch with Dekker, whom she had last seen two days earlier. On Sunday morning, she rushed over to his apartment at 1731 North Normandie Street in Hollywood and found several notes on the door from friends trying to reach him. She slipped her own message under the locked door. That evening, when she still had heard nothing from him, she returned. Accompanied by the manager, they entered the locked, but unbolted front door of the apartment. When the manager forced open the bathroom door, the sight was so horrifying, Saunders fainted.

The once-distinguished actor was found kneeling naked in the bath tub. A dirty hypodermic needle was stuck in each arm. Around his neck was a hangman's noose, loose enough not to strangle him. There was a scarf wrapped around his eyes and a rubber ball bit in his mouth with metal chains tied firmly behind his head. His body was trussed in several leather belts fastened around his body halter-fashion, with the end of a belt rope (tied around his middle) leading to the rope's end clutched in his hand. His wrists were each handcuffed separately. Obscene writings and symbols covered his body. On his chest was written "cocksucker" and "slave" and on his throat was "make me suck."

The police investigation uncovered no signs of forced entry or a struggle, although several thousands dollars in cash and camera equipment were missing. While admitting this was "quite an unusual case" the official verdict was "accident death, not a suicide." Los Angeles County Coroner Thomas T. Noguchi had his own opinion. He theorized that the sophisticated Dekker had died of the not uncommon autoerotic asphyxia in which heightened orgasm is achieved by risking death. Friends insisted that they had never known the scholarly Dekker to be kinky nor

did they think him a closeted gay man. (For a brief period, the police speculated that Dekker may have been killed by a male hustler who had been involved in a ritual gone bad and then had left the apartment quickly, taking valuables with him.)

While the case has long been closed, it still remains a confusing Hollywood mystery.

Mario Lanza

[Alfred Arnold Cocozza]

January 31, 1921 - October 7, 1959

Everything about Mario Lanza was enormous: his talent, his ego, his lifestyle and often his weight. In his relatively short career, he made only eight feature films. However, the legacy of his powerful, golden operatic tenor voice is guaranteed by his many recordings which, to date, have sold over 50 million copies. His untimely death was brought on by a reckless living style and his irresolute battle to curb his ever-ballooning figure.

He was born in South Philadelphia in 1921. His father was disabled in World War I, and the family survived on the meager earnings of Mrs. Cocozza, a seamstress. His father was an avid opera fan and instilled a love of music in his son. Alfred—known as Freddie—listened to Enrico Caruso recordings constantly on a neighbor's phonograph and grew up idolizing Caruso. Freddie had little interest in academics but enjoyed school sports, chasing girls, and taking vocal lessons for which his mother had to scrape to pay. A few months before graduation he was expelled from high school and went to work at his grandfather's grocery shop. He stayed there for three years, until his voice coach (Irene Williams) arranged an audition at the

Philadelphia Academy of Music. This audition led to a scholarship at the Berkshire Music Center in Tanglewood, based in Lenox, Massachusetts. By now, he had adopted his mother's maiden name of Lanza and adapted her first name of Maria, changing it into Mario.

Mario made his Tanglewood debut in the opera *The Merry Wives of Windsor* in the summer of 1942 and then went on concert tour. His promising career was cut short when he was drafted into World War II duty the next January. Because of his singing skills, he was assigned to the Army's Special Services and was cast in their productions of *On the Beam* and *Winged Victory*. He toured with the latter show on the West Coast where actress Irene Manning was so impressed with his talent that she had him audition for Jack Warner. Because Lanza then weighed over 250 pounds, the Warner Bros. chief dismissed his screen potential. Later, Lanza sang at a party hosted by Frank Sinatra and found himself an agent (Art Rush) who got him a RCA Victor recording contract. By early 1945, Lanza had been discharged from the service, and, by that April, he had married Betty Hicks, the sister of an Army friend. (They would have four children: Colleen, Ellisa, Damon and Marc.)

In 1947 Lanza gave a sensational concert at the Hollywood Bowl. After enjoying the performance, MGM head, Louis B. Mayer, signed Lanza to a seven-year movie contract starting at $750 a week. His screen debut was in *That Midnight Kiss* (1949), followed by *The Toast of New Orleans* (1950), both opposite Kathryn Grayson. Inflated with the progress of his career so far, ego-inflated Mario insisted that his next vehicle must be based on the life of the legendary Caruso. And so it was. *The Great Caruso* (1951) grossed $4.5 million at the box-office. However, by now, Lanza was becoming increasing temperamental and so crude at times that actresses shuddered at the thought of working with him.

The studio announced that Lanza would next star in the Sigmund Romberg operetta, *The Student Prince* (1954). However, after pre-recording his songs, Mario got into a dispute with the studio and left the film. MGM sued him and when a new regime came onto the lot, a compromise was reached. Filming began, but more bad words were exchanged and Lanza again left the project. Eventually, Mario (who by now had become grossly overweight), agreed to permit his singing voice to be used, while handsome, thin Edmund Purdon mouthed the words as the on-screen lead. Lanza's studio contract was ended and the hot-tempered star pounted, "I rebelled because of my sincerity to the public and my career."

In October 1954, Mario made his dramatic debut on TV in "*Lend an Ear*." Because of his crash dieting (usually just grapefruit and booze), his voice had grown weak, and it was decided to dub him using his own recordings. When word of this circulated in the industry, Lanza lost out on the starring role in *The Vagabond King* (1956) and suffered the humility of being replaced by Oreste, a relative unknown. Mario's career was not helped when he suddenly cancelled a Las Vegas club engagement in the mid-Fifties because his habit of mixing champagne and tranquilizers had gotten the better of him.

Needing fresh cash to support his luxuriant lifestyle, the "reformed" Lanza convinced Warner Bros. to hire him at $150,000 a picture. After the moderately successful *Serenade* (1956), the studio decided it could do without the troublesome Lanza and cancelled the remaining pictures. Mario went on concert tours, but they weren't sufficient to support his family and himself.

If the Hollywood studios had washed their hands of him, Lanza's name was still magic in Europe, and he signed a two-picture deal with an Italian company. Buoyed by the turn-of-events, Mario grandiosely rented a luxurious Rome villa, reasoning, "I'm a movie star and I think I should live like one." *Seven Hills of Rome* (1958) had gorgeous, colorful scenery plus Mario singing "Come Prima" and "Arriverderci Roma." Incongruously, that—and his next picture (*For the First Time*, 1959)— were released by Mario's old studio, MGM, which had a distribution deal with the Italian company.

The peaks and valleys of his flamboyant career and indulgent personal life had taught Mario little. He was convinced he could continue his eating/drinking binges and then compensate by going on crash diets, aided by food depressant drugs. However, the cumulative strain on his heart was getting serious. About this time, he met exiled gangster Lucky Luciano who "suggested" that Mario sing at an upcoming charity gala in Naples. When Lanza failed to attend a scheduled rehearsal, two thugs visited him to convince him not to back out. Determined not to perform, Mario checked into a Rome clinic, ostensibly for a new weight-loss regimen. Doctors there insisted his heart had gone bad, while his wife was informed that he was suffering from the combined effects of pneumonia and phlebitis. When Lanza's driver came to visit, he found the singer comatose and an empty intravenous tube pumping air into his veins. On October 7, 1959, Lanza died. The official cause was listed as

a heart attack, but no one was certain (or saying) what was the true cause of death. Lanza was only thirty-eight years old.

On March 11, 1960, Betty Lanza, who had been in a constant depression since Lanza's death, died of asphyxiation, brought on by a regimen of alcohol and pills. She was buried at Los Angeles' Holy Cross Cemetery together with Mario, whose body had previously rested at Calvary Cemetery.

After their parents deaths, the four Lanza children were temporarily cared for by Kathryn Grayson, and then were made wards of Lanza's parents. However, they were actually raised by Lanza's personal manager Terry Robinson. Lanza's daughter Colleen was the only offspring to become a singer. The Lanzas' last-born child, Marc, died in Los Angeles on June 27, 1991 at the age of thirty-seven. The cause of death was not disclosed.

Bruce Lee

[Li Yuen Kam]

November 27, 1940 - July 20, 1973

To master the art of kung fu requires tremendous dedication, concentration and discipline. Handsome Bruce Lee (promoted as the Oriental Clint Eastwood) displayed all these qualities in his meteoric TV and movie career. His international success was cut short by his sudden death. However, as with other twentieth century icons (Elvis Presley, Marilyn Monroe), the cloudy circumstances of Bruce's passing only fueled his mystique. A hero in his lifetime, the magnetic martial arts expert became a legend in death.

He was born Li Yuen Kam in San Francisco in 1940, the fourth child of

Eurasians parents: Li Hoi-chuen and his Shanghai-born wife. The father was a veteran of the Cantonese (vaudeville) Opera and was touring the West Coast as a singer and comic. When the boy—soon nicknamed Li Siu-lung (Little Dragon)—was three, the family returned to Hong

BRUCE LEE

Kong. Having already made his movie debut in the San Francisco-shot *Golden Gate Girl* (1941), Li Siu-lung made a series of feature films in Hong Kong, usually cast as a short-fused, scowling ruffian. Off screen, the actor had a reputation as a tough young man always in search of a street fight. Later, while attending the Saint Francis Xavier College, he studied martial arts. The peace of mind he found within the discipline helped to end his years as a troublemaking punk.

In 1958, the slight but muscular young man returned alone to San Francisco. Later, he attended the Edison Vocational School in Seattle and then Washington University where he met his wife-to-be, medical student Linda Emery. To support himself, he taught kung fu and then opened his own martial arts academy. Hoping to break into films in Hollywood, he competed in marital arts tournaments. He was spotted at a Long Beach, California competition which led to his being cast in the action TV series, "*The Green Hornet*" (1966-67). Now known professionally as Bruce Lee, he played Kato, the faithful manservant who employed martial art and nanchukkas (fighting sticks) to subdue villains.

When "*The Green Hornet*" was cancelled, Bruce opened another kung fu school, where his celebrity clients included James Coburn, James Garner, Kareem Abdul-Jabbar, Lee Marvin and Steve McQueen. It was Garner who got him a small role in *Marlowe* (1969). Another "student," scripter Sterling Silliphant wrote Lee into a new TV show, "*Longstreet*" (1971-72), starring James Franciscus. Bruce campaigned for the role of Kwai Chang Caine in the TV series "*Kung Fu*" (1972- 75), but it was an Occidental actor (David Carradine) who won the part. Bent on proving himself to be a box-office commodity, Bruce accepted the offer of Hong Kong filmmaker Raymond Chow to star in the low-budget *The Big Boss* (1971). The slam-bang action picture did very well in its U.S. release. Always eager to improve himself physically, Lee studied other forms of self-defense which he used in his future films. With the increased worldwide profits of each new Lee picture, Warner Bros. signed Bruce (billed as "the fastest fist in the east") to star in the American-produced *Enter the*

Dragon (1973), with John Saxon and Jim Kelly. Years earlier Lee had said, "Hollywood is like a magic kingdom. It's beyond everyone's reach." Now, with his fourth- starring adult role, he was fulfilling his dream. Enter the Dragon was a huge box-office success everywhere.

By now Bruce and his wife Linda, and their two children (Brandon— who would become an actor—and Shannon) were living in a plush Hong Kong mansion. Lee went to India with James Coburn and Stirling Silliphant to work on the concept of an upcoming film, *Silent Flute* (which eventually would be made in 1979 as *Circle of Iron*, with David Carradine). Back in Hong Kong, in May 1973, he collapsed on the set of *Game of Death*. Physicians determined that he had suffered a mild seizure as the result of a epileptic-like disorder. Several weeks later, on July 20, 1973, while at the apartment of actress Betty Ting Pei with producer Raymond Chow, Bruce experienced a severe headache. The Taiwanese actress offered Bruce a prescribed pain killer (Equagesic) containing aspirin and meprobanate. He took it, then lay down to rest. Chow left. Later, Betty tried to awaken Lee and when she couldn't, she phoned Chow. He rushed back and, in turn, summoned a doctor. Bruce was rushed to Queen Elizabeth Hospital where he died that night. He was only 32 years old.

It seemed incongruous that the world's fittest man had "just" died. Some sources insisted that Lee's strict "health diet" (including eggs, raw beef, beef blood) had finally shocked his system. Other rumors exploded when initial newspaper accounts of Bruce's last day (in which it was claimed he was found at home nearly comatose by his wife) were discovered to be a cover-up. An au-topsy revealed that for some unknown reason, Lee's brain had swollen abnormally, although a brain hemorrhage was ruled out. When traces of cannabis were detected in his stomach, the media began crying about drug abuse. Some insisted that he had been poisoned (with a nontraceable drug) or had been the victim of "the vibrating hand" death touch. The murder theory was based on the rationale that Bruce had angered martial arts lords by revealing too many trade secrets of the ancient fighting arts in his pictures.

Meanwhile, on July 25, 1973, Bruce was given a royal funeral in Hong Kong with hysterical fans parading through the streets in the hopes of walking by his open coffin at the funeral parlor. Six days later, the body was flown to Seattle, where it was buried at the Lake View Cemetery. Pallbearers at the Washington funeral included James Coburn and Steve McQueen. At the service, Coburn said, "As a friend and teacher you brought my physical, spiritual, and psychological being together. Thank you and peace be with you."

When several empty parcels (with messages pointing to Betty Ting Pei as the holder of vital information) came to the attention of the Hong Kong police, they conducted an inquest, which began on September 3, 1973. The actress admitted the truth about Bruce being in her apartment on the fatal day. When she explained about giving him Equagesic, the coroner brought in a verdict of "death by misadventure," concluding that Lee had died from a strong reaction to ingredients in the medication which caused brain swelling. Despite the "evidence," many fans have refused to accept the final verdict as the truth and stick firmly to their wild speculations.

Bruce's untimely death only increased his box-office appeal and everyone seemed to jump on the financial bandwagon. His earlier movies were re-issued; TV appearances were re-edited into features; the merchandizing of memorabilia was enormous. Specious documentaries were produced on his life. Several imitation kung fu stars (including Bruce Li) suddenly appeared to star in rip-off kung fu entries, with promotional campaigns that insisted, "Bruce Lee Lives!" Lee's footage from the interrupted *Game of Death*—touted to be more than a 100 minutes—was used for the 1978 release of that name. However, in the revamped plotline, Bruce was only seen in a few minutes of fight footage, with obvious doubles padding out his long-delayed last "appearance."

Marilyn Monroe

[Norma Jean Mortensen Baker]
June 1, 1926 - August 5, 1962

Few twentieth century personalities have generated as much enthusiasm, analysis and worship as Marilyn Monroe. She was a vulnerable little lost girl who became a legendary screen star, blessed with a startling figure, a captivating walk and a whispery, childish voice. Her life was full of contradictions. She was a tremendous sex symbol who had grave misgivings about her sexual appeal and abilities, and far more wanted to be a mother than just another screen siren. Some of the sharpest commentary about this confusing blonde bombshell originated from fellow artists:

"There were two entirely unrelated sides to Marilyn. You would not be far out if you described her as schizoid; the two people that she was could hardly have been more different..she was so adorable, so witty, such incredible fun and more physically attractive than anyone I could have imagined, apart from herself on the screen."—Laurence Olivier

"For what you finally got on the screen she was worth every hour you had to wait for her. I wish she was around today. How often do you have a face like hers that lights up a screen?"—[director] Billy Wilder

"What she wanted most was not to judge but to win recognition from a sentimentally cruel profession, and from men blinded to her humanity by her perfect beauty. She was part queen, part waif, sometimes on her knees before her own body and sometimes despairing because of it."—[playwright and ex-husband] Arthur Miller

"I always felt insecure and in the way—but most of all I felt scared. I guess I wanted love more than anything else in the world."—Marilyn Monroe

Certainly a portion of Monroe's enduring fame stems from her sudden death at age thirty-six. At first, much of the public agreed with the official verdict that her death was most probably a suicide. It was simpler to accept that this love goddess was another victim of career and personal insecurities, and, thus, label her a casualty of her profession.

However, as years passed and the persistent probing into Marilyn's clouded passing refused to disappear, an increasing number of people have come to believe that her romantic relationship with Kennedy clan members—first with then Senator John F. and later with Attorney General Robert F. Kennedy—might well have played a far greater role than many ever suspected in her (accidental) "self- induced" death from a pill overdose. Many people who insist Marilyn Monroe was murdered, also insist that a conspiracy existed to cover- up the homicide.

She was born Norma Jean Baker in 1926 in Los Angeles, an illegitimate child. Her mother, Gladys Pearl Monroe Mortenson (who had two children by a previous marriage) was a 25-year-old film lab worker, who would spend most of her subsequent life in mental institutions. Norma Jean's unhappy childhood was played out in a succession of foster homes and orphanages. At the age of eight, in one of these temporary set-ups, she was raped. One of the side effects of her emotional scarring during childhood was her tendency to stutter.

In June, 1942, sixteen-year-old Norma Jean married 21-year-old James Dougherty, an aircraft factory worker, to escape being sent to yet another foster home. While Dougherty was serving in the Merchant Marines in World War II, she was employed in a San Fernando Valley defense plant and began posing for local photographers, typically in form-fitting sweaters. Further modeling work led to national (mostly girlie) magazine layouts, which, in turn, brought her to the attention of Twentieth Century-Fox. Outfitted with a new name, Marilyn Monroe, she was signed by the studio. This same year, she divorced Dougherty.

At Fox, Marilyn appeared in *Dangerous Years* (1947) before she was dropped, and, then, she made *Ladies of the Chorus* (1948) at Columbia. During this period, she dated vocal coach Fred Karger and, when he dropped her, she attempted suicide. Because of a good friend, John Hyde (her agent and boyfriend), she won small but showy screen roles *The Asphalt Jungle* (1950) and *All About Eve* (1950). Next, Hyde (already dy-

ing) engineered her return to Twentieth Century-Fox.

Monroe had a talent for promoting herself with the correct people. She soon had made a blase Fox studio interested in prompting her career, at a renegotiated $500 per week contract. Also, her 1949 nude calendar pose photo surfaced, giving her career a surprise boost. She proved to be more than a bust line with her dramatic work in *Don't Bother to Knock* (1952) and *Niagara* (1953). By *How to Marry a Millionaire* (1953), Marilyn was the queen of the Fox lot. However, on the set Monroe was a problem, addicted to temperament and tardiness. At this stage, she was controlled by her acting coach, Natasha Lytess.

In 1954, Marilyn married Joe Di-Maggio, the celebrated 38-year-old

MARILYN MONROE

baseball player. He hoped she would abandon her career to become a housewife, and he grew frustrated and jealous being Mr. Monroe. They soon divorced. Now single, Monroe resisted her studio and, despite a seven-year contract, departed for New York. Amid much public ridicule, the "dumb blonde" studied at the Actor's Studio, becoming a discipline of Lee Strasberg's method acting. Soon, Strasberg's wife, Paula, became her manipulative acting coach.

The "new" Marilyn debuted in *Bus Stop* (1956) to terrific reviews. Increasingly unmanageable, she rejected a rash of movie projects, despite a newly-revised Fox contract. Meanwhile, her dependency on pills and drink (especially Dom Perignon champagne) accelerated. In June 1956, Marilyn married much older, famous playwright Arthur Miller in White Plains, New York. It was a case of an intellect in love with a culture-hungry sex goddess. For her own production company, she traipsed to England to co-star with Laurence Olivier (!) in *The Prince and the Showgirl* (1958). The finished film proved to be a semi-dud. The next year, Monroe bounced back with the classic *Some Like It Hot*.

Unfortunately, her next picture was *Let's Make Love* (1960), where Monroe and French co-star, Yves Montand, exhibited far more chemistry off camera than on. The movie flopped. Miller had written and (re)written *The Misfits* (1961) as a vehicle for Marilyn. By now, the combined effects of pills, drink, emotional breakdowns, miscarriages, etc. had weighed the actress down. She looked and acted forlorn, much like her co-star Montgomery Clift (who would die of a drug overdose in 1966). The making of the arty *The Misfits* (which was a commercial disappointment) was a saga unto itself.

Not long after its completion, Clark Gable died in November 1960 of a heart attack, having suffered from Monroe's on-set artistic temperament and the rough desert location filming. In January 1961, Monroe and Miller divorced. A distraught Marilyn underwent psychiatric treatment at Manhattan's Payne Whitney clinic.

By 1962, Marilyn had settled into a modest one-story stucco ranch-style house at 12305 Fifth Helena Drive in Brentwood. It was the first place she ever owned. She lived there alone except for her housekeeper (Mrs. Eunice Murray) and her little white dog. Her closest friend at the time was said to be long-time pal Robert F. Slatzer, alleged to have been married secretly to her at one brief point in the Fifties.

Monroe was starting *Something's Got To Give* with Dean Martin at Fox. Although physically in peak form, emotionally it was the same sad story: she frequently was absent from the set, claiming illness. However, when she appeared in New York to sing "Happy Birthday" to President John F. Kennedy at Madison Square Garden, the studio was livid. They were appeased, however, when Marilyn returned to the lot and was more cooperative than usual.

On June 1, she celebrated her thirty-sixth birthday with an on- the-set party. However, by the following Thursday (June 7) she was fired from the picture for unprofessional antics. Fox filed a $750,000 law suit against her, but later, agreed quietly to have her complete the project, once co-star Dean Martin completed other commitments. Meanwhile, Marilyn was contemplating movie and stage (including Las Vegas) offers, as well as the possibility of a Playboy magazine layout. After a short visit to New York City and Mexico City, the actress returned home. (Supposedly in this period, she underwent an abortion.)

The very lonely Monroe spent her last days holed up at home. Her romance with the married Robert Kennedy had supposedly reached a stalemate. He refused to accept her phone calls. She remained persistent in her romantic demands, threatening to make public her romance with him.

On Saturday, August 4, 1962, Marilyn was home all day, her "only" guest Pat Newcomb, her publicist. (Later reports hinted that Robert Kennedy might have visited her during the afternoon.) About 5 p.m. her psychoanalyst, Dr. Ralph R. Greenson came for her therapy session. He suggested she go for a drive to relax. Instead, she remained at home, and retired to her bedroom around 8 p.m. taking the phone from the hall into the room with her.

She made several phone calls that evening. One was to Joe DiMaggio, Jr. in San Francisco to discuss his break-up with a recent girlfriend. She also talked with actor Peter Lawford, who, in past years, had introduced her to his brothers-in-laws, John F. and Robert Kennedy. That call "was" about 6 p.m. and its subject was to cancel a dinner invitation. Allegedly, she said to Lawford, "Peter, I don't think I'm going to make it tonight because I just don't feel well.... Will you say goodbye to Pat [Lawford's wife] and to Jack and to yourself, because you're a nice guy." Supposedly, Lawford became concerned about her "goodbye" message and wanted to rush over there, but was advised not to, because of the adverse publicity it could generate (being the President's brother-in-law) if something was amiss. Lawford later claimed he contacted Monroe's agent who, in turn, called Monroe's house. Mrs. Murray answered the 9:30 p.m.

call and said that the telephone cord was still in Marilyn's room and that she must be okay. (Because Monroe had difficulty sleeping—even with sleeping pills—she typically placed the phone outside her room, so once she went to bed for the night she would not be disturbed.) What other calls Monroe made this crucial night is unknown, because telephone records for her last evening mysteriously disappeared after being taken by authorities from the phone company office.

According to the "official" story of Marilyn's death, after midnight (later said to be 3:25 a.m.) on August 6, 1962, Mrs. Murray noticed a light shining from under Marilyn's bedroom door. When Marilyn didn't respond to her knocking, she went outside and peered through the closed French window doors. When she saw Monroe on her bed, looking "peculiar," she phoned Dr. Greenson. When he arrived, he broke a pane in the French window and opened the door. He, in turn, called her personal physician, Dr. Hyman Engelberg, who pronounced Monroe dead. Thereafter, about 4:20 p.m., the police were called. When Los Angeles Police Department Sergeant Jack Clemmons arrived, he found several people there, including the two doctors, Mrs. Murray, Mrs. Murray's son-in-law (Marilyn's gardener), Pat Newcomb and Inez Melson (the legal guardian of Marilyn's mother). In Clemmons's words, "it looked like a convention" and something "wasn't kosher."

Clemmons stated that he found the movie star lying naked—face down and cater-cornered—on her bed in the sparsely-furnished master bedroom with her outstretched arm apparently reaching for a nearby phone. An empty bottle of sleeping pills was found next to her bed, with ten to fourteen other bottles on the night stand, including one containing ten capsules of Choloral Hydrate. Her body was taken to Westwood Village Mortuary, while the house was sealed and placed under guard. Later, the corpse was transferred to the county morgue where Los Angeles County Deputy Medical examiner and pathologist, Dr Thomas T. Noguchi, conducted the high profile autopsy. (In his book, Coroner, 1983, he plead naivete in the case due to his youth and inexperience; at another time he indicated being pressured by his superiors into signing his questionable original autopsy report on Monroe's death.)

The investigation listed her death as the result of a lethal overdose of Nembutal and from Chloral Hydrate. It was determined a probable suicide. Joe DiMaggio, who, after their divorce, had stayed in touch, flew down from San Francisco to supervise the funeral arrangements. At the service, Lee Strasberg delivered the eulogy. Marilyn was buried at Westwood (Village) Memorial Park where, to this day, red roses are placed in a vase attached to the crypt (courtesy of DiMaggio).

In her will, Marilyn left a $100,000 trust fund for her mother (who was institutionalized at the time; she died at age eighty-three in March 1984.) Marilyn bequeathed another portion of a trust and a quarter of the residuary estate to her then psychotherapist, Dr. Marianne Kris. (Dr. Kris died in 1980, leaving her estate share to what became the Anna Freud Center for the Psychoanalytic Study and Treatment of Children in London). A large portion of Monroe's estate went to her acting mentor, Lee Strasberg. When he died in 1982, his estate portion passed to his widow, Anna. However, due to tax and other debts outstanding at the

time of her death, it was not until seven years after Monroe's passing that her estate was straightened out. Now, through proceeds from her films and the merchandizing of her image, the Monroe estate earns over $1 million annually, most of the proceeds going to Anna Strasberg.

A year after her death, Monroe's studio issued a documentary Marilyn (1963). It contained footage of her aborted final movie which Fox revamped into a Doris Day vehicle, Move, Over Darling (1963).

Increasingly, over the years, observers have wondered about the puzzling, contradictory case facts/speculations about her death: (1) indications that Marilyn's body had been moved from somewhere else and re-positioned on the bed; (2) the peculiar delay—ranging from a few minutes to four hours —before the two physicians on the scene summoned the police (the doctors claimed there was a brief lag time because of a discussion whether to first notify the police or a mortuary; (3) there was no drink glass near the dead actress, with which she could have washed down the 47-pills which "killed" her; (4) mortuary workers who transported Marilyn's corpse from her house that morning were surprised to be told that she had died only a few hours earlier, since advance rigor mortis had set in; (5) the autopsy revealed a high barbiturate level in her blood stream (as the result of ingesting forty to fifty pills), but peculiarly no test was made of her small intestine for traces of unabsorbed pills and no pill residue was found on internal organs or in the stomach; (6) Monroe usually swallowed pills with milk, but there were no milk traces in her stomach lining, (7) bruises on her left hip gave rise to the theory that she might have been injected with a lethal dosage (another conjecture was she had been given a fatal suppository or enema as Monroe took enemas as a way to diet); (8) post-mortem symptoms indicated that, for a period after death, she had been lying on her back, but the police found her lying flat on her stomach; (9) Monroe's diary disappeared after being taken to the coroner's office with other pertinent possessions; (10) Robert Kennedy, who claimed to have been in northern California with his family on the night of August 4 and the day of August 5, supposedly made a secret trip to Los Angeles on that Saturday and then flew back up north by helicopter, and, of course (11) the lack of any found suicide note by the victim.

Despite the wealth of contradictory facts and testimony recorded or covered up at the time of Marilyn Monroe's death, no charges were ever pressed in the matter. During the intervening years, many of the major knowledgeable parties have died (Peter Lawford; Los Angeles Police Department chief, William H. Parker; FBI chief, J. Edgar Hoover), been assassinated (John F. Kennedy, Robert F. Kennedy) and much evidence has simply vanished. In 1985, from pressure publicity of new books on Monroe and TV documentaries, the Los Angeles County grand jury was asked again to re-examine Marilyn's death. However, the jury's criminal justice committee recommended against reopening the still controversial case.

And so the myth continues.

Elvis Presley

January 8, 1935 - August 16, 1977

Even now, years after Elvis Presley's documented death, many fans refuse to accept that the "King" is gone.

The phenomenon of "Elvis sightings" is more cause for astonishment than ridicule. It is but one of many manifestations of global Elvis-mania, along with the enshrinement of his Graceland estate, continued high sales of his albums and movies, and mass merchandizing of Presley memorabilia. Obviously, the public deeply misses this beloved singer and no other twentieth century icon is so revered by so many.

He was born Elvis Aron Presley on January 8, 1935 in Tupelo, Mississippi, the son of a farm laborer, Vernon Elvis Presley, and his sewing machine operator wife, Gladys (Smith) Presley. A twin brother died at birth. From an early age, the extremely polite boy was more drawn to singing than school studies and began vocalizing at church (the Assembly of God camp meetings which his family attended). For his twelfth birthday, he wanted a bicycle. However, his doting mother couldn't afford one, but did manage to buy him a $12.95 guitar. He taught himself to play it and soon became fascinated with the blues and country music he heard on the radio. By 1948, the family had moved to Memphis, Tennessee, where Vernon worked at a paint factory and Elvis went to Humes High School. After graduation, Elvis had a variety of jobs, including ones as factory worker and truck driver (at $35 a week). At one time, he thought of becoming an electrician.

In mid-1953, Elvis paid $4 to record two songs for his mother at the Memphis Recording Service, one of the stops on his truck route. One of the Service's employees took a shine to the handsome, shy young man and mentioned his singing ability to her boss, Sam Phillips who also owned Sun Records. Phillips finally listened to Elvis and was impressed by his in-

ELVIS PRESLEY

novative mix of black blues and white hillbilly sounds. He recorded Elvis whose first songs were popular with teenagers, if not with shocked disc jockeys. Presley gave up truck driving, focusing on personal appearances as well as performing on radio shows like *"Grand Ole Opry."* Before long, Colonel Tom Parker—an expert showman and career organizer—began managing the gyrating young Presley, and soon negotiated a RCA recording contract for him. Elvis's first new single, "Heartbreak Hotel," was an instant hit, leading to Presley's TV debut (on Tommy and Jimmy Dorsey's *"Stage Show"*) and Las Vegas club appearances. It would later be suggested that during this early period Elvis first became addicted to drugs, especially amphetamines and Benzedrine, to give him energy boosts.

Love Me Tender (1956) was Elvis's first movie and teenagers flocked to see "Elvis the Pelvis." By the time of *King Creole* (1958), he was among the top ten box-office stars and earning $250,000 plus fifty percent of the movie's profits. With some of his earnings, he purchased Graceland, his soon-to-be extravagant Memphis mansion, whose driveways were lined with Presley's Cadillacs. Also by now, his many romances (including Natalie Wood) had added to his growing legend.

In the spring of 1958, Elvis was drafted into the U.S. Army and his salary dropped from over $100,000 a month to $78. He served most of his two years with an armored unit in West Germany. (During this period his mother died of a heart attack.) To celebrate his service release in 1960, Sergeant Elvis Presley returned to Hollywood for *G.I. Blues* (1960) and two of his new recordings (including "Are You Lonesome Tonight?") became gold records.

During the Sixties, Elvis's annual movie excursions developed a casual formula that made their simple plots and songs interchangeable. However, they continued to earn money, even as his first fans grew into middle-age and new singers (especially the Beatles and the British Invasion) vied for audience attention. Well-known for his extravagant lifestyle and assorted romances, Elvis finally married on May 1, 1967. (One source insists that Elvis, dreading the confines of matrimony, took an overdose of barbiturates shortly before the nuptial day.) He had first met 21-year-old Priscilla Beaulieu when he was based in West Germany, and she was the teen-aged daughter of an U.S Army major stationed in Frankfurt. Their high-profile Las Vegas marriage did nothing to diminish his popularity. On February 1, 1968, their daughter Lisa Marie was born.

By the late 1960s, Elvis's career was dragging badly and his movies' budgets were cut to keep the profits up, which, in turn, only reduced audience interest. A comeback TV special ("*Singer Presents Elvis*") in December 1968 re-sparked his professional as did his return to performing in Las Vegas (in the summer of 1969) and Lake Tahoe. By 1970, he had stopped making feature films (except for career documentaries) and begun a heavy concert tour schedule. Back in touch with his public, his album sales increased and he had several more gold records. In October 1973, he and Priscilla divorced. She explained later, "I realized I couldn't give him the kind of adulation he got from his fans, and he needed that adulation desperately. Without it he was nothing."

By the mid-1970s, the sagging Elvis had changed considerably from the slim man of two decades ago. His indulgent, excessive lifestyle and tantrums were legendary, as was the "Memphis Mafia"— his coterie of bodyguards and helpers who had constantly surrounded him since 1960. Elvis had an array of health problems and his increased dependency on prescribed medications was enough to kill most normal human beings. Frequently after his near-overdosing on drugs, he would attempt to kick the habit, but always failed. By now, he weighed nearly 250 pounds and was dying his gray hair black. Nevertheless, his devout fans remained supportive: a one-night engagement in Detroit in late 1975 earned him $816,000. At one point, Presley was considered as co-star to Barbra Streisand in *A Star Is Born* (1976), but Kris Kristofferson got the assignment. Several associates in this period reported Presley's fascination with death, and

his ambigious remarks about not having much longer to live.

In 1977, one live-in girlfriend (Linda Thompson—a former Miss Tennessee) had departed and another (23-year-old Ginger Alden) had become her replacement. At the end of June he returned to Graceland after a midwestern tour, during which a network special was taped of his concertizing. His young daughter Lisa Marie had flown out from Los Angeles for a lengthy stay at Graceland.

On Monday, August 15, Presley was in residence at Graceland preparing to leave the next day for Portland, Maine for another tour. (Colonel Parker was already in Maine organizing the opening show.) As was typical due to his performing schedule, his days were the reverse of most people: sleeping in the days, up at night. More recently, he had become more reclusive and sedentary, especially in his drug- induced stupors.

At 4 p.m. that Monday, he awoke and had breakfast, later playing with his daughter as she raced about the ground in her blue electric cart. (She was to return the next day to California and her mother, Priscilla.) Original plans for the evening included renting the local movie theatre for a special showing of *MacArthur*, but that fell through. About 10:30 p.m., Presley, with his retinue in tow, visited his dentist so the star could have two cavities filled.

The group returned home about 2:00 a.m. on Tuesday, August 16. Around 4:00 a.m., Elvis summoned a few associates to join he and Ginger for racquetball at the estate's indoor court. About 6 a.m., Presley retired with Ginger. She soon fell asleep. Meanwhile, Elvis took another volley of pills to help him get to sleep. About 9:00 a.m., clad in his gold pa-

197

jamas, he grabbed a book about psychic energy (some insists it was a raunchy astrology study) to read in his extravagant bathroom on his cushiony chair "throne." Around 2:00 p.m., Ginger awoke and, after searching for Elvis, found him lying in a fetal position on the bathroom floor. It was later estimated that during the final seizure he had thrown the book in a spasm and then lurched forward a few steps before collapsing some four feet from the toilet. In the process he bit down on his tongue.

All attempts by Ginger, Vernon Presley, the bodyguards, etc. to revive Elvis—including mouth-to-mouth resuscitation—proved useless. An ambulance was summoned and arrived at 2:33 p.m. The paramedics, after putting a life-support mask on the singer's face, examined the prostrate Presley for vital signs. None were apparent, but they prepared to take him to the hospital. Just as the vehicle was about to leave Graceland's gates, Dr. George Nichopolous, Elvis's personal physician, arrived and jumped into the ambulance. En route, the doctor massaged Presley's heart, all the while yelling, "Breathe, Presley! Come on! Breathe for me!" The ambulance reached Memphis' Baptist Memorial Hospital at 2:56 p.m. There the medical trauma team worked on Elvis, attempting to revive him. (After performing a thoractomy to perform open-heart massage, they forced breathing tubes down his throat, in the process having to knock out his front teeth.) The emergency efforts failed to revive the patient. At 3:30 p.m., Dr. Nichopolous pronounces him dead.

The autopsy initially "suggested" that Elvis had died of an erratic heartbeat and it was hurriedly announced to the press that Elvis suf-

fered "cardiac arrhythmia due to undetermined causes." (This is what those close to Presley wanted the public to believe. As part of the "cover-up," by the time the Medical Examiner could examine Elvis's bedroom and bathroom at Graceland to reconstruct events leading up to his death, the rooms had been cleaned up and rearranged to a degree.) Later, more complete tests revealed there were at least ten drugs in his blood, including Quaaludes, codeine and morphine. Some time later, Dr. Nichopolous was tried, but acquitted of illegally prescribing drugs to the star. (On August 15, he had written eight prescriptions for Presley including two for Dilaudid, a strong narcotic. In the last seven months of Elvis's life, the doctor had prescribed nearly 5,000 pills; an estimated 19,000 in the last two-and-a-half years). Later theories about Presley's death would conclude that (1) Elvis had committed suicide, or (2) that he was murdered or (3), the most wish-fulfilling of all, that he was not dead, but merely in hiding.

There was worldwide mourning in the wake of Elvis's death. President Jimmy Carter stated that Elvis's "death deprives our country of a part of itself. His music and his personality changed the face of American popular culture. His following was immense and he was a symbol to the people the world over of the vitality, rebelliousness and good humor of this country." Tennessee Governor Ray Blanton ordered all flags to fly at half mast at state buildings; the same was done at the county and city level. RCA Records shut down all of its offices to commemorate its leading star's death.

Thousands of fans as well as worldwide media representatives rushed to Memphis for his funeral on Thursday, August 18, prompting the National Guard to be called out to maintain order. As the mourners lined up in the heat waiting to parade through Graceland for a final view of Presley, two young women from Louisiana were killed when a car ran out of control into the crowd, one man suffered a heart attack and a woman went into labor. During the several hours of public viewing at Graceland, it was estimated that 100,000 passed by the open coffin where Elvis lay, wearing a white suit and tie and a blue shirt. Thousands others jammed up along Elvis Presley Boulevard where the hearse had brought Elvis back from the Memphis Funeral Home in his copper-lined, 900-pound coffin.

The service was conducted at 2:00 p.m. that Thursday in the music room at Graceland by Reverend C. W. Bradley, pastor of the local Whitehaven Church of Christ. Two quartets, the Stamps and the Statesmen, who had performed in concert with Presley, sang (including "How Great Thou Art"). Final remarks were offered by comedian Jackie Kahane and the eulogy was delivered by TV evangelist Reverend Rex Humbard. Among celebrity attendees were: Sammy Davis Jr., Ann-Margret and her husband Roger Smith, George Hamilton, Burt Reynolds and Caroline Kennedy (whose account of the event was later published in *Rolling Stone*).

After the service, his coffin, covered with hundreds of red rosebuds was transported by hearse in a fifty-car procession down Elvis Presley Boulevard to the Forest Hills Cemetery four miles away. The procession contained, as Presley had requested, sixteen white Cadillacs and one white hound dog. At the cemetery, his body was placed inside a white marble mausoleum in a six-crypt family chamber next to his mother. (Ironically, Elvis's mother had also been forty-two when she died, nineteen years and two days before her famous son.)

At the time of his death, Elvis was survived by his father, his grandmother (Minnie Mae Presley), and nine-year old Lisa Marie. His will, signed in March 1977, left the bulk of his multi-million dollar estate for the benefit of these three relatives, with Vernon appointed as estate trustee. In 1989, ten years after Vernon Presley's death, the estate was concluded with all property being held in trust for Elvis's daughter until she reached the age of twenty-five. (Also in 1989, Lisa Marie, married to musician Danny Keough, became a mother when she gave birth to daughter Danielle.)

Remarkably, after his death, Elvis's career continued on as if he were alive. Albums, movies, merchandising, impersonators, books, documentaries continued to trade on the Elvis legend. There was even a 1991 TV—*The Elvis Files*—which insisted that the singer didn't die at Graceland in 1977, but was alive and living in anonymity.

Obviously, for many, Elvis still lives.

George Reeves

[George Besselo]
April 6, 1914 - June 16, 1959

It is not just wishful thinking that many insist George Reeves— best known for playing TV's caped crusader "*Superman*" (1951-57)—did not commit suicide on June 16, 1959. The Beverly Hills police ruled that his death "indicated suicide." However, Reeves's mother insisted, "I had just spoken to him, he was in a splendid frame of mind." She could not accept that he had shot himself while in a drunken, depressed stupor. George's pal, Gig Young, protested, "He was a clean guy, in no way capable of bumping himself off." Alan Ladd contended, "he was never happier." (Ironically Young would commit suicide and Ladd's death from pills and alcohol was believed to be more suicidal than accidental.)

Decades later, Reeves's agent, Arthur Weissman argued that George Reeves's death was not suicide. According to Weissman, what mostly likely happened was that someone—most likely at the direction of Eddie Mannix or his wife Toni who had had a long affair with George—had replaced the blank in George's favorite gun with a real bullet, knowing that sooner or later he would play his usual exhibitionist game of Russian roulette.

The true facts in the case may never be known publicly.

Reeves was born George Bessolo in 1914 in Ashland, Kentucky (or Idaho). He was athletic as a youngster and as a strapping 6' 2" adult became a contender as a Golden Gloves boxer, but his possessive mother feared he would get injured. During junior college he had developed a liking for acting, which his overly-possessive mother fostered and led to them moving to Los Angeles. He took acting classes at Pasadena Playhouse, and eventually was spotted by a movie talent scout. He had several movie bits before he was launched in 1939's most prestige feature film, *Gone with the Wind*, playing one of the frisky Tarleton twins. In 1940 he married Eleanora Needles, another fledgling actor, whom he met while they were both at the Pasadena Playhouse. (They would divorce in 1949).

George's screen career, un-

fortunately, never really took off. He had small roles in several major features, and was cast in several Hopalong Cassidy Westerns in the early 1940s. His most impressive role was as Claudette Colbert's romantic interest in *So Proudly We Hail* (1943). He was in World War II service for a few years, but by the time he returned to the screen, he was on a downhill cycle. The best he could get was playing the lead in a serial (*Adventures of Sir Galahad*, 1949).

Reeves turned to TV work in the late 1940s. In 1951, he appeared in the low-budget *Superman and the Mole Men*, which served as the pilot for a forthcoming TV series. The first batch of 26 segments were shot that year but did not reach the air until 1952. They were an enormous hit with youngsters (and adults) and, between 1953-57, seventy-eight other episodes were filmed. The series made George a well-known personality worldwide, and he had occasional screen roles during this time.

Once the series went off the air, George continued with personal appearances as the invincible Superman. However, he was typecast by his TV work and frustrated by the stalemate it had created in his career. Then, things turned around professionally. At the time of his death, he was scheduled to start an Australian personal appearance tour worth $20,000. In addition, he was contracted to begin a new "Superman" TV series in 1960, and to participate in a televised exhibition boxing match with light heavyweight champion Archie Moore. He was very upbeat about his future.

At the time he died, Reeves was living in Los Angeles on Benedict Canyon in a home bought for him by Toni Mannix. She was the wife of Loew's, Inc. vice president, Eddie Mannix (a man with an unsavory past and sinister connections, who once had been #3 man at Louis B. Mayer's MGM studio). George and Toni had had an on-again off-again romance for nearly fifteen years. During the last months of his life, George had received many death threats on his (unlisted) phone. He reported the calls to local authorities, only to learn that both he and Toni were recipients of telephone threats. George had also been involved in several recent traffic mishaps, which in retrospect, could have been murder attempts.

By June 1959, Reeves was engaged to marry Lenore Lemmon, a New York show girl who had once been barred from several elite Manhattan clubs for causing trouble. On June 15, three days before he and Lenore were to marry, he and Lenore—along with house guest Robert Condon, a writer—were home celebrating the couple's future. About 12:30 a.m. on June 16, the three went to bed. Around 1 a.m., two pals (Carol Von Ronkel and William Bliss), in a partying mood, came by the house to partake in the usual drinking and merriment for which host Reeves was well-known. Lemmon admitted the noisy visitors, only to have Reeves stomp downstairs and argue with them for having shown up at such a late hour. Soon afterwards, the sulking Reeves went upstairs. In a joking mood, Lenore quipped, "He'll probably go up to his room and shoot himself!" A few minutes later, they heard a shot from Reeves's bedroom. When they reached the room upstairs, they found Reeves on his bed. He had shot himself in the head with his .30 caliber Luger pistol, but no suicide note was found.

The police investigation concluded that his death was an "indicated suicide," insisting that the confusing reports of the intoxicated house guests made it difficult to draw a cohesive picture of the events. Besides, they added, Reeves was known for playing with his Luger gun, simulating a game of Russian roulette. While speculation ran high about the "suicide" theory, no one who might have had the real answers was talking. Reeves—wearing his gray double-bresated suit he used as Clark Kent on "Superman"—was buried at Forest Lawn Memorial Parks in Glendale. When his will was probated, most of his $71,000 assets, including his house, was left not to his fiancee, but to Toni Mannix.

Mrs. Besselo, convinced that her son had been murdered, hired private detectives to investigate the case. They concluded that the death was not suicide, based on the position of the body (with the empty cartridge found under the corpse), the lack of powder burns on the victim's body, and from the angle of entry-exit of the bullet wound in Reeves's head. However, no official charges were ever brought against anyone. George's mother died in 1964.

After George's death, the production company that was to make the new "Superman" series wanted to piece together new episodes using outtakes from earlier Reeves footage and by employing a double. However, a very depressed Jack Larson (cub reporter Jimmy Olson of the original TV series) refused to make the new segments and the deal fell apart.

Years later, long after Eddie Mannix had died, Reeves's one-time agent, Arthur Weissman, called on Toni Mannix, by then a reclusive Beverly Hills widow. He recalls that during most of the visit she insisted that they watch re-runs of George's "Superman" series. A few years later she, in turn, died.

Romy Schneider

[Rosemarie Albach-Retty]

September 23, 1938 - May 29, 1982

As a teenage actress, she was known as the Shirley Temple of German movies. As an adult, she was a talented, beautiful star of the international cinema, making her Hollywood debut opposite Jack Lemmon in *Good Neighbor Sam* (1964). In the late 1970s, a series of catastrophes turned everything sour for Romy. When she died suddenly in 1982, the media initially concluded that she had killed herself. Later reports "insisted" that it was a heart attack which ended her life.

She was born in 1938 into a theatrical family. Her father was well-known Austrian actor Wolf Albach-Retty; her mother was Magda Schneider, the famous German singing star of many movies. At fourteen, Romy (a contractor of Rosemarie) made her screen debut in one of her mother's movies. She continued making pictures and throughout the Fifties was particularly popular in a series of saccharine movies featuring her as "Sissi" (Empress Elizabeth). She changed her screen image in 1962 by starring in a segment of Luchino Visconti's *Boccaccio '70* and in Orson Welles's *The Trial*. She played a whore in *The Victors* (1963) but showed a comic touch in *What's New Pussycat* (1965) with Peter O'Toole.

Romy married West German actor-director Harry Meyen-Haubenstock in 1966 and the next year their son, David, was born. Most of her filmmaking in the 1970s was done in France where she became a star with such pictures as *The Things of Life* (1970), *Cesar et Rosalie* (1971) and *Dirty Hands* (1974). For *The Most Important Thing: Love* (1974) she won France's equivalent to the Academy Award as Best Actress. By this time, Schneider was divorced from Haubenstock and she had married (in 1975) photographer Daniel Biasini. Their daughter Sarah was born in 1978.

In 1979, the misfortunes began. Soon after breaking up her marriage to Biasini, her first husband, Harry, committed suicide. Only a few weeks later, Romy underwent surgery for the removal of a kidney. In July 1981, her fourteen-year-old son died when he impaled himself accidentally on a wrought-iron fence. Romy went into deep despondency, particularly over the death of her boy. However, she continued making movies, finally making *La Passante Du Sans-Souci,* which had been postponed several times because of the various tragedies in her life. Based on Joseph Kessel's novel, the movie dealt with a mother grieving for her dead son. The picture was dedicated to her late son and his father.

By 1982, Romy had contracts to make three more new movies. However, on May 29, 1982, while *La Passante Du Sans-Souci* was enjoying a popular release, the 43-year-old actress was found dead in her Paris apartment. The Public Prosecutor's office reported that. "Apparently she suffered some kind of cardiac arrest." Other less official sources preferred the more dramatic theory that unable to cope with life's sadness, Romy had killed herself. (Initial news headlines detailed that the actress had died from an overdose of barbituates.)

On June 2, 1982, Romy was buried in the village of Boissy-Sans-Avoir (outside of Paris) where she had purchased a home and a cemetery plot recently. Among the three hundred people who attended the private service at a local fourteenth century church there were film directors Claude Berri and Roman Polanski, actors Jean-Claude Brialy and Michel Piccoli, and Monique Lang, the wife of the French culture minister.

Jean Seberg

November 13, 1938 - August 30, 1979

In 1974, writer, diplomat and occasional filmmaker, Romain Gary said of his ex-wife, Jean Seberg:

"To understand Jean, you have to understand the mid-West. She emerged from it intelligent, talented, beautiful but with the naivete of a child. She has the kind of goodwill that to me is infuriating—persistent, totally unrealistic idealism. It has made her totally defenseless. In the end it came between us."

On August 30, 1979, she was found dead in her car in a Paris suburb, an apparent suicide. On November 2, 1980 the despondent Romain Gary killed himself in his Paris apartment by shooting himself in the mouth with his Smith and Wesson .38 caliber gun. The source of this double tragedy can be traced back to 1956 when filmmaker Otto Preminger conducted a nationwide talent search for his upcoming *St. Joan* (1957) and cast Iowa-born Jean Seberg in the lead.

Jean Dorothy Seberg was born in Marshalltown, Iowa in 1938. She was one of five children—there were two brothers and two sisters — of pharmacist Edward and school teacher Dorothy (Benson) Seberg Jr. As an adolescent, seeing a Marlon Brando movie (*The Men*, 1950) convinced her that she wanted to be an actress. As a teenager, she did summer stock in Massachusetts and New Jersey and reluctantly attended the University of Iowa for a semester. She

was among the regional candidates tested by Otto Preminger for St. Joan. She won the coveted movie role which proved to be a nightmare. During production Preminger tormented her for the very qualities that made him hire Jean—her inexperience and naivete. When released, the drama was badly panned, with much criticism levelled at inept Seberg. Nevertheless, the sadistic Preminger used Jean for his next movie, *Bonjour Tristese* (1958).

While filmmaking in France, Jean met French attorney Francois Moreuil and they married in September 1957 in her hometown. The union lasted less than two years. However, it was Moreuil who introduced her to avant-garde moviemaker Jean-Luc Godard who, in turn, cast Jean in *Breathless* (1959) with Jean-Paul Belmondo. The New Wave picture was a hit and Jean with it. She moved back and forth during the 1960s between Hollywood and European film projects.

In 1963, 25-year-old Seberg married Romain Gary, who was twice her age. They already had a son, Alexandre born in July 1962. Now an international star, Seberg made one movie after another; one of her best was as the disturbed *Lilith* (1964) opposite Warren Beatty. In 1968, her 18-year-old brother David died in a car crash. *Airport* (1970) proved to be Seberg's last American-made feature.

Years later, Gary would say that the F.B.I. unfairly sought retaliation on Jean because of her financial donations and political support of assorted black liberal groups (such as the Black Panthers) during the 1960s. It was Gary's contention that the Federal Bureau planted Hollywood gossip column stories in 1970 that Jean, who was in the midst of divorcing Gary, was pregnant by a

Black Panther leader. In actuality, stated Romain, he was the father. Seberg became so distressed by the perpetuating "stories," that she attempted suicide with pills. This action on her part led to pre-mature labor and her Caucasian girl baby died two days after being born in August 1970. Both Gary and Seberg sued the various publications which had picked up the damaging rumor and received minimal damages for their legal efforts. Thereafter, according to Gary, each year on the anniversary of the baby's stillbirth, the perpetually depressed actress attempted suicide.

Seberg continued moviemaking throughout the early and mid-1970s, none of which added to her laurels (including her last, *The Wild Duck*, 1977). By then, she had developed a severe drinking problem which made her appear bloated at times. She married film director Dennis Berry in 1972, but they separated in 1978. The next year, she wed a young Algerian, Ahmed Hasni in Paris. However, because her divorce from Berry had never been official, the new marriage was not legal.

Less than two weeks before she died, Jean attempted suicide at a French train station by throwing herself on the tracks. Hasni, with whom she had been arguing, rescued her in time. According to Ahmed, he last saw Jean on August 30 when she left their Rue de Longchamps apartment naked under a blanket and carrying a bottle of barbituates. On September 8, her white Renault car was found on the street nearby to her apartment. Her decomposing, naked body was lying on the back seat of the car. The autopsy determined she died from a mixture of pills and alcohol and that she probably died the night she left her apartment. The distraught actress left a farewell note for her son, Alexandre:

Diego, my dear son, forgive me. I can't live any longer. I can't deal with a world that beats the weak, puts down the blacks and women, and massacres infants. Understand me, I know that you can, and you know that I love you. Be strong. Your mother who loves you. Jean

Jean was buried on September 14, 1979 at Montparnasse Cemetery in Paris. Her three ex-husbands and Ahmed Hasni were at the services, as was Jean-Paul Belmondo.

To his dying day a year later, Gary insisted that the facts surrounding Seberg's death suggested foul play. He cited as evidence that thee police later discovered a suitcase at her apartment containing her driver's license (reported stolen months before), money and her eyeglasses (which she needed for driving). He also noted that the liquor level in her bloodstream had been medically determined to be above the point where a person would fall into a coma. (Because no liquor bottles were found in her car, the police had ruled out the possibility that she started drinking after she parked the car). Years have passed and no satisfactory solution to the case has ever been reached.

Natalie Wood

[Natasha Nikolaevna Zacharenko Gurdin]

July 20, 1938 - November 29, 1981

When Natalie Wood died tragically in November 1981, it was a shocking coda to an erratic life. Highly emotional both on and off screen, Natalie had gone through periods of great professional popularity and then relative inactivity. Marrying the same man (actor Robert Wagner) twice was only one unique aspect of her highly-charged love life during her decades in the movie colony.

There were many complicated layers to Natalie Wood. Equally so, there were great ambiguities and contradictions concerning her sudden death—officially designated an "accidental" drowning. To this day, the case remains puzzling, further confused by the contradictory statements of the three individuals present on the night she died, especially by the later theories as to her death stated by the boat's captain, Dennis Davern. Since providing their statements to the police at the time of the tragedy, both Robert Wagner and Christopher Walken have remained silent about that fateful weekend.

Natalie's death marked the fourth disastrous end to a co-star of *Rebel without a Cause* (1955). James Dean died in a car crash in 1955, Nick Adams died from a drug overdose in 1968, and Sal Mineo was murdered in 1976.

She was born in San Francisco in 1938 to Russian immigrant parents, Nikolai and Maria Kuleff (Zacharenko), who changed their surname to Gurdin when he became an American citizen. Maria, had a daughter (Olga) by a previous marriage; there would be a third daughter, Lana, born in 1946. When Natalie was four, she and her mother were among extras used for *Happy Land* (1943), which filmed on location in northern California. Convinced her daughter had a potential screen career, Maria moved the household to Los Angeles and changed Natasha's name to Natalie Wood. Irving Pichel, who had directed *Happy Land*, remembered the expressive, bright youngster when he was casting *Tomorrow Is Forever* (1945) and he gave her a key role. By the time she was nine, Natalie was co-starred in *Miracle on 34th Street* (1947) and sometimes earned

$1,000 a week. For the rigidly controlled Natalie, it was not a happy period. "I spent practically all of my time in the company of adults. I was very withdrawn, very shy, I did what I was told and I tried not to disappoint anybody. I knew I had a duty to perform, and I was trained to follow orders."

One of Natalie's more terrifying (and prophetic) moviemaking moments occurred during the making of Bette Davis's *The Star* (1952) when the script called for her to dive into the water. The director told the frightened Natalie he would use a double. At the last minute, he changed his mind and instructed Wood to do the stunt. She went into hysterics. Thanks to Davis's intervention, a double was employed for the shot.

The ex-child star went through an awkward adolescence in the mid-Fifties. However, as the result of playing a mixed-up teenager in *Rebel without a Cause* (1955) opposite James Dean, she was Oscar- nominated as Best Supporting Actress. Suddenly, Natalie was a hot box-office property whose hectic romantic life ranged from dating Raymond Burr to Elvis Presley. Her studio tried to manufacture an on- and off-screen romance between she and Tab Hunter, her co-star of *The Burning Hills* (1956) and *The Girl He Left Behind* (1956). However, in "real" life, she had fallen in love with young leading man/playboy, Robert Wagner. They married in Arizona at the Scottsdale Methodist Church on December 28, 1957. Meanwhile, Natalie was shoved into big, if unsuccesful, movies such as *Marjorie Morningstar* (1958). She and her husband co-starred in *All the Fine Young Cannibals* (1961). By then, the couple's "dream" marriage had fallen apart. Their relationship was

THE HOLLYWOOD DEATH BOOK

not helped by her romance with Warren Beatty while the two of them were making a picture together. Natalie and Robert divorced in 1962. It began a period of several highly-chronicled romances for Wood.

In the early Sixties, Natalie blossomed into a major star. She was Oscar-nominated for both *Splendor in the Grass* (1961) and *Love with the Proper Stranger* (1962), and played the leads in two major musicals—*West Side Story* (1961) and *Gypsy* (1962). However, by the mid-Sixties, her career had slipped again and she made no movies between 1966-69. In May 1969, she married British scriptwriter/agent Richard Gregson and their daughter (Natasha) was born in September 1970. Her career rose—briefly—when she was one of the spouse-swapping characters in *Bob & Carol & Ted & Alice* (1969). Then she announced her retirement, insisting, "Let's face it, acting is not really important.... I know they're not going to send my latest movie up in a time capsule." In the summer of 1971, she and Gregson filed for divorce and, a year later, she and Robert Wagner re-married, aboard his yacht Rambling Rose, anchored off of Catalina Island. (Between marriages to Natalie, Wagner had also married again and had a child from that union.) Natalie and Robert had their own child, Courtney Brooke, in 1974.

From the mid-Seventies onward, her best acting was done on TV. She and Wagner co-starred in *The Affair* (1973), *Cat on a Hot Tin Roof* (1976) with Laurence Oliver, and she was a guest on the pilot (1979) of his popular series, "Hart to Hart." When questioned about her diminished screen career, she reasoned, "I am a woman, a wife, a mother, and a working actress, in that order." In 1980, she had the title role in *The Memory of Eve Ryker*, an oversized TV movie. In November 1981, Wood was co-starring in *Brainstorm* and was scheduled to make her stage debut in a Los Angeles production of *Anastasia* in February 1982, while Robert was launching into the third season of "Hart to Hart." However, when William Holden, the one-time intimate of his co-star, Stephanie Powers, died in a drunken fall on November 16, 1981, production on teleseries halted while Powers coped with the tragedy. Robert spent several days comforting his co-star, which did nothing to soothe the highly jealous Natalie.

On Thanksgiving day, November 26, 1981, the Wagners hosted an informal party. One of the guests was Christopher Walken, Natalie's co-star—and some insisted new romantic interest—in *Brainstorm*. (For some reason, Walken's wife had returned alone to her family in Connecticut.) Natalie invited Walken to spend Thanksgiving weekend with she and Wagner aboard their 55-foot cabin cruiser, *The Splendour*. On Friday, November 27, the three actors boarded the yacht at Marina del Rey, skippered by a one-man crew, Dennis Davern, and the quartet headed for Catalina Island. That evening, after anchoring, the four came ashore to Avalon in the yacht's dinghy, *The Valiant*. After dinner, because of rough waters, Wagner decided to move the yacht to a safer mooring. The others remained ashore at a local hotel. The next day, November 28, they returned to *The Splendour*, now anchored at Isthmus Cover. At about 4 p.m. they went ashore in the dinghy for dinner. They remained at the restaurant, drinking several bottles of wines. Reportedly, Natalie was both intoxicated and flirtatious (with Walken).

Once back on the yacht that night,

the skipper retired, while Natalie, Robert and Christopher continued—as one account has it—the festivities in the main cabin. About midnight, Natalie left to change clothes. A few minutes later, about 12:20 a.m., Davern made his last rounds and noted the dinghey, *The Valiant*, was gone. He assumed that Natalie must have taken the boat, as was her occasional custom, to view the evening stars. When she didn't return in the next several minutes, a concerned Wagner began a search for her in another boat. By 1:00 a.m., on November 29, Robert had requested the harbor patrol to scout for Natalie; and at 3:26 a.m., the Coast Guard was added to the search party. Helicopters joined in the task. At 7:44 a.m. her body—face down—was found floating beneath the water's surface some 200 yards from the isolated Blue Cavern Point. *The Valiant*, with four life jackets aboard, was 200 yards away. From the evidence, it appeared she had never gone aboard the small craft that night. Because of scratches on her hands and wrists, it was concluded she had attempted to cling to the cove rocks before drowning.

In the ensuing police investigation, it was decided that after changing clothes (at the time of her death, she was wearing a blue nightgown, knee-length socks and a red down jacket), Natalie had decided to go out on the ten-foot inflatable dinghy, perhaps to go to the hotel ashore. However, while untying it, she had fallen, struck her cheek in the process, and then fallen into the extremely cold water. She soon drowned, dragged down by her water-soaked jacket.

Controversial Los Angeles County coroner Thomas T. Noguchi was in charge of the much-publicized case and his investigation of the freak accident brought forth the speculation—refuted by some—that Wagner and Walken had argued that night and Natalie may or may not have attempted to leave the boat to get away from the two antagonistic men. As Noguchi wrote in *Coroner* (1983), "There's a lot of room left for further investigation...." There was one "witness" to Natalie's mishap. A Los Angeles businesswoman whose own boat was anchored 300 feet from *The Splendour* testified that around midnight, she heard a woman's voice—sounding quite sober—shouting for help. However, she soon heard another voice responding, "Take it easy. We'll be over to get you." Thereafter, silence, and she assumed the matter was resolved satisfactorily.

Natalie's gardenia-draped coffin was buried at Westwood (Village) Memorial Park on December 2, 1981. Her simple bronze marker plate reads "Natalie Wood Wagner." Among the celebrities attending her

NATALIE WOOD

funeral were: Fred Astaire, Rock Hudson, Laurence Olivier, Gregory Peck, Elizabeth Taylor, as well as Christopher Walken and Stephanie Powers. Three of Natalie's best friends—Hope Lange, Roddy McDowall and author/screenwriter Tommy Thompson—delivered eulogies. Father Stephen Fitzgerald (of the Russian Orthodox Church of the Holy Virgin Mary) officiated at the brief services. In her will, Natalie requested that Wagner be appointed guardian of her daughter Natasha (by Richard Gregson) so that the three girls could be brought up together. She left $15,000 to her stepsister, Olga Viripaeff; and all her clothing and furs to her sister, Lana Wood. Much of her jewelry and interests in works of arts, household furnishings, etc. were bequeathed to Wagner as well as a portion of her residual estate. The balance of the estate was to be held in trust for her parents and children.

After being shelved for several months, *Brainstorm* finally was completed, working around Natalie's unfinished scenes. When released in 1983, it was a sad anti-climax to her lengthy acting career. Ironically, in the face of what happened, a few years before her death, Natalie Wood was asked what she thought she would be like when she grew old, "I don't really think that far ahead."

Ross Alexander

July 27, 1907 - January 2, 1937

Tall and lanky Ross Alexander was born in Brooklyn, New York and began his stage career at age eighteen, appearing with Blanche Yurkain. Enter Madame. His first screen appearance was with Paramount Pictures in *The Wiser Sex* (1932). However, he gained his fame as a contract leading man at Warner Bros. He supported Dick Powell and Ruby Keeler in two musicals: *Flirtation Walk* (1934) and *Shipmates Forever* (1935). In the studio's all-star version of *A Midsummer Night's Dream* (1935) he played Demetrius.

Then life took a turn for the worse for soulful-looking Alexander. On December 6, 1935, four months after his marriage to stage actress, Aleta Freile, she shot herself in the yard of their home. Reportedly, she was unhappy by her failure to build her own screen career and by the fact that Ross was dating other women.

Although Alexander appeared in six programmers in 1936, the studio was no longer grooming him for stardom. In September of that year, Ross wed starlet Anne Nagel, with whom he had co-starred in three 1936 features, including *Here Comes Carter*. Exactly four months into this second marriage, he shot himself in his home near Hollywood. His despondency over Aleta's death was the "official" reason for his suicide. His final picture—ironically titled *Ready,Willing and Able*—was released several months after his passing. In this mediocre musical, he supported Ruby Keeler and Lee Dixon.

Pier Angeli

[Anna Maria Pierangeli]

June 19, 1932 - September 10, 1971

In the early 1950s, Sardinia-born Pier Angeli had a most promising show business future. After two Italian-made movies, she had been signed by Metro-Goldwyn-Mayer to play the sensitive Italian bride of a G.I. (John Ericson) in *Teresa* (1951). She and her twin-sister Marisa Luisa (who became screen actress Marisa Pavan) were brought to Hollywood. There 5', 100-pound, raven-haired Pier was proclaimed a Star of Tomorrow. While her film assignments were non-spectacular, she began dating (with much publicity) an array of notable Hollywood figures: Kirk Douglas, James Dean and Vic Damone. It was Damone, the Brooklyn-born Italian singer also under MGM contract, whom she wed in 1954. Their son Perry was born in 1955. The next year—during which she suffered a miscarriage—Pier enjoyed her best screen assignment, as the soulful wife of boxer Rocky Graziano (Paul Newman) in *Somebody Up There Likes Me* (1956).

By 1957, the combative Damones had separated. By the following year, Pier, who had never been comfortable with film stardom, made her final MGM film, Danny Kaye's *Merry Andrew* (1958). She and Damone were divorced in 1959, with the crooner blaming her domineering widowed mother for most of their problems.

The next several years were spent in court as Pier and Vic battled over custody of their son. In 1962, Pier, whose screen career had dimmed badly, married much-older Italian band leader Armando Travajoli. Soon after their son was born in 1963, the couple separated. The distraught Pier now admitted publicly, "I am still in love, deeply and eternally with Jimmy Dean." (Dean's business manager, Pier's mother, and MGM had strongly disapproved of the couple's relationship. Dean died in a car crash in 1955.)

R.I.P.

SUICIDES

By 1971, the near-manic Angeli, who had attempted suicide four times, was reportedly broke. Her sister Marisa (and her husband Jean Pierre Aumont) came to her rescue. The almost-forgotten Pier confessed, "It would be better if I was already dead. I can't go on anymore." In mid-year, she returned to Hollywood where Debbie Reynolds—her best friend from her studio years—tried to help Pier find work. Meanwhile, an Italian-made exploitation picture, *Addio Alexandra* (1971), which featured Pier in several semi-nude scenes, was about to be released in the U.S. over Angeli's objections. (When she had made the film, it had been agreed that such scenes would be deleted for any American release.)

On September 10, 1971, the 39-year-old Pier died from an overdose of barbituates in the Beverly Hills apartment she was sharing with drama coach Helena Correll. Unknown to the actress, she just had been approved for a guest-role on the TV series, "Bonanza." Debbie Reynolds offered to adopt Pier's younger son, then attending private school in London. However, Angeli's mother announced angrily, "The boy is mine." Pier's dreadful final movie, *Octaman*, a monster picture with Kerwin Matthews, was released after her death.

To the end, the volatile Pier had two great regrets: losing her beloved James Dean and not being given the screen roles she most coveted: *Lili* (1953—Leslie Caron played the carnival girl) and *Green Mansions* (1959—Audrey Hepburn was cast as Rima, the Bird Girl).

Pedro Armendariz

May 9, 1912 - June 18, 1963

Eccentric movie maker Howard Hughes's *The Conqueror* (1956) proved to be a bomb in many senses of the word. The costume "epic"—featuring John Wayne as Genghis Khan!—was a ludicrous period production filled with atrocious dialogue and was severely panned by critics. More devastatingly, it had been shot on location in St.George, Utah, close to the Nevada border. Nearby, the U.S. government was then conducting A-bomb testing, and one such blast (nicknamed "Dirty Harry"), which registered 32.4 kiloton, passed directly over the town, contaminating the whole locale. Since that time, nearly half of the 220 cast and crew of *The Conqueror* have developed some form of cancer. Among the more than 46 people from the movie who died from cancer were John Wayne, Susan Hayward, Agnes Moorehead and Dick Powell.

The Conqueror co-star Pedro Armendariz had become a major stage and film star in his native Mexico during the 1930s and 1940s. The swarthy, intense actor had come to Hollywood in the mid-1940s where he appeared in such John Ford-directed pictures as *The Fugitive* (1947). Failing to break out of his stereotype, the moustachiod Armendariz returned to his homeland, occasionally traveling to Europe or Hollywood for screen assignments. (He made several films with his pal John Wayne: *Fort Apache* (1948), *Three Godfathers* (1948), *The Conqueror*.)

In early 1963, he was diagnosed as having lymph cancer. His scenes as Karim Bey in the James Bond thriller, *From Russia with Love* (1964), were rushed to completion. That June he was admitted to UCLA Medical Center in Los Angeles with an advanced case of neck cancer. On June 18, 1963, he shot himself with a gun he had snuck into his room. He was survived by his wife, two daughters, and his actor son, Pedro Armendariz, Jr.

Don "Red" Barry

[Donald Barry de Acosta]

January 11, 1911 - July 17, 1980

For a compact actor, Don Barry packed a lot of living into his sixty-nine years.

Born in Houston Texas, he was a high school athlete and was selected for the Texas All-Stars in 1929, having already attended the Texas School of Mines. He migrated to Los Angeles where he worked for an ad agency. A fling at summer stock led him to an acting career, and he played a high school student in Cecil B. DeMille's movie, *This Day and Age* (1933). After touring in a road edition of Tobacco Road he returned to Hollywood and made his official movie debut in *Night Waitress* (1936). His breakthrough roles came in 1939 when he appeared in *Only Angels Have Wings* and played a fugitive in *Wyoming Outlaw*, one of Republic's The Three Mesquiteers series.

In 1940 Don was cast in the lead of *The Adventures of Red Ryder*. The serial and he were so popular that he starred in several more entries of the Western series. (Although Barry did not have red hair, playing the comic strip hero led to his professional nickname of "Red.") By 1942, Barry had his own Western series at Republic and in the next three years he was voted one of the top ten Western stars in the *Motion Picture Herald* annual poll.

Wanting more demanding assignments, in 1949 he joined Robert L. Lippert's budget releasing company where he frequently produced his own pictures. In 1951 Barry moved over to TV and it was not until three years later that he returned to filmmaking with the privately- financed *Jesse James' Women*, which was not successful. He continued in supporting roles in pictures, while joining the cast of the TV series "Sugarfoot" in the late 1950s. He played a police detective on television's "Surfside Six" (1960-61) and was Mr. Gallo on "Mr. Novak" (1963-64). He made three Westerns for Twentieth Century-Fox in 1965, one of which—*Convict Stage*—he also scripted. In 1970. Don announced his return to making low-budget Westerns and asked fans to send in "loans" to finance the project. (The film never happened.) Thereafter, he continued in supporting roles in film, on TV and in making guest appearances as Western film buff conventions.

The feisty, short-statured Barry was noted as one of Hollywood's principal ladies' men. Despite being married three times—including actress Peggy Stewart—he dated some of Hollywood's leading beauties, ranging from Joan Crawford to Linda Darnell and Ann Sheridan. In 1956, he made headlines when he and *I'll Cry Tomorrow* co-star Susan Hayward were caught together one early morning at his home by his then girlfriend, starlet Jill Jarmyn.

By 1980, Barry was separated from his latest wife, the mother of their two children. Late on the evening of July 17, 1980, the police were called to his North Hollywood, California home where he was having a domestic scuffle with his estranged wife. Thinking they had solved the situation, the police were returning to their squad car, when Barry rushed out of the house wielding a .38 caliber revolver. He shot himself in the head before the officers could stop

THE HOLLYWOOD DEATH BOOK

him. He was declared dead at ten p.m. that night at nearby Riverside Hospital. His final film, *Back Roads*, starring Sally Field, was released in March 1981.

Scotty Beckett

October 4, 1929 - May 10, 1968

Professional success can be difficult at any age; but it is really tough on child actors, especially when they cannot duplicate their professional popularity in adult years. Becoming a has-been at age fifty is bad enough; to do so in one's twenties is far worse.

Born in Oakland, California, Scotty and his parents moved to Los Angeles when he was three. He made his screen debut in *Gallant Lady* (1933) and, the next year, producer Hal Roach signed him to co-star in the *Our Gang* movie series. Undeniably cute, Beckett projected a wistful look in the series wearing his trademark oversized turtleneck sweater and askew baseball cap. He left the series in late 1935 to pursue more dramatic roles. In his film assignments, he often played the hero as a youth or the leading man's son: *Dante's Inferno* (1935), *Marie Antoinette* (1938), *Kings Row* (1941). He attended Los Angeles High School, did some stage work, played on radio in *"The Life of Riley"* and on screen was seen in *The Jolson Story* (1946), *A Date with Judy* (1948) and *Battleground* (1949).

Although he appeared on screen in *The Happy Years* (1950), his off camera life was far from that. In 1948 he was arrested for alleged drunk driving. The next year he married tennis star Beverly Baker, but their marriage fell apart in months. (A longer-lasting second marriage resulted in a son, Scott, Jr.) In 1954, he

was in the news again for carrying a concealed weapon, and then for passing a bad check. That same year he was cast as the sidekick of the syndicated TV series, *"Rocky Jones, Space Ranger"* although he was out of the cast before the series finished in 1955.

The final decade of Scotty's life was the chronicle of a desperate man involved with drugs, violence, arrests and divorce. In 1962, he slit his wrists, but recovered. He failed in his efforts to find a new career selling cars or real estate, or completing his school studies to become a doctor. On May 18, 1968, he admitted himself to a Hollywood rest home to receive treatment for a severe beating. Two days later he was dead. Although a bottle of barbituates and a farewell note were found nearby, the coroner refused to state a specific cause of death. Ironically, Scotty's last TV work had been on an episode of TV's *"The George Sanders Mystery Theatre"* entitled *"The Night I Died."*

Clara Blandick

June 4, 1880 - April 15, 1962

To film buffs, Clara Blandick will always remain the wise, kindly Auntie Em of Judy Garland's *The Wizard of Oz* (1939). However, in cinema history, she has earned another footnote—for committing suicide.

Born aboard a U.S. ship harbored in Hong Kong, she was reared in Boston. She made her acting debut there with E. H. Sothern in a stage production of *Richard Lovelace*. During the 1910s she made a few forays into silent films, including: *The Maid's Double* (1911) and The *Stolen Triumph* (1916). She much preferred playing ingenues on the stage.

When talkies came in, Clara returned to picture-making. She proved to be a very reliable character performer, useful for her stalwart, Midwestern looks. She was Aunt Polly in *Tom Sawyer* (1930) and *Huckleberry Finn* (1931) and played a score of practical women throughout the thirties. She beat out several other actresses for the plum role of Auntie Em in *The Wizard of Oz*, and continued into the next decade with roles in *One Foot in Heaven* (1941), *Gentleman Jim* (1942), *Frontier Gal* (1945), *Life with Father* (1947), *Mr. Soft Touch* (1949) and what proved to be her final film, *Love that Brute* (1950) with Paul Douglas.

By 1962, the 81-year-old Clara was suffering from failing eyesight and increasingly crippling arthritis. To avoid further agony she decided to end her life. On April 15, 1962, she had her hair done and then returned to her modest Hollywood hotel apartment. Garbed in her best dress and surrounded by memorabilia from her lengthy career, she took an overdose of sleeping pills. To ensure that she would die, she fastened a plastic bag over her head, and then lay down waiting for the end. She was survived by a niece.

John Bowers

December 25, 1899 - November 17, 1936

Although it was never officially conceded, it has been long accepted in the film industry that the suicide of Norman Maine (Fredric March) in *A Star Is Born* (1937) was based on the tragic end of actor John Bowers.

John was born in Garrett, Indiana and began in films in 1916 as a teenager. By the early 1920s he was an established if not famous leading man, playing opposite some of Hollywood's loveliest actresses in such films as *Roads of Destiny* (1921), *Lorna Doone* (1922) and *Divorce* (1923). He co-starred with gorgeous brunette Marguerite de la Motte in *Richard, the Lion-Hearted* (1923) and *What a Wife Learned* (1923) and they married in real life. Although he made seven features in 1927, Hollywood's transition to talkies nearly halted his career. In 1929, he had supporting roles in *Skin Deep* and *Say it with Songs* and in 1931 he was barely in the cast of *Mounted Fury*.

By 1932, he was a has-been and soon developed into an alcoholic. Now divorced, he ended his traumatic life in November 1936 by walking into the Pacific Ocean and deliberately drowning. His finish was said to have been witnessed by journalist/scripter Adela Rogers St. John, thus paving the way for its use in the plotline of *A Star Is Born* and the subsequent remakes in 1954 and 1976.

Charles Boyer

August 28, 1897 - August 26, 1978

As Pepe Le Moko in *Algiers* (1938), he never said "Come with me to ze Casbah." However, for years, female filmgoers would have followed him anywhere. Always the polished gentleman, his sizzling, sophisticated screen image as the "great lover" was based more on illusion than reality: he was not tall (5' 9"), he was somewhat bald (he always wore a toupee in his movies) and his stomach protruded. Despite his physical limitations, on camera, he was indelible as the Gallic lover with deep-set, brooding eyes and a most engaging French accent.

He was born in Figeac in southwest France, the son of a farm machinery dealer. He began acting in school

CHARLES BOYER

productions and would use his dad's granary as a theater to perform his own plays. He studied at the Sorbonne and the Paris Conservatory. He made his stage debut in Paris in *Les Jardins des Marcie* (1920), the same year he bowed in films in *L'Homme du Large*. Not considered particularly photogenic by French filmmakers, he accepted a contract from MGM to come to Hollywood to make French versions of English-language hits. (This was the era before dubbing was used.) In 1932, he made his first major film in English, playing opposite Claudette Colbert in *The Man from Yesterday*. After a small role in Jean Harlow's *Red-Headed Woman* (1932), he returned to France, thinking he had no Hollywood future.

After doing more plays and pictures

in his homeland, he was brought back to the States by Fox Films to be the "new Valentino." He soon gravitated to other studios, and, eventually, a new contract with producer Walter Wanger. Charles made a name for himself opposite Claudette Colbert as the intense physician in *Private Worlds* (1935). Afterwards, he alternated between making pictures in Europe and America. In Hollywood, he gained acclaim—and Oscar nominations—for *Conquest* (1937—opposite Greta Garbo), *Algiers* (1938—opposite Hedy Lamarr), and *Gaslight* (1944—opposite Ingrid Bergman). He won a special Oscar in 1942 for "his progressive cultural achievement in establishing the French Research Foundation in Los Angeles as a source of reference for the Hollywood motion picture industry."

In the latter 1940s, the free-lancing Boyer re-teamed with Ingrid Bergman for *Arch of Triumph* (1948), which flopped. He abandoned Hollywood to do a Broadway play, *Red Gloves* (1948). When he returned again to the screen, it was as a character star, playing a variety of nationalities and professions in *The Thirteenth Letter* (1951), etc. He joined with Dick Powell, David Niven and Ida Lupino to form TV's "Four Star Playhouse" in the early Fifties. Boyer received his fourth and final Oscar nomination for *Fanny* (1961). During this period, Charles returned to Broadway in *Kind Sir* (1953— with Mary Martin), *The Marriage-Go-Round* (1958—with Claudette Colbert) and *Lord Pengo* (1963).

Boyer made his London stage bow in *Man and Boy* (1964) and continued to accept character leads—often as the roue—in international co-productions such as *The Four Horsemen of the Apocalypse* (1961) and *How to Steal a Million* (1965). He returned to Hollywood for the gloomy musical version of *Lost Horizon* (1973), playing the high lama with great dignity. Back in Europe he was in *Stavisky* (1974) and supported Liza Minnelli in *A Matter of Time* (1976), his final picture.

Charles had married British-born actress Pat(ricia) Paterson on February 14, 1934 by eloping to Yuma, Arizona. They had an extremely happy marriage. Their son Michael Charles was born on December 10, 1943. At the age of twenty-one, in September 1965, Michael killed himself with a gun. It was a grief the parents could never overcome. In the late 1970s, the Boyers were living mostly in Europe. When Pat developed cancer, the couple relocated to a ranch in Paradise Valley (a suburb of Phoenix, Arizona), where she could undergo special medical treatment. She died on August 24, 1978 at the age of sixty- seven. Two days later, the distraught Boyer was found unconscious in his home, having taken an overdose of Seconal. He died at a Phoenix hospital that day. On what would have been his eighty-first birthday, he was buried at Holy Cross Cemetery in Culver City, California. His grave is next to his wife and that of their son, whose marker reads "Our Beloved Son, Michael Charles Boyer."

Capucine

[Germaine Lefebvre]

January 6, 1933 - March 17, 1990

For the longest time the most intriguing aspects of this chic, enigmatic French model-turned-actress were (1) was she really a transsexual as rumor long insisted (the answers appears to be no) and (2) how could her professional connections be that strong to overcome her wooden screen performances (obviously there is no accounting for the power of physical attraction). Then, at age fifty-seven, the tall, lanky Capucine added a fresh wrinkle to her strange career. She plunged to her death from her eighty-floor apartment in Lausanne, Switzerland.

She was born into a middle-class family in Toulon, France in 1933. As a teenager, she worked as a model in Parisian haute couture fashion houses before making her screen bow in Jacques Becker's *Les Rendez-Vous De Juillet* (1949), a study of postwar youth. She made a few additional French films. By age twenty she was married and, by the time producer Charles K. Feldman "discovered her," she was single. As a new face in Hollywood, the self-christened Capucine (pronounced Kap-u-Seen) was touted as the latest successor to Greta Garbo. She learned English and studied acting with Gregory Ratoff. She was cast as Princess Carolyne in *Song Without End* (1960) with Dirk Bogarde trying to be Franz Liszt. For many, this ponderous biography was a "film without end." A brave Capucine admitted that in the course of making this bore she had honed her new-found craft, adding, "As the scenes warmed up, so did I."

Thereafter, she jetted back and forth between making American and European films. Among her efforts were playing the love interest of a bordello madam (Barbara Stanwyck) in *A Walk on the Wild Side*. William Holden became absorbed with her and left his actress wife Brenda Marshall to be with his new love. Together they made *The Lion* (1962) and *The Seventh Dawn* (1964). Although eventually their romance ended and he returned to Marshall, Holden nevertheless left Capucine $50,000 in his will when he died in 1981.

By the mid-1960s, Capucine was acting mostly in Europe, cropping up in *Fellini's Satyricon* (1969). Blake Edwards, who had used her patrician image to satisfactory advantage in *The Pink Panther* (1963), brought her back to American screens in *Trail of the Pink Panther* (1982) and *Curse of the Pink Panther* (1984). Occasionally, she returned to the U.S. for TV work. In 1980, she was in an episode of Robert Wagner's *"Hart to Hart,"* a detective series which co-starred Stephanie Powers (William Holden's last major love). In 1985, she was among the parade of once-names who popped up in a segment of *"Murder, She Wrote."* Her final work was in 1989's *My First 40 Years*.

A few years before the end, Capucine sighed to a reporter, "I'm weary, always weary, these days. I'd like to work, but the enthusiasm is gone. But then, so are the opportunities." In the following months she grew more depressed. On March 17, 1990, she jumped from the window of her attic apartment. Her only known survivors were her three cats.

Dennis M. Crosby

July 13, 1934 - May 7, 1991

Lindsay Crosby

January 5, 1938 - December 12, 1989

During his lifetime, crooner-actor Bing Crosby was a major success in every entertainment medium he tackled, even winning an Academy Award for *Going My Way* (1944). On October 14, 1977, the 76-year old superstar had just completed eighteen holes of golf at the La Moraleja Golf Club in Madrid, Spain. He complimented his pals, "That was a great game of golf, fellers." Then he col-

lapsed and died of a heart attack. What a wonderful way to go, everyone thought. Two of his children were not so lucky.

Harry Lillis "Bing" Crosby and his actress-wife, Dixie Lee, married in 1930 and had four children: Gary (born in 1933), the twins, Dennis and Philip (born in 1934), and Lindsay (born in 1938). Dixie died of cancer on November 1, 1952. Five years later, Bing eloped to Las Vegas where, on October 24, 1957, he married much younger starlet Kathryn Grant. They would have three children: Harry, Jr. (born in 1958), Mary Frances (born in 1959) and Nathaniel (born in 1961). With his offspring by Kathy Grant, Crosby was loving, thoughtful and accessible. Such had not been the case with the four boys by Dixie Lee. Their family life was made vividly clear to the public when Gary wrote his revealing memoirs *Going My Own Way*. Some insisted Gary was bitter because Bing had tied up any inheritance to his first family until they reached the age of sixty-five.

Nevertheless, Dixie's children grew up under their father's shadow in a stern household where the hard-drinking Bing showed scant affection to his needy sons. As the years passed, the boys all tried show business, but only Gary succeeded to a small degree as a second banana in some 1950s and 1960s movies.

By 1989, Lindsay, Dixie's youngest, was fifty-one years old and had been twice divorced. He was then separated from his third wife, former Miss Alaska, Susan Marlin, by whom he had two of his four sons. Over the years, Lindsay had suffered nervous breakdowns, been arrested for drunken driving and battery, and was currently undergoing treatment for alcoholism. At the end of November, 1989, he had learned some additional bad news. The trust funds Dixie had established for her sons—mostly oil investments—had dried up. There would be no more monthly four figure checks. This was the final straw for manic depressive Lindsay. On December 12, 1989, he killed himself in the bedroom of his Calabasas, California home with a blast from a small caliber rifle.

Two years later, the horrible legacy repeated itself. Dennis, one of Bing's twin sons, shot himself in the head with a 12-gauge shotgun at the boarding house where he was staying at Novato in northern California. The 56-year old Dennis had always been shy about his show business efforts. He admitted once, "I guess I wasn't cut out to be an entertainer. I was always painfully self-conscious out there in the spotlight with my brothers." The quietest of Crosby's sons by Dixie, he too suffered from alcoholism, and had barely survived several failed business enterprises. Two weeks earlier, the second of his two broken marriages had ended in divorce. (He had five children). According to family friends, Dennis had never recovered from the death of his favorite brother, Lindsay. Dennis was cremated and his ashes strewn in the northern California Novato area. The family asked that in lieu of flowers, donations be made to TASK (Take a Stand for KIDS), an organization for abused children.

It appeared that only in death could some of Der Bingle's brood find peace at last.

Bella Darvi

[Bayla Wegier]

October 23, 1928 - September 11, 1971

She was born in Sosnowiec, Poland in 1928, but grew up in France. During World War II, she was imprisoned in a concentration camp. On one of his frequent safaris to Europe in the early 1950s searching for talent and fun, married movie mogul Darryl Zanuck met Bayla and became captivated with her exotic beauty. He escorted the young woman back to Hollywood where he gave her a studio contract at Twentieth Century-Fox. He christened her Bella Darvi, the new surname a combination of his and his wife's (Virginia) first names.

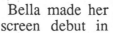

BELLA DARVI

Bella made her screen debut in *Hell and High Water* (1954), a spy story in wide screen but set in a claustrophobia-inducing submarine. Marlon Brando had walked off the set of *The Egyptian* (1954), but Bella was not so lucky. As the prostitute-temptress in this overripe costume epic, she received more notice for her outre outfits and colored wigs than for her acting. After *The Racers* (1955), Bella suffered the same fate as Zanuck's other European imports—i.e., when he tired of them and/or they failed at picture-making, he dropped them.

Darvi returned to Europe where she gamely found work in Continental films such as *Je Suis un Sentimental* (1955) and *Lipstick* (1965). She tried marriage to a French businessman, Alban Cavalade; but that failed. She attempted suicide several times in the 1960s, having also developed a strong liking for gambling, drink and drugs. By 1971, she was living in Monte Carlo. There, on September

11, 1971, she turned on the gas jets of her apartment stove and let nature take its course. Her corpse was not discovered for six days.

So much for being a Hollywood "star."

Peter Duel

[Peter Deuel]

February 24, 1940 - December 31, 1971

Whenever a celebrity, especially one in the prime of life and career, commits suicide, everyone becomes a Monday morning quarterback. Suddenly, a lot of people who knew the victim "well" insist there were telltale signs that should have been heeded. There were some warnings with handsome, six-foot Peter Duel who was riding high in a successful TV series when he placed a .38 caliber gun to his temple and killed himself.

He was born in Penfield, New York in 1940, the oldest of three children (Geoffrey was born in 1943 and Pamela in 1945) born to Dr. and Mrs. Ellsworth Deuel. Always creative, Peter had no interest in becoming a doctor and gravitated to the arts. He graduated from the American Theatre Wing in New York City in 1961 and toured in the national company of the comedy, *Take Her, She's Mine* with Tom Ewell. By 1964 he was in Hollywood and was an occasional guest on TV shows. By the fall of 1965 he was a series regular in Sally Field's sitcom *"Gidget,"* playing her brother-in-law. He did well in the job and was hired for his second series, *"Love on a Rooftop"* (1966-67). Although the show and Peter got good reviews, it was cancelled in the rating wars.

With a good professional track record, Peter signed a seven-year contract with Universal Pictures. As such, he appeared in studio series (*"The Virginian," "Ironside," "The Name of the Game"*) and began having roles in TV movies (*Marcus Welby, M.D.: A Matter of Humanity*, 1969) and feature films (*Cannon for Cordoba*, 1970) shot on the home lot. While making *Generation* (1969) on loan-out, he had a romance with co-star Kim Darby as well as officially changing his professional name to Peter Duel. Then he was signed for his third series, *Alias Smith and Jones*, about two congenial ex-outlaws (Duel, Ben Murphy) trying to go straight in the old West. The comedy-buddy show debuted in January 1971 to good notices. It returned that fall for a second season, with Sally Field now added to give the show additional appeal.

Everything was going well—or so it seemed. However, when one backtracks the picture was not so rosy. When Peter first arrived in Hollywood, he set a timetable for himself. He wanted to be making feature films full time within five years (that never really happened). A year before he died, he said, "After two or three interviews, talking about pictures and how they're made and what I do in them and what I'm going to do next, there's nothing more to say." He became very concerned about ecology and environmental pollution, reasoning, "there isn't much to smile about anymore." He had also become a concerned citizen, having traveled around the country in 1968 working for Senator Eugene McCarthy's presidential bid. Duel was in Chicago during the Democratic Convention that year and witnessed firsthand the nasty riots that occurred. More recently, Peter had signed with a celebrity speakers' bureau to speak out about his convictions.

Duel, a perfectionist performer, was not particularly happy about making "*Alias Smith and Jones*," but Universal offered him a salary increase and he accepted reluctantly. He told a reporter friend, "Contractually, I have to do this series—or some other trash." For serious-minded Duel, doing a weekly show was "a big fat drag to any actor with interest in his work. It's the ultimate trap." He also insisted that—thanks to the series—his private life had fallen apart and he was trying to "patch" it together.

By August 1971 the working pressures got to him and he collapsed on the set (due to a flu bug) and was sent home by ambulance. In November 1971, the activist actor lost his bid for a board seat at the Screen Actors Guild. Supposedly, he shot a bullet through the telegram bringing him the defeat notice. (Other friends say he immediately began planning for the next election). That December, he volunteered to work two weekends at out-of-state Toys for Tots telethons. (A photo taken of Peter at one of the charity events showed him holding a toy pistol to his head. It was a stunt he pulled occasionally while sitting in the make-up chair at the studio, holding his prop gun to his head and going "click, click, click.") Also in December 1971 he found himself in court dealing with a October 1970 traffic accident that injured two people. This being his third "driving while under the influence" charge, he lost his license.

On Thursday night, December 30, 1971, Peter planned to go with a friend to see the movie *A Clockwork Orange* after finishing work on the "*Alias Smith and Jones*" sound stage. However, he was called back to do some looping on the set. When his friends left, he said, "I'll see you tomorrow." Peter returned to his Holly-wood Hills home in time to watches his 8-9 p.m. show (the particular episode of "*Alias Smith and Jones*" dissatisfied him). Then he switched channels to a Lakers basketball game. During the evening, he drank heavily, leading to an argument with his girlfriend, Diana Ray. Later, she retired for the night, while Duel stayed up to watch more TV. About 12:30 a.m., the actor came into the bedroom and removed his revolver from a table drawer. Diana awakened. He said, "I'll see you later," and left the room. A few minutes went by and she heard a single shot. When she rushed into the living room, she found Peter dead, nude beneath the Christmas tree. The shot had entered Duel's right temple and exited the left side. It had then traveled through the front window of

PETER DUEL

uel's home, leaving a small hole. Police investigation revealed that a second spent shot in the gun chamber had been discharged a week or so earlier.

A memorial service was held in Los Angeles at the Hindu- Christian temple in the Santa Ynez Canyon near the Pacific Ocean. Peter was not a temple member, but his manager was. Duel's body was flown back to Penfield, New York where, after a service at the Baptist Church on January 5, 1972, Peter was buried in the Penfield Cemetery.

Wanting to keep "*Alias Smith and Jones*" going, Universal replaced Peter in his recurring role with actor Roger Davis, but the program folded in early 1973. Ironically, the acting work of which Peter was most proud—playing Squire Talbot in "*The Scarecrow*"—was telecast on "*Hollywood TV Theatre*" on January 10, 1972, several days after Peter's death.

Two decades after Peter's tragic end, people are still asking "Why?"

Peg Entwistle

[Lillian Millicent Entwistle]
1908 - September 18, 1932

No study of Hollywood heartbreak would be complete without mention of blonde, blue-eyed Peg Entwistle, who earned a permanent place in movie trivia the hard way. She was the ex-Broadway actress who became so depressed when screen success eluded her, that she jumped to her death from the five-story high "Hollywoodland" sign on Mt. Lee in Hollywood.

Born in London, England in 1908, Lillian Millicent (known as Peg) had come to the United States where, at age seventeen, she made her stage debut with a Boston repertory company. She proved a talented find and soon was working on Broadway in Theater Guild productions. She married actor Robert Keith in 1927, but they divorced in 1929. She was with Dorothy Gish in *Getting Married* (1931) and with Laurette Taylor in *Alice-Sit-By-the-Fire* (1932). However, the Depression hit the New York theater scene badly, so out-of-work Peg decided to try the movies.

She arrived in Los Angeles in April 1932 and moved in with her Uncle Harold. His home was at 2428 Beachwood Canyon Drive in Hollywood, not far from the "Hollywoodland" sign that been erected in 1923 to promote a new (unsuccessful) 500-acre real estate development. She found stage work with Billie Burke in *The Mad Hopes*. However, the play folded after a brief run. Dejected by this latest setback, Peg was elated when RKO optioned her for a picture role— although small—in a murder mystery, *Thirteen Women* (1932), starring Irene Dunne and Myrna Loy. By August that year the movie had been previewed. However, the reaction was so poor the studio held back release to re-cut the film which would not be released officially until after her death. Meanwhile, Entwistle's studio option was dropped, leaving her extremely despondent.

Her uncle later recalled that Peg tried desperately to raise the train fare to return to Broadway, but could not get a loan. On September 18, 1932, after dinner, wearing a dress that stage actress Effie Shannon had lent her, she left the Beachwood Canyon house. She told her relative that she was going to the local Hollywoodland drugstore. Instead, she walked up the nearby road that led to the big electric-light sign. Reaching the towering letters, she stopped by

220

the "H." She removed her jacket and placed it next to her purse. Then, she slowly maneuvered up the electrician's ladder on the 50- foot high "H." Part way up, one of her shoes fell off. Finally reaching the top, she jumped off. Several days later, a hiker came across her mangled corpse. A note was found inside Peg's purse, which read: "I am afraid I am a coward. I am sorry for everything. If I had done this a long time ago, it would have saved a lot of pain. P.E."

At first, authorities could not identify the body. When news of the suicide by "P. E." made the headlines, Harold Entwistle— distraught about the vanished Peg—read the account and hastened to the morgue. After identifying the victim as Peg, he told the press, "Although she never confided her grief to me, I was somehow aware that she was suffering intense mental anguish.... It is a great shock to me that she gave up the fight as she did."

In death, Peg finally gained the fame she had craved so much when alive.

Jon Hall

[Charles Hall Locher]

February 23, 1913 - December 13, 1979

Over the decades, Hollywood and the public has always been fond of screen love teams, such as: Janet Gaynor/Charles Farrell, Ginger Rogers/Fred Astaire, Jeanette MacDonald/Nelson Eddy, June Allyson/Van Johnson, etc. And then there was exotic Maria Montez and handsome Jon Hall. Together, these two stars sashayed through several wonderfully absurd and colorful movie romps, including *Arabian Nights* (1942), *Cobra Woman* (1944) and *Sudan* (1945). These escapist pictures were the pinnacle of both stars'

JON HALL

careers. Montez would die of a heart attack in her bath tub in 1951; Hall would die by his own hands in 1979.

Charles Hall Locher's father was Swiss-born skating champ- turned-character actor Felix Locher; his mother was Tahitian. Charles was born in Fresno, California in 1916 because his mother's train happened to be stopped there when she went into labor. He spent part of his childhood in Tahiti and then was educated in England and Switzerland. By 1935, Charles, now 6' 2", had appeared on stage and made his screen debut in Hollywood. Later, changing his name to Lloyd Crane, he performed in *Mind Your Own Business* (1936) and *The Girl from Scotland Yard* (1937). Samuel Goldwyn cast him in *The Hurricane* (1937), a spectacle which co-starred him as a Polynesian in love with Dorothy Lamour. A proficient swimmer, he did his own aquatic stunts in the picture. His new screen name, Jon Hall, came from the surname of a relative (Norman Hall) who had co-authored the novel on which the epic was based. He was promoted as "Goldwyn's Gift to Women."

Thereafter, he was off the screen for three years, returning in *Kit Carson* (1940). Once under contract to Universal in the early 1940s, he made his mark in six Technicolor fantasies opposite beguiling Maria Montez. Off camera he was married to vocalist-actress Frances Langford from 1939 to 1955. By the early Fifties, Hall's waist had thickened and he transferred his presence to TV in a highly popular adventure series "*Ramar of the Jungle*" (1952-54). Then he left acting and became involved in lucrative underwater photography equipment firms. Meanwhile, he married and divorced ex-actress Raquel Torres twice. Finally, he both directed and starred in his final film, *The Beach Girls and the Monster* (1965). Looking back on his movie career, he explained, "I never liked acting. I don't like to be told what to do and what to say and how to say it....as a profession, it's a bore."

For the last decade of his life, Hall was much out of the news. When Dino De Laurentiis produced an elaborate (but empty) remake of *The Hurricane* (1979), Jon was among the many celebrities persuaded to attend the Los Angeles premiere that spring. When interviewed, he looked extremely gaunt. Unknown to the general public, he was suffering from bladder cancer. On December 13, 1979, Hall's married sister returned to her North Hollywood home where Jon was staying. She found that Hall had shot himself in the head with a single bullet that morning (later estimated at 7 a.m.). He had been bed-ridden for several months, suffering from his terminal disease, and had tired of being a burden to others.

Rusty Hamer

February 15, 1947 - January 18, 1990

The relatively short, unhappy life of Russell Craig Hamer began in Tenafly, New Jersey where he was born in 1947. He was the third son of parents who were active in little theater. His father, a salesman with the Manhattan Shirt Company, was relocated to Los Angeles in 1951. Once there, Rusty began his acting career by being cast in a stage production of *On Borrowed Time*. At the same time, his parents took

him to an open audition call to play Danny Thomas's son in a new TV comedy series. Thomas was impressed with the boy and hired the youth from among 500 applicants. After seeing Rusty perform in the stage play, the comic visited the young actor backstage and told him, "I picked you because you were so cute. And now I find out you're a great little actor, too."

"*Make Room for Daddy*" (a.k.a. "*The Danny Thomas Show*") debuted in September 1953 and became a hit series, lasting through 1964. On the surface it appeared that Hamer had an ideal life. However, it was far from that. Rusty's father died when he was six, and, as a TV show co-star, he became the family's financial mainstay. His education was a mixture of on-the-set tutors and brief stays at a Roman Catholic School where the other children refused to accept him as a peer. Then, at age twenty-one, Rusty discovered that much of his trust fund, invested in stocks, had evaporated. Typecast by playing Rusty Williams on TV for so many years, he found it difficult to gain other acting work, especially as his weight fluctuated upward. In the late 1960s he married, but that marriage ended in divorce after a year.

In 1970, Danny Thomas, who labeled Rusty "the best boy actor I ever saw in my life" and had been his surrogate father, came to his professional rescue. He reassembled some of the original series cast for TV's "*Make Room for Grandaddy*" the storyline of which now had Hamer twenty-three and married. Unfortunately, that show lasted one season. Thereafter, Rusty never earned more than $10,000 a year, working in L.A. for a messenger service and other catch-can jobs.

Unable to cope in a town which had rejected him, the bitter and disillusioned Hamer moved to southwest Louisiana to DeRidder, a town forty miles north of Lake Charles. Sometimes, he worked at his brother John's restaurant, other times he worked off-shore for Exxon, occasionally seeking employment delivering newspapers. On January 18, 1990, John came to Rusty's trailer and found him dead. The ex-actor had shot himself in the head with a .357 caliber Magnum revolver. The brother told the press of Rusty, "He hasn't really been happy since his early 20s. But he didn't show any signs of this happening. It was just all of a sudden."

Carole Landis

[Frances Lillian Mary Ridste]

January 1, 1919 - July 5, 1948

Dearest Mommie: I'm sorry, really sorry to put you through this. But there is no way to avoid it. I love you darling. You have been the most wonderful Mom ever. Everything goes to you. Look in the files and there is a will which decrees everything. Good-bye, my angel. Pray for me. Your Baby.

Having written this touching farewell note, pretty 29-year old actress Carole Landis, who had tried suicide several times before, finally succeeded in ending her life with an overdose of sleeping pills.

She was born in Fairchild, Wisconsin to parents of Polish and Norwegian descent. She had an older brother and sister. Soon after her birth, her father abandoned the family, and Clara (Stentek) Ridste took her three youngsters to live in California. As a child, Frances was starstruck; Kay Francis was one of her favorite movie stars. Frances was fifteen and attending San Bernardino High School when she eloped with 19-year-old Irving Wheeler to Yuma, Arizona. After a few weeks, they separated and she went back to school. She and Wheeler reconciled later in the year, but, by 1935 the marriage had again fallen apart. She bused to San Francisco where rumor later had it that she lived a very fast life. Now known as Carole Landis, she worked first at the Royal Hawaiian Club and then sang with Carl Ravazza and His Orchestra at an exclusive Santa Cruz country club.

Anxious to break into movies, the very shapely Carole moved to Hollywood and was soon joined by both her mother and Wheeler. The ambitious actress was spotted in several 1937 features, including: *A Day at the Races* and *A Star Is Born*. She was featured far more prominently in the Busby Berkeley musical *Varsity Show* (1937). Thanks to choreographer-director Berkeley, she gained a Warner Bros. contract (at $50 per week) and did more bits in studio pictures. However, there were no headlines when Warners let her option lapse in 1938. But there were several items published a few weeks later when Irving Wheeler brought

action against Busby Berkeley for $250,000, claiming that the director had alienated Carole's affections from him. The suit was dismissed and Landis divorced Irving. After a failed pre-Broadway tour with Ken Murray in *Once Upon a Night*, she returned to picture-making in 1939.

It was pioneering film director D. W. Griffith who helped re- discover Carole for movies. He was engaged to help on *One Million B.C.* (1940) and chose her to be the prehistoric heroine. By the time filming had begun, she had had her nose reshaped surgically, become a blonde, and had gone on a severe diet. The film surprised everyone by being a hit and her new boss, producer Hal Roach, promoted Carole as "The Ping Girl." Also in 1940, Carole married again—this time to wealthy yacht broker, Willis Hunt, Jr. When they divorced that November, Carole commented, "We should have just remained good friends."

After a few more Roach pictures, half of Carole's contract was purchased by Twentieth Century-Fox. In both *Moon over Miami* (1941) and *I Wake Up Screaming* (1941) she received much attention as Betty Grable's sister. Thereafter, as Fox head Darryl F. Zanuck's infatuation with Landis ended, her studio status dropped and she was reduced to pictures like *Manilla Calling* (1942). In the fall of 1942, Carole joined with Kay Francis, Martha Raye and Mitzi Mayfair for a Hollywood Victory Committee tour to Northern Ireland and England. On January 5, 1943 she impulsively wed naval flier Captain Thomas Wallace. Returning to the States she co-starred with Francis, Raye and Mayfair in *Four Jills in a Jeep* (1944), a fictionalized version of their USO trek. On a further tour, Carole contracted malaria and dysentery. By the fall of 1944, she and

Wallace had separated and they divorced in Reno in mid-1945. Wallace said, "I've had enough of being the guy Carole Landis married."

In early 1945 Carole reached Broadway in the short-lived musical, *A Lady Says Yes*. Later that year, Carole married wealthy Broadway producer W. Horace Schmidlapp, whom she had met through a new actress friend of hers, Jacqueline Susann (the future best-selling author of *Valley of the Dolls*). Still under Fox contract, Carole made two deplorable minor films there in 1946 and was loaned to United Artists for *A Scandal in Paris* (1946). The next year, she met British actor Rex Harrison, then married (to actress Lilli Palmer) and under Fox contract. "Sexy Rexy" quickly became infatuated with the spunky American actress. Meanwhile, with no Hollywood work, Carole went to England for two pictures and to be with Harrison who was making a movie in his homeland.

He was back in Hollywood by early 1948 starring in the ironically titled *Unfaithfully Yours* (1948). He insisted to the press that he and Carole were "great friends and that is all." Landis returned to California in 1948 and started divorce proceedings against Schmidlapp. Meanwhile, Carole and Rex continued their steamy affair. On July 3, 1948, Harrison joined Carole for dinner at her new home in Pacific Palisades. Carole mentioned that she had severe financial problems, but he was too excited about returning to Broadway (*Anne of the Thousand Days*) to pay much attention. Rex left about 9 p.m. to visit actor Roland Culver and his wife. Later that evening, Landis phoned New York to speak with long-time friend Marguerite Haymes (the mother of crooner-actor Dick Haymes). By the time Marguerite returned home, it was too late at night to return the California call. Several other calls by Carole to friends went unheeded because of the July 4th holiday.

The next afternoon, Harrison phoned Carole's house and was told by the maid that there was no answer when she knocked on the bedroom door. The actor hastily went to her home where about 3 p.m. he found Landis dead on the bathroom floor. The actress was curled on her side, with her cheek resting on a jewel box. She had taken an overdose of Seconal. The autopsy revealed a high alcohol content in her bloodstream and that, just before she passed out, she had been trying to raise herself off the floor (perhaps in attempt to get help). That night, when a distraught Rex went to the Culvers to spend the night, they handed him a small suitcase which Carole must have left outside their home the prior night. It contained Rex's love letters to her.

Carole's funeral took place at Forest Lawn Memorial Parks in Glendale where she was buried in an evening gown with an orchid pinned to each shoulder strap. Among the attendees were Rex Harrison and Lilli Palmer (who had flown back from New York). The pallbearers included Dick Haymes, Pat O'Brien and Cesar Romero. When Carole's estate was tallied, the debts outweighed the $150,000 assets. Her memorabilia was auctioned off to cut the deficit.

As for Harrison, he "claimed" to feel no guilt over the tragic situation, but later admitted he spent several months in therapy. Branded the villain of the piece, his Fox contract was terminated, and he retreated to Broadway to star as the philandering Henry VIII in *Anne of a Thousand Days* (1948).

After the fact it was recalled that when movie star Lupe Velez had taken her own life in 1944, Carole had said, "I know how she felt. You fight just so long and then you begin to worry about being washed up. You fear there's one way to go, and that's down."

Ona Munson

[Ona Wolcott]
June 16, 1906 - February 11, 1955

Most moviegoers recall her as the genteel Belle Watling, the full-figured, red-headed Atlanta madam who befriends Rhett Butler in *Gone with the Wind* (1939). The real-life actress was actually a petite blonde who began her career in vaudeville dancing and singing. However, like the shadowy Belle whose life held many, many heartaches, Ona Munson's last years were tinged with sorrow, illness and, finally, escape in the form of suicide.

She was born in 1906 in Portland, Oregon and started her show business career in 1922 in a musical revue playing the Orpheum vaudeville circuit. By 1926, she had taken over the title role in the Broadway musical comedy *No, No Nanette*. Her early film roles were in fast-paced comedies (*The Hot Heiress*, 1931, *Broadminded*, 1931). During the mid-Thirties she spent most of her time on the Broadway stage and touring, before she returned to movies in *Dramatic School* (1938). Several name stars (Marlene Dietrich, Mae West) had been considered for the Belle Watling role before Ona was cast as the good-hearted prostitute in *Gone with the Wind*. She should have been Oscar-nominated for her poignant performance and her career should have escalated. However, it didn't. The one highlight of her 1940s movies was her portrayal

225

FREDDIE PRINZE

of the vengeful Mother Gin Sling in *The Shanghai Gesture* (1941). Her final screen part was as Lon McCallister's mother in *The Red House* (1947).

By the early 1950s, Ona was living in New York with her second husband, artist-designer, Eugene Berman. (She had previously married and divorced movie director Eddie Buzzell, whom she had met when they both were on the Broadway stage). In 1952 she survived major surgery, but, thereafter, grew increasingly despondent. The next year, she appeared in a revival production of *First Lady* at the City Center.

On February 11, 1955, at about 1 p.m., Ona was found dead in her Manhattan apartment by her husband. Next to an empty packet of sleeping pills was a note which read "This is the only way I know to be free again.... Please don't follow me." She is buried at Ferncliff Cemetery in Hartsdale, New York.

Freddie Prinze

[Freddie Preutzel]

June 22, 1954 - January 29, 1977

For two-and-a-half years Freddie Prinze was the enormously popular star of TV's hit comedy, *"Chico and the Man."* At age 22, he had risen from the New York slums and a crummy childhood to becoming a show business phenomenon. However, beneath the surface, he was under tremendous self-pressure. Always insecure, his meteoric fame had only intensified his vulnerability. His fifteen-month marriage had fallen apart. He was dependent on drugs and had a death wish. Finally unable to "take it any longer," the brilliant performer shot himself. Poof! The end of a short-lived legend.

He was born in New York City in 1954, the son of a Puerto Rican mother and a Jewish-Hungarian father. (He joked that his mixed parentage made him a "Hungar-ican.") He grew up in the tough Spanish Ghetto area of Washington Heights. Because he was fat as a child, his mother sent him to dance school, which did not endear him to the neighborhood kids. After being mugged, he switched from dance school to karate. Like his hybrid heritage, much of his childhood was a pull in different directions. He attended a Lutheran elementary school, but went to Catholic mass on Sunday. As a youngster he was fantasy- prone; as a teenager he became addicted to drugs. (He often pushed marijuana to earn extra money.) With his gift for imitations and comic jibing at his bizarre childhood, he gravitated to New York's High School for Performing Arts. After leave there in 1973, he performed with the New York City Street Theatre, appearing in *Bye Bye Birdie* and *West Side Story*. However, rather than singing and dancing, it was in comedy that he excelled. He haunted Manhattan's Improv Club, hoping for a spot on their new talent nights. He was seen performing there and booked on Jack Paar's ABC-TV talk show. That success led to Johnny Carson putting him on his "*The Tonight Show*" for several appearances.

Producer Jimmie Komack saw Freddie on the Carson outing and signed him to co-star with veteran Jack Albertson in "*Chico and the Man*." The sitcom was set in the East Los Angeles barrio and dealt with two persons of contrasting backgrounds who learn to respect one another. The network series debuted in September 1974 and was a hit. Perhaps only Prinze saw the bitter ironies of a Hungarian-Puerto Rican playing a Chicano, and that a year ago he had been nearly broke and now he was a well-paid star.

After his first TV season, Prinze, who wrote his own material, took his comedy act on the road, and he made his first comedy album, "*Looking Good*." In Jackson Hole, Wyoming he fell in love with travel agency worker Katherine Cochran. They married in Las Vegas in October 1975 and their child, Freddie Jr. was born in March 1976. Besides his "*Chico*" duties in 1976, Freddie did several TV specials that year and made a dramatic appearance in a TV movie (*The Million Dollar Rip-Off*). In the fall of 1976 Freddie began the third season of "*Chico*." He occasionally was a guest host on "*The Tonight Show*" and frequently performed in Las Vegas. He was the idol of every kid who wanted to make it big in show business. He moved his parents to a house in North Hollywood, California. He had a new multi-million dollar pact at NBC and a deal to perform at Caesar's Palace in Las Vegas. There was talk of his starring in a remake of the classic *It Happened One Night* (1934). In January 1977 he performed at President Jimmy Carter's Inaugeral Ball at the Kennedy Center in Washington, D.C.

In his personal life, however, everything started to come apart; he was full of pain. He was sued successfully by his ex-manager for breaking a contract, and his wife, four years older than he, began divorce proceedings. He was seeing a variety of women, and he was arrested for driving under the influence of drugs. He relied on heavy therapy, liquor and drugs (cocaine, Quaaludes), but nothing seemed to put his chaotic life back in order. He began telling his friends that "Life isn't worth living." He would shock them by pulling out a .357 magnum gun, pointing it at his temple, and squeezing the trigger.

On Wednesday, January 26, 1977, his secretary, Carol Novak, was with hyperactive Freddie when he was served with a restraining order from his soon-to-be ex-wife. The legal document made Prinze crazed and he phoned his attorneys in a highly erratic frame of mind. He drew out his gun and, after toying with it, charged into a nearby room, shouting "I'm gonna do it!" It discharged, but the bullet went into a wall. The next day, Prinze went through an assortment of activities including a visit to his psychiatrist. Early on Friday morning, the 28th, his manager (Marvin "Dusty" Snyder) responded to a frantic call from Freddie and rushed over at 3:00 a.m. to his Wilshire Boulevard hotel apartment west of Beverly

Hills. As Snyder walked in, Prinze was standing with the phone in one hand, his gun in the other. Snyder tried to reason with him, but to no avail. A frantic Freddie called his mother, then his lawyer and next his estranged wife. When he finally hung up, he sat down on the sofa and then, suddenly, raised the weapon to his head. Before the manager, who had spent hours trying to reassure Prinze, could stop him, Freddie had shot himself. (A note from Freddie was found in the suite. It stated, "I must end it. There's no hope left. I'll be at peace. No one had anything to do with this. My decision totally. Freddie Prinze.")

He was rushed to UCLA Medical Center where, already brain dead, he lingered on. He died at 1 p.m. on Saturday, September 29. He was buried in the Court of Remembrance at Forest Lawn—Hollywood Hills after services at that cemetery's Old North Church. Among the celebrity pallbearer were his good friends Tony Orlando and Paul Williams. Co-star Jack Albertson and TV show producer Jimmie Komack were among those to read eulogies. Freddie's crypt contains a plaque reading, "We love you. Psalm 23." As for *Chico and the Man*," it continued through the rest of the 1976-77 season without Freddie. For the final TV year, 1977-78, a new youngster (Gabriel Melgar) was added to the cast as a foil for Jack Albertson.

Perhaps veteran entertainer Albertson said it best about Freddie: "He was a strange boy. He was a barrel of laughs. A real good kid, but at 22 he may have run into problems he just couldn't handle." On the other hand, his bereaved mother told the press, "If anyone killed him, it was Hollywood and all the things that made him show off.... What's my boy got? Just a grave and people who say he killed himself. He wouldn't do that to me." In 1981-82, Prinze's widow and son received nearly $1 million to settle assorted malpractice suits against the late performer's psychiatrist (for allowing him access to the death weapon) and internist (for over-prescribing Quaaludes). In January 1983, a jury confirmed the contention of Freddie's mother, that Prinze, at the time of his death, was acting under the influence of drugs. In short, he had been playing a prank with the gun when it went off. As a result of the verdict, the family received the proceeds of a $200,000 life insurance policy.

David Rappaport

November 23, 1952 - May 2, 1990

British-born David Rappaport may have stood only 3' 11", but he was oversized in talent and died in a big way.

Born in Hackney, London in 1952, he was the son of a Jewish taxi driver who changed careers late in life and became a teacher. David was a victim of achondroplasia at birth, and physically stopped growing when he was seven. With a psychology degree from Bristol University, David became a teacher in Yorkshire. His first real acting job was doing a 45-minute monologue in *Illuminatus*, an eight-hour play at the Liverpool Everyman Theatre. The production moved on to the National Theatre, which led Rappaport to playing the dwarf in *Volpone* (1976) with John Gielgud. On television, he became popular as the host of *"Grapevine"* and as a cast member of the *"Robin of Sherwood"* and other series. Always working, David did the cabaret circuit with his one-man show, *Little Brother Is Watching You*. He had been offered a part in *Star Wars*

(1977), but he rejected the role because he "did not want to play a puppet or a robot." His screen debut came in the Dutch film *Mysteries* (1979). Then David was in *Cuba* (1979), *Time Bandits* (1981), and *Sword of the Valiant* (1982), all with Sean Connery. In *The Bride* (1985)—in which rock star Sting was Dr. Frankenstein—Rappaport stole the limelight as the midget who befriends the doctor's monstrous creation.

In 1986, Rappaport—who had been married and divorced and had a son Joseph—came to America for the TV series *"The Wizard."* He had the lead as a diminutive toymaker recruited by the government to make high tech contraptions for their agencies' needs. He received good reviews and a much higher salary that he had earned abroad. However, the show lasted less than a season (1986-87), a fact which depressed the actor greatly. He remained in the U.S. doing both movie and TV projects—including Blake Edwards's TV movie *Peter Gunn* (1989). He also played the drums semi-professionally, performing with a New Age jazz band in Los Angeles.

His greatest recent success came in late 1988 with a recurring role on TV's *"L.A. Law."* He was the sharp-witted lawyer, nicknamed "Mighty Mouth," who always outmaneuvered his courtroom rival (Jimmy Smits). Again in the limelight, Rappaport told the press that he craved to be a "boring, normal person....I look at boring people every day and I say, 'God, I wish I could be like that,' but my lot is to be unique, special, so I have to put up with it. It's a hard life."

On March 4, 1990, David was hospitalized at Queens of Angels-Hollywood Presbyterian Medical Center with carbon monoxide poisoning. Police had found him unconscious in Hollywood in his 1982 Volkswagen. The motor was running and a hose from the exhaust pipe was pumping fumes into the idling car. Although he recovered physically, he remained depressed, despite the fact that he was to shoot a film in Ireland in September and was involved in a new syndicated TV series (*"Beyond the Groove"*).

On May 2, 1990, David drove off from his house to take his Labrador dog, Rickie, for a walk in Laurel Canyon Park in the San Fernando Valley. When he didn't return that day, his business manger filed a missing person's report. On May 3, police found his car at the park with the dog inside. By a nearby bush, they located Rappaport's body. He had shot himself in the chest with a .38 caliber pistol. The 38-year-old actor left no suicide note, although friends mentioned his unhappiness over an on-again, off-again recent romance. David's body was returned to London for burial.

Rappaport's death was reminiscent of another diminutive actor who died unnaturally seventeen years previous. Oklahoma-born dwarf actor Michael Dunn—who earned an Oscar-nomination for his movie debut in *The Ship of Fools* (1965)—died in his London hotel room in 1973 while onlocation for the film, The Abdication. His abrupt passing was listed officially as "a possible suicide."

George Sanders

July 3, 1906 - April 25, 1972

Urbane and cynical in life, Academy Award-winning actor George Sanders left this Earth the same way. His suicide note read:

Dear World: I am leaving because I am bored. I feel I have lived long enough. I am leaving you with your worries in this sweet cesspool—good luck.

He was born in 1906 in St. Petersburg, Russia to British parents: his father manufactured rope and his mother was a famed horticulturist. (There was an older brother, who became actor Tom Conway, and a sister, Margaret.) In 1917 due to the Communist revolution, the family left Russia for England where he attended Brighton College and the Manchester Technical School. Next, he sailed for South America to work in the tobacco industry in Argentina. However, he refused to take the business seriously, preferring to develop his reputation as a young rake. Back in England, a producer heard George singing at a party and hired him for a musical revue, *Ballyhoo* (1933). This job led to more stage work (usually as an understudy), radio dramas and cabaret work. In 1934, George made his screen debut in *Love, Life and Laughter.* By 1936, he was under contract to a British film company. When that studio burned to the ground, Twentieth Century-Fox took over its assets, including options on its players. Fox's chief, Darryl F. Zanuck, brought Sanders to Hollywood for the role of a haughty, cold-hearted lord in Tyrone Power's *Lloyds of London* (1936).

The 6' 3" actor soon specialized in playing good-looking, cultured cads. He quipped to the press, "I find it so pleasant to be unpleasant." Moviegoers enjoyed him as the new Simon Templar, the debonair sleuth in the Saint series (1939-41), but for Sanders it was "the nadir of my career." He wasn't much happier when RKO switched him, in 1941, to the role of a similar detective, The Falcon. After four such episodes, he relinquished the series to his brother, Tom, in *The Falcon's Brother*

(1942). Meanwhile, in October 1940, the sophisticated, iconoclastic actor married Elsie Poole, known professionally as Susan Larson. For his own offbeat reasons, the wedding was not made pubic until 1942. (Once when asked why he hadn't brought Susan to a party, he replied, "Oh I can't bring her. She bores people.") The mismatched couple divorced in 1948.

Sanders proved a busy actor in the 1940s, often playing conquest-hungry Nazis in World War II thrillers or fops in costume pictures. In 1949, he married actress Zsa Zsa Gabor in Las Vegas. Sanders remarked of their years in her Beverly Hills mansion, "I lived there as a sort of paying guest." After their 1954 divorce, Zsa Zsa said of her ex-husband that the trouble with their marriage had been that they both had loved the same person—George Sanders.

Sanders's screen career peaked when he won an Oscar as the dapper, vicious theater critic of *All About Eve* (1950). He decided against replacing Ezio Pinza on Broadway in *South Pacific*, but demonstrated his excellent singing voice opposite Ethel Merman in the screen musical, *Call Me Madam* (1953). In 1959, he married Benita Hume, the widow of actor Ronald Colman; they remained together until her death in 1967. On TV, Sanders had hosted an anthology series in 1957, although he was at his best as a supercilious guest villain, Mr. Freeze, on TV's "Batman" series in 1966.

His last major screen role was as an aged drag queen in the spy thriller, *The Kremlin Letter* (1970). He now claimed that it was time for him to retire. That same year he married Zsa Zsa Gabor's much- married older sister, Magna. Magna's mother, Jolie, insisted, "He just wanted to get back in the family. He missed me. I always liked George...." Several weeks later they divorced. Thereafter, Sanders's health declined. He entered into another romantic relationship, most notable for making him do foolish things (like selling his beloved house in Majorca.) After visiting his sister Margaret in England in April 1972, George—looking exceedingly ill and seeming on the verge of a nervous breakdown—departed for Barcelona. On April 23, he registered at a hotel in the seaside resort of Castelldefels, ten miles south of Barcelona. He drank heavily that day and the next. When he retired on the night of April 24, he left a request to be called early the next morning. When the staff could not contact him the next morning, the manager investigated. He found Sanders dead, the actor having taken an overdose of Nembutal, washed down with vodka. Among George's effects, besides his suicide message, was a note to his sister, "Dearest Margoolinka. Don't be sad. I have only anticipated the inevitable by a few years."

Dreading the horror of growing sicker, older and poorer, cultured George Sanders had created his own exit scene and played it perfectly.

Lupe Velez

[Guadalupe Velez de Villalobos]
July 18, 1908 - December 14, 1944

Like Maria Montez, petite screen star Lupe Velez was an exotic fireball with tremendous self-confidence, a knack for self-promotion, and a vulnerability masked as sexual aggressiveness. Variously known as the Hot Tamale, the Mexican Wildcat, the Queen of the Hot-Cha, madcap Velez ended her life as tempestuously as she had lived it—in a blaze of scandalous headlines.

She was born in 1908 in San Luis de Potosi, a suburb of Mexico City. Her father was an officer in the Mexican Army; her mother had been an opera singer. The Villalobos clan had three other children: Emigdio, Mercedes, Josefina. Being rambunctious, Lupe was sent to a convent school in San Antonio, Texas. When her father died a few years later, she returned home to help support the family. With her shapely figure, she soon turned to show business and in 1924 was cast in the musical revue, *Ra-Ta-Plan*. She arrived penniless in Hollywood in 1926. but found work dancing in the local *Music Box Revue*, which starred Fanny Brice. This stint led to Broadway offers, but Lupe rejected them, wanting to break into movies instead. Producer Hal Roach put her in a comedy short (1927), but she did much better as the wild mountain girl in Douglas Fairbanks's *The Gaucho* (1928), a role originally thought of for another Mexican actress, Dolores Del Rio (who would remain Velez's screen rival for years). She made an accented talkie film debut in the abysmal *Lady of the Pavements* (1929), co-directed by D. W. Griffith.

It was while filming *Wolf Song* (1929) that Lupe began a passionate romance with handsome co-player Gary Cooper, with whom she lived in a Spanish-styled house on Laurel Canyon Boulevard in Hollywood. When Cooper's studio and his parents broke up their romance, Velez turned to other stars (including John Gilbert), and then fixated on muscular swimmer-actor Johnny Weissmuller whom she married in October 1933. Meanwhile, she played fascinating spitfires on screen: a half-caste Oriental (*East Is West*, 1930), an Indian maiden (*The Squaw Man*, 1931), a flashy Latin American dancer (*Cuban Love Song*, 1931), etc. She went to Broadway for two musicals: *Hot-Cha!* (1932) with Bert Lahr and *Strike Me Pink* (1933) with Jimmy Durante. She then returned to Los Angeles now under contract to MGM where her husband was making Tarzan jungle adventures. Her resultant films were tame, but she made wild headlines from her ongoing spats and dramatic separations from Weissmuller (whom she would divorce in 1938).

RKO rescued Lupe's career from its decline by starring her in the tailor-made *Girl from Mexico* (1939). With rubber-legged comedian Leon Errol as co-star, the film set the tone for seven later episodes in the popular *Mexican Spitfire* series through 1943. That year, she met 27-year old French actor, Harold Ramond, and Lupe cooed, "I've always been used to controlling men, but I try it with Harold and he tells me where to go." After the Mexican-made *Nana* received poor reviews in June 1944, Lupe announced plans to return to the stage that fall, but they fell through.

On November 27, Lupe excitedly announced that she and the unemployed Ramond would marry. However, by December 10, the temperamental actress had called off the planned nuptials. Unknown to the public at the time, Lupe was already four months pregnant and in a desperate quandary. A devout Catholic, she dreaded the thought of her child being born illegitimate, but she was unconvinced that Harold loved her for herself. In desperation, Velez even thought of giving birth to the child and then having one of her sisters (who lived with her) claim the infant as her own. Given her religion and the moral climate of the times, she never considered the possibility of an unlawful abortion.

On December 13, Lupe attended the Hollywood premiere of *Nana*. She told her good friend, actress Estelle Taylor, "I am getting to the place where the only thing I am afraid of is life itself.... People think that I like to fight. I have to fight for everything. I'm so tired of it all.... I've never met a man with whom I didn't have to fight to exist." Later that Wednesday night, Velez returned alone to her Beverly Hills mansion on North Rodeo Drive. (Her family was away at the time.) Putting on her favorite blue silk pajamas, she sat down on her oversized bed and swallowed an overdose of sleeping pills. The following morning, a doctor was called when her housekeeper couldn't awaken her. He pronounced Lupe dead. Two notes were found by the bed. One, addressed to Ramond, stated, "You know the facts for the reason I am taking my life." The other letter was to her housekeeper-companion, Mrs. Beulah Kinder: "My faithful friend, you and only you know the fact for the reason I am taking my life. May God forgive me, and don't think bad of me.... Say goodbye to all my friends and the American press that were always so nice to me." A postscript begged her friend to take care of her pet dogs, Chips and Chops.

(A much-circulated apocryphal account of Lupe's final day had her exiting in a grand manner. According to this story, after having her hair done and being made-up, she put on a flamboyant dress and ate a solitary banquet. Later, having dismissed the servants, she went to the master bedroom where she swallowed Seconal tablets and lay down to await the end. However, the mix of Seconal and the spicy food brought on an upset stomach. As she raced to the bathroom toilet bowl, she slipped on the marble titles. She fell head-first into the commode and broke her neck. According to this unconfirmed report, she died and was found later, half-submerged in the bowl.)

After a dispute between the Beverly Hills coroner and the city's district attorney, it was decided not to do an autopsy. A non- denominational church service was provided for Lupe at the Church of the Recessional at Forest Lawn Memorial Parks in Glendale. Some 4,000 friends, fans, and curiosity-seekers passed by her casket. Pallbearers included Johnny Weissmuller, Gilbert Roland and Arturo de Cordova. Lupe was buried at the Pateon Delores Cemetery in Mexico City.

Lupe's estate was estimated at between $160,000 to $200,000. She bequeathed approximately one-third of the assets to Mrs. Kinder (the executrix) with the remainder placed in a trust fund for her family. One of Lupe's sisters contested the will and, at the hearing, proudly told the judge how she had saved the estate over $20,000 by vetoing her sister's burial in an expensive bronze casket and not permitting a $16,000 diamond ring nor a $15,00 ermine cape to be interred with the body. In June 1945 Lupe's Beverly Hills home was sold at auction and the highly-publicized over-sized death bed went for $45.

Such was the end of Lupe Velez who said shortly before her needless death, "I just want to have a little fun! I know I'm not worth anything. I can't sing well. I can't dance well. I've never done anything like that [well]...."

Gig Young

[Byron Elsworth Barr]

November 4, 1913 - October 19, 1978

In his prime he was handsome, deb-onair and ever so charming—at least on camera. Away from the limelight, he endured tremendous insecurity, always feeling second-rate (a life-long situation first developed when his father showed preference for his older brother). Seeking escape and validation in drink, drug, romances and marriages, Gig hid behind a well-practiced smiling mask. One friend at the end observed, "I think he probably had his own private hell going on inside him." Co-player Red Button observed, "Beneath that light-hearted sophistication, Gig was a big baby needing an arm around him." A cynical Young once summed up his professional life with: "thirty years and 55 pictures—not more than five that were any good, or any good for me."

He was born in St. Cloud, Minnesota in 1913, the third child—there was already brother Donald and sister Genevieve—of a dour Scotsman who founded the J. E. Barr Pickling and Preserving Company and his ex-schoolteacher wife, Emma. By 1932, with the Depression ruining J. E.'s business, the parents and Gig (the only child still at home) relocated to Washington, D.C. When his parents next moved to North Carolina, Byron remained in Washington. Through the encouragement of his landlady, he fulfilled his childhood desires for attention and fantasy by acting with the Phil Hayden Players. His efforts to please his father by working at a local car agency ended in failure, and he chose to try Hollywood.

Having hitchhiked to California, the handsome young man worked at a gas station and other odd jobs to keep going while he studied at the Pasadena Playhouse. In addition to acting in plays there, he auditioned for the new talent departments at the movie studios. At the Playhouse he

**GIG
YOUNG**

met actress Sheila Stapler, whom he married in Las Vegas on August 2, 1940. That same year, he was signed by Warner Bros. where he did assorted bits in various pictures. As he described it, his speciality was "corpses, unconscious bodies and people snoring in spectacular epics." Spotted as a "new" young Cary Grant, Byron received his best role to date as the dashing young artist in Barbara Stanwyck's *The Gay Sisters* (1942). He got good notices for his performance and he took the name of his character, Gig Young, as his new professional name. (He had been known briefly as Bryant Fleming in his first film days.)

On screen, Bette Davis was the star of *Old Acquaintances* (1943), but off camera the married Davis and the

married Young had a brief affair. It was one of several that mother-fixated Gig had with older women over the years. In *Air Force* (1943), he was a flyer; in real life, he was drafted into the U.S. Coast Guard during World War II. By the fall of 1945, he was a civilian again and back at Warner Bros., where he continued in supporting roles, eventually earning $500 weekly. Frustrated by Warners' failure to push his career, he sought comfort from studio drama teacher-turned-friend, Sophie Rosenstein, who was already married. She bolstered him when Warners dropped his contract in 1947. The relationship added to the growing rift between Gig and Sheila and they divorced in 1949. The next year. he and the now-single Rosenstein, six years his senior, married.

Young's screen career was stagnating until—thanks to Sophie and other contacts—Gig got a breakthrough dramatic role in James Cagney's *Come Fill the Cup* (1951), as a dissolute, drunken composer. This role earned him an Academy Award nomination for Best Supporting Actor. However, Young had little opportunity to rejoice, for Sophie developed cancer and died in November 1952. To mask his grief and the boredom from his dull movie roles, he turned increasingly to drink. He branched out into other mediums, acting on TV anthology series and appearing in the sophisticated comedy, *Oh Men! Oh Women!* (1953) on Broadway. While in the stage hit, he dated well-known, busty stripper Sherry Britton. However, their masochistic relationship ended with her refusal to marry him. He next turned to actress Elaine Stritch, but that relationship fizzled, although they remained lifelong friends.

While hosting the TV series "*Warner Bros. Presents*" (1955-56), Gig met Elizabeth Montgomery, the actress daughter of screen-stage star Robert Montgomery. Much against her father's wishes, she and the twenty-years-older Gig wed in late 1956. By now, Young was entrenched as a polished second banana on camera. For a typical such chore— Doris Day's *Teacher's Pet* (1958)—he was again Oscar-nominated as Best Supporting Actor and again lost. Unable to break into leading man movie roles, he again retreated to Broadway, this time as the lecherous lead of the sex comedy, *Under the Yum Yum Tree* (1960). By now, Gig was a very heavy drinker, which was a prime reason for fights between he and his wife, Elizabeth, who also had to compete with his recurring interest in older women authority figures. Young and Montgomery divorced in 1963. Now middle-aged and alone—again— Gig turned not only to drink, but also to drugs and to assorted young women—anything to bolster his need not to feel old.

Young married real estate agent Elaine Young in September 1963 and their daughter, Jennifer, was born the next April. To pay for his new family, Gig accepted the co-lead in *"The Rogues"* (1964-65) with Charles Boyer and David Niven. Anticipating a successful TV run, he expanded his lifestyle, only to have the series flop after one season. He and Elaine bickered increasingly; their relationship unaided by Young's LSD therapy phase. The couple divorced in November 1966.

By now, Gig was in his fifties, puffy-faced and flabby. He no longer had illusions about Hollywood starring roles. However, on Broadway he could still be a star; he accepted the lead in the sex farce, *There's a Girl in My Soup* (1967) and dated actress Skye Aubrey, 31-years his junior.

She wanted to marry him, but he refused. With his career heading downhill, his ex-agent, Martin Baum, now a film executive, won him the role of the dissolute master of ceremonies in *They Shoot Horses, Don't They?* (1969). This time Gig won an Oscar. As he insisted, "This is the greatest moment of my life."

However, Young's career did not accelerate after his Academy Award. He played a grandfather (!) in *Lovers and Other Strangers* (1970) and other lesser TV and film assignments. When not battling his ex-wife Elaine in court over their property settlement, he was involved in backstage cast bickering during a stage revival of *Harvey* (1971) and then was dropped from *Blazing Saddles* (1974), only to be replaced by Gene Wilder. Innocent or guilty in all these highly-touted escapades, he had gained an industry reputation of being unreliable.

When Bruce Lee died in 1973, he was in the midst of a new film. Wanting to exploit his footage, the storyline was restructured and Gig Young, among others were hired in 1977 to pad out the new scenario of *Game of Death* (1978). On the set of this paste-together project in Hong Kong, he met young German actress Kim Schmidt. It was the start of an on-again, off-again "romantic" relationship. Meanwhile, Young's own career slipped further downhill. In 1978, he played on stage in *Nobody Loves an Albatross in Canada*, hoping it would lead to a national tour, but the production was a fiasco. Thereafter, he and 31-year old Kim finalized their live-in relationship by marrying at New York City Hall on September 27, 1978.

By early October 1978, neighbors at Manhattan's fashionable Osborne Apartments on West 57th Street (across the street from Carnegie

Hall) reported that they heard daily arguments from apartment #1BB, shared by Gig and his new wife, Kim. Gig's friends noted that he had become increasingly secretive and withdrawn. seemingly preoccupied with his shaky finances, his aging, and the many ill-turns of his life. Despite friends' prompting, he still refused to go to Alcoholic Anonymous. Meanwhile, he and Kim argued about his latest drafted will, which left half his estate to her and half to his sister, Genevieve. She wanted it altered in her behalf.

On Wednesday night, October 18, 1978, Gig called long-time friend Harriette Vine Douglas in Los Angeles. (She was a 58-year-old married woman he had known for ten years. She later claimed they had a romantic relationship during this period.) He asked her to fly to New York and take him back to Hollywood. He said he needed to recoup his self-esteem after battling so much with his very moody new wife. Harriette refused, trying to exhibit "tough love" to her good friend. The next morning, Young called down to the doorman to check about the weather; Kim telephoned a local grocery store with a small order. Some time around 2:30 p.m. Gig took a .38 caliber Smith & Wesson gun he had hidden in the apartment and shot Kim in the head in their bedroom. Whether it was a pre-meditated or a spontaneous act is unknown. Seeing his wife dead, he placed the barrel of the gun in his mouth, and pulled the trigger. The fully-clothed bodies were discovered five hours later by the building manager who wondered why the Youngs' grocery order standing in the lobby had not been collected. In the death room, a blood-soaked diary was opened to September 27, 1978, the day the couple had married. The police uncovered three additional revolvers in the posh duplex apartment as well as 350 rounds of ammunitions.

At the request of Gig's sister, Harriette Douglas, flew to New York to claim Gig's body. A service was held at Pierce Brothers Mortuary in Beverly Hills on October 26, 1978. As he had requested, Young's body was cremated. Gig's estate was valued at approximately $200,000.

Gig Young's death revealed just how much of a dual, Jekyll-and-Hyde existence he had endured for so many years. Shocked that a seemingly gentle, now-content man could commit such acts, long-time friend and mentor Martin Baun said, "He seemed like a man who had everything going for him. How little we know." It appeared that Gig Young's best acting job was his private life, where he had hidden his overwhelming doubts and fears from even his "closest" associates.

SPECIAL FEATURE: ADDITIONAL CELEBRITIES NOT INCLUDED IN THE FIRST EDITION

ACCIDENTS

Brandon Lee

February 1, 1965 - March 31, 1993

Rising film actor Brandon Lee once said, "I don't want to be known only as Bruce Lee's son. When you have a built-in comma after your name, it makes you sensitive." However, in many ironic ways the phrase "like father, like son" certainly applied to martial arts screen idol Bruce Lee and his only son, Brandon. As fate would prove, there were too many coincidental parallels between the two generations of Lees: both were anti-establishment rebels who boasted a reckless regard for safety and each shared a near fanatical determination to succeed in show business under their own terms.

Charismatic kung fu expert Bruce died in Hong Kong on July 20, 1973 at the age of 32 while making an action movie, *Game of Death*. Although the coroner's verdict insisted he died of a cerebral edema, wild rumors of how the world's fittest man "really" expired have endured for decades and new ones continue to be hypothesized. In March 1993, almost twenty years after Lee's demise, Brandon, 28, would die in a tragic accident on the North Carolina movie set of his own starring vehicle, *The Crow*.

The tumult following Brandon's untimely death seemed a replay of the circumstances involving Bruce's sudden end. Because of the bizarre facts surrounding Brandon's freak mishap, there was immediate speculation that Brandon, like his father, had been a victim of foul play. Others reasoned that Brandon's tragic end had been pre-ordained by fate, a fulfillment of the young actor's premonition that "I'm going to die young just like Dad."

Brandon Bruce Lee was born on February 1, 1965 (the first day of the Chinese New Year) in Oakland, California. He was the son of San Francisco-born Eurasian Bruce Lee and Linda (Emery) Lee, his Caucasian blonde American wife of Swedish heritage. (The Lees had married in 1964 and would have a second child, Shannon, born in 1965.) The year following Brandon's birth, Bruce gained a modest degree of show business

BRANDON LEE

fame by being cast as "Kato" in the Hollywood TV series "The Green Hornet" (1966-67), followed by a small role in the James Garner detective movie, *Marlowe* (1969). Then, after many months of professional struggle, Bruce was teamed with James Franciscus in a short-lasting TV series, "Longstreet" (1971-72). By the time of Bruce's hit action features—such as *The Big Boss* (1971) and *Enter the Dragon* (1973)—the Lees were enjoying the good life, living in an expensive Hong Kong mansion. (According to the Bruce Lee "legend," when Bruce, whose Chinese name Lee Siu-lung meant Little Dragon, bought the house in the Hong Kong suburb called Lowloon-Tong [Pond of the Nine Dragon] he incurred the jealous wrath of the neighborhood's resident demons. The curse, per the tradition, lasts, three generations.)

Meanwhile, five-year-old Brandon appeared in one of his father's films, *Legacy of Rage* (1970), which contained a clip of a Hong Kong TV appearance young Brandon had made with his famous father. By the time Brandon was eight, he could speak Cantonese fluently.

Following Bruce's death in 1973, Linda took Brandon and Shannon back to the United States to live in Los Angeles. The trauma of his father's death had a strong effect on Brandon who became a rebellious loner. He was obsessed by his celebrated parent, determined to follow in his father's show business foot-

steps and convinced that he would die much like his dad had. At age nine, when Linda enrolled Brandon for martial arts lessons, the boy spotted a picture of his father on the wall. He started to cry and ran from the training studio. Martial arts star Chuck Norris, a friend of Bruce's, would recall about the troubled, teenaged Brandon: "He never really knew his dad. One day when he was about 12 or 14 he came out and we talked for a few hours about his dad—the man I knew and the father he didn't get a chance to know.... He wanted to be his own man which is good. He didn't want to be just Bruce Lee's son. He wanted to be Brandon Lee, the star."

Strong-willed Brandon proved to be a difficult teenager. In the spring of 1983, he was expelled from the private Chadwick School in Palos Verdes, for misbehaving. He received his diploma at nearby Miraleste High School. Actor Lou Diamond Phillips, a close friend of Brandon in this period, would remember that his pal was "a boiling mass of energy." Deciding to fulfill his destiny to become an actor, Brandon enrolled at Emerson College in Boston majoring in theatre. He also took acting classes at the Strasberg Academy in Manhattan and studied dramatics in Los Angeles.

On his twenty-first birthday, Brandon made his professional acting debut in *Kung Fu: The Movie*. In this made-for-television movie, David Carradine reprised the role of Kwai Chang Caine from his hit

1972-75 TV series, "Kung Fu." (Ironically, Bruce Lee had been a contender for the 1970s television series lead, before Carradine won the assignment.) Brandon was cast in the storyline as an assassin, leading *Daily Variety* to report, "It's a pro acting debut, not auspicious." The next year, CBS-TV aired a failed series pilot, "Kung Fu: The Next Generation," an abortive attempt to update the old Carradine program. David Darlow appeared as the contemporary counterpart to Carradine who attempts to lure his wayward son (Brandon Lee) into the family enterprise of fighting injustice. *Variety* rated Brandon's appearance as "animated and okay."

In the next few years, acting jobs eluded Brandon. He spent much of his free time racing his motorcycle recklessly around the Los Angeles turf. He refused to wear a helmet, insisting, "If I want to put my head in a brick wall, it's my business." Then his acting career took an upward turn. In the cheaply-assembled *Laser Mission* (1990), he played a government agent who must kidnap a Soviet scientist who has developed a new high-tech offensive weapon. Much more mainstream and popular was *Showdown in Little China* (1991), a violent actioner which teamed Brandon (as a pop culture American) as the partner of a Los Angeles cop/martial arts master (Dolph Lundgren). Together, on-camera they battled a gang of Japanese dope smugglers. Kevin

Thomas (*Los Angeles Times*) rated the picture "smart, fast-moving" and thought Brandon was humorously effective in his latest screen assignment.

With his movie career finally accelerating, 6', 155-pound Lee was cast by Twentieth Century-Fox (in the first of a three-picture deal with the studio) as the lead in *Rapid Fire* (1992). He played a pacifistic college student pressured into becoming a killing machine. Critics rated the action entry schlocky, but most noted that Brandon had a definite exotic charisma as the wiry, muscular lead player.

By this point in life, Brandon had come to terms with the fact that, unlike his father, he would never be a world-class martial artist. Insistent on establishing his own identity, he turned down a fat role in an upcoming screen biography of his dad—*Dragon: The Bruce Lee Story* (1993). Off-camera, Brandon was known to some of his California peers as a comedian. He was the type of jokster who once drove around Los Angeles in a hearse. Other contemporaries said he could act "wild and weird." For example, he was the sort who, instead of knocking at a friend's door, would "climb up the wall of your house and go in through your window just for the fun of it."

By early 1993, Brandon's life was in high gear both professionally and romantically. Lee, 28, was sharing a Beverly Hills home with year-older Eliza (Lisa Hutton), a

SPECIAL ADDITIONS

Hollywood casting assistant. The couple planned to be married in Ensenada, Mexico on April 17. First, however, he was scheduled to star in *The Crow*, based on a high-tech action comic book. Lee was to play a rock star who is murdered by a gang and comes back in the persona of a bird to avenge his and his girlfriend's deaths. Producer Ed Pressman intended this movie to be the first in a series of movies starring Lee as The Crow.

The movie was shot on location at the Carolco Studio in Wilmington, North Carolina. Almost from the start, the action entry was jinxed with production problems. On February 1, 1993, the first day of filming, a carpenter on the shoot received severe shock and extensive burns when the crane he was riding struck high-power lines. On March 13, a storm destroyed some of the movie sets. Then, there was the occasion when an actor on the set went to check his gun before the cameras began rolling, only to find a live bullet in the firearm. Adding to the production chaos, a disgruntled set sculptor drove his car through the studio's plaster shop. Still later, another crew member slipped and drove a screwdriver through his hand.

By the end of March, *The Crow* was eight days away from the end of the filming. The cast and crew were working extremely long hours without sufficient breaks to finish the movie on time. On March 31, shortly after midnight, Brandon reported to sound stage #4 to shoot a flashback scene depicting how his screen character had died. In the storyline, a drug dealer (Michael Massee) fires a .44 Magnum revolver at Brandon's character as the latter enters his apartment. In the set-up, Lee opens the door, carrying a grocery bag in his arms. The package hid a trigger mechanism he was to pull which would set off a small dummy explosive charge just as the on-camera villain fired the blank shot.

As the film scene played out, Massee, standing approximately fifteen feet away from the star, aimed his firearm at Lee and shot. According to plan, Brandon triggered the charge. However, contrary to the stunt routine, Lee collapsed (at 12:30 AM) on the set, profusely bleeding from the right side of his abdomen. Immediate investigation revealed that he had a hole the size of a quarter in his lower right abdomen. While crew members phoned for help, the emergency medical technician assigned to the set began CPR on the injured star.

Within minutes, Lee was rushed by ambulance to the New Hanover Regional Medical Center in Wilmington. Upon arrival, he still had detectable vital signs. After the staff stabilized him, he was taken into emergency surgery. During the five-hour procedure sixty units of blood were used on the patient. Shortly after 7 AM he was placed in the Center's Trauma-Neuro Intensive Care Unit. His condition deteriorated progressively until finally his heart stopped and he could not be resuscitated. He was pronounced dead at 1:04 PM. At the time of his passing, his fiancee was with him, while his mother, Linda, had flown in from Boise, Idaho where she lived with her businessman husband Bruce Cadwell.

The media had a field day with this freak accident, pointing up the parallels of Brandon's death with that of his famous dad. Soon after the mystifying tragedy, Detective Rodney Simmons of the Wilmington Police Department (the first officer at the scene of the accident) examined the video of the fatal final footage. In explaining the tragic mishap, he suggested that "One of the lead slugs could have come off its casing and lodged in the gun." (According to this theory, when the gun was reloaded after the close-up shot, the metal tip had remained behind in the gun's cylinder. When the blank went off, it was speculated, the explosive force propelled the dummy tip through the gun barrel and lodged in Brandon's body near his spine.)

However, an autopsy performed on the actor's body on Thursday, April 1, in Jacksonville, North Carolina revealed (or confirmed) the alternative theory that Lee had been shot accidentally with a "live" .44 caliber bullet. How such a thing happened remained unexplained as did the fact that protocol had been broken by having Massee point (and fire) the gun directly at Lee, rather than "faking" the shot as was

industry tradition. (It also brought back memories of the 1984 death of actor Jon-Erik Hexum on the set of his TV series "Cover-Up" when he had "accidentally" shot himself with a blank charge.) Following Brandon's autopsy, the Wilmington, North Carolina district attorney, Jerry Spivey, stated: "In my opinion, I don't think there was any doubt there was negligence on several occasions [on *The Crow* set].... [We] are looking at the written investigative report for the purpose of deciding if there will be criminal charges [of negligence] and, if so, against whom." Spivey added, "there is no indication anybody was trying to hurt Brandon." Thus, whether any of *The Crow* crew members would be charged with criminal negligence remained an open issue, pending further investigation.

While the media began building a legend about the latest Lee family member to die "mysteriously," reporters queried the film's production executives whether *The Crow* could/would be finished and be released posthumously (as had been the case after Natalie Wood's death during the shooting of *Brain Storm* a decade earlier). Indications were that the movie would somehow be completed and released as a tribute to the late young star-in-the-making.

On April 3, 1993, Brandon was laid to rest beside his father in Lake View Cemetery in Seattle, Washington. Among family members and friends attending the services was Brandon's sister, Shannon, 23, who lived in New Orleans and was a singer. Linda Lee Cadwell did her best to keep up everyone's spirits at the funeral. Said one attendee, "She told us Brandon would have wanted this to be a joyful occasion." Another guest remarked to the press, "We're here to be happy, to celebrate his life."

On the following day, Sunday, April 4, a memorial service was conducted at actress Polly Bergen's home in the Hollywood Hills. Among the two hundred who attended were action stars Steven Seagal and David Carradine, actors David Hasselhoff and Lou Diamond Phillips, as well as Brandon's close friend, Jeff Imada (who had been the stunt coordinator on *The Crow*). Linda and Shannon led the tribute services.

Not long after Brandon's death a portion of Lee and Lisa's wedding invitation found its way to media reporters. In the invite, the couple had quoted from a passage from the novel, *The Sheltering Sky*: "Because we don't know when we will die, we get to think of life as an inexhaustible well...." For Brandon Lee, who lived his brief life with the fear of dying young, his prophecy of doom came all too true.

Wednesday, April 28, 1993 was declared Bruce Lee Day in Los Angeles by Mayor Tom Bradley. There was a special ceremony to unveil a star on the Hollywood Walk of Fame for Bruce Lee. That evening, at Mann's Chinese Theatre in Hollywood, *Dragon: The Bruce Lee Story* premiered. On hand for the bittersweet occasion, Linda Lee Cadwell told the press that she felt it important for her to attend because the screen biography "is a tribute to our family's life and for that reason I thought I should be here. I feel the film is a tribute to Bruce as a father and to Brandon as a son."

A special end title had been added to *Dragon: The Bruce Lee Story*, dedicating the movie to Brandon Bruce Lee. The tribute quote, which applied to both Brandon and Bruce Lee, read, "The key to immortality is first living a life worth remembering."

ALCOHOL AND DRUGS

Judy Garland

[Frances Ethel Gumm]

June 10, 1922 - June 22, 1969

"Judy! Judy! Judy!"

There probably will never be another personality like her. Judy Garland had a magical way of interpreting a song with a consummate skill possessed by few other performers before or since. On stage and off, she could be wicked-

JUDY GARLAND-Metro Goldwyn-Mayer   J.GXX-54

ly funny and she proved in *A Star Is Born* (1954) and *Judgment at Nuremberg* (1961) that she had great depth as a dramatic actress. On screen—but more so in live concerts—this versatile entertainer revealed an electric vibrancy and touching vulnerability that endeared her to audiences no matter what she was (or was not) accomplishing in the spotlight. She may have been less than five-foot tall, but on screen and stage, she was a giant embued with tremendous energy and incredible talent.

Like several other twentieth century legends (such as Marilyn Monroe or Elvis Presley), Garland became pill-addicted to compensate for personal insecurities and career instabilities. More so than most performers, she constantly exposed her raw emotions, one of the several qualities that made her performing so truly unique. She wore her heart on her proverbial sleeve, constantly asking the public to bolster her sagging courage and recharge her creative juices. With the evidence of her several suicide attempts before her tragic end, many commentators insist that Judy's drug overdosing finale was self-engineered.

She was born Frances Ethel Gumm in 1922 in Grand Rapids, Minnesota, the third daughter of struggling Irish tenor Frank Avent Gumm and vaudeville house pianist Ethel Marion (Milne) Gumm. Frances' parents ran the New Grand Theatre there. Frances was born with scoliosis, a slight curvature of the spine condition which compounded later insecurities about her feminine allure. At age two-and-a-half, she made her show business bow by joining her parents on stage in singing "Jingle Bells," a "spontaneous" event orchestrated by her ambitious mother.

Ethel Gumm was so determined to get her children into the movies, that the family moved to California, first settling in Lancaster, seventy miles north of Los Angeles where Frank ran a movie theatre. After many auditions, the Gumm girls signed with the Meglin Kiddies, a talent agency specializing in child acts. From 1929-31 the girls appeared in four movie short sub-

SPECIAL ADDITIONS

jects and toured with their singing act. They performed at the Chicago World's Fair in 1934, which led to a local engagement at the Oriental Theatre. Headliner George Jessel christened the girls with a new surname, Garland, taken from the last name of columnist Robert Garland who had phoned Jessel that night at the theatre. Frances chose "Judy" for herself, drawing on the title of a favorite song. By now, Judy Garland was the focal point of the family act.

The sisters—Judy in particular—auditioned unsuccessfully for several studios. However, it was Judy's test for MGM musical arranger, Roger Edens, which led to her being signed by the elite studio. Years later Garland claimed of her new affiliation, "I was very thrilled by it, though I actually didn't sign the contract. nobody asked me. That should be the title of my life: Nobody Asked Me." It was during 1935, Judy's first year with the studio, that her father died. Thus, her $150 weekly salary became the basis of the family's livelihood.

MGM was unsure how to showcase their new plump young talent. Finally, they cast her in a short subject (*Every Sunday*, 1936) with another young player, Deanna Durbin. Next, MGM sent Garland over to Twentieth Century-Fox to co-star in *Pigskin Parade* (1936), figuring that if her first feature flopped, the blame could be placed on the rival studio. However, despite wearing unbecoming coveralls and pigtails in the musical,

Judy was a vocal delight belting out such numbers as the "Balboa" swing selection.

Only when MGM couldn't borrow Shirley Temple from Twentieth Century-Fox did Judy inherit the career-shaping role of Dorothy in *The Wizard of Oz* (1939). She sang what became her signature tune ("Over the Rainbow") and won a special Academy Award Oscar-ette. Riding the crest of her popularity, she churned out several let's-put-on-the-show musicals, such as *Babes in Arms* (1939), with frequent co-star, pint-sized Mickey Rooney.

Rebelling at the control exercised by her mother and the studio, Judy asserted her independence by eloping to Las Vegas in July 1941 with composer David Rose, twelve years her senior. The marriage was troublesome and they soon separated, divorcing in 1945. Meanwhile, Judy pursued a hectic movie-making pace, teaming with a new partner, Gene Kelly in *For Me and My Gal* (1942). By now, bad habits had set in: pills to see her through the busy days, downers to get her through the restless nights, and a repeat of the cycle the next day. Soon alcohol would be added to the damaging regimen. (It has been speculated that the studio actually started her dependency upon drugs in order to keep their star "active" in all her film dates and at the pace the studio wished.)

MGM scriptwriter Joseph L. Mankiewicz encouraged her to seek psychiatric help. Her mom and the studio were incensed at the idea that anyone was tampering mentally with their prize property, fearful that Judy might rebel even more. (A long-bitter Judy often referred to her mother as "the real-life Wicked Witch of the West." They were still battling when Mrs. Gumm died in 1953.)

Judy brightened several memorable 1940s musicals: *Meet Me In St. Louis* (1944) and *The Harvey Girls* (1946). Her frequent director, Vincente Minnelli, became her second husband in June 1945 and their daughter, Liza May, was born in May 1946. By the time of *Words and Music* (1948), Garland was edgy and thin; off screen she was increasingly suicidal. Her mood swings were severe: she was wildly temperamental during the making of *The Pirate* (1948) with Gene Kelly, and very winning during production of *Easter Parade* (1948) with Fred Astaire. Her increasing instability caused her to be dropped from *The Barkleys of Broadway* and Ginger Rogers replaced her. Judy was unhappy and ill through much of *In The Good Old Summertime* (1949) and was a wreck by the time she pre-recorded her numbers for *Annie Get Your Gun* (1950). While she was shipped to Boston, Massachusetts for a rest cure, Betty Hutton replaced her in the big-budgeted musical.

Released from treatment, Garland returned to MGM for the musical, *Summer Stock* (1950). Her bizarre behavior and weight is very evident in the final product. When June Allyson's pregnancy caused her to drop out of *Royal Wedding* (1951), Garland was rushed in as a substitute. However, Judy collapsed and Jane Powell, in turn, took over the assignment.

Struggling with escalating professional and domestic turmoil, Judy attempted suicide on June 20, 1950 by cutting her throat with a piece of glass. Katharine Hepburn advised her, "your ass has hit the gutter. There's no place to go but up. Now, goddamit, do it!" However, Garland was too much of an emotional mess by now to heed the suggestion. MGM decided to call it quits with Judy Garland.

Judy and Vincente Minnelli divorced in March 1951. At this juncture, Michael Sidney Luft, the ex-husband of movie actress Lynn Bari, came into Garland's life. A strong controller, he engineered her sensational appearance at the London Palladium in 1951. Later that year, she played New York's Palace Theatre to equal acclaim, proving she was no has-been. She and Luft married in June 1952. Their daughter Lorna was born that November and their son, Joseph, in March 1955.

The second peak of Judy's roller coaster career came with her show-stopping *A Star Is Born* (1954) in which she sang, danced and acted memorably. She was Oscar-nominated for her tour-de-force performance, but lost to Grace Kelly. Then the downhill slide began in

SPECIAL ADDITIONS

earnest. She was a guest several times on TV before gaining her own series (1963-64) which displayed Judy at her vocal best and undisciplined worst (especially when she became the victim of TV network politics). The trouble-plagued series sadly lasted only one season. She made occasional movies, her most effective being *Judgment at Nuremberg* (1961) in which she played a plump German hausfrau. Whenever things got rough financially, she returned to the stage. However, sadly, by now, her on-stage banter was often the best part of the evening's entertainment.

Garland and Luft divorced in 1965 leading to bitter custody fights over their children. Later that year, she wed young actor Mark Herron, but they soon separated and divorced in 1967. Meanwhile, she was hired and then let go from *Harlow* (1965) and *Valley of the Dolls* (1967). She checked in and out of hospitals for "rests" faster than she and her children moved from hotel to hotel (often one step ahead of creditors). At the end of 1968, she made yet another comeback, this time at London's Talk of the Town Club. As had become customary with Judy, frequently she was late for performances or merely talked her way through her act. On March 15, 1969 in London, she married her fifth husband—discotheque manager Mickey Deans, twelve years her junior.

On June 20, 1969, Judy lunched with her London press agent and, despite being thin and run-down, insisted she wanted fresh work. The next day, Judy and Deans remained at their London flat, nursing an onslaught of strep throat. Later that evening, a London theatrical agent came by to visit. Later, while he and Deans chatted, Judy excused herself and went to bed. She was still awake when Mickey came up at midnight. Hoping to go to the country the next day, Judy took a healthy number of sleeping pills to get through the night.

The next morning, June 22, 1969, Deans was awakened about 11 a.m. by a phone call. When he looked about, Judy was not in the bedroom. Investigating, he found the bathroom door locked. He knocked on the door, but there was no answer. Increasingly worried, he climbed onto the roof and looked down through the bathroom window. There was Judy seated on the toilet. Her head was cradled in her arms which were resting on her lap. Mickey smashed the window and once inside, tried to revive her. Unfortunately, she was already dead.

The autopsy revealed that Judy's system was full of barbiturates and that the final dosage of sleeping pills (taken sometime in the early morning) had been the last straw, crippling her body's breathing mechanism. Despite much speculation of suicide, the coroner insisted "there is absolutely no evidence that this was intentional." Judy's body was flown back to New York City where the open casket was placed on display at Frank E. Campbell's Funeral Home, the same establishment where, decades before, Rudolph Valentino had lain in state. Thousands of people lined the streets to offer their farewells to Judy. Of those commenting on Garland's sudden passing, perhaps Judy's *The Wizard of Oz* co-star, Ray Bolger, said it best: "Judy didn't die. She just wore out."

At the funeral service on June 27, 1969, her *A Star Is Born* co-star, James Mason, delivered a touching eulogy. He said, "the thing about Judy Garland was that she was so alive. You close your eyes and you see a small vivid woman sometimes fat, sometimes thin, but vivid. Vivacity, vitality...that's what our Judy had, and still has as far as I'm concerned." Other celebrities attending the funeral included Lauren Bacall, Sammy Davis Jr., Katharine Hepburn, Lana Turner, Patricia Kennedy Lawford, and New York City Mayor and Mrs. John Lindsay. Judy's white metal casket—covered with yellow roses purchased by her children—was carried from the chapel to the tune of "The Battle Hymn of the Republic."

Judy's body was interred at Ferncliff Cemetery in Hartsdale, New York, with a much-publicized flurry about the many unpaid bills Garland had left behind. (Liza, who had organized the funeral, was left to cope with the huge debts.) Originally, Garland was placed in a modest, small crypt at Ferncliff. Later, when Liza could afford it,

Judy was transferred to a much larger crypt in the main mausoleum near to a magnificent stained glass window. A bouquet of flowers are always to be found in front of her marker.

In death, Judy no longer had to prove anything to anyone, least of all to herself. She had become a show business immortal.

William Holden

[William Franklin Beedle, Jr.]

April 17, 1918 - November 16, 1981

A few years after William Holden's grotesque death, a psychotherapist who once had treated the movie star, stated, "in my sixteen years of dealing with chronic drug and alcohol abusers, Bill was the sickest person I ever treated. He was the sweetest, classiest guy you could ever want to meet, but when he was strung out on drugs and alcohol, he could be a monster."

All his life, Holden brooded because "Dad never showed me any love or caring." Despite his material success, he was generally an unhappy man. He was convinced he had constantly to prove his manliness, that he was as bad a father as his own had been, and that his life would end disastrously. William's misery fueled his wanderlust, as his substance abuse turned him both obnoxious and physically abusive. Holden's life ended violently and pathetically

WILLIAM HOLDEN

ing in high school and at South Pasadena Junior College. However, while at the Junior College, he got talked into working on a campus stage production. A Paramount talent scout spotted the young man during a performance, which led to a $50-a-week studio contract, plus a new name, William Holden. Columbia Pictures borrowed him for the lead in *Golden Boy* (1939). His co-star was veteran actress Barbara Stanwyck, who took a great liking to Holden and helped him tremendously throughout the production. (Thereafter, William would always send her a bouquet of flowers on the anniversary of the first day of shooting that movie.)

Columbia was so impressed with Holden that it made a deal with Paramount to share the actor's contract. During the shooting of *Arizona* (1941), he wed actress Brenda Marshall, who had a daughter, Virginia, by a previous marriage. The Holdens would have two children: Peter (born: 1943) and Scott (born: 1946). During World War II, William served in the military—largely making Defense Department documentaries. The polished actor returned to Hollywood for such pictures as *Dear Ruth* (1947). He was Oscar-nominated for his heavily dramatic role in *Sunset Boulevard* (1950), and won an Academy Award for his performance as the cynical war camp prisoner in *Stalag 17* (1953). During the Fifties, the hard-drinking Holden, with a reputation for violent outbursts and for being a

alone: while drunk he tripped on a bedroom scatter rug, banged his head against a night table, gashed his skull and bled to death. When his corpse was finally found, this deeply-shy man had been dead some four to five days.

At one point in his successful career, William was known as "Golden Holden" and, to outsiders, it certainly seemed that he had a charmed existence. He was born William Franklin Beedle, Jr. in 1918 in O'Fallon, Illinois. At age four, the family, which included two younger brothers, moved to Monrovia, California where the father had gotten a new job as a chemical analyst. William was more interested in sports than act-

moody loner, became involved romantically with two of his co-stars: Audrey Hepburn (*Sabrina*, 1954) and Grace Kelly (*The Bridges at Toko-Ri*, 1954, and *Country Girl*, 1954).

By the late 1950s, weather-beaten Holden moved to Switzerland for tax purposes and was making most of his pictures abroad. He invested his salaries in several overseas business projects, including the founding of the Mount Kenya Safari Club near Nairobi. He became a devout African wildlife preservationist and spent much of his free time traveling around the globe. In 1966, he was convicted of vehicular manslaughter in Italy, in which the other driver died. He received a fine and a suspended sentence. He and Brenda Marshall divorced finally in the early 1970s and, during much of the decade, he was involved romantically with actress Stefanie Powers. His movie choices seemed capricious, and with rare exceptions—*The Wild Bunch* (1969) and *Network* (1976—for which he was Oscar-nominated)—they were beneath him. His last feature appearance was in the cynical comedy *S.O.B.* (1981). He was to have starred in *That Championship Season*, but didn't live to take that 1982 assignment, which was given to Robert Mitchum.

By 1981, Holden, when in the U.S., divided his California time between a Palm Springs home and a Santa Monica apartment on the fifth floor of the Shorecliff Towers on Ocean Avenue. He held an ownership interest in the latter twelve-story building for years. No one thought much of it when loner Holden disappeared from his desert residence and wasn't heard of for days. However, the star's butler, Brian Keating became concerned. At the urging of Patricia Stauffer (an on-again, off-again romance who insisted they were to marry in a few weeks), Keating drove to Santa Monica to check the apartment. When the building manager wouldn't admit Keating to Holden's apartment, the police were summoned. Upon entering the actor's dwelling, they found him sprawled on the bedroom floor in a large pool of blood. He had been dead some four or five days.

Because of the importance of the case, Los Angeles County Coroner Thomas T. Noguchi ("coroner to the stars") took charge. As Noguchi's investigation uncovered, the star had been drunk at the time of his death. He evidently had tripped on a bedroom scatter rug. In his fall, he banged his head against a night table, gashing the right side of his forehead. Holden had attempted to stem the blood flow with Kleenex. Some five to ten minutes later he had passed out, never reaching for the bedside telephone. The Coroner assumed that the drunken star had not realized the severity of his wound and/or that his deep sense of privacy prevented him from calling for help. As fate would have it, Holden's maid had been on vacation that week, or she might have discovered the dying actor.

As often happens when a celebrity dies under peculiar circumstances, rumors abounded that Holden's death might not have been accidental. It was conjectured that he was a victim of organized crime (there were alleged "links" between the underworld and some of his business enterprises) or that his friendships with Ronald Reagan and Richard Nixon had led him into covert government work and that he had accidentally talked too much about his C.I.A.-type activities.

The bulk of Holden's estate was placed in trust for his ailing mother, his ex-wife, their two sons and his step-daughter. He bequeathed his African property to the Kenya government to establish a wildlife preserve. He gave $50,000 to actress Capucine, a former romance (who later killed herself), and the same amount to Patricia Stauffer. He left $250,000 to Stefanie Powers.

Director Billy Wilder, a long-time pal, sighed: "If someone had said to me, 'Holden's dead,' I would have assumed that he had been gored by a water buffalo in Kenya, that he had died in a plane crash approaching Hong Kong, that a crazed jealous woman had shot him and he drowned in a swimming pool. But to be killed by a bottle of vodka and a night table—what a lousy fadeout for a great guy...."

NATURAL CAUSES

Marlene Dietrich

[Maria Magdalena Dietrich]
December 27, 1901 - May 6, 1992

I know that I, myself, could never see Marlene without her moving me and making me happy. If that's what makes her mysterious, it's a beautiful mystery.

—(Ernest Hemingway)

Aside from Joan Crawford, no film star of Hollywood's golden age worked harder than Marlene Dietrich to retain her glamorous allure for so many decades. Illusion was the essential ingredient of the legendary Marlene and she craftily maintained the facade of exotic beauty well into her seventies. Bursting upon the international film scene with *The Blue Angel* (1930), she spent the next 40 or 50 years reshaping her public image to suit the changing times. Throughout these decades, she continued to perform successfully in all types of media: film, radio, recordings and onstage.

But there was much more to shrewd, complex Dietrich than her public facade suggested. She understood herself far better than her adoring fans. Once, after a retrospective showing of her pictures at New York City's Museum of Modern Art, she told the agog audience: "I don't ask whom you are applauding—the legend, the performer or me. I personally liked the legend. Not that it was easy to live with, but I liked it." On another occasion, she confided to her Beverly Hills neighbor, actor Van Johnson: "I'm a hausfrau, a cook—not that sequined clown you see on the stage." A highly intelligent realist and humanist, she acknowledged frequently that her arduous years of entertaining Allied troops during World War II was "the only important thing I've done."

Another of Marlene's intriguing facets was her long-standing reputation as a temptress. (Filmmaker Garson Kanin once insisted, "She was the most experienced and seductive flirt of her time, turning that heady activity into an art form.") Over the years, the long-married Marlene—who lived apart from her accommodating spouse—boasted such lovers as actors Maurice Chevalier, Douglas Fairbanks Jr., George Raft, Jean Gabin, Yul Brynner as well as novelist Erich Maria Remarque. Her sexual liaisons ranged from Edith Piaf to Edward R. Murrow and General George Patton to John F. Kennedy and Joe DiMaggio. However, for the charismatic actress, it was the attention of the famous, the powerful and the intellectual that appealed to her

appetite, not sexual satisfaction. (After all, it was Dietrich who observed, "When people start sleeping with one another, it ruins things. Kaput!")

Having devoted many years to fabricating and orchestrating the myths surrounding her life, it is characteristic of hedonistic Marlene that when advancing years forced her to retire from show business in the late 1970s, she should embark with gusto on a final new phase of her life—seclusion. As with everything else she did, perfectionistic Marlene undertook her new role with unswerving determination.

MARLENE DIETRICH

Once Marlene abandoned her public life, she remained sequestered in her Paris apartment, unlike her long-time movie rival Greta Garbo who ventured out into the Manhattan streets until near the end of her life in 1990.

In complete retirement, Dietrich permitted only a chosen few to visit her in her final twelve years. Highly manipulative and controlling until the end, she was determined that the world should remember her as the sophisticated, seductive Dietrich, not as a frail old woman.

Maria Magdalena Dietrich was born on December 27, 1901 in Schoneberg, Germany, a suburb of Berlin. She was the second daughter (there was year-older Elizabeth) of Prussian policeman Louis Erich Otto Dietrich and Wilhelmina Elisabeth Josephine Felsing. Maria's father, a former cavalry lieutenant turned police officer, died when she was nine, and his widow soon remarried, to Edouard von Losch, an officer in the German army. Throughout her highly-disciplined childhood, it was her mother (Maria called her "the good General") who exerted the most influence upon her younger daughter. She was always exhorting the girl to "Do something" with your life. Looking back on these formative years, Dietrich admitted once, "My whole upbringing... [forced me] to mask my feelings."

From an early age, Maria was fascinated with motion pictures and determined to one day be part of the acting profession. Meanwhile, as a teenager, Maria took violin lessons and, at age sixteen, had her first affair with her considerably older music teacher. Post-World War I Berlin was disrupted by riots and revolution, so Maria went to Weimar in 1919 to study violin at the Konservatorium. However, a wrist injury ended her musical ambitions and she turned to her first love, acting.

By 1921 she was studying drama in Berlin and began winning minor roles in stage dramas and revues. Still fascinated with movies, Maria, who had changed her first name to Marlene, haunted the film studios seeking acting assignments. One of her earliest screen parts was in *Die Tragodie der Liebe* (1923) starring Emil Jannings. She was given a small role by assistant director Rudolf Sieber, who had become fascinated with the plump, vivacious young actress.

On May 17, 1924 Marlene married Sieber (four years her senior) in Berlin. The following January, their only child, Maria, was born. However, the conventions of marriage and motherhood did not change Dietrich, who was gaining a reputation as a fun-loving, bisexual jazz baby. In 1927, she was in the Berlin cast of the American musical, Broadway. When that show went on tour to Vienna, she was given a larger role, perhaps as a result of her attachment to the play's star, Willi Forst. Once back in Berlin, it was Forst, her co-star in the movie *Cafe Electric* (1927), who introduced her to the city's young intelligentsia, including

SPECIAL ADDITIONS

future film director Billy Wilder and novelist Erich Maria Remarque.

Marlene was appearing in a Berlin musical revue, *Two Bow Ties* (1929), when Hollywood director Josef von Sternberg arrived in Germany to film *Der Blaue Engel* (The Blue Angel). In this Paramount movie—shot in German, French and English language versions—Emil Jannings starred as the middle-aged professor who is brought to ruination by a seductive cabaret singer. Von Sternberg saw Dietrich perform on stage and cast her as the decadent Lola Lola, who in the course of the drama sings "Falling in Love Again" and "Lola." The night the movie premiered in Berlin to enthusiastic response, Dietrich, buoyed by a Paramount contract, left Germany for Hollywood. Both her husband and young daughter remained in Berlin.

Paramount envisioned Dietrich as the rival to MGM's Greta Garbo and immediately Americanized their much-touted fraulein contractee. By the time she appeared in her first American-made feature, *Morocco* (1930), Dietrich had thinned down considerably, revamped her hair style and make-up, and created the exotic image that was to remain her trademark for the next several decades. With her Svengali director, von Sternberg, Marlene made four other features, which ranged from the deliciously ridiculous (*Shanghai Express*, 1932) to the completely dreary (*The Devil Is a Woman*, 1935).

In her first Hollywood year, Marlene maintained a bachelor life. However, in the spring of 1931, she brought her daughter Maria to Hollywood, telling the press that her 6-year old girl was just four. As for her absent husband, Rudi, he moved the next year to Paris to be with Tamara Matul, a Russian dancer. (Rudi and Tamara would remain together till her death in 1968.)

When von Sternberg's wife, Riza, divorced her husband in later 1931, Paramount had to pay her off as she had filed charges of libel and alienation of affection against Dietrich. Meanwhile, Marlene, who, both onscreen and in real life, preferred the androgynous look of wearing trousers, had an assortment of affairs. These included lesbian socialite/author Mercedes d'Acosta and, later in 1935, with ex-silent screen star John Gilbert. Both of these people had been former lovers of Dietrich's great rival, Greta Garbo.

By the mid-1930s, Dietrich had broken her professional ties with von Sternberg. She refused Adolph Hilter's blandishments to return to Germany to star in movies for the Third Reich. Instead, she appeared to good advantage with Gary Cooper (her one-time lover and co-star of *Morocco*) in *Desire* (1936). However after the tiresome *Angel* (1937), Paramount and Marlene called it quits. She was branded

SPECIAL ADDITIONS

box-office poison.

Always the survivor, she made a stunning comeback in Universal's comic western, *Destry Rides Again* (1939), cast opposite Jimmy Stewart. The new Marlene was an earthy saloon chanteuse who could get rough and dirty (i.e., her classic barroom brawl with Una Merkel). The movie was a great hit and Marlene was again a saleable Hollywood commodity. She spent the early Forties making a series of raucous romantic entries, often teamed with John Wayne: *Seven Sinners* (1940), *The Spoilers* (1942) and *Pittsburgh* (1942). Reportedly, Wayne rebuffed her advances, not wanting to be part of her stable.

Marlene had become an American citizen in 1938 and, by 1940, daughter Maria had returned from schooling abroad. That year, as Maria would reveal years later in her bittersweet autobiography, the teenager was raped by her governess. However, she could not confide the trauma to her mother because Marlene was in seclusion recuperating from an abortion.

When the U.S. entered World War II, Marlene became one of Hollywood's most active entertainers in the war effort. She worked tirelessly at the Hollywood Canteen, participated in war bond drives, made radio broadcasts in assorted languages for the government to air in Europe, and made recordings (including "Lili Marlene") in German, which were dropped behind enemy lines. She entertained for the USO both in America and in Europe, selling $100,000 worth of her jewelry to finance her expedition. For uplifting the spirits of Allied fighting men during World War II, she later received the U.S. Defense Department's Medal of Freedom. (She had already been given the French Legion of Honor.)

After the war, Marlene went to France where she and her on-again, off-again lover, French film star Jean Gabin, co-starred in *Martin Roumagnac* (1946). It made little impact when released in a censored version in the U.S. as *The Room Upstairs*. After lesser co-starring roles in *Golden Earrings* (1947—with Ray Milland), *A Foreign Affair* (1948—with Jean Arthur) and *Stage Fright* (1950—with Jane Wyman), Dietrich accepted that her leading-lady days in movies were nearly through. By now, daughter Maria, who had gone through eating and drinking binges, had found happiness with a second husband (William Riva) who was fostering her acting career. In 1948 Maria had her first child, which led the ever-enterprising Marlene to create a new role for herself as "The World's Most Glamorous Grandmother."

In the early 1950s, Dietrich starred in a radio series "Cafe Istanbul" (later reformatted to "Time for Love"), made recordings, and an occasional movie (*Rancho Notorious*, 1952). More importantly, she turned to cabaret performing throughout the world, proving to be a sensation in her provocative see-through shimmering gowns and singing in that inimitable throaty voice of hers. In 1957 she enjoyed a dramatic success on screen in the courtroom thriller, *Witness for the Prosecution*. Her last sizeable screen assignment was in the all-star *Judgment at Nuremberg* (1961). In 1962, when daughter Maria quit acting and moved to Europe with her husband and four boys, Marlene purchased a Paris apartment for herself.

Throughout the 1960s and early 1970s, Marlene continued her one-woman show, bringing the stylized production to Broadway in 1967. To the public at large, Marlene was defying the laws of nature and gravity by maintaining her glamorous illusion well into her seventies. However, she carefully kept secret her various face lifts and junkets to Switzerland for youth rejuvenation treatments. The public was never made aware of the elaborate undergarments she wore beneath her "form-fitting" gown to retain the semblance of a seductive figure, or that she pulled her hair into a painfully tight bun beneath her wig to give her face a youthful appearance.

As the 1960s progressed, Marlene suffered increasingly from hardening of the arteries which made standing for long periods (as required by her show) an agonizing ordeal. Then too, she became increasingly deaf which caused her to often sing flat as she could not hear the orchestra properly. Bette Davis, herself a champion survivor, would recount visiting the aged Dietrich one evening backstage and being bowled over by the sharp contrast between the magnetic legend in the spotlight and the tired figure who greeted her in her dressing room. Davis recalled, "She was this old, old woman. I asked, 'Marlene, why do you go on?' She replied, 'Because I need the money.'"

Marlene continued undaunted through the early 1970s, being paid $5,000 a performance. However, in 1972 she began suffering a series of mishaps. That year, during a curtain call at the Queen's Theatre in London, she fell on stage, partially caused by the confining flesh-colored sheath she wore beneath her magnificent dress. It was the first of several falls. After another tumble in 1974, she went to Houston, Texas for skin grafts to repair the gash to one of her famous gams. Thereafter, she returned to Paris where she fell in her bedroom and broke her hip. A steel ball was inserted in her hip socket and a bar riveted through the bone of her upper thigh.

Her final stage appearance in Britain was in 1975 when she had to leave the stage in mid-performance due to excruciating pain in her bad leg. Some eight months later, her cabaret career ended in Sydney, Australia. While making her entrance, she stumbled over a cable backstage and fell backwards to the floor. Thereafter she was hospitalized for months, first in Los

SPECIAL ADDITIONS

Angeles and then in New York.

Returning to Paris, Marlene was too ill to accept the role of an actress who appears to be eternally young in Billy Wilder's *Fedora* (1978); the part was taken by Hildegarde Knef. However, Dietrich did play a Prussian madam in David Bowie's *Just a Gigolo* (1979) because her brief scenes could be shot at a makeshift studio a few blocks from Dietrich's apartment. Appearing enfeebled (daughter Maria insists that her mother was drunk on the sound stage), Dietrich made her final screen appearance, earning $250,00 for two days of work. She wore a wide-brimmed hat pulled down over one eye, with a heavy veil in place to distort the ravages of time. She sang, rather weakly, a rendition of the title tune.

Thereafter, Marlene became a recluse at her high-rise apartment at 12 Avenue Montaigne across the street from the Plaza Athenee Hotel. She refused to deal with the press. When enterprising reporters left notes at her door begging for an audience, she would leave typed notes that Marlene Dietrich no longer lived in Paris. Often when long-time friends came to France, they would call the star, coaxing her to allow them to visit. Occasionally she would relent and agree, but usually at the last minute she would phone, pretending to be Dietrich's maid, and insisting that the star had been called out of town.

Actor Maximilian Schell, Dietrich's *Judgment at Nurenberg* co-star, had become so fascinated with the legendary actress that he produced a documentary of her career. After much persuasion, Marlene agreed to allow him to interview her at her apartment, on condition that she only provide occasional off-camera commentary. In the highly-regarded results, *Marlene* (1984), Dietrich refused to acknowledge any chronological facts or events which contradicted her carefully engineered mythology.

If Marlene refused to go out in public, her fans around the world were still fascinated to learn how the reclusive superstar spent her days of seclusion. It leaked out that Marlene maintained a very simple regimen. She would typically awake at 5:30 AM, and blow her police whistle to let her live-in secretary, Bernard Hall, know she wanted her cup of Earl Grey tea. According to Hall: "At 6 AM, the Scotch would be going down. I didn't know what to do. I gave it to her—it was impossible saying no.... Anyway, she had two bottles under her bed. She was brilliant until 10 AM, then zonk—she'd collapse.... Until then she would be marvelous. She had a wonderful brain. It was so sad to watch, heartbreaking." The star spent much of her waking hours reading (newspapers and sometimes murder mysteries) or watching TV news programs. (She hated her old movies on TV, insisting "It bores me to see them. They were terrible, terrible kitsch.")

One of her frequent distractions

was making her famous calls to friends (and strangers) around the globe, often tallying up a $5,000 monthly phone bill as she chatted about world events or discussed (usually in the third person) remarks she had read in the media about herself. Actor/friend Tony Perkins would observe, "She didn't like to receive calls. She liked to make them. It was her way of reaching out."

Her self-indulgent autobiography, *Marlene*, was published in 1987. In that year, she became completely bed-ridden, remaining so for her final five years. She kept to her rigid daily schedule, allowing only a few chosen souls to visit and do her bidding. (Even her dominated daughter Maria was supposed to make an appointment before arriving at Chez Dietrich.) Marlene would often complain about her grandsons' inattention, yet when they came to visit, she would pretend not to be home.

Although she still received royalties from her recordings, finances proved pressing. When most all of her jewelry had been auctioned off, she would sell a piece of art, such as a Picasso painting which went for $750,000 in 1988.

In December 1991, Marlene celebrated her ninetieth birthday. Long-alerted that the star was in failing health, the media kept a watch on her apartment, waiting for the inevitable to happen. But she remained in control until the very last. Her grandson Peter, a New York City literary agent, would say,

"Until the very end she was her own creation, keeping out what she called the wolves at the door." In early 1992, Burt Bacharach who had been her cabaret tour accompanist and confidante several years earlier, reported, "I received my last call from her in January and her voice was the saddest I'd ever heard." In March 1992, Marlene suffered a stroke. She completely lost her appetite and soon was weighing only seventy pounds.

In May 1992, grandson Peter flew to Paris to be at Marlene's bedside. On May 6th, when he arrived, she was dressed in a white nightgown and pink bed jacket. He inquired if she would like to go into the living room of her three-room apartment. It would be her first time in there in five years. She nodded yes. He carried her to the sofa, where she gazed at the many celebrity photos on the walls. Later, she spoke briefly to her daughter by phone, even swallowing a scant spoonful of soup. According to Peter, after saying "Maria," she closed her eyes "as if she wanted to have her afternoon nap. And she was gone." The following day, May 7, the Cannes International Film Festival opened with the year's events dedicated to Marlene Dietrich.

In her final years, Dietrich had been obsessed by her death. She once told her daughter that when she died she was to remove her body in a garbage bag so the press would not see her. Instead, Dietrich's body was taken from her fashionable apartment draped in the French Tricolor. On May 14, 1992, a simple memorial service was held at Paris' Church of Madeleine. Among the attendants were Maria, her husband and their four sons, as well as two of Marlene's great-grandsons. In eulogizing her, Reverend Philippe Brizzard commented, "She was a woman of unflinching moral principle who lived like a soldier and would have liked to die like a soldier. Marlene was highly discreet, secretive. Her secret belongs to her alone. She will share it with God."

Maria placed a wooden crucifix, a St. Christopher's medal, a star of David and a locket enclosing photos of Dietrich's grandsons in the casket beside her mother. The lid was then sealed and the French flag draped across its mahogany surface. Marlene was sent home to Germany to be buried, with an American flag draped on her coffin. In Berlin, the city's flag was placed on the casket. On May 16, 1993 she was buried in the Friedenau cemetery in Schoneberg next to her mother's grave. Among the mourners attending was Maximilian Schell. As she was laid to rest he said, "Dear Marlene, welcome home." Among the floral tributes was a wreath from German movie director Wim Wenders, inscribed with the words "Angels Don't Die."

Typically Marlene had the final word on this occasion. Back in September 1984 she had written, "When they finally close the coffin on me the world will be crying and sighing for me. Forget the sighing and crying. It's only one sighing that matters to me. Of someone who's watching over me."

In the months following Marlene's death, several biographies of the screen legend were published, including Maria's 790-page memoir: *Marlene Dietrich by Her Daughter*. (A few years earlier when Dietrich had learned that her daughter was writing a tell-all book she had threatened to sue her to prevent its publication.) Attempting to explain her enigmatic parent, Riva wrote in her tome, "I don't use the word 'mother' for Dietrich. That is a special word that implies love shown to one person, and that is not what I remember." In the course of her gossipy, detailed book, Riva also recalls her mother urging her on one occasion to have an abortion, reasoning that "Children are nothing but trouble." In analyzing the subservient roles both she and her father (who died in 1976 at his California chicken farm) endured, Maria summarized, "If you adored her, you took whatever she had to give you."

Most thought-provoking of all was Maria's analysis of Dietrich, the famed goddess of love. On a 1993 U.S. TV interview with commentator Diana Sawyer, Maria said, "I don't think my mother knew what love was, and that was her tragedy." Amplifying that comment, she added, "I can't help thinking her life was a kind of tragedy. I wish her life had been fuller. Dietrich believed that she invented love, but I don't think she really knew what love was."

Audrey Hepburn

[Edda van Heemstra Hepburn-Ruston]

May 4, 1929 - January 20, 1993

Slender, doe-eyed Audrey Hepburn was a unique personality in many ways. Few actresses have gained success so quickly in Hollywood. With her debut American feature, *Roman Holiday* (1953), she won an Academy Award and established herself as a major leading lady of the cinema. Initially, she was compared to other waifish movie types, such as Leslie Caron and Maggie McNamara. However, she soon established that she had a very special personality all to herself. (At 5'7" and 110 pounds she was a distinct contrast to the curvaceous screen bombshells of the day such as Marilyn Monroe, Elizabeth Taylor and Sophia Loren.)

On-camera, Audrey most frequently and successfully played Cinderella roles, demonstrating repeatedly her knack for portraying the perfect gamine. Yet Hepburn was far more complex than that stereotype. She had a civilized, aristocratic look which, in conjunction with her hard-to-place accent, gave her a sophisticated undertone. This elegance was heightened by her penchant for wearing high fashion clothes (usually designed by Hubert de Givenchy and which often established new styling fads).

SPECIAL ADDITIONS

Entertainment Weekly would analyze in retrospect that Audrey was the "screen's most enduring symbol of graceful self-possession.... Her long, sculpted neck was the kind budding ballerinas—as the adolescent Hepburn herself had been—pray for. Her velvety voice, which barely made the acquaintance of consonants, purred elegance." Peter Bogdanovich, who directed her in *They All Laughed* (1981) would rapsodize, "Looking back now, we can see clearly that in the last decade and a half of the golden age of Hollywood, Audrey Hepburn became the last true innocent of the American screen."

Part of Audrey's appeal both on-camera and in person was her staunch modesty. With utter sincerity she remarked once: "I've never understood what makes me so special." She also observed, "Let me say that the so-called glamour in the movies wasn't me...It was the movies. That was a job, not reality." During the latter part of the 1960s, as she reached the age (forty) when substantial screen roles are notoriously difficult for women to win, she retired from movies to devote herself to a fresh stab at domesticity with her second husband. She would return to films occasionally over the next decades, however. Her greatest role would be as the selfless UNICEF goodwill ambassador who took as a personal cause the plight of malnourished, sickly children of third world nations. They became her cause celebre and, in her devotion to their welfare, she gained yet a new generation of admirers.

When Audrey Hepburn developed cancer in 1992, the world took her misfortune to heart, especially when she displayed great courage in the face of tremendous pain, refusing to become a martyr. Her untimely death pricked the conscience of devotees around the world.

Audrey Hepburn once remarked, "I could never be cynical [onscreen]. I wouldn't dare. I'd roll over and die before that. After all, I've been so fortunate in my own life. I feel I've been born under a lucky star." However, her early years seemed often quite the opposite. She was born Edda van Heemstra Hepburn-Ruston on May 4, 1929 in Brussels, Belgium. Her mother—wealthy Dutch Baroness Ella van Heemstra—had two sons from the first of two earlier marriages, each of which had ended in divorce. Edda's father, Joseph Hepburn-Ruston, was an Irish businessman who managed his wife's finances through the Brussels' branch of the Bank of England. As a youngster, Audrey was a sickly girl, disturbed by her gawky looks and especially by her nose. Because her parents quarreled so much, the child became very introverted. When she was six, her parents separated and. then, divorced three years later. Years later, Audrey would say that "losing" her father, whom she worshipped, was "one of the traumas that left a very deep mark on me."

SPECIAL ADDITIONS

One of the stipulations of the divorce decree was that Edda be schooled near London so her father might visit her frequently. She was just adjusting to the girls' school there when England declared war against Nazi Germany in September 1939. The Baroness, on holiday in Arnhem, Holland where her family had an estate, thought it would be safer for Edda to live there, since Holland was neutral in the growing conflict. With her propensity for languages the youngster quickly learned Dutch so she could converse with her class-mates.

In early 1940, eleven-year-old Edda anounced she wanted to become a dancer and started classes at the Arnhem Conservatory of Music. However, a few weeks later—in May 1940—the Germans invaded and occupied the Netherlands. During the subsequent four years of enemy regime, Edda attended school infrequently and hardly had the opportunity to practice dancing. Because of insufficient food, milk, vitamins, etc. she became extreme-ly thin and developed anemia. (There were times when Edda and her family survived by eating flour made from tulip bulbs.)

During the occupation, one of her half-brothers was carted away to a German labor camp, while an uncle and a cousin were executed as ene-mies of the Third Reich. Meanwhile, the van Heemstra estate and much of their funds were confiscated. The Baroness, who had a part-Jewish heritage, joined the underground and staged ama-teur shows as fund-raisers. Edda occasionally carried messages for the Resistance hidden in her shoes.

At the time of the liberation of the Netherlands in 1945, sixteen-year-old Edda suffered from acute ane-mia, respiratory problems and edema (the swelling of the limbs). She was one of those who received food and medicine from the newly-formed United Nations Children's Fund (UNICEF), a debt she vowed to repay one day.

Following World War II, Edda studied ballet diligently for three years in Amsterdam. In 1948, she made her film debut in a brief bit in the Dutch-British documentary-style travelogue, *Dutchat the Double*. Also that year, she and her mother returned to England. By then, her father was residing in Ireland and he and his daughter never reestablished a rapport. To pay for her London dancing class-es, Edda became a part-time model as well as haunted movie casting offices hoping for work. Because of her wartime deprivations, she lacked the stamina ever to be a suc-cessful ballerina. Instead, she turned to dance jobs in nightclubs and West End revues (including *Sauce Tartare*, 1949). By now, she had anglicized her first name to Audrey and had assumed part of her father's hyphenated surname as her last name. A few subordinate movie roles convinced Associated British Films to sign her to a con-tract in 1951

SPECIAL ADDITIONS

In the summer of 1951, Audrey traveled to the French Riviera to film *Nous Irons a Monte Carlo* (Monte Carlo Baby). During the shooting of a scene at the Hotel Paris, 78-year-old novelist Colette, a hotel guest, was wheeled past the cast of actors as they rested between takes. The famed author spotted Hepburn and knew immediately that she had found the right actress to play the lead in a pending Broadway version of her popular work, *Gigi*. Within weeks, Audrey, accompanied by the ever-vigilant Baroness, was whisked off to the United States. When *Gigi* debuted in November 1951, the critics had reservations about the adaptation, but they were unanimous in their delight at newcomer Audrey Hepburn. Almost overnight she was the toast of Broadway, and, in her new posture, decided against marrying young trucking company executive James Hansen whom she had first met in London.

Just before Audrey left for New York, she had tested for director William Wyler who was planning a new Paramount picture, to be shot in Italy. He was so delighted with Hepburn's screen charisma, that she was signed by the studio to a four-picture deal. After a six-month run in *Gigi*, Audrey flew to Rome to co-star with Gregory Peck in *Roman Holiday* (1953). She was the incognito European princess who falls in love with a newspaper correspondent (Peck), only to realize she must abandon him in the face of regal duty. At a party cele-brating the London premiere of *Roman Holiday*, Peck introduced Audrey to Mel Ferrer, an actor twelve years older than she and then co-starring in the movie *Lili* (1953). Hepburn and Ferrer were smitten at once and promptly agreed that they would like to do a play together.

Meanwhile, Paramount cast Audrey in *Sabrina* (1954). During the course of the moviemaking, co-star William Holden fell madly in love with her, much to the chagrin of the jealous third lead in the movie, Humphrey Bogart. It was for this romantic comedy that Hepburn convinced young coutourier, Hubert de Givenchy to design her wardrobe. It was the start of a long-lasting relationship. After this picture, Audrey joined Mel Ferrer in the allegorical play, *Ondine*, which opened to much acclaim on Broadway in February 1954. A few weeks later she won an Academy Award for *Roman Holiday* and, a week thereafter, she was given a Tony Award for *Ondine*. After the play's close, Audrey and Mel were married on September 24, 1954 in Switzerland. The following February she suffered the first of several miscarriages.

She and Ferrer labored for months in a staggering film version of *War and Peace* (1956), a project more noteworthy for its epic scope than its dramatic integrity. Among the many scripts she was offered was *The Diary of Anne Frank*, which she rejected as it hit too closely to her World War II traumas.

SPECIAL ADDITIONS

Continuing a trend of her movies, she was again teamed with a (much) older leading man, Fred Astaire, in a musical, *Funny Face* (1957). The movie proved to be an elegant diversion and while Hepburn was no threat to Judy Garland or Doris Day, she proved to have an intriguing light singing voice. By choice, Audrey continued to revolve in Ferrer's orbit and together they co-starred in a TV special of *Mayerling* (1957), a tale of nineteenth century regal tragedy. She rounded off the year with *Love in the Afternoon* (1957), teamed with 56-year-old Gary Cooper who looked far too old to play her on-camera lover.

Ferrer had long harbored a desire to film the classic nature novel, *Green Mansions*, by William H. Hudson. With compliant Audrey agreeing to star as the ethereal bird girl Rima, MGM backed the problematic project with Ferrer assigned as director. The high-faluting picture was a critical and commercial flop, despite Audrey's performance and the exotic movie score by the Brazilian composer Heitor Villa-Lobos. As Audrey continued to reject projects that either did not co-star Ferrer or please him, the industry pondered her self-destructive path. (Her rationalization was, "He takes care of me in every sense. I enjoy that.") Her professional slide was reversed by *The Nun's Story* (1959) which earned her another Academy Award nomination.

Audrey had already agreed (for $300,000) to star in the adult western *The Unforgiven* (1960), when she learned she was again pregnant. During the shoot she was thrown from a horse, fracturing four vertebrae and requiring filming to halt for three weeks. After the movie was completed she returned to Switzerland where she had another miscarriage in July 1959. That December she was again pregnant and this time remained in seclusion at the Swiss villa the Ferrers had purchased in Tolochenaz, a lakeside village fifteen miles from Lausanne. On July 17, 1960, Audrey finally gave birth to a son, Sean.

Thereafter, Hepburn quickly reestablished herself on-screen as Holly Golightly, the free spirited heroine of *Breakfast at Tiffany's* (1961). She was far less successful in a new version of *The Children's Hour* (1961) co-starring Shirley MacLaine as the school teacher who discovers she has a hidden, "forbidden" love for Hepburn. Much more popular and in the Hepburn fashion was the modish thriller *Charade* (1963), co-starring her with a dapper Cary Grant. A decade after she had first teamed with William Holden in *Sabrina*, the two were reunited for *Paris When It Sizzles* (1964), a high-concept spoof that fizzled. Observers noted that Holden still retained a passion for Hepburn that she did not return.

Perhaps the most controversial Hollywood movie casting of the 1960s concerned the screen musical version of the hit Broadway musical *My Fair Lady* (1964). While Rex Harrison was signed to recreate his role of Professor Henry Higgins, Julie Andrews, the stage production's Eliza Doolittle, was overlooked for the film role in favor of Audrey. Although Hepburn diligently studied with a vocal coach, director George Cukor et al decided to dub her singing with the voice of Marni Nixon. Audrey was profoundly disturbed by the corporate decision, but the movie proved to be a large moneymaker and garnered several Oscar nominations/awards. However, Audrey was snubbed by the Academy and, ironically, it was Julie Andrews who won the Best Actress Oscar that year for *Mary Poppins*.

Thereafter, Audrey was touted to star in a screen musical version of *Goodbye, Mr. Chips* and/or a new version of *Peter Pan*. However, she chose to make the sophisticated *Two for The Road* (1967), dealing with a couple's twelve years of marriage during which both are adulterous. With Mel Ferrer away on another film project, Audrey and co-star Albert Finney became the talk of the French Riviera more for their unabashed togetherness away from the filming rather than on-camera. (Her final words on the subject were, "Albie's just plain wonderful, that's all there is to it.") With that relationship cooled, she returned to Hollywood for *Wait Until Dark* (1967), in which she played a blind woman terrorized by

a trio of crooks in her Greenwich Village apartment. Ferrer produced the project and there was much on-set tension.

Audrey gained her fifth Oscar nomination for *Wait Until Dark*, but in the process lost her marriage. In late 1967 she filed for divorce citing "incompatibility." The next summer she met and fell in love with wealthy Italian psychiatrist Andrea Dotti, nine years her junior. They wed on January 18, 1969. Her second son, Luca was born in February 1970.

Having drifted away from filmmaking, Audrey did a few TV commercials and then sought the lead role in *Forty Carats* (1972) but lost the part to Liv Ullmann when she refused to come to Hollywood for the filming. After several abortive movie projects, Hepburn made her comeback in *Robin and Marion* (1976), co-starred with Sean Connery in the bittersweet account of a middle-aged Robin Hood and his Maid Marion. The movie failed to win over critics or the public. However, it was far superior to her high-toned trash *Bloodline* (1979), based on a Sidney Sheldon thriller. On that set, Audrey, tired of her womanizing spouse, had set her romantic sights on co-star Ben Gazzara. He was then married to actress Janice Rule and rebuffed her advances, as he did again during the making of their next joint venture, *They All Laughed* (1981).

Admitting defeat with Gazzara, Audrey finally terminated her tattered marriage to Dotti. (She would reflect, "You always hope that if you love somebody enough, everything will be all right—but it isn't always true.") At a dinner party in 1981, she met Dutch actor Robert Wolders, 46, who was the widower of movie star Merle Oberon (who died in 1979). After a few meetings, Hepburn became attracted to the eight-year-younger Wolders, commenting, "I discovered that Robbie was solid in every way." They became constant companions, but never married, with the reasoning that marriage "wouldn't contribute anything to what we already have."

Professionally, Hepburn nearly abandoned her career, except for a TV movie (*Love Among Thieves*, 1987) and playing an angel in *Always* (1989). Between domesticity with Wolders and her two sons, she began devoting increasing time and energy to UNICEF charity work. By 1988 she had taken on a full-time task as a UNICEF volunteer, jetting from Ethiopia to Ireland, Turkey, Venezuela and Ecuador. She explained her devotion to the cause with, "Now, forty years later [after her horrible World War II experiences], I can get some relief from the knot in my stomach, the pain of watching children starving to death."

Based at her Swiss villa in Tolochenaz, the extremely private and shy Audrey made occasional forays to the United States, such as attending a film tribute gala in her honor at Lincoln Center on April

22, 1991. In the late summer of 1992 she was scheduled to visit Somalia in East Africa as part of her UNICEF duties. She began experiencing excrucitiating stomach pains, but refused to deal with the matter until after the high-profile trek. In late September she returned from Somalia and, after undergoing medical tests to diagnose the cause of her severe stomach pains, entered Cedars-Sinai Medical Center in Los Angeles. There, on November 2, 1992, she underwent intestinal surgery, with the physicians initially optimistic about her full recovery. However, they discovered she had a cancerous tumor necessitating that part of her colon be removed, as well as having her undergo a hysterectomy. The next day she was told that the cancer had spread throughout her stomach and that, at best, she had three months to live.

Refusing to surrender to the grim news, she announced, "The thousands of starving children need me. I've got to get back on my feet for them—even if it takes a miracle!" The medical team implanted a Hichman catheter in her chest for administering chemoterapy and pain-killing medicines. Some days later, she left the hospital. However, she was back again by December 9 and new exploratory surgery revealed that nothing further could be done.

Accepting the inevitable, she told Wolders that she wished to return to her villa, La Plaisance, her home for the last 26 years. "I want to see the snow on the mountains one more time.... I want to pet my dogs and feel them lick my face.... Please take me home." Putting on a brave face, she insisted to well-wishers that "It's not that bad," but the pain was horrific. It was so severe that, toward the end, she could only speak in barely audible whispers. Meanwhile, President George Bush announced on December 11 that he had awarded Audrey the Presidential Medal of Freedom, the nation's highest civilian honor, for her UNICEF work. The Screen Actors Guild extended the Lifetime Achievement Award to Audrey, which was to be presented at a January 10, 1993 tribute.

On the weekend of December 19, Audrey accompanied by the ever-present Wolders returned to Switzerland aboard a private jet courtesy of Gregory Peck. She now weighed only 83 pounds, and was unable to keep down any solid foods. She received pain-killing morphine intravenously. Wolders, her sons, and friends did their best to make the dying star comfortable at her villa retreat. One of her last outings was on January 10, 1993 to pay a final visit to the adjacent flower garden she had tended for years. She was now down to 75 pounds. She said, "I want to feel alive one more time before I die." Supported by two nurses, she painfully took a fifteen-minute trek outside before the exhausted woman was returned to her bedroom. There her bed was so positioned that she could look out her

window and view the snowcapped mountains in the distance. Unable to attend the Screen Actors Guild festivities in her honor in Los Angeles, she sent a message thanking all her directors and co-stars for their good thoughts.

On Janury 20, 1993, Audrey passed away without fanfare. Among her final words were "Remember the children when I'm gone. Please make sure those poor starving babies get enough to eat." In a simple statement to the press, son Sean said, "Mother believed in one thing above all. She believed in love." On Sunday, January 24, she was buried in the cemetery at Tolochenaz. Seven hundred villagers stood outside as 120 invited guests attended the services. Among those on hand were Prince Sadruddin Aga Khan, actors Roger Moore and Alain Delon. Other guests included Doris Brynner, as well as Audrey's first spouse, Mel Ferrer. Pallbearers for her unadorned oak coffin included sons Sean and Luca, Robert Wolders, designer Hubert de Givenchy and ex-husband Andrea Dotti. Local mayor Pierre-Alain Mercier stated, "She was a star in France, England, the U.S., Italy. But here she was just another neighbor. I used to see her working on her flowers, like anyone else, and we'd say hello. Everyone knew the same thing about her: she was a person like any other—not at all a star." Audrey's grave, atop a small knoll, was marked by a simple pinewood cross reading "Audrey Hepburn,

1929-1993."

On January 21, 1993, the day following her death, Audrey could be seen on television in the first of a six-part PBS-TV documentary series, "Gardens of the World with Audrey Hepburn," taped in 1992. On March 29, 1993, she posthumously received the Jean Hersholt Humanitarian Award shared with Liz Taylor. Audrey's award was accepted in a moving speech by her son Sean. Several tributes in Hepburn's honor followed thereafter, with proceeds donated to UNICEF. April 1993 saw the release of one of her last projects (done in May 1992), "Audrey Hepburn's Enchanted Tales" recorded for Dove Audio Tapes, as well as a re-issue of her 1974, Grammy-winning recording of "The Little Prince."

Perhaps the best tribute to this beloved star came from columnist Rex Reed who voiced, "In a cruel and imperfect world she was living proof that God could still create perfection." Finally, as Elizabeth Taylor observed so aptly, "God has a most beautiful new angel."

Anthony Perkins

April 4, 1932 - September 12, 1992

Most actors spend their entire careers hoping vainly for that special "role of a lifetime" to establish them as a major name in their profession. Early in his screen career, tall (6' 2"), lanky Anthony Perkins, who had made a specialty of playing gawky, mumbling Jimmy Stewart-type leading men, achieved that dream. He was lucky enough to be chosen by Alfred Hitchcock to star as mother-fixated, homicidal Norman Bates in the classic thriller, *Psycho* (1960). It proved to be the magic movie part that launched Tony as an international star. However, it also led the film industry to typecast him thereafter in a series of highly neurotic movie assignments. Generally, Perkins was stuck playing tormented (even deranged) characters forever at odds with themselves and the world. (En route. Tony would also star in three film sequels to *Psycho*.) While fully aware that Hollywood's early pigeonholing of him had often obscured his real acting talents, Perkins acknowledged late in life: "Without *Psycho*, who's to say if I would have endured?"

As events in Perkins' own life would prove, there were several amazing parallels between the real-life actor and *Psycho*'s nutty Norman Bates. These resemblances once again prove that art often does imitate life and that it was no wild decision that led astute Alfred Hitchcock to hire Tony for *Psycho*.

Anthony Perkins was born in New York City on April 4, 1932, the only child of Osgood and Janet (Rane) Perkins. His father was a noted stage and film actor who was frequently away on theatre tours or making movies in Hollywood. Because of this situation, Tony became extremely devoted to his mother. Perkins would say later, "I became abnormally close to my mother and when my father came home, I was jealous.... I loved him, but I also wanted him to be dead so I could have her all to myself."

When Tony was five, his dad, age 45, died of a heart attack. The son confessed years later, "I was horrified. I assumed that my wanting him to be dead had actually killed him.... I prayed and prayed for my father to come back. I remember long nights of crying in bed. For years I nursed the hope that he wasn't really dead. Because I'd see him on film, it was as if he were still alive. He became a mythic being to me, to be dreaded and appeased."

Equally damaging to Tony's psyche, his widowed mother suffocated him with a love which often veered toward sexuality. "She was constantly touching and caressing me.... She wasn't ill-tempered or mean. Just a strong-willed, dominant, New England kind of woman. She controlled everything about my life, including my thoughts and feelings.... She felt she was taking responsibility, but she was really taking control."

Initially brought up in Manhattan, Tony and Mrs. Perkins (who never remarried) moved later to Brookline, Massachusetts where, during World War II, she managed the Boston Stage Door Canteen. A lonely youth, Perkins sought escape and life-justification in acting. As he explained, "...all my life, I'd

ANTHONY PERKINS

heard glory stories about my father. What a wonderful actor he was, how everybody loved him, how he went everywhere and did everything he wanted. I longed for that glory, that adoration, that freedom.... I made up my mind to be a great actor—greater than my father." In becoming a fledgling actor, Perkins analyzed, "There was nothing about me I wanted to be. But I felt happy being somebody else."

He began his professional career at age fourteen in 1946, playing a role in *Junior Miss* in summer stock in Brattleboro, Vermont. After graduating from private high school in Cambridge, Massachusetts, he started college at Rollins College in Winter Park, Florida, later transfer-

SPECIAL ADDITIONS

ring to Columbia University. Meanwhile, he continued working in summer stock and on TV. He made his movie debut in *The Actress* (1953) as Jean Simmons' young suitor. He next auditioned for the lead in *East of Eden* (1954) but lost the screen part to James Dean. Shortly before he was to graduate from Columbia in 1954, Perkins left college to make his Broadway debut in *Tea and Sympathy*. He took over for John Kerr in the role of the mother-devoted collegian bewildered by his homosexual tendencies. (The stage part had tremendous simularities to Perkins' offstage life, as he was coping with his own gay inclinations.)

As a result of his *Tea and Sympathy* acclaim, Tony became much in demand in Hollywood. He was cast as Gary Cooper's son in *Friendly Persuasion* (1956), receiving a Best Supporting Actor Oscar nomination for his performance. This acclaimed performance led to *Fear Strikes Out* (1957), in which Tony played baseball player Jim Piersall, whose father fixation leads to a nervous breakdown. That same year Tony returned to Broadway for the drama *Look Homeward, Angel* in which his character must break free of a grasping, materialistic mother.

Being a closet gay created trying movie-making situations for Tony. Frequently on the sets of his pictures, Perkins' sexy leading ladies—including Sophia Loren in *Desire Under the Elms* (1958), Jane Fonda in *Tall Story* (1960), Ingrid

Bergman in *Goodbye Again* (1961) and Brigitte Bardot in *A Ravishing Idiot* (1964)—attempted to seduce their handsome, bachelor co-star. He made every excuse possible to escape these heterosexual seductions. On the other hand, he would later acknowledge that he was equally unhappy with his clandestine gay experiences.

In 1960, dissatisfied with his screen assignments, Perkins returned to Broadway in the short-lived Frank Loesser musical *Greenwillow*. Then came the enormously successful *Psycho*. Tony created such an indelible impression as the deranged killer that Hollywood forever dropped any conventional leading man plans for him. Said Perkins, "For about ten years after I made the movie, Norman [Bates] dominated my life. I always liked Norman, but it was a fact that if someone approached me, I could be pretty sure it was a question about *Psycho*—even years later. I resented it, I really did."

During the 1960s Perkins made his home in Paris and most of his films were shot abroad. He returned to the U.S. occasionally: e.g., to appear in a Neil Simon Broadway comedy (*The Star-Spangled Girl*, 1966), to star in Hollywood as the highly disturbed arsonist in *Pretty Poison*, etc. In 1970 he turned down a starring role in a Stephen Sondheim musical (*Company*) because the lead character (as conceived originally) was sexually ambivalent, instead directing an off-Broadway drama, *Steambath*.

SPECIAL ADDITIONS

By 1971, Perkins had undergone aversion therapy to "rid" himself of his homosexuality. Bolstered by his new sexual re-orientation, the once confirmed bachelor reported for the filming of *The Life and Times of Judge Roy Bean* (1972), playing a shifty-eyed preacher. On the set, the 39-year-old actor had his first heterosexual experience, reportedly with co-star Victoria Principal.

In the early 1970s Perkins had seen a picture of photographer Berry Berenson (the sister of actress/model Marisa Berenson) in *Vogue* magazine. Tony and Berry (sixteen years his junior) met at a New York City party thereafter, and, by 1973, had become lovers. When she became pregnant, they decided to marry. Just before the August 9, 1973 nuptials on Cape Cod, the frightened actor confessed, "I wanted to walk into the ocean and dive to the bottom." However, he later conceded that one of the many benefits of his marriage was that it made him "not nearly so grasping and ambitious. Not so paranoid. Not so fearful." Their first child, Osgood, was born in 1974, and two years later, came their second son, Elvis. Apparently content with domesticity, Perkins told the press, "I've dropped all my ambitious characteristics. I turn down work that will take me away from home."

After twenty years in the movies, Perkins' screen career had stagnated. By now he could walk through such roles as the mad fashion photographer in Diana Ross' *Mahogany* (1975) or as the obsessed police man Javert in a TV movie version of *Les Miserables* in 1978. It was a telling note of Tony's career rut that in 1983 he returned to the role of Norman Bates in *Psycho II* (with his son Osgood playing the young Norman). The sequel was a thin echo of its predecessor. In 1984, the year Perkins played a psychotic preacher pursuing prostitute Kathleen Turner in the bizarre *Crimes of Passion*, the actor was ordained a minister of the Universal Life Church of America. Then came *Psycho III* (1986), in which Perkins not only reprised his "reformed" psychotic, but directed the ify proceedings. However, Tony refused to participate in the low-grade TV movie sequel (*Bates Motel*, 1987) which found the creepy motel turned over to a new young crazy (Bud Cort). Nevertheless, Perkins participated in the made-for-cable movie *Psycho IV: The Beginning* (1990). In this latest installment, the paranoid Norman recalls life with his unbalanced mother (Olivia Hussey) and how her influence abnormally twisted his existence.

A new off-screen drama occurred in 1990 when Perkins was hospitalized for a temporary facial palsy. Unknown to him, someone took the liberty of testing his blood for the HIV virus and leaked the results to a supermarket tabloid paper. In a twist of irony, Tony first learned that he was HIV positive by reading about it in the scandal newspaper. He immediately underwent new blood tests which confirmed the published results. However, fearful that he would never work again in Hollywood if he admitted he had AIDS, he denied to everyone except his close family that he had the disease. (To date, no one has publicly revealed how the actor contracted AIDS.)

Determined to provide financially for his wife and sons, the ailing Perkins embarked on a strenuous career path, including lecture tours discussing his lengthy film career, and making movies abroad (e.g., *A Demon in My View*, 1991, *The Naked Target*, 1992). Publicly he spent what would be his last two years working with the AIDS organization, Project Angel Food (a charitable organization founded by Marianne Williamson, Perkins' spiritual advisor). In between screen projects, he coped privately with his ravaging disease. To avoid public awareness of his plight, he had to check into hospitals for treatment under assumed names. (Berry Berenson would later reflect bitterly about this closeted situation: "You think that this man has spent his entire life giving people so much pleasure in show business and this is his reward. He can't even be himself at the end.")

In mid-1992, Tony was set to direct a play called *Together*, which was to have a pre-Broadway tryout in Chicago. However, his physical condition suddenly worsened. By July 1992, Tony could no longer hide his terminal state from the press or friends. Due to the wasting syndrome he now weighed a frail 120 pounds. When sent home from Los Angeles' Midway Hospital, he admitted, "I have finally accepted the fact that I'm dying." In the final weeks, pals such as Mike Nichols, Richard Benjamin, Paula Prentiss and Roddy McDowall came to say painful farewells at his Hollywood Hills home. Fashion photographer Paul Jasmin, a longtime friend (and the person who provided the voice of Norman Bates' mother in *Psycho*), would share memories of the dying star: "Those last few days we tried to go up and show him all that love he gave us.... Berry was with him every moment. She slept in a little bed she set up by Tony's sickbed, and she'd go lay her head on his shoulders and just lie next to him. When he got his strength up, his friends came in and they shared experiences. The boys called their friends and told them that their father was dying of HIV, and they came to be with him also."

Of the final ordeal, Berry has said, "He was in and out of a coma. On his last day [September 12, 1992], he woke up only once. His eyes opened and he looked to me holding his hand and at his beloved sons sitting at the foot of his bed.... He tried to talk but he was so weak his voice wasn't even a whisper. We could see his lips move as he breathed, 'I love you.' Then he closed his eyes and went back to sleep. He died a few hours later."

In the month following his death, Perkins could constantly be seen in posthumous media appearances. On October 14, 1992, American Movie Classics aired Perkins' final interview in which he evaluated the ups and downs of his career. Later in the month, the new TV movie, *In the Deep Woods*, aired. Tony played a mysterious private detective who spends the plotline stalking heroine Rosanna Arquette. His final feature film, *A Demon in My View*, in which he played—surprise, surprise—a former serial killer, was released on home video at the end of October 1992.

Haunted throughout the decades by personal demons and his on-screen characterization of cinema's arch crazy, Perkins found solace in his belated family life. As one friend observed, "There was such love and such warmth, always. The Perkins home was where you came for family love." Examining his own life choices, sixty-year-old Tony left a message for his sons, given to them after his death: "...boys, don't try to find a woman as wonderful as your mother to marry because if you do, you'll stay single your whole lives."

NECROLOGY
Notable Actors and Directors Through 4/30/93

Abbott, Bud: Oct 2, 1895—Apr 24, 1974
Abbott, Dawn: Sep 21, 1930—May 7, 1985
Abel, Walter: Jun 6, 1898—Mar 26, 1987
Acker, Jean: 1893—Aug 16, 1978
Ackles, Kenneth: 1916—Nov 5, 1986
Acord, Art: 1890—Jan 4, 1931
Acosta, Rodolfo: 1920—Nov 7, 1974
Acuff, Eddie: 1908—Dec 17, 1956
Acuff, Roy: Sep 15, 1903—Nov 23, 1992
Adams, Claire: c. 1900—Sep 25, 1978
Adams, Dorothy: 1899—Mar 16, 1988
Adams, Ernest S.: 1885—Nov 26, 1947
Adams, Kathryn: 1894—Feb 17, 1959
Adams, Nick: Jul 10, 1931—Feb 7, 1968
Adams, Peter: Sep 22, 1917—Jan 8, 1987
Adams, Stanley: 1915—Apr 27, 1977
Adamson, Victor: 1890—Nov 9, 1972
Addams, Dawn: Sep 9, 1930—May 7, 1985
Ades, Daniel: 1933—May 30, 1992
Adler, Luther: May 4, 1903—Dec 8, 1984
Adler, Stella: Feb 10, 1902—Dec 21, 1992
Adolfi, John G.: Feb 19, 1888—May 10, 1933
Adoree, Renee: Sep 1, 1898—Oct 5, 1933
Adrian, Max: Nov 1, 1903—Jan 19, 1973
Agnew, Robert "Bobby": 1899—Nov 8, 1983
Ahearne, Tom: 1906—Jan 5, 1969
Ahern, Gladys: c. 1910—Jun 12, 1992
Aherne, Brian: May 2, 1902—Feb 10, 1986
Aherne, Patrick: 1901—Sep 30, 1970
Ahn, Philip: Mar 29, 1911—Feb 28, 1978
Aikins, Spottiswoode: 1869—1933
Alberni, Luis: 1887—Dec 23, 1962
Albert, Elsie: 1888—Oct 7, 1981
Albertson, Frank: Feb 2, 1909—Feb 29, 1964
Albertson, Jack: Jun 16, 1907—Nov 25, 1981
Albertson, Mabel: 1901—Sep 28, 1982
Albright, Hardie: Dec 16, 1903—Dec 7, 1975
Alda, Robert: Feb 26, 1914—May 3, 1986
Alden, Mary: 1883—1946
Alderman, John: 1934—Jan 12, 1987
Alderson, Floyd Taliaferro: 1896—Feb 12, 1980
Aldrich, Robert: Aug 9, 1918—Dec 5, 1983
Alex, Robert: 1959—Aug 6, 1990
Alexander, Ben: May 26, 1911—Jul 5, 1969
Alexander, John: Nov 29, 1897—Jul 13, 1982
Alexander, Richard: 1903—Aug 9, 1989
Alexander, Ross: Jul 27, 1907—Jan 2, 1937
Alexander, Tom: 1963—Jun 24, 1992
Alinder, Dallas: 1932—Jul 14, 1990
Alison, Dorothy: 1925—Jan 17, 1992
Allbritton, Louise: Jul 3, 1920—Feb 16, 1979
Allen, Chet: Aug 17, 1932—Jun 17, 1984
Allen, Fred: May 31, 1894—Mar 17, 1956
Allen, Gracie: Jul 26, 1902—Aug 27, 1964

Allen, Irving: Nov 24, 1905—Dec 17, 1987
Allen, Irwin: Jun 12, 1916—Nov 2, 1991
Allen, Lester: 1891—Nov 6, 1949
Allen, Peter: Feb 10, 1944—Jun 18, 1992
Allen, Ronald: 1935—Jun 18, 1991
Allgood, Sara: Oct 31, 1883—Sep 13, 1950
Allison, May: Jun 14, 1895—Mar 27, 1989
Allister, Claud: Oct 3, 1891—Jul 26, 1970
Allman, Elvia: 1905—Mar 6, 1992
Allwyn, Astrid: Nov 27, 1909—Mar 31, 1978
Allyn, Alyce: _____—Feb 11, 1976
Almendros, Nestor: Oct 30, 1930—Mar 4, 1992
Alpar, Gita: 1900—Feb 12, 1991
Alvarado, Don: Nov 4, 1900—Mar 31, 1967
Alzado, Lyle: Apr 3, 1949—May 14, 1992
Ames, Adrienne: Aug 3, 1907—May 31, 1947
Amy, George: 1903—Dec 18, 1986
Anders, Chris: 1937—Aug 28, 1991
Anders, Glenn: Sep 1, 1890—Oct 26, 1981
Anders, Irene: 1929—Dec 7, 1988
Anders, Laurie: 1922- Oct 1, 1992
Anderson, Claire: 1894—Mar 23, 1964
Anderson, Eddie "Rochester":
                Sep 18, 1905—Feb 28, 1977
Anderson, Gilbert "Bronco Billy": Mar 21, 1882—
Jan 20, 1971
Anderson, John: Oct 20, 1922—Aug 7, 1992
Anderson, Judith (Dame):
                Feb 10, 1898—Jan 3, 1993
Anderson, Warner: Mar 10, 1911—Aug 26, 1976
Andor, Lotte Palfi: 1904—Jul 8, 1991
Andor, Paul: 1901—Jun 26, 1991
Andre, Gwili: Feb 24, 1908—Feb 5, 1959
Andre, Lona: Mar 2, 1915—Sep 18, 1992
Andre, Monya: _____—Jan 5, 1981
Andrews, Ann: 1891—Jan 23, 1986
Andrews, Dana: Jan 1, 1909—Dec 17, 1992
Andrews, Edward: Oct 9, 1914—Mar 9, 1985
Andrews, LaVerne: Jul 6, 1915—May 8, 1967
Andrews, Lloyd "Slim": 1907—Apr 3, 1992
Andrews, Lois: Mar 24, 1924—Apr 4, 1968
Andrews, Nancy: Dec 16, 1924—Jul 29, 1989
Andrews, Stanley: 1892—Jun 23, 1969
Angel, Heather: Feb 9, 1909—Dec 13, 1986
Angeli, Pier: Jun 19, 1932—Sep 10, 1971
Angold, Edit: 1895—Oct 4, 1971
Ankers, Evelyn: Aug 17, 1918—Aug 28, 1985
Anson, Laura: 1892—Jul 15, 1968
Anthony, Joseph: May 24, 1912—Jan 20, 1993
Antrim, Harry: 1895—Jan 18, 1967
Apfel, Oscar C.: c. 1880—Mar 21, 1938
Appleby, Dorothy: 1906—Aug 9, 1990
Aragon, Jesse: 1936—Nov 8, 1988
Arbuckle, Roscoe "Fatty":
                Mar 24, 1887—Jun 29, 1933
Archainbaud, George: May 8, 1890—Feb 20, 1959
Arden, Eve: Apr 30, 1908—Nov 12, 1990
Arden, Jane: 1905—Mar 21, 1981
Arkin, David: 1942—Jan 14, 1991
Arledge, John: Mar 12, 1906—1947
Arlen, Richard: Sep 1, 1898—Mar 28, 1976
Arliss, George: Apr 10, 1868—Feb 5, 1946
Armendariz, Pedro: May 9, 1912—Jun 18, 1963
Armetta, Henry: Jul 4, 1888—Oct 21, 1945
Armstrong, Louis "Satchmo": Jul 4, 1900—Jul 6, 1971

Armstrong, Robert: Nov 20, 1890—Apr 20, 1973
Armstrong, Todd: 1937—Nov 16, 1992
Arnaz, Desi: Mar 2, 1917—Dec 2, 1986
Arno, Sig: 1895—Aug 17, 1975
Arnold, Edward: Feb 18, 1890—Apr 26, 1956
Arnold, Jack: Oct 14, 1912—Mar 17, 1992
Arnt, Charles: Aug 20, 1908—Aug 6, 1990
Arquette, Cliff: Dec 28, 1905—Sep 23, 1974
Arteago, Mario: _____—Jan 9, 1990
Arthur, Jean: Oct 17, 1900—Jun 19, 1991
Arthur, Johnny: May 10, 1883—Dec 31, 1951
Arvan, Jan: 1913—May 24, 1979
Arvidson, Linda: 1884—Jul 26, 1949
Arzner, Dorothy: Jan 3, 1897—Oct 1, 1979
Ashby, Hal: 1929—Dec 27, 1988
Ashcroft, Ronnie: 1923—Dec 14, 1988
Ashe, Martin: 1911—Apr 15, 1991
Asher, Max: 1880—Apr 15, 1957
Astaire, Fred: May 10, 1899—Jun 22, 1987
Asther, Nils: Jan 17, 1897—Oct 13, 1981
Astor, Gertrude: Nov 9, 1887—Nov 9, 1977
Astor, Mary: May 3, 1905—Sep 25, 1987
Astor, Philip: 1944—Oct 19, 1991
Atchley, Hooper: 1887—Nov 16, 1943
Ates, Roscoe: Jan 20, 1892—Mar 1, 1962
Attaway, Ruth: 1910—Sep 21, 1987
Atterbury, Malcolm: Feb 20, 1907—Aug 23, 1992
Atwater, Edith: Aug 22, 1911—Mar 14, 1986
Atwill, Lionel: Mar 1, 1885—Apr 22, 1946
Aubrey, Jimmy: Oct 23, 1887—Sep 2, 1983
Aubuchon, Jacques: 1924—Dec 28, 1991
Audley, Eleanor: 1905—Nov 25, 1991
Auer, Mischa: Nov 17, 1905—Mar 5, 1967
August, Edwin: 1883—Mar 4, 1964
Aylesworth, Arthur: Aug 12, 1884—Jun 26, 1946
Aylmer, Felix: Feb 21, 1889—Sep 2, 1979
Ayres, Agnes: Apr 4, 1898—Dec 25, 1940
Babbitt, Art: 1907—Mar 4, 1992
Baccaloni, Salvatore: 1900— Dec 31, 1969
Bach, Robin: 1948—Aug 10, 1991
Backus, Jim: Feb 25, 1913—Jul 3, 1989
Baclanova, Olga: 1899—Sep 6, 1974
Bacon, Irving: Sep 6, 1893—Feb 5, 1965
Bacon, Lloyd: Jan 16, 1890—Nov 15, 1955
Baddeley, Hermione: Nov 13, 1906—Aug 19, 1986
Badger, Clarence: Jun 8, 1880—Jun 17, 1964
Baer, Max: 1909—Nov 21, 1959
Bagdasarian, Ross: Jan 27, 1919—Jan 16, 1972
Baggot, King: 1874—Jul 11, 1948
Bailey, Pearl: Mar 29, 1918—Aug 17, 1990
Bailey, Raymond: 1904—Apr 15, 1980
Bailey, Sherwood: Aug 6, 1923—Aug 6, 1987
Bainter, Fay: Dec 7, 1891—Apr 16, 1968
Baird, Leah: Jun 20, 1883—Oct 3, 1971
Baker, Art: Jan 7, 1898—Aug 26, 1966
Baker, Bob: Nov 8, 1914—Aug 29, 1975
Baker, Dorothy Helen: 1914—Oct 15, 1992
Baker, Eddie: 1898—Feb 4, 1968
Baker, Kenny: Sep 30, 1912—Aug 10, 1985
Baker, Lance: 1960—Oct 23, 1991
Baker, Lenny: Jan 17, 1945—Apr 12, 1982
Baker, Russell 1916—Jun 20, 1982
Baker, Tom: 1940—Sep 2, 1982
Bakewell, William: May 2, 1908—Apr 15, 1993
Baldwin, Walter S.: 1887—Jan 27, 1977

Balfour, Katharine: 1921—Apr 3, 1990
Balin, Ina: Nov 12, 1937—Jun 20, 1990
Ball, Lucille: Aug 6, 1911—Apr 26, 1989
Ball, Suzan: Feb 3, 1933—Aug 5, 1955
Ball, William: Apr 29, 1931—Jul 30, 1991
Ballin, Hugo: 1880—Nov 27, 1956
Ballin, Mabel: 1885—Jul 24, 1958
Bancroft, George: Sep 30, 1882—Oct 2, 1956
Bankhead, Tallulah: Jan 31, 1902—Dec 12, 1968
Banks, Monty: 1897—Jan 7, 1950
Banky, Vilma: Jan 2, 1898—Mar 18, 1991
Banner, John: Jan 28, 1910—Jan 28, 1973
Bara, Nina: 1924—Aug 15, 1990
Bara, Theda: Jul 29, 1890—Apr 7, 1955
Baragrey, John: Apr 15, 1918—Aug 4, 1975
Barbier, George W.: Nov 9, 1865—Jul 19, 1945
Barcroft, Roy: Sep 7, 1902—Nov 28, 1969
Bardette, Trevor: Nov 19, 1902—Nov 28, 1977
Barfield, Eddie: 1910—Jan 3, 1991
Bari, Lynn: Dec 18, 1913—Nov 20, 1989
Barker, Lex: May 8, 1919—May 11, 1973
Barker, Reginald: 1886—Sep 25, 1937
Barlett, Scott: 1943—Sep 29, 1991
Barlow, Reginald: 1866—Jul 6, 1943
Barnett, Vince: Jul 4, 1902—Aug 10, 1977
Barney, Jay: Mar 14, 1918—May 19, 1985
Barr, Leonard: 1903—Nov 22, 1980
Barrat, Robert: Jul 10, 1891—Jan 7, 1970
Barrett, Edith: 1913—Feb 22, 1977
Barrie, Wendy: Apr 18, 1912—May 8, 1919
Barrier, Edgar: Mar 4, 1906—Jun 20, 1964
Barriscale, Bessie: 1884—Jun 30, 1965
Barry, Donald "Red": Jan 11, 1911—Jul 17, 1980
Barry, J. J.: 1932—Jan 26, 1990
Barrymore, Diana: Mar 3, 1921—Jan 25, 1960
Barrymore, Ethel: Aug 15, 1879—Jun 18, 1959
Barrymore, John: Feb 15, 1882—May 29, 1942
Barrymore, Lionel: Apr 28, 1978—Nov 15, 1954
Barsi, Judith: 1977—Jul 27, 1988
Barthelmess, Richard: May 9, 1897—Aug 17, 1963
Bartholomew, Freddie: Mar 28, 1924—Jan 23, 1992
Barton, Charles T.: May 25, 1902—Dec 5, 1981
Barton, James: Nov 1, 1890— Feb 19, 1962
Barton, Larry: 1910—Apr 10, 1990
Basehart, Richard: Aug 31, 1914—Sep 17, 1984
Bassermann, Albert: Sep 7, 1865—May 15, 1952
Bates, Barbara: Aug 6, 1925—Mar 18, 1969
Bates, Florence: Apr 15, 1888—Jan 31, 1954
Bates, Granville: Jan 7, 1882—Jul 8, 1940
Bauer, Charita: Dec 20, 1923—Feb 28, 1985
Baum, Siegfried: 1918—Mar 3, 1992
Baumberger, Tamera: 1962—Apr 19, 1993
Bavier, Frances: 1903—Dec 6, 1989
Baxley, Barbara: Jan 1, 1925—Jun 7, 1990
Baxter, Alan: Nov 19, 1908—May 8, 1976
Baxter, Anne: May 7, 1923—Dec 12, 1985
Baxter, Warner: Mar 29, 1891—May 7, 1951
Bayne, Beverly: Nov 11, 1894—Aug 18, 1982
Bazlen, Brigid: 1945—May 25, 1989
Beal, Royal: 1900—May 20, 1969
Beal, Scott: 1890—Jul 10, 1973
Beard, Matthew "Stymie", Jr.:
                          Jan 1, 1925—Jan 8, 1981
Beatty, Clyde: Jun 10, 1903—Jul 19, 1965
Beatty, Robert: Oct 19, 1909—Mar 3, 1992

Beaudine, William: Jan 15, 1892—Mar 18, 1970
Beaumont, Harry: Feb 10, 1888—Dec 22, 1966
Beaumont, Hugh: Feb 16, 1909—May 14, 1982
Beavers, Louise: Mar 8, 1902—Oct 26, 1962
Becher, John C.: Jan 13, 1915—Sep 20, 1986
Beckett, Scotty: Oct 4, 1929—May 10, 1968
Beddoe, Don: Jul 1, 1903—Jan 19, 1991
Beebe, Marilyn Elizabeth: 1926—Oct 25, 1992
Beecher, Janet: Oct 21, 1884—Aug 6, 1955
Beery, Noah, Sr.: Jan 17, 1883—Apr 1, 1946
Beery, Wallace: Apr 1, 1885—Apr 15, 1949
Begley, Ed: Mar 25, 1901—Apr 28, 1970
Belasco, Leon: Oct 11, 1902—Jun 1, 1988
Belgado, Maria: 1906—Jun 24, 1969
Bell, David: 1937—Jun 9, 1990
Bell, Hank: 1892—Feb 4, 1950
Bell, James: Dec 1, 1891—Oct 26, 1973
Bell, Monta: Feb 5, 1891—Feb 4, 1958
Bell, Rex: Oct 16, 1905—Jul 4, 1962
Bellamy, Madge: Jun 30, 1900—Jan 24, 1990
Bellamy, Ralph: Jun 17, 1904—Nov 29, 1991
Bellini, Mario: ____—Mar 4, 1991
Belmore, Lionel: 1867—1953
Belushi, John: Jan 24, 1949—Mar 5, 1982
Benaderet, Bea: Apr 4, 1906—Oct 13, 1968
Benchley, Robert: Sep 15, 1889—Nov 21, 1945
Bender, Russell: 1910—Aug 16, 1969
Bendix, William: Jan 14, 1906—Dec 14, 1964
Benedek, Laslo: Mar 5, 1907—Mar 11, 1992
Benedict, Richard: 1920—Apr 25, 1984
Benet, Brenda: Aug 1945—Apr 7, 1982
Benner, Richard: 1943—Dec 2, 1990
Bennet, Spencer Gordon: Jan 5, 1893—Oct 8, 1987
Bennett, Barbara: Aug 13, 1906—Aug 8, 1958
Bennett, Belle: 1891—Nov 4, 1932
Bennett, Constance: Oct 22, 1904—Jul 24, 1965
Bennett, Enid: Jan 2, 1895—May 14, 1969
Bennett, Joan: Feb 27, 1910—Dec 7, 1990
Bennett, Marjorie: 1895—Jun 14, 1982
Bennett, Richard: May 21, 1873—Oct 22, 1944
Benny, Jack: Feb 14, 1894—Dec 26, 1974
Benson, Lucille: Jul 17, 1914—Feb 17, 1984
Beranger, George Andre: Mar 27, 1895—1973
Beresford, Harry: Nov 4, 1864—Oct 4, 1944
Berg, Gertrude: Oct 3, 1899—Sep 14, 1966
Bergen, Edgar: Feb 16, 1903—Sep 30, 1978
Berger, Ludwig: Jan 6, 1892—May 17, 1969
Bergere, Ouida: 1886—Nov 29, 1974
Berghof, Herbert: Sep 13, 1909—Nov 5, 1990
Bergman, Ingrid: Aug 29, 1915—Aug 29, 1982
Bergner, Elisabeth: Aug 22, 1900—May 12, 1986
Berke, William: Oct 3, 1903—Feb 15, 1958
Berkeley, Busby: Nov 29, 1895—Mar 14, 1976
Berkeley, George: 1922—Feb 1, 1992
Berlin, Abby: 1907—Aug 19, 1965
Bernardi, Herschel: Oct 30, 1923—May 9, 1986
Bernhard, Dorothy: 1890—Dec 14, 1955
Bernhardt, Curtis: Apr 15, 1899—Feb 22, 1981
Berti, Dehl: 1921—Nov 26, 1991
Bertram, Bert: 1894—Oct 31, 1991
Besser, Joe: 1907—Mar 1, 1988
Besserer, Eugenie: 1870—May 30, 1934
Best, Edna: Mar 3, 1900—Sep 18, 1974
Best, Willie: May 27, 1913—Feb 27, 1962
Betz, Carl: Mar 9, 1920—Jan 18, 1978

Bevan, Billy: Sep 29, 1897—Nov 26, 1957
Bevans, Clem: Oct 16, 1879—Aug 11, 1963
Beyers, Bill: 1955—May 29, 1992
Biberman, Abner: Apr 1, 1909—Jun 20, 1977
Biberman, Herbert: Mar 4, 1900—Jun 30, 1971
Bickford, Charles: Jan 1, 1889—Nov 9, 1967
Big Tree, John (Chief): 1865—Jul 5, 1967
Bing, Herman: Mar 30, 1889—Jan 9, 1947
Binns, Edward: 1916—Dec 4, 1990
Binyon, Claude: Oct 17, 1902—Feb 14, 1978
Bishop, William: Jul 16, 1917—Oct 3, 1959
Blackmer, Sidney: Jul 13, 1894—Oct 5, 1973
Blackton, J. Stuart: Jan 4, 1875—Aug 13, 1941
Blackwell, Carlyle, Jr.: 1912—Sep 20, 1974
Blackwell, Carlyle (Sr.): 1888—Jun 17, 1955
Blackwood, Christian: Jul 7, 1942—Jul 22, 1992
Blagoi, George: 1898—Jun 23, 1971
Blaire, Sallie: 1924—Feb 17, 1992
Blake, Amanda: Feb 20, 1929—Aug 16, 1989
Blake, Arthur: 1915—Mar 24, 1985
Blake, Larry J.: 1914—May 25, 1982
Blake, Madge: 1900—Feb 19, 1969
Blake, Marie: Aug 21, 1896—Jan 14, 1978
Blake, Oliver: Apr 5, 1905—Feb 12, 1992
Blanc, Mel: May 30, 1908—Jul 10, 1989
Blanchard, Mari: Apr 13, 1927—May 10, 1970
Blandick, Clara: Jun 4, 1880—Apr 15, 1962
Bletcher, Arline: 1893—Jul 3, 1992
Blocker, Dan: Dec 10, 1929—May 13, 1972
Blondell, Joan: Aug 30, 1906—Dec 25, 1979
Bloom, George "Tex": 1894—May 5, 1989
Blore, Eric: Dec 23, 1887—Mar 2, 1959
Blue, Ben: Sep 12, 1901—Mar 7, 1975
Blue, Monte: Jan 11, 1890—Feb 18, 1963
Blyden, Larry: Jun 23, 1925—Jun 6, 1975
Blystone, John G.: Dec 2, 1892—Aug 7, 1938
Blystone, Stanley: Aug 1, 1894—Jul 16, 1956
Blythe, Betty: Sep 1, 1893—Apr 7, 1972
Boardman, Eleanor: Aug 19, 1898—Dec 12, 1991
Boardman, Virginia True: 1889—Jun 10, 1971
Bogart, Humphrey: Dec 25, 1899—Jan 14, 1957
Bois, Curt: Apr 5, 1901—Dec 25, 1991
Boland, Joseph: 1904—Jun 21, 1987
Boland, Mary: Jan 28, 1880—Jun 23, 1965
Boles, Jim: 1914—May 26, 1977
Boles, John: Oct 28, 1895—Feb 27, 1969
Boleslawski, Richard: Feb 4, 1889—Jan 17, 1937
Boley, May: 1882—Jan 6, 1963
Bolger, Ray: Jan 10, 1904—Jan 15, 1987
Bonanova, Fortunio: Jan 13, 1893—Apr 2, 1969
Bonar, Ivan: ____—Dec 8, 1988
Bond, David: 1915—Feb 16, 1989
Bond, Lillian: Jan 18, 1908—Jan 18, 1991
Bond, Raleigh V.: 1935—Aug 10, 1989
Bond, Rudy: 1914—Mar 29, 1982
Bond, Sudie: Jul 13, 1928—Nov 10, 1984
Bond, Ward: Apr 9, 1903—Nov 5, 1960
Bondi, Beulah: May 3, 1888—Jan 11, 1981
Bonnell, Lee: 1919—May 12, 1986
Bonner, Margerie: 1905—Sep 28, 1988
Booker, Bernice Ingalls: 1895—Feb 25, 1987
Boone, Richard: Jun 18, 1916—Jan 10, 1981
Booth, Edwina: Sep 13, 1909—May 18, 1991
Booth, Shirley: Aug 30, 1897—Oct 16, 1992
Borden, Eugene: Mar 21, 1897—Jul 21, 1972

Borden, Olive: Jul 14, 1906—Oct 1, 1947
Borden, Renee: 1908—Sep 8, 1992
Borg, Sven-Hugo: 1896—Feb 19, 1981
Borg, Veda Ann: Jan 11, 1915—Aug 16, 1973
Borzage, Frank: Apr 23, 1893—Jun 19, 1962
Bostwick, Dorothy Davis: ____—May 25, 1991
Boswell, Connee: Dec 3, 1907—Oct 10, 1976
Boswell, Martha: 1905—Jul 2, 1958
Boswell, Vet: 1911—Nov 12, 1988
Bosworth, Hobart: Aug 11, 1867—Dec 30, 1943
Boteler, Wade: 1891—May 7, 1943
Bothwell, John F.: 1923—Mar 8, 1967
Bouchey, Willis: 1895—Sep 28, 1977
Bourneuf, Philip: 1908—Mar 23, 1979
Bovasso, Julie: Aug 1, 1930—Sep 14, 1991
Bow, Clara: Aug 25, 1905—Sep 27, 1965
Bow, Simmy: 1922—Dec 21, 1988
Bowers, John: Dec 25, 1899—Nov 17, 1936
Bowman, Lee: Dec 28, 1914—Dec 25, 1979
Boxer, Warren Neal: 1958—May 17, 1992
Boyd, Stephen: Jul 4, 1928—Jun 2, 1977
Boyd, William "Stage":
                    Dec 18, 1890—Mar 20, 1935
Boyd, William: Jun 5, 1895—Sep 12, 1972
Boyer, Charles: Aug 28, 1897—Aug 26, 1978
Brabin, Charles J.: Apr 17, 1883—Nov 3, 1957
Bracey, Sidney: 1877—Aug 5, 1942
Bradford, Lane: 1923—Jun 7, 1973
Bradley, Estelle: 1908—Jun 28, 1990
Bradley, Truman: 1905—Jul 28, 1974
Brady, Alice: Nov 2, 1892—Oct 28, 1939
Brady, Pat: Dec 31, 1914—Feb 27, 1972
Brady, Scott: Sep 13, 1924—Apr 16, 1985
Brahm, John: Aug 17, 1893—Oct 11, 1982
Brand, Neville: Aug 13, 1921—Apr 16, 1992
Branda, Richard: 1936—Jan 7, 1993
Brandon, Henry: Jun 18, 1912—Feb 15, 1990
Brasselle, Keefe: Feb 7, 1923—Jul 7, 1981
Bray, Robert: Oct 23, 1917—Mar 7, 1983
Bray, Stephen: 1959—Jun 10, 1990
Breakston, George P.: Jan 22, 1920—May 21, 1973
Brecher, Egon: Feb 16, 1880—Aug 12, 1946
Breeding, Larry 1946—Sep 28, 1982
Breese, Edmund: Jun 18, 1871—Apr 6, 1936
Bremen, Lennie: 1915—Mar 21, 1986
Brendel, El: Mar 25, 1890—Apr 9, 1964
Brennan, Walter: Jul 25, 1894—Sep 21, 1974
Brenner, Glenn: 1948—Jan 14, 1992
Brenon, Herbert: Jan 13, 1880—Jun 21, 1958
Brent, Evelyn: Oct 20, 1899—Jun 4, 1975
Brent, George: Mar 15, 1904—May 26, 1979
Brent, Romney: Jan 26, 1902—Sep 24, 1976
Breon, Edmund: Dec 12, 1882—1951
Bressan, Arthur J., Jr.: 1943—Jul 29, 1987
Bressart, Felix: Mar 2, 1880—Mar 17, 1949
Bretherton, Howard: Feb 13, 1896—Apr 12, 1969
Brewster, Diane: 1931—Nov 12, 1991
Brice, Fanny: Oct 29, 1891—May 29, 1951
Bridge, Alan: Feb 26, 1891—Dec 27, 1957
Briggs, Charles: 1933—Feb 6, 1985
Briggs, Donald P.: Jan 28, 1911—Feb 3, 1986
Briggs, Harlan: 1880—Jan 26, 1952
Briggs, Richard R.: 1919—Jul 12, 1990
Brill, Patti: Mar 8, 1923—Jan 18, 1963
Briscoe, Lottie: 1883—Mar 19, 1991

Brissac, Virginia: c. 1895—1979
Brisson, Carl: Dec 24, 1895—Sep 26, 1958
Britton, Barbara: Sep 26, 1919—Jan 17, 1980
Britton, Pamela: 1923—Jun 17, 1974
Brocco, Peter: 1903—Jan 3, 1993
Brockwell, Gladys: 1894—Jul 2, 1929
Broderick, Helen: Aug 11, 1891—Sep 25, 1959
Broderick, James: Mar 7, 1927—Nov 1, 1982
Brodie, Steve: Nov 25, 1919—Jan 9, 1992
Brody, Ronnie: 1919—May 8, 1991
Bromberg, J. Edward: Dec 25, 1903—Dec 6, 1951
Bronson, Betty: Nov 17, 1906—Oct 19, 1971
Brook, Clive: Jun 1, 1887—Nov 17, 1974
Brooke, Tyler: Jun 6, 1891—Mar 2, 1943
Brooke, Van Dyke: 1859—Sep 17, 1921
Brookner, Howard: 1955—Apr 27, 1989
Brooks, Geraldine: Oct 29, 1925—Jun 19, 1977
Brooks, Louise: Nov 14, 1906—Aug 8, 1985
Brooks, Richard: May 18, 1912—Mar 11, 1992
Brooks, Walter: 1915—Aug 20, 1986
Brophy, Edward: Feb 27, 1895—May 30, 1960
Brotherson, Eric: 1911—Oct 21, 1989
Brown, Barry: Apr 19, 1951—Jun 25, 1978
Brown, Cassandra: 1896—Sep 12, 1981
Brown, Clarence: May 10, 1890—Aug 17, 1987
Brown, Georgia: Oct 21, 1933—Jul 5, 1992
Brown, Harry Joe: Sep 22, 1890—Apr 28, 1972
Brown, James L.: Mar 22, 1920—Apr 11, 1992
Brown, Joe E.: Jul 28, 1892—Jul 6, 1973
Brown, Johnny Mack: Sep 1, 1904—Nov 14, 1974
Brown, Joseph: 1923—Apr 9, 1982
Brown, Karl: 1895—Mar 25, 1990
Brown, Lucille E.: 1918—Aug 21, 1992
Brown, Ritchard (Dick): 1925—Jan 21, 1993
Brown, Rowland C.: Nov 6, 1900—May 6, 1963
Brown, Russ: 1892—Oct 19, 1964
Brown, Tom: Jan 6, 1913—Jun 3, 1990
Brown, Wally: Oct 9, 1904—Nov 13, 1961
Browne, Coral: Jul 23, 1913—May 29, 1991
Browne, Reno: 1921—May 15, 1991
Browning, Tod: Jul 12, 1882—Oct 6, 1962
Bruce, Betty: 1920—Jul 18, 1974
Bruce, David: Jan 6, 1914—May 3, 1976
Bruce, Kate: 1858—Apr 2, 1946
Bruce, Nigel Feb 4, 1895—Oct 8, 1953
Bruce, Virginia: Sep 29, 1910—Feb 24, 1982
Bruckman, Clyde: 1894—1955
Brumer, Martin: 1961—Jul 18, 1989
Brummer, Howard: 1940—Nov 12, 1991
Bruni, Peter: 1932—May 3, 1992
Brunner, Howard: 1940—Nov 12, 1991
Bryant, John: 1917—Jul 13, 1989
Bryant, Nana: 1888—Dec 24, 1955
Bryceland, Yvonne: Nov 18, 1925—Jan 13, 1992
Brynner, Yul: Jul 12, 1915—Oct 10, 1985
Bryson, Winifred: 1897—Aug 20, 1987
Bubbles, John W.: Feb 19, 1902—May 18, 1986
Buchanan, Edgar: Mar 21, 1903—Apr 4, 1979
Buchowetzki, Dimtri: 1895—1932
Buck, Frank: Mar 17, 1888—Mar 25, 1950
Bucquet, Harold S.: Apr 10, 1891—Feb 13, 1946
Buetel, Jack: Sep 5, 1917—Jun 27, 1989
Bull, Peter: Mar 21, 1912—May 21, 1984
Buloff, Joseph: Dec 6, 1907—Feb 27, 1985
Bunker, Ralph: 1889—Apr 28, 1966

Bunny, John: Sep 21, 1863—Apr 26, 1915
Buono, Victor: Feb 3, 1938—Jan 1, 1982
Burgess, Dorothy: Mar 4, 1907—Aug 20, 1961
Burke, Alan: 1923—Aug 25, 1992
Burke, Billie: Aug 7, 1885—May 14, 1970
Burke, James: 1886—May 28, 1968
Burke, Kathleen: Sep 5, 1913—Apr 9, 1980
Burke, Walter: 1909—Aug 4, 1984
Burks, Stephen: 1956—Nov 26, 1992
Burnell, Peter: 1933—Jan 5, 1987
Burnette, Smiley: Mar 18, 1911—Feb 16, 1967
Burns, Bob "Bazooka": Aug 6, 1890—Feb 2, 1956
Burns, David: Jun 22, 1902—Mar 12, 1971
Burns, Paul E.: Jan 26, 1881—May 17, 1967
Burns, Stephan: 1955—Feb 22, 1990
Burton, Frederick: Oct 20, 1871—Oct 23, 1957
Burton, Miriam: 1927—Jan 27, 1991
Burton, Richard: Nov 10, 1925—Aug 5, 1984
Burton, Robert: Aug 13, 1895—Sep 29, 1964
Busch, Mae: Jan 20, 1891—Apr 19, 1946
Bushman, Francis X., Jr.:
                    May 1, 1903—Apr 16, 1978
Bushman, Francis X. (Sr.):
                    Jan 10, 1883—Aug 23, 1966
Buster, Budd: Jun 14, 1891—Dec 22, 1965
Butler, David: Dec 17, 1889—Jun 15, 1979
Butler, Royal: 1893—Jul 28, 1973
Butrick, Merritt: 1960—Mar 17, 1989
Butterworth, Charles: Jul 26, 1896—Jun 14, 1946
Buzzell, Edward "Eddie":
                    Nov 13, 1897—Jan 11, 1985
Byington, Spring: Oct 17, 1893—Sep 7, 1971
Byrd, Ralph: Apr 22, 1909—Aug 18, 1952
Byron, Arthur: Apr 3, 1872—Jul 17, 1943
Byron, Marion: 1912—Jul 5, 1985
Byron, Walter: Jun 11, 1899—1972
Cabanne, William Christy:
                    Apr 16, 1888—Oct 15, 1950
Cabot, Bruce: Apr 20, 1904—May 3, 1972
Cabot, Sebastian: Jul 6, 1918—Aug 22, 1977
Cabot, Susan: Jul 9, 1927—Dec 10, 1986
Caesar, Adolph: 1934—Mar 6, 1986
Cagney, James: Jul 17, 1899—Mar 30, 1986
Cagney, Jeanne: Mar 25, 1919—Dec 7, 1984
Cagney, William J.: Mar 26, 1905—Jan 3, 1988
Cahn, Edward L.: Feb 2, 1899—Aug 25, 1963
Cain, Robert: 1887—Apr 27, 1954
Caine, Georgia: 1876—Apr 4, 1964
Calhern, Louis: Feb 19, 1895—May 12, 1956
Calhoun, Alice: Nov 24, 1901—Jun 3, 1966
Calleia, Joseph: Aug 14, 1897—Oct 31, 1975
Calthrop, Donald: Apr 11, 1888—Jul 15, 1940
Calve, Olga: 1900—May 12, 1982
Calvert, E. H.: Jun 27, 1873—Oct 5, 1941
Calvert, Steve: ____—Mar 5, 1991
Calvin, Henry: 1918—Oct 6, 1975
Cambridge, Godfrey: Feb 26, 1933—Nov 29, 1976
Cameron, Donald: 1889—Jul 11, 1955
Cameron, Donald A:. 1926—Dec 16, 1987
Cameron, Rod: Dec 7, 1910—Dec 21, 1983
Camp, Helen Page: 1930—Aug 2, 1991
Campbell, Colin: 1880—Mar 25, 1966
Campbell, Emma: 1942—Jul 30, 1991
Campbell, Mrs. Patrick: Feb 9, 1865—Apr 9, 1940
Campbell, Muriel: 1911—Jul 1, 1986

Campbell, Webster: 1893—Aug 28, 1972
Campeau, Frank: Dec 14, 1864—Nov 5, 1943
Campos, Rafael: 1936—Jul 9, 1985
Canova, Judy: Nov 20, 1916—Aug 5, 1983
Cantor, Eddie: Jan 31, 1892—Oct 10, 1964
Cantor, Max: ____—Oct 3, 1991
Canutt, Yakima: Nov 29, 1895—May 24, 1986
Capellani, Albert: 1870—1931
Capra, Frank: May 18, 1897—Sep 3, 1991
Caprice, June: 1899—1936
Capucine: Jan 6, 1933—Mar 17, 1990
Carew, Arthur Edmund: 1894—Apr 23, 1937
Carew, Ora: 1893—Oct 26, 1955
Carewe, Edwin: Mar 5, 1883—Jan 22, 1940
Carey, Harry: Jan 16, 1878—Sep 21, 1947
Carey, Mary Jane: 1924—Jan 11, 1990
Carey, Olive: Jan 31, 1896—Mar 13, 1988
Caristi, Vincent: 1948—Sep 20, 1990
Carle, Richard: Jul 7, 1871—Jun 28, 1941
Carlin, Thomas A.: 1929—May 6, 1991
Carlson, Richard: Apr 29, 1912—Nov 25, 1977
Carmel, Roger C.: 1932—Nov 11, 1986
Carmichael, Hoagy: Nov 22, 1899—Dec 27, 1981
Carmichael, Katherine: 1919—May 20, 1992
Carminati, Tullio: 1894—Feb 26, 1971
Carmine, Michael: 1959—Oct 7, 1989
Carney, Alan: Dec 22, 1911—May 2, 1973
Carnovsky, Morris: Sep 5, 1898—Sep 1, 1992
Carol, Sue: Oct 30, 1907—Feb 4, 1982
Carpenter, Charles: 1913—Nov 12, 1990
Carpenter, Constance: Apr 19, 1906—Dec 26, 1992
Carr, Mary K.: 1874—Jun 24, 1973
Carradine, John: Feb 5, 1906—Nov 27, 1988
Carrillo, Leo: Aug 6, 1880—Sep 10, 1961
Carrol, Regina: 1943—Nov 4, 1992
Carroll, Dee: 1926—Apr 28, 1980
Carroll, John: Jul 17, 1905—Apr 24, 1979
Carroll, Leo G.: Oct 25, 1892—Oct 16, 1972
Carroll, Madeleine: Feb 26, 1906—Oct 2, 1987
Carroll, Nancy: Nov 19, 1904—Aug 6, 1965
Carson, Jack: Oct 27, 1910—Jan 2, 1963
Carson, Sunset: Nov 12, 1922—May 1, 1990
Carson, Wayne: 1929—Jul 4, 1982
Carter, Beverly: 1941—Jun 8, 1992
Carter, Lynne: 1925—Jan 11, 1985
Carter, Nellie Bell: 1902—May 1, 1981
Carver, Louise: Jun 6, 1869—Jan 18, 1956
Carver, Lynn: Sep 13, 1909—Aug 12, 1955
Carver, Tina: 1924—Feb 18 1982
Carville, Virginia: 1895—Feb 18, 1982
Casey, Kenneth: 1899—Aug 10, 1965
Cason, Barbara: Nov 15, 1929—Jun 18, 1990
Cass, Maurice: Oct 12, 1884—Jun 8, 1954
Cassavetes, John: Dec 9, 1929—Feb 3, 1989
Cassidy, Ed: 1893—Jan 19, 1968
Cassidy, Jack: Mar 5, 1927—Dec 12, 1976
Cassidy, Ted: 1932—Jan 16, 1979
Castellano, Richard: Sep 4, 1933—Dec 10, 1988
Castle, Don: 1919—May 26, 1966
Castle, Irene: 1893—Jan 25, 1969
Castle, Peggy (Peggie):
                    Dec 22, 1926—Aug 11, 1973
Catlett, Walter: Feb 4, 1889—Nov 14, 1960
Caulfield, Joan: Jun 1, 1922—Jun 18, 1991
Cavanagh, Paul: Dec 8, 1895—Mar 15, 1964

Cavanaugh, Hobart: Sep 22, 1896—Apr 27, 1950
Cawthorn, Joseph: Mar 29, 1868—Jan 21, 1949
Cazale, John: 1936—Mar 12, 1978
Chadwick, Helen: Nov 25, 1897—Sep 4, 1940
Chaffey, Don: Aug 5, 1917—Nov 9, 1990
Chaliapin, Feodor, Jr.: 1905—Sep 17, 1992
Challee, William: 1905—Mar 18, 1989
Chalmers, Thomas: 1884—Jun 12, 1966
Chamberlin, Howland: 1911—Sep 1, 1984
Chambers, J. Wheaton: 1888—Jan 31, 1958
Champion, Gower: Jun 22, 1919—Aug 25, 1890
Champlin, Irene: 1931—Jul 10, 1990
Chandet, Louis W.: 1884—May 10, 1965
Chandler, Chick: Jan 18, 1905—Sep 30, 1988
Chandler, George: Jun 30, 1898—Jun 10, 1985
Chandler, Helen: Feb 1, 1906—Apr 30, 1965
Chandler, James: 1922—Jun 14, 1988
Chandler, Jeff: Dec 15, 1918—Jun 17, 1961
Chandler, Lane R.: Jun 4, 1899—Sep 14, 1972
Chaney, Lon, Jr.: Feb 10, 1906—Jul 12, 1973
Chaney, Lon (Sr.): Apr 1, 1883—Aug 26, 1930
Chaney, Norman "Chubby":
                    Jan 18, 1918—May 30, 1936
Chaplin, Charles, Jr.: May 5, 1925—Mar 20, 1968
Chaplin, Charles (Sr.): Apr 16, 1889—Dec 25, 1977
Chaplin, Sydney: Mar 17, 1885—Apr 16, 1965
Chapman, Edythe: Oct 8, 1863—Oct 15, 1948
Charles, Anthony: 1945—Dec 3, 1987
Charleston, Mary: 1885—Dec 3, 1961
Charters, Spencer: 1875—Jan 25, 1943
Chase, Charley: Oct 20, 1893—Jun 20, 1940
Chase, Ilka: Apr 8, 1903—Feb 15, 1978
Chase, Stephen Alden: ____—Apr 1, 1982
Chassey, Don: 1917—Nov 13, 1990
Chatterton, Ruth: Dec 24, 1893—Nov 24, 1961
Chautard, Emile: 1865—Apr 24, 1934
Chefee (Chefe), Jack: Apr 1, 1894—Dec 1, 1975
Chekhov, Michael: Aug 29, 1891—Sep 30, 1955
Chesebro, George: Jul 29, 1888—May 28, 1959
Cheshire, Harry V.: 1892—Jun 16, 1968
Chevalier, Maurice: Sep 12, 1888—Jan 1, 1972
Childers, Naomi: 1892—May 9, 1964
Childress, Alvin: 1908—Apr 19, 1986
Ching, William: Oct 2, 1913—Jul 1, 1989
Christensen, Benjamin: Sep 28, 1879—1959
Christi, Panos: 1938—Apr 25, 1992
Christian, Robert: 1941—Jan 27, 1983
Christians, Mady: Jan 19, 1900—Oct 28, 1951
Christy, Ann: May 31, 1909—Nov 14, 1987
Churchill, Berton: Dec 9, 1876—Oct 10, 1940
Ciannelli, Eduardo (Edward):
                    Aug 30, 1887—Oct 8, 1969
Clair, Rene: Nov 11, 1898—Mar 15, 1981
Claire, Carleton: 1913—Dec 11, 1979
Claire, Ina: Oct 15, 1892—Feb 21, 1985
Claire, Ludi: 1922—Jul 3, 1990
Clark, Bobby: Jun 16, 1888—Feb 12, 1960
Clark, Cliff: 1893—Feb 8, 1953
Clark, Dort: 1918—Mar 30, 1989
Clark, Eddie: 1879—Nov 18, 1954
Clark, Fred: Mar 9, 1914—Dec 5, 1968
Clark, Harvey: 1886—Jul 19, 1938
Clark, Mamo: 1914—Dec 18, 1986
Clark, Marguerite: Feb 22, 1883—Sep 25, 1940
Clarke, Gordon: 1907—Jan 11, 1972

Clarke, Mae: Aug 16, 1910—Apr 29, 1992
Clayton, Ethel: 1884—Jun 11, 1966
Clayton, Jan: Aug 26, 1917—Aug 28, 1983
Clayworth, June: 1913—Jan 1, 1993
Clement, Marc: 1951—Feb 18, 1990
Clements, Stanley: Jul 16, 1926—Oct 16, 1981
Cleveland, George: 1883—Jul 15, 1957
Clift, Denison: May 3, 1892—Dec 17, 1961
Clift, Montgomery: Oct 17, 1920—Jul 23, 1966
Clifton, Elmer: 1892—Oct 15, 1949
Cline, Edward F. "Eddie":
                    Nov 7, 1892—May 22, 1948
Clive, Colin: Jan 20, 1898—Jun 25, 1937
Clive, E. E.: Aug 28, 1879—Jun 6, 1940
Clive, Henry: 1881—Dec 12, 1960
Clute, Chester L:. 1891—Apr 5, 1956
Clute, Sidney: Apr 21, 1916—Oct 2, 1985
Clyde, Andy: Mar 25, 1892—May 18, 1967
Clyde, June: Dec 2, 1909—Oct 1, 1987
Cobb, Edmund F.: Jun 23, 1892—Aug 15, 1974
Cobb, Irvin S.: Jun 23, 1876—Mar 11, 1944
Cobb, Lee J.: Dec 8, 1911—Feb 11, 1976
Coburn, Charles: Jun 19, 1877—Aug 30, 1961
Coburn, Dorothy "Doddie": 1905—May 15, 1978
Cochran, Steve: May 25, 1917—Jun 15, 1965
Coco, James: Mar 21, 1929—Feb 25, 1987
Codee, Ann: 1890—May 18, 1961
Cody, Bill, Sr.: Jan 5, 1891—Jan 24, 1948
Cody, Lew: Feb 22, 1884—May 31, 1934
Cody, Wild Bill: 1913—Oct 25, 1988
Coe, Peter: Apr 18, 1929—May 25, 1987
Coffield, Peter: 1945—Nov 19, 1983
Coffin, Tristram 1910—Mar 26, 1990
Colasanto, Nicholas: Jan 19, 1924—Feb 12, 1985
Colby, Anita: 1915—Mar 27, 1992
Cole, Nat "King": Mar 17, 1919—Feb 15, 1965
Coleman, Charles: Dec 22, 1885—Mar 8, 1951
Colleano, Bonar: Mar 14, 1924—Aug 17, 1958
Collier, Constance: Jan 22, 1878—Apr 25, 1955
Collier, James F.: 1929—May 27, 1991
Collier, William "Buster", Jr.:
                    Feb 12, 1902—Feb 6, 1987
Collier, William, Sr.: Nov 12, 1866—Jan 13, 1944
Collinge, Patricia: Sep 20, 1892—Apr 10, 1974
Collins, G. Pat: Dec 16, 1895—Aug 5, 1959
Collins, Lewis D.: Jan 12, 1899—Aug 24, 1954
Collins, Ray: Dec 10, 1889—Jul 11, 1965
Collins, Russell: Oct 8, 1897—Nov 14, 1965
Collyer, June: Aug 19, 1907—Mar 16, 1968
Colman, Ben: 1907—Feb 22, 1988
Colman, Ronald: Feb 9, 1891—May 19, 1958
Colonna, Jerry: Sep 17, 1904—Nov 21, 1986
Columbo, Russ: Jan 14, 1908—Sep 2, 1934
Combs, Frederick: 1935—Sep 19, 1992
Comingore, Dorothy: Aug 24, 1913—Dec 30, 1971
Compson, Betty: Mar 18, 1897—Apr 18, 1974
Condos, Nick: 1915—Jul 8, 1988
Conklin, Charles "Heinie": 1880—Jul 30, 1959
Conklin, Chester: Jan 11, 1888—Oct 11, 1971
Conlin, Jimmy: Oct 14, 1884—May 7, 1962
Connelly, Bobby: Apr 4, 1909—Jul 6, 1922
Connelly, Christopher: 1941—Dec 7, 1988
Connolly, Walter: Apr 8, 1887—May 28, 1940
Connor, Whitfield: 1917—Jul 16, 1988
Connors, Chuck: Apr 10, 1921—Nov 10, 1992

Conrad, Michael: Oct 16, 1921—Nov 22, 1983
Conried, Hans: Apr 15, 1917—Jan 5, 1982
Conroy, Frank: Oct 14, 1890—Feb 24, 1964
Constantine, Eddie: Oct 29, 1917—Feb 25, 1993
Conte, Richard: Mar 24, 1910—Apr 15, 1975
Conti, Albert: Jan 29, 1878—Jan 18, 1967
Convy, Bert: Jul 23, 1933—Jul 15, 1991
Conway, Curt: 1916—Apr 11, 1974
Conway, Jack: Jul 17, 1887—Oct 11, 1952
Conway, Morgan: Mar 16, 1903—Nov 16 1981
Conway, Tom: Sep 15, 1904—Apr 22, 1967
Coogan, Jackie: Oct 24, 1914—Mar 1, 1984
Cook, Clyde: Dec 16, 1891—Aug 13, 1984
Cook, Donald: Sep 26, 1900—Oct 1, 1961
Cook, Roderick: 1932—Aug 17, 1990
Coolidge, Phil: 1909—May 23, 1967
Cooper, Albert Raymond: 1900—Jan 9, 1989
Cooper, Clancy: 1907—Jun 14, 1975
Cooper, Dorothy J.: Aug 9, 1906—Dec 7, 1988
Cooper, Dulcie: 1904—Sep 3, 1981
Cooper, Edna Mae: 1901—Jun 27, 1986
Cooper, Gary May 7, 1901—May 13, 1961
Cooper, Gladys Dec 18, 1888—Nov 17, 1971
Cooper, Melville G.: Oct 15, 1896—Mar 29, 1973
Cooper, Merian C.: Oct 24, 1893—Apr 21, 1973
Cooper, Miriam: 1892—Apr 12, 1976
Cooper, Olive: 1893—Jun 12, 1987
Cooper, Ralph: c. 1910—Aug 4, 1992
Coote, Robert: Feb 4, 1909—Nov 25, 1982
Corbett, Glenn: 1934—Jan 16, 1993
Corbett, Leonora: Jun 28, 1909—Jul 29, 1960
Corbett, Ruth: 1914—Dec 7, 1992
Corday, Rita (Paula): Oct 20, 1924—Nov 23, 1992
Cording, Harry: Apr 29, 1891—Sep 1, 1954
Corey, Wendell: Mar 20, 1914—Nov 8, 1968
Correll, Charles: Feb 3, 1890—Sep 26, 1972
Corrigan, Lloyd: Oct 16, 1900—Nov 5, 1969
Corrigan, Raymond "Crash":
                    Feb 14, 1902—Aug 10, 1976
Cortez, Ricardo: Sep 19, 1899—Apr 28, 1977
Cossart, Ernest: Sep 24, 1876—Jan 21, 1951_
Costello, Anthony: 1941—Aug 15, 1983
Costello, Dolores: Sep 17, 1905—Mar 1, 1979
Costello, Helene: Jun 21, 1903—Jan 26, 1957
Costello, Lou: Mar 6, 1906—Mar 3, 1959
Costello, Maurice: Feb 22, 1877—Oct 28, 1950
Coston, Ann Sorg: 1929—Dec 6, 1991
Coughlin, Kevin: 1945—Jan 19, 1976
Coulouris, George: Oct 1, 1903—Apr 25, 1989
Courtland, Nicholas: 1941—Aug 21, 1988
Courtney, Inez: Mar 12, 1908—Apr 5, 1975
Cowan, Jerome: Oct 6, 1897—Jan 24, 1972
Coward, Noel: Dec 16, 1899—Mar 26, 1973
Cowl, Jane: 1887—Jun 22, 1950
Cox, Robert: 1895—Sep 8, 1974
Cox, Wally: Dec 6, 1924—Feb 15, 1973
Crabbe, Larry "Buster":
                    Feb 17, 1907—Apr 23, 1983
Craig, Alec: 1885—Jun 25, 1945
Craig, Edith: 1908—Mar 2, 1979
Craig, Helen: May 13, 1912—Jul 20, 1986
Craig, James: Feb 4, 1912—Jul 8, 1985
Craig, Nell: 1891—Jan 5, 1965
Crane, Bob: Jul 13, 1928—Jun 29, 1978
Crane, Norma: 1931—Sep 28, 1973

Crane, Richard O.: 1918—Mar 9, 1969
Craven, Edward 1908—May 14, 1991
Craven, Frank: Aug 24, 1875—Sep 1, 1945
Craven, John Edward: 1908—May 14, 1991
Crawford, Broderick: Dec 9, 1911—Apr 26, 1986
Crawford, Joan: Mar 23, 1904—May 10, 1977
Crawford, Timothy: 1904—Jun 13, 1978
Cregar, Laird: Jul 28, 1916—Dec 9, 1944
Crehan, Joseph: Jul 12, 1886—Apr 15, 1966
Crews, Laura Hope: Dec 12, 1879—Nov 13, 1942
Crisp, Donald: Jul 27, 1880—May 25, 1974
Cromwell, John: Dec 23, 1887—Sep 26, 1979
Cromwell, Richard: Jan 8, 1910—Oct 11, 1960
Cronin, Laurel: 1939—Oct 26, 1992
Crosby, Bing: May 2, 1901—Oct 14, 1977
Crosby, Bob: Aug 25, 1913—Mar 9, 1993
Crosby, Dennis: Jul 13, 1934—May 4, 1991
Crosby, Lindsay: Jan 5, 1938—Dec 11, 1989
Crosby, Wade: 1911—Oct 11, 1976
Crosland, Alan: Aug 10, 1894—Jul 16, 1936
Cross, Allan: 1895—Mar 4, 1993
Crossman, Henrietta: Sep 2, 1861—Oct 31, 1944
Crothers, Scatman: May 23, 1910—Nov 26, 1986
Cruze, James: Mar 27, 1884—Aug 4, 1942
Cuevas, Jose Luis (Joey): 1958—May 2, 1992
Cugat, Xavier: Jan 1, 1900—Oct 27, 1990
Cukor, George: Jul 7, 1899—Jan 24, 1983
Culver, Cal: 1944—Aug 10, 1987
Cummings, Dorothy: 1899—Dec 10, 1983
Cummings, Irving, Sr.: Oct 9, 1888—Apr 18, 1959
Cummings, Robert "Bob":
                    Jun 10, 1908—Dec 2, 1990
Cummings, Ruth Sinclair: 1984—Dec 6, 1984
Cummings, Sandy: 1914—Jan 14, 1982
Cunard, Grace: 1894—Jan 19, 1967
Cuneo, Lester: 1888—Nov 21, 1925
Cunningham, Cecil: Aug 2, 1888—Apr 17, 1959
Cunningham, Sarah: 1909—Mar 24, 1986
Cunningham, Zamah: 1893—Jun 2, 1967
Currie, Finlay: Jan 20, 1878—May 9, 1968
Currier, Frank: 1857—Apr 22, 1928
Curtis, Alan: Jul 24, 1909—Feb 1, 1953
Curtis, Billy: 1909—Nov 9, 1988
Curtis, Dick: May 11, 1902—Jan 3, 1952
Curtis, Jackie: 1947—May 15, 1985
Curtis, Ken: Jul 2, 1916—Apr 28, 1991
Curtiz, Michael: Dec 24, 1888—Apr 11, 1962
Curtright, Jorja: ____—May 11, 1985
Custer, Bob: Oct 18, 1898—Dec 27, 1974
Cutts, Patricia: 1926—Sep 6, 1974
Da Costa, Morton: Mar 7, 1914—Jan 29, 1989
Dailey, Dan: Dec 14, 1914—Oct 16, 1978
D'Albrook, Sidney: May 3, 1886—May 30, 1948
Dale, Bobby: 1899—May 21, 1991
Dale, Charlie: 1881—Nov 16, 1971
Dale, Esther: Nov 10, 1885—Jul 23, 1961
Daley, Cass: Jul 17, 1915—Mar 23, 1975
Dalio, Marcel: Jul 17, 1900—Nov 20, 1983
Dall, John: 1918—Jan 15, 1971
Dallimore, Maurice: c. 1900—Mar 5, 1973
Dalton, Dorothy: Sep 22, 1893—Apr 12, 1972
Daly, James: Oct 23, 1918—Jul 3, 1978
Dalzell, Lyda St. Clair: ____— Mar 28, 1974
D'Ambricourt, Adrienne: 1888—Dec 6, 1957
Damon, Cathryn: Sep 11, 1930—May 4, 1987

Dana, Leora: Apr 1, 1923—Dec 13, 1983
Dana, Viola: Jun 28, 1897—Jul 3, 1987
Dandridge, Dorothy: Nov 9, 1923—Sep 8, 1965
Dandridge, Ruby: Mar 3, 1900—Oct 17, 1987
Dane, Karl: Oct 12, 1886—Apr 15, 1934
Daniell, Henry: Mar 5, 1894—Oct 31, 1963
Daniels, Bebe: Jan 14, 1901—Mar 16, 1971
Danova, Cesare: Mar 1, 1926—Mar 19, 1992
Dantine, Helmut: Oct 7, 1917—May 3, 1982
Danton, Ray: Sep 19, 1931—Feb 11, 1992
D'Arcy, Peter A.: 1914—May 31, 1991
D'Arcy, Roy: Feb 10, 1894—Nov 15, 1969
Darin, Bobby: May 14, 1936—Dec 20, 1973
Darmond, Grace: 1894—Oct 7, 1963
Darnell, Linda: Oct 16, 1923—Apr 10, 1965
D'Arrast, Harry d'Abbadie: 1897—Mar 17, 1968
Darro, Frankie: Dec 22, 1918—Dec 25, 1976
Darvas, Lili: Apr 10, 1902—Jul 22, 1974
Darvi, Bella: Oct 23, 1928—Sep 11, 1971
Darwell, Jane: Oct 15, 1879—Aug 13, 1967
Dash, Pauly: 1919—Feb 2, 1974
Da Silva, Howard: May 4, 1909—Feb 16, 1986
Dauphin, Claude: Aug 19, 1903—Nov 17, 1978
Davenport, Dorothy: 1895—Aug 17, 1977
Davenport, Harry: Jan 19, 1866—Aug 9, 1949
Daves, Delmer: Jul 24, 1904— Aug 17, 1977
David, Thayer: Mar 4, 1927—Jul 17, 1978
Davidson, John: Dec 25, 1886—Jan 15, 1968
Davidson, William B.: Jun 16, 1888—Sep 28, 1947
Davies, Marion: Jan 3, 1897—Sep 22, 1961
Davis, Art: 1914—Jan 16, 1987
Davis, Bette: Apr 5, 1908—Oct 6, 1989
Davis, Brad: Nov 6, 1949—Sep 8, 1991
Davis, Colleen: 1962—Jan 16, 1992
Davis, Jim: Aug 26, 1915—Apr 26, 1981
Davis, Joan: Jun 29, 1907—May 23, 1961
Davis, John H: 1914—Nov 3, 1992
Davis, Johnny "Scat": May 11, 1910—Nov 24, 1983
Davis, Mildred: Jan 1, 1900—Aug 18, 1969
Davis, Rufus: 1908—Dec 13, 1974
Davis, Sammy, Jr.: Dec 8, 1925—May 16, 1990
Daw, Evelyn: 1912—Nov 30, 1970
Dawn, Hazel: 1890—Aug 28, 1988
Dawn, Isabel: 1904—Jun 29, 1966
Dawson, Hal K.: 1897—Feb 17, 1987
Day, Dennis: May 21, 1917—Jun 22, 1988
Day, Josette: 1915—Jun 29, 1978
Deacon, Richard: May 14, 1922—Aug 8, 1984
Dean, James: Feb 6, 1931—Sep 30, 1955
Dean, Julia: May 12, 1878—Oct 17, 1952
Dean, Priscilla: Nov 25, 1896—Dec 27, 1988
Deane, Palmer: 1934—Apr 23, 1990
Dearing, Edgar: May 4, 1893—Aug 17, 1974
DeAubrey, Diane: 1890—May 23, 1969
De Brulier, Nigel: 1878—Jan 30, 1948
De Cordoba, Pedro: Sep 28, 1881—Sep 17, 1950
De Cordova, Arturo: May 8, 1907—Nov 3, 1973
De Corsia, Ted: Sep 29, 1903—Apr 12, 1973
Deering, Olive: 1919—Mar 22, 1986
Deghy, Guy: 1913—Feb 25, 1992
De Grasse, Joseph: 1873—May 24, 1940
De Grasse, Sam: 1875—Nov 29, 1953
de Groot, Katherine Hynes: 1905—Mar 27, 1993
De Haven, Carter, Sr.: 1886—Jul 20, 1977
Dehner, John: Nov 23, 1915—Feb 4, 1992

Dekker, Albert: Dec 20, 1904—May 5, 1968
De Kova, Frank: 1910—Oct 15, 1981
DeKoven, Roger: Oct 22, 1907—Jan 28, 1988
De La Motte, Marguerite:
                    Jun 22, 1902—Mar 10, 1950
Del Rio, Dolores: Aug 3, 1905—Apr 11, 1983
Del Ruth, Roy: Oct 18, 1895—Apr 27, 1961
Del Vando, Amapola: 1909—Feb 25, 1988
Delaney, Charles: 1892—Aug 31, 1959
Delauder, Doug: 1954—Jun 30, 1992
Delevanti, Cyril: 1887—Dec 13, 1975
Dell, Dorothy Jan 30, 1915— Jun 8, 1934
Dell, Gabriel: Oct 7, 1919—Jul 3, 1988
Delmar, Kenny: 1910—Jul 14, 1984
Demarest, William: Feb 27, 1892—Dec 28, 1983
DeMille, Cecil B.: Aug 12, 1881—Jan 21, 1959
DeMille, William C.: Jun 25, 1878—Mar 18, 1955
Dempster, Carol: 1902—Feb 1, 1991
Demyan, Lincoln: 1925—Oct 6, 1991
Dennis, Sandy: Apr 27, 1937—Mar 2, 1992
Denny, Reginald: Nov 20, 1891—Jun 16, 1967
Dent, Vernon: 1900—Nov 5, 1963
Depew, Joseph: Jul 11, 1912—Oct 30, 1988
De Putti, Lya: 1901—Nov 27, 1931
Derr, Richard: 1918—May 8, 1992
DeRue, Carmen: 1908—Sep 28, 1986
De Sales, Francis: 1912—Sep 25, 1988
De Santis, Joe: 1909—Aug 30, 1989
Desmond, Florence: 1906—Jan 16, 1993
Desmond, Johnny: Nov 14, 1920—Sep 6, 1985
Desmond, William: Jan 1878—Nov 3, 1949
DeSoto, Henry: 1888—Sep 9, 1963
De Vega, Jose, Jr.: 1936—Apr 8, 1990
Deveau, Jack: 1936—Dec 2, 1982
Devine, Andy: Oct 7, 1905—Feb 18, 1977
DeVore, Dorothy: 1899—Sep 10, 1976
Dewhurst, Colleen: Jun 3, 1924—Aug 22, 1991
De Wilde, Brandon: Apr 9, 1942—Jul 6, 1972
De Wolfe, Billy: Feb 18, 1907—Mar 5, 1974
Dexter, Elliott (Sr.): 1870—Jun 23, 1941
Dhiegh, Khigh: 1916—Oct 25, 1991
Dial, Dick: 1932—Jan 17, 1992
Diamond, Selma: Aug 5, 1920—May 14, 1985
Dierkes, John: Feb 10, 1908—Jan 8, 1975
Dieterle, William: Jul 15, 1893—Dec 9, 1972
Dietrich, Marlene: Dec 27, 1901—May 6, 1992
Digges, Dudley: Jun 9, 1879—Oct 24, 1947
Dillaway, Donald: 1904—Nov 18, 1982
Dillin, Edward: 1880—Jul 11, 1933
Dillon, John (Jack) T.: Jul 13, 1886—Dec 29, 1937
Dillon, John Francis: Nov 28, 1884—Apr 4, 1934
Dinehart, Alan, Jr.: 1918—Mar 14, 1992
Dinehart, Alan (Sr.): Oct 3, 1889—Jul 17, 1944
Dingle, Charles W.: Dec 28, 1887—Jan 19, 1956
Divine: 1945—Mar 7, 1988
Dix, Constance: 1922—Feb 1, 1982
Dix, Richard: Aug 8, 1894—Sep 20, 1949
Dixon, Denver: 1890—Nov 9, 1972
Dixon, Jean: 1896—Feb 12, 1981
Dixon, Joan: 1931—Feb 20, 1992
Dobson, James: 1920—Dec 6, 1987
Dodd, Claire: Dec 29, 1908—Nov 23, 1973
Dodd, Jimmie: 1910—Nov 10, 1964
Dodd, Neal (Rev.): 1878—May 26, 1966
Doherty, Charla: 1947—May 29, 1988

Donahue, Maugene: 1928—Apr 1, 1993
Donahue, Vincent J.: 1916—Jan 17, 1966
Donat, Robert: Mar 18, 1905—Jun 9, 1958
Donath, Ludwig: Mar 5, 1900—Sep 29, 1967
Donlevy, Brian: Feb 9, 1899—Apr 5, 1972
Donnell, Jeff: Jul 10, 1921—Apr 11, 1988
Donnelly, Ruth: May 17, 1896—Nov 17, 1982
Donovan, King: 1918—Jun 30, 1987
Donovan, Warde: 1916—Apr 16, 1988
Dorn, Philip: Sep 30, 1901—May 9, 1975
Doro, Marie: 1882—Oct 9, 1956
Dors, Diana: Oct 23, 1932—May 4, 1984
D'Orsay, Fifi: Apr 16, 1904—Dec 2, 1983
Dorsey, Jimmy: Feb 29, 1904—Jun 12, 1957
Dorsey, Tommy: Nov 19, 1905—Nov 26, 1956
Doucet, Catherine: Jun 20, 1875—1958
Douglas, Don: 1905—Dec 31, 1945
Douglas, Melvyn: Apr 5, 1901—Aug 4, 1981
Douglas, Paul: Nov 4, 1907—Sep 11, 1959
Douglas, Tom: 1896—May 4, 1978
Dowell, Clifton: 1948—May 10, 1992
Dowling, Constance: 1920—Oct 28, 1969
Dowling, Joseph J.: 1848—Jul 10, 1928
Downs, Cathy: Mar 3, 1924—Dec 8, 1976
Drake, Alfred: Oct 1, 1914—Jul 25, 1992
Drake, Oliver: 1903—Aug 5, 1991
Drake, Tom: Aug 5, 1918—Aug 11, 1982
Drayton, Noel: 1913—Dec 7, 1981
Dresser, Louise: Oct 5, 1880—Apr 24, 1965
Dressler, Marie: Nov 9, 1869—Jul 28, 1934
Drew, Ann: 1889—Feb 6, 1974
Drew, Roland: 1901—Mar 17, 1988
Drew, Sidney: Aug 28, 1864—Apr 9, 1919
Drew, Sidney (Mrs.): Apr 18, 1890—Nov 3, 1925
Driggers, Donald: 1893—Nov 19, 1972
Driscoll, Bobby: Mar 3, 1937—Mar 1968
Drivas, Robert: Nov 21, 1936—Sep 28, 1986
Du Pont, Miss: 1894—1973
Dubbins, Don: Jun 28, 1929—Aug 17, 1991
Dudgeon, Elspeth: Dec 4, 1871—Dec 11, 1955
Dudley, Lynn: 1927—Dec 24, 1991
Duel, Peter: Feb 24, 1940—Dec 31, 1971
Duff, Howard: Nov 24, 1917—Jul 8, 1990
Dugan, Tom: 1889—Mar 6, 1955
Duggan, Andrew: Dec 28, 1923—May 15, 1988
Dumbrille, Douglas: Oct 13, 1888—Apr 2, 1974
Dumont, Gordon: 1896—Mar 1966
Dumont, Margaret: Oct 20, 1889—Mar 6, 1965
Duna, Steffi: Feb 18, 1913—May 1992
Dunbar, Dixie: Jan 19, 1919—Aug 20, 1992
Dunbar, Dorothy: 1902—Oct 30, 1992
Duncan, Bud: Oct 31, 1883—Nov 25, 1960
Duncan, Kenne: Feb 17, 1902—Feb 5, 1972
Duncan, Rosetta: 1901—Dec 4, 1959
Duncan, Vivian: 1902—Sep 19, 1986
Duncan, William: 1880—Feb 8, 1961
Dunlap, Scott R.: Jun 20, 1892—Mar 30, 1970
Dunn, Edward F. "Eddie": 1896—May 5, 1951
Dunn, Emma: Feb 26, 1875—Dec 14, 1966
Dunn, James: Nov 2, 1901—Sep 1, 1967
Dunn, Josephine: May 1, 1906—Apr 1983
Dunn, Liam: 1917—Apr 11, 1976
Dunn, Michael: Oct 20, 1934—Aug 29, 1973
Dunn, Peter: 1922—Apr 14, 1990
Dunn, Ralph: 1902—Feb 19, 1968

Dunne, Dominque: 1959—Nov 4, 1982
Dunne, Irene: Dec 20, 1898—Sep 4, 1990
Dunne, Philip: Feb 11, 1908—May 10, 1992
Dunne, Steve: 1918—Aug 27, 1977
Dunnock, Mildred: Jan 25, 1900—Jul 5, 1991
Dupont, E. A.: Dec 25, 1891—Dec 12, 1956
Duprez, June: May 14, 1918—Oct 30, 1984
Durante, Jimmy: Feb 10, 1893—Jan 28, 1980
Durfee, Minta: 1890—Sep 9, 1975
Duryea, Dan: Jan 23, 1907—Jun 7, 1968
Duval, Jose F.: 1921—Feb 27, 1993
Duvivier, Julien: Oct 8, 1896—Oct 31, 1967
Dvorak, Ann: Aug 2, 1912—Dec 10, 1979
Dwan, Allan: Apr 3, 1885—Dec 2, 1981
Eagels, Jeanne: Jun 26, 1894—Oct 3, 1929
Eagle, James "Jimmy": Sep 10, 1907—Dec 15, 1959
Eames, Virginia: 1889—Jun 10, 1971
Earle, Edward: Jul 16, 1882—Dec 15, 1972
Earle, Merie: May 13, 1889—Nov 4, 1984
Earle, William P. S.: Dec 28, 1882—Nov 30, 1972
Eason, B. Reeves: Oct 2, 1886—Jun 10, 1956
Eaton, Dorothy M.: 1914—Jan 7, 1988
Eaton, Jay: 1900—Feb 5, 1970
Eaton, Marjorie: 1900—Apr 25, 1986
Eburne, Maude: 1875—Oct 15, 1960
Eckhardt, John: 1909—Jan 5, 1991
Eddy, Helen Jerome: 1898—Jan 27, 1990
Eddy, Nelson: Jun 29, 1901—Mar 6, 1967
Edwards, Cliff "Ukulele Ike":
                    Jun 14, 1895—Jul 17, 1971
Edwards, Edna Park: 1895—Jun 5, 1967
Edwards, Gloria: 1945—Feb 12, 1988
Edwards, J. Gordon: 1867—Dec 31, 1925
Edwards, James: 1912—Jan 4, 1970
Edwards, Sarah: 1883—Jan 7, 1965
Edwards, Snitz: 1862—May 1, 1937
Egan, Richard: Jul 29, 1921—Jul 20, 1987
Eilers, Sally: Dec 11, 1908—Jan 5, 1978
Eldridge, Florence: Sep 5, 1901—Aug 1, 1988
Eldridge, John: Aug 30, 1904—Sep 23, 1961
Ellerbe, Harry: 1901—Dec 2, 1992
Ellington, Duke: Apr 29, 1899—May 24, 1974
Elliott, Denholm: May 31, 1922—Oct 6, 1992
Elliott, Dick: Apr 30, 1886—Dec 22, 1961
Elliott, Gordon "Wild Bill":
                    Oct 15, 1903—Nov 26, 1965
Elliott, John H.: Jul 5, 1876—Dec 12, 1956
Elliott, Robert: Oct 9, 1879—Nov 15, 1951
Elliott, William David: 1934—Sep 30, 1983
Ellis, Edward: 1873—Jul 26, 1952
Ellis, Patricia: May 20, 1916—Mar 26, 1970
Ellis, Robert: 1933—Nov 23, 1973
Ellis, Robert Reel: Jun 27, 1892—Dec 29, 1974
Elsom, Isobel: Mar 16, 1893—Jan 12, 1981
Emerson, Faye: Jul 8, 1917—Mar 9, 1983
Emerson, Hope: Oct 29, 1897—Apr 25, 1960
Emerson, John: May 29, 1878—Mar 8, 1956
Emery, Gilbert: Jun 11, 1875—Oct 26, 1945
Emery, John: 1905—Nov 16, 1964
Emmett, Fern: Mar 22, 1896—Sep 3, 1946
Engel, Roy: 1914—Dec 29, 1981
Engle, Dale C.: 1922—May 16, 1990
English, John W.: 1903—Oct 11, 1969
Enright, Ray: Mar 25, 1896—Apr 3, 1965
Enriquez, Rene: Nov 25, 1933—Mar 23, 1990

Entwistle, Peg: 1908—Sep 18, 1932
Epper, John: 1906—Dec 3, 1992
Epstein, David S.: 1919—Jul 7, 1992
Epstein, Jerry: 1922—Nov 16, 1991
Erickson, Leif: Oct 27, 1911—Jan 29, 1986
Errol, Leon: Jul 3, 1881—Oct 12, 1951
Erwin, June: 1918—Dec 28, 1965
Erwin, Stuart: Feb 14, 1902—Dec 21, 1967
Essler, Fred: 1896—Jan 17, 1973
Ethier, Alphonse: 1875—Jan 4, 1943
Etting, Ruth: Nov 23, 1896—Sep 23, 1978
Evans, Douglas: 1904—Mar 25, 1968
Evans, John Morgan: 1942—Dec 27, 1991
Evans, Madge: Jul 1, 1909—Apr 26, 1981
Evans, Maurice: Jun 3, 1901—Mar 12, 1989
Evans, Rex: 1903—Apr 3, 1969
Evelyn, Judith: Mar 13, 1913—May 7, 1967
Everest, Barbara: 1891—Feb 9, 1968
Evers, Ann: ____—Jun 4, 1987
Eythe, William: Apr 7, 1918—Jan 26, 1957
Fair, Elinor: Dec 21, 1903—Apr 26, 1957
Fairbanks, Douglas, Sr.:
                        May 23, 1883—Dec 12, 1939
Faire, Virginia Browne: Jun 26, 1906—Jun 30, 1980
Falat, Stephen J.: 1957—Oct 10, 1991
Farley, Dot: Feb 6, 1881—May 2, 1971
Farley, James Lee "Jim": Jan 8, 1882—Oct 12, 1947
Farley, Morgan: Oct 3, 1898—Oct 11, 1988
Farmer, Frances: Sep 19, 1914—Aug 1, 1970
Farmer, Virginia: 1898—May 19, 1988
Farnum, Dustin: May 27, 1874—Jul 3, 1929
Farnum, Franklyn: Jun 5, 1876—Jul 4, 1961
Farnum, William: Jul 4, 1876—Jun 5, 1953
Farrar, Geraldine: Feb 28, 1882—Mar 11, 1967
Farrell, Charles: Aug 9, 1901—May 6, 1990
Farrell, Glenda: Jun 30, 1904—May 1, 1971
Farrell, Timothy: 1923—May 9, 1989
Farrow, John: Feb 10, 1904—Jan 27, 1963
Faulkner, Ralph: 1892—Jan 19, 1987
Fawcett, George D.: Aug 25, 1860—Jun 6, 1939
Fawcett, William: ____—Jan 25, 1974
Fay, Frank: Nov 17, 1894—Sep 25, 1961
Fay, Sheldon, Jr.: 1937—Mar 12, 1990
Faye, Frances: ____—Nov 8, 1991
Faye, Herbie: 1899—Jun 28, 1980
Faye, Julia: Sep 24, 1896—Apr 6, 1966
Faylen, Frank: Dec 8, 1907—Aug 2, 1985
Fazenda, Louise: Jun 17, 1889—Apr 17, 1962
Fealy, Maude: 1881—Nov 9, 1971
Feddon, Margaret: 1873—Apr 17, 1968
Feist, Felix E.: Feb 28, 1906—Sep 3, 1965
Fejos, Paul: Jan 24, 1897—Apr 24, 1963
Feldman, Andrea: ____—Aug 8, 1972
Feldman, Marty: Jul 8, 1933—Dec 2, 1982
Fellowes, Rockliffe: 1885—Jan 28, 1950
Felton, Verna: Jul 20, 1890—Dec 14, 1966
Fennelly, Parker: 1896—Jan 22, 1988
Fenton, Frank: Apr 9, 1906—Jul 24, 1957
Fenton, Leslie C.: Mar 12, 1902—Mar 25, 1978
Fenwick, Irene: 1887—Dec 24, 1936
Ferguson, Al: Apr 19, 1888—Dec 4, 1971
Ferguson, Elsie: 1883—Nov 15, 1961
Ferguson, Frank: Dec 25, 1899—Sep 12, 1978
Ferguson, Helen: Jul 23, 1901—Mar 14, 1977
Fernandez, Emilio: Mar 26, 1904—Aug 6, 1986

Ferrer, Jose: Jan 8, 1912—Jan 26, 1992
Fetchit, Stepin: May 30, 1902—Nov 19, 1985
Fetherstone (Featherstone) Eddie:
                        ____—Jun 12, 1965
Feury, Peggy: ____—Nov 20, 1985
Feyder, Jacques: Jul 21, 1885—May 25, 1948
Field, Betty: Feb 8, 1918—Sep 13, 1973
Field, Virginia: Nov 4, 1917—Jan 2, 1992
Field, Walter: 1875—Jun 5, 1976
Fields, Gracie: Jan 9, 1898—Sep 27, 1979
Fields, Stanley: May 20, 1883—Apr 23, 1941
Fields, W. C.: Jan 29, 1880—Dec 25, 1946
Fillmore, Clyde: Oct 25, 1874—Dec 19, 1946
Finch, Flora: Jun 17, 1869—Jan 4, 1940
Finch, Peter: Sep 28, 1916—Jan 14, 1977
Fine, Larry: Oct 5, 1911—Jan 24, 1975
Finlayson, James: Aug 27, 1887—Oct 9, 1953
Finley, Evelyn: 1915—Apr 7, 1989
Finley, Ned: ____—Sep 27, 1920
Fiske, Richard: Nov 20, 1915—Aug 1944
Fiske, Robert L.: Oct 20, 1889—Sep 12, 1944
Fitzgerald, Barry: Mar 10, 1888—Jan 4, 1961
Fitzgerald, Neil: 1892—Jun 15, 1982
Fitzmaurice, George: Feb 13, 1885—Jun 13, 1940
Fitzroy, Emily: 1861—Mar 3, 1954
Fix, Paul: Mar 13, 1901—Oct 14, 1983
Flaherty, Pat J., Sr.: Mar 8, 1903—Dec 2, 1970
Flaherty, Robert J.: Feb 16, 1884—Jul 23, 1951
Flaum, Mayer: 1901—Apr 26, 1990
Flavin, James: May 14, 1906—Apr 23, 1976
Fleming, Eric: 1925—Sep 28, 1966
Fleming, Victor: Feb 23, 1883—Jan 6, 1949
Fletcher, Bramwell: Feb 20, 1904—Jun 22, 1988
Flint, Helen: 1898—Sep 9, 1967
Flint, Sam: Oct 19, 1882—Oct 24, 1980
Flippen, Jay C.: Mar 6, 1898—Feb 3, 1971
Flowers, Bess: Nov 23, 1898—Jul 28, 1984
Flowers, Wayland: Nov 19, 1939—Oct 11, 1988
Fluellen, Joel: 1909—Feb 2, 1990
Flynn, Errol: Jun 20, 1909—Oct 14, 1959
Flynn, Joe: Nov 8, 1924—Jul 19, 1974
Flynn, Sean: May 10, 1941—Missing in Action
Fonda, Henry: May 16, 1905—Aug 12, 1982
Fong, Benson: Oct 10, 1916—Aug 1, 1987
Fontaine, Eddie: 1934—Apr 13, 1992
Fontaine, Frank: Apr 19, 1920—Aug 4, 1978
Fontaine, Lilian: 1887—Feb 20, 1975
Fontanne, Lynn: Dec 6, 1887—Jul 30, 1983
Foran, Dick: Jun 18, 1910—Aug 10, 1979
Foran, Mary: 1920—Apr 10, 1981
Forbes, Mary: Jan 1, 1880—Jul 22, 1974
Forbes, Ralph: Sep 30, 1902—Mar 31, 1951
Ford, Constance: Jul 1, 1924—Feb 26, 1993
Ford, Francis: Aug 15, 1882—Sep 5, 1953
Ford, Harrison: Mar 16, 1894—Dec 2, 1957
Ford, John: Feb 1, 1895—Aug 31, 1973
Ford, Lloyd: 1911—May 8, 1991
Ford, Paul: Nov 2, 1901—Apr 12, 1976
Ford, Ross: 1923—Jun 22, 1988
Ford, Tennessee Ernie: Feb 13, 1919—Oct 17, 1991
Ford, Victoria: 1897—Jul 24, 1964
Ford, Wallace: Feb 12, 1898—Jun 11, 1966
Forde, Eugenie: Nov 8, 1898—Sep 5, 1940
Foreman, Carl: Jul 23, 1914—Jun 26, 1984
Forman, Tom: Feb 22, 1893—Nov 7, 1926

Forrest, William H.: 1902—Jan 26, 1989
Forte, Joe: 1896—Feb 22, 1967
Fosse, Bob: Jun 23, 1927—Sep 23, 1987
Foster, Lewis R.: Aug 5, 1900—Jun 10, 1974
Foster, Norman: Dec 13, 1900—Jul 7, 1976
Foster, Phil: Mar 29, 1914—Jul 8, 1985
Foster, Preston: Aug 24, 1900—Jul 14, 1970
Foster, Skip: 1952—Sep 5, 1992
Foulger, Byron: 1899—Apr 4, 1970
Fowler, Brenda: 1883—Oct 27, 1942
Fox, Mickey: 1916—Mar 9, 1988
Fox, Virginia: 1903—Oct 14, 1982
Fox, Wallace W.: Mar 9, 1895—Jun 30, 1958
Foxe, Earle A.: Dec 25, 1888—Dec 10, 1973
Foxx, Redd: Dec 9, 1922—Oct 11, 1991
Foy, Bryon: Dec 8, 1896—Apr 20, 1977
Foy, Eddie, Jr.: Feb 4, 1905—Jul 15, 1983
Francen, Victor: Aug 5, 1888—Nov 18, 1977
Franchi, Sergio: 1933—May 1, 1990
Francis, Alec B.: 1869—Jul 6, 1939
Francis, Ivor: 1918—Oct 22, 1986
Francis, Kay: Jan 13, 1903—Aug 26, 1968
Francis, Noel: 1911—Oct 30, 1959
Francis, Robert Feb 26, 1930—Jul 31, 1955
Francisco, Betty: 1900—Nov 25, 1950
Franciscus, James: Jan 31, 1934—Jul 8, 1991
Franck, Edward A.: 1920—Jul 12, 1990
Franey, William "Billy": 1885—Dec 9, 1940
Frank, Ben: Sep 2, 1934—Sep 11, 1990
Frank, Melvin: Aug 13, 1913—Oct 13, 1988
Franklin, Alberta: 1897—Mar 14, 1976
Franklin, Chester M.: Sep 1, 1890—1948
Franklin, Sidney A.: Mar 21, 1893—May 18, 1972
Franz, Eduard: Oct 31, 1902—Feb 10, 1983
Fraser, Harry: 1889—Apr 8, 1974
Fraser, Tom: 1932—Feb 10, 1992
Frawley, William: Feb 26, 1887—Mar 3, 1966
Frazee, Jane: Jul 18, 1918—Sep 6, 1985
Frazer, Robert W.: Jun 29, 1891—Aug 17, 1944
Frechette, Mark: 1948—Sep 27, 1975
Frederici (Friderici), Blanche: 1878—Dec 24, 1933
Frederick, Pauline: Aug 12, 1883—Sep 19, 1938
Fredericks, Charles: 1920—May 14, 1970
Freeman, Howard: Dec 9, 1899—Dec 11, 1967
Fregonese, Hugo: Apr 18, 1908—Jan 18, 1987
French, Charles K.: 1860—Aug 2, 1952
French, George B.: Apr 14, 1883—Jun 9, 1961
French, Valerie: Mar 11, 1932—Nov 3, 1990
French, Victor: Dec 4, 1934—Jun 15, 1989
Freund, Karl: Jan 16, 1890—May 3, 1969
Frey, Arno: Oct 11, 1900—Jun 26, 1961
Frey, Leonard: Sep 4, 1938—Aug 24, 1988
Friebus, Florida: Oct 10, 1909—May 27, 1988
Friganza, Trixie: Nov 29, 1870—Feb 27, 1955
Frome, Milton: 1911—Mar 21, 1989
Frommer, Ben: 1913—May 5, 1992
Frost, Terry: 1906—Mar 1, 1992
Frye, Dwight: Feb 22, 1899—Nov 9, 1943
Fung, Willie: Mar 3, 1896—Apr 16, 1945
Furthman, Jules: Mar 5, 1888—Sep 22, 1966
Gabel, Martin: Jun 19, 1912—May 22, 1986
Gable, Clark: Feb 1, 1901—Nov 16, 1960
Gade, Sven: Feb 9, 1879—Jun 25, 1952
Gaines, Richard H.: Jul 23, 1904—Jul 20, 1975
Gall, Ray: 1950—Sep 27, 1992

Gallagher, Richard "Skeets":
                Jul 28, 1890—May 22, 1955
Gammill, Noreen: 1898—Dec 20, 1988
Gan, Chester: 1909—Jun 30, 1959
Garbo, Greta: Sep 18, 1905—Apr 15, 1990
Garcia, Cecilla A.: 1957—Jan 3, 1989
Garcia, Henry: 1904—Nov 3, 1970
Garde, Betty: Sep 19, 1905—Dec 25, 1989
Garden, Mary: 1875—Jan 3, 1967
Gardenia, Vincent: Jan 7, 1922—Dec 9, 1992
Gardiner, Reginald: Feb 27, 1903—Jul 7, 1980
Gardner, Ava: Dec 24, 1922—Jan 25, 1990
Gardner, Helen: 1885—Nov 20, 1968
Gardner, Jack: 1900—Feb 13, 1977
Gardner, Joan: 1926—Dec 10, 1992
Garfield, John: Mar 4, 1912—May 21, 1952
Gargan, Edward: 1901—Feb 19, 1964
Gargan, William: Jul 17, 1905—Feb 17, 1979
Garland, Judy: Jun 10, 1922—Jun 22, 1969
Garner, Peggy Ann: Feb 3, 1931—Oct 16, 1984
Garner, Ray C.: 1923—Jul 20, 1989
Garnett, Tay: Jun 13, 1893—Oct 3, 1977
Garon, Pauline: Sep 9, 1901—Aug 27, 1965
Garrett, Joy: 1948—Feb 11, 1993
Garroway, Dave: Jul 13, 1913—Jul 21, 1982
Gasnier, Louis: Sep 15, 1878—1948
Gates, Maxine: 1917—Jul 27, 1990
Gateson, Marjorie: Jan 17, 1891—Apr 17, 1977
Gauguin, Lorraine: 1924—Dec 22, 1974
Gauthier, Suzanne: 1927—Jan 26, 1988
Gaynor, Janet: Oct 6, 1906—Sep 14, 1984
Geary, Bud: 1899—Feb 22, 1946
Geer, Lenny: 1914—Jan 9, 1989
Geer, Will: Mar 9, 1902—Apr 22, 1978
Gehrig, Earle: 1906—May 20, 1982
Geil, Joe (Corky): 1928—Jan 1, 1992
Genn, Leo: Aug 9, 1905—Jan 26, 1978
Gentry, Britt Nilsson: 1943—Jul 27, 1989
George, Christopher: Feb 25, 1929—Nov 29, 1983
George, Dan (Chief): Jul 24, 1899—Sep 23, 1981
George, George L.: Jul 31, 1907—Dec 31, 1992
George, Gladys: Sep 13, 1900—Dec 8, 1954
George, John: Jan 21, 1898—Aug 25, 1968
George, Joseph L.: 1927—Jul 31, 1992
George, Mary: 1902—Dec 22, 1987
George, Virginia: 1915—Jan 5, 1993
Geraghty, Carmelita: 1901—Jul 7, 1966
Geraghty, Maurice: Sep 29, 1908—Jun 30, 1987
Geray, Steven: Nov 10, 1898—Dec 26, 1973
Gerberg, Gary: 1943—Dec 29, 1992
Gering, Marion: Jun 9, 1901—Apr 19, 1977
Gerrard, Douglas 1888—Jun 5, 1950
Gerry, Toni: 1926—Jul 25, 1991
Gerson, Jeanne: 1905—Feb 7, 1992
Gerstle, Frank: Sep 27, 1915—Feb 23, 1970
Gest, Inna: 1923—Jan 1, 1965
Gibson, Edward "Hoot":
                Aug 6, 1892—Aug 23, 1962
Gibson, Wynne: Jul 3, 1905—May 15, 1987
Gifford, Alan: 1910—Mar 20, 1989
Gilbert, Billy: Sep 12, 1894—Sep 23, 1971
Gilbert, Jody: 1916—Feb 3, 1979
Gilbert, John: Jul 10, 1897—Jan 9, 1936
Gilford, Jack: Jul 25, 1907—Jun 4, 1990
Gillingwater, Claude: Aug 2, 1870—Oct 31, 1939

Gillmore, Margalo: May 31, 1897—Jun 30, 1986
Gilmore, Virginia: Jul 26, 1919—Mar 28, 1986
Gingold, Hermione: Dec 9, 1897—Apr 30, 1987
Girard, Joe: Apr 2, 1871—Aug 12, 1949
Girardot, Etienne: 1856—Nov 10, 1939
Girdler, William: 1948—Jan 21, 1978
Gish, Dorothy: Mar 11, 1898—Jun 4, 1968
Gish, Lillian: Oct 14, 1893—Feb 27, 1993
Gist, Rod: Nov 11, 1947—Sep 29, 1991
Givney, Kathryn: 1897—Mar 16, 1978
Glass, Everett: 1891—Mar 22, 1966
Glass, Gaston: Dec 31, 1898—Nov 11, 1965
Glass, Ned: 1906—Jun 15, 1984
Glaum, Louise: 1900—Nov 26, 1970
Gleason, Jackie: Feb 26, 1916—Jun 24, 1987
Gleason, James "Jimmy":
                May 23, 1882—Apr 12, 1959
Gleason, Lucille: Feb 6, 1888—May 18, 1947
Gleason, Russell: Feb 6, 1908—Dec 26, 1945
Gleckler, Robert P.: Jan 11, 1890—Feb 26, 1939
Glenn, Raymond: 1898—Dec 27, 1974
Glenn, Roy: 1915—Mar 11, 1971
Gliona, Michael: 1947—Jun 2, 1992
Gobel, George: May 20, 1919—Feb 24, 1991
Goddard, Paulette: Jun 3, 1905—Apr 23, 1990
Godfrey, Arthur: Aug 31, 1903—Mar 16, 1983
Godfrey, Peter: Oct 16, 1899—Mar 4, 1970
Godowsky, Dagmar: 1897—Feb 13, 1975
Golden, Murray: 1912—Aug 5, 1991
Golm, Lisa: _____—Jan 6, 1964
Gombell, Minna: May 28, 1892—Apr 14, 1973
Gomez, Thomas: Jul 10, 1905—Jun 18, 1971
Gonzales, Myrtle: Sep 28, 1891—Oct 22, 1918
Goode, Jack: 1908—Jun 24, 1971
Goodrich, Bert: 1907—Dec 6, 1991
Goodwin, Bill: Jul 28, 1910—May 9, 1958
Goodwin, Harold: Dec 1, 1902—Jul 13, 1987
Goodwin, Leslie: Sep 17, 1889—Jan 8, 1970
Goodwin, Thomas, Jr.: 1941—Dec 11, 1992
Gorcey, Bernard: 1888—Sep 11, 1955
Gorcey, David: Feb 6, 1921—Oct 23, 1984
Gorcey, Leo B.: Jun 3, 1915—Jun 2, 1969
Gordon, Bert: 1898—Nov 30, 1974
Gordon, C. Henry: Jun 17, 1883—Dec 3, 1940
Gordon, Gavin: 1901—Apr 7, 1983
Gordon, Huntley: 1897—Dec 7, 1956
Gordon, James: 1881—May 12, 1941
Gordon, Julia Swayne: Oct 29, 1878—May 28, 1933
Gordon, Kitty: 1878—May 26, 1974
Gordon, Mary: 1882—Aug 23, 1963
Gordon, Maud Turner: May 10, 1868—Jan 12, 1940
Gordon, Michael: Sep 6, 1909—Apr 29, 1993
Gordon, Robert: 1895—Oct 26, 1971
Gordon, Ruth: Oct 30, 1896—Aug 28, 1985
Gordon, Steve: Oct 10, 1938—Nov 27, 1982
Gordon, Vera: Jun 11, 1886—May 8, 1948
Gordon, William D.: 1908—Aug 12, 1991
Gorss, Saul: 1908—Sep 10, 1966
Gosden, Freeman: May 5, 1899—Dec 10, 1982
Gosfield, Maurice: c. 1913—Oct 19, 1964
Gottschalk, Ferdinand: 1969—Nov 17, 1944
Goudal, Jetta: Jul 18, 1898—Jan 14, 1985
Gough, John: 1894—Jun 30, 1968
Goulding, Alfred: 1896—Apr 25, 1972
Goulding, Edmund: Mar 30 1891—Dec 24, 1959

Gowland, Gibson: Jan 4, 1872—Sep 9, 1951
Grable, Betty: Dec 18, 1916—Jul 2, 1973
Graf, Louis C.: 1890—Jul 21, 1967
Graff, Wilton: 1903—Jan 13, 1969
Graham, Fred: 1918—Oct 10, 1979
Grahame, Gloria: Nov 28, 1925—Oct 5, 1981
Gran, Albert: 1862—Dec 16, 1932
Granach, Alexander: Apr 18, 1890—Mar 14, 1945
Granby, Joseph: 1885—Sep 22, 1965
Grandin, Ethel: 1894—Sep 28, 1988
Grange, Harold "Red": 1904—Jan 28, 1991
Grant, Cary: Jan 18, 1904—Nov 29, 1986
Grant, Earl: 1931—Jun 10, 1970
Grant, Frances: 1910—Feb 22, 1982
Grant, Kirby: Nov 24, 1911—Oct 30, 1985
Grant, Lawrence: Oct 31, 1869—Feb 19, 1952
Granville, Bonita: Feb 2, 1923—Oct 11, 1988
Granville, Louise: 1895—Dec 22, 1968
Grapewin, Charles "Charlie":
                Dec 20, 1875—Feb 2, 1956
Gravers, Steve: 1922—Aug 26, 1978
Graves, Ralph: Jan 23, 1900—Feb 18, 1977
Gravet (Gravey), Fernand: Dec 25, 1904—Nov 2, 1970
Gray, Gilda: Oct 24, 1896—Dec 22, 1959
Gray, Lawrence: Jul 28, 1898—Feb 2, 1970
Gray, Mack: 1906—Jan 17, 1981
Greaza, Walter: Jan 1, 1897—Jun 1, 1973
Green, Alfred E.: 1889—Sep 4, 1960
Green, Dorothy: 1892—Nov 16, 1963
Green, Harry: 1898—Feb 16, 1958
Green, Kenneth: 1908—Feb 24, 1969
Green, Mitzi: Oct 22, 1920—May 24, 1969
Green, Nigel: 1924—May 25, 1972
Greene, Angela: 1923—Feb 9, 1978
Greene, Harrison: 1884—Sep 28, 1945
Greene, Herbert Stanton: 1906—Aug 5, 1991
Greene, Lorne: Feb 12, 1915—Sep 11, 1987
Greene, Richard: Aug 25, 1918—Jun 1, 1985
Greene, Stanley: 1911—Jul 4, 1981
Greenleaf, Raymond: 1892—Oct 29, 1963
Greenstreet, Sydney: Dec 27, 1879—Jan 18, 1954
Greenway, Tom: 1910—Feb 8, 1985
Greenwood, Charlotte: Jun 25, 1893—Jan 18, 1978
Gregg, Virginia: 1917—Sep 15, 1986
Gregory, Mercedes: 1936—Feb 10, 1992
Greig, Robert: Dec 27, 1880—Jun 27, 1958
Grey, Olga: 1897—Apr 25, 1973
Gribbon, Edward T. "Eddie":
                Jan 3, 1890—Sep 29, 1965
Gribbon, Harry: 1886—Jul 28, 1961
Gries, Tom: Dec 20, 1922—Jan 3, 1977
Griffies, Ethel: Apr 26, 1878—Sep 9, 1975
Griffith, Corinne: Nov 24, 1894—Jul 13, 1979
Griffith, D. W.: Jan 22, 1875—Jul 23, 1948
Griffith, Hugh: May 30, 1912—May 14, 1980
Griffith, Linda: 1884—Jul 26, 1948
Griffith, Raymond: Jan 23, 1890—Nov 25, 1957
Grossmith, Lawrence: Mar 29, 1877—Feb 21, 1944
Guard, Kit: May 5, 1894—Jul 18, 1961
Guhl, George: _____—Jun 27, 1943
Guilfoyle, Paul: Jul 14, 1902—Jun 27, 1961
Guinan, Texas: _____—Nov 5, 1933
Gurie, Sigrid: May 18, 1911—Aug 14, 1969
Gwenn, Edmund: Sep 26, 1875—Sep 6, 1959

Haade, William: Mar 2, 1903—Nov 15, 1966
Haas, Hugo: Feb 19, 1903—Dec 1, 1968
Hackathorne, George: Feb 13, 1896—Jun 25, 1940
Hackett, Florence: 1882—Aug 21, 1954
Hackett, Joan: May 1, 1942—Oct 8, 1983
Hackett, Raymond: Jul 15, 1902—Jul 7, 1958
Haden, Sara Nov 17, 1897—Sep 15, 1981
Hadley, Reed: 1911—Dec 11, 1974
Hage, Frank: 1956—Mar 9, 1990
Hagen, Jean: Aug 3, 1923—Aug 29, 1977
Haggerty, Don: 1914—Aug 19, 1988
Hagney (Hagny), Frank S.: 1884—Jun 25, 1973
Haines, William: Jan 1, 1900—Dec 26, 1973
Hakins, Dick: 1903—Feb 22, 1990
Hale, Alan, Jr.: Mar 8, 1918—Jan 2, 1990
Hale, Alan (Sr.): Feb 10, 1892—Jan 22, 1950
Hale, Creighton: May 24, 1882—Aug 9, 1965
Hale, Jonathan: 1891—Feb 28, 1966
Hale, Louise Closser: Oct 13, 1872—Jul 26, 1933
Haley, Jack: Aug 10, 1898—Jun 6, 1979
Hall, Alexander: 1894—Jul 30, 1968
Hall, Charles D. "Charlie":
                          Aug 18, 1899—Dec 7, 1959
Hall, Ed: Jan 11, 1931—Jul 30, 1991
Hall, Geraldine : 1905—Sep 18, 1970
Hall, Grayson: 1927—Aug 7, 1985
Hall, James: Oct 22, 1900—Jun 7, 1940
Hall, Jon: Feb 23, 1913—Dec 13, 1979
Hall, Juanita: Nov 6, 1901—Feb 28, 1968
Hall, Porter: Sep 19, 1888—Oct 6, 1953
Hall, Thurston: May 10, 1882—Feb 20, 1958
Hall, Winter: Jun 21, 1878—Feb 10, 194
Halliday, Gardner: 1910—Sep 6, 1966
Halliday, John: Sep 14, 1880—Oct 17, 1947
Halligan, William: Mar 29, 1884—Jan 28, 1957
Halls, Ethel May: 1882—Sep 16, 1967
Halop, Billy: Feb 11, 1920—Nov 9, 1976
Halop, Florence: Jan 23, 1923—Jul 15, 1986
Halton, Charles: Mar 16, 1876—Apr 16, 1959
Hamer, Rusty: Feb 15, 1947—Jan 18, 1990
Hamilton, John: 1887—Oct 15, 1958
Hamilton, Kipp: 1936—Jan 29, 1981
Hamilton, Lloyd: Aug 19, 1891—Jan 19, 1935
Hamilton, Mahlon: Jun 15, 1889—Jun 20, 1960
Hamilton, Margaret: Dec 9, 1902—May 16, 1985
Hamilton, Murray: Mar 24, 1923—Sep 1, 1986
Hamilton, Neil: Sep 9, 1899—Sep 24, 1984
Hammer, Peter: 1939—Apr 27, 1993
Hammerstein, Elaine: 1897— Aug 13, 1948
Hammond, Kay: 1902—Jan 7, 1982
Hammond, Ruth: 1896—Apr 9, 1992
Hammond, Virginia: 1894—Apr 6, 1972
Hampden, Walter: Jun 30, 1979—Jun 11, 1955
Hampton, Deborah: 1958—Feb 25, 1990
Hampton, Grayce: 1876—Dec 20, 1963
Hampton, Hope: ____—Jan 23, 1982
Hancock, John: Feb 12, 1939—Oct 12, 1992
Haney, Carol: Dec 24, 1924—May 10, 1964
Hannes, Art: 1920—Mar 30, 1992
Hansen, William: 1911—Jun 23, 1975
Hanson, Arthur: ____—Feb 21, 1991
Hanson, Juanita: 1895—Sep 26, 1961
Hanson, Lars: Jul 26, 1886—Apr 8, 1965
Harcourt, David: 1900—Feb 27, 1993
Hardie, Russell: 1904—Jul 21, 1973

Hardin, Ken: 1929—Oct 30, 1992
Harding, Ann: Aug 7, 1902—Sep 1, 1981
Hardwicke, Cedric (Sir):
                          Feb 19, 1893—Aug 6, 1964
Hardy, Oliver: Jan 18, 1892—Aug 7, 1957
Hardy, Sam: Mar 21, 1883—Oct 16, 1935
Hare, Lumsden: Oct 2, 1875—Aug 28, 1964
Harlan, Kenneth: Jul 26, 1895—Mar 6, 1967
Harlan, Otis: Dec 29, 1864—Jan 20, 1940
Harlan, Russell B.: Sep 16, 1903—Feb 28, 1974
Harlow, Jean: Mar 3, 1911—Jun 7, 1937
Harmon, Pat: Feb 3, 1888—Nov 26, 1958
Harmon, Tom: 1920—Mar 15, 1990
Harolde, Ralf: 1899—Nov 1, 1974
Harrigan, Nedda: 1900-'Apr 1, 1989
Harrigan, William: 1877—Feb 1, 1966
Harris, Cassandra: 1952—Dec 28, 1991
Harris, Mildred: Nov 29, 1901—Jul 20, 1944
Harris, Robert H.: Jul 15, 1909—Nov 30, 1981
Harris, Robin: 1954—Mar 18, 1990
Harris, William E. 1955—Jun 25, 1992
Harrison, June: 1926—Mar 10, 1974
Harrison, Rex: Mar 5, 1908—Jun 2, 1990
Harron, Bobby: Apr 24, 1893—Sep 6, 1920
Harron, John: Mar 31, 1903—Nov 24, 1939
Hart, Neal: 1879—Apr 2, 1949
Hart, Richard: Apr 14, 1915—Jan 3, 1951
Hart, William S.: Dec 6, 1862—Jun 23, 1946
Harte, Betty: 1883—Jan 3, 1965
Hartigan, Pat: Dec 21, 1881—May 8, 1951
Hartman, Don: Nov 18, 1900—Mar 23, 1958
Hartman, Elizabeth: Dec 23, 1941—Jun 10, 1987
Hartman, Paul: Mar 1, 1904—Oct 2, 1973
Hartog, Simon: 1940—Aug 18, 1992
Harvey, Don C.: Dec 12, 1911—Apr 23, 1963
Harvey, Forrester: 1880—Dec 14, 1945
Harvey, Harry, Sr.: 1901—Nov 27, 1985
Harvey, Laurence: Oct 1, 1928—Nov 25, 1973
Harvey, Lilian: Jan 19, 1906—Jul 27, 1968
Harvey, Paul: Sep 10, 1883—Dec 14, 1955
Haskin, Byron: Apr 22, 1899—Apr 16, 1984
Hasse, O. E.: Jul 11, 1903—Sep 12, 1978
Hathaway, Henry: Mar 13, 1898—Feb 11, 1985
Hatton, Raymond: Jul 7, 1887—Oct 21, 1971
Hatton, Rondo: Apr 29, 1894—Feb 2, 1946
Haupt, Ullrich: Aug 8, 1887—Aug 5, 1931
Hausner, Jerry: 1910—Apr 1, 1993
Haver, Phyllis: Jan 6, 1899—Nov 19, 1960
Hawley, Wanda: Jul 30, 1895—Mar 18, 1963
Hay, Mary: 1901—Jun 4, 1957
Hayakawa, Sessue: Jun 10, 1889—Nov 23, 1973
Hayden, Harry: 1882—Jul 24, 1955
Hayden, Russell: Jun 12, 1912—Jun 10, 1981
Hayden, Sterling: Mar 26, 1916—May 23, 1986
Haydn, Richard: 1905—Apr 23, 1985
Hayes, Allison: Jan 6, 1930—Feb 27, 1977
Hayes, Christopher: ____—Nov 12, 1991
Hayes, George "Gabby": May 7, 1885—Feb 9, 1969
Hayes, Grace: 1896—Feb 1, 1989
Hayes, Helen: Oct 10, 1900—Mar 17, 1993
Hayes, Margaret: Dec 5, 1924—Jan 26, 1977
Hayes, Sam: 1905—Jul 28, 1958
Haymer, Johnny: 1920—Nov 18, 1989
Haymes, Dick: Sep 13, 1916—Mar 28, 1980
Haynes, Hilda: 1914—Mar 4, 1986

Haynes, Lloyd: Oct 19, 1934—Dec 31, 1986
Hayward, Louis: Mar 19, 1909—Feb 21, 1985
Hayward, Susan: Jun 30, 1917—Mar 14, 1975
Hayworth, Rita: Oct 17, 1918—May 14, 1987
Hazlett, Marlene: 1927—Jun 9, 1992
Healy, Ted: Oct 1, 1896—Dec 21, 1937
Hearn, Edward "Eddie": Sep 6, 1888—Apr 15, 1963
Heath, Gordon: 1919—Aug 27, 1991
Hecht, Ben: Feb 28, 1894—Apr 18, 1964
Hecht, Ted: 1908—Jun 24, 1969
Heflin, Van: Dec 13, 1910—Jul 23, 1971
Heggie, O. P.: Sep 17, 1876—Feb 7, 1936
Heider, Frederick: Apr 9, 1917—May 17, 1992
Heigh, Helene: 1905—Dec 20, 1991
Heisler, Stuart: 1894—Aug 21, 1979
Helton, Percy: 1894—Sep 11, 1971
Heming, Violet: Jan 27, 1895—Jul 4, 1981
Hemsley, Estelle: 1887—Nov 5, 1968
Henabery, Joseph E.: 1888—Feb 18, 1976
Henderson, Del (Dell): Jul 5, 1883—Dec 2, 1956
Henderson, Marcia: Jun 22, 1929—Nov 30, 1987
Hendricks, Ben, Jr.: Nov 2, 1893—Aug 15, 1938
Hendrix, Wanda: Nov 3, 1928—Feb 1, 1981
Henie, Sonja: Apr 8, 1912—Oct 12, 1969
Henley, Hobart: Nov 23, 1891—May 22, 1964
Hennecke, Clarence R.: 1895—Aug 28, 1969
Henning, Pat: 1911—Apr 28, 1973
Henreid, Paul: Jan 10, 1908—Mar 29, 1992
Henry, Charlotte: Mar 3, 1913—Apr 11, 1980
Henry, Robert "Buzz": Sep 4, 1931—Sep 30, 1971
Henson, Jim: Sep 24, 1936—May 16, 1990
Hepburn, Audrey: May 4, 1929—Jan 20, 1993
Herbert, Holmes E.: Jul 3, 1882—Dec 26, 1956
Herbert, Hugh: Aug 10, 1887—Mar 13, 1952
Herbert, Pitt: 1915—Jun 23, 1989
Herbert, Tim: 1915—Jun 20, 1986
Hernandez, Juan (Juano): 1896—Jul 17, 1970
Hernandez, Wilfredo: ____—Feb 19, 1990
Hersholt, Jean: Jul 12, 1886—Jun 2, 1956
Herzberg, Jack L.: 1917—Apr 23, 1992
Hewitt, Alan: Jan 21, 195—Nov 7, 1986
Hexum, Jon-Erik: Nov 5, 1957—Oct 18, 1984
Heyburn, Weldon: 1905—May 18, 1951
Heydt, Louis Jean: Apr 17, 1905—Jan 29, 1960
Heyes, Herbert: Aug 3, 1889—May 30, 1958
Heywood, Herbert: Feb 1, 1881—Sep 15, 1964
Hibbs, Jesse: Jan 11, 1906—Feb 4, 1985
Hickman, Howard C.: Feb 9, 1880—Dec 31, 1949
Hicks, Joe: 1927—Jan 7, 1991
Hicks, Russell: Jun 4, 1895—Jun 1, 1957
Hiers, Walter: Jul 18, 1893—Feb 27, 1933
Higby, Mary Jane: 1916—Feb 1, 1986
Higgins, Colin: Jul 28, 1941—Aug 5, 1988
Hill, Al: Jul 14, 1892—Jul 14, 1954
Hill, George William: 1894—Aug 10, 1934
Hill, Phyllis: 1921—Jan 1, 1993
Hill, Ramsey: 1891—Feb 3, 1976
Hill, Robert F.: Apr 14, 1886—Mar 18, 1966
Hilliard, Ernest: Feb 1, 1890—Sep 3, 1947
Hilo Hattie: 1901—Dec 12, 1979
Hinds, Samuel S.: Apr 4, 1875—Oct 13, 1948
Hines, Harry: 1889—May 3, 1967
Hines, Johnny: Jul 25, 1897—Oct 24, 1970
Hinton, Ed: 1928—Oct 12, 1958
Hitchcock, Alfred: Aug 13, 1899—Apr 29, 1980

Hitchcock, Keith: 1887—Apr 11, 1966
Hobbes, Halliwell: Nov 16, 1877—Feb 20, 1962
Hodge, Al: Apr 18, 1913—Mar 19, 1979
Hodgins, Earl: 1899—Apr 14, 1964
Hodgson, Leland: ____—Mar 16, 1949
Hodiak, John: Apr 16, 1914—Oct 19, 1955
Hoey, Dennis: Mar 30, 1893—Jul 25, 1960
Hoff, Louise: 1923—Jun 1, 1992
Hoffman, Otto: May 2, 1879—Jun 23, 1944
Hogan, James P.: c. 1891—Nov 4, 1943
Hohl, Arthur: May 21, 1889—Mar 10, 1964
Holden, Fay: Sep 26, 1895—Jun 23, 1973
Holden, Gloria: Sep 5, 1908—Mar 22, 1991
Holden, William: Apr 17, 1918—Nov 16, 1981
Holdren, Judd: Oct 16, 1915—Mar 11, 1974
Hole, William J., Jr.: 1919—Feb 11, 1990
Holland, Anthony: 1928—Jul 9, 1988
Holliday, Judy: Jun 21, 1923—Jun 7, 1965
Holliday, Marjorie: 1920—Jun 16, 1969
Hollister, Alice: Sep 1886—Feb 24, 1973
Holloway, Stanley: Oct 1, 1890—Jan 30, 1982
Holloway, Sterling: Jan 14, 1905—Nov 22, 1992
Holman, Harry: 1874—May 2, 1947
Holmes, Burton: Jan 8, 1870—Jul 22, 1958
Holmes, George: 1919—Feb 19, 1985
Holmes, Helen: 1892—Jul 8, 1950
Holmes, Phillips: Jul 22, 1909—Aug 12, 1942
Holmes, Stuart: Mar 10, 1887—Dec 29, 1971
Holmes, Taylor: May 16, 1872—Sep 30, 1959
Holt, Jack: May 31, 1888—Jan 18, 1951
Holt, Tim: Feb 5, 1918—Feb 15, 1973
Homans, Robert E.: Nov 8, 1874—Jul 28, 1947
Homolka, Oscar: Aug 12, 1898—Jan 27, 1978
Hood, Darla: Nov 4, 1931—Jun 13, 1979
Hood, Joseph, Sr.: 1894—Jun 23, 1965
Hope, Harry: 1926—Nov 16, 1988
Hopkins, Arthur: Oct 4, 1878—Mar 22, 1950
Hopkins, Miriam: Oct 18, 1902—Oct 9, 1972
Hopper, De Wolf: Mar 30, 1858—Sep 23, 1935
Hopper, E. Mason: Dec 6, 1885—Jan 3, 1967
Hopper, Hedda: Jun 2, 1890—Feb 1, 1966
Hopper, Jerry: Jul 29, 1907—Dec 17, 1988
Hopper, William: Jan 26, 1915—Mar 6, 1970
Hopton, Russell: Feb 18, 1900—Apr 7, 1945
Horne, James W.: Dec 14, 1881—Jun 30, 1942
Horton, Edward Everett:
                    Mar 18, 1886—Sep 29, 1970
Horvath, Charles: 1921—Jul 23, 1978
Hoshelle, Marjorie: 1918—Apr 5, 1989
Hoskins, Allen "Farina": Aug 9, 1920—Jul 26, 1980
Houdini, Harry: Mar 24, 1874—Oct 31, 1926
House, Billy: 1890—Sep 23, 1961
Houseman, Arthur: 1890—Apr 7, 1942
Houseman, John: Sep 22, 1902—Oct 31, 1988
Houston, George: 1898—Nov 12, 1944
Hovey, Tim: Jun 1945—Sep 9, 1989
Howard, Booth: 1889—Oct 4, 1936
Howard, David: Oct 6, 1896—Dec 21, 1941
Howard, Esther: 1893—Mar 8, 1965
Howard, Frances: 1903—Jul 2, 1976
Howard, Jerome "Curly":
                    Oct 22, 1903—Jan 18, 1952
Howard, Kathleen Jul 17, 1880—Apr 15, 1956
Howard, Leslie: Apr 3, 1893—Jun 2, 1943
Howard, Mary: 1913—Dec 13, 1989

Howard, Moe: Jun 19, 1897—May 4, 1975
Howard, Noel: 1920—Feb 7, 1986
Howard, Samuel "Shemp":
                    Mar 17, 1900—Nov 22, 1955
Howard, William K.: Jun 16, 1899—Feb 21, 1954
Howard, Willie: 1883—Jan 14, 1949
Howes, Reed: Jul 5, 1900—Aug 6, 1964
Howland, Jobyna: Mar 31, 1880—Jun 7, 1936
Howlin, Olin: Feb 10, 1896—Sep 20, 1959
Hoxie, Al: 1902—Apr 6, 1982
Hoxie, Jack: Jan 24, 1885—Mar 28, 1965
Hoyos, Rudolfo, Sr.: 1896—May 24, 1980
Hoyt, Arthur: Mar 19, 1873—Jan 4, 1953
Hoyt, John: 1904—Sep 15, 1991
Hubbard, John: 1914—Nov 6, 1988
Huber, Harold: 1910—Sep 29, 1959
Hudnut, Bill: 1945—Oct 24, 1992
Hudson, Rochelle: Mar 6, 1914—Jan 17, 1972
Hudson, Rock: Nov 17, 1925—Oct 2, 1985
Huff, Louise: 1896—Aug 22, 1973
Huffman, David: 1946—Feb 27, 1986
Hughes, Gareth: Aug 23, 1894—Oct 1, 1965
Hughes, Howard: Dec 24, 1905—Apr 5, 1976
Hughes, Joseph Anthony:
                    May 2, 1904—Feb 11, 1970
Hughes, Lloyd: Oct 21, 1897—Jun 6, 1958
Hugo, Mauritz: 1909—Jun 16, 1974
Hull, Henry: Oct 3, 1890—Mar 8, 1977
Hull, Josephine: Jan 3, 1884—Mar 12, 1957
Hull, Warren: Jan 17, 1903—Sep 14, 1974
Humberstone, H. Bruce:
                    Nov 18, 1903—Oct 11, 1984
Hume, Benita: Oct 14, 1906—Nov 1, 1967
Humphrey, William J.: Jan 2, 1874—Oct 4, 1942
Hunnicutt, Arthur: Feb 17, 1911—Sep 27, 1979
Hunt, Eleanor: 1910—Jun 12, 1981
Hunt, Richard: 1952—Jan 7, 1992
Hunter, Ian: Jun 13, 1900—Sep 24, 1975
Hunter, Jeffrey: Nov 23, 1925—May 27, 1969
Hurst, Brandon: Nov 30, 1866—Jul 15, 1947
Hurst, Paul C.: 1888—Feb 27, 1953
Huston, John: Aug 5, 1906—Aug 28, 1987
Huston, Walter: Apr 6, 1884—Apr 7, 1950
Hutton, Jim: Mar 31, 1934—Jun 2, 1979
Hutton, Marion: Mar 10, 1919—Jan 9, 1987
Hyams, Leila: May 1, 1905—Dec 4, 1977
Hyde, Jacquelyn: 1931—Feb 23, 1992
Hyde-White, Wilfrid: May 12, 1903—May 6, 1991
Hyland, Diana: 1936—Mar 27, 1977
Hymer, Warren: Feb 25, 1906—Mar 25, 1948
Hytten, Olaf: 1888—Mar 11, 1955
Ihnat, Steve: 1935—May 12, 1972
Imboden, David C.: 1887—Mar 18, 1974
Imhof, Roger: Apr 15, 1875—Apr 15, 1958
Ince, John E.: 1877—Apr 10, 1947
Ince, Ralph Waldo: Jan 16, 1882—Apr 11, 1937
Ince, Thomas Harper: Nov 6, 1882—Nov 19, 1924
Indrisano, John "Johnny": 1906—Jul 9, 1968
Inescort, Frieda: Jun 29, 1900—Feb 21, 1976
Ingraham, Lloyd: 1885—Apr 4, 1956
Ingram, Jack: 1903—Feb 20, 1969
Ingram, Rex (actor): Oct 20, 1895—Sep 19, 1969
Ingram, Rex (director): Jan 15, 1892—Jul 21, 1950
Ireland, Jill: Apr 24, 1936—May 18, 1990
Ireland, John: Jan 30, 1914—Mar 21, 1992

Irving, George: Oct 5, 1874—Sep 11, 1961
Irving, Margaret: 1898—Mar 5, 1988
Irving, William J.: 1893—Dec 25, 1943
Irwin, Boyd: Mar 12, 1880—Jan 22, 1957
Irwin, Charles W.: 1888—Jan 12, 1969
Irwin, Horace:, ____—Feb 4, 1991
Irwin, May: Jun 27, 1862—Oct 22, 1938
Iturbi, Jose: Nov 28, 1895—Jun 28, 1980
Ivan, Rosalind: 1884—Apr 6, 1959
Jabara, Paul: 1948—Sep 29, 1992
Jackson, Mahlia: Oct 25, 1911—Jan 27, 1972
Jackson, Selmer: May 7, 1888—Mar 30, 1971
Jackson, Thomas E.: 1886—Sep 8, 1967
Jacobson, Henrietta: 1906—Oct 11, 1988
Jaffe, Sam: Mar 8, 1891—Mar 24, 1984
Jagger, Dean: Nov 7, 1903—Feb 5, 1991
James, Claire: 1921—Jan 18, 1986
James, Gladden: 1892—Aug 28, 1948
James, Harry: Mar 15, 1916—Jul 1, 1983
James, Jessica: 1930—May 7, 1990
James, Ralph: 1925—Mar 14, 1992
Jameson, Joyce: Sep 26, 1932—Jan 16, 1987
Jamison, William "Bud": 1894—Sep 30, 1944
Janney, Leon: Apr 1, 1917—Oct 28, 1980
Janney, William: 1908—Dec 27, 1992
Jannings, Emil: Jul 23, 1984—Jan 3, 1950
Janssen, David: Mar 27, 1931—Feb 13, 1980
Jaquet, Frank: Mar 16, 1885—May 11, 1958
Jarvis, Scott: 1952—Feb 26, 1990
Jason, Leigh: Jul 26, 1904—Feb 19, 1979
Jeans, Isabel: Sep 16, 1891—Sep 4, 1985
Jefferson, Thomas: 1859—Apr 2, 1932
Jenkins, Allen: Apr 9, 1990—Jul 20, 1974
Jenks, Frank: 1902—May 13, 1962
Jenks, Si: Sep 23, 1876—Jan 6, 1970
Jennings, Al: 1864—Dec 26, 1961
Jennings, Claudia: 1950—Oct 3, 1979
Jennings, De Witt: Jun 21, 1879—Mar 1, 1937
Jessel, George: Apr 3, 1898—May 24, 1981
Jewell, Isabel: Jul 19, 1909—Apr 5, 1972
Jimindez, Soledad: 1874—Oct 17, 1966
Joel, Thelma: 1916—Nov 23, 1992
Johnson, Arthur: Feb 2, 1876—Jan 17, 1916
Johnson, Brad: 1926—Apr 4, 1981
Johnson, Chic: Mar 5, 1891—Feb 28, 1962
Johnson, Chubby: 1903—Oct 31, 1974
Johnson, Emory: 1894—Apr 18, 1960
Johnson, Kay: Nov 29, 1904—1975
Johnson, Kevin: 1918—Jul 12, 1992
Johnson, Martin E: Oct 9, 1884—Jan 13, 1937
Johnson, Nunnally: Dec 5, 1897— Mar 25, 1977
Johnson, Osa: Mar 14, 1894—Jan 7, 1953
Johnson, Rita: Aug 13, 1913—Oct 31, 1965
Johnson, Rome: 1917—Jan 3, 1993
Johnson, Sunny: 1954—Jun 20, 1984
Johnson, Teddy: Sep 23, 1887—Oct 1956
Johnson, Tor: Oct 19, 1903—May 12, 1971
Johnstone, Julanne: 1900—Dec 30, 1989
Jolley, I. Stanford: 1900—Dec 7, 1978
Jolson, Al: May 26, 1886—Oct 23, 1950
Jones, Allan: Oct 14, 1908—Jun 27, 1992
Jones, Anissa: 1958—Aug 29, 1976
Jones, Bobby: Mar 17, 1902—Dec 18, 1971
Jones, Buck: Dec 4, 1889—Nov 30, 1942
Jones, Carolyn: Apr 28, 1929—Aug 3, 1983

Jones, Charlotte: 1916—Nov 6, 1992
Jones, Darby: 1910—Nov 30, 1986
Jones, Gordon: Apr 5, 1911—Jun 20, 1963
Jones, Spike: Dec 14, 1911—May 1, 1965
Jones, T. C.: 1921—Sep 25, 1971
Jonson, Kevin Joe: 1918—Jul 12, 1992
Jordan, Dorothy: Aug 9, 1908—Dec 7, 1988
Jordan, Jim: 1897—Apr 1, 1988
Jordan, Marian: Apr 15, 1897—Apr 7, 1961
Jordan, Robert "Bobby": Apr 1, 1923—Sep 10, 1965
Jory, Victor: Nov 28, 1902—Feb 11, 1982
Jose, Edward: c. 1880—Deceased
Joslin, Thomas H.: 1947—Jul 1, 1990
Joslyn, Allyn: Jul 21, 1901—Jan 21, 1981
Joy, Leatrice: Nov 7, 1896—May 13, 1985
Joy, Nicholas: Jan 31, 1892—Mar 16, 1964
Joyce, Alice: Oct 1, 1890—Oct 9, 1955
Joyce, Eileen: 1913—Mar 25, 1991
Joyce, Natalie: 1900—Nov 9, 1992
Joyce, Patrick: 1908—Jul 21, 1990
Joyce, Peggy Hopkins: 1893—Jun 12, 1957
Judel, Charles: Aug 17, 1882—Feb 14, 1969
Judge, Arline: Feb 21, 1912—Feb 7, 1974
Julian, Rupert: Jan 25, 1889—Dec 30, 1943
Jurgens, Curt: Dec 13, 1912—Jun 18, 1982
Kadar, Jan: Apr 1, 1918—Dec 4, 1979
Kahanamoku, Duke P.: Aug 24, 1890—Jan 22, 1968
Kallman, Richard "Dick": 1934—Feb 22, 1980
Kaminska, Ida: Sep 4, 1899—May 21, 1980
Kane, Dennis: 1923—May 12, 1992
Kane, Eddie: Aug 12, 1889—Apr 30, 1969
Kane, Helen: Aug 4, 1903—Sep 26, 1966
Kane, Joseph: Mar 19, 1897—Aug 25, 1975
Karloff, Boris: Nov 23, 1887—Feb 2, 1969
Karlson, Phil: Jul 2, 1908—Dec 12, 1985
Karnes, Robert: 1917—Dec 4, 1979
Karns, Roscoe: Sep 7, 1893—Feb 6, 1970
Kasha, Lawrence: Dec 3, 1933—Sep 29, 1990
Kasznar, Kurt: Aug 12, 1913—Aug 6, 1979
Katch, Kurt: Jan 28, 1896—Aug 14, 1958
Katzka, Gabriel: 1932—Feb 19, 1990
Kaufman, Andy: Jan 17, 1948—May 16, 1984
Kay, Beatrice: Apr 21, 1907—Nov 8, 1986
Kaye, Danny: Jan 18, 1913—Mar 3, 1987
Kaye-Martin, Edward: 1939—Aug 13, 1989
Kean, Betty: Dec 15, 1920—Sep 29, 1986
Keane, Edward: May 28, 1884—Oct 12, 1959
Keane, Joe: 1924—Jan 4, 1993
Keane, Raymond: 1907—Aug 31, 1973
Keane, Robert Emmett: Mar 4, 1883—Jul 2, 1981
Keane, Tom: Dec 20, 1898—Aug 4, 1963
Keating, Larry: 1896—Aug 26, 1963
Keaton, Buster: Oct 4, 1895—Feb 1, 1966
Keefe, Zena: Jun 26, 1896—Nov 16, 1977
Keeler, Ruby: Aug 25, 1909—Feb 28, 1993
Keenan, Paul: 1956—Dec 11, 1986
Keene, Tom: Dec 20, 1898—Aug 6, 1963
Keene, William Joseph: 1916—May 23, 1992
Keighley, William: Aug 4, 1889—Jun 24, 1984
Keith, Ian: Feb 27, 1899—Mar 26, 1960
Keith, Robert: Feb 10, 1898—Dec 22, 1966
Kellaway, Cecil: Aug 22, 1893—Feb 28, 1973
Keller, Harry: Feb 22, 1913—Feb 19, 1987
Kellerman, Annette: 1887—Nov 5, 1975
Kelley, Barry: 1909—Jun 15, 1991

Kellin, Mike: Apr 26, 1922—Aug 26, 1983
Kelljan, Robert: 1930—Nov 25, 1982
Kellogg, Ray: ____—Sep 26, 1981
Kelly, Craig: ____—Feb 9, 1991
Kelly, Dorothy: Feb 12, 1894—May 31, 1966
Kelly, Grace: Nov 12, 1929—Sep 14, 1982
Kelly, Jack: Sep 16, 1927—Nov 7, 1992
Kelly, Kitty: 1902—Jun 29, 1968
Kelly, Lew: 1879—Jun 10, 1944
Kelly, Patsy: Jan 12, 1910—Sep 24, 1981
Kelly, Paul: Aug 9, 1899—Nov 6, 1956
Kelly, Paula: 1920—Apr 2, 1992
Kelsey, Fred A.: Aug 20, 1884—Sep 2, 1961
Kelso, Mayme: Feb 28, 1867—Jun 5, 1946
Kelton, Pert: Oct 14, 1907—Oct 30, 1968
Kendall, Cy: Mar 10, 1898—Jul 22, 1953
Kendall, Kay: May 21, 1926—Sep 6, 1959
Kendrick, Henry: 1934—Apr 12, 1990
Kennedy, Arthur: Feb 17, 1914—Jan 5, 1990
Kennedy, Douglas: Sep 14, 1915—Aug 10, 1973
Kennedy, Edgar: Apr 26, 1890—Nov 9, 1948
Kennedy, Madge: Apr 19, 1891—Jun 9, 1987
Kennedy, Merna: Sep 7, 1908—Dec 20, 1944
Kennedy, Tom: 1884—Oct 6, 1965
Kent, Charles: Jun 18, 1852—May 21, 1923
Kent, Crauford: 1881—May 14, 1953
Kent, Robert: Dec 3, 1980—May 4, 1955
Kenton, Erle C.: Aug 1, 1896—Jan 28, 1980
Kenyon, Doris: Sep 12, 1897—Sep 1, 1979
Kerman, David: ____—Feb 18, 1990
Kern, James V.: 1909—Nov 9, 1966
Kerr, Donald: ____—Jan 25, 1977
Kerrigan, J(ack) Warren: Jul 25, 1889—Jun 9, 1947
Kerrigan, J(oseph) M.: Dec 16, 1887—Apr 29, 1964
Kerry, Norman: Jun 16, 1889—Jan 12, 1956
Kibbee, Guy: Mar 6, 1882—May 24, 1956
Kibbee, Milton: Jan 27, 1896—Apr 17, 1970
Kibrick, Leonard: 1925—Jan 1993
Kidd, Jonathan: 1914—Dec 15, 1987
Kilbride, Percy: Jul 16, 1888—Dec 11, 1964
Kilgalllen, Dorothy: Jul 3, 1913—Nov 8, 1965
Kilian, Victor: Mar 6, 1891—Mar 11, 1979
Killmond, Francis Xavier (Frank):
                                  ___ 1934—Apr 17, 1992
King, Anita: 1889—Jun 10, 1963
King, Charles: Oct 31, 1889—Jan 11, 1944
King, Charles L., Sr.: Feb 21, 1895—May 7, 1957
King, Claude: Jan 15, 1879—Sep 18, 1941
King, Dennis, Jr.: ____—Aug 24, 1986
King, Dennis (Sr.): Nov 2, 1897—May 21, 1971
King, Henry: Jun 24, 1888—Jun 29, 1982
King, Joe: Feb 9, 1883—Apr 11, 1951
King, John "Dusty": Jul 11, 1909—Nov 11, 1987
King, Louis: Jun 28, 1898—Sep 7, 1962
King, Michael: 1923—Jun 1, 1992
King, Walter Woolf: Nov 2, 1899—Oct 24, 1984
Kingsford, Walter: Sep 20, 1881—Feb 7, 1958
Kingston, Winifred: 1895—Feb 3, 1967
Kinison, Sam: 1954—Apr 10, 1992
Kinsolving, Lee: 1938—Dec 4, 1974
Kirby, Johanna Denise: 1973—Dec 29, 1992
Kirk, Jack "Pappy": 1895—Sep 3, 1948
Kirkland, Muriel: Aug 19, 1904—Sep 26, 1971
Kirkwood, James: Feb 22, 1883—Aug 21, 1964
Kirschner, Claude: 1916—Mar 8, 1993

Kirsten, Dorothy: Jul 6, 1910—Nov 18, 1992
Kissinger, Charles: 1925—Jan 21, 1991
Kjellin, Alf: Feb 28, 1920—Apr 5, 1988
Knapp, Evelyn: Jun 17, 1908—Jun 10, 1981
Knight, Fuzzy: May 9, 1901—Feb 23, 1976
Knight, June: Jan 22, 1913—Jun 16, 1987
Knight, Ted: Dec 7, 1923—Aug 26, 1983
Knopf, Edwin H.: Nov 11, 1899—Dec 27, 1981
Kohler, Fred, Sr.: Apr 20, 1888—Oct 28, 1938
Kolb, Clarence: 1875—Nov 25, 1964
Kolker, Henry: Nov 13, 1874—Jul 15, 1947
Korda, Alexander: Sep 16, 1893—Jan 23, 1956
Korjus, Miliza: Aug 18, 1900—Aug 26, 1980
Kornman, Mary: 1917—Jun 1, 1973
Kortman, Robert F.: Dec 24, 1887—Mar 13, 1967
Kortner, Fritz: May 12, 1892—Jul 22, 1970
Kosloff, Theodore: 1882—Nov 22, 1956
Koster, Henry: May 1, 1905—Sep 21, 1988
Kovacs, Ernie: Jan 23, 1919—Jan 12, 1962
Kramer, Sy: 1933—Apr 4, 1992
Krasna, Norman: Nov 7, 1909—Nov 1, 1984
Krebs, Nita: 1906—Jan 18, 1991
Kroeger, Berry: Oct 16, 1912—Jan 4, 1991
Krueger, Michael: ____— Aug 27, 1990
Kruger, Alma: Sep 13, 1868—Apr 5, 1960
Kruger, Otto: Sep 6, 1885—Sep 6, 1974
Krugman, Lou: 1914—Aug 9, 1992
Krupa, Gene: Jan 15, 1909—Oct 16, 1973
Kulky, Henry: Aug 11, 1911—Feb 12, 1965
Kulp, Nancy: Aug 28, 1921—Feb 3, 1991
Kuluva, Will: 1917—Nov 6, 1990
Kupcinet, Karyn: Mar 6, 1941—Nov 28, 1963
Kusell, Maurice L.: 1903—Feb 2, 1992
Kuwa, George K.: Apr 7, 1885—Oct 13, 1931
Kyser, Kay: Jun 18, 1897—Jul 23, 1985
La Badie, Florence: 1893—Oct 13, 1917
La Cava, Gregory: Mar 10, 1892—Mar 1, 1952
Lachman, Harry: Jun 29, 1886—Mar 19, 1975
Lackteen, Frank: Aug 29, 1894—Jul 8, 1968
Ladd, Alan: Sep 3, 1913—Jan 29, 1964
Lahr, Bert: Aug 13, 1895—Dec 4, 1967
Laidlaw, Ethan: Nov 25, 1899—May 25, 1963
Lake, Alice: 1896—Nov 15, 1967
Lake, Arthur: Apr 17, 1905—Jan 9, 1987
Lake, Florence: 1905—Apr 11, 1980
Lake, Veronica: Nov 14, 1919—Jul 7, 1973
La Marr, Barbara: Jul 28, 1896—Jan 30, 1926
Lamas, Fernando: Jan 9, 1915—Oct 8, 1982
Lampkin, Charles: 1913—Apr 17, 1989
Lanchester, Elsa: Oct 28, 1902—Dec 26, 1986
Landau, David: 1878—Sep 20, 1935
Landers, Lew: Jan 2, 1901—Dec 16, 1962
Landi, Elissa Dec 6, 1904—Oct 21, 1948
Landin, Hope: 1893—Feb 28, 1973
Landis, Carole: Jan 1, 1919—Jul 5, 1948
Landis, Cullen: Jul 19, 1898—Aug 26, 1975
Landis, Jessie Royce: Nov 25, 1904—Feb 2, 1972
Landis, Joseph P.: 1919—Sep 13, 1986
Landis, Walter James: 1926—Dec 17, 1991
Landon, Michael: Oct 31, 1937—Jul 1, 1991
Lane, Allan "Rocky": Sep 22, 1901—Oct 27, 1973
Lane, Lola: May 21, 1906—Jun 22, 1981
Lane, Lupino: Jun 16, 1892—Nov 10, 1959
Lane, Richard: May 28, 1899—Sep 5, 1982
Lane, Rosemary: Apr 4, 1914—Nov 25, 1974

Lanfield, Sidney: Apr 20, 1899—Jun 30, 1972
Lang, Fritz: Dec 5, 1890—Aug 2, 1976
Lang, Walter: Aug 10, 1898—Feb 7, 1972
Langan, Glenn: Jul 8, 1918—Jan 19, 1991
Langdon, Harry: Jun 15, 1884—Dec 22, 1944
Langton, Paul: Apr 17, 1913—Apr 15, 1980
Lansing, Joi: Apr 6, 1928—Aug 7, 1972
Lanza, Mario: Jan 31, 1921—Oct 7, 1959
La Plance, Rosemary: 1925—May 6, 1979
Largay, Raymond: 1886—Sep 28, 1974
Larkin, George: Nov 11, 1888—Mar 27, 1946
Larkin, John: 1874—Mar 19, 1936
La Rocque, Rod: Nov 28, 1898—Oct 15, 1969
La Roy, Rita: Oct 2, 1907— Feb 18, 1993
Larrimore, Francine: Aug 22, 1898—Mar 7, 1975
La Rue, Bart: 1923—Jan 5, 1990
La Rue, Frank H.: Dec 5, 1878—Sep 26, 1960
LaRue, Jack: May 3, 1900—Jan 11, 1984
Latell, Lyle: Apr 9, 1905—Oct 24, 1967
La Torre, Charles: 1895—Feb 1, 1990
Latz, Elaine: 1917—Oct 6, 1988
Lau, Wesley: c. 1921—Aug 30, 1984
Lauck, Chester H.: 1901—Feb 21, 1980
Laughlin, Billy: Jul 5, 1932—Aug 31, 1948
Laughton, Charles: Jul 1, 1899—Dec 15, 1962
Laurel, Stan: Jun 16, 1890—Feb 23, 1965
Lauter, Harry: 1914—Oct 30, 1990
La Verne, Lucille: Nov 8, 1872—Mar 4, 1945
Law, Walter: 1876—Aug 8, 1940
Lawford, Peter: Sep 7, 1923—Dec 24, 1984
Lawrence, Florence: 1886—Dec 27, 1938
Lawrence, Gertrude: Jul 4, 1898—Sep 6, 1952
Lawrence, Jody: Oct 19, 1930—Jul 10, 1986
Lawrence, John: Jul 1910—Jun 26, 1974
Lawrence, John: 1932—Mar 21, 1992
Lawrence, Keith: 1951—Jul 25, 1990
Lawrence, Lillian: 1870—May 7, 1926
Lawrence, Mary: 1918—Sep 24, 1991
Lawrence, William E. "Babe": 1896—Nov 28, 1947
Lawton, Frank: Sep 30, 1904—Jun 10, 1969
Leacock, Philip: 1922—Jul 14, 1990
Leaming, Chet: 1926—Feb 19, 1992
Lease, Rex: Feb 11, 1901—Jan 3, 1966
Lebedeff, Ivan: Jun 18, 1899—Mar 31, 1953
LeBorg, Reginald: Dec 11, 1902—Mar 25, 1989
Lederer, Charles: Dec 31, 1910—Mar 5, 1976
Lederer, Gretchen: 1891—Dec 30, 1955
Lederer, Otto: Apr 17, 1886—Sep 3, 1965
Lederman, D. Ross: Dec 11, 1895—Aug 24, 1972
Lee, Annabelle: ____—Sep 8, 1989
Lee, Billy: Sep 12, 1930—Nov 17, 1989
Lee, Brandon: Feb 1, 1965—Mar 31, 1993
Lee, Bruce: Nov 27, 1940—Jul 20, 1973
Lee, Canada: Mar 2, 1907—May 9, 1952
Lee, Dixie: Nov 4, 1911—Nov 1, 1952
Lee, Duke R.: 1881—Apr 1, 1959
Lee, Florence: 1888—Sep 1, 1962
Lee, Gwen: Nov 12, 1904—Aug 20, 1961
Lee, Gypsy Rose: Feb 9, 1914—Apr 26, 1970
Lee, Jane: 1913—Mar 17, 1957
Lee, Johnny: Jul 4, 1898—Dec 12, 1965
Lee, Lila: Jul 25, 1901—Nov 13, 1973
Lee, Pinky: 1908—Apr 3, 1993
Lee, Raymond: 1910—Jun 26, 1974
Lee, Rowland V.: Sep 6, 1891—Dec 21, 1975

Lee, Ruth: 1896—Aug 3, 1975
Leeds, Andrea: Aug 18, 1914—May 21, 1984
Leeds, Herbert I.: 1900—1954
Le Gallienne, Eva: Jan 11, 1899—Jun 3, 1991
Leiber, Fritz: Jan 31, 1882—Oct 14, 1949
Leigh, Vivien: Nov 5, 1913—Jul 8, 1967
Leighton, Margaret: Feb 26, 1922—Jan 13, 1976
Leighton, Merrill: 1940—Jul 5, 1991
Leisen, Mitchell: Oct 6, 1898—Oct 28 1972
Lembeck, Harvey: Apr 15, 1923—Jan 5, 1982
Lemkow, Tutte: 1918—Nov 10, 1991
Leni, Paul: Jul 8, 1885—Sep 2, 1929
Lenya, Lotte: Oct 18, 1900—Nov 27, 1981
Leonard, Gus: 1856—Mar 27, 1939
Leonard, Jack E.: Apr 24, 1911—May 9, 1973
Leonard, Marion: 1880—Jan 9, 1956
Leonard, Robert Z.: Oct 7, 1889—Aug 27, 1968
Leontovich, Eugenie: Mar 21, 1900—Apr 2, 1993
Lerner, Irving: Mar 7, 1909—Dec 25, 1976
LeRoy, Hal: 1914—May 2, 1985
LeRoy, Mervyn: Oct 15, 1900—Sep 13, 1987
Le Saint, Edward J.: 1871—Sep 10, 1940
Leslie, Bob: 1927—Feb 4, 1991
Leslie, Gladys: Mar 5, 1899—Oct 2, 1976
Leslie, Lilie "Lila": 1892—Sep 8, 1940
Lessey, George A.: ____—Jun 3, 1947
Lester, Kate: ____—Oct 12, 1924
L'Estrange, Dick: Dec 27, 1889—Nov 19, 1963
L'Estrange, Julian: 1880—Oct 22, 1918
Lettieri, Al: 1928—Oct 18, 1975
Levant, Oscar: Dec 27, 1906—Aug 14, 1972
Levene, Sam: Aug 28, 1907—Dec 1980
LeVeque, Edward: 1896—Jan 28, 1989
Levin, Henry: Jun 5, 1909—May 1, 1980
Lewin, Albert: Sep 23, 1894—May 9, 1968
Lewis, Buddy: 1917—Nov 22, 1986
Lewis, Cathy: 1918—Nov 20, 1968
Lewis, David P.: 1909—Oct 25, 1992
Lewis, Elliot: 1917—May 20, 1990
Lewis, Forrest: 1900—Jun 2, 1977
Lewis, Jarma: 1931—Nov 11, 1985
Lewis, Mitchell J.: Jun 26, 1880—Aug 24, 1956
Lewis, Ralph: 1872—Dec 4, 1937
Lewis, Robert Q.: Apr 5, 1921—Dec 11, 1991
Lewis, Sheldon: 1869—May 7, 1958
Lewis, Ted: Jun 6, 1891—Aug 25, 1971
Lewis, Vera: Jun 10, ____—Feb 8, 1956
Lewis, Walter P.: Jun 1871—Jan 30, 1932
Liberace, Lee: May 16, 1919—Feb 4, 1987
Lightner, Winnie: Sep 17, 1901—Mar 5, 1971
Lillie, Beatrice: May 29, 1894—Jan 20, 1989
Lincoln, E. K.: ____—Jan 9, 1958
Lincoln, Elmo: 1889—Jun 27, 1952
Linder, Max: Dec 16, 1883—Nov 2, 1925
Lindsay, Lois: 1917—Apr 21, 1982
Lindsay, Margaret: Sep 19, 1910—May 9, 1981
Lindsay, Phillip: 1924—Oct 22, 1988
Lingham, Thomas J.: Apr 7, 1874—Feb 19, 1950
Linton, Philip: 1964—Feb 16, 1992
Lion, Margo: 1899—Feb 25, 1989
Liss, Ted: 1920—Mar 3, 1992
Litel, John: Dec 30, 1894—Feb 3, 1972
Little, Ann: 1891—May 21, 1984
Little, Cleavon: Jun 1, 1939—Oct 22, 1992
Littlefield, Lucien: Aug 16, 1895—Jun 4, 1960

Litvak, Anatole: May 10, 1902—Dec 15, 1974
Livesey, Jack: 1901—Oct 12, 1961
Livingston, Robert: Dec 9, 1908—Mar 7, 1988
Lloyd, Doris: Jul 3, 1896—May 21, 1968
Lloyd, Frank: Feb 2, 1886—Aug 10, 1960
Lloyd, Harold, Jr.: Jan 25, 1931—Jun 9, 1971
Lloyd, Harold (Sr.): Apr 20, 1893—Mar 8, 1971
Lloyd, Jimmy: 1919—Aug 25, 1988
Lloyd, Ray: 1946—Oct 3, 1990
Lloyd, Rollo: Mar 22, 1883—Jul 24, 1938
Locher, Felix: Jul 16, 1882—Mar 13, 1969
Lockhart, Gene: Jul 18, 1891—Apr 1, 1957
Lockhart, Kathleen: 1887—Feb 18, 1978
Lockwood, Harold A.: Apr 12, 1887—Oct 19, 1918
Lockwood, King: 1898—Feb 23, 1971
Lockwood, Margaret: Sep 15, 19.16—Jul 15, 1990
Loden, Barbara: 1932—Sep 5, 1980
Loder, John: Jan 3, 1898—Dec 1988
Lodge, John: Oct 20, 1903—Oct 29, 1985
Loft, Arthur: May 25, 1897—Jan 1, 1947
Loftus, Cecilia: Oct 22, 1876—Jul 12, 1943
Logan, Ella: Mar 6, 1913—May 1, 1969
Logan, Jacqueline: Nov 30, 1901—Apr 4, 1983
Logan, Joshua: Oct 5, 1908—Jul 12, 1988
Logan, Stanley: Jun 12, 1885—Jan 30, 1953
Lombard, Carole: Oct 6, 1908—Jan 16, 1942
Lombardi, Paul Michael: 1960—Sep 9, 1991
London, Jean "Babe": 1901—Nov 29, 1980
London, Tom: Aug 24, 1893—Dec 5, 1963
Lonergan, Lenore: Jun 2, 1928—Aug 31, 1987
Long, Avon: Jun 18, 1910—Feb 15, 1984
Long, Richard: Dec 17, 1927—Dec 22, 1974
Long, Walter: Mar 5, 1879—Jul 4, 1952
Lontoc, Leon: 1909—Jan 22, 1974
Loo, Richard: 1903—Nov 20, 1983
Loos, Anne: 1916—May 3, 1916
Lorch, Theodore A.: 1873—Nov 12, 1947
Lord, Pauline: Aug 8, 1890—Oct 11, 1950
Lorentz, Pare: Dec 11, 1905—Mar 4, 1992
Lormer, Jon: 1906—Mar 19, 1986
Lorne, Marion: Aug 12, 1888—May 9, 1968
Lorraine, Lillian: Jan 1, 1892—Apr 17, 1955
Lorraine, Louise: Oct 1, 1901—Feb 2, 1981
Lorre, Peter: Jun 26, 1904—Mar 23, 1964
Losch, Tilly: Nov 15, 1902—Dec 24, 1975
Losee, Frank: 1856—Nov 14, 1937
Losey, Joseph: Jan 14, 1909—Jun 22, 1984
Lott, Lawrence: 1951—Jan 24, 1991
Louden, Thomas: 1874—Mar 15, 1948
Louis, Willard: 1886—Jul 22, 1926
Louise, Anita: Jan 9, 1915—Apr 25, 1970
Love, Bessie: Sep 19, 1898—Apr 26, 1986
Love, Edward M.: 1948—Dec 27, 1991
Love, Montagu: Mar 15, 1877—May 17, 1943
Lovejoy, Frank: Mar 28, 1914—Oct 2, 1962
Low, Carl: 1917—Oct 19, 1988
Low, Warren: 1906—Jul 27, 1989
Lowe, Edmund: Mar 5, 1890—Apr 21, 1971
Lowenstein, Cary Scott: 1962—Nov 29, 1992
Lowery, Margerie Bonner: 1905—Sep 28, 1988
Lowery, Robert: 1914—Dec 26, 1971
Lowry, Judith: Jul 27, 1890—Nov 29, 1976
Lubitsch, Ernst: Jan 28, 1892—Nov 30, 1947
Lucas, Gail: 1953—Jan 7, 1990
Lucas, Wilfred: Jan 30, 1871—Dec 13, 1940

Luce, Claire: Oct 15, 1901—Aug 31, 1989
Ludwig, Edward: 1899—Aug 20, 1982
Lugosi, Bela: Oct 20, 1882—Aug 16, 1956
Lukas, Paul: May 26, 1895—Aug 15, 1971
Luke, Keye: Jun 18, 1904—Jan 12, 1991
Lumet, Baruch: 1899—Feb 8, 1992
Lund, Art: Apr 1, 1915—May 31, 1990
Lund, John: Feb 6, 1911—May 10, 1992
Lundigan, William "Bill":
                Jun 12, 1914—Dec 20, 1975
Lunt, Alfred: Aug 19, 1892—Aug 3, 1977
Luther, Anna: 1893—Dec 16, 1960
Lynch, Helen: Apr 6, 1900—Mar 2, 1965
Lynch, Ken: 1911—Feb 13, 1990
Lynde, Paul: Jun 13, 1926—Jan 11, 1982
Lynn, Diana: Oct 7, 1926—Dec 18, 1971
Lynn, Emmett: Feb 14, 1897—Oct 20, 1958
Lynn, Sharon E.: 1904—May 26, 1963
Lyon, Ben: Feb 6, 1901—Mar 22, 1979
Lyons, Cliff "Tex": 1902—Jan 6, 1974
Lyons, Eddie: Nov 25, 1886—Aug 30, 1926
Lyons, Fred: ____—Mar 16, 1921
Lys, Lya: 1908—Jun 2, 1986
Lytell, Bert: Feb 24, 1885—Sep 28, 1954
Lytell, Wilfred: 1892—Sep 10, 1954
Lytton, L. Rogers: 1867—Aug 9, 1924
Mabley, Jackie "Moms": 1897—May 23, 1975
MacArthur, Charles: Nov 5, 1895—Apr 21, 1956
MacBride, Donald: 1894—Jun 21, 1957
MacDonald, Edmund: May 7, 1908—Sep 1951
MacDonald, J. Farrell: Jun 6, 1875—Aug 2, 1952
MacDonald, Jeanette: Jun 18, 1901—Jan 14, 1965
MacDonald, Katherine: 1891—Jun 4, 1956
MacDonald, Wallace: 1891—Oct 30, 1978
MacDowell, Melbourne: 1857—Feb 18, 1941
Mace, Fred: 1879—Feb 21, 1917
MacFadden, Gertrude "Mickey": 1900—Jun 3, 1967
MacGibbon, Harriet: 1906—Feb 8, 1987
MacGowran, Jack: Oct 13, 1918—Jan 31, 1973
MacGrath, Leueen: Jul 3, 1914—Mar 27, 1992
MacGregor, Lee: ____—Jun 1961
Machaty, Gustav: May 9, 1901—Dec 14, 1963
Mack, Cactus: Aug 9, 1899—Apr 17, 1962
Mack, Charles E.: Nov 22, 1887—Jan 11, 1934
Mack, Charles Emmett: 1900—Mar 17, 1927
Mack, Marion: 1902—May 1, 1989
Mack, Russell: 1983—Jun 1, 1972
Mack, Wilbur: 1873—Mar 13, 1964
Mackaill, Dorothy: Mar 4, 1903—Aug 12, 1990
Mackaye, Dorothy: 1898—Jan 5, 1940
MacKaye, Norman: 1906—Apr 24, 1968
MacLane, Barton: Dec 25, 1900—Jan 1, 1969
MacLaren, Mary: 1900—Nov 9, 1985
MacLean, Douglas: Jan 14, 1890—Jul 9, 1967
MacMahon, Aline: May 3, 1899—Oct 12, 1991
MacMurray, Fred: Aug 30, 1908—Nov 5, 1991
MacPherson, Jeanie: 1884—Aug 26, 1946
MacQuarrie, Murdock:
                Aug 26, 1878—Aug 22, 1942
MacRae, Gordon: Mar 12, 1921—Jan 24, 1986
Macready, George: Aug 29, 1909—Jul 2, 1973
Madison, Cleo: 1883—Mar 11, 1964
Madison, Noel N.: 1898—Jan 6, 1975
Magginetti, William Shaw: 1894—Feb 21, 1992
Magnani, Anna: Mar 7, 1908—Sep 26, 1973

Magrill, George: Jan 5, 1900—May 31, 1952
Maguire, Kathleen: 1925—Aug 9, 1989
Mahoney, Jock: Feb 7, 1919—Dec 14, 1989
Mailes, Charles Hill: May 25, 1870—Feb 17, 1937
Main, Marjorie: Feb 24, 1890—Apr 10, 1975
Mala, Ray: 1906—Sep 23, 1952
Malatesta, Fred: Apr 18, 1889—Apr 8, 1952
Maler, Tom: ____—Jan 23, 1990
Mallory, Patricia "Boots":
                Oct 22, 1913—Dec 1, 1958
Maloney, Joan: 1935—Oct 28, 1992
Maloney, Leo D.: 1888—Nov 2, 1929
Malyon, Eily: Oct 30, 1879—Sep 26, 1961
Mamoulian, Rouben: Oct 8, 1898—Dec 4, 1987
Manders, Miles: Nov 14, 1888—Feb 8, 1946
Mandy, Jerry: 1893—May 1, 1945
Mankiewicz, Joseph L.: Feb 11, 1909—Feb 5, 1993
Mann, Anthony: Jun 30, 1906—Apr 29, 1967
Mann, Daniel: Aug 8, 1912—Nov 21, 1991
Mann, Hank: 1887—Nov 25, 1971
Mann, Jerry: 1910—Dec 6, 1987
Mann, Margaret: Apr 4, 1868—Feb 4, 1941
Manning, Aileen: 1886—Mar 25, 1946
Manning, Knox: 1904—Aug 26, 1980
Mansfield, Jayne: Apr 19, 1933—Jun 29, 1967
Mansfield, Marian: 1906—Nov 16, 1989
Mansfield, Martha: 1900—Nov 30, 1923
Mantz, Paul: 1904—Jul 8, 1965
March, Alex: 1921—Jun 11, 1989
March, Fredric: Aug 31, 1897—Apr 14, 1975
March, Hal: Apr 22, 1920—Jan 19, 1970
Marcus, James A.: Jan 21, 1868—Oct 15, 1937
Marcuse, Theodore: 1920—Nov 29, 1967
Marden, Adrienne: 1909—Nov 9, 1978
Margo: May 10, 1917—Jul 17, 1985
Maricle, Leona: 1907—Mar 25, 1988
Marin, Edwin L.: Feb 21, 1899—May 2, 1951
Marion, Frances: Nov 18, 1888—May 12, 1973
Marion, George F., Sr.: Jul 16, 1860—Nov 30, 1945
Marion, Sid: 1900—Jun 29, 1965
Maris, Mona: 1903—Mar 23, 1991
Mark, Michael: Mar 15, 1889—Feb 3, 1975
Markey, Enid: Feb 22, 1890—Nov 15, 1981
Markle, Fletcher: Mar 27, 1921—May 22, 1991
Marks, Willis: Aug 20, 1865—Dec 6, 1952
Marley, John: 1907—May 22, 1984
Marlow, Jo Ann: 1936—Jan 2, 1991
Marlowe, Frank: 1904—Mar 30, 1964
Marlowe, Hugh: Jan 30, 1911—May 2, 1982
Marlowe, June: 1903—Mar 10, 1984
Marlowe, Louis J.: 1906—Jan 19, 1991
Marlowe, Nora: ____—Dec 31, 1977
Marly, Florence: Jun 2, 1918—Nov 9, 1978
Marquard, Yvonne Peattie: 1917—Jan 10, 1990
Marrero, Ralph: 1958—Nov 16, 1991
Marsh, Mae: Nov 9, 1895—Feb 13, 1968
Marsh, Marguerite: 1892—Dec 8, 1925
Marshal, Alan: Jan 29, 1909—Jul 9, 1961
Marshall, Boyd: 1885—Nov 9, 1950
Marshall, Brenda: Sep 29, 1915—Jul 30, 1992
Marshall, George: Dec 29, 1891—Feb 17, 1975
Marshall, Herbert: May 23, 1890—Jan 22, 1966
Marshall, Tully: Apr 13, 1864—Mar 10, 1943
Marston, Merlin: 1945—Aug 22, 1990
Martel, Alphonse: Mar 27, 1890—Mar 18, 1976

Martin, Chris-Pin: 1893—Jun 27, 1953
Martin, Dean Paul: Nov 17, 1951—Mar 21, 1987
Martin, Kiel: Jul 26, 1944—Dec 27, 1990
Martin, Marion: Jun 7, 1908—Aug 13, 1985
Martin, Mary: Dec 1, 1913—Nov 3, 1990
Martin, Ross: Mar 22, 1920—Jul 3, 1981
Martin, Strother: Mar 26, 1919—Aug 1, 1980
Martin, Vivian: 1894—Mar 16, 1987
Martindel, Edward B.: Jul 8, 1876—May 4, 1955
Martini, Nino: Jul 8, 1904—Dec 9, 1976
Marton, Andrew: Jan 26, 1904—Jan 7, 1992
Marvin, Lee: Feb 19, 1924—Aug 29, 1987
Marx, Chico: Mar 22, 1886—Oct 11, 1961
Marx, Groucho: Oct 2, 1890—Aug 19, 1977
Marx, Harpo: Nov 21, 1888—Sep 28, 1964
Marx, Zeppo: Feb 25, 1901—Nov 30, 1979
Mason, Dan: 1853—Jul 6, 1929
Mason, James (American): 1890—Nov 7, 1959
Mason, James (British): May 15, 1909—Jul 27, 1984
Mason, Leroy: 1903—Oct 13, 1947
Mason, Linn: 1930—Jul 3, 1992
Mason, Shirley: Jun 6, 1901—Jul 27, 1979
Mason, William C. "Smiling Billy":
                1888—Jan 24, 1941
Massey, Curt: 1910—Oct 20, 1991
Massey, Edith: 1918—Oct 24, 1984
Massey, Ilona: Jun 16, 1910—Aug 20, 1974
Massey, Raymond: Aug 30, 1896—Jul 19, 1983
Mate, Rudolph: Jan 21, 1898—Oct 26, 1964
Mather, Jack: 1908—Aug 15, 1966
Matheson, Murray: Apr 11, 1912—Apr 25, 1985
Mathiesen, Otto: Mar 27, 1873—Feb 20, 1932
Matray, Ernst: 1891—Nov 12, 1978
Matthews, Lester: Dec 3, 1900—Jun 6, 1975
Mattox, Martha: 1879—May 2, 1933
Matts, Tom: 1924—Apr 28, 1990
Matuszak, John: 1951—Jun 17, 1989
Maurice, Mary Birch: Nov 15, 1844—Apr 30, 1918
Maxey, Paul: 1908—Jun 3, 1963
Maxwell, Edwin: 1886—Aug 12, 1948
Maxwell, Elsa: May 24, 1883—Nov 1, 1963
Maxwell, Marilyn: Aug 3, 1921—Mar 20, 1972
May, Doris: ____—May 12, 1984
May, Joe: Nov 7, 1880—May 5, 1954
Mayall, Hershell: 1863—Jun 10, 1941
Mayehoff, Eddie: Jul 7, 1911—Nov 12, 1992
Mayer, Ken: 1919—Jan 30, 1985
Mayer, Ray: 1901—Nov 22, 1948
Maynard, Ken: Jul 21, 1895—Mar 23, 1973
Maynard, Kermit: Sep 20, 1902—Jan 16, 1971
Mayne, Eric: 1866—Feb 10, 1947
Mayo, Archie: 1891—Dec 4, 1968
Mayo, Edna: 1893—May 5, 1970
Mayo, Frank: 1886—Jul 9, 1963
Mazurki, Mike: Dec 25, 1909—Dec 9, 1990
McAvoy, May: Sep 8, 1901—Apr 26, 1984
McCall, William: May 19, 1879—Jan 10, 1938
McCallion, James: 1919—Jul 11, 1991
McCarey, Leo: Oct 3, 1898—Jul 5, 1969
McCarey, Ray: Sep 6, 1904—Dec 8, 1948
McCarthy, John P.: Mar 17, 1885—Sep 4, 1962
McCom, Tim: Apr 10, 1891—Jan 28, 1978
McConnell, Gladys: Oct 22, 1907—Mar 1979
McCormack, William M.: 1891—Aug 19, 1953
McCormick, Myron: Feb 8, 1907—Jul 30, 1962

McCoy, Gertrude: 1896—Jul 17, 1967
McCoy, Harry: 1894—Sep 1, 1937
McCoy, Tim (Colonel): Apr 10, 1891—Jan 29, 1978
McCrea, Joel: Nov 5, 1905—Oct 20, 1990
McCullough, Philo: Jun 16, 1890—Jun 5, 1981
McDaniel, Etta: Dec 1, 1890—Jan 13, 1946
McDaniel, Hattie: Jun 10, 1895—Oct 26, 1952
McDaniel, Sam: Jan 28, 1886—Sep 24, 1962
McDermott, Marc: 1881—Jan 5, 1929
McDevitt, Ruth: Sep 13, 1895—May 27, 1976
McDonald, Francis J.: Aug 22, 1891—Sep 18, 1968
McDonald, Frank: Nov 9, 1899—Mar 8, 1980
McDonald, Marie: Jul 6, 1923—Oct 21, 1965
McDonald, William: 1927—Dec 19, 1992
McDowell, Claire: Nov 2, 1877—Oct 23, 1966
McFadden, Ivor: Aug 6, 1887—Aug 14, 1942
McGann, Wiliam H.: Apr 5, 1895—Nov 15, 1977
McGill, Moyna: 1895—Nov 25, 1975
McGinn, Walter: 1939—Mar 30, 1977
McGiveney, Maura: 1939—Nov 10, 1990
McGiver, John: Nov 5, 1913—Sep 9, 1975
McGlynn, Frank, Sr.: Oct 26, 1866—May 17, 1951
McGowan, J. (John) P.:
                    Feb 24, 1880—Mar 26, 1952
McGowan, Oliver F.: 1907—Aug 23, 1971
McGrail, Walter B.: 1899—Mar 19, 1970
McGrath, Frank: 1903—May 13, 1967
McGrath, Paul: 1904—Apr 13, 1978
McGraw, Charles: May 10, 1914—Jul 30, 1980
McGregor, Malcolm: Oct 13, 1892—Apr 29, 1945
McGuinn, Joseph Ford: Jan 21, 1904—Sep 22, 1971
McGuire, Kathryn: Dec 6, 1904—Oct 10, 1978
McGuire, Tom: 1874—May 6, 1954
McHugh, Frank: May 23, 1899—Sep 11, 1981
McHugh, John: 1914—Jan 13, 1983
McHugh, Matt: 1894—Feb 22, 1971
McIntire, John: Jun 27, 1907—Jan 30, 1991
McIntire, Tim: 1943—Apr 15, 1986
McIntosh, Burr: Aug 21, 1862—Apr 28, 1942
McIntyre, Christine: ____—Jul 8, 1984
McIntyre, Leila: 1882—Jan 9, 1953
McKay, George W.: 1880—Dec 3, 1945
McKay, Scott: May 28, 1915—Mar 16, 1987
McKee, Lafe: Jan 23, 1872—Aug 10, 1959
McKenzie, Eva B.: 1889—Sep 15, 1967
McKenzie, Ida Mae: ____—Jun 29, 1986
McKenzie, Robert B.: Sep 22, 1883—Jul 8, 1949
McKim, Robert: Aug 26, 1887—Jun 2, 1927
McLaglen, Victor: Dec 11, 1886—Nov 7, 1959
McLaren, Wayne: 1941—Jul 22, 1992
McLaughlin, Don: 1907—May 28, 1986
McLaughlin, Emily: 1930—Apr 26, 1991
McLeod, Norman Z.: Sep 20, 1898—Jan 26, 1964
McMahon, Horace: May 17, 1907—Aug 17, 1971
McMillan, Kenneth: Jul 2, 1932—Jan 8, 1989
McNamara, Edward C.: 1884—Nov 9, 1944
McNamara, Maggie: Jun 18, 1928—Feb 18, 1978
McNear, Howard: 1905—Jan 3, 1969
McPhillips, Hugh: 1920—Oct 31, 1990
McQueen, Steve: Mar 24, 1930—Nov 7, 1980
McRae, Henry: 1876—Oct 2, 1944
McVey, Patrick: 1910—Jul 6, 1973
McWade, Edward: Jan 14, 1865—May 16, 1943
McWade, Margaret: Sep 3, 1872—Apr 1, 1956
McWade, Robert, Jr.: 1882—Jan 20, 1938

Meader, George: Jul 6, 1888—Dec 1963
Medford, Kay: Sep 14, 1920—Apr 10, 1980
Meek, Donald: Jul 14, 1880—Nov 18, 1946
Meeker, Ralph: Nov 21, 1920—Aug 5, 1988
Megowan, Don: 1922—Jun 26, 1981
Mehaffey, Blanche: Jul 28, 1907—Mar 31, 1968
Meighan, Thomas: Apr 9, 1879—Jul 8, 1936
Melchior, Lauritz: Mar 20, 1890—Mar 18, 1973
Melesh, Alex: Oct 21, 1890—Mar 5, 1949
Melford, George: c. 1877—Apr 25, 1961
Mell, Marisa: Feb 24, 1939—May 16, 1992
Mellish, Fuller, Jr.: 1895—Feb 8, 1930
Mellish, Fuller (Sr.): Jan 3, 1865—Dec 7, 1936
Melton, Frank: Dec 6, 1907—Mar 19, 1951
Melville, Rose: Jan 30, 1873—Oct 8, 1946
Melville, Sam: Aug 20, 1940—Mar 9, 1989
Mendenhall, Jim: 1928—Dec 1, 1990
Menjou, Adolphe: Feb 18, 1890—Oct 29, 1963
Menzies, Lothar: May 19, 1894—Feb 25, 1974
Menzies, William Cameron:
                    Jul 29, 1896—Mar 5, 1957
Merande, Doro: ____—Nov 1, 1975
Mercer, Beryl: Aug 13, 1882—Jul 28, 1939
Meredith, Charles: 1894—Nov 28, 1964
Meredith, Iris: 1916—Jan 22, 1980
Merivale, John: 1918—Feb 6, 1990
Merivale, Philip: Nov 2, 1880—Mar 12, 1946
Merkel, Una: Dec 10, 1903—Jan 2, 1986
Merlo, Anthony "Tony": 1887—Apr 25, 1976
Merman, Ethel: Jan 16, 1909—Feb 15, 1984
Merrill, Frank: 1894—Feb 12, 1966
Merrill, Gary: Aug 2, 1914—Mar 5, 1990
Merrill, Joan: 1918—May 10, 1992
Merry, Eleanor: 1907—Aug 28, 1991
Merton, John: 1901—Sep 19, 1959
Messenger, Buddy: Oct 26, 1909—Oct 25, 1965
Metaxa, Georges: Sep 11, 1899—Dec 8, 1950
Metcalfe, Gordon: 1947—Aug 6, 1990
Metcalfe, James: 1901—Apr 2, 1960
Methot, Mayo: Mar 3, 1904—Jun 9, 1951
Meyer, Emile G.: 1916—Mar 19, 1987
Meyer, Greta: 1883—Oct 8, 1965
Meyer, Torben: Dec 1, 1884—May 22, 1975
Meyers, Sidney: 1906—1969
Michael, Gertrude: Jun 1, 1911—Dec 31, 1964
Micheaux, Oscar: 1884—Apr 1, 1951
Middlemass, Robert M.: Sep 3, 1885—Sep 10, 1949
Middleton, Charles B.: Oct 3, 1879—Apr 22, 1949
Middleton, Robert: May 13, 1911—Jun 14, 1977
Midgely, Fannie: Nov 26, 1877—Jan 4, 1932
Milestone, Lewis: Sep 30, 1895—Sep 25, 1980
Miljan, John: Nov 9, 1892—Jan 24, 1960
Milland, Ray: Jan 3, 1905—Mar 10, 1986
Millarde, Harry: Nov 12, 1885—Nov 2, 1931
Miller, Cameron: 1909—Jun 22, 1991
Miller, Carl: Aug 9, 1893—Dec 7, 1979
Miller, Charles B.: 1891—Jun 5, 1955
Miller, David: Nov 28, 1909—Apr 14, 1992
Miller, Glenn: Mar 1, 1904—Dec 15, 1944
Miller, Hope: 1929—Jul 25, 1992
Miller, Marilyn: Sep 1, 1898—Apr 7, 1936
Miller, Marvin: Jul 18, 1913—Feb 8, 1985
Miller, Max: 1918—Oct 24, 1992
Miller, Ruth: 1903—Jun 13, 1981
Miller, W. Christy: 1843—Sep 23, 1922

Miller, Walter: Mar 9, 1892—Mar 30, 1940
Millican, James: 1910—Nov 24, 1955
Milligan, Andy: Feb 12, 1929—Jun 3, 1991
Milton, Robert: Jan 24, 1885—Jan 13, 1956
Mims, William R.: ____—Apr 9, 1991
Mineo, Sal: Jan 10, 1939—Feb 12, 1976
Miner, Worthington "Tony":
                    Nov 13, 1900—Dec 11, 1982
Minnelli, Vincente: Feb 28, 1903—Jul 25, 1986
Minner, Kathryn: 1892—May 26, 1969
Minter, Mary Miles: Apr 1, 1902—Aug 4, 1984
Mintz, Eli: Aug 1, 1904—Jun 8, 1988
Miranda, Carmen: Feb 9, 1904—Aug 5, 1955
Miranda, Isa: Jul 5, 1909—Jul 8, 1982
Mitchell, Belle: 1888—Feb 12, 1979
Mitchell, Bruce: Nov 16, 1883—Sep 26, 1952
Mitchell, Charles (Chuck): 1928—Jun 22, 1992
Mitchell, Coleman: 1944—Nov 17, 1992
Mitchell, Frank: 1906—Jan 21, 1991
Mitchell, Geneva: Feb 3, 1907—Mar 10, 1949
Mitchell, Grant: Jun 17, 1874—May 1, 1957
Mitchell, Millard: Aug 14, 1900—Oct 12, 1953
Mitchell, Rhea "Ginger": 1905—Sep 16, 1957
Mitchell, Thomas: Jul 11, 1892—Dec 17, 1962
Mix, Tom: Jan 6, 1880—Oct 12, 1940
Mohr, Gerald: Jun 11, 1914—Nov 10, 1968
Molinari, Antoinette (Toni): 1929—Oct 16, 1992
Mong, William V.: 1875—Dec 10, 1940
Monica, Maria: 1899—Oct 29, 1991
Monroe, Marilyn: Jun 1, 1926—Aug 5, 1962
Montague, Frederick: 1864—Jul 3, 1919
Montague, Monte: 1892—Apr 6, 1959
Montalban, Carlos: 1903—Mar 28, 1991
Montana, Bull: May 16, 1887—Jan 24, 1950
Montand, Yves: Oct 13, 1921—Nov 9, 1991
Montez, Maria: Jun 6, 1918—Sep 7, 1951
Montgomery, Douglass: Oct 29, 1908—Jul 23, 1966
Montgomery, Goodee: 1906—Jun 5, 1978
Montgomery, Robert: May 21, 1904—Sep 27, 1981
Montoya, Alex P.: Oct 19, 1907—Sep 25, 1970
Moody, Ralph: Nov 5, 1887—Sep 16, 1971
Moore, Brian: 1933—May 8, 1992
Moore, Carlyle, Jr.: 1909—Mar 3, 1977
Moore, Carlyle (Sr.): 1875—Jun 26, 1924
Moore, Cleo: Oct 31, 1928—Oct 25, 1973
Moore, Colleen: Aug 19, 1900—Jan 25, 1988
Moore, Del: 1917—Aug 30, 1970
Moore, Dennis: 1914—Mar 1, 1964
Moore, Eleanor: 1907—Aug 28, 1991
Moore, Eva: Feb 9, 1870—Apr 27, 1955
Moore, Ida: 1883—Sep 1964
Moore, Matt: Jan 8, 1888—Jan 21, 1960
Moore, Owen: Dec 12, 1886—Jun 9, 1939
Moore, Robert: Aug 17, 1927—May 10, 1984
Moore, Tom: Jan 1885—Feb 12, 1955
Moore, Victor: Feb 24, 1876—Jul 23, 1962
Moorehead, Agnes: Dec 6, 1906—Apr 30, 1974
Moorhead, Natalie: 1901—Oct 6, 1992
Moran, Dolores: 1926—Feb 5, 1982
Moran, Frank: Mar 18, 1887—Dec 14, 1967
Moran, George: 1882—Aug 1, 1949
Moran, Jackie: 1923—Sep 20, 1990
Moran, Lee: Jun 23, 1890—Apr 24, 1961
Moran, Lois: Mar 1, 1907—Jul 13, 1990
Moran, Patsy: 1905—Dec 10, 1968

Moran, Polly: Jun 28, 1883—Jan 25, 1952
Morante, Milburn: Apr 6, 1887—Jan 28, 1964
Moreland, Mantan: Sep 4, 1901—Sep 28, 1973
Moreno, Antonio: Sep 26, 1887—Feb 15, 1967
Morgan, Boyd "Red": 1916—Jan 8, 1988
Morgan, Frank: Jul 1, 1890—Sep 18, 1949
Morgan, Gene: 1892—Aug 13, 1940
Morgan, Helen: Aug 2, 1900—Oct 9, 1941
Morgan, Joan Virginia: 1918—Jun 30, 1991
Morgan, Lee: Jun 12, 1902—Jan 30, 1967
Morgan, Ralph: Jul 6, 1883—Jun 11, 1956
Morgan, Russ: 1904—Aug 7, 1969
Morley, Robert: May 25, 1908—Jun 3, 1992
Morrell, George: 1873—Apr 28, 1955
Morris, Adrian: 1903—Nov 30, 1941
Morris, Chester: Feb 16, 1901—Sep 11, 1970
Morris, Glenn: 1912—Jan 31, 1974
Morris, Jack Julius: 1904—Apr 21, 1990
Morris, Johnnie: 1886—Oct 7, 1969
Morris, Margaret: Nov 7, 1903—Jun 7, 1968
Morris, Philip: Jan 20, 1893—Dec 18, 1949
Morris, Rolland "Rusty": 1923—May 14, 1986
Morris, Wayne: Feb 17, 1914—Sep 14, 1959
Morrison, Ann: 1916—Apr 18, 1978
Morrison, Barbara: Oct 1, 1907—Mar 12, 1992
Morrison, Ernie "Sunshine Sammy":
                    Dec 20, 1912—Jul 24, 1989
Morrison, George "Pete": Aug 8, 1891—Feb 5, 1973
Morrison, James W.: Nov 15, 1888—Nov 15, 1974
Morrison, Louis "Lou": Feb 8, 1876—Apr 22, 1940
Morrison, Michael David: 1960—Feb 18, 1993
Morrow, Doretta: Jan 27, 1928—Feb 28, 1968
Morrow, Vic: Feb 14, 1932—Jul 23, 1982
Morton, Charles S.: Jan 28, 1907—Oct 26, 1966
Morton, James C.: 1884—Oct 24, 1942
Moscovitch, Maurice: Nov 23, 1871—Jun 18, 1940
Moss, Arnold: Jan 28, 1910—Dec 15, 1989
Mostel, Zero: Feb 28, 1915—Sep 8, 1977
Mowbray, Alan: Aug 18, 1896—Mar 25, 1969
Mower, Jack: 1890—Jan 6, 1965
Mower, Margaret: 1896—Sep 1, 1989
Mudie, Leonard: Apr 11, 1884—Apr 14, 1965
Muir, Gavin: Sep 8, 1907—May 24, 1972
Mulhall, Jack: Oct 7, 1887—Jun 1, 1979
Mullaney, Jack: 1931—Jun 27, 1982
Mundin, Herbert: Aug 21, 1898—Mar 4, 1939
Muni, Paul: Sep 22, 1895—Aug 25, 1967
Munier, Ferdinand: Dec 3, 1889—May 27, 1945
Munro, Janet: 1934—Dec 6, 1972
Munshin, Jules: 1915—Feb 19, 1970
Munson, Ona: Jun 16, 1906—Feb 11, 1955
Murdock, Ann: Nov 10, 1890—Apr 22, 1939
Murnau, F. W.: Dec 28, 1888—Mar 11, 1931
Murphy, Audie: Jun 20, 1924—May 28, 1971
Murphy, Edna: Nov 17, 1904—Aug 3, 1974
Murphy, George: Jul 4, 1902—May 2, 1992
Murphy, Maurice: 1913—Nov 23, 1978
Murray, Charlie: Jun 22, 1872—Jul 29, 1941
Murray, James: Feb 9, 1901—Jul 11, 1936
Murray, John T.: 1886—Feb 12, 1957
Murray, Ken: Jul 14, 1903—Oct 12, 1988
Murray, Mae: May 10, 1885—Mar 23, 1965
Murray, Mary Phillips: _____—May 26, 1990
Murray, Tom: 1875—Aug 27, 1935
Murrow, Edward R.: Apr 25, 1908—Apr 27 1965

Muse, Clarence: Oct 7, 1889—Oct 13, 1979
Mustin, Burt: Feb 8, 1882—Jan 28, 1977
Myers, Carmel: Apr 4, 1899—Nov 9, 1980
Myers, Harry: 1882—Dec 26, 1938
Myhers, John: 1922—May 27, 1992
Mylong, John: 1893—Sep 8, 1975
Myrtil, Odette: Jun 28, 1898—Nov 18, 1978
Nadel, Arthur H.: 1922—Feb 22, 1990
Nagel, Anne: Sep 30, 1912—Jul 6, 1966
Nagel, Conrad: Mar 16, 1897—Feb 24, 1970
Naish, J. Carrol: Jan 21, 1897—Jan 24, 1973
Nalder, Reggie: c. 1901—Nov 19, 1991
Naldi, Nita: Apr 1, 1899—Feb 17, 1961
Napier, Alan: Jan 7, 1903—Aug 8, 1988
Nash, June: 1911—Oct 8, 1979
Nash, Mary: Aug 15, 1885—Dec 3, 1976
Natheaux, Louis: 1898—Aug 23, 1942
Nazarro, Ray: Sep 25, 1902—Sep 8, 1986
Nazimova, Alla: Jun 4, 1879—Jul 13, 1945
Neagle, Anna (Dame): Oct 20, 1904—Jun 3, 1986
Neal, Tom: Jan 28, 1914—Aug 7, 1972
Nedell, Bernard: Oct 14, 1897—Nov 23, 1973
Negri, Pola: Dec 31, 1894—Aug 1, 1987
Neilan, Marshall A.: Apr 11, 1891—Oct 27, 1958
Neill, James: Dec 28, 1860—Mar 16, 1931
Neill, Richard B.: 1876—Apr 8, 1970
Neill, Roy William: 1886—Dec 14, 1946
Nelson, Ozzie: Mar 20, 1906—Jun 3, 1975
Nelson, Ralph: Aug 12, 1916—Dec 21, 1987
Nelson, Rick (Ricky): May 8, 1940—Dec 31, 1985
Nelson, Ruth: 1905—Sep 12, 1992
Nesbitt, Cathleen: Nov 24, 1889—Aug 2, 1982
Nesbitt, Frank M.: 1942—Jul 15, 1990
Nesbitt, Miriam: Sep 14, 1873—Aug 11, 1954
Nesmith, Ottola: 1888—Feb 7, 1972
Neumann, Kurt: Apr 5, 1980—Aug 21, 1958
Newberg, Frank: 1886—Nov 11, 1969
Newell, David: 1905—Jan 25, 1980
Newell, William "Billy": 1894—Feb 21, 1967
Newfield, Sam: Dec 6, 1899—Nov 10, 1964
Newman, Thomas: 1931—Dec 20, 1991
Newton, Robert: Jun 1, 1905—Mar 25, 1956
Niblo, Fred: Jan 6, 1874—Nov 11, 1948
Nichols, Barbara: Dec 30, 1929—Oct 5, 1976
Nichols, Dudley: Apr 6, 1895—Jan 4, 1960
Niesen, Gertrude: Jul 8, 1910—Mar 27, 1975
Nilsson, Anna Q.: Mar 30, 1888—Feb 11, 1974
Nissen, Greta: Jan 30, 1906—May 15, 1988
Niven, David: Mar 1, 1909—Jul 29, 1983
Nixon, Marion: Oct 20, 1904—Feb 13, 1983
Nolan, Bob: 1908—Jun 16, 1980
Nolan, James F.: Nov 29, 1913—Jul 29, 1985
Nolan, Lloyd: Aug 11, 1902—Sep 27, 1985
Nolan, Mary: Dec 18, 1905—Oct 31, 1948
Noonan, Tommy: Apr 29, 1922—Apr 24, 1968
Normand, Mabel: Nov 10, 1894—Feb 23, 1930
North, Wilfrid: Jan 16, 1863—Jun 3, 1935
Northrup, Harry S.: Jul 31, 1875—Jul 2, 1936
Norton, Barry: Jun 16, 1905—Aug 24, 1956
Norton, Edgar: Aug 11, 1868—Feb 6, 1953
Norton, Jack: 1889—Oct 15, 1958
Norworth, Jack: Jan 5, 1879—Sep 1, 1959
Novak, Eva: 1899—Apr 17, 1988
Novak, Jane: 1896—Feb 6, 1990
Novarro, Ramon: Feb 6, 1899—Oct 31, 1968

Novello, Jay: 1904—Sep 2, 1982
Novello, Roselle: 1897—Jan 16, 1992
Nugent, Elliott: Sep 20, 1899—Aug 9, 1980
Nugent, J. C.: Apr 6, 1875—Apr 21, 1947
Nureyev, Rudolf: Mar 17, 1938—Jan 6, 1993
Nye, Carroll: Oct 4, 1901—Mar 17, 1974
Oakie, Jack: Nov 12, 1903—Jan 23, 1978
Oakland, Simon: Aug 28, 1922—Aug 29, 1983
Oakland, Vivien: 1895—Aug 1, 1958
Oakman, Wheeler: 1890—Mar 19, 1949
Oates, Warren: Jul 5, 1928—Apr 3, 1982
Ober, Philip: Mar 23, 1902—Sep 13, 1982
Ober, Robert: 1882—Dec 7, 1950
Oberon, Merle: Feb 19, 1911—Nov 23, 1979
Oboler, Arch: Dec 7, 1909—Mar 19, 1987
O'Brien, David "Dave":
                    May 13, 1912—Nov 8, 1969
O'Brien, Edmond: Sep 10, 1915—May 8, 1985
O'Brien, Eloise Taylor: 1903—Dec 16, 1987
O'Brien, Eugene: Nov 14, 1882—Apr 29, 1966
O'Brien, Pat: Nov 11, 1899—Oct 15, 1983
O'Brien, Richard: 1918—Mar 29, 1983
O'Brien, Tom: Jul 25, 1891—Jun 9, 1947
O'Brien-Moore, Erin: May 2, 1903—May 3, 1979
Ocko, Daniel: 1913—Aug 29, 1991
O'Connell, Arthur: Mar 29, 1908—May 18, 1981
O'Connell, Hugh: Aug 4, 1898—Jan 19, 1943
O'Connor, Edward: Feb 20, 1862—May 15, 1932
O'Connor, Frank: Apr 11, 1888—Nov 22, 1959
O'Connor, Harry M.: 1873—Jul 10, 1971
O'Connor, Kevin: May 7, 1937—Jun 22, 1991
O'Connor, Robert Emmett: 1885—Sep 4, 1962
O'Connor, Una: Oct 23, 1880—Feb 4, 1959
O'Davoren, Vesey: 1889—May 30, 1989
O'Day, Nell: 1910—Jan 3, 1989
O'Donnell, Cathy: Jul 6, 1925—Apr 11, 1970
O'Donnell, Gene: 1911—Nov 22, 1992
Offerman, George, Jr.: Mar 14, 1917—Jan 14, 1963
Ogle, Charles: Jun 5, 1865—Oct 11, 1940
O'Hanlon, George: 1913—Feb 11, 1989
O'Hara, Shirley: 1911—May 5, 1979
O'Keefe, Dennis: Mar 28, 1908—Aug 31, 1968
O'Keefe, James Winston "Win":
                    1910— Aug 4, 1991
Oland, Warner: Oct 3, 1880—Aug 5, 1938
Olcott, Sidney: Sep 20, 1873—Dec 16, 1949
Oldfield, Barney: Jan 29, 1878—Oct 4, 1946
Oliver, David: 1962—Nov 12, 1992
Oliver, Edna May: Nov 9, 1883—Nov 9, 1942
Oliver, Guy: 1875—Sep 1, 1932
Oliver, Ruth: 1910—Oct 3, 1989
Oliver, Susan: Feb 13, 1937—May 10, 1990
Oliver, Virgil, Jr.: 1916—Jun 3, 1988
Olivier, Laurence (Sir): May 22, 1907—Jul 11, 1989
Olmstead, Gertrude: Nov 10, 1904—Jan 18, 1975
Olmsted, Nelson: 1914—Apr 8, 1992
Olsen, Moroni: Jul 27, 1889—Nov 22, 1954
Olsen, Ole: Nov 6, 1892—Jan 26, 1963
O'Malley, J. Pat: 1901—Feb 27, 1985
O'Malley, Pat: Sep 3, 1892—May 21, 1966
O'Malley, Rex: Jan 2, 1901—May 1, 1976
O'Moore, Patrick: 1909—Dec 10, 1983
O'Neal, Anne: Dec 23, 1893—Nov 24, 1971
O'Neal, Frederick: Aug 27, 1905—Aug 25, 1992
O'Neil, Barbara: Jul 10, 1909—Sep 3, 1980

O'Neill, Henry: Aug 10, 1891—May 18, 1961
O'Neill, Nance: Oct 8, 1874—Feb 7, 1965
O'Neill, Peggy: 1924—Apr 13, 1945
O'Neill, Sally: Oct 23, 1910—Jun 18, 1968
Ophuls, Max: May 6, 1902—Mar 26, 1957
Orlando, Don: 1912—Dec 10, 1987
O'Rourke, Heather: Dec 27, 1975—Feb 1, 1988
Orth, Frank: Feb 21, 1880—Mar 17, 1962
Osborne, Jefferson: 1871—Jun 11, 1932
Osborne, Lennie "Bud": Jul 20, 1881—Feb 2, 1964
Osborne, Vivienne: Dec 10, 1896—Jun 10, 1961
O'Shea, Michael: Mar 17, 1906—Dec 3, 1973
O'Shea, Oscar: 1882—Apr 6, 1960
Ostriche, Muriel: 1897—May 3, 1989
Oswald, Gerd: Jun 9, 1916—May 22, 1989
O'Toole, Ollie: 1913—Feb 25, 1992
Ottiano, Rafaela: Mar 4, 1894—Aug 18, 1942
Ouspenskaya, Maria: Jul 29, 1876—Dec 3, 1949
Overman, Jack: 1916—Jan 4, 1950
Overman, Lynne: Sep 19, 1887—Feb 19, 1943
Overton, Evart Emerson: 1889—Jan 27, 1949
Overton, Frank: 1918—Apr 24, 1967
Ovey, George: Dec 13, 1870—Sep 13, 1951
Owen, Catherine Dale: Jul 28, 1900—Sep 7, 1965
Owen, Garry: Dec 18, 1902—Jun 1, 1951
Owen, Reginald: Aug 5, 1887—Nov 5, 1972
Owen, Seena: 1894—Aug 15, 1966
Owsley, Monroe: 1901—Jun 7, 1937
Padden, Sarah: ____—Dec 4, 1967
Paddock, Charles: Nov 8, 1900—Jul 21, 1943
Padula, Vincent: 1900—Jan 16, 1967
Page, Gale: Jul 23, 1913—Jan 8, 1983
Page, Geraldine: Nov 22, 1924—Jun 13, 1987
Page, Paul: May 13, 1903—Apr 28, 1974
Paget, Alfred: 1880—1925
Paige, Jean: 1895—Dec 15, 1990
Paige, Mabel: 1880—Feb 8, 1954
Paige, Robert: Dec 2, 1910—Dec 21, 1987
Paiva, Nestor: Jun 30, 1905—Sep 9, 1966
Pal, George: Feb 1, 1908—May 2, 1980
Palange, Inez: 1889—Oct 16, 1962
Pale, Edward Lionel: 1867—Oct 24, 1944
Pallette, Eugene: Jul 8, 1889—Sep 3, 1954
Palmer, Lilli: May 24, 1914—Jan 27, 1986
Palmer, Maria: Sep 5, 1924—Sep 6, 1981
Palmer, Patricia: Sep 14, 1895—Oct 21, 1964
Pangborn, Franklin: Jan 23, 1893—Jul 20, 1958
Panzer, Paul Wolfgang: Nov 3, 1872—Aug 16, 1958
Parfrey, Woodrow: 1923—Jul 29, 1984
Paris, Freddie: 1928—May 15, 1991
Paris, Jerry: Jul 25, 1925—Mar 31, 1986
Parker, Barnett: Sep 11, 1886—Aug 5, 1941
Parker, Eddie: Dec 12, 1900—Jan 20, 1960
Parker, Lew: Oct 28, 1907—Oct 27, 1972
Parker, Vivian: 1897—Feb 2, 1974
Parks, Bert: Dec 30, 1914—Feb 2, 1992
Parks, Larry: Dec 13, 1914—Apr 13, 1975
Parks, Mama Lu: 1929—Sep 23, 1990
Parkyakarkus: 1904—Nov 24, 1958
Parnell, Emory: 1894—Jun 22, 1979
Parnell, James: 1923—Dec 27, 1961
Parrish, Helen: Mar 12, 1922—Feb 22, 1959
Parrott, James: 1892—May 10, 1939
Parry, Harvey: 1900—Sep 18, 1985
Parsons, Milton: May 19, 1904—May 15, 1980

Pasha, Kalla: 1877—Jun 10, 1933
Paterson, Pat: Apr 7, 1911—Aug 24, 1978
Patrick, Dorothy: 1922—May 31, 1987
Patrick, Gail: Jun 20, 1911—Jul 6, 1980
Patrick, Lee: Nov 22, 1911—Nov 25, 1982
Patricola, Tom: Jan 27, 1894—Jan 1, 1950
Patterson, Elizabeth: Nov 22, 1874—Jan 31, 1966
Patterson, Hank: Oct 9, 1888—Aug 23, 1975
Patton, William "Bill": 1894—Dec 12, 1951
Pawle, J. Lennox: Apr 27, 1872—Feb 22, 1936
Pawley, Edward: 1904—Jan 27, 1988
Pawley, William: Jul 21, 1905—Jun 15, 1952
Paxinou, Katina: Dec 17, 1900—Feb 22, 1973
Paxton, Sidney: 1861—Oct 13, 1930
Payne, Edna: Dec 5, 1891—Jan 31, 1953
Payne, John: May 23, 1912—Dec 6, 1989
Payne, Louis "Lou": Jan 13, 1876—Aug 14, 1953
Payson, Blanche: 1881—Jul 3, 1964
Payton, Barbara: Nov 16, 1927—May 8, 1967
Payton, Claude: Mar 30, 1882—Mar 1, 1955
Peacock, Lillian: Oct 23, 1890—Aug 18, 1918
Pearce, Alice: Oct 16, 1913—Mar 3, 1966
Pearce, George C.: 1865—Aug 12, 1940
Peardon, Patricia: 1924—Apr 22, 1993
Pearson, Melissa C.: 1963—Jul 18, 1992
Pearson, Virginia: Mar 7, 1888—Jun 6, 1958
Peary, Harold: Jul 25, 1908—Mar 30, 1985
Peck, Ed: 1917—Sep 12, 1992
Peckinpah, Sam: Feb 21, 1925—Dec 28, 1984
Peers, Joan: 1911—Jul 11, 1975
Pegg, Vester: May 28, 1889—Feb 19, 1951
Peil, Edward, Jr.: 1908—Nov 7, 1962
Peil, Edward (Sr.): 1888—Dec 29, 1958
Peixoto, Mario: 1909—Feb 3, 1992
Pelicer, Pina: 1940—Dec 10, 1964
Pelish, Thelma: 1938—Mar 6, 1983
Pelletier, Denise: 1929—May 24, 1976
Pemberton, Brock: Dec 14, 1885—Mar 11, 1950
Pendleton, Nat: Aug 9, 1895—Oct 11, 1967
Penn, Leonard: 1907—May 20, 1975
Penner, Joe: Nov 11, 1905—Jan 10, 1941
Pennick, Jack: Dec 7, 1895—Aug 16, 1964
Pennington, Ann: Dec 23, 1892—Nov 4, 1971
Pepper, Barbara: May 31, 1912—Jul 18, 1969
Pepper, Buddy: Apr 21, 1922—Feb 7, 1993
Percival, Walter C.: 1887—Jan 28, 1934
Percy, Eileen: 1901—Jul 29, 1973
Periolat, George: 1876—Feb 20, 1940
Perkins, Anthony (Tony): Apr 4, 1932—Sep 12, 1992
Perkins, Osgood: May 16, 1892—Sep 21, 1937
Perkins, Voltaire: 1897—Oct 10, 1977
Perrin, Jack: Jul 25, 1896—Dec 17, 1967
Perrin, Vic: 1916—Jul 4, 1989
Perry, Robert E. "Bob": 1879—Jan 8, 1962
Perry, Walter: Sep 14, 1868—Jan 22, 1954
Perry, Wanda: 1918—Feb 17, 1985
Peters, House, Sr.: Mar 12, 1879—Dec 7, 1967
Peters, Ralph: 1903—Jun 5, 1959
Peters, Susan: Jul 3, 1921—Oct 23, 1952
Peterson, Alan: 1938—Dec 30, 1992
Peterson, Dorothy: c. 1900—1979
Peterson, Skip: 1940—May 18, 1992
Petrie, Howard A.: 1907—Mar 26, 1968
Petrova, Olga: 1886—Nov 30, 1977

Petrushka, Gina: __—Nov 20, 1991
Pettyjohn, Angelique: 1944—Feb 14, 1992
Peyton, Lawrence R. "Larry": ____—Oct 1918
Phelps, Lee: 1894—Mar 19, 1953
Philbrook, James: 1924—Oct 24, 1982
Philips, Mary: Jan 23, 1901—Apr 22, 1975
Phillips, Barney: Oct 20, 1913—Aug 17, 1982
Phillips, Dorothy: Oct 30, 1889—Mar 1, 1980
Phillips, Edward N.: Aug 14, 1899—Feb 22, 1965
Phillips, Edward R.: ____—Aug 29, 1915
Phillips, Wendell K.: 1908—Oct 13, 1991
Phipps, Sally: 1911—Mar 17, 1978
Piazza, Ben: Jul 30, 1934—Sep 7, 1991
Pichel, Irving: Jun 24, 1891—Jul 13, 1954
Pickens, Jane: 1909—Feb 20, 1992
Pickens, Slim: Jun 29, 1919—Dec 8, 1983
Pickford, Jack: Aug 18, 1896—Jan 3, 1933
Pickford, Mary: Apr 9, 1893—May 29, 1979
Picon, Molly: Jun 1, 1898— Apr 5, 1992
Pidgeon, Walter: Sep 23, 1897—Sep 25, 1984
Pierce, Arthur C.: 1923—Nov 17, 1987
Pierce, Hugh Preston: 1940—Dec 12, 1992
Pierlot, Francis: 1876—May 11, 1955
Pierret, Leonce: May 13, 1880—Aug 15, 1936
Pierson, Arthur: 1902—Jan 1, 1975
Pigott, Tempe: 1884—Oct 13, 1962
Pinero, Miguel: 1947—Jun 16, 1988
Pinza, Ezio: May 8, 1892—May 9, 1957
Piteoff, Sacha: 1920—Jul 21, 1990
Pitts, Zasu: Jan 3, 1898—Jun 7, 1963
Platt, Edward: Feb 14, 1916—Mar 30, 1974
Poff, Lon: Feb 8, 1870—Aug 8, 1952
Pollack, Ben: 1904—Jun 7, 1971
Pollard, Harold "Snub": 1886—Jan 19, 1962
Pollard, Harry A.: Jan 23, 1879—Jul 6, 1934
Polo, Eddie: 1875—Jun 14, 1961
Pond, Barbara: ____—Jun 16, 1990
Pons, Lily: Apr 12, 1898—Feb 13, 1976
Poole, Roy: 1924—Jul 1, 1986
Porcasi, Paul: 1880—Aug 8, 1946
Porter, Edwin Stratton: Apr 21, 1869—Apr 30, 1941
Post, Charles A. "Buddy":
                    Nov 3, 1897—Dec 20, 1952
Post, Guy Bates: Sep 22, 1875—Jan 16, 1968
Potel, Victor: 1889—Mar 8, 1947
Potter, H. C.: Nov 18, 1904—Aug 31, 1977
Powell, David: 1885—Apr 16, 1925
Powell, Dick: Nov 14, 1904—Jan 2, 1963
Powell, Eleanor: Nov 21, 1912—Feb 11, 1982
Powell, Lee B.: May 15, 1908—Jul 8, 1944
Powell, Russ(ell): Sep 16, 1875—Nov 28, 1950
Powell, William: Jul 29, 1892—Mar 5, 1984
Power, Hartley: Mar 14, 1894—Jan 29, 1966
Power, Tyrone (Jr.): May 5, 1913—Nov 15, 1958
Power, Tyrone (Sr.): May 2, 1869—Dec 30, 1931
Powers, Tom: Jul 7, 1890—Nov 9, 1955
Prager, Stanley: Jan 8, 1917—Jan 18, 1972
Pratt, Purnell B.: Oct 20, 1886—Jul 25, 1941
Preisser, June: 1923—Sep 19, 1984
Preminger, Otto: Dec 5, 1906—Apr 23, 1986
Prentice, Keith: 1940—Sep 27, 1992
Presley, Elvis: Jan 8, 1935—Aug 16, 1977
Preston, Robert: Jun 8, 1917—Mar 21, 1987
Preston, Wayde: 1930—Feb 6, 1992
Pretty, Arline: Sep 5, 1893—Apr 14, 1978

Prevost, Marie: Nov 8, 1893—Jan 21, 1937
Price, Hal: Jun 14, 1886—Apr 15, 1964
Price, Kate: Feb 13, 1872—Jan 4, 1943
Price, Stanley L.: 1900—Jul 13, 1955
Prickett, Maudie: 1915—Apr 14, 1976
Priestley, Thomas A: 1918—Jan 28, 1993
Pringle, Aileen: Jul 23, 1895—Dec 16, 1989
Prinze, Freddie: Jun 22, 1954—Jan 29, 1977
Prosser, Hugh: 1906—Nov 8, 1952
Prouty, Jed: Apr 6, 1879—May 10, 1956
Provenza, Sal D.: 1946—Dec 25, 1991
Prud'Homme, Cameron:
                Dec 16, 1892—Nov 27, 1967
Prud-Homme, George: 1901—Jun 11, 1972
Pryor, Roger: Aug 27, 1901—Jan 31, 1974
Puglia, Frank: 1892—Oct 25, 1975
Purcell, Irene: Aug 7, 1903—Jul 9, 1972
Purcell, Richard "Dick":
                Aug 6, 1908—Apr 10, 1944
Purdy, Constance: c. 1885—Apr 1, 1960
Purviance, Edna: Oct 21, 1894—Jan 13, 1958
Qualen, John: Dec 8, 1899—Sep 17, 1987
Quigley, Charles: Feb 12, 1906—Aug 5, 1964
Quillan, Eddie: Mar 31, 1907—Jul 19, 1990
Quine, Richard: Nov 12, 1920—Jun 10, 1989
Quinn, Louis: 1915—Sep 14, 1988
Quinn, James "Jimmie": 1885—Aug 22, 1940
Quirk, William "Billy": 1881—Apr 20, 1926
Radner, Gilda: Jun 28, 1946—May 20, 1989
Rafferty, Chips: 1909—May 27, 1971
Raffetto, Michael: 1899—May 31, 1990
Raft, George: Sep 26, 1895—Nov 24, 1980
Ragland, Rags: Aug 23, 1905—Aug 20, 1946
Raine, Jack: May 18, 1897—May 30, 1979
Raine, Jennifer: 1932—Jan 5, 1993
Raines, Ella: Aug 6, 1921—May 30, 1988
Rains, Claude: Nov 10, 1889—May 30, 1967
Raker, Lorin: May 8, 1891—Dec 25, 1959
Ralph, Jessie: Nov 5, 1864—May 30, 1944
Ralston, Howard: 1905—Jun 1, 1992
Ralston, Jobyna: Nov 24, 1902—Jan 22, 1967
Rambeau, Marjorie: Jul 15, 1889—Jul 7, 1970
Rambo, Dirk: Nov 13, 1941—Feb 5, 1967
Ramirez, Carlos: 1913—Dec 11, 1986
Ramos, Lou: 1941—Jul 31, 1992
Ramsey, Anne: 1929—Aug 11, 1988
Rand, Sally: Jan 2, 1903—Aug 30, 1979
Randall, Addison "Jack": 1907—Jul 16, 1945
Randolph (Randolf), Anders:
                Dec 18, 1876—Jul 3, 1930
Randolph, Amanda: 1902—Aug 24, 1967
Randolph, Lillian: 1915—Sep 12, 1980
Rankin, Arthur: Aug 30, 1900—Mar 23, 1947
Rankin, Doris: 1880—1946
Rappaport, David: Nov 23, 1952—May 2, 1990
Rappe, Virginia: 1896—Sep 9, 1921
Rasulala, Thalmus: Nov 16, 1939—Oct 9, 1991
Ratcliffe, E. J.: 1863—Sep 28, 1948
Rathbone, Basil: Jun 13, 1892—Jul 21, 1967
Ratoff, Gregory: Apr 20, 1897—Dec 14, 1960
Rattenberry, Harry: 1860—Dec 10, 1925
Rawlins, Lester: Sep 24, 1924—Mar 22, 1988
Rawlinson, Herbert: Nov 15, 1885—Jul 12, 1953
Ray, Aldo: Sep 25, 1926—Mar 27, 1991
Ray, Charles: Mar 15, 1891—Nov 23, 1943

Ray, Harry Milton: 1947—Oct 1, 1992
Ray, Jack: 1917—Nov 1, 1975
Ray, James: 1932—Dec 3, 1989
Ray, Johnnie: 1927—Feb 24, 1990
Ray, Nicholas: Aug 7, 1911—Jun 15, 1979
Raymond, Frances "Frankie": 1869—Jun 18, 1961
Raymond, Jack: Dec 14, 1901—Dec 5, 1951
Razetto, Stella: 1881—Sep 21, 1948
Read, Barbara: Dec 29, 1917—Dec 12, 1963
Reade, Charles A.: 1910—Aug 29, 1992
Reardon, Michael T., Jr.: 1942—May 26, 1991
Red Wing: 1884—Mar 12, 1974
Redfield, William "Billy":
                Jan 26, 1927—Aug 17, 1976
Redgrave, Michael: Mar 20, 1908—Mar 21, 1985
Redwing, Rodd: 1905—May 30, 1971
Reed, Alan: Aug 20, 1907—Jun 14, 1977
Reed, Donald: Jul 23, 1902—Feb 27, 1973
Reed, Donna: Jan 27, 1921—Jan 14, 1986
Reed, Florence: Jan 10, 1883—Nov 21, 1967
Reed, George H.: Nov 27, 1866—Nov 6, 1952
Reed, Jay Theodore: 1887—Feb 24, 1959
Reed, Luther: Jul 14, 1888—Nov 16, 1961
Reed, Marshall: May 28, 1917—Apr 15, 1980
Reed, Robert: Oct 19, 1932—May 12, 1992
Reed, Vivian: 1894—Jul 19, 1989
Reeves, George: Apr 6, 1914—Jun 16, 1959
Reeves, Richard: Aug 10, 1912—Mar 17, 1967
Regas, George: Nov 9, 1890—Dec 13, 1940
Regas, Pedro: Apr 12, 1882—Aug 10, 1974
Reichenbach, Francois: 1922—Feb 2, 1993
Reicher, Frank: Dec 2, 1875—Jan 19, 1965
Reichert, Kittens: 1911—Jan 11, 1990
Reid, Carl Benton: 1893—Mar 16, 1973
Reid, Kate: Nov 4, 1930—Mar 28, 1993
Reid, Wallace, Jr.: 1917—Feb 26, 1990
Reid, Wallace (Sr.): Apr 15, 1891—Jan 18, 1923
Reis, Irving: May 7, 1906—Jul 3, 1953
Remick, Lee: Dec 14, 1935—Jul 2, 1991
Remme, John: 1936—Jan 18, 1992
Remus, Romoloa: _____—Feb 17, 1987
Renaldo, Duncan: Apr 23, 1904—Sep 3, 1980
Renavent, George: Apr 23, 1894—Jan 2, 1969
Renick, Ruth: _____—May 7, 1984
Rennie, James: 1890—Jul 31, 1965
Rennie, Michael: Aug 29, 1909—Jun 10, 1971
Renoir, Jean: Sep 15, 1904—Feb 12, 1979
Repp, Stafford: Apr 26, 1918—Nov 5, 1974
Revere, Anne: Jun 25, 1903—Dec 18, 1990
Rey, Alejandro: Feb 8, 1930—May 21, 1987
Reynolds, Adeline DeWalt:
                Sep 19, 1862—Aug 13, 1961
Reynolds, Craig: Jul 15, 1907—Oct 22, 1949
Reynolds, Helen: 1925—Mar 28, 1990
Reynolds, Jack: 1907—Sep 30, 1990
Reynolds, Quentin: 1903—Mar 17, 1965
Reynolds, Vera: Nov 25, 1899—Apr 22, 1962
Rhodes, "Little" Billy: Aug 15, 1894—Jul 24, 1967
Rhodes, Billie: 1895—Mar 12, 1988
Rhodes, Erik: Feb 10, 1906—Feb 17, 1990
Rhodes, Grandon: 1905—Jun 9, 1987
Rhodes, Hari: Apr 10, 1932—Jan 14, 1992
Riano, Renie: _____—Jul 3, 1971
Rice, Florence: Feb 14, 1911—Feb 22, 1974
Rice, Frank: May 13, 1892—Jan 9, 1936

Rice, Grantland: 1881—Jul 13, 1954
Rice, Jack: May 14, 1893—Dec 14, 1968
Rich, Irene: Oct 13, 1891—Apr 22, 1988
Rich, Lillian: 1900—Jan 5, 1954
Rich, Vernon: 1906—Feb 7, 1978
Rich, Vivian: May 1893—Nov 17, 1957
Richards, Addison W.: Oct 20, 1887—Mar 22, 1964
Richards, Cully: 1910—Jun 17, 1978
Richards, Frank: Sep 15, 1909—Apr 15, 1992
Richards, Gordon: Oct 27, 1893—Jan 13, 1964
Richards, Grant: 1916—Jul 4, 1963
Richards, Keith: 1915—Mar 23, 1987
Richards, Paul: 1924—Dec 10, 1974
Richardson, Frankie: Sep 6, 1898—Jan 30, 1962
Richardson, James G.: Aug 22, 1945—Feb 20, 1983
Richardson, Tony: Jun 5, 1928—Nov 14, 1991
Richetts, Thomas "Tom": 1853—Jan 20, 1939
Richman, Charles: Jan 12, 1865—Dec 1, 1940
Richmond, Kane: Dec 23, 1906—Mar 22, 1973
Richmond, Warner: Jan 11, 1895—Jun 19, 1948
Rickson, Joe: Sep 6, 1880—Jan 8, 1958
Ridgely, Cleo: 1894—Aug 18, 1962
Ridgely, John: Sep 6, 1909—Jan 18, 1968
Ridges, Stanley: Jul 17, 1891—Apr 22, 1951
Riehl, Kate (Kay): 1899—Jan 8, 1988
Riga, Nadine: 1909—Dec 11, 1968
Riley, Alice Mary: 1941—Apr 19, 1992
Riley, Larry: Jun 20, 1953—Jun 6, 1992
Ring, Blanche: Apr 24, 1876—Jan 13, 1961
Ring, Cyril: 1893—Jul 17, 1967
Rini, David: 1952—Jul 20, 1992
Ripley, Robert L.: Dec 25, 1893—May 27, 1949
Risdon, Elisabeth: Apr 26, 1887—Dec 20, 1958
Riss, Dan: 1910—Aug 28, 1970
Ritchard, Cyril: Dec 1, 1897—Dec 18, 1977
Ritchie, Billie: 1877—Jul 6, 1921
Ritchie, Franklin: _____—Jan 26, 1918
Ritt, Martin: Mar 2, 1920—Dec 8, 1990
Ritter, Tex: Jan 12, 1906—Jan 2, 1974
Ritter, Thelma: Feb 14, 1905—Feb 5, 1969
Ritz, Al: Aug 27, 1901—Dec 22, 1965
Ritz, Harry: May 22, 1906—Mar 29, 1986
Ritz, Jimmy: Oct 5, 1903—Nov 17, 1985
Rivero, Julian: Jul 25, 1891—Feb 24, 1976
Roach, Bert: Aug 21, 1891—Feb 16, 1971
Roach, Hal: Jan 14, 1892—Nov 2, 1992
Robards, Jason, Sr.: Dec 31, 1892—Apr 4, 1963
Robbins, Duke: 1921—Sep 16, 1992
Robbins, Fred: Sep 28, 1919—Jun 23, 1992
Robbins, Gale: May 7, 1922—Feb 18, 1980
Robbins, Roy "Skeeter Bill": _____—Nov 29, 1933
Rober, Richard: May 14, 1906—May 26, 1952
Roberson, Chuck: 1919—Jun 8, 1988
Roberti, Lyda: May 20, 1906—Mar 12, 1938
Roberts, Edith: 1899—Aug 20, 1935
Roberts, Florence: Mar 16, 1861—Jun 6, 1940
Roberts, Leona: 1880—Jan 30, 1954
Roberts, Rachel: Sep 20, 1927—Nov 27, 1980
Roberts, Roy: Mar 19, 1900—May 28, 1975
Roberts, Stephen: Nov 23, 1895—Jul 18, 1936
Roberts, Theodore: Oct 2, 1861—Dec 14, 1928
Robertson, Hugh A: 1932—Jan 10, 1988
Robertson, John Stuart: Jun 14, 1878—Nov 7, 1964
Robertson, Willard: Jan 1, 1886—Apr 5, 1948
Robeson, Paul: Apr 9, 1898—Jan 23, 1976

Robinson, Bartlett: c. 1912—Mar 28, 1986
Robinson, Bill "Bojangles":
May 25, 1878—Nov 25, 1949
Robinson, Dewey: 1898—Dec 11, 1950
Robinson, Edward G., Jr.:
Mar 19, 1933—Feb 26, 1974
Robinson, Edward G. (Sr.):
Dec 12, 1893—Jan 26, 1973
Robinson, Gertrude R.: 1891—Mar 19, 1962
Robles, Rudy: Apr 28, 1910—Aug 1970
Robson, Flora: Mar 28, 1902—Jul 7, 1984
Robson, Mark: Dec 4, 1913—Jun 20, 1978
Robson, May: Apr 19, 1858—Oct 20, 1942
Roche, John: Feb 6, 1896—Nov 10, 1952
Rochelle, Claire: c. 1910—May 23, 1981
Rodgers, Walter: 1887—Apr 24, 1951
Rodriguez, Estelita: Jul 2, 1913—Mar 12, 1966
Rogell, Albert S.: Aug 1, 1901—Apr 7, 1988
Rogers, Eugene C.: 1867—Mar 9, 1919
Rogers, Jean: Mar 25, 1916—Feb 24, 1992
Rogers, Rena: 1901—Feb 19, 1966
Rogers, Will: Nov 4, 1879—Aug 15, 1935
Roland, Ruth: Aug 26, 1892—Sep 22, 1937
Rolf, Erik: ____—May 28, 1957
Roman, Paul Reid: 1936—Nov 17, 1991
Romanoff, Michael: Feb 21, 1890—Sep 1, 1971
Romanov, Natasha Galitzine: 1907—Mar 28, 1989
Rooney, Pat, II: Jul 4, 1880—Sep 9, 1962
Roope, Fay: 1893—Sep 13, 1961
Roosevelt, Buddy: Jun 25, 1898—Oct 6, 1973
Roper, Jack: Mar 25, 1904—Nov 28, 1966
Roquemore, Henry: Mar 13, 1888—Jun 30, 1943
Rork, Ann: 1909—Jan 23, 1988
Rorke, Hayden: Oct 23, 1910—Aug 19, 1987
Roscoe, Alan: Aug 23, 1887—Mar 8, 1933
Rose, Blanche: 1878—Jan 5, 1953
Rose, Bob: 1902—Mar 8, 1993
Rose, George: Feb 19, 1920—May 1, 1988
Rose, Jane: Feb 7, 1912—Jun 29, 1979
Rosemond, Clinton: 1883—Mar 10, 1966
Rosen, Philip E.: May 8, 1888—Oct 22, 1951
Rosenblatt, Martin: 1917—Jun 24, 1991
Rosenbloom, "Slapsie" Maxie:
Sep 6, 1903—Mar 6, 1976
Rosing, Bodil: 1878—Jan 1, 1942
Rosley, Adrian: 1890—Mar 5, 1937
Ross, Anthony: 1906—Oct 26, 1955
Ross, Betty: 1880—Feb 1, 1947
Ross, Frank: Aug 12, 1904—Feb 18, 1990
Ross, Joe E.: Mar 15, 1905—Aug 13, 1982
Ross, Shirley: Jan 7, 1909—Mar 9, 1975
Ross, Thomas W.: Jan 22, 1875—Nov 14, 1959
Rossen, Robert: May 16, 1908—Feb 18, 1966
Rossitto, Angelo: 1908— Sep 21, 1991
Rosson, Arthur H.: 1887—Jun 17, 1960
Rosson, Richard "Dick":
Apr 4, 1893—May 31, 1953
Roth, Gene: 1903—Jul 19, 1976
Roth, Lillian: Dec 13, 1910—May 12, 1980
Rouse, Russell: 1916—Oct 2, 1987
Rousimoff, Andre: 1947—Jan 27, 1993
Rowan, Dan: Jul 2, 1922—Sep 22, 1987
Rowan, Donald W.: 1906—Feb 17, 1966
Rowland, Henry: 1914—Apr 26, 1984
Royce, Lionel: Mar 30, 1891—Apr 1, 1946

Royle, Selena: Nov 6, 1904—Apr 23, 1983
Rub, Christian: Apr 13, 1887—Apr 14, 1956
Ruben, J. Walter: Aug 14, 1899—Sep 18, 1942
Rubens, Alma: 1897—Jan 21, 1931
Rubenstein, Phil: 1941—Jun 26, 1992
Rubin, Benny: Feb 2, 1899—Jul 15, 1986
Ruby, Mary: 1894—Dec 13, 1987
Rudolph, Oscar: 1912—Feb 1, 1991
Ruggles, Charles: Feb 8, 1886—Dec 23, 1970
Ruggles, Wesley: Jun 11, 1889—Jan 8, 1972
Ruick, Barbara: 1932—Mar 3, 1974
Rumann, Sig (Siegfried):
Oct 11, 1884—Feb 14, 1967
Rusinow, Irving: 1915—Aug 2, 1990
Russell, Andy: Sep 16, 1920—Apr 16, 1992
Russell, Byron: 1884—Sep 4, 1963
Russell, Craig: 1948—Oct 30, 1990
Russell, Don: 1927—May 27, 1981
Russell, Gail: Sep 23, 1924—Aug 26, 1961
Russell, J. Gordon: Jan 11, 1883—Apr 21, 1935
Russell, John: Jan 3, 1921—Jan 19, 1991
Russell, Rosalind: Jun 4, 1907—Nov 28, 1976
Russell, William: Apr 12, 1886—Feb 18, 1929
Rutherford, Jack: 1893—Aug 21, 1982
Ruysdael, Basil: 1888—Oct 10, 1960
Ryan, Dick: 1897—Aug 12, 1969
Ryan, Edmon: 1905—Aug 4, 1984
Ryan, Frank: Oct 18, 1907—Dec 31, 1947
Ryan, Irene: Oct 17, 1903—Apr 26, 1973
Ryan, Joe: 1887—Dec 23, 1944
Ryan, Robert: Nov 11, 1909—Jul 11, 1973
Ryan, Sheila: Jun 8, 1921—Nov 4, 1975
Ryan, Tim: Jul 5, 1899—Oct 22, 1956
Sabu: Jan 27, 1924—Dec 2, 1963
Sachs, Scotty: 1953—Jun 11, 1992
Sagal, Boris: Oct 18, 1923—May 22, 1981
Sage, Willard: Aug 13, 1922—Mar 17, 1974
St. Clair, Malcolm: May 17, 1897—Jun 1, 1952
St. Jacques, Raymond: Mar 1, 1930—Aug 27, 1990
St. John, Al "Fuzzy" Sep 10, 1893—Jan 21, 1963
St. John, Howard: 1905—Mar 13, 1974
St. Polis, John: Nov 24, 1873—Oct 10, 1946
Sais, Marin: Aug 2, 1890—Dec 31, 1971
Sakall, S. Z. "Cuddles": Feb 2, 1884—Feb 12, 1955
Sakata, Harold "Oddjob": 1926—Jul 29, 1982
Sale, Charles "Chic": Aug 25, 1885—Nov 7, 1936
Sale, Richard: Dec 17, 1911—Mar 4, 1993
Sale, Virginia: 1900—Aug 23, 1992
Salmi, Albert: Mar 11, 1928—Apr 22, 1990
Salter, Thelma: ____—Nov 17, 1953
Sampson, Will: 1935—Jun 3, 1987
Samuel, Andrew: 1910—Mar 5, 1992
Sande, Walter: 1906—Feb 22, 1972
Sanders, Denis: Jan 21, 1929—Dec 10, 1987
Sanders, George: Jul 3, 1906—Apr 25, 1972
Sandford, "Tiny": Feb 26, 1894—Oct 29, 1961
Sandford, Ralph: May 21, 1899—Jun 20, 1963
Sandrich, Mark: Oct 26, 1900—Mar 5, 1945
Sands, Diana: Aug 22, 1934—Sep 21, 1973
Sansberry, Hope: 1896—Dec 14, 1990
Santell, Alfred: Sep 14, 1895—Jul 30, 1981
Santley, Frederic: Nov 28, 1888—May 14, 1953
Santley, Joseph: Jan 10, 1889—Aug 8, 1971
Santoro, Dean: Jan 30, 1938—Jun 10, 1987
Santschi, Tom: Oct 14, 1878—Apr 9, 1931

Sarno, Hector V.: 1880—Dec 16, 1953
Sasha, Kenny: 1953—Aug 1, 1992
Sato, Isao: 1950—Mar 9, 1990
Saum, Clifford: Dec 18, 1882—Mar 1943
Saunders, Jackie: Oct 6, 1892—Jul 14, 1954
Savalas, George: Dec 5, 1926—Oct 2, 1985
Saville, Ruth: 1893—Mar 31, 1985
Saville, Victor: Sep 15, 1897—May 8, 1979
Sawyer, Joseph: 1901—Apr 21, 1982
Sawyer, Laura: 1885—Sep 7, 1970
Saxe, Templar: Aug 22, 1865—Mar 23, 1935
Saxon, Hugh A.: Jan 14, 1869—May 14, 1945
Saylor, Syd: Mar 24, 1895—Dec 21, 1962
Sayre, Jeffrey: 1901—Sep 26, 1974
Scala, Gia: Mar 3, 1934—Apr 30, 1972
Scardon, Paul: May 6, 1874—Jan 17, 1954
Schable, Robert: 1873—Jul 1, 1947
Schaefer, Ann: 1870—May 3, 1957
Schaefer, Armand L.: Aug 5, 1898—Sep 26, 1967
Schaeffer, Rebecca: Nov 6, 1967—Jul 18, 1989
Schafer, Natalie: Nov 5, 1900—Apr 10, 1991
Schaffner, Franklin J.: May 30, 1920—Jul 2, 1989
Schary, Dore: Aug 31, 1905—Jul 7, 1980
Schertzinger, Victor: Apr 8, 1889—Oct 26, 1941
Schildkraut, Joseph: Mar 22, 1895—Jan 21, 1964
Schildkraut, Rudolph: 1862—Jul 15, 1930
Schilling, August E. "Gus":
Jun 20, 1908—Jun 16, 1957
Schneider, James: 1882—Feb 14, 1967
Schneider, Romy: Sep 23, 1938—May 29, 1982
Schnur, Jerome: 1924—Mar 12, 1990
Schoedsack, Ernest B. Jun 8, 1893—1979
Schorr, William: 1901—Jun 18, 1989
Schultz, Harry: 1883—Jul 5, 1935
Schumann-Heink, Ferdinand:
Aug 9, 1893—Sep 15, 1958
Schumm, Hans: 1897—Feb 2, 1990
Schunzel, Rheinhold: Nov 7, 1886—Sep 11, 1954
Schuster, Harold: Aug 1, 1902—Jul 19, 1986
Scott, Daniel: 1920—Dec 11, 1991
Scott, Fred: Feb 14, 1902—Dec 16, 1991
Scott, Hazel: Jun 11, 1920—Oct 2, 1981
Scott, Ken: 1928—Dec 2, 1986
Scott, Mabel Juliene: Nov 2, 1893—Oct 1, 1976
Scott, Randolph: Jan 23, 1898—Mar 3, 1987
Scott, Simon: 1920—Dec 11, 1991
Scott, Zachary: Feb 24, 1914—Oct 3, 1965
Scourby, Alexander: Nov 13, 1913—Feb 23, 1985
Seabury, Ynez: 1909—Apr 11, 1973
Seales, Franklyn, V.: Jul 15, 1953—May 13, 1990
Sears, Allan: 1887—Aug 18, 1942
Sears, Fred F. Jul 7, 1913—Nov 30, 1957
Seastrom (Sjostrom), Victor:
Sep 20, 1879—Jan 3, 1960
Seaton, George: Apr 17, 1911—Jul 28, 1979
Seaton, Scott: Mar 11, 1878—Jun 3, 1968
Sebastian, Dorothy: Apr 26, 1903—Apr 8, 1957
Seberg, Jean: Nov 13, 1938—Aug 30, 1979
Sedan, Rolfe: Jan 21, 1896—Sep 16, 1982
Seddon, Margaret: Nov 18, 1872—Apr 17, 1968
Sedgwick, Edward: Nov 7, 1892—May 7, 1953
Sedgwick, Josie: 1898—Apr 30, 1973
Seegar, Sara: 1914—Aug 12, 1990
Segal, Vivienne: Apr 19, 1897—Dec 29, 1992
Segwick, Edie: 1943—Nov 16, 1971

Segwick, Edward, Jr.: Nov 7, 1889—May 7, 1953
Seiter, William A.: Feb 8, 1895—Jul 26, 1964
Seitz, George B.: Jan 3, 1888—Jul 8, 1944
Selbie, Evelyn: Jul 6, 1882—Dec 7, 1950
Selby, Norman "Kid McCoy":
                 Oct 13, 1873—Apr 18, 1940
Selby, Sarah: 1906—Jan 7, 1980
Sellers, Peter: Sep 8, 1925—Jul 24, 1980
Sellon, Charles: Aug 24, 1878—Jun 26, 1937
Selwyn, Clarissa: Feb 26, 1886—Jun 13, 1948
Selwyn, Edgar: Oct 12, 1875—Feb 13, 1944
Semels, Harry: Nov 20, 1887—Mar 2, 1946
Semon, Larry: Jul 16, 1889—Oct 8, 1928
Sen Yung, Victor: 1915—Nov 9, 1980
Sennett, Mack: Jan 17, 1880—Nov 5, 1960
Senson, Karl: Jul 23, 1908—Oct 8, 1978
Servoss, Mary: 1888—Nov 20, 1968
Sessions, Almira: 1888—Aug 3, 1974
Sevareid, Eric: Nov 26, 1912—Jul 9, 1992
Seymour, Anne: Sep 11, 1909—Dec 8, 1988
Seymour, Harry: 1890—Nov 11, 1967
Shaiffer, Howard Charles "Tiny":
                 1918—Jan 24, 1967
Shannon, Cora: Jan 30, 1869—Aug 27, 1957
Shannon, Effie: May 13, 1867—Jul 24, 1954
Shannon, Ethel: 1898—Jul 14, 1951
Shannon, Frank Connolly: 1875—Feb 1, 1959
Shannon, Harry: Jun 13, 1890—Jul 27, 1964
Shannon, Peggy: Jan 10, 1909—May 11, 1941
Sharland, Reginald: 1887—Aug 21, 1944
Sharpe, David: 1910—Mar 30, 1980
Shaughnessy, Mickey: 1920—Jul 23, 1985
Shaw, C. Montague: Mar 23, 1884—Feb 6, 1968
Shaw, Reta: Sep 13, 1912—Jan 8, 1982
Shaw, Robert: Aug 9, 1925—Aug 27, 1978
Shaw, Steve: 1965—Dec 5, 1990
Shaw, Victoria: 1935—Aug 17, 1988
Shaw, Winifred: Feb 25, 1899—May 2, 1982
Shawlee, Joan: Mar 5, 1926—Mar 22, 1987
Shawley, Robert: 1927—May 9, 1990
Shawn, Dick: Dec 1, 1923—Apr 17, 1987
Shay, Dorothy: 1921—Oct 22, 1978
Shayne, Robert: Oct 4, 1900—Nov 29, 1992
Shayne, Tamara: 1903—Oct 23, 1983
Shdanoff, Elsa Schreiber: 1901—Jan 9, 1982
Shea, William: ____—Nov 5, 1918
Shean, Al: May 12, 1868—Aug 12, 1949
Shear, Barry: 1923—Jun 13, 1979
Shearer, Norma: Aug 10, 1900—Jun 12, 1983
Sheehan, John J.: Oct 22, 1890—Feb 15, 1952
Sheffield, Reginald: Feb 18, 1901—Dec 8, 1957
Shelby, Margaret: 1900—Dec 21, 1939
Sheldon, Richard: 1933—Feb 22, 1992
Shelly, Joshua: ____—Feb 16, 1990
Shelton, Don: 1912—Jun 19, 1976
Shelton, John: May 18, 1917—May 16, 1972
Shenar, Paul: Feb 12, 1936—Oct 11, 1989
Sher, Jack: Mar 16, 1913—Aug 23, 1988
Sheridan, Ann: Feb 21, 1915—Jan 21, 1967
Sheridan, Frank: Jun 11, 1869—Nov 24, 1943
Sherman, Fred E.: 1905—May 20, 1969
Sherman, George: Jul 14, 1908—Mar 15, 1991
Sherman, Hiram: Feb 11, 1908—Apr 11, 1989
Sherman, Lowell: Oct 11, 1885—Dec 28, 1934
Sherry, J. Barney: 1872—Feb 22, 1944

Shields, Arthur: Feb 15, 1896—Apr 27, 1970
Shirley, Bill: 1921—Aug 27, 1989
Shoemaker, Ann: Jan 10, 1891—Sep 18, 1978
Short, Antrim: 1900—Nov 23, 1972
Short, Gertrude: Apr 6, 1902—Jul 31, 1968
Shotwell, Marie: ____—Sep 18, 1934
Shriner, Herb: May 29, 1918—Apr 23, 1970
Shubert, Eddie: Jul 11, 1898—Jan 23, 1937
Shumway, Lee: 1884—Jan 4, 1959
Shumway, Walter: Aug 26, 1884—Jan 13, 1965
Shutta, Ethel: 1897—Feb 5, 1976
Sidney, George: Mar 18, 1876—Apr 29, 1945
Siegel, Bernard: Apr 19, 1868—Jul 9, 1940
Siegel, Don: Oct 26, 1912—Apr 20, 1991
Siegmann, George: 1883—Jun 22, 1928
Siegrist, Jeremy: 1973-Mar 30, 1993
Siletti, Mario G.: 1904—Apr 19, 1964
Sills, Milton: Jan 10, 1882—Sep 15, 1930
Silva, Trinidad, Jr.: 1950—Jul 31, 1988
Silver, Joe: Sep 28, 1922—Feb 27, 1989
Silvera, Frank: Jul 24, 1914—Jun 11, 1970
Silverheels, Jay: May 26, 1919—Mar 5, 1980
Silvers, Phil: May 11, 1912—Nov 1, 1985
Silvers, Sid: Jan 1, 1904—Aug 20, 1976
Simon, Robert F: Dec 2, 1909—Nov 29, 1992
Simon, S. Sylvan: Mar 9, 1910—May 17, 1951
Simpson, Ivan: Feb 4, 1875—Oct 12, 1951
Simpson, Mickey: 1913—Sep 23, 1985
Simpson, Russell: Jun 17, 1880—Dec 12, 1959
Sinclair, Robert B.: May 24, 1905—Jan 3, 1970
Sinclair, Ronald: Jan 21, 1924—Nov 21, 1992
Singleton, Catherine: 1904—Sep 9, 1969
Siodmak, Robert: Aug 8, 1900—Mar 10, 1973
Sirk, Douglas: Apr 26, 1900—Jan 14, 1987
Sisson, Vera: Jul 31, 1891—Aug 6, 1954
Skelly, Hal: May 31, 1891—Jun 16, 1934
Skinner, Cornelia Otis: May 30, 1901—Jul 9, 1979
Skipworth, Alison: Jul 25, 1863—Jul 5, 1952
Sleeper, Martha: Jun 24, 1907—Mar 25, 1983
Slezak, Walter: May 3, 1902—Apr 22, 1983
Sloane, Everett: Oct 1, 1909—Aug 6, 1965
Slyter, Fred: 1936—Feb 4, 1992
Smalley, Phillips: Aug 7, 1875—May 2, 1939
Smart, J. Scott: 1903—Jan 15, 1960
Smiley, Joseph W.: 1881—Dec 2, 1945
Smith, Albert J.: 1894—Apr 12, 1939
Smith, Art: 1900—Feb 24, 1973
Smith, C. Aubrey: Jul 21, 1863—Dec 20, 1948
Smith, Charles B.: ____—Dec 26, 1988
Smith, Clifford S.: Aug 22, 1894—Sep 17, 1937
Smith, Gerald: Jun 26, 1896—May 28, 1974
Smith, Harry: 1923—Nov 27, 1991
Smith, Howard I.: Aug 12, 1893—Jan 10, 1968
Smith, Jack: 1932—Sep 25, 1989
Smith, Kate: May 1, 1907—Jun 17, 1986
Smith, Kent: Mar 19, 1907—Apr 23, 1985
Smith, Pete: Sep 4, 1892—Jan 12, 1979
Smith, Queenie: Sep 8, 1902—Aug 5, 1978
Smith, Samantha: Jun 29, 1972—Aug 25, 1985
Smith, Stanley: 1905—Apr 13, 1974
Snegoff, Leonid: May 15, 1883—Feb 22, 1974
Snow, Marguerite: Sep 9, 1889—Feb 17, 1958
Snowden, Leigh: 1931—May 11, 1982
Soderling, Walter: Apr 13, 1872—Apr 10, 1948
Sofaer, Abraham: Oct 1, 1896—Jan 21, 1988

Sojin: Jan 30, 1891—Jul 28, 1954
Sokol, Mike: 1894—Aug 24, 1991
Sokoloff, Vladimir: Dec 26, 1889—Feb 14, 1962
Somerset, Paul: Feb 28, 1897—Apr 20, 1974
Sommer, Bert: 1948—Jul 23, 1990
Sondergaard, Gale: Feb 15, 1899—Aug 14, 1985
Soo, Jack: 1915—Jan 11, 1979
Sothern, Hugh: Jul 20, 1881—Apr 13, 1947
Soussanin, Nicholas: 1909—Apr 27, 1975
Space, Arthur: 1909—Jan 13, 1983
Spacey, John G.: 1895—Jan 2, 1940
Spain, Fay: 1933—May 1983
Sparks, Ned: 1883—Apr 2, 1957
Spear, Harry: Dec 16, 1921—Feb 10, 1969
Spencer, Douglas: 1910—Oct 10, 1960
Spinell, Joe: 1937—Jan 13, 1989
Spivy, Madame: 1907—Jan 7, 1971
Spratley, Thomas: 1913—Jun 10, 1967
Springsteen, R. G.: Sep 8, 1904—Dec 9, 1989
Stab, Ralph B.: Jul 21, 1899—Oct 22, 1969
Stafford, Hanley: Sep 22, 1898—Sep 9, 1968
Stahl, John M.: Jan 21, 1886—Jan 12, 1950
Stalker, John: 1923—Aug 23, 1990
Standing, Guy (Sir): Sep 1, 1873—Feb 24, 1937
Standing, Herbert, Jr.: 1884—Sep 23, 1955
Standing, Jack: 1886—Oct 26, 1917
Standing, Joan: Jun 21, 1903—Feb 3, 1979
Standing, Wyndham: Aug 23, 1880—Feb 1, 1963
Stanger, Hugo L.: ____—Jan 29, 1990
Stanlaws, Penrhyn: Mar 19, 1877—May 20, 1923
Stanley, Edwin: 1880—Dec 24, 1944
Stanley, Forrest: Aug 21, 1889—Aug 27, 1969
Stanton, Paul: Dec 21, 1884—Oct 9, 1955
Stanton, Will: Sep 18, 1885—Dec 18, 1969
Stanwyck, Barbara: Jul 16, 1907—Jan 20, 1990
Stark, Pauline: Jan 10, 1901—Feb 3, 1977
Starrett, Charles: Mar 28, 1903—Mar 22, 1986
Starrett, Jack: Nov 2, 1936—Mar 27, 1989
Steadman, John: 1910—Jan 28, 1993
Steadman, Vera: Jun 23, 1900—Dec 14, 1966
Stedman, Lincoln: 1907—Mar 22, 1948
Stedman, Myrtle: Mar 3, 1888—Jan 8, 1938
Steele, Bob: Jan 23, 1906—Dec 21, 1988
Steele, Vernon: 1883—Jul 23, 1955
Steele, William "Bill": 1889—Feb 13, 1966
Steers, Larry: 1881—Feb 15, 1951
Stein, Paul L.: Feb 4, 1892—May 1951
Stein, Robert M: 1951—Jun 13, 1991
Stephens, Harvey: 1901—Dec 22, 1986
Stephenson, Henry: Apr 16, 1871—Apr 24, 1956
Stephenson, James: Apr 14, 1888—Jul 29, 1941
Steppling, John C.: 1869—Apr 5, 1932
Sterling, Ford: Nov 3, 1880—Oct 13, 1939
Stevens, Charles: May 26, 1893—Aug 22, 1964
Stevens, Fran: 1919—Nov 2, 1991
Stevens, George: Dec 18, 1904—Mar 8, 1975
Stevens, Inger: Oct 18, 1934—Apr 30, 1970
Stevens, Landers: Feb 17, 1877—Dec 19, 1940
Stevens, Onslow: Mar 29, 1902—Jan 5, 1977
Stevens, Robert: 1921—Aug 7, 1989
Stevenson, Houseley: Jul 30, 1879—Aug 6, 1953
Stevenson, Robert: Mar 31, 1905—Apr 30, 1986
Stewart, Anita: Feb 7, 1895—May 4, 1961
Stewart, Fred: 1906—Dec 5, 1970
Stewart, Paul: Mar 13, 1908—Feb 17, 1986

Stewart, Roy: Oct 17, 1889—Apr 26, 1933
Stiller, Mauritz: Jul 17, 1883—Nov 8, 1928
Stockdale, Carl: Feb 19, 1874—Mar 15, 1953
Stone, Arthur: 1884—Sep 4, 1940
Stone, Fred: Aug 19, 1873—Mar 6, 1959
Stone, George E.: May 1, 1904—May 26, 1967
Stone, Lewis: Nov 15, 1878—Sep 12, 1953
Stone, Milburn: Jul 5, 1904—Jun 12, 1980
Stonehouse, Ruth: Oct 24, 1893—May 12, 1941
Storey, Edith: Mar 18, 1892—Sep 23, 1955
Storey, June: 1918—Dec 18, 1991
Stossell, Ludwig: Feb 12, 1883—Jan 29, 1973
Stowell, William H.: Mar 13, 1885—Dec 1919
Stradner, Rose: 1913—Sep 27, 1958
Strait, Ralph: 1936—Jul 31, 1992
Strange, Glenn: Aug 16, 1899—Sep 20, 1973
Strange, Robert: 1882—Feb 22, 1952
Strasberg, Lee: Nov 17, 1901—Feb 17, 1982
Stratton, Chester: 1913—Jul 7, 1970
Strauch, Joseph, Jr.: 1930—May 31, 1986
Strauss, Robert: Nov 8, 1913—Feb 20, 1975
Strauss, William H.: Jun 13, 1885—Aug 5, 1943
Strayer, Frank R.: Sep 21, 1891—Feb 2, 1964
Strickland, Helen 1863—Jan 11, 1938
Striker, Joseph: 1900—Feb 24, 1974
Strong, Leonard: Aug 12, 1908—Jan 23, 1980
Stroud, Claude: 1907—Oct 16, 1985
Strudwick, Shepperd: Sep 22, 1907—Jan 15, 1983
Stuart, Donald: 1898—Feb 22, 1944
Stuart, Nick: Apr 10, 1904—Apr 7, 1973
Stubbs, Harry: Sep 7, 1874—Mar 9, 1950
Sturges, John: Jan 3, 1911—Aug 18, 1992
Sturges, Preston: Aug 29, 1898—Aug 6, 1959
Sturgis, Eddie: Oct 22, 1881—Dec 13, 1947
Stussy, Jan: 1922—Jul 31, 1990
Sudlow, Joan: 1892—Feb 1, 1970
Sullavan, Margaret: May 16, 1911—Jan 1, 1960
Sullivan, Ed: Sep 28, 1901—Oct 13, 1974
Sullivan, Elliott: Jul 4, 1907—Jun 2, 1974
Sullivan, Francis L.: Jan 6, 1903—Nov 19, 1956
Sullivan, Marie: 1911—Jan 5, 1991
Sullivan, William A. "Billy": 1891—May 23, 1946
Sully, Frank: 1908—Dec 17, 1975
Summers, Hope: 1901—Jul 22, 1979
Summerville, Slim: Jul 10, 1892—Jan 6, 1946
Sundberg, Clinton: Dec 7, 1906—Dec 14, 1987
Sunshine, Marion: May 15, 1894—Jan 25, 1963
Sutherland, A. Edward "Eddie":
                     Jan 5, 1895—Jan 1, 1974
Sutherland, Dick: 1882—Feb 3, 1934
Sutherland, Esther: 1932—Dec 31, 1986
Sutherland, Victor: 1889—Aug 29, 1968
Sutton, Frank: 1923—Jun 28, 1974
Sutton, Paul: 1912—Jan 31, 1970
Swain, Mack: Feb 16, 1876—Aug 25, 1935
Swanson, Gloria: Mar 27, 1897—Apr 4, 1983
Swarthout, Gladys: Dec 25, 1904—Jul 7, 1969
Sweeney, Bob: 1919—Jun 7, 1992
Sweet, Blanche: Jun 18, 1895—Sep 6, 1986
Sweet, Dolph: Jul 18, 1920—May 10, 1985
Swenson, Karl: 1908—Oct 8, 1978
Swickard, Joseph: 1866—Feb 29, 1940
Switzer, Carl "Alfalfa": Aug 8, 1927—Jan 21, 1959
Swor, Bert: 1878—Nov 30, 1943
Swor, John: Apr 7, 1883—Jul 15, 1965

Tabler, P. Demsey: Nov 23, 1876—Jun 7, 1956
Taft, Sara: _____—Sep 24, 1973
Taggart, Ben L.: Apr 5, 1889—May 17, 1947
Taliaferro, Mabel: May 21, 1887—Jan 24, 1979
Tallichet, Margaret: 1914—May 3, 1991
Talmadge, Constance: Apr 18, 1898—Nov 23, 1973
Talmadge, Natalie: 1899—Jun 19, 1969
Talmadge, Norma: May 26, 1893—Dec 24, 1957
Talmadge, Richard: Dec 3, 1892—Jan 25, 1981
Talman, William: Feb 4, 1915—Aug 30, 1968
Talton, Alix: 1920—Apr 7, 1992
Tamiroff, Akim: Oct 29, 1899—Sep 17, 1972
Tanguay, Eva: Aug 1878—Jan 11, 1947
Tannen, Charles D.: 1915—Dec 28, 1980
Tannen, Julius: 1881—Jan 3, 1965
Tannen, William "Bill": 1911—Dec 2, 1976
Tapley, Rose: Jun 30, 1881—Feb 23, 1956
Tarlow, Florence; 1922—Feb 10, 1992
Tarron, Elsie: 1903—Oct 24, 1990
Tashlin, Frank: Feb 19, 1913—May 5, 1972
Tashman, Lilyan: Oct 23, 1900—Mar 21, 1934
Tate, Dennis: 1931—Jan 1993
Tate, Sharon: Jan 24, 1943—Aug 9, 1969
Taurog, Norman: Feb 23, 1899—Apr 7, 1981
Tavares, Albert: 1953—Jul 28, 1992
Tayback, Vic: Jan 6, 1930—May 25, 1990
Taylor, Avonne: 1899—Mar 20, 1992
Taylor, Donald F.: 1919—Jan 3, 1966
Taylor, Estelle: May 20, 1899—Apr 15, 1958
Taylor, Ferris: 1893—Mar 6, 1961
Taylor, Forrest: 1884—Feb 19, 1965
Taylor, John: 1921—Apr 9, 1982
Taylor, Kent: May 11, 1907—Apr 11, 1987
Taylor, Laurette: Apr 1, 1884—Dec 7, 1946
Taylor, Ray: Dec 1, 1888—Feb 15, 1952
Taylor, Robert: Aug 5, 1911—Jun 8, 1969
Taylor, Ruth: 1908—Apr 12, 1984
Taylor, Sam: Aug 13, 1895—Mar 6, 1958
Taylor, Vaughn: 1911—May 3, 1983
Taylor, William Desmond:
                     Apr 26, 1877—Feb 1, 1922
Teal, Ray: Jan 12, 1902—Apr 2, 1976
Teale, Sir Godfrey: Oct 12, 1884—Jun 8, 1953
Tearle, Conway: May 17, 1878—Oct 1, 1939
Teasdale, Verree: Mar 15, 1905—Feb 17, 1987
Teitel, Carol: Aug 1, 1929—Jul 27, 1986
Tell, Olive: 1894—Jun 8, 1951
Tellegen, Lou: Nov 26 1881—Nov 1, 1934
Tenbrook, Harry: Oct 9, 1897—Sep 14, 1960
Terhune, Max "Alibe": Feb 12, 1891—Jun 5, 1973
Terris, Norma: Nov 13, 1904—Nov 15, 1989
Terry, Alice: Jul 24, 1899—Dec 22, 1987
Terry, Don: Aug 8, 1902—Oct 6, 1988
Terry, Ethel Grey: _____—Jan 6, 1931
Terry, Tex: 1903—May 18, 1985
Tessier, Robert: 1924—Oct 11, 1990
Tetley, Walter: 1915—Sep 4, 1975
Tetzel, Joan: Jun 21, 1923—Oct 31, 1977
Thatcher, Heather: 1898—Feb 1987
Thatcher, Torin: Jan 15, 1905—Mar 4, 1981
Thaw, Evelyn Nesbit: 1885—Jan 18, 1967
Thelma, Melva: 1897—Jan 21, 1991
Thesiger, Ernest: Jan 15, 1879—Jan 14, 1961
Thiele, Wilhelm (William):
                     May 10, 1890—Sep 7, 1975

Thomas, Ann: 1914—Apr 28, 1989
Thomas, Billy "Buckwheat":
                  Mar 12, 1931—Oct 10, 1980
Thomas, Danny: Jan 6, 1912—Feb 6, 1991
Thomas, David: 1908—Jan 27, 1981
Thomas, Jameson: Mar 24, 1889—Jan 10, 1939
Thomas, Olive: Oct 29, 1884—Sep 10, 1920
Thompson, Carlos: Jun 7, 1916—Oct 10, 1990
Thompson, Marshall: Nov 27, 1925—May 18, 1992
Thomson, Fred: Apr 28, 1890—Dec 25, 1928
Thomson, Frederick A.:
                  Aug 7, 1869—Jan 23, 19125
Thomson, Kenneth: Jan 7, 1899—Jan 27, 1967
Thordsen, Kelly: 1917—Jan 23, 1978
Thorpe, Jim: May 28, 1886—Mar 28, 1953
Thorpe, Richard: Feb 24, 1896—May 1, 1991
Thundercloud, Chief (Daniels, Victor): Apr 12,
1889—Nov 30, 1955
Thurman, Mary: Apr 27, 1894—Dec 22, 1925
Tibbett, Lawrence: Nov 16, 1896—Jul 15, 1960
Tierney, Gene: Nov 20, 1920—Oct 6, 1991
Tilbury, Zeffie: Nov 20, 1863—Jul 24, 1950
Tinling, James: May 8, 1889—1967
Titus, Lydia Yeamans: 1866—Dec 30, 1929
Tobias, George: Jul 14, 1901—Feb 27, 1980
Tobin, Dan: 1910—Nov 26, 1982
Todd, Christopher: 1962—Aug 9, 1992
Todd, Thelma: Jul 29, 1905—Dec 18, 1935
Toler, Sidney: Apr 28, 1874—Feb 12, 1947
Tomack, Sid: 1907—Nov 12, 1962
Tomlin, Pinky: 1907—Dec 12, 1987
Tone, Franchot: Feb 27, 1905—Sep 18, 1968
Tong, Kam: 1907—Nov 8, 1969
Tong, Sammee: 1901—Oct 27, 1964
Toomey, Regis: Aug 13, 1898—Oct 12, 1991
Toren, Marta: May 21, 1926—Feb 19, 1957
Torrence, David: Jan 17, 1864—Dec 26, 1951
Torrence, Ernest: Jun 16, 1878—May 15, 1933
Torres, Raquel: Nov 11, 1908—Aug 10, 1987
Tors, Ivan: Jun 12, 1916—Jun 4, 1983
Touchstone, John: 1933—Jan 25, 1992
Tourneur, Jacques: Nov 12, 1904—Dec 19, 1977
Tourneur, Maurice: Feb 2, 1876—Aug 4, 1961
Tozere, Frederic: 1901—Aug 5, 1972
Tracy, Emerson: Sep 7, 1905—Jan 10, 1967
Tracy, Lee: Apr 14, 1898—Oct 18, 1968
Tracy, Spencer: Apr 5, 1900—Jun 10, 1967
Tracy, William: Dec 1, 1917—Jun 18, 1967
Traeger, Kim Patrick: 1951—Nov 12, 1987
Traeger, Rick: 1915—Nov 14, 1987
Trask, Wayland: Jul 16, 1887—Nov 11, 1918
Traube, Shepard: Feb 27, 1907—Jul 23, 1983
Traubel, Helen: Jun 16, 1903—Jun 28, 1972
Travers, Henry: Mar 5, 1874—Oct 18, 1965
Travers, Richard C.: Apr 15, 1890—Apr 20, 1935
Traverse, Madelaine: 1876—Jan 7, 1964
Travis, Richard: Apr 7, 1913—Jul 11, 1989
Treacher, Arthur: Jul 23, 1894—Dec 14, 1975
Treadwell, Laura: 1879—Nov 22, 1960
Tree, Dorothy: May 21, 1909—Feb 12, 1992
Treen, Mary: Mar 27, 1907—Jul 20, 1989
Trevor, Hugh: Oct 28, 1903—Nov 10, 1933
Triesault, Ivan: 1900—Jan 3, 1980
Trimble, Lawrence: Feb 15, 1885—Feb 8, 1954
Trop, J. D.: Apr 28, 1901—May 17, 1992

Troubetzkoy, Youcca: 1906—Apr 22, 1992
Trowbridge, Charles: Jan 10, 1882—Oct 30, 1967
Truesdale, Howard: Jan 3, 1861—Dec 8, 1941
Truex, Ernest: Sep 19, 1889—Jun 27, 1973
Tryon, Glenn: Sep 14, 1899—Apr 18, 1970
Tryon, Thomas: Jan 14, 1926—Sep 4, 1991
Tsiang, H. T.: 1899—Jul 16, 1971
Tubb, Ernest: Feb 9, 1914—Sep 6, 1984
Tucker, Forrest: Feb 12, 1919—Oct 25, 1986
Tucker, George Loane: 1881—Jun 21, 1921
Tucker, Harland: ____—Mar 22, 1949
Tucker, Lorenzo: Jun 27, 1907—Aug 19, 1986
Tucker, Paul: 1951—May 25, 1991
Tucker, Richard: Jun 4, 1884—Dec 5, 1942
Tucker, Sophie: Jan 13, 1884—Feb 9, 1966
Tufts, Sonny: Jul 16, 1911—Jun 5, 1970
Tully, Tom: Aug 21, 1896—Apr 27, 1982
Turich, Felipe F: 1899—Mar 9, 1992
Turner, Florence: 1885—Aug 28, 1946
Turpin, Ben: Sep 17, 1869—Jul 1, 1940
Tuttle, Frank: Aug 6, 1892—Jan 6, 1963
Tuttle, Lurene: Aug 29, 1906—May 28, 1986
Twelvetrees, Helen: Dec 25, 1908—Feb 14, 1958
Twitchell, A. R. "Archie":
                    Nov 28, 1906—Jan 31, 1957
Tyler, Harry: 1888—Sep 15, 1961
Tyler, Judy: c. 1932—Jul 3, 1957
Tyler, Tom: Aug 8, 1903—May 1, 1954
Tynan, Brandon: 1879—Mar 19, 1967
Tyrell, John E.: Dec 7, 1902—Sep 19, 1949
Ulmer, Edgar G.: Sep 17, 1900—Sep 30, 1972
Ulric, Lenore: Jul 21, 1892—Dec 30, 1970
Unger, Bertil: 1921—Apr 22, 1990
Urecal, Minerva: 1894—Feb 26, 1966
Usher, Guy: 1875—Jun 16, 1944
Vague, Vera: Sep 2, 1904—Sep 14, 1974
Vail, Lester: 1900—Nov 28, 1959
Vale, Louise: ____—Oct 28, 1918
Valentino, Rudolph: May 6, 1895—Aug 23, 1926
Valenty, Lily: 1901—Mar 11, 1987
Valerie, Joan: ____—Jan 30, 1983
Vallee, Rudy: Jul 28, 1901—Jul 3, 1986
Valli, June: 1929—Mar 12, 1993
Valli, Virginia: Jun 10, 1895—Sep 24, 1968
Vallin, Richard "Rick": 1920—Aug 31, 1977
Van Buren, Mabel: 1879—Nov 4, 1947
Van Cleef, Lee: Jan 9, 1925—Dec 16, 1989
Van Dyke, W. S., II: Mar 26, 1889—Feb 5, 1943
Van Dyke, Willard: Dec 5, 1906—Jan 23, 1986
Van Rooten, Luis: Nov 29, 1906—Jun 17, 1973
Van Sickel, Dale: 1907—Jan 25, 1977
Van Sloan, Edward: Nov 1, 1881—May 6, 1964
Van Zandt, Philip: Oct 3, 1904—Feb 16, 1958
Van, Bobby: Dec 6, 1930—Jul 31, 1980
Van, Gus: 1888—Mar 13, 1968
Van, Wally: Sep 27, 1880—May 9, 1974
Vance, Vivian: Jul 26, 1907—Aug 17, 1979
Vane, Denton: 1890—Sep 17, 1940
Varconi, Victor: Mar 31, 1891—Jun 16, 1976
Varden, Evelyn: Jun 12, 1893—Jul 11, 1958
Varden, Norma: Jan 20, 1898—Jan 19, 1989
Varsi, Diane: Feb 23, 1938—Nov 19, 1992
Vaughan, Dorothy: Nov 5, 1889—Mar 15, 1955
Vaughn, Alberta: 1905—Apr 26, 1992
Veidt, Conrad: Jan 22, 1893—Apr 3, 1943

Velez, Lupe: Jul 18, 1908—Dec 14, 1944
Venable, Reginald: 1926—Jun 28, 1974
Vera, Axel: 1952—Feb 7, 1993
Vera-Ellen: Feb 16, 1926—Aug 30, 1981
Verne, Karen: 1918—Dec 23, 1967
Vernon, Bobby: Mar 9, 1897—Jun 28, 1939
Vernon, Dorothy: Nov 11, 1875—Oct 28, 1970
Vernon, Wally: 1904—Mar 7, 1970
Vickers, Martha: May 28, 1925—Nov 2, 1971
Victor, Henry: Oct 2, 1898—May 15, 1945
Vidor, Charles: Jul 27, 1900—Jun 4, 1959
Vidor, Florence: Jul 23, 1895—Nov 3, 1977
Vidor, King: Feb 8, 1894—Nov 1, 1982
Viertel, Berthold: Jun 28, 1885—Sep 25, 1953
Vignola, Robert G.: Aug 5, 1882—Oct 25, 1953
Vigran, Herbert: 1910—Nov 28, 1986
Vincent, "Sailor" Billy: 1896—Jul 12, 1966
Vincent, Chuck: 1940—Sep 23, 1991
Vincent, James: 1897—May 29, 1957
Vincent, Romo: 1909—Jan 16, 1989
Vinton, Arthur Rolfe: ____—Feb 26, 1963
Viotti, Domenic (John): 1931—Oct 27, 1992
Visaroff, Michael: Nov 18, 1892—Feb 27, 1951
Vitte, Raymond: Nov 20, 1949—Feb 20, 1983
Vivyan, John: May 31, 1916—Dec 20, 1983
Vogan, Emmett: Sep 27, 1893—Nov 13, 1969
Vogeding, Fredrick: Mar 28, 189—Apr 18, 1942
Von Brincken, Wilhelm:
                    May 27, 1891—Jan 18, 1946
Von Eltz, Theodore: Nov 5, 1894—Oct 6, 1964
Von Meter, Harry: Mar 29, 1871—Jun 2, 1956
Von Seyffertitz, Gustav: 1863—Dec 25, 1943
Von Sternberg, Josef: May 29, 1894—Dec 22, 1969
Von Stroheim, Erich, Jr.:
                    Aug 25, 1916—Oct 26, 1968
Von Stroheim, Erich (Sr.):
                    Sep 22, 1885—May 12, 1957
Von Stroheim, Valerie: 1897—Oct 22, 1988
Von Twardowski, Hans: 1898—Nov 19, 1958
Von Zell, Harry: Jul 11, 1906—Nov 21, 1981
von Zerneck, Peter: Jun 17, 1908—Jun 10, 1992
Voskovec, George: Jun 19, 1905—Jul 1, 1981
Vye, Murvyn: Jul 15, 1913—Aug 17, 1976
Waddington, Patrick: 1900—Feb 4, 1986
Wadsworth, Henry: 1902—Dec 5, 1974
Wadsworth, William: 1873—Jun 6, 1950
Wagenheim, Charles: c. 1895—Mar 6, 1979
Waggner, George: Sep 7, 1894—Dec 12, 1984
Wagner, Jack: 1897—Feb 6, 1965
Wagner, Max: Nov 28, 1901—Nov 16, 1975
Wagner, William: 1885—Mar 11, 1964
Wakely, Jimmy: Feb 16, 1914—Sep 23, 1982
Walburn, Raymond: Sep 9, 1887—Jul 26, 1969
Waldis, Otto: 1906—Mar 25, 1904
Waldron, Charles D.: Dec 23, 1874
Wales, Ethel: 1881—Feb 15, 1952
Wales, Wally: 1896—Feb 12, 1980
Walker, Betty: 1928—Jul 26, 1982
Walker, Charlotte: Dec 29, 1878—Mar 24, 1958
Walker, Hal: Mar 20, 1896—Jul 3, 1972
Walker, Helen: 1920—Mar 10, 1968
Walker, Johnnie Jan 7, 1894—Dec 4, 1949
Walker, June: Jun 14, 1904—Feb 3, 1966
Walker, Lillian "Dimples":
                    Apr 21, 1887—Oct 10, 1975

Walker, Nancy: May 10, 1921—Mar 22, 1992
Walker, Nella: Mar 6, 1886—Mar 21, 1971
Walker, Ray W.: Aug 10, 1904—Oct 6, 1980
Walker, Robert: Oct 13, 1918—Aug 27, 1951
Walker, Robert "Bob": Jun 18, 1888—Mar 1954
Walker, Stuart C.: Mar 4, 1888—Mar 13, 1941
Walker, William (Bill): 1897—Jan 27, 1992
Walker, William Arlen: 1918—Jan 4, 1992
Wallace, Jean: Oct 12, 1923—Feb 14, 1990
Wallace, May: 1877—Dec 11, 1938
Wallace, Morgan: Jul 26, 1888—Dec 12, 1953
Wallace, Regina: 1892—Feb 13, 1978
Wallace, Richard: Aug 26, 1894—Nov 3, 1951
Wallack, Roy Homer: 1928—Mar 10, 1992
Waller, Eddy C.: 1889—Aug 20, 1977
Walling, William "Will": Jun 2, 1872—Mar 5, 1932
Walsh, George: Mar 16, 1892—Jun 13, 1981
Walsh, James: 1923—Jun 20, 1991
Walsh, Raoul: Mar 11, 1887—Dec 31, 1980
Walters, Casey: 1916—Dec 3, 1991
Walters, Charles: Nov 17, 1911—Aug 13, 1982
Walthall, Henry B.: Mar 16, 1878—Jun 17, 1936
Walton, Douglas: Oct 17, 1909—Nov 15, 1961
Walton, Fred: 1865—Dec 28, 1936
Warburton, John: Jun 18, 1899—Oct 27, 1981
Ward, Carrie: 1862—Feb 6, 1926
Ward, Charles: 1905—Jan 14, 1992
Ward, Fannie: Feb 22, 1872—Jan 27, 1952
Ward, Lucille: 1880—Aug 8, 1952
Warde, Anthony: 1909—Jan 8, 1975
Warde, Harlan: ____—Mar—1980
Warfield, Irene: 1896—Apr 10, 1961
Warhol, Andy: Aug 8, 1927—Feb 21, 1987
Waring, Richard: May 27, 1911—Jan 18, 1993
Warner, Gertrude: 1918—Jan 26, 1986
Warner, H. B.: Oct 26, 1876—Dec 24, 1958
Warren, Charles Marquis:
                    Dec 16, 1917—Aug 13, 1990
Warren, E. Alyn: 1875—Jan 22, 1940
Warren, Fred H.: Sep 16, 1880—Dec 5, 1940
Warren, Jerry: 1923—Aug 21, 1988
Warwick, Robert: Oct 9, 1878—Jun 4, 1964
Washburn, Bryant, Jr.: ____—1960
Washburn, Bryant (Sr.):
                    Apr 23, 1889—Apr 30, 1963
Waters, Ethel: Oct 31, 1896—Sep 1, 1977
Waters, John: 1894—May 1, 1965
Watkin, Pierre: Dec 29, 1889—Feb 3, 1960
Watson, Bobby: 1888—May 22, 1965
Watson, Lucile: May 27, 1879—Jun 24, 1962
Watson, Minor: Dec 22, 1889—Jul 28, 1965
Watters, John S.: 1894—May 4, 1965
Watts, Charles: ____—Dec 13, 1966
Wayne, John: May 26, 1907—Jun 11, 1979
Weaver, Doodles: May 11, 1911—Jan 15, 1983
Weaver, June "Elviry": 1891—Nov 27, 1977
Webb, Alan: Jul 2, 1906—Jun 22, 1982
Webb, Clifton: Nov 19, 1889—Oct 13, 1966
Webb, Harry S.: Oct 15, 1891—Deceased
Webb, Jack: Apr 2, 1920—Dec 23, 1982
Webb, Millard: Dec 6, 1893—Apr 21, 1935
Webb, Robert D.: Jan 3, 1903—Apr 18, 1990
Webb, Roy: Oct 3, 1888—Dec 10, 1982
Webber, Robert: Oct 14, 1924—May 17, 1989
Webber, Ronald: 1932—Jul 26, 1992

Weber, Joe: Aug 11, 1867—May 10, 1942
Weber, Karl: 1916—Jul 30, 1990
Weber, Lois: 1882—Nov 13, 1939
Webster, Ben: Jun 2, 1864—Feb 26, 1947
Webster, Byron: 1933—Dec 1, 1991
Weed, Leland T.: 1901—Aug 29, 1975
Weeks, Marion: 1887—Apr 20, 1968
Weidler, Virginia: Mar 21, 1927—Jul 1, 1968
Weigel, Paul: Feb 18, 18, 1867—May 25, 1951
Weisenborn, Gordon: 1923—Oct 4, 1987
Weissmuller, Johnny: Jun 2, 1904—Jan 20, 1984
Weist, Dwight: 1910—Jul 16, 1991
Welch, Niles: Jul 29, 1895—Nov 21, 1976
Welford, Nancy: 1904—Sep 30, 1991
Welk, Lawrence: Mar 11, 1903—May 17, 1992
Welles, Orson: May 6, 1915—Oct 10, 1985
Wellesley, Charles: 1875—Jul 24, 1946
Wellman, William A.: Feb 29, 1896—Dec 9, 1975
Welsh, Ronnie: 1941—Jan 5, 1993
Welsh, William: Feb 9, 1870—Jul 16, 1946
Wengraf, John E.: 1897—May 4, 1974
Wentworth, Martha: ____—Mar 8, 1974
Wescoatt, Rusty: 1911—Sep 3, 1987
Wessel, Richard "Dick": 1913—Apr 20, 1965
Wesson, Dick: Feb 20, 1919—Jan 27, 1979
West, Billy: Sep 21, 1893—Jul 21, 1975
West, Brooks: c. 1916—Feb 7, 1984
West, Madge: c. 1891—May 29, 1985
West, Mae: Aug 17, 1892—Nov 22, 1980
West, Pat: 1889—Apr 10, 1944
West, Roland: 1887—Mar 31, 1952
West, William: ____—Sep 23, 1918
Westerfield, James: 1912—Sep 20, 1971
Westley, Helen: Mar 28, 1875—Dec 12, 1942
Westman, Nydia: Feb 19, 1902—May 23, 1970
Weston, Doris: 1918—Jul 27, 1960
Westover, Winifred: 1900—Mar 19, 1978
Whale, James: Jul 22, 1896—May 29, 1957
Whalen, Michael: Jun 30, 1902—Apr 14, 1974
Wheat, Lawrence "Larry": 1876—Aug 7, 1963
Wheatcroft, Stanhope: May 11, 1888—Feb 12, 1966
Wheeler, Bert: Apr 7, 1895—Jan 18, 1968
Whelan, Arleen: Sep 16, 1915—Apr 8, 1993
Whelan, Tim: Nov 2, 1893—Aug 12, 1957
Whipper, Leigh: 1877—Jul 26, 1975
Whitaker, Charles "Slim":
                              Jul 29, 1893—Jun 27, 1960
White, Alice: Aug 28, 1907—Feb 19, 1983
White, David: 1916—Nov 27, 1990
White, Glenn: 1950—May 27, 1992
White, John I.: 1900—Nov 26, 1990
White, Lee "Lasses": Aug 22, 1888—Dec 16, 1949
White, Leo: 1880—Sep 21, 1948
White, Pearl: Mar 4, 1889—Aug 4, 1938
White, Ruth: Apr 24, 1914—Dec 3, 1969
Whiting, Jack: Jun 22, 1901—Feb 15, 1961
Whitley, Crane: ____—Feb 28, 1958
Whitley, Ray: 1902—Feb 21, 1979
Whitlock, T. Lloyd: Jan 2, 1891—Jan 8, 1966
Whitman, Gayne: Mar 19, 1890—Aug 31, 1958
Whitney, Claire: 1890—Aug 27, 1969
Whitney, Peter: 1916—Mar 30, 1972
Whittell, Josephine: ____—Jun 1, 1961
Whitty, May (Dame): Jun 19, 1865—May 29, 1948
Whorf, Richard: Jun 4, 1906—Dec 14, 1966

Wiard, William: 1928—Jul 2, 1987
Wiecks, Dorothea: Jan 3, 1905—Feb 23, 1986
Wiere, Sylvester: 1910—Jul 7, 1970
Wilbur, Crane: Nov 17, 1889—Oct 18, 1973
Wilcox, Frank: Mar 13, 1907—Mar 3, 1974
Wilcox, Fred M.: 1905—Sep 24, 1964
Wilcox, Robert: May 19, 1910—Jun 11, 1955
Wilcoxon, Henry: Sep 8, 1905—Mar 6, 1984
Wilde, Cornel: Oct 13, 1915—Oct 16, 1989
Wilder, Marshall P.: 1860—Jan 10, 1915
Wilding, Michael: Jul 23, 1912—Jul 7, 1979
Wilke, Robert: 1915—Mar 28, 1989
Wilkerson, Guy: 1898—Jul 15, 1971
Willes, Jean: 1924—Jan 3, 1989
Willey, Margaret: ____—Feb 19, 1991
William, Warren: Dec 2, 1895—Sep 24, 1948
Williams, Bert: 1877—Mar 5, 1922
Williams, Bill: May 15, 1916—Sep 21, 1992
Williams, Charles B.: Sep 27, 1898—Jan 3, 1958
Williams, Charlie: 1930—Oct 15, 1992
Williams, Clark: 1906—Feb 13, 1989
Williams, Cora: 1871—Dec 1, 1927
Williams, Earle: Feb 28, 1880—Apr 25, 1927
Williams, Grant: Aug 18, 1930—Jul 28, 1985
Williams, Guinn "Big Boy":
                              Apr 26, 1899—Jun 6, 1962
Williams, Guy: Jan 14, 1924—May 6, 1989
Williams, Hope: Aug 11, 1897—May 3, 1990
Williams, John: Apr 15, 1903—May 5, 1983
Williams, Kathlyn: May 31, 1888—Sep 23, 1960
Williams, Mack: 1907—Jul 29, 1965
Williams, Rhys: 1892—May 28, 1969
Williams, Spencer: Jul 14, 1893—Dec 13, 1969
Williams, Tex: Aug 23, 1917—Oct 11, 1985
Willis, Matt: 1914—Mar 30, 1989
Willock, Dave: 1909—Nov 12, 1990
Wills, Beverly: Aug 6, 1933—Oct 24, 1963
Wills, Bob: 1905—May 13, 1975
Wills, Chill: Jul 18, 1903—Dec 15, 1978
Wilson, Benjamin F.: 1876—Aug 25, 1930
Wilson, Charles Cahill: 1894—Jan 7, 1948
Wilson, Clarence H.: 1877—Oct 5, 1941
Wilson, Dooley: Apr 3, 1894—May 30, 1953
Wilson, Frank: 1955—Feb 6, 1992
Wilson, Lois: Jun 28, 1894—Mar 3, 1988
Wilson, Margery: 1898—Jan 21, 1986
Wilson, Marie: Aug 19, 1916—Nov 23, 1972
Wilson, Richard: 1916—Aug 21, 1991
Wilson, Stu: 1904—Aug 1, 1991
Wilson, Theodore R.: Dec 10, 1943—Jul 21, 1991
Wilson, Tom: 1880—Feb 19, 1965
Wilson, Trey: 1949—Jan 16, 1989
Wilson, Whip: Jul 16, 1919—Oct 23, 1964
Winchell, Walter: Apr 7, 1897—Feb 20, 1972
Winckler, Robert: 1927—Dec 28, 1989
Windsor, Claire: Apr 14, 1897—Oct 24, 1972
Windust, Bretaigne: Jan 20, 1906—Mar 18, 1960
Winninger, Charles: May 26, 1884—Jan 27, 1969
Winters, Roland: Nov 22, 1904—Oct 22, 1989
Winton, Jane: 1908—Sep 22, 1959
Winwood, Estelle: Jan 24, 1883—Jun 20, 1984
Wisbar, Frank: 1899—Mar 17, 1967
Withers, Grant: Jun 17, 1904—Mar 27, 1959
Withers, Isabel: Jan 20, 1896—Sep 3, 1968
Witherspoon, Cora: Jan 5, 1890—Nov 17, 1957

Wix, Florence E.: 1883—Nov 23, 1956
Wolfe, Ian: Nov 4, 1896—Jan 23, 1992
Wolheim, Louis: Mar 23, 1880—Feb 18, 1931
Wong, Anna May: Jan 3, 1907—Feb 3, 1961
Wong, Iris: 1921—Sep 2, 1989
Wood, Britt: 1895—Apr 13, 1965
Wood, Douglas: 1880—Jan 13, 1966
Wood, Edward, Jr.: Jul 5, 1905—Oct 8, 1989
Wood, Edward D., Jr.: 1922—1978
Wood, Freeman N.: 1897—Feb 19, 1956
Wood, George: 1936—Jul 22, 1990
Wood, Natalie: Jul 20, 1938—Nov 29, 1981
Wood, Peggy: Feb 9, 1892—Mar 18, 1978
Wood, Sam: Jul 10, 1883—Sep 22, 1949
Woodbury, Joan: Dec 17, 1915—Feb 22, 1989
Woods, Harry Lewis, Sr.: 1889—Dec 28, 1968
Woodward, Robert "Bob": 1909—Feb 7, 1972
Wooland, Norman: 1906—Apr 3, 1989
Woollcott, Alexander: Jan 19, 1887—Jan 23, 1943
Woolley, Monty: Aug 17, 1888—May 6, 1963
Woolsey, Robert: Aug 14, 1889—Oct 31, 1938
Worden, Hank: 1901—Dec 6, 1992
Worlock, Frederick: Dec 14, 1886—Aug 1, 1973
Worth, Constance: 1915—Oct 18, 1963
Wray, John Griffith: Feb 13, 1888—Apr 5, 1940
Wright, Mack V.: 1895—1963
Wright, Will: Mar 26, 1891—Jun 19, 1962
Wright, William: 1912—Jan 19, 1949
Wrightson, Earl: Jan 1, 1916—Mar 7, 1993
Wu, Honorable: 1903—Mar 1, 1945
Wunderlee, Frank: 1875—Dec 11, 1925
Wurschmidt, Sigrid: 1953—Mar 24, 1990
Wyatt, Allan, Sr.: 1920—Aug 12, 1992
Wycherly, Margaret: Oct 26, 1881—Jun 6, 1956
Wyler, William: Jul 1, 1902—Jul 27, 1981
Wynn, Ed: Nov 9, 1886—Jun 19, 1966
Wynn, Keenan: Jul 27, 1916—Oct 14, 1986
Wynn, Nan: 1916—Mar 21, 1971
Wynters, Charlotte: 1900—Jan 7, 1991
Wynyard, Diana: Jan 16, 1906—May 13, 1964
Yaconelli, Frank: Oct 2, 1898—Nov 19, 1965
Yarborough, Barton: 1900—Dec 19, 1951
Yarmy, Dick: 1933—May 5, 1992
Yearsley, Ralph: 1897—Dec 4, 1928
York, Dick: Sep 4, 1928—Feb 20, 1992
York, Duke: 1902—Jan 24, 1952
Yorke, Edith: 1872—Jul 28, 1934
Yost, Herbert A.: 1880—Oct 23, 1945
Young, Carleton: 1907—Jul 11, 1971
Young, Clara Kimball: Sep 6, 1890—Oct 15, 1960
Young, Clifton: 1917—Sep 10, 1951
Young, Gig: Nov 4, 1913—Oct 19, 1978
Young, Roland: Nov 11, 1887—Jun 5, 1953
Young, Skip: 1930—Mar 17, 1993
Young, Tammany: 1887—Apr 26, 1936
Youngson, Robert: Nov 27, 1917—Apr 8, 1974
Yowlachie, Chief: Aug 15, 1891—Mar 7, 1966
Yule, Joe: Apr 30, 1894—Mar 30, 1950
Yurka, Blanche: Jun 18, 1887—May 30, 1974
Zaremba, John: 1908—Dec 15, 1986
Zucco, George: Jan 11, 1886—May 28, 1960

Abel's Hill Cemetery (Chilmark, MA)
John Belushi

Arlington National Cemetery (Arlington, VA)
Fay Bainter, Constance Bennett, Lee Marvin, Ilona Massey, Audie Murphy, Wayne Morris,

Beaverdale Memorial Park (Hamden, CT)
Raymond Massey

Beth David Cemetery (Elmont, Long Island, NY)
Andy Kaufman

Beth El Cemetery (Brooklyn, NY)
Edward G. Robinson

Beth Olam Cemetery (Hollywood, CA)
Mel Blanc, Andrew Samuel

Calvary Cemetery (Los Angeles, CA)
Ethel Barrymore, Lionel Barrymor, Lou Costello, John Hodiak, Pola Negri, Mabel Normand, Ramon Novarro

Calvary Cemetery (Woodside, NY)
Nita Naldi

Cemetery of the Gate of Heaven (Hawthorne, NY)
Fred Allen, James Cagney, Dorothy Kilgallen, Sal Mineo

Chapel of the Pincs Crematory (Los Angeles, CA)
G. M. "Broncho Billy" Anderson, Lionel Atwill, Nigel Bruce, Edmund Gwenn, Ann Sheridan

Cypress Hills Cemetery (Brooklyn, NY)
Mae West

Eden Memorial Park (San Fernando, CA)
Groucho Marx

BURIAL SPOTS

Elmira Cemetery (Elmira, NY)
Hal Roach

Evergreen Cemetery/Crematory (Los Angeles, CA)
Eddie "Rochester" Anderson

Ferncliff Cemetery and Mausoleum (Hartsdale, NY)
Richard Barthelmess, Connee Boswell, Joan Crawford, Lya de Putti, Judy
Garland, Jackie "Moms" Mabley", Hugh Marlowe, Elsa Maxwell, Ona Munson,
Basil Rathbone, Paul Robeson, Diana Sands, Preston Sturges, Ed Sullivan ,
Conrad Veidt

Flushing Cemetery (Flushing, NY)
Louis "Satchmo" Armstrong, May Robson, Hazel Scott, Ernest Truex

Forest Lawn—Hollywood Hills (Los Angeles, CA)
Lucille Ball, Judith Barsi, Clyde Beatty, Ralph Bellamy, Pamela Britton, Smiley
Burnette, Godfrey Cambridge, Bert Convy, Benjamin Sherman "Scatman"
Crothers, Bette Davis, Sammy Davis, Jr., Marty Feldman, Reginald Gardiner,
John Hancock, George "Gabby" Hayes, Marlene Hazlett, Wanda Hendrix, Rex
Ingram *, Buster Keaton, Ernie Kovacs, Otto Kruger, Fritz Lang, Charles
Laughton, Stan Laurel, "Lee" Liberace, Marjorie Main, Strother Martin, John
Myhers, Ozzie Nelson, Rick[y] Nelson, David Oliver, Paul Panzer, Snub Pollard,
Freddie Prinze, George Raft, Jason Robards, Sr., Lynne Roberts, Sabu, Jack Soo,
William Talman, Forrest Tucker, Jack Webb, Bill Williams, Marie Wilson

the black actor (1895-1969) not the director/actor (1892-1950)

Forest Lawn Memorial Parks (Glendale, CA)
Art Acord, Robert Alda, Ross Alexander, Gracie Allen, LaVerne Andrews,
Robert Armstrong, Roscoe Ates, Susan Ball, Theda Bara, Warner Baxter, Wallace
Beery, Rex Bell, Richard Bennett, Clara Blandick, Joan Blondell, Monte Blue,
Humphrey Bogart, May Boley, Olive Borden, Frank Borzage, Hobart Bosworth,
Clara Bow, William "Hopalong Cassidy" Boyd, Charles J. Brabin, Edmund
Breese, Clarence Brown, Joe E. Brown, Johnny Mack Brown, Helen Burgess,
Bob Burns, Francis X. Bushman, Ralph M. Byrd, Godfrey Cambridge, Judy
Canova, Sue Carol, Jack Carson, Lon Chaney, Sr., Charley Chase, Spencer
Charters, George Cleveland, Elmer Clifton, Andy Clyde, Nat "King" Cole,
William Collier, Sr., Russ Columbo, James Craig, Laird Cregar, George Cukor,
Michael Curtiz, Fifi D'Orsay, Dan Dailey, Dorothy Dandridge, Jane Darwell,
Alice Davenport, Alan Dinehart, Walt Disney, Richard Dix, Marie Dressler,
Vivian Duncan, Rosetta Duncan, Minta Durfee, Junior Durkin, W. C. Fields,
Larry Fine, Errol Flynn, Wallace W. Fox, Robert Francis, George B. French,

BURIAL SPOTS

Clark Gable, John Gilbert, Hermione Gingold, Huntly Gordon, Sydney Greenstreet, Alan Hale, Sr., Charles Halton, Hale Hamilton, Sam Hardy, Jean Harlow, Harry Hayden, Sam Hearn, Holmes Herbert, Jean Hersholt, Fay Holden, Edward Everett Horton, Jobyna Howland, Lloyd Hughes, Rex Ingram*, Rupert Julian, J. Warren Kerrigan, Ted Knight, Henry Kolker, Alan Ladd, Carole Landis, Rosemary Lane, Ivan Lebedeff, Mitchell Lewis, Frank Lloyd, Arthur Loft, Carole Lombard, Tom London, Anita Louise, Ernst Lubitsch, Jeanette MacDonald, Charles E. Mack, Chico Marx, Gummo Marx, Marie McDonald, Victor McLaglen, Beryl Mercer, Tom Mix, Alla Nazimova, Fred Niblo, Sr., George Nichols, Jr., Jack Oakie, Merle Oberon, Edna May Oliver, Moroni Olsen, Monroe Owsley, Lilli Palmer, Franklin Pangborn, Joe Penner, Susan Peters, Jack Pickford, Mary Pickford, Francis Pierlot, Harry A. Pollard, Dick Powell, Richard Powell, Addison Randall, Charles Ray, George Reeves, Wallace Reid, Addison Richards, Florence Roberts, Ruth Roland, Bodil Rosing, Charlie Ruggles, Wesley Ruggles, S. Z. "Cuddles" Sakall, Charles "Chic" Sale, Victor Schertzinger, Ruth Selwyn, Norma Shearer, Lowell Sherman, John M. Stahl, James Stephenson, Landers Stevens, Anita Stewart, Fred Stone, Robert Taylor, Chief Thundercloud, Lawrence Tibbett, Ernest Torrence, Raquel Torres, Spencer Tracy, Leonard E. Trainor, Henry Travers, Ben Turpin, Lurene Tuttle, Woody S. Van Dyke, II, Bobby Vernon, Charles Waldron, Ethel Waters, Earle Williams, Grant Withers, Sam Wood, Robert Woolsey, William Wyler, Ed Wynn, Keenan Wynn, Joe Yule

the director/actor (1892-1950) not the black actor (1895-1969)

Fort Sam Houston National Cemetery (San Antonio, TX)
Glenn Corbett

The Friends Cemetery (Brooklyn, NY)
Montgomery Clift

Graceland (Memphis, TN)
Elvis Presley

Greenwood Cemetery (Brooklyn, NY)
William S. Hart, Frank Morgan, Edward R. Murrow

Hillside Memorial Park (Los Angeles, CA)
Jack Benny, Eddie Cantor, Jeff Chandler, David Janssen, George Jessel, Al Jolson, Michael Landon, Mary Livingstone, Vic Morrow, Dick Shawn

Hollywood Memorial Park (Hollywood, CA)
Renee Adoree, Agnes Ayres, Felix Bressart, Peter Bruni, Louis Calhern, Charles Chaplin, Jr., James Cruze, Bebe Daniels, Marion Davies, Cecil B. DeMille,

BURIAL SPOTS

William DeMille, Nelson Eddy, Douglas Fairbanks, Sr., Peter Finch, Victor
Fleming, Sidney Franklin, Janet Gaynor, Joan Hackett, Darla Hood, John Huston,
Arthur Lake, Barbara LaMarr, Henry Lehrman, Peter Lorre, John Lund, Ben
Lyon, Jayne Mansfield [headstone only], Adolphe Menjou, Paul Muni, Eleanor
Powell, Tyrone Power, Virginia Rappe, Edward G. Robinson, Jr., Joseph
Schildkraut, Carl "Alfalfa" Switzer, Constance Talmadge, Natalie Talmadge,
Norma Talmadge, Eva Tanguay, William Desmond Taylor, Rudolph Valentino,
Clifton Webb

Holy Cross Cemetery (Calumet City, IL)
Gene Krupa

Holy Cross Cemetery-Mausoleum (Culver City, CA)
Frank Albertson, Sara Allgood, Richard Arlen, Henry Armetta, Mary Astor, Ray
Bolger, Charles Boyer, Scott Brady, Keefe Brasselle, Jackie Coogan, Charles
Correll, Bing Crosby, Dixie Lee Crosby, Joan Davis, Dennis Day, Constance
Dowling, Tom Drake, Jimmy Durante, Richard Egan, Joe Flynn, John Ford,
Bonita Granville, Jack Haley, Rita Hayworth, Jose Iturbi, Spike Jones, James
Jordan, Marion Jordan, Edgar Kennedy, Mario Lanza, Jack LaRue, Margaret
Lindsay, Gene Lockhart, Frank Lovejoy, Bela Lugosi, William Lundigan, Marion
Martin, Edmund O'Brien, Pat O'Brien, Barney Oldfield, Pat Paterson, Zasu Pitts,
Alejandro Rey, Rosalind Russell, Gia Scala, Mack Sennett, Sharon Tate

Holy Sepulcher Cemetery (Costa Mesa, CA)
Ruby Keeler

Home of Peace Cemetery (Palm Springs, CA)
Virginia Valli

Home of Peace Memorial Park (Los Angeles, CA)
Fanny Brice, Jerome "Curly" Howard, Shemp Howard, Charles Vidor

Inglewood Park Cemetery (Inglewood, CA)
Edgar Bergen, Hoot Gibson, Betty Grable, Gypsy Rose Lee, William
"Buckwheat" Thomas

Kensico Cemetery (Valhalla, NY)
Tommy Dorsey

Lake View Cemetery (Seattle, WA)
Brandon Lee, Bruce Lee

BURIAL SPOTS

Machpelah Cemetery (Ridgewood, Queens, NY)
Harry Houdini

Mission Hills Cemetery (Mission Hills, CA)
Edward Arnold, William Bendix, Frank Faylen, William Frawley

Mt. Sinai Memorial Park (Los Angeles, CA)
Herschel Bernardi, Georgia Brown, Lee J. Cobb, Billy Halop, Lou Krugman, Phil Silvers

Mt. Tabor United Methodist Church (Crestwood, KY)
D. W. Griffith

Mt. Vernon Cemetery (Philadelphia, PA)
John Barrymore

Oak Hill Cemetery (Nyack, NY)
Helen Hayes

Oakwood Memorial Park, (Chatsworth, CA)
Fred Astaire, Bob Crane, John Epper, Robert F. Simon

Our Lady of Perpetual Help Church (Carrollton, GA)
Susan Hayward

Pacific View Memorial Park (Newport Beach, CA)
John Wayne

Park Cemetery, (Fairmount, IN)
James Dean

Pasadena Cemetery (Altadena, CA)
Carolyn Jones

Prospect Hill Cemetery (Towson, MD)
Divine

Rose Hill Cemetery (Altoona, PA)
Hedda Hopper

Rosedale Cemetery (Los Angeles, CA)
Hattie McDaniel, Anna May Wong

BURIAL SPOTS

Sacred Heart Cemetery (Southampton, Long Island, NY)
Gary Cooper

San Bruno/Golden Gate National (San Bruno, CA)
Percy Kilbride

San Fernando Mission Cemetery (Mission Hills, CA)
Chuck Connors, Francis Xavier Killmond, Joan Maloney

Santa Barbara Cemetery (Santa Barbara, CA)
Heather Angel, John Ireland

Spring Hill Cemetery (Nashville, TN)
Roy Acuff

SS. Cyril And Methodius Cemetery (Briar Creek, PA)
Nick Adams

Union Field Cemetery (Queens, NY)
Bert Lahr

Valhalla Memorial Park (Burbank, CA)
Bea Benaderet, Cliff Edwards, Oliver Hardy, Gail Russell

West Point Military Academy Cemetery (West Point, NY)
Glenda Farrell

Westchester Hills Cemetery (Hastings-On-Hudson, NY)
John Garfield, Judy Holliday

Westwood (Village) Memorial Park (Los Angeles, CA)
Jim Backus, Edgar Barrier, Richard Basehart, John Boles, Sebastian Cabot, John Cassavetes, Richard Conte, Norma Crane, Helmut Dantine, Philip Dorn, Dominique Dunne, Jay C. Flippen, Christopher George, Thomas Gomez, Percy Helton, Steve Ihnat, Victor Jory, Cecil Kellaway, Victor Kilian, Oscar Levant, Andrew Marton, Edith Massey, Marvin Miller, Marilyn Monroe, William Newell, Lloyd Nolan, Heather O'Rourke, Donna Reed, Adeline De Walt Reynolds, Jack Roper, Richard Rosson, Franklin J. Schaffner, Dorothy Shay, Dorothy Stratten, Marshall Thompson, Helen Traubel, Frank Tuttle, John Vivyan, Charles Wagenheim, June Walker, Sylvester Wiere, Estelle Winwood, Natalie Wood

Will Rogers Memorial (Claremore, OK)
Will Rogers

BURIAL SPOTS

Woodlawn Cemetery (Bronx, NY)
Diana Barrymore, Irene Castle, Vernon Castle, George M. Cohan, Duke Ellington, Marilyn Miller, Laurette Taylor

ORDER FORM

_____ Trek Crew Book $9.95	_____ Number Six: The Prisoner Book $14.95
_____ Best Of Enterprise Incidents $9.95	_____ Gerry Anderson: Supermarionation $17.95
_____ Trek Fans Handbook $9.95	_____ Addams Family Revealed $14.95
_____ Trek: The Next Generation $14.95	_____ Bloodsucker: Vampires At The Movies $14.95
_____ The Man Who Created Star Trek: $12.95	_____ Dark Shadows Tribute $14.95
_____ 25th Anniversary Trek Tribute $14.95	_____ Monsterland Fear Book $14.95
_____ History Of Trek $14.95	_____ The Films Of Elvis $14.95
_____ The Man Between The Ears $14.95	_____ The Woody Allen Encyclopedia $14.95
_____ Trek: The Making Of The Movies $14.95	_____ Paul Mccartney: 20 Years On His Own $9.95
_____ Trek: The Lost Years $12.95	_____ Yesterday: My Life With The Beatles $14.95
_____ Trek: The Unauthorized Next Generation $14.95	_____ Fab Films Of The Beatles $14.95
_____ New Trek Encyclopedia $19.95	_____ 40 Years At Night: The Tonight Show $14.95
_____ Making A Quantum Leap $14.95	_____ Exposing Northern Exposure $14.95
_____ The Unofficial Tale Of Beauty And The Beast $14.95	_____ The La Lawbook $14.95
_____ Complete Lost In Space $19.95	_____ Cheers: Where Everybody Knows Your Name $14.95
_____ ..doctor Who Encyclopedia: Baker $19.95	_____ SNL! The World Of Saturday Night Live $14.95
_____ Lost In Space Tribute Book $14.95	_____ The Rockford Phile $14.95
_____ Lost In Space With Irwin Allen $14.95	_____ Encyclopedia Of Cartoon Superstars $14.95
_____ Doctor Who: Baker Years $19.95	_____ How To Create Animation $14.95
_____ Doctor Who: Pertwee Years $19.95	_____ How To Draw Art For Comic Books $14.95
_____ Batmania Ii $14.95	_____ King And Barker:an Illustrated Guide $14.95
_____ The Green Hornet $14.95 _____ Special Edition $16.95	_____ King And Barker: An Illustrated Guide II $14.95

100% Satisfaction Guaranteed.

We value your support. You will receive a full refund as long as the copy of the book you are not happy with is received back by us in reasonable condition. No questions asked, except we would like to know how we failed you. Refunds and credits are given as soon as we receive back the item you do not want.

BORING, BUT NECESSARY ORDERING INFORMATION

Payment:

Use our new 800 # and pay with your credit card or send check or money order directly to our address. All payments must be made in U.S. funds and please do not send cash.

Shipping:

We offer several methods of shipment. Sometimes a book can be delayed if we are temporarily out of stock. You should note whether you prefer us to ship the book as soon as available, send you a merchandise credit good for other goodies, or send your money back immediately.

Normal Post Office: $3.75 for the first book and $1.50 for each additional book. These orders are filled as quickly as possible. Shipments normally take 5 to 10 days, but allow up to 12 weeks for delivery.

Special UPS 2 Day Blue Label Service or Priority Mail: Special service is available for desperate Couch Potatoes. These books are shipped within 24 hours of when we receive the order and normally take 2 to 3 three days to get to you. The cost is $10.00 for the first book and $4.00 each additional book .

Overnight Rush Service: $20.00 for the first book and $10.00 each additional book.

U.s. Priority Mail: $6.00 for the first book and $3.00.each additional book.

Canada And Mexico: $5.00 for the first book and $3.00 each additional book.

Foreign: $6.00 for the first book and $3.00 each additional book.

Please list alternatives when available and please state if you would like a refund or for us to backorder an item if it is not in stock.

COUCH POTATO INC.   5715 N. Balsam Rd   Las Vegas, NV 89130   (702)658-2090

Use Your Credit Card 24 HRS — Order toll Free From: **(800)444-2524** Ext 67